SOURCE

JAE K. SHIM JOEL G. SIEGEL

SOURCE

The Complete Guide to

INVESTMENT INFORMATION

Where to Find It and How to Use It

International Publishing Corporation
Chicago

Library of Congress Number: 92-70720

ISBN 0-942641-32-9

TO

Dr. Bill F. Roberts and Professor C. B. McGuire
Former mentors at University of California, Berkeley

Table of Contents

Chapter 2: General Market Information/Benchmarks   13

Chapter 4: Industry Information   59

Chapter 5: Company Information   75

Chapter 6: How To Analyze Financial Statements   109

Chapter 7: Common Stocks and Preferred Stocks   133

Chapter 8: Fixed-Income Securities 173

Chapter 11: Tangibles: Real Estate and Other Real Assets 293

Chapter 12: On-Line Data Service & Investment Software 305

Chapter 13: Investment Newsletters and Advisories   343

Chapter 14: Investment Information Grids   381

Glossary   387

Index   407

About the Authors

Jae K. Shim, Ph.D., is Professor of Finance and Accounting at California State University, Long Beach, and President of National Business Review Foundation, an investment consulting and training firm. He is also Chief Investment Officer (CIO) of a Lawndale-based investment firm. Dr. Shim received his M.B.A. and Ph.D. degrees from the University of California at Berkeley. He has published numerous articles in academic and professional journals.

Among 32 professional and college books to his credit, are *Personal Finance, The Personal Financial Planning and Investment Guide, Investments: A Self-Teaching Guide, Encyclopedic Dictionary of Accounting and Finance, Financial Management, Managerial Finance, Dictionary of Personal Finance,* and the best-selling *The Vest-Pocket MBA.*

Dr. Shim was the 1982 recipient of the *Credit Research Foundation Award* for his article on investment management.

Joel G. Siegel, Ph.D., CPA, is an active consultant in investment analysis and Professor of Finance and Accounting at Queens College of the City University of New York. Previous employers include Coopers, Lybrand, and Arthur Anderson. Dr. Siegel is a personal financial analyst and planning consultant. He has acted as an investment consultant to Citicorp, ITT, United Technologies, AICPAs, and Person-Wolinsky Associates.

Dr. Siegel is the author of 34 books and 200 articles on financial topics. His books have been published by International Publishing, Macmillan, Prentice-Hall, McGraw-Hill, Harper and Row, John Wiley, Barron's, and the AICPAs. He has been published in many financial journals, including the *Financial Analysts Journal, Financial Executive,* and the *CPA Journal.*

In 1972 he received the Outstanding Educator of America Award. Dr. Siegel is listed in *Who's Where Among Writers* and *Who's Who in the World.*

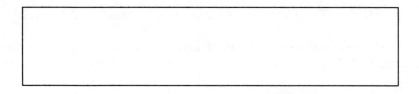

Preface

Knowledge is of two kinds. We know a subject ourselves,
or we know where we can find information upon it.
—Samuel Johnson (1709-1784)

Labor generates income; investment creates wealth.
—Anonymous

As the title indicates, this book is an investment information *source*book, a reference that investors can use to make informed investment decisions. In an environment where investment vehicles expand constantly in number and variety, acquiring the right information at the right time is a must for successful investing.

Lack of information would increase the chance for ill-informed decisions and therefore cost money—not only in terms of potential income but in terms of money invested. Not only must an investor choose the right investments, he or she must learn where to find relevant information on specific investments.

SOURCE: The Complete Guide to Investment Information is designed primarily for students of finance and investments as well as practical investors. It shows where to find information and advice on different types of investment instruments and how to read and interpret the various sources of data. Chapters consist of an overview, a look at how to choose the right kind of security in each investment category, how to read related information given for each source, and how to interpret newspaper quotations.

The book includes a discussion on:

• How key information elements (for example, risk-adjusted yield, discount yield, dividend yield, current yield, beta, P/E ratio, and 7-day compound yield) are calculated, with numerical examples;
   • What each element means, and
   • How each can be used for investment decision making.

Main chapter titles are classified by investment categories—for example, mutual funds; common and preferred stock; warrants, options, and futures. Within each chapter a particular topic is reviewed in an easily understood format. Sources of information for that specific investment instrument follow with excerpts and sample pages.

The appendix at the end of the book contains a quick-reference matrix and names and addresses of data sources. A glossary is also provided.

The quality of future revisions of the guide will depend largely upon the input and constructive suggestions we receive from readers. With this in mind, we respectfully request that readers submit their comments directly to the publisher. Any errors or omissions are the responsibility of the authors.

We wish to express our deep gratitude to Barbara Craig, Editor-in-Chief, and Ronald J. Liszkowski of International Publishing Corporation for their outstanding editorial assistance during the project; their input and efforts are recognized and greatly appreciated. Special thanks to our graduate assistants Titi Sunardi and Sherri Hwang and our school secretaries Janie Daly and Gina Trinh for their library research and word processing.

Los Alamitos, California   Jae K. Shim

Wantagh, New York   Joel G. Siegel

Acknowledgments

We are indebted to many people for ideas and assistance. Our primary obligation is to Professor C. B. McGuire and Dr. B. F. Roberts at the University of California at Berkeley to whom this book is dedicated. For those who know them, no words are necessary; for those who do not know them, no words will suffice.

It is with gratitude that we acknowledge the many sources from which the data in this book have been compiled.

All quotation examples and samples are reproduced with permission from the following sources:

The *Wall Street Journal* and *Barron's* (Dow Jones & Co., Inc., 200 Liberty St. New York, NY 10281 (800) 841-8000).

Money (Time Inc., Box 2500, Boulder, CO 80302 (800) 621-8200).

Fortune (Time Inc., Time & Life Building, Rockefeller Center, New York, NY 10020).

Business Week (McGraw-Hill Company, 1221 Avenue of the Americas, New York, NY 10002).

The Outlook, Analyst's Handbook, Stock Guide, Bond Guide, Industry Surveys and *Corporate Records* (Standard & Poor's Corporation, 345 Hudson St., New York, NY 10014).

The *Value Line Investment Survey,* Ratings & Report (Value Line Services, Arnold Bernhard Co., 5 E. 44th St., New York, NY 10017).

Technical Analyses of Industry (Merrill Lynch Capital Markets, Equity Research Department).

Moody's Handbook and *Moody's Bond Record* (Moody's Investment Service, 99 Church St., New York, NY 10007).

Annual Chart Book and *Quarterly Chart Book* (Board of Governors, Federal Reserve System, Washington, DC 20551).

Monetary Trends, National Economic Trends, U.S. Financial Data and *Review* (Federal Reserve Bank of St. Louis).

Business Conditions Digest (U.S. Department of Commerce Bureau of Economic Analysis).

Commodity Price Charts (219 Parkade, Cedar Falls, IA 50613).

Wiesenberger Investment Companies Service Report (Wiesenberger Investment Companies Service, Warren, Gorham & Lamont, 210 South St., Boston, MA 02111 (619) 423-2020).

Mutual Fund Values (Morningstar, Inc., 53 W. Jackson Blvd., Chicago, IL 60604).

The Individual Investor's Guide to No-Load Mutual Funds, The Individual Investor's Guide to Computerized Investing, The Individual Investor's Guide to Investment Publications, and *The Complete Guide to Closed-End Funds* (International Publishing Corp., 625 North Michigan Avenue, Suite 1920, Chicago, IL 60611).

Donoghue's Money Market Fund Report (The Donoghue Organization, P.O. Box 411, Holliston, MA 01746).

An Investor's Guide to Reading A Mutual Fund Prospectus (Investment Company Institute, 1600 M St., NW, Suite 600, Washington, DC 20036).

Kiplinger's Personal Investing (formerly *Changing Times*) (Kiplinger Washington Editors, Inc., 1729 H St., NW, Washington, DC 20006 (202) 887-6400).

Investor's Business Daily (Investor's Business Daily, P.O. Box 25970, Los Angeles, CA 90025 (800) 223-1673).

Every effort has been made to identify and give proper credit to the sources of information in this book. We apologize if we inadvertently overlooked anyone and would like to hear from you so that we can give you proper credit in future editions. Also, as we stated in the Preface, ''The quality of future revisions of the guide will depend largely on the input and constructive suggestions we receive from readers. With this in mind, we respectfully request that readers submit their comments directly to the publisher.''

1

Investment Information in General

OVERVIEW

Most investments involve risk, but you can control the degree of risk you undertake by carefully diversifying your funds and investments. Information and advice can certainly help in this effort, and you can learn more about investment opportunities from any of these sources (besides your broker):

- **Publications**

Newspapers; business, consumer, finance magazines; books; and tapes provide a wealth of information on investing and consumer news and are often written with the beginning investor in mind. Major newspapers, available in public and college libraries, quote market prices for stocks, bonds, mutual funds, and commodities.

- **TV and radio programs**

In a world of mass communication and high-tech media, television and radio provide up-to-date consumer, business, and financial news. Interviews with experts provide investment advice via local and national broadcasts. Examples include **Consumer News and Business Channels and Financial News Network (CNBC and FNN), The Business Channel, Financial News Network (FNN), Nightly Business Report (NBR)**, and the program **Wall Street Week**.

- **Courses on investments and personal finance**

Adult/continuing education programs and colleges offer a variety of classes on investments and personal finance. Telecourses—TV classrooms—are also available.

- **Prospectuses**

These documents, furnished on request from offering corporations, describe their securities for sale to the public. The initial offering, however, is generally announced in a financial newspaper such as the *Wall Street Journal*.

- **Annual reports**

Annual reports, which show a company's collective financial statements and other operating features, are issued by the corporation.

- **Brokers, financial planners, insurance agents, lawyers, accountants**.

These professionals offer financial, investment, and legal information and advice, generally for a fee. Make sure the adviser you select specializes in the investment area of your interest. Brokers generally have access to research data on which to base their advice. Financial planners, especially those with the CFA (Chartered Financial Analyst), CFP (Certified Financial Planner), or CLU/ChFC (Chartered Life Insurance Underwriter/Chartered Financial Consultant) designation, review your assets/financial goals; provide written investment plans and help you implement them.

- **Investment clubs and associations**

Members of investment clubs meet to pick investments and pool resources. These clubs can help you learn more about the capital market, especially if membership includes experienced investors or brokers who can give market guidance. Associations (such as the American Association of Individual Investors) offer seminars and training materials (books and tapes).

- **Investment advisory services and newsletters**

These entities track investment performance and market trends. Subscription fees vary widely. For a few dollars, many of these services will send a sample issue or two.

WHAT INFORMATION MOVES THE MARKET?

What information do you need before making an investment? To answer this question, you need to understand what really moves the market for a particular investment vehicle. In the stock market, for example, experts consider the following 10 factors to be major movers:

Earnings

The bottom line here is that if a company is doing well (i.e., earnings are growing), so will its stock price. Some things do not change.

Rumors

A whole industry of people makes a living by guessing where stock prices will go. Many make their trades based on rumors gleaned from other traders, corporate sources, bankers, or lawyers. In particular, takeover gossip can send a stock flying; rumors of a possible bankruptcy filing can make a stock nose-dive. *NOTE: No matter how woeful or wonderful the rumor, never buy or sell an investment solely on the basis of a story. By the time you read or hear about a company, many professional investors have already acted on the information and have bought or sold the stock. Consequently, the news is already discounted in the price.*

Corporate Announcements

Traders usually know what's going on with a company, so announcements of contracts, new products, or promotions do not always affect stock prices. But if an important announcement is a surprise, watch out.

Other Stocks

If stocks of competing companies are doing well, chances are your stock will ride coattails. For example, stocks in computer companies often move up or down together in waves.

Interest Rates

If rates are falling, chances are investors will do better by shifting into stocks. As the economy ebbs and flows each day, so does cash move into and out of the stock market. In this way, stock prices can jump even if there is nothing unusual going on at the company.

Cycles

Many traders base their stock purchases *not* on the strength of underlying companies but on market cycles. This strategy is called *technical analysis*, one of a host of theories on how the patterns of stock trading work.

Who Knows?

The market can take on a life of its own. A trader will sell or buy merely because a neighboring trader does so. Or, analysts will read profound meanings into mundane announcements. Or, it is snowing in Las Vegas. *Who knows?*

Club Member

If your stock is part of a stock index, such as one of the Dow Jones averages or the Standard and Poor's 500, professional traders will buy or sell it applying complicated formulas that also involve futures and options. Program trading, which allows the rapid buying and selling of baskets of stocks and futures, is often blamed for sharp price movement of stocks and the market. Program trades are made independently of the fundamental strengths or weaknesses of the underlying stocks.

Unexpected World Events

Sudden news, such as the war in the Persian Gulf, would certainly impact the market. After all, the stock market has a heart, reflecting consumer psychology.

Buy or Sell Recommendations

Earnings forecasts made by analysts or brokerage houses often shake up traders. For example, a lower earnings estimate or loss expectation may put a dent on the stock concerned. Buy-or-sell recommendations in investment newsletters sometimes make a difference.

BASIC ANALYSIS FOR INVESTMENT DECISIONS

Before investing, take note of economic conditions, political environment, market status, industry surroundings, and company performance. Ideally, the intelligent investor obtains answers to four basic questions:

What is the State of the Economy?

In view of economic conditions, is it a good time to invest? Where are we in the *business cycle*? Is the boom likely to top out shortly? Is a recession near at hand? Questions in this area will vary with the stage of the business cycle.

What is the State of the Market?

Are we in the early stages of a bull market? Has the low point of a bear market been reached? Is the bull market about to top out? Questions will vary with the state of the market.

What is the State of the Industry?

If answers to the preceding questions seem favorable, then there must be an investment selection. What industries are likely to grow most rapidly? Are there any special factors that favor a particular industry?

Which Company is Desirable?

Which company (or companies) within the industry are likely to be the best performers? Which should be avoided because of poor prospects?

Table 1-1 summarizes a number of factors—not all—that will go into your investment decision-making process, ranging from economics and the external environment surrounding the investment vehicle to the company's performance measures.

BENEFITS AND COSTS OF INVESTMENT INFORMATION

A number of benefits can be derived from investment information. For example, it allows you to develop expectations of the risk–return behavior of potential investments. With better estimates of risk and return, you should be able to select investment products that demonstrate behaviors consistent with your investment goals. Access to investment information should help in making more informed and more intelligent judgments.

Investment resources may help you avoid the undesirable consequences of misrepresentation of facts by the issuer and/or underwriter of an investment vehicle.

TABLE 1-1: Factors Affecting Investment Decision-Making

Economic Analysis

Business cycles, monetary and fiscal policy, economic indicators, government policy, world events, and foreign trade, public attitude (optimism or pessimism), domestic legislation, inflation, GNP growth, unemployment, productivity, capacity utilization, interest rates

Market Analysis

Market forecasting, stock averages, stock volume, trading diary, bond indicators, short sales, open market indexes, mutual fund indicators

Industry Analysis

Industry structure, industry growth, competition, product quality, cost elements, government regulations, labor position, business cycle exposure, financial norms and standards

Company Analysis

Sales growth, earnings, dividends, quality of earnings, position in the industry, discount rates, fundamental analysis (balance sheet, income statement, and cash flow analyses), analysis of accounting policy and footnotes, management, research and development, return and risk, brands, patents, goodwill, diversification

---

Before making a decision it is often beneficial to obtain and evaluate information provided by an independent source.

Investment information costs money—despite "almost free" information from newspapers and magazines. However, chances are you'll have to pay for additional information from a financial advisory service publication such as *Value Line, Moody's,* and *Standard & Poor's.* Luckily, local public and college libraries usually have these publications. Many other sources include market data and indexes, economic and current events, and industry and company data and can be obtained from local newspapers and magazines. *NOTE: Financial advisory services can cost money, but obtaining, reading, and analyzing free information can cost time. Do a cost/benefit analysis to calculate the worth of potential information in terms of your investment program.*

DESCRIPTIVE VERSUS ANALYTICAL INFORMATION

In general, investment information is either descriptive or analytical. **Descriptive information** explains prior behavior of the economy, politics, the market, and a particular investment. **Analytical information** encompasses current data, including forecasts and recommendations about specific securities. Both kinds of information help you assess the risk and return of a particular choice to determine whether the investment conforms to your objectives.

TYPES OF INFORMATION

Investment information can be broadly divided into three categories, each covering a phase of your decision process.

Economic Trends and Current Events

Provide background and forecast data that relate to economic, political, and social trends (domestic as well as international). Such information is useful in that it provides a basis for assessing the environment in which decisions are made. As indicated earlier, rumors and news on the domestic and world fronts tend to move various investment markets.

By studying and analyzing economic trends and current events, you can learn to predict national and international economic movements. Make a habit of reading *USA Today, Wall Street Journal, Investor's Business Daily, Barron's National Business and Financial Weekly*, or the business section of your local newspaper. Also, read business magazines such as *Money, Forbes, Fortune, Business Week, U.S. News and World Report, Dun's Review*, and *Financial World*.

To learn how the national economy is doing, you might also read the *Federal Reserve Bulletin*, which includes a summary of business conditions; statistics on employment, retail prices, and other relevant trends; and the Federal Reserve Board index of industrial production. The *Bulletin* also gives information about gross national product and national income as well as interest rates and yields.

Every month the U.S. Department of Commerce issues the *Survey of Current Business* and *Business Conditions Digest*. The *Survey* includes a monthly update by industry of business information about exports, inventories, personal consumption, and labor market statistics. The *Digest* publishes cyclical indicators of economic activity, including leading indicators.

Subscription services—for example the *Blue Chip Consensus* and the *Kiplinger Washington Letter*—provide data on economic and corporate developments. They also publish forecasts of business trends and detailed economic data and analyses.

Market Information and Indexes

Market price information provides past, current, and projected prices of securities. Data on current and recent stock price behavior are contained in price quotations, available directly from your broker or from a **ticker**—an automated quotation device with a screen on which stock transactions on the exchange floor are immediately reported.

Price quotations also appear in newspapers, electronic data bases, and on TV and radio networks.

Stock market indexes show how the market is doing, and they help you pick the right stocks at the proper time. Market behavior is important: if the market is down, a particular company—even though it is financially sound—may not do well.

Stock market averages are the mathematical average prices of a group of stocks for a specified time period. These indexes measure the present price behavior of a group of stocks relative to a base value established at an earlier time. To evaluate the strength of the market, compare the averages and indexes at various times. A **bull market** exists when prices are rising; a **bear market** exists when prices are falling.

The **Dow Jones Industrial Average (DJIA)** is a measure of the performance ratings of 30 industrial stocks having wide ownership and volume activity as well as significant market value. Dow Jones calculates separate averages for public utilities, transportation, and the composite average, made up of the 30 industrials plus 20 transportations and 15 public utilities. The DJIA shows market trends, is the stock market average most commonly referred to and is often called the blue chip indicator.

Standard & Poor's has five common stock indexes: industrial (400 companies), financial (40 companies), transportation (20 companies), public utility (40 companies), and composite (500 companies). S&P also has indexes for consumer and capital goods companies as well as low-grade and high-grade common stocks. It recently introduced the Midcap 400.

The **New York Stock Exchange (NYSE) Index** includes all stocks on the exchange. The **American Stock Exchange (AMEX) Index** reflects price changes of its stocks. The **National Association of Securities Dealers Automated Quotation (NASDAQ) Index** shows over-the-counter (OTC) market activity. Its composite index consists of approximately 2,300 companies traded on the NASDAQ system.

Barron's puts out a 50-stock average as well as the average price of the 20 most active and 20 lowest priced stocks. Other averages and indexes are published by **Moody's** and **Value Line**. Value Line includes a composite of 1,700 companies as an illustration of the overall behavior of the stock market or its particular segments. Indicators of bond performance state bond prices as a percent of par. Bond yields show the return the bondholder receives if he or she holds the bond to maturity. Bond yields are generally quoted for a group of bonds that are of similar type and quality. You'll find bond yield information in various sources including the *Federal Reserve Bulletin*, the *Wall Street Journal*, *Standard & Poor's*, and *Barron's*.

Industry and Company Analysis

Provide background as well as forecast data on specific industries and companies. This type of information is used by securities investors to assess the outlook in a given industry and/or company. Because it is company oriented, this category of data is most relevant to stock, bond, or option investments.

Investment analysts—or securities analysts as they are sometimes called—furnish recommendations to clients for a fee. Some also manage their clients' investment portfolios and give tax advice.

Investment advisers include stockbrokers, trust department bank officers (who invest funds held in trust for clients), employees of subscription services, and investment advisory firms. Most advisory firms employ specialists in certain industries or types of portfolios.

Before they pick a particular company, investment analysts usually select an industry that looks good. You can get data on a particular industry from trade publications, such as *Public Utilities Fortnightly*.

Financial services provide financial information and analysis, but most do not make recommendations. Financial advisory reports from **Standard & Poor's**, **Moody's**, and **Value Line** usually present one company's financial history, current financial position, and future expectations; supplements are issued periodically. Examples include:

- Standard & Poor's: Publishes *Corporate Records, Stock Guide, Bond Guide, Analysts Handbook, Industry Survey*, the *Outlook*, and *Opportunities in Convertible Bonds*.
- Moody's: Publishes manuals (**Bond Record, Bond Survey,** *Manuals,* and **Stock Survey**).
- Value Line Investor Service: Publishes the *Value Line Investment Survey*.
- Morningstar, Inc.: Publishes one of the best-known sources of information on Mutual Funds, *Mutual Fund Values.*
- Dun & Bradstreet: Issues *Key Business Ratios, Million Dollar Directory*, and *Billion Dollar Directory*.
- Dow Jones-Irwin: Publishes the *Business Almanac.*

Brokerage reports analyze companies and make recommendations to buy, hold, or sell certain stocks. They also offer investment strategies and analyze specific industries and companies.

As mentioned, you can find corporate financial data in a company's annual report in the form of financial statements and disclosures. Securities and Exchange Commission (SEC) *Form 10-K* contains detailed information on companies that have securities listed on the stock exchanges. For a public offering of a new issue, you must obtain the *prospectus*. Various company reports and SEC requirements will be discussed in Chapter 5.

MICROCOMPUTERS AND ELECTRONIC DATA BASES

A microcomputer can give you immediate access to business data. It will also enable you to analyze that data quickly and to compute a rating for all of your funds or stocks. Programs are available for recordkeeping, graphics (for plotting prices), and portfolio management. Software helps identify securities that meet specific criteria and improves the timing of buys and sells. Specific software features include:

- Programs that allow you to perform sophisticated fundamental and technical analyses.
- Investment maintenance that helps you to keep track of your investments in terms of shares, cost, and revenue.

• Programs equipped with the price and dividend history of certain securities. This software can handle stock splits, dividends, distributions, and fractional shares.

• Investment monitoring that helps you decide whether to purchase or sell a stock. This software lets you keep track of your portfolio by using investment information in data bases. You can add new prices to the files or modify old ones. Dividend information is also available.

• On-line broker access. Some brokers are on line so that a client can buy and sell securities from the comfort of home.

• Tax investment assistance so you can consider the tax aspects of certain securities. For example, this software can record transactions and assist in matching sell transactions with existing positions to minimize the tax liability applicable to capital gains and losses. The software also helps you prepare tax schedules and reports, such as Schedule D of IRS Form 1040.

Dow Jones News/Retrieval contains many data bases including current and historical Dow Jones Quotes, Corporate Earnings Estimator (earnings per share estimates), Disclosure II (corporate financial statements and footnote data), Media General Financial Services (stock performance–related ratios; comparisons-to-market indicators; bond, mutual fund, and money market information), Merrill Lynch Research Service, Weekly Economic Survey and Update (economic data, trends, and analysis), and Wall Street Highlights.

CompuServe's Executive Information Service, published by Investors Management Science Company (a subsidiary of Standard & Poor's), provides financial data on companies; economic information and projections; money market trends; and price, dividend, and earnings results and forecasts (including Value Line and Standard and Poor's information). CompuServe's **MicroQuote** provides a record of market prices, dividends, and interest paid on securities. CompuServe's mainframe will figure the worth of a portfolio for transfer to your terminal.

Most investment programs communicate through computer terminals with outside data bases such as Dow Jones News/Retrieval and various brokerage houses. To take advantage of these sources you will need a **modem**—a device that lets you communicate with other computers. Some programs analyze and create charts of the technical behavior of price movements as well as support and resistance lines; others evaluate the financial statements. These computerized investment programs can accommodate and track stocks, bonds, Treasury securities, options, warrants, mutual funds, commodities. Some of the popular programs include the **Dow-Jones Market Analyzer**, the **Dow-Jones Microscope**, the **Dow-Jones Investment Evaluator,** and **Value Line's Value/Screen and ValuePak.**

CompuStat provides 20 years of annual financial data for over 3,000 companies. Most balance sheet and income statement items are available. CompuStat tapes are compiled by Standard & Poor's. **Interactive Data Corporation** also provides the same information found on CompuStat tapes. **CRSP tapes**, maintained by the University of Chicago's Center for Research in Security Prices (CRSP), provide information on earnings, dividends, stock prices, dates of mergers, stock splits, stock dividends, and the like. Value Line also has made computer tapes of its 1,700 companies available.

Datext, Inc., offers corporate financial information on compact disks, including financial statements, SEC documents, and investment analysts' reports.

For real estate investments, **Howard Soft's Real Estate Analyzer** can make property projections based on considerations of changes in interest rates, inflation, and rental payments. Included is an after-tax analysis of cash flow and profitability.

The **Federal Trade Commission (FTC)** has aggregate industry data, and the **Federal Reserve Bank of St. Louis** has tapes of monetary data that are available to analysts and investors.

You can find a detailed list of investment software in chapter 12 of this book and in the **Individual Investor's Guide to Computerized Investing,** by the American Association of Individual Investors (International Publishing Corporation).

NONTRADITIONAL MARKETS

For purposes of this section, we define *nontraditional* as being outside the realm of stocks, bonds, and government securities. A major area that received increased attention during the 1980s was commodities and financial futures.

Commodity Yearbook, a yearly publication, is a key source of information on commodity futures. The *Yearbook* runs several feature articles of investment interest, covering commodities or situations currently in the forefront of commodities trading. It also covers each traded commodity, from alcohol to zinc. For example, corn is covered in six pages, the first of which is a description of the corn crop and occurrences for the current year; the next five pages cover data in tabular form for the past 13 years. The tables show world production of corn, acreage, supply in the United States, and, of course, the weekly high-low-close of the nearest month's futures price. Each commodity has a similarly detailed evaluation and statistical summary. The *Yearbook* is supplemented three times a year by the *Commodity Yearbook Statistical Abstract.*

Other publications about commodities come from mainline brokerage houses and specialty commodities brokers. In addition, the commodities exchanges publish informative booklets and newsletters. The International Monetary Market publishes the *I.M.M. Weekly Report,* which discusses the interest rate markets, the foreign exchange markets, and gold. It also presents weekly prices for all interest rate futures, foreign exchange markets, gold, and selected cash market information such as the federal funds rate and the prime rate. The Chicago Board of Trade publishes the *Interest Rate Futures Newsletter.* As investors (speculators) continue to become active in these markets, they can be sure to find more available data.

The Scott Publishing Company, long involved in the philatelic (stamp) market, turns out annual stamp catalogs, complete with pictures. Recently, Scott added *Stamp Market Update*, a quarterly report on current Philatelic trends and prices. It features prices of major U.S. stamps and popular foreign stamps; information for specialized collectors; investment opportunities and strategies as disclosed by recognized experts; and special articles, statistical tables, and graphs.

Appendix to Chapter 1

General Investment Publications

Following is a representative list of information sources in the field of investments. Mailing information can be found in Chapter 13.

Investor's Business Daily

Published by William O'Neil & Co., Inc., *Investor's Business Daily* reports daily coverage of: "The Top Story" (most important news event of the day); "The Economy" (sophisticated analysis of current economic topics and government economic reports); "National Issue/Business" (major national business issue); "Leaders and Success" (profiles of successful people and companies); "Investor's Corner" (wide variety of personal finance topics including investment ideas); "Today's News Digest" (35-40 brief but important news items of the day).

Among other things, *Investor's Business Daily* provides what they call "Smarter Stock Tables" that feature *three* key rankings on all 6,000 publicly-traded issues They are: "Earnings Per Share Rank" (compares a company's 5-year earnings growth record to all other publicly-traded corporations; "Relative Strength Rank" (measures a stock's price performance over the past year compared to all other stocks); "Volume % Change" (measures a stock's trading volume over the last 50 days to alert an investor to any unusual trading activity).

Wall Street Journal

Published by Dow Jones, the *Wall Street Journal* is read by millions of investors who want to keep up with the economy and business environment. Virtually all "market movers," as discussed in Chapter 1, are covered. The *Journal* reports daily comprehensive coverage of: regular feature articles on labor, business, economics, personal investing, technology, world events, and taxes; corporate announcements of all kinds; new offerings of stock and bonds as advertised by investment bankers; prices of actively traded securities, presented by the market in which they trade; common and preferred stock prices, organized by exchange and over-the-counter markets; many other price data, such as prices of government Treasury bills, notes and bonds, mutual funds, put and call prices from option exchanges, government agency securities, foreign exchange prices, and commodities futures prices, all of which are listed by category and exchange. Finally, the *Journal* publishes an educational edition that explains how to read it and interprets some of the data.

Barron's National Business and Financial Weekly

Also published by Dow Jones (every Monday), *Barron's* contains regular features on dividends, put and call options, international stock markets, commodities, a review of the stock market, and many pages of prices and financial statistics. *Barron's* takes a weekly perspective and summarizes the previous week's market behavior. It also regularly analyzes several companies in its "Investment News and Views" section. The common stock section provides high-low-close prices and volume; it also informs investors as to the latest earnings per share, dividends declared, dividend record, and payable dates. The "Market Laboratory" fills the last eight pages of each issue. Data on major stock and bond markets are presented with the week's market statistics.

Forbes

Forbes is a biweekly magazine featuring several corporate management interviews. This management-oriented approach showcases various management styles and provides a look into the qualitative factors of securities analysis. Several regular columnists discuss investment topics from a diversified perspective.

Business Week

Somewhat broader in nature than *Forbes*, *Business Week* magazine, published weekly by McGraw-Hill, Inc., is widely circulated and includes an update on a number of economic variables. These include interest rates, electricity consumption, and market prices; also featured are articles on specific industries and companies. The "Corporate Strategy" section, which discusses a company's future direction, is first-rate.

Fortune

Published biweekly and known for its coverage of industry problems and specific company analysis, *Fortune* has several regular features that make interesting reading. The "Business Roundup" section usually deals with a major business concern—the federal budget, inflation, or productivity. "Personal Investing" is always thought provoking and presents ideas and analyses for the average investor.

Money

Money magazine, a monthly with an additional special issue in December, covers broad areas of personal finance—investments, credit management, money management, insurance, taxes, college education, and retirement planning. Its well-known "Small Investor's Index" tracks the performance of a typical investor's holdings.

2

General Market Information/Benchmarks

OVERVIEW

Market price information provides past, current, and projected prices of securities. As mentioned in Chapter 1, data on current and recent stock price behavior are contained in price quotations, available from your broker, the business pages of local newspapers, the financial section of national newspapers (such as *USA Today*), financial and investment dailies (such as the *Wall Street Journal* and *Investor's Business Daily*), a ticker, and TV networks.

STOCK MARKET AVERAGES AND INDEXES

Market indexes and averages are gauges used to track performance for stocks and bonds. In *theory*, an **average** is the simple or appropriately weighted arithmetic mean, whereas, an **index** is an average expressed in percentage changes from a base year or from the previous month. In *practice*, however, the distinction is not all that clear.

A number of stock market indexes and averages are available. Each market has several indexes published by Dow Jones, Standard & Poor's, and other financial services. Different investors prefer different indexes. Indexes and averages are also used as the underlying value of index futures and index options.

Many indexes and averages track the performance of groups of securities. Each national and regional stock exchange has its own index. The major reporting companies (e.g., Standard & Poor's and Value Line) have long-established indexes. Specific industry sectors (e.g., utilities, health care, transportation, financial services) have their own indexes.

Of all indexes and averages pertaining to the stock market, none receives as much financial news attention as the Dow Jones Industrial Average.

Dow Jones Averages

The **Dow Jones Industrial Average (DJIA)** is the most widely used and watched market index of four stock averages compiled by the *Wall Street Journal*. This average

FIGURE 2-1: The Dow Jones Averages

INDUSTRIALS—30

Allied Sig.	Goodyear
Alum Co	IBM
Amer Exp	Int'l Paper
AT&T	McDonald's
Beth Steel	Merck
Boeing	Minn M&M
Caterpillar	Morgan (J.P.)
Chevron	Phillip Morris
Coca-Cola	Proc Gamb
Disney(Walt)	Sears
Du Pont	Texaco
Eastman	Union Carbide
Exxon	United Tech
Gen Electric	Westinghouse
Gen Motors	Woolworth

TRANSPORTATION—20

AMR Corp.	Fed Express
Airbrn Freigt	Norfolk So
Alaska Air	Roadway Svcs
Amer Pres	Ryder System
Burlington	Santa Fe
Caro Freight	Southwest Airl
Cons Freight	UAL Corp.
Cons Rail	Union Pac
CSX Corp.	USAir
Delta Air	Xtra Corp.

UTILITIES—15

Am El Power	Niag Mohawk
Arkla Inc.	Pacific G&E
Centerior	Panhandle
Comwl Edis	Peoples En
Cons Edison	Phila Elec
Cons N Gas	Pub Serv E
Detroit Edis	SCEcorp
Houston Ind	

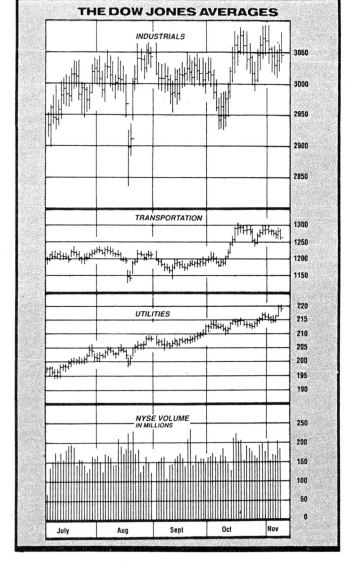

THE DOW JONES AVERAGES

consists of 30 large companies and is considered a "blue chip" (stocks of very high quality) index. Figure 2-1 lists the stocks that make up three of the Dow Jones stock averages.

FIGURE 2-2: Stock Market Data Bank—*Wall Street Journal*

| STOCK MARKET DATA BANK | | | | | | 5/2/91 | | | | |

MAJOR INDEXES

HIGH	LOW (12 MOS)		CLOSE	NET CHG	% CHG	12 MO CHG	% CHG	FROM 12/31	% CHG
DOW JONES AVERAGES									
3004.46	2365.10	30 Industrials	2938.61 +	8.41 +	0.29	+ 242.44	+ 8.99	+ 304.95	+ 11.58
1212.77	821.93	20 Transportation	x1168.37 +	4.23 +	0.36	+ 27.90	+ 2.45	+ 258.14	+ 28.36
220.89	190.96	15 Utilities	211.90 −	0.19 −	0.09	+ 5.79	+ 2.81	+ 2.20	+ 1.05
1070.03	839.00	65 Composite	x1051.80 +	2.65 +	0.25	+ 59.18	+ 5.96	+ 131.19	+ 14.25
364.73	272.91	Equity Mkt. Index	355.27 +	0.30 +	0.08	+ 42.87	+13.72	+ 49.68	+ 16.26
NEW YORK STOCK EXCHANGE									
213.21	162.20	Composite	208.26 +	0.23 +	0.11	+ 24.29	+13.20	+ 27.77	+ 15.39
267.25	200.80	Industrials	260.97 +	0.32 +	0.12	+ 35.22	+15.60	+ 37.37	+ 16.71
95.87	80.96	Utilities	92.43 −	0.39 −	0.42	+ 2.60	+ 2.89	+ 1.13	+ 1.24
182.55	127.25	Transportation	170.93 +	0.46 +	0.27	+ 1.56	+ 0.92	+ 29.44	+ 20.81
158.19	103.26	Finance	153.44 +	0.97 +	0.64	+ 16.42	+11.98	+ 31.37	+ 25.70
STANDARD & POOR'S INDEXES									
390.45	295.46	500 Index	380.52 +	0.23 +	0.06	+ 44.95	+13.40	+ 50.30	+ 15.23
463.12	346.86	Industrials	451.51 +	0.44 +	0.10	+ 60.39	+15.44	+ 64.09	+ 16.54
291.30	208.77	Transportation	283.05 +	0.24 +	0.08	+ 11.70	+ 4.31	+ 48.38	+ 20.62
147.30	124.60	Utilities	141.81 −	1.04 −	0.73	+ 3.69	+ 2.67	− 1.78	− 1.24
31.69	18.80	Financials	30.41 +	0.24 +	0.80	+ 3.26	+12.01	+ 6.98	+ 29.79
NASDAQ									
511.31	325.44	Composite	491.13 +	3.28 +	0.67	+ 65.69	+15.44	+ 117.29	+ 31.37
575.67	344.11	Industrials	545.57 +	4.92 +	0.91	+ 98.69	+22.08	+ 139.52	+ 34.36
585.08	379.36	Insurance	552.86 +	1.07 +	0.19	+ 76.97	+16.17	+ 101.02	+ 22.36
357.28	235.25	Banks	331.24 +	1.13 +	0.34	− 15.38	− 4.44	+ 76.33	+ 29.94
225.92	142.41	Nat. Mkt. Comp.	216.62 +	1.49 +	0.69	+ 30.37	+16.31	+ 51.45	+ 31.15
229.93	135.93	Nat. Mkt. Indus.	217.25 +	2.03 +	0.94	+ 40.96	+23.23	+ 54.91	+ 33.82
OTHERS									
373.40	287.79	Amex	363.54 +	1.57 +	0.43	+ 18.57	+ 5.38	+ 55.43	+ 17.99
250.56	179.55	Value-Line (geom.)	240.61 +	1.03 +	0.43	+ 5.93	+ 2.53	+ 44.62	+ 22.77
178.70	118.82	Russell 2000	173.64 +	1.44 +	0.84	+ 13.92	+ 8.72	+ 41.45	+ 31.36
3731.48	2772.31	Wilshire 5000	3636.42 +	7.59 +	0.21	+ 421.15	+13.10	+ 535.07	+ 17.25

30 Industrials
20 Transportation
15 Utility

1,700 Companies

The DJIA represents about 20 percent of the market value of the New York Stock Exchange (NYSE) stocks. In addition to the three averages represented in Figure 2-1 is a fourth average, a composite of the 30 industrials, 20 transportations, and 15 utilities. Thus, this composite average, called the **Dow Jones Composite** or **65 Stock Average** or **65 Composite**, totals 65 stocks (see Figure 2-2). The DJIA would have been a simple average of 30 blue chip stocks, but when a firm split its stock price, the average had to be adjusted in some manner. In fact, the divisor is changed from time to time to maintain continuity of the average. The Dow Jones averages are designed to indicate broad movements in the securities markets.

The *Dow Jones Equity Market Index* is a broad-based index of the share prices of about 750 companies. These companies were chosen to reflect the movements of over 80 percent of the broad stock market, including NYSE, American

Stock Exchange, and over-the-counter (OTC) issues. The index is subdivided into 82 industry groups clustered into nine Sectors that represent larger segments of the U.S. economy. Unlike Dow Jones Averages, the index is capitalization-weighted, and its based level of 100 was assigned on June 30, 1982.

Barron's Indexes

Barron's, also a publication of Dow Jones, compiles **Barron's Low Price Stock Index** (Figure 2-3) and **Barron's 50 Stock Average** (Figure 2-4), which meets the needs of small investors. *Barron's* also publishes a weekly average, **Barron's Group Stock Averages**, covering 32 industry groups. These averages are useful to the investor who follows the performance of a specific industry relative to the general market.

Standard & Poor's (S&P) Indexes

Standard & Poor's Corporation publishes several indexes, including the two most widely used —the **S&P 400 Stock Index** and the **S&P 500 Stock Index**, shown in Figure 2-5. The S&P 400 is composed of 400 industrial common stocks of companies listed on the NYSE, and the S&P 500 Stock Index consists of the 400 industrials, 60 utilities and transportation stocks, and 40 financial issues. These two indexes, used as broad measures of the market direction, are also frequently used as proxies for market return when the systematic risk measure (beta) of individual stocks and portfolios is computed. *Beta* will be discussed in Chapter 7 (Common Stocks and Preferred Stocks) and Chapter 9 (Mutual Funds). The S&P 500 Stock Index is one of the U.S. Commerce Department's 11 leading economic indicators, representing some 80 percent of the market value of all issues traded on the NYSE. The purpose of the S&P 500 is to portray the pattern of common stock price movement. For this reason, many investors use the S&P 500 as a yardstick to help evaluate the performance of mutual funds.

The Standard & Poor's 100 Stock Index consists of stocks for which options are listed on the Chicago Board Options Exchange (CBOE). The S&P 100 Stock Index and the S&P Midcap Index are shown in Figures 2-5 and 2-6.

The S&P's newly created index, the S&P MidCap Index, became available June 19, 1991. The index is a market-valued index and tracks the market behavior of 400 medium-sized U.S. companies with a median market capitalization of $610 million, where market capitalization is defined as stock price times shares outstanding. About 62 percent of the companies in the MidCap Index are listed on the NYSE; 35 percent on the NASDAQ; and 3 percent on the AMEX. The list of stocks included in the index appears in Figure 2-6. *NOTE: This index fills a void in that it provides investors and investment managers with a new analytical tool for a potentially lucrative but volatile sector of the market. You can find the best values in small and medium stocks because they have lower price/earnings (P/E) ratios and large growth rates. The popular S&P 500 Index tracks only large companies.*

FIGURE 2-3: *Barron's* "Market Laboratory" —Stocks

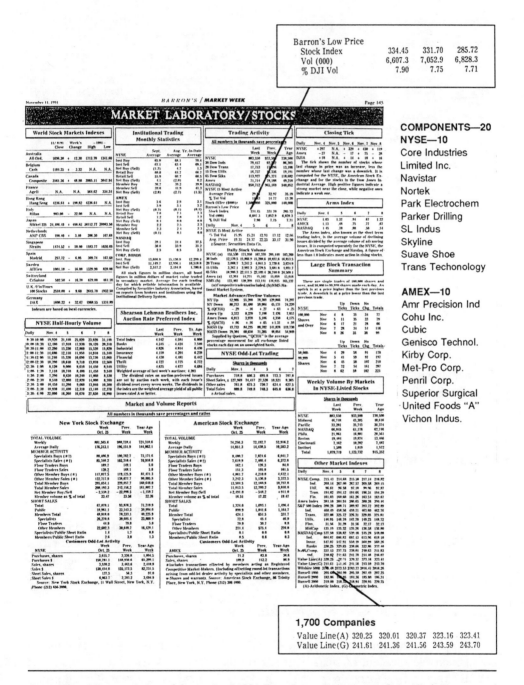

Barron's Low Price			
Stock Index	334.45	331.70	285.72
Vol (000)	6,607.3	7,052.9	6,828.3
% DJI Vol	7.90	7.75	7.71

COMPONENTS—20

NYSE—10

Core Industries
Limited Inc.
Navistar
Nortek
Park Electrochem
Parker Drilling
SL Indus
Skyline
Suave Shoe
Trans Techonology

AMEX—10

Amr Precision Ind
Cohu Inc.
Cubic
Genisco Technol.
Kirby Corp.
Met-Pro Corp.
Penril Corp.
Superior Surgical
United Foods "A"
Vichon Indus.

1,700 Companies					
Value Line(A)	320.25	320.01	320.37	323.16	323.41
Value Line(G)	241.61	241.36	241.56	243.59	243.70

FIGURE 2-4: *Barron's* 50-Stock Average

COMPONENTS—50

Allied Signal	Gannett Co.	PPG
Amer. Brands	Gen Elec.	Pfizer
Amer. T&T	Gen Mills	Proc & Gam
Amoco	Gen Motors	Raytheon
Baxter Trav	Goodyear	Schlumberger
Bell South	Hewlett Pack	Sou Call Edis
Boeing	IBM	Timken
CPC Int'l	Inco Ltd.	TRW
CSX	Inland Steel	Union Carbide
Caterpillar	James River	Union Pac
Citicorp	Kellog	United Tech
Coca Cola	Merck	VulcanMat
Delta Air	Minn Mng M	Westinghouse
Detroit Edis	Mobil	Weyerhaeusr
Donnelly,RR	Monsanto	Wisc Energy
Du Pont	Motorola	Wrigley
GATX	Norfolk So	

	Oct. 31 1991	Oct. 24 1991	Oct. 1990
Average price index	1566	1550	1222
Projected quarterly earn	17.76	19.57	28.79
Annualized projected earn	71.04	78.28	115.16
Annualized projected P/E	22.0	19.8	10.6
Five-year average earn	100.15	99.92	96.94
Five-year average P/E	15.6	15.5	12.6
Year-end earn	74.29	83.19	109.62
Year-end P/E	21.1	18.6	11.1
Year-end earns yield, %	4.7	5.4	9.0
Best grade bond yields, %	8.41	8.44	9.41
Bond yields/stock ylds, %	1.79	1.56	1.05
Actual year-end divs	53.08	53.08	48.32
Actual yr-end divs yld, %	3.39	3.42	3.95

Value Line Average

The Value Line average is a measure of some 1,700 companies (included in the *Value Line Survey*) from the NYSE, AMEX, and OTC market. The *Wall Street Journal* shows the Value Line Geometric Index (Figure 2-2), whereas *Barron's* shows both the Geometric Index and the Arithmetic Index (Figure 2-3). Some individual investors use these indexes, because they more closely correspond to the variety of stocks small investors may have in their portfolios.

Other Market Indexes

Each exchange publishes its own market indexes. The NYSE publishes a composite index as well as an industrial, utility, transportation, and financial index. AMEX compiles two major indexes—the **AMEX Market Value Index (AMVI)** (Figure 2-2) and the **AMEX Major Market Index**. The **National Association of Securities Dealers (NASD)** also publishes several indexes—**NASDAQ OTC** composite, insurance, industrial, and banking indexes—that represent companies in the OTC market.

The NYSE Composite Stock Index

The **NYSE Composite Stock Index** (Figure 2-2), established in 1966, provides a comprehensive measure of market trends on the New York Stock Exchange. The NYSE Composite is made up of four subindexes: industrials, transportation, utilities, and financials. This index is based on multiplying the per share price of the stock by the number of shares outstanding. Thus the total amount of equity dollars represented

---

FIGURE 2-5: S&P Indexes

Standard & Poor's indexes	High	Low	Close	Chg.
Indust	456.84	454.58	454.70	—0.32
Transpt	292.67	290.97	291.20	—1.47
Utilities	137.18	136.59	136.64	—0.07
Financl	30.48	30.35	30.37	—0.08
MidCap 400	126.12	125.73	126.05	+0.20
500 Stocks	382.86	381.13	381.18	—0.36
100 Stocks	365.11	362.95	363.11	—0.25

400 Industrials
40 Utilities
40 Financials
20 Transportation

---

by all shares of each issue can be determined. This total market value (the sum of the total market value of all common stock issues listed on the NYSE) is then expressed relative to the market value at the time the index was initiated in 1966. An arbitrary value of 50 is taken as the base value for that year, and the movement of stock prices is measured from there. The arithmetic procedure—grossly oversimplified here—is to take the current total market value of all listed securities, divide that sum by the market value of all listed securities in 1966, and multiply the result by 50.

Changes in the NYSE Composite Index are reported every half-hour on ticker tape and are available to traders even more frequently. Besides a general pulse of the market, the index also provides the base for options written on the index and for futures contracts.

Wilshire 5000 and 6000 Equity Indexes; Russell 1000, 2000, and 3000 Indexes

Wilshire indexes, published by Wilshire Associates of Santa Monica, California, represent the market value of 5,000 or 6,000 NYSE, AMEX, and OTC issues. *NOTE: One point in this index is equivalent to $1 billion. For example, a 700-point increase means that $700 billion is poured into the stock market or economy, which is considered positive for the economy.*

Russell indexes, developed by Frank Russell Co., Tacoma, Washington, are value-weighted indexes consisting of 1,000, 2,000, or 3,000 small market value stocks. Both the Wilshire and Russell indexes are shown in Figure 2-2.

Bond Market Indicators

Barron's publishes an index of 20 bonds, 10 utility bonds, and 10 industrial bonds as an average of the bond market. These averages are shown in *Barron's* **"Market Laboratory"** section (see Figure 2-7). Dow Jones also publishes two major bond

FIGURE 2-6: S&P's MidCap Index Components

Stock index list

Stocks in 400 domestic companies included in the Standard & Poor's MidCap Index, a new indicator designed to track the performance of medium-capitalization stocks. OC companies are in bold.

NYSE—62%
NASDAQ—35%
AMEX—3%

Federal Home Loan Mort.	GBI Industries	LEGENT Corp.	LSI Logic
Burlington Resources	Centocor Inc.	SouthTrust Corp.	Cross (A.T.) Class "A"
General Motors Cl. "E"	BMC Software	CalMat Co.	Cordis Corp.
McCaw Cellular Cl. "A"	Manufacturers National	Affiliated Publications "A"	Dauphin Deposit
Novell Inc.	Provident Life & Acc. "B	GATX Corp.	Gibson Greetings
Wachovia Corp.	First Financial Mgt.	Noble Affiliates	Vanguard Cellular Sys.
Sun Microsystems	Comdisco Inc.	NCH Corp.	Neutrogena Corp.
Costco Wholesale	First of America Bank	Crompton & Knowles	Arvin Industries
Morgan Stanley Group	Multimedia Inc.	Bob Evans Farms	Carpenter Technology
U.S. Surgical	Avnet Inc.	Critical Care America	Symantec Corp.
Great Lakes Chemical	Carter-Wallace	Crestar Financial	City National
Tyson Foods Class "A"	Delmarva Power & Light	Silicon Graphics	Smith International
Laidlaw Inc. Class "B"	Valero Energy	XOMA Corp.	Dreyer's Grand Ice Cr.
American Barrick Res.	Policy Management Sys.	Family Dollar Stores	Mid-Amer. Waste Sys.
Medco Containment	Cintas Corp.	Dell Computer Corp.	Sanford Corp.
Aon Corp.	Fruit of the Loom "A"	International Multifoods	Wausau Paper Mills
Washington Post "B"	Pinnacle West Capital	Service Merchandise	West One Bancorp
U.S. HealthCare Inc.	Witco Corp.	Leggett & Platt	Westmark International
Castle & Cooke	Olin Corp.	Belo (A.H.) Class "A"	Octel Communications
Northeast Utilities	Bergen Brunswig "A"	Cetus Corp.	Lawter International
Tambrands Inc.	Cisco Systems	Savannah Foods & Ind.	Durr-Fillauer Medical
Wisconsin Energy Corp.	Minnesota Power & Light	Church & Dwight	PacifiCare Health Sys.
Freeport McMoRan	Idaho Power	Golden Nugget	Puritan-Bennett
Potomac Electric Power	Mylan Labs	Stewart & Stevenson	Air & Water Tech. "A"
Florida Progress	LG&E Energy	Nevada Power	Chesapeake Corp.
Bank of New York	Rochester Telephone	Commun. Satellite	Tidewater Inc.
Coca-Cola Enterprises	Allegheny Ludlum	Washington Gas Light	American President Cos.
Allegheny Power System	Portland General Corp.	Diamond Shamrock	Atlantic Southeast Air
CMS Energy	Wilmington Trust	HON Industries	Lincoln Telecom.
So. New Eng. Telecom	LAC Minerals	Iowa-Illinois Gas & El. •	MAXXAM Inc.
Circus Circus Enterprises	Omnicom Group	Duty Free International	Federal-Mogul
Sigma-Aldrich	Varian Associates	Georgia Gulf Corp.	VeriFone Inc.
TECO Energy	Century Telephone Ent.	Battle Mountain Gold	Houghton Mifflin
Fifth Third Bancorp	Tiffany & Co.	Rollins Inc.	Lands' End
Lyondell Petrochemical	Marshall & Ilsley	Dexter Corp.	Lawson Products
Lubrizol Corp.	Thermo Electron	Sbarro Inc.	Convex Computer
N. England Elec.Sys.	Transatlantic Holdings	Hancock Fabrics	TCA Cable TV
American Family	First Alabama Banc.	Unifi Inc.	Standard Register
Flight Safety International	Mercantile Bankshares	Diebold Inc.	MIPS Computer Systems
Cincinnati Gas & Electric	Atlantic Energy	Wallace Computer Svs.	Kennametal Inc.
Consolidated Papers	Brooklyn Union Gas	Micron Technology	Pic'n'Save
Kemper Corp.	CUC International	Sensormatic Electronics	MNC Financial
Sinroge Technology	Edwards (AG) Inc.	Trinity Industries	Intelligent Electronics
Interpublic Gr. Cos.	Edison Brothers Stores	Universal Corp.	Measurex Corp.
State St. Boston	Office Depot	Schwab (Chas) Corp.	Kaydon Corp.
HAPCO Inc.	Horsco Corp.	Amtek Inc.	Banta Corp.
New York State E&G	Wellman Inc.	UJB Financial	Linear Technology Corp.
Pioneer Hi-Bred Intl.	Hawaiian Electric Ind.	Caesars World	Exabyte Corp.
Sonoco Products	Surgical Care Affiliates	Central Fidelity Banks	Albany International "A"
KeyCorp	Borland International	Illinois Central Corp.	Leslie Fay Companies
SCANA Corp.	Shaw Industries	MCN Corp.	Michael Foods
McCormick & Co.	FHP International Corp.	Federal Signal	Pentair Inc.
Forest Labs	Aldus Corp.	Central Maine Power	Morrison Inc.
Oklahoma Gas & Electric	Genzyme Corp.	Beckman Instruments	Network Systems
First Bank System	SciMed Life Systems	Colonial Companies "B"	Cleveland-Cliffs
Betz Laboratories	Longview Fibre	Kansas City So. Ind.	KnowledgeWare Inc.
Bear Stearns Companies	Questar Corp.	CPI Corp.	Datascope Corp.
Equifax Inc.	Atlanta Gas Light	Danaher Corp.	Lukens Inc.
Anadarko Petroleum	National Fuel Gas	First Security	Heilig-Meyers
Illinois Power	Schulman (A.)	Toleflex Inc.	Angelica Corp.
Allergan Inc.	Biogen Inc.	Analog Devices	Parker Drilling
NIPSCO Industries	Mentor Graphics	Global Marine	Nabors Industries
United Healthcare	Magma Power	Miller (Herman)	National Pizza
Franklin Resources	Lance Inc.	NovaCare	Anthem Electronics
Willamette Industries	Cracker Bar. Old Co.	Waban Inc.	OEA Inc.
Molex Inc.	Chris-Craft Industries	Barod Corp.	National Presto Ind.
Progressive Corp., Ohio	Ivax Corp.	Applied Materials	Applied Bioscience
Dreyfus Corp.	Brinker International	Xilinx Inc.	Toradyne Inc.
Hartford Steam B. Ins.	Cadence Des. Sys.	ADC Telecom.	Donaldson Co.
Northern Trust	AST Research	Home Shopping	Liberty National Bancorp
Dean Foods	Cypress Semiconductor	HEALTHSOUTH Rehab	Claire's Stores
Puget Sound Power & L.	WPL Holdings	Flowers Industries	Black Hills Corp.
Stryker Corp.	T2 Medical Inc.	Clayton Homes	Indiana Energy
Bancorp Hawaii	Ranger Oil Ltd.	Sizzler International	
Acuson Corp.	Tosco Corp.	PHH Corp.	A & W Brands
Alexander & Baldwin	SynOptics Commun.	INB Financial Corp	Seagull Energy
Murphy Oil	Meridian Bancorp	Genetics Institute	Altera Corp.
Sowest. Public Service	Seagate Technology	Ferro Corp.	BJ Services
Conner Peripherals	Apache Corp.	Advanced Telecom.	Sealed Air
Sundstrand Corp.	Topps Co.	Sequa Corp. Class "A"	Duriron Co.
Public Service of Colo.	UtiliCorp United	Information Resource	Thiokol Corp.
Kelly Services "A"	RPM Inc.	Media General Class "A"	Nellcor Inc.
Kansas City Power & L.	First Virginia Banks	Mercantile Bancorp	Parametic Technology
Montana Power	First Brands Corp.	Goulds Pumps	Ennis Business Forms
Penn Central	Corona Corp. "A"	First Tennessee National	MagneTek Inc.
Vons Companies	Smucker (J.M.)	Quantum Corp.	Modine Manufacturing
Comerica Inc.	Stratum Computer	Diagnostic Product	Brush Wellman
Loctite Corp.	Harley-Davidson	HealthCare COMPARE	Sterling Chemicals
Merry-Go-Round Ent.	Precision Castparts	Nordson Corp.	Varco International
Calgon Carbon	Continental Bank	Jacobs Eng. Group	Alaska Air Group
Adobe Systems	Stanhome Inc.	Airborne Freight	Sequent Computer Sys.
Keystone International	Hanna (M.A.) Co.	Symbol Technologies	Quaker State Corp.
Medical Care Intl.	U.S. Shoe	Structural Dynamics Res.	GonCorp
Chiron Corp.	Immunex Corp.	Central Louisiana Electric	International Technology
IPALCO Enterprises	Sotheby's Holding Cl. "A"	Enterra Corp.	Western Publishing
Southwest Airlines	Overseas Shipholding	Rohr Industries	Southdown Inc.
Universal Foods	Watts Industries "A"	Synergen Inc.	Cirrus Logic
Bowater Inc.	Oregon Steel Mills	Continental Medical Sys.	Carlisle Companies
Telephone & Data Sys.	Intl. Game Tech.	Public Serv. N. Mexico	Reynolds & Reynolds "A"
IMC Fertilizer Group	Intl. Dairy Queen "A"	Fuller (HB)	American Waste Svs.

Source: The Associated Press

averages—the **Dow Jones 20 Bond Average,** representative of six different bond groups, and the **Dow Jones Municipal Bond Yield Average** (Figure 2-8). **Bond yields** are key measures of bond performance. Indexes are published by Shearson Lehman Hutton, Merrill Lynch, and others (Figure 2-8).

Mutual Fund Averages

Lipper Analytical Services compiles the **Lipper Mutual Fund Performance Averages,** published weekly in *Barron's.* As shown in Figure 2-9, the performance of all mutual funds is ranked quarterly and annually by type of fund. Observe how certain types of funds did better or worse and how their performance changed with differing periods of measurement. Lipper publishes many basic fund indexes including ones for growth funds, growth and income funds, and balanced funds. Mutual fund managers attempt to outperform the average as well as all other funds in each category.

International Stock Averages

The *Wall Street Journal* provides daily information on stock market averages around the globe. Figure 2-10 shows different market indicators for price changes in foreign markets, such as the **Tokyo Nikkei Average.** *Forbes* provides **AMEX International Market Index,** which is a value-weighted index comprising 50 largest **American Deposit Receipts (ADRs).**

Commodity Research Bureau (CRB) Composite Futures Index

The **CRB Composite Futures Index** tracks the volatile behavior of commodity futures prices. (See Figures 2-11 and 2-12). Figure 2-11 represents a one-year perspective on prices of gold, oil, wheat, and steers, and thus an idea of inflationary trends. Higher commodity prices, for example, can signal inflation, which in turn can lead to higher interest rates and yields and lower bond prices. The CRB index consists of 20 commodities.

SPECIALIZED INDEXES

The *Money* Small Investor Index

The **Small Investor Index,** developed by *Money* magazine, measures gains and losses of the average investor relative to a base valued at 100, set on December 31, 1990. It is based on a portfolio that includes categories of investments held by average small investors. This index, which can be used to measure the average investor's gains and losses, is reported each Monday in newspaper dailies such as *USA Today* and the *Orange County Register.* It is likewise reported monthly as part of *Money* magazine's "Investor's Scorecard." The Small Investor Index is based on a portfolio

FIGURE 2-7: *Barron's* "Market Laboratory"—Bonds

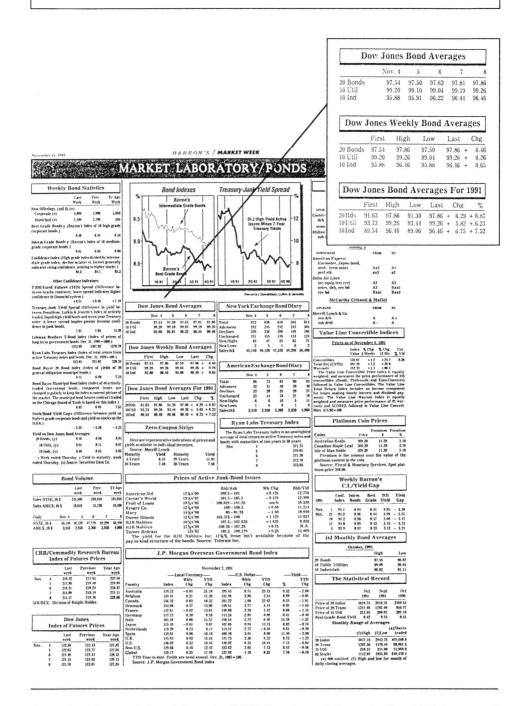

FIGURE 2-8: Bond Market Indexes Examples

BOND MARKET DATA BANK   **5/13/91**

MAJOR INDEXES

HIGH	LOW (12 MOS)		CLOSE	NET CHG	% CHG	12-MO CHG	% CHG	FROM 12/31	% CHG

U.S. TREASURY SECURITIES (Lehman Brothers indexes)

HIGH	LOW	Name	CLOSE	NET CHG	% CHG	12-MO CHG	% CHG	FROM 12/31	% CHG
3220.02	2868.68	Intermediate	3217.05 +	5.41 +	0.17 +	340.40 +	11.83 +	102.58 +	3.29
3815.81	3277.64	Long-term	3768.01 +	15.97 +	0.43 +	411.86 +	12.27 +	98.99 +	2.70
1356.57	1218.60	Long-term (price)	1316.53 +	4.66 +	0.36 +	37.62 +	2.94 −	5.79 −	0.44
3354.26	2970.65	Composite	3340.54 +	7.97 +	0.24 +	356.29 +	11.94 +	101.22 +	3.12

U.S. CORPORATE DEBT ISSUES (Merrill Lynch)

HIGH	LOW	Name	CLOSE	NET CHG	% CHG	12-MO CHG	% CHG	FROM 12/31	% CHG
508.15	448.59	Corporate Master	506.47 +	0.59 +	0.12 +	57.88 +	12.90 +	25.47 +	5.30
383.02	340.85	1-10 Yr Maturities	382.82 +	0.48 +	0.13 +	41.97 +	12.31 +	19.11 +	5.25
376.55	326.63	10+ Yr Maturities	374.07 +	0.44 +	0.12 +	44.96 +	13.66 +	19.52 +	5.51
205.99	169.08	High Yield	205.99 +	0.16 +	0.08 +	25.96 +	14.42 +	31.61 +	18.13
366.07	322.56	Yankee Bonds	364.68 +	0.33 +	0.09 +	41.48 +	12.83 +	16.66 +	4.79

TAX-EXEMPT SECURITIES (Bond Buyer; Merrill Lynch: Dec. 31, 1986 = 100)

HIGH	LOW	Name	CLOSE	NET CHG	% CHG	12-MO CHG	% CHG	FROM 12/31	% CHG
93-11	87-21	Bond Buyer Municipal	92-30 +	-2 +	0.07 +	1-18 +	1.71 +	1-21 +	1.82
130.55	110.82	New 10-yr G.O. (AA)	129.30 +	0.06 +	0.05 +	13.24 +	11.41 +	6.30 +	5.12
134.84	117.43	New 20-yr G.O. (AA)	132.83 +	0.08 +	0.06 +	12.89 +	10.75 +	5.57 +	4.38
151.53	129.65	New 30-yr revenue (A)	150.71 +	0.09 +	0.06 +	17.55 +	13.18 +	9.45 +	6.69

MORTGAGE-BACKED SECURITIES (current coupon; Merrill Lynch: Dec. 31, 1986 = 100)

HIGH	LOW	Name	CLOSE	NET CHG	% CHG	12-MO CHG	% CHG	FROM 12/31	% CHG
149.65	129.85	Ginnie Mae (GNMA)	149.63 +	0.58 +	0.39 +	19.65 +	15.12 +	6.19 +	4.32
149.56	130.43	Fannie Mae (FNMA)	149.10 +	0.25 +	0.17 +	18.40 +	14.08 +	5.62 +	3.92
149.72	130.12	Freddie Mac (FHLMC)	149.08 +	0.25 +	0.17 +	18.66 +	14.31 +	5.96 +	4.16

CONVERTIBLE BONDS (Merrill Lynch: Dec. 31, 1986 = 100)

HIGH	LOW	Name	CLOSE	NET CHG	% CHG	12-MO CHG	% CHG	FROM 12/31	% CHG
137.87	115.06	Investment Grade	137.15 +	0.08 +	0.06 +	10.94 +	8.67 +	13.90 +	11.28
125.09	93.43	High Yield	124.33 +	0.41 +	0.33 +	13.47 +	12.15 +	23.13 +	22.86

INDEX	FRI	FRI YIELD	THU	THU YIELD	YR AGO	12-MO HIGH	12-MO LOW
Lehman Brothers Long T-Bond	3780.20	8.36%	3815.81	8.26%	3286.69	3815.81	3276.93
DJ 20 Bond (Price Return)	94.76	9.07	94.64	9.07	88.83	94.86	88.44
Salomon mortgage-backed	596.39	9.01	597.27	8.98	520.45	597.27	517.79
Bond Buyer municipal	92-28	7.26	93	7.24	89-20	93-11	87-21
Merrill Lynch corporate	506.67	9.13	508.15	9.08	442.19	508.15	442.19

that includes 10 types of investments held in proportions consistent with Federal Reserve data on what the average household owns. The investments and their proportions are shown in Table 2-1 (page 28). The value of the index on March 1, 1991, was 104.93, which reflected a 0.22 percent gain for the week and a 9.40 percent gain over the preceding year. Although this index is not widely used on Wall Street, its importance lies in the fact that it provides the individual investor with a standard against which he or she can assess portfolio composition and performance.

The Sotheby Art Index

Not to be outdone by its counterparts, the **Sotheby Art Index** (Table 2-2), consists of more than 400 individual items grouped into 12 "market baskets." The index was developed by Jeremy Eckstein. Items have been handpicked by Sotheby's experts to represent categories routinely brought to market by the superwealthy, instead of the infrequent "supersales" that make the evening news. The index is reported in *Barron's*. Data reflected in the Sotheby Index are based on the result of auction sales

FIGURE 2-9: Lipper Mutual Fund Performance Averages

Weekly Summary Report
July 3, 1991
Please see page 93 for a listing of the Special Quarterly Summary Report.

General Equity Funds   Dividends Reinvested Cumulative Performances

NAV Mil. $	No. Funds		10/11/90- 7/03/91	7/12/90- 7/03/91	7/05/90- 7/03/91	12/31/90- 7/03/91	6/27/91- 7/03/91
20,201.7	141	Capital Appreciation	+ 31.46%	+ 2.55%	+ 4.96%	+ 18.03%	+ 0.28%
84,175.3	277	Growth Funds	+ 31.08%	+ 3.09%	+ 5.68%	+ 16.84%	+ 0.05%
13,031.6	91	Small Company Growth	+ 42.48%	+ 3.34%	+ 5.37%	+ 24.07%	+ 0.34%
87,139.3	220	Growth and Income	+ 26.53%	+ 4.64%	+ 6.81%	+ 14.23%	− 0.15%
24,552.0	72	Equity Income	+ 22.37%	+ 5.04%	+ 6.44%	+ 12.25%	− 0.12%
229,099.9	801	Gen. Equity Funds Avg.	+ 30.45%	+ 3.61%	5.89%	+ 16.75%	+ 0.05%

Other Equity Funds

NAV Mil. $	No. Funds		10/11/90- 7/03/91	7/12/90- 7/03/91	7/05/90- 7/03/91	12/31/90- 7/03/91	6/27/91- 7/03/91
2,814.8	9	Health/Biotechnology	+ 51.73%	+ 27.70%	+ 31.77%	+ 27.71%	+ 0.22%
1,985.3	19	Natural Resources	+ 1.60%	− 6.35%	− 3.74%	+ 3.24%	− 0.03%
293.5	7	Environmental	+ 20.72%	− 13.13%	− 10.10%	+ 7.86%	+ 0.01%
2,040.9	21	Science & Technol.	+ 41.06%	− 1.87%	+ 0.25%	+ 16.88%	− 0.28%
1,600.4	31	Specialty/Misc.	+ 31.21%	+ 1.08%	+ 3.15%	+ 17.99%	+ 0.54%
7,356.7	23	Utility Funds	+ 13.51%	+ 7.86%	+ 8.27%	+ 4.64%	+ 0.09%
309.1	10	Financial Services	+ 50.20%	+ 12.15%	+ 12.99%	+ 28.89%	− 0.01%
152.4	5	Real Estate	+ 26.51%	+ 1.72%	+ 2.60%	+ 20.37%	− 0.33%
1,782.0	9	Option Income	+ 23.34%	+ 4.53%	+ 5.74%	+ 11.07%	+ 0.01%
15,061.4	51	Global Funds	+ 10.86%	− 7.74%	− 6.26%	+ 7.83%	− 0.61%
10,617.7	68	International Funds	+ 2.70%	− 12.53%	− 11.31%	+ 3.63%	− 1.23%
3,917.6	23	European Region Fds	− 6.04%	− 19.06%	− 18.65%	− 4.97%	− 2.30%
1,563.9	18	Pacific Region Funds	+ 8.33%	− 9.29%	− 7.54%	+ 11.52%	− 0.30%
2,954.1	37	Gold Oriented Funds	+ 3.10%	− 2.59%	− 2.81%	+ 4.83%	+ 5.66%
281,256.2	1125	All Equity Funds Avg.	+ 25.78%	+ 1.39%	+ 3.41%	+ 14.39%	+ 0.08%

Other Funds

NAV Mil. $	No. Funds		10/11/90- 7/03/91	7/12/90- 7/03/91	7/05/90- 7/03/91	12/31/90- 7/03/91	6/27/91- 7/03/91
4,444.9	54	Flexible Portfolio	+ 19.59%	+ 4.99%	+ 6.35%	+ 10.13%	+ 0.09%
1,454.2	13	Global Flex Port.	+ 8.84%	− 1.01%	+ 0.14%	+ 4.69%	− 0.18%
15,031.1	62	Balanced Funds	+ 20.01%	+ 6.73%	+ 8.05%	+ 10.48%	+ 0.15%
581.9	6	Balanced Target	+ 20.08%	+ 7.61%	+ 8.41%	+ 8.63%	+ 0.46%
2,215.2	31	Conv. Securities	+ 22.21%	+ 3.51%	+ 4.72%	+ 15.30%	+ 0.19%
4,194.5	13	Income Funds	+ 16.45%	+ 7.76%	+ 8.24%	+ 9.52%	+ 0.22%
17,594.7	74	World Income Funds	+ 0.75%	+ 6.77%	+ 7.12%	− 0.22%	+ 0.01%
164,259.0	566	Fixed Income Funds	+ 11.23%	+ 9.24%	+ 9.16%	+ 7.03%	+ 0.69%
491,325.2	1951	Total Long-Term Funds					
		Long-Term Average	+ 20.20%	+ 4.14%	+ 5.43%	+ 11.41%	+ 0.25%
		Long-Term Median	+ 18.50%	+ 6.20%	+ 7.70%	+ 10.70%	+ 0.20%
		Funds with % Change	1793	1746	1746	1840	1899

Lipper Indexes

NAV Mil. $	No. Funds		10/11/90- 7/03/91	7/12/90- 7/03/91	7/05/90- 7/03/91	12/31/90- 7/03/91	6/27/91- 7/03/91
295.17	30	Capital Apprec Index	+ 30.08%	+ 3.22%	+ 5.95%	+ 17.93%	+ 0.24%
535.35	30	Growth Fund Index	+ 30.67%	+ 3.03%	+ 5.71%	+ 15.97%	− 0.06%
267.84	30	Small Co Growth Index	+ 37.62%	+ 0.64%	+ 2.71%	+ 17.32%	+ 0.25%
816.53	30	Growth & Income Index	+ 25.64%	+ 4.61%	+ 6.67%	+ 13.97%	− 0.27%
527.14	30	Equity Income Index	+ 22.22%	+ 6.42%	+ 7.64%	+ 12.82%	− 0.13%
191.97	10	Sci & Tech Index	+ 39.51%	− 2.97%	− 0.73%	+ 16.58%	− 0.14%
268.66	30	Global Fund Index	+ 6.54%	− 11.30%	− 9.62%	+ 0.60%	− 0.60%
320.89	10	International Index	+ 1.53%	− 13.17%	− 11.71%	+ 3.08%	− 1.23%
152.28	10	Gold Fund Index	+ 7.46%	+ 1.00%	+ 0.81%	+ 9.22%	+ 5.44%
637.16	10	Balanced Fund Index	+ 21.60%	+ 7.24%	+ 8.78%	+ 11.63%	− 0.02%
135.04	10	Conv. Secur. Index	+ 19.65%	+ 3.73%	+ 4.94%	+ 12.36%	+ 0.08%

Value 6/30/91			6/30/81- 6/30/91	6/30/86- 6/30/91	6/30/90- 6/30/91	12/31/90- 6/30/91	3/31/91- 6/30/91
371.16		S&P 500 Reinvested	+ 324.60%	+ 75.55%	+ 7.38%	+ 14.24%	− 0.23%
2,906.75		Dow Jones Reinvested	+ 362.24%	+ 84.70%	+ 4.64%	+ 12.23%	+ 0.55%

FIGURE 2-10: Foreign Market Indicators

EXCHANGE	5/1/91 CLOSE	NET CHG	PCT CHG
Tokyo Nikkei Average	26489.00 +	377.75 +	1.45
Tokyo Topix Index	1998.45 +	35.03 +	1.78
London FT 30-share	1966.7 +	13.0 +	0.67
London 100-share	2508.4 +	22.2 +	0.89
London Gold Mines	139.9 −	2.2 −	1.55
Frankfurt DAX	closed		
Zurich Credit Suisse	closed		
Paris CAC 40	closed		
Milan Stock Index	closed		
Amsterdam ANP-CBS General	200.9 +	0.2 +	0.10
Stockholm Affarsvarlden	closed		
Brussels Bel-20 Index	closed		
Australia All Ordinaries	1532.4 −	1.8 −	0.12
Hong Kong Hang Seng	3631.23 +	42.87 +	1.19
Singapore Straits Times	closed		
Johannesburg J'burg Gold	closed		
Madrid General Index	closed		
Toronto 300 Composite	3493.06 +	24.25 +	0.70
Euro, Aust, Far East MSCI-p	865.5 +	14.5 +	1.70

p-Preliminary
na-Not available

FIGURE 2-11: Commodity Price Behavior over Time

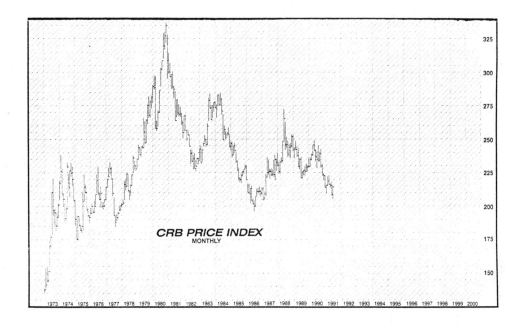

FIGURE 2-12: CRB Composite Futures Index

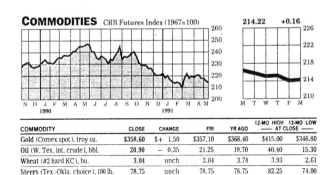

COMMODITIES CRB Futures Index (1967=100)   214.22   +0.16

COMMODITY	CLOSE	CHANGE	FRI	YR AGO	12-MO HIGH — AT CLOSE — 12-MO LOW	
Gold (Comex spot), troy oz.	$358.60	$+ 1.50	$357.10	$368.40	$415.00	$346.80
Oil (W. Tex. int. crude), bbl.	20.90	− 0.35	21.25	19.70	40.40	15.30
Wheat (#2 hard KC), bu.	3.04	unch	3.04	3.74	3.93	2.61
Steers (Tex.-Okla. choice), 100 lb.	78.75	unch	78.75	78.75	82.25	74.00

by Sotheby's affiliated companies and other information deemed relevant by Sotheby's. Sotheby's does warrant the accuracy of the data reflected therein. However, neither commentary furnished by Sotheby's nor any of its indexes is intended to be relied on for investment advice or used as a predictor, warranty, or guarantee of performance. All individual prices quoted in the review are aggregate prices, inclusive of the buyer's premium.

Stamp Indexes

Scott Philatelic Corporation, an affiliate of Scott Publishing Company, computes the **Scott Index** values. These values are for "fine" stamps and are used as a basis for comparison in a study of quality-adjusted rates of return in stamp auctions. *Linn's Stamp News* publishes the *U.S. Stamp Market Index*, a weighted average of U.S. 19th- and 20th-century stamps and air mails. This index also keeps track of prices in the stamp market.

Real Estate Performance Averages

Developed by the Frank Russell Co. of Tacoma, Washington, **Real Estate Performance Averages** are market value-driven property performance averages (in millions of dollars), broken down by regions. These data appear in *Barron's*, and an example is shown in Figure 2-13.

HOW TO READ TICKER TAPE QUOTATIONS

Ticker tape is an electronic device that shows a running report of the stock symbol, latest price, and volume of trades on the exchanges. With the recent growth of cable

---

FIGURE 2-13: Russell's Real Estate Performance Averages

Annual Performance
Years Ending June 30

Period	Total	Income	Capital
1979	18.56	8.85	9.12
1980	20.43	8.67	11.06
1981	17.30	8.26	8.53
1982	13.91	7.84	5.74
1983	9.31	8.05	1.20
1984	15.68	7.40	7.85
1985	10.60	7.42	3.02
1986	8.96	7.46	1.42
1987	4.68	7.04	-2.24
1988	6.99	7.05	-0.06
1989	6.69	6.91	-0.20
1990	5.37	6.58	-1.15
1991	-1.10	6.81	-7.53

---

television, more and more investors pick up financial and investment news from cable networks that cover the securities and commodities markets throughout the business day. What is known as the ticker tape can be seen moving constantly across the lower portion of the TV screen, which rapidly transmits the symbols and figures.

The most frequent display is the consolidated tape, a combination of two networks that report all transactions from the following exchanges (Components of the consolidated tape are explained in the following sections):

Network A New York Stock Exchange

Network B American Stock Exchange

Other markets (Instinet)
OTC market and others

Boston Stock Exchange
Cincinnati Stock Exchange
Midwest Stock Exchange
Pacific Stock Exchange
Philadelphia Stock Exchange

Stock Symbol

The first letters are the stock ticker symbols—*XON* for Exxon, *CCI* for Citicorp, and *IBM* for International Business Machines, for example. (One exception is the prefix *Q*, which is used when a company is in receivership or bankruptcy.) The ticker symbol may be followed by an abbreviation designating a type of issue, such as *Pr* to signify preferred stock, which may in turn be followed by a letter indicating a class of preferred.

For example, *XYZPrE.cv* means XYZ Corporation's preferred stock series E was convertible (the abbreviation *.cv*). Common stock classes, if any, are indicated

TABLE 2-1: Investments in *Money's* Small Investor Index

(Final week of February 1991)

Category	Current	Percent of Portfolio A Year Ago
NYSE stocks	18.11%	20.83%
AMEX/OTC stocks	5.72	6.58
Equity funds	3.78	3.60
Taxable bonds	17.11	15.61
Municipals	4.76	4.66
Bond funds	4.31	3.88
CDs	22.31	22.02
Cash	22.53	21.33
Real estate	0.80	0.81
Gold	0.57	0.69

Source: *Money* magazine, March 1991.

TABLE 2-2: Sotheby's Art Index

Category	Weight	Sept. 1, 1986	Sept. 1, 1985	Sept. 1, 1984
Old master paintings	17	303	289	251
19th century European paintings	12	250	249	220
Impressionist & post-Imp. paintings	18	432	371	317
Modern paintings (1900–1950)	10	429	342	301
American paint. (1800–pre-WWII)	3	687	635	589
Continental ceramics	3	290	284	284
Chinese ceramics	10	486	486	482
English silver	5	338	298	237
Continental silver	5	192	178	161
American furniture	3	380	324	241
French continental furniture	7	285	273	270
English furniture	7	447	382	360
Weighted Aggregate Sept. 1975 = 100		369	336	302

Source: Sotheby Art Index.

by a period plus a letter following the ticker symbol. Thus, XYZ's class B common would be designated by XYZ.B.

Other applicable abbreviations placed after the ticker symbol are:

rt = rights
wi = when issued
.WD = when distributed

.WS = warrants (The abbreviation may be preceded by another period and letter to identify the particular issue of warrant.)

.XD = ex-dividend

Market Identifiers

If information about the stock is followed by an ampersand (&) and a letter, the transaction took place in a market other than the New York Stock Exchange, if you are looking at Network B. The letter identifies the market as follows:

A   American Stock Exchange
B   Boston Stock Exchange
C   Cincinnati Stock Exchange
M   Midwest Stock Exchange
N   New York Stock Exchange
O   Other Markets (mainly Instinet)
P   Pacific Stock Exchange
T   Third Market (mainly NASDAQ)
X   Philadelphia Stock Exchange

Volume

The next portion of the transaction information provided on a ticker tape may appear below, or to the right of, the above stock symbol and market designation. It reports the number of shares traded. However, if the trade is in a round lot (100 shares), which it usually is, no volume is indicated and the tape shows the issue and the price. For example, the designation "XYZ 34 1/2" simply means that 100 shares of XYZ were traded at $34.50 a share.

Where larger round-lot transactions take place, the number of round lots is indicated by the letter *s* followed by the price. "XYZ 15 s 34 1/2" means that 1,500 shares were traded at $34.50 a share. If the volume is 10,000 shares or more, the full number is given: "XYZ 25,000 s 34 1/2."

Some stocks, because of their price or infrequency of transaction, are traded in fewer than 100 shares per round lot. Transactions on these round lots are indicated by the following symbol: $\overset{s}{s}$.

On the NYSE, these lots are always made up of 10 shares. Therefore: "XYZ PrB 2 $\overset{s}{s}$ 36" means two 10-share lots (20 shares) of XYZ preferred stock B were traded at $36.

Abbreviated Forms of Ticker Quotations

If trading becomes sufficiently heavy to cause the tape to run more than a minute behind, shortcuts are used. Several key shortcuts are explained below.

Digits and Volume Deleted

This means that only the initial price digit is deleted and thus the unit price digit and fraction are printed (for example, 5 1/4 instead of 15 1/4). Digits and volume are never deleted if

- the price ends in zero; or
- the trade is an opening transaction; or
- the trade exceeds 10,000 shares.

Repeat Prices Omitted

Trades will not be displayed unless there is a price change—i.e., if it takes place at the same price as the immediately preceding transaction in that stock. Exceptions occur when the trade:

- is an opening transaction; or
- exceeds 10,000 shares.

Trading Delayed or Halted

This notice will appear if the trading of a stock is halted for any reason.

Minimum Price Changes Omitted

This notice will appear unless the price difference exceeds 1/8 of a point. Again, exceptions occur when

- the price is for an opening transaction; or
- the trade is 10,000 shares or more.

Digits and Volume Resumed

This notice will appear when trading activity slackens to a more normal level.

Other Abbreviations

Other important abbreviations to be noted are:

- **.SLD** = sold. This is used if a transaction is displayed out of its proper order (i.e., it occurred at some point in the past and was not reported). For example, *XYZ .SLD 2 s 34 1/2* means that sometime in the past XYZ sold 200 shares at $34.50.
  - **CORR** = A correction of information follows.
  - **ERR** or **CXL** = A print is to be ignored.

- **OPD** = An opening transaction is delayed.
- **.16** = Sixteenths (For example, "9.16" on the ticker means 9/16.)

Bonds and Treasury Bills on the AMEX

Bonds are traded on both the NYSE and AMEX. Whereas the NYSE has a separate ticker for bonds, the AMEX includes bonds within its stock quotations. For example, "ABC.D 10s.20s451/2" means ABC bond "D" has 10% coupon rate, 20 bonds at 45 1/2. Or, "TBIL 8.11.92s.10s10.55.." means: This Treasury bill is due 8/11/1992, 10 bills at 10.55%.

3

General Economic
Information

OVERVIEW

An investor analyzes the economy primarily to determine investment strategy. It is not necessary for the investor to formulate his or her own economic forecasts because published forecasts can be relied on to identify trends in the economy and adjust an investment position accordingly.

     The investor must keep abreast of the economic trend and direction in an attempt to see how they affect the securities market. As noted earlier, important sources of economic information include the *Wall Street Journal, Barron's, Business Week, Federal Reserve Bulletin*, and *Current Business Conditions*. Unfortunately, there are too many economic indicators and variables to be analyzed. Each has its own significance and in many cases could give *mixed* signals about the economy's future, therefore misleading the investor. Table 3-1 summarizes the types of economic variables and their probable effect on the securities market and the economy in general. Table 3-2 provides a brief yet concise list of significant economic indicators, how they affect bond yields, and why they occur.

ECONOMIC FORECASTING SERVICES

Examination of economic variables will help investors interpret the direction of the economy and the securities market. This, along with expert economic opinion and projection in newspapers, magazines, and newsletters, should lead to the formulation of a sound investment policy. (Figure 3-1 and Table 3-3 show examples of economic forecasts.) Other projections can be found in publications such as *Blue Chip Consensus* and the *Kiplinger Washington Letter*.

     The **Blue Chip Indicators** are based on a poll of 50 business economists working for investment houses, banks, and businesses. The **National Association of Business Economists (NABE)** conducts a similar survey on the future economic condition of the nation. A thriving industry of private consulting firms—like **DRI/McGraw-Hill, Inc.**, and **Evans Economics**—provides economic forecasts based on their own econometric models.

TABLE 3-1: Economic Variables and Their Effect on the Economy and the Securities Market

Variables	Effect
Real growth in GNP (without inflation)	Positive
Industrial production	Consecutive drops are a sign of recession.
Inflation	Detrimental to equity and bond prices
Capacity utilization	A high percentage is positive, but full capacity is inflationary.
Durable goods orders	Consecutive drops signal recession.
Increase in business investment, consumer confidence, personal income, etc.	Positive
Leading indicators	A rise is bullish for the economy and the market; consecutive drops signal bad times ahead.
Housing starts	A rise is positive, and vice versa.
Corporate profits	Strong corporate earnings are positive for the market, and vice versa.
Unemployment	Unfavorable for the market and economy
Increase in business inventories	Positive for the inflationary economy; negative for the stable economy
Federal deficit	Inflationary and negative; positive for the depressed economy
Deficit in trade and balance of payment	Negative
Weak dollar	Negative for the market
Interest rates	Rising rates depress the value of fixed income; securities such as bonds tend to fall, and vice versa.

Privately constructed forecasting indexes are available from **Composite Forecasting Index** (Safian Investment Research, White Plains, N.Y.), and from **Macro-Economic Index** (Jesup, Josephal & Company).

KEEPING TRACK OF THE ECONOMY WITH ECONOMIC AND MONETARY INDICATORS

To sort out the confusing mix of statistics that flow almost daily from the government and to help you keep track of what goes on in the economy, this section will examine various economic and monetary indicators that you should watch. Economic and monetary indicators attempt to determine where the economy seems to be headed and

TABLE 3-2: Effect of Economic Indicators on Bond Yields

Indicators*	Effect**	Reasons
Business Activity		
GNP and industrial production falls.	Fall	As economy slows, Fed may ease credit by allowing rates to fall.
Unemployment rises.	Fall	High unemployment indicates lack of economic expansion; Fed may loosen credit.
Inventories rise.	Fall	Inventory levels are good indicators of duration of economic slowdown.
Trade deficit rises.	Fall	Dollar weakens.
Leading indicators rise.	Rise	Advance signals about economic health; Fed may tighten credit.
Housing starts rise.	Rise	Growing economy due to increased new housing demand; Fed may tighten; mortgage rates rise.
Personal income rises.	Rise	Higher income means higher consumer spending, thus inflationary; Fed may tighten.
Inflation		
Consumer price index rises.	Rise	Inflationary
Producer price index rises.	Rise	Early signal for inflation
Monetary Policy		
Money supply rises.	Rise	Excess growth in money supply is inflationary; Fed may tighten.
Discount rate rises.	Rise	Causes increase in business and consumer loan rates; used to slow economic growth and inflation.
Fed buys (sells) bills.	Rise (fall)	Adds (deducts) money to the economy; interest rates may go down (up).
Required reserve rises.	Rise	Depresses bank lending.

* A fall in any of these indicators will have the opposite effect on bond yields.
**The effects are based on yield and therefore will have the opposite effect on bond prices.

---

where it's been. Each month, government agencies (including the Federal Reserve) and several economic institutions publish various indicators that can be broken down into six broad categories: measures of overall economic performance, price indexes, indexes of labor market conditions, index of leading indicators, money and credit market indicators, and measures for major product markets.

TABLE 3-3: Sample Econometric Forecasts

Forecast for 1991:

Percent Change (1991 over 1990)

	Real GNP	GNP Deflator	Consumer Prices	Full Year % Unemployment
Leonard Silk, New York Times	0.3%	3.8%	4.5%	6.7%
Fortune Magazine	-0.0	3.9	4.3	6.7
Standard & Poor's Corp.	-0.1	3.7	4.2	6.8
First Fidelity Bank Corp.	-0.3	4.1	4.3	6.8
Wells Fargo Bank	-0.3	4.1	4.4	6.8
Peter Bernstein	-0.8	4.0	4.3	6.7
Business Economics	-1.0	3.7	4.3	6.9
Compare: Blue Chip Consensus	-0.2	3.9	4.2	6.7

Additional Indicators: Industrial Production -1.6%; Housing Starts 1.05 mil.; Auto Sales 8.7 mil.

Forecast for 1992:

Percent Change (1992 over 1991)

	Real GNP	GNP Deflator	Consumer Prices	Full Year % Unemployment
Leonard Silk, New York Times	2.8%	3.4%	3.6%	6.2%
Fortune Magazine	3.3	4.3	4.6	6.2
Standard & Poor's Corp.	3.0	2.9	3.3	6.4
First Fidelity Bankcorp.	2.6	4.0	3.8	6.2
Wells Fargo Bank	2.6	4.1	4.0	6.5
Peter Bernstein	2.9	3.5	3.8	6.2
Business Economics	-0.7	3.7	3.9	7.3
Compare: Blue Chip Consensus	2.7	3.5	3.7	6.5

Additional Indicators: Industrial Production 4.0%; Housing Starts 1.26 mil.; Auto Sales 9.5 mil.

Source: *Blue Chip Economic Indicators,* published by Eggert Economic Enterprises, Inc., Jordan Road, Sedona Building—North, Suite B, Box 2243, Sedona, AZ 86366 (602) 282-4882, September 10, 1991.

Measures of Overall Economic Performance

Overall economic performance is measured by gross national product (GNP), industrial production, personal income, housing starts, unemployment rate, and retail sales.

Gross National Product (GNP)

GNP measures the value of all goods and services produced in the economy and is the nation's broadest gauge of economic health. GNP is normally stated in annual terms, although quarterly data are also available. GNP is often a measure of the state of the economy. For example, many economists speak of recession if there has been a decline in GNP for two consecutive quarters. Unfortunately, there is no way of measuring, based on the GNP, whether we are currently in a recession or state of prosperity. Only after the quarter is over can it be determined whether there was growth or decline. In addition, an increasing number of analysts say the GNP criteria for a recession are actually no longer valid. Instead, they look to other measures—unemployment rate, industrial production, durable orders, corporate profits, retail sales, and housing activity—for signs of recession. The following diagram charts a series of events leading from a declining GNP to lower securities prices.

GNP down —> Corporate profits down —> Dividends down —> Securities prices down

Gross Domestic Product (GDP)

Unlike GNP, GDP only includes the values of goods and services earned by a nation *within* its boundaries. Thus, it includes only the income derived from factories within the country (and *not* without). For example, when General Motor's British unit repatriates dividends, profits, or interest on loans, the money is counted as part of GNP, whereas British GM profits is not included in GDP. *NOTE: In December 1991, the Department of Commerce began focusing on GDP instead of GNP when reporting the nation's economic condition.* Economists agree GDP is a better measure of how the whole economy is doing than GNP.

Industrial Production

The industrial production index shows changes in the output of U.S. plants, mines, and utilities. Detailed breakdowns of the index provide a reading on how individual industries are faring. The index is issued monthly by the Federal Reserve Board.

Personal Income

The personal income index shows the before-tax income, such as wages and salaries, rents, interest and dividends, and other payments (such as unemployment and Social Security) received by individuals and unincorporated businesses. This index represents consumers' spending power. When personal income rises, it usually means that consumers will buy more, which in turn will favorably affect the investment climate. Personal income data are released monthly by the U.S. Commerce Department.

Figure 3-1: Economic Forecast Example

FORTUNE FORECAST

By Vivian Brownstein

WHY STATE BUDGETS ARE A MESS

■ Life in the executive suite may get a bit easier when the economy finally picks up, but not for many state and local budget planners—nor for most taxpayers. Governors and mayors, facing growing demands to fix neglected bridges and roadways, make streets safer, improve education, and take care of the sick and homeless, are threatening drastic cutbacks. At the same time, taxes are headed up (see table, following page). The seeds of the trouble were planted well before the recession, and the problems will remain with us for years, through bad times and good alike.

Part of the public dissatisfaction comes from expectations built up during the past decade. Until last year, most state and local governments were healthy enough to cope with whatever problems came their way, especially compared with big brother in Washington. While the federal government plunged ever deeper into red ink, states and municipalities ran a combined operating surplus that reached 3% of receipts in 1984-85. Counting the excess in their social insurance funds—just as the

federal budget includes the Social Security surplus—they were in the black by more than $60 billion. Even late in the decade, state and local deficits—including both current and capital spending—were modest. Meantime, the federal deficit soared past the $200 billion mark.

The states did not stint on spending, either. Real outlays for payrolls, goods, and purchased services grew an average of 3% a year. Welfare and other transfer payments expanded at an even faster 4.5% pace. And public works projects financed by borrowing—school buildings, water treatment plants, and the like—seemed to be in progress everywhere.

THE STATES and localities managed this fiscal performance even as they were losing support from the federal government. With the demise of revenue sharing, among other Reagan-era cutbacks, total grants fell from 23% of receipts in 1980 to 16% last year. What's more, the cost of federally mandated programs grew faster than the grants earmarked to pay for them. As a result, income and health programs such as Aid to Families With Dependent Children and Medicaid now absorb

OVERVIEW

■ Twenty-three governors plan to raise taxes so far, and others are likely to follow.

■ State and local spending will grow just 1.5%.

■ Budget woes will slow the economic recovery.

60 cents of each dollar in grant money, compared with less than 40 cents a decade ago.

This forced devolution unleashed a lot of energy at the state and local level, says Steven Gold, who heads a think tank for studying states at the Nelson A. Rockefeller Institute of Government in Albany, New York. Largely as a result, says Gold, "states are where the action is for domestic policy." He points out that innovative programs on the environment, economic development, and education are coming out of the states, not Washington.

All that creative energy is sure to pay more dividends in the long run, but right now the crisis is overwhelming it. States can no longer shrug off reduced federal aid. By the first quarter of this year, operating deficits—leaving aside *continued on page 30*

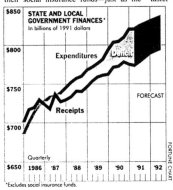

State and Local Government Finances
In billions of 1991 dollars
- $850
- $800 — Expenditures / Deficit
- $750 — FORECAST
- $700 — Receipts
- $650 — Quarterly — 1986 '87 '88 '89 '90 '91 '92

FORTUNE CHART

*Excludes social insurance funds.

TAXPAYERS AREN'T TAKING IT WELL
Speaking for millions, a Houston woman shows how she feels about higher state and local taxes and shrinking services. The deficits here include spending on public works that are financed largely by borrowing.

JUNE 3, 1991 **FORTUNE** 21

Housing Starts

Housing starts, or new construction, are an important indicator followed by investors and economists that estimates the number of dwelling units on which construction has begun during a stated period. Whenever an economy takes a downturn, the housing sector is the first to decline. This indicates the future strength of the housing sector of the economy. At the same time, this indicator is closely related to interest rates and other basic economic factors. Housing figures are issued monthly by the U.S. Bureau of Census.

Unemployment Rate

No one indicator can point to the direction in which an economy is headed. Many indicators commonly give mixed signals regarding, for example, the possibility of a recession. When faced with mixed leading indicators, many analysts look to the unemployment rate.

Retail Sales

The estimate of total sales at the retail level includes everything from groceries to durable goods (automobiles for example). It is used as a measure of future economic conditions—long slowdown in sales could spell cuts in production. Because they represent about one-half of overall consumer spending, retail sales are a major concern to analysts. Consumer spending in turn accounts for about *two-thirds* of the nation's GNP so any sharp change could be an important factor in an overall turnaround. Retail sales volume depends heavily on consumer confidence in the economy. Retail sales data are issued monthly by the U.S. Commerce Department.

Price Indexes

Price indexes are designed to measure the rate of economic inflation. Three indexes measure living costs, price level changes, and inflation. They are, respectively, the consumer price index, producer price index, and GNP deflator.

Consumer Price Index (CPI)

The consumer price index (CPI), the most familiar inflation gauge, is used as the cost-of-living index, to which labor contracts and Social Security are tied. The CPI measures the cost of buying a fixed basket of goods (some 400 consumer goods and services), representative of the purchase of the typical working-class urban family. The fixed basket is divided into the following categories: food and beverages, housing, apparel, transportation, medical care, entertainment, and other. The CPI is widely used for escalation clauses. The base year for the CPI was 1982–1984, at which time it was assigned 100. The following diagram charts a chain of events leading from lower rates of inflation to increased consumer spending and, possibly, the up securities market.

CPI down —> Real personal income up —> Consumer confidence up —> Consumer spending up (Retail sales up + Housing starts up + Auto sales up) —> Securities market up

Generally referred to as a cost-of-living index, the CPI is published monthly by the Bureau of Labor Statistics of the U.S. Department of Labor.

Producer Price Index (PPI)

Like the CPI, the producer price index (PPI) is a measure of the cost of a given basket of goods priced in wholesale markets, including raw materials, semifinished goods, and finished goods at the early stage of the distribution system. The PPI signals changes in the general price level, or the CPI, some time before they actually materialize. (Because the PPI does not include services, caution should be exercised when the principal cause of inflation is service prices.) For this reason, the PPI and especially some of its subindexes, such as the index of sensitive materials, serve as one of the leading indicators that are closely watched by policymakers. The PPI is published monthly by the Bureau of Labor Statistics of the Department of Commerce.

GNP Deflator (Implicit Price Index)

The GNP implicit deflator is the third index of inflation that is used to separate price changes in GNP calculations from real changes in economic activity. The GNP deflator is a weighted average of the price indexes used to deflate the components of GNP. Thus, it reflects price changes for goods and services bought by consumers, businesses, and governments. The GNP deflator is found by dividing current GNP in a given year by constant (real) GNP. Because it covers a broader group of goods and services than the CPI and PPI, the GNP deflator is a popular price index for measuring inflation. Unlike the CPI and PPI, available monthly, the GNP deflator is available quarterly, published also by the U.S. Department of Commerce.

Indexes of Labor Market Conditions

Indicators covering labor market conditions are unemployment rate, average workweek of production workers, applications for unemployment compensation, and hourly wage rates.

Money and Credit Market Indicators

Most widely reported in the media are money supply, consumer credit, the DJIA, and the Treasury bill rate.

Index of Leading Indicators

The leading indicators index, the most widely publicized signal caller, is made up of 11 data series: money supply, stock prices, vendor performance, average workweek, new orders, contracts, building permits, inventory change, consumer confidence, change in sensitive prices, and change in total liquid assets. These components monitor certain business activities that can signal a change in the economy. A more detailed discussion appears below.

Measures for Major Product Markets

Major product market indicators are designed to measure specific segments of the economy—housing, retail sales, steel, automobiles, and such. Examples are 10-day auto sales, advance retail sales, housing starts and construction permits. It is important to note that indicators are signals *only*. They tell an investor something about economic conditions in the country or a particular area; about an industry; and, over time, about emerging trends.

INDEXES OF LEADING, COINCIDENT, AND LAGGING ECONOMIC INDICATORS

Leading Indicators

Published monthly by the U.S. Department of Commerce, **the Index of Leading Economic Indicators** is a series of 11 signals that tend to predict future changes in economic activity. (Officially, it is called the **Composite Index of 11 Leading Indicators**.) Designed to reveal the direction of the economy in the next six to nine months (1982=100), this series is the government's main barometer for forecasting business trends. Each component has shown a tendency to change before the economy makes a major turn—hence, the term *leading indicators. NOTE: If the index rises consistently, even slightly, the economy is chugging along and a setback is unlikely. If the indicators drop for three or more consecutive months, look for an economic slowdown and possibly a recession in the next year or so.*

The 11 indicators, each of which is discussed below, are subject to revision. For example, petroleum and natural gas prices were found to distort the data from crude material prices and were subsequently dropped from that category.

1.   Average workweek of production workers in manufacturing. Employers find it a lot easier to increase the number of hours worked in a week than to hire more employees.

2.   Initial claims for unemployment insurance. The number of people signing up for unemployment benefits signals changes in present/future economic activity.

3.   Change in consumer confidence. Asset changes is based on the University of Michigan's survey of consumer expectations. The index measures

consumers' optimism regarding the present and future state of the economy and is based on an index of 100 in 1966.

4.   Percent change in prices of sensitive crude materials. Rises in prices of such critical materials as steel and iron usually mean factory demands are going up, which means factories plan to step up production.

5.   Contracts and orders for plant and equipment. Heavier contracting and ordering usually lead economic upswings.

6.   Vendor performance. Vendor performance represents the percentage of companies reporting slower deliveries. As the economy grows, firms have more trouble filling orders.

7.   Stock prices. A rise in the common stock index indicates expected profits and lower interest rates. Stock market advances usually precede business upturns by three to eight months.

8.   Money supply. A rising money supply means easy money that sparks brisk economic activity. This usually leads recoveries by as much as 14 months.

9.   New orders for manufacturers of consumer goods and materials. New orders mean more workers hired, more materials and supplies purchased, and increased output. Gains in this series usually lead recoveries by as much as four months.

10.   Residential building permits for private housing. Gains in building permits signal business upturns.

11.   Factory backlogs of unfilled durable goods orders. Backlogs signify business upswings.

NOTE: These 11 index components are adjusted for inflation. Rarely do all of them go in the same direction at once. Each factor is weighted. The composite figure is designed to tell only in which direction business will go, not to forecast the magnitude of future ups and downs.

Coincident Indicators

Coincident indicators are the types of economic indicator series that tend to move up and down in line with the aggregate economy and, therefore, are measures of current economic activity. Examples are gross national product (GNP) and gross domestic product (GDP), employment, retail sales, and industrial production.

Lagging Indicators

Lagging indicators trail aggregate economic activity. Currently six lagging indicators are published by the government: unemployment rate, labor cost per unit, loans outstanding, average prime rate charged by banks, ratio of consumer installment credit outstanding to personal income, and ratio of manufacturing and trade inventories to sales.

Business Conditions Digest routinely charts leading, coincident, and lagging indicators (see Figure 3-2).

FIGURE 3-2: Leading, Coincident, and Lagging Indicators

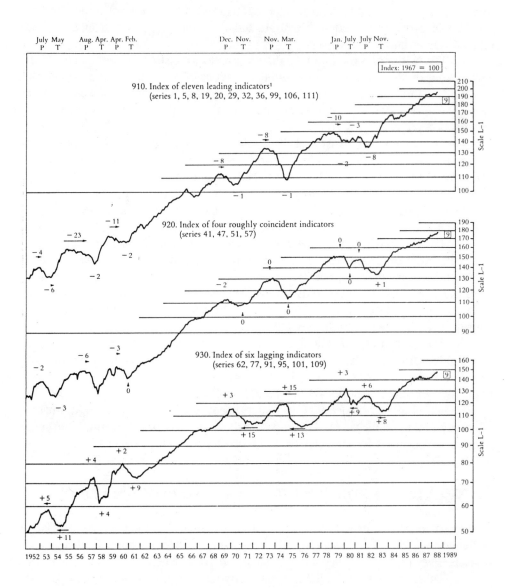

Source: *Business Conditions Digest* (U.S. Department of Commerce Bureau of Economic Analysis).

OTHER IMPORTANT INDEXES

Forbes publishes **The Forbes Index**. This index (1976=100) is a measure of U.S. economic activity composed of 8 equally weighted elements: total industrial production, new claims for unemployment compensation, the cost of services relative to all consumer prices, new housing starts, total retail sales, the level of new orders for durable goods compared with manufactures' inventories, personal income, and total consumer installment credit.

The **National Association of Purchasing Management** releases its monthly **Purchasing Index**, which discloses buying intentions of corporate purchasing agents. The **Dodge Index**, prepared by the F. W. Dodge Division of McGraw-Hill, is a monthly market index that assesses the building industry in terms of the value of new construction projects.

The Conference Board of New York, an industry-sponsored, nonprofit economic research institute, publishes two indexes. The **Help-Wanted Advertising Index** measures the volume of help-wanted advertising in 51 newspapers and reports changes in labor market conditions. The **Consumer Confidence Index** measures consumer optimism and pessimism about general business conditions, jobs, and total family income.

The University of Michigan Survey Research Center compiles its own index, called the **Index of Consumer Sentiment**. It measures consumers' personal financial circumstances and their outlook for the future. The survey is compiled through a telephone survey of 500 households. The index is used by the Commerce Department in its monthly **Index of Leading Economic Indicators** and regularly charted in the Department's **Business Conditions Digest**.

The University of Michigan Survey Research Center also releases the **Investor Sentiment Index**, based on a survey conducted for Fidelity Investments. The index, an indicator of the overall sentiment of U.S. investors, measures consumer plans for their investment dollars and their overall confidence level.

The National Federation of Independent Business, a Washington-based advocacy group, publishes the **Optimism Index**, which is based on small-business owners' expectations for the economy. The benchmark year is 1978.

CONVENIENT SOURCES OF ECONOMIC INFORMATION

Numerous sources of general economic information provide a convenient overview of the current state of the economy, showing many of these economic statistics and indexes. They also provide economic commentary, raw statistics, and even forecasts.

These sources are available by subscription or can be found in local public and college libraries. They include daily local and national newspapers, such as *USA Today*, the *Wall Street Journal*, *Investor's Business Daily*, the *Los Angeles Times,* and the *New York Times*, as well as periodicals, such as *Business Week* (see Figure 3-3), *Forbes, Fortune, Money, Barron's, Nation's Business*, and *U.S. News and World Report*.

ECONOMIC VARIABLES AND INVESTMENT DECISIONS

Economic indicators apply to business outlook. A growing economy will lead to improved profitability and dividends; thus it is bullish for stocks. A decline in real GNP or GDP will result in lower profits and dividends, causing a decline in stock prices. Economic indicators can be used to confirm market direction. For example, if the economy is contracting at an unsustainable rate, stock prices will immediately do better to reflect the better business environment that will emerge. Once the stock market no longer reacts to bad news, the market has already discounted the bad news and stock prices should start to move upward.

A low inflation rate is better for equity securities. During the bull market period of 1984, the yearly percent increases in the consumer price index (CPI) were 4.0 percent, 3.8 percent, and 1.1 percent.

Monetary indicators apply to Federal Reserve actions and the demand for credit. They involve consideration of long-term interest rates, which are important in that bond yields compete with stock yields. Monetary and credit indicators are often the first signs of market direction. If monetary indicators move favorably, this is an indication that a decline in stock prices may be over. A stock market top may be ready for a contraction if the Federal Reserve tightens credit, making consumer buying and corporate expansion more costly and difficult.

Monetary indicators regularly watched are:

- Dow Jones 20-bond index
- Dow Jones utility average
- NYSE utility average
- T-bill yield
- 30-year T-bond yield

Bonds and utilities are yield instruments and therefore money-sensitive. They are impacted by changing interest rates. If the above monetary indicators are active and pointing higher, it is a sign that the stock market will start to take off. In other words, an upward movement in these indicators takes place in advance of a stock market increase.

Following is a brief description of economic variables that should be carefully watched by investors.

Money Supply

The money supply is the level of funds available at a given time for conducting transactions in an economy, as reported by the Federal Reserve. The Federal Reserve system can influence money supply through its monetary policy measures. Several other definitions relate to the money supply: *M1* is currency in circulation, such as demand deposits, traveler's checks, and, that in interest-bearing NOW accounts; *M2*, the most widely followed measure, equals M1 plus savings deposits, money market deposit accounts, and money market funds; and *M3* is M2 plus large CDs. Moderate

Figure 3-3: Source of Economic Information Example

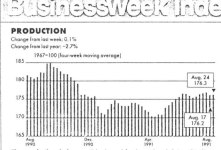

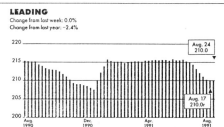

PRODUCTION

Change from last week: 0.1%
Change from last year: -2.7%

1967=100 (four-week moving average)

Aug. 24
176.3

Aug. 17
176.2

The production index was little changed for the week ended Aug. 24. On a seasonally adjusted basis, output of lumber, rail-freight traffic, paperboard, coal, and electric power increased. Truck, steel, and paper production declined. Auto and crude-oil refining output levels were unchanged from the previous week. Before calculation of the four-week moving average, the index advanced strongly, to 177.9, from 176.5 in the prior week.

BW production index copyright 1991 by McGraw-Hill Inc.

LEADING

Change from last week: 0.0%
Change from last year: -2.4%

Aug. 24
210.0

Aug. 17
210.0r

The leading index was flat during the week ended Aug. 24, as the index continued to signal sluggish economic growth in the coming months. Stock prices were lower, and the growth in real estate loans has fallen sharply since early July. On the plus side were lower bond yields, a smaller rate of decline in materials prices, a drop in the number of business failures, and an increase in M2. Prior to calculation of the four-week moving average, the index dropped to 209.8, from 210.5.

Leading index copyright 1991 by Center for International Business Cycle Research

PRODUCTION INDICATORS

	Latest week	Week ago	% Change year ago
STEEL (8/31) thous. of net tons	1,599	1,583#	-16.1
AUTOS (8/31) units	107,788	111,948r#	-14.2
TRUCKS (8/31) units	75,996	70,691r#	2.2
ELECTRIC POWER (8/31) millions of kilowatt-hours	65,905	62,667#	1.0
CRUDE-OIL REFINING (8/31) thous. of bbl./day	14,099	13,873#	-0.5
COAL (8/24) thous. of net tons	20,837#	20,388	-0.2
PAPERBOARD (8/24) thous. of tons	820.1#	789.0r	10.8
PAPER (8/24) thous. of tons	771.0#	771.0r	0.0
LUMBER (8/24) millions of ft.	515.3#	488.7	7.4
RAIL FREIGHT (8/24) billions of ton-miles	20.2#	19.9	-3.8

Sources: American Iron & Steel Institute, Ward's Automotive Reports, Edison Electric Institute, American Petroleum Institute, Energy Dept., American Paper Institute, WWPA¹, SFPA², Association of American Railroads.

FOREIGN EXCHANGE

	Latest week	Week ago	Year ago
JAPANESE YEN (9/4)	135	137	141
GERMAN MARK (9/4)	1.74	1.74	1.56
BRITISH POUND (9/4)	1.69	1.69	1.89
FRENCH FRANC (9/4)	5.90	5.90	5.23
CANADIAN DOLLAR (9/4)	1.14	1.14	1.16
SWISS FRANC (9/4)	1.52	1.52	1.30
MEXICAN PESO (9/4)³	3,034	3,034	2,892

Sources: Major New York banks. Currencies expressed in units per U. S. dollar, except for British pound expressed in dollars.

PRICES

	Latest week	Week ago	% Change year ago
GOLD (9/4) $/troy oz.	348.700	354.500	-9.0
STEEL SCRAP (9/3) #1 heavy, $/ton	97.00	94.00	-16.0
FOODSTUFFS (8/30) index, 1967=100	202.5	204.9	-4.8
COPPER (8/31) ¢/lb.	107.5	104.8	-19.5
ALUMINUM (8/31) ¢/lb.	58.1	57.9	-29.1
WHEAT (8/31) #2 hard, $/bu.	3.21	3.07	12.6
COTTON (8/31) strict low middling 1-1/16 in., ¢/lb.	65.19	65.36	-13.0

Sources: London Wednesday final setting, Chicago market, Commodity Research Bureau, Metals Week, Kansas City market, Memphis market.

LEADING INDICATORS

	Latest week	Week ago	% Change year ago
STOCK PRICES (8/30) S&P 500	395.09	386.40	22.8
CORPORATE BOND YIELD, Aaa (8/30)	8.70%	8.68%	-9.0
INDUSTRIAL MATERIALS PRICES (8/30)	97.0	96.6	-7.9
BUSINESS FAILURES (8/23)	339	355	16.1
REAL ESTATE LOANS (8/21) billions	$398.2	$399.7	3.9
MONEY SUPPLY, M2 (8/19) billions	$3,407.0	$3,400.4r	2.9
INITIAL CLAIMS, UNEMPLOYMENT (8/17) thous.	421	430	10.2

Sources: Standard & Poor's, Moodys, Journal of Commerce (index: 1980=100), Dun & Bradstreet (failures of large companies), Federal Reserve Board, Labor Dept. CIBCR seasonally adjusts data on business failures and real estate loans.

MONTHLY ECONOMIC INDICATORS

	Latest month	Month ago	% Change
CONSTR. SPENDING (July) annual rate, billions	$404.9	$398.7r	-10.6
PERSONAL INCOME (July) annual rate, billions	$4,807.7	$4,813.3r	3.1
12 LEADING INDICATORS COMPOSITE (July) index	145.4	143.7	-0.5
NEW HOME SALES (July) annual rate. thous.	472	516r	-12.8

Sources: Census Bureau, Commerce Dept.

MONETARY INDICATORS

	Latest week	Week ago	% Change year ago
MONEY SUPPLY, M1 (8/19)	$864.9	$862.8r	5.7
BANKS' BUSINESS LOANS (8/21)	299.8	299.9	-6.9
FREE RESERVES (8/21)	656r	171r	NM
NONFINANCIAL COMMERCIAL PAPER (8/21)	139.7	140.7	-3.7

Sources: Federal Reserve Board (in billions, except for free reserves, which are expressed for a two-week period in millions).

MONEY MARKET RATES

	Latest week	Week ago	Year ago
FEDERAL FUNDS (9/3)	5.82%	5.59%	8.25%
PRIME (9/4)	8.50	8.50	10.00
COMMERCIAL PAPER 3-MONTH (9/3)	5.76	5.74	7.85
CERTIFICATES OF DEPOSIT 3-MONTH (9/4)	5.60	5.66	7.94
EURODOLLAR 3-MONTH (8/31)	5.64	5.58	8.08

Sources: Federal Reserve Board, First Boston

#Raw data in the production indicators are seasonally adjusted in computing the BW index (chart); other components (estimated and not listed) include machinery and defense equipment. 1=Western Wood Products Assn.   2=Southern Forest Products Assn.   3=Free market value   NA=Not available   r=revised   NM=Not meaningful

Reprinted from September 16, 1991 of *Business Week* by special permission. ©1991 by McGraw-Hill, Inc.

growth is thought to have a positive impact on the economy; rapid growth is viewed as inflationary; a sharp drop in the money supply is considered recessionary.

Interest Rates

Interest rates represent the costs of borrowing and the value of fixed-income investments such as bonds. Rising interest rates depress values of fixed-income securities, whereas falling rates boost their prices. *NOTE: Remember the basic rule of investing in fixed-income securities such as bonds: prices move inversely to movement in rates.*

High interest rates tend to adversely affect the equity market as well. Rising rates send stock prices down for two reasons. First, higher rates mean bigger borrowing expenses for companies, which erode corporate profits and in turn depress stock prices. Second, share values fall because high interest rates lure investors away from stocks and into interest-paying investments such as money market funds.

You can discern broad trends by focusing on two rates. One is the *prime rate*, the rate banks charge their best customers for short-term loans. When the prime rate is climbing, it means companies are borrowing heavily and the economy is still on an upward swing. The second rate is the **yield on 90-day Treasury bills**. When yields on 90-day bills rise sharply, this may signal a resurgence of inflation, after which the economy could slow down.

Interest rates are controlled by the Fed's monetary policy, which changes the required reserve ratio, changes the discount rate, and affects open market operations—that is, purchase and sale of government securities. For example, cuts in the discount rate are aimed at stimulating the economy—a positive development for stocks. Table 3-4 summarizes the effect of cutting the discount rate on the economy. NOTE: The size of the cut is a critical consideration. For example, a half-point discount rate in itself is not strong enough to get the economy moving fast. External political conditions (such as the crisis in the Middle East), the federal deficit, and bank and S&L problems would make companies hesitant to expand again and also keep consumers and investors nervous longer than the Fed would anticipate. The following diagram summarizes the impact of open market operations on the money supply, level of interest rates, and loan demand.

Easy Money Policy

Fed buys securities —> Bank reserve up —> Bank lending up —> Money supply up —> Interest rates down —> Loan demand up

Tight Money Policy

Fed sells securities —> Bank reserve down —> Bank lending down —> Money supply down —> Interest rates up —> Loan demand down

---

TABLE 3-4: Effects of Lowering the Discount Rate

—**The players:** The Federal Reserve is the nation's central bank. It regulates the flow of money through the economy.

—**The action:** Discount rate is what the Federal Reserve charges on short-term loans to member banks. When the Fed cuts the discount rate, it means banks can get cash more cheaply and thus charge less on loans.

—**The first effect:** Within a few days, banks are likely to start passing on the discounts by cutting their prime rate, which is what banks charge on loans to their best corporate customers.

—**Impact:** Businesses are more likely to borrow. Second, adjustable consumer loans are tied to the prime. These become cheaper, which stimulates spending.

—**The second effect:** Within a few weeks, rates drop on mortgages, auto loans, and construction loans.

—**The third effect:** The lower the rates, the more investors move their cash to stocks, thus creating new wealth.

—**The goal:** To jump start the economy. If lower interest rates cause businesses to start growing, laid-off workers get jobs, retailers start selling, and the economy starts to roll again.

Some of the more important rates are explained below. The *Wall Street Journal* carries key interest rates (see Figures 3-4 and 3-5). The **Federal Reserve Bank of St. Louis** charts these key rates and others (see Figures 3-6 and 3-7).

Prime rate—the rate banks charge their best customers for short-term loans. This is a bellwether rate in that it is construed as a sign of rising or falling loan demand and economic activity.

Federal funds rate—the rate on short-term loans among commercial banks for overnight use. The Fed influences this rate by open market operations and by changing the bank's required reserve.

Discount rate—the charge on loans to depository institutions by the Fed. A change in the discount rate is considered a major economic event and is expected to have an impact on security prices, especially bonds. A change in the prime rate usually follows the change in the discount rate.

90-day Treasury bills—yield representing the direction of short-term rates, a closely watched indicator.

5-year and 10-year Treasury notes—yields indicating the prevailing interest rates for intermediate-term fixed-income securities.

30-year Treasury bonds—also called the long bond yield, a closely watched indicator of long-term interest rates because the entire bond market (and sometimes the stock market) often moves in line with this rate.

Figure 3-4: Key Interest Rates

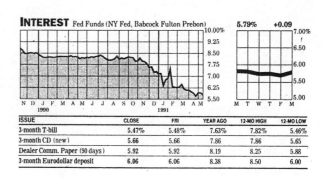

Key Interest Rates

Annualized interest rates on certain investments as reported by the Federal Reserve Board on a weekly-average basis:

	Week Ended: July 12, 1991	July 5, 1991
Treasury bills (90 day)-a	5.57	5.58
Commrcl paper (Dealer, 90 day)-a	6.13	6.13
Certfs of Deposit (Resale, 90 day)	6.02	6.04
Federal funds (Overnight)-b	5.79	6.34
Eurodollars (90 day)-b	6.06	6.06
Treasury bills (one year)-c	6.30	6.40
Treasury notes (three year)-c	7.44	7.42
Treasury notes (five year)-c	7.97	7.95
Treasury notes (ten year)-c	8.32	8.28
Treasury bonds (30 year)-c	8.50	8.45

a-Discounted rates. b-Week ended Wednesday, July 10, 1991 and Wednesday July 3, 1991. c-Yields, adjusted for constant maturity.

INTEREST Fed Funds (NY Fed, Babcock Fulton Prebon) 5.79% +0.09

ISSUE	CLOSE	FRI	YEAR AGO	12-MO HIGH	12-MO LOW
3-month T-bill	5.47%	5.48%	7.63%	7.82%	5.46%
3-month CD (new)	5.66	5.66	7.86	7.86	5.65
Dealer Comm. Paper (90 days)	5.92	5.92	8.19	8.25	5.88
3-month Eurodollar deposit	6.06	6.06	8.38	8.50	6.00

Inflation

Inflation is the general rise in prices of consumer goods and services. The federal government measures inflation by comparing prices today—measured in terms of the CPI, PPI, and/or GNP deflator—to a two-year period, 1982–1984. Rising prices are public enemy number one for stocks and bonds. Inflation usually hurts stock prices since higher consumer prices lessen the value of future corporate earnings, which make shares of those companies less appealing to investors. By contrast, when prices rocket ahead, investors often flock to long-term inflation hedges such as real estate and gold. *NOTE: Check to see whether the inflation rate has been rising (a negative, or bearish, sign for stock and bond investors) or falling (a bullish sign).*

Most likely, the Federal Reserve will tighten the money supply and raise interest rates (such as discount rate or federal funds rate). The underlying idea is that if it costs too much to borrow money, then there is less demand for products, which in turn pushes prices down. The following diagram shows how inflation affects the price of products.

Inflation —>Fed raises discount rate —> Interest rates up —> Demand for money down —> Demand for products down —> Prices down

In economic theory, interest rates are no more than a reflection of what expectations are for inflation. Inflation therefore means higher interest rates.

Productivity and Unit Labor Costs

Data on productivity and unit labor costs are released by the U.S. Labor Department. Increased productivity, or getting more worker output per hour on the job, is consi-

FIGURE 3-5: Key Interest Rates—Daily Money Rates

Wednesday, May 1, 1991

The key U.S. and foreign annual interest rates below are a guide to general levels but don't always represent actual transactions.

PRIME RATE: 8½%–9%. The base rate on corporate loans at large U.S. money center commercial banks.

FEDERAL FUNDS: 6⅛% high, 2% low, 5% near closing bid, 6% offered. Reserves traded among commercial banks for overnight use in amounts of $1 million or more. Source: Babcock Fulton Prebon (U.S.A.) Inc.

DISCOUNT RATE: 5½%. The charge on loans to depository institutions by the New York Federal Reserve Bank.

CALL MONEY: 7½% to 8½%. The charge on loans to brokers on stock exchange collateral.

COMMERCIAL PAPER placed directly by General Motors Acceptance Corp.: 5.80% 15 to 56 days; 5.50% 57 to 63 days; 5.80% 64 to 119 days; 5.825% 120 to 179 days; 5.80% 180 to 270 days.

COMMERCIAL PAPER: High-grade unsecured notes sold through dealers by major corporations in multiples of $1,000: 5.90% 30 days; 5.90% 60 days; 5.90% 90 days.

CERTIFICATES OF DEPOSIT: 5.66% one month; 5.69% two months; 5.69% three months; 5.74% six months; 6.13% one year. Average of top rates paid by major New York banks on primary new issues of negotiable C.D.s, usually on amounts of $1 million and more. The minimum unit is $100,000. Typical rates in the secondary market: 5.80% one month; 5.90% three months; 6% six months.

BANKERS ACCEPTANCES: 5.69% 30 days; 5.69% 60 days; 5.69% 90 days; 5.69% 120 days; 5.69% 150 days; 5.69% 180 days. Negotiable, bank-backed business credit instruments typically financing an import order.

LONDON LATE EURODOLLARS: 6% – 5⅞% one month; 6% – 5⅞% two months; 6 1/16% – 5 15/16% three months; 6 1/16% – 5 15/16% four months; 6⅛% – 6% five months; 6⅛% – 6% six months.

LONDON INTERBANK OFFERED RATES (LIBOR): 5 15/16% one month; 6 1/16% three months; 6⅛% six months; 6 9/16% one year. The average of interbank offered rates for dollar deposits in the London market based on quotations at five major banks. Effective rate for contracts entered into two days from date appearing at top of this column.

FOREIGN PRIME RATES: Canada 9.75%–10.25%; Germany 10.50%; Japan 7.88%; Switzerland 10.63%; Britain 12%. These rate indications aren't directly comparable; lending practices vary widely by location.

TREASURY BILLS: Results of the Monday, April 29, 1991, auction of short-term U.S. government bills, sold at a discount from face value in units of $10,000 to $1 million: 5.60% 13 weeks; 5.68% 26 weeks.

FEDERAL HOME LOAN MORTGAGE CORP. (Freddie Mac): Posted yields on 30-year mortgage commitments for delivery within 30 days. 9.40%, standard conventional fixed-rate mortgages; 6.625%, 2% rate capped one-year adjustable rate mortgages. Source: Telerate Systems Inc.

FEDERAL NATIONAL MORTGAGE ASSOCIATION (Fannie Mae): Posted yields on 30 year mortgage commitments for delivery within 30 days (priced at par). 9.33%, standard conventional fixed rate-mortgages; 7.10%, 6/2 rate capped one-year adjustable rate mortgages. Source: Telerate Systems Inc.

MERRILL LYNCH READY ASSETS TRUST: 5.76%. Annualized average rate of return after expenses for the past 30 days; not a forecast of future returns.

PRIME RATE: 8½%–9%. The base rate on corporate loans at large U.S. money center commercial banks.

FEDERAL FUNDS: 6⅛% high, 2% low, 5% near closing bid, 6% offered. Reserves traded among commercial banks for overnight use in amounts of $1 million or more. Source: Babcock Fulton Prebon (U.S.A.) Inc.

DISCOUNT RATE: 5½%. The charge on loans to depository institutions by the New York Federal Reserve Bank.

---

dered vital to increasing the nation's standard of living without inflation. Meanwhile, unit labor costs is a key gauge of future price inflation, along with the CPI, PPI, and GNP deflator.

Recession

Recession means a sinking economy. Unfortunately, there is no consensus definition and measure of recession, but three or more straight monthly drops of the Index of

FIGURE 3-6: Key Interest Rates Charted

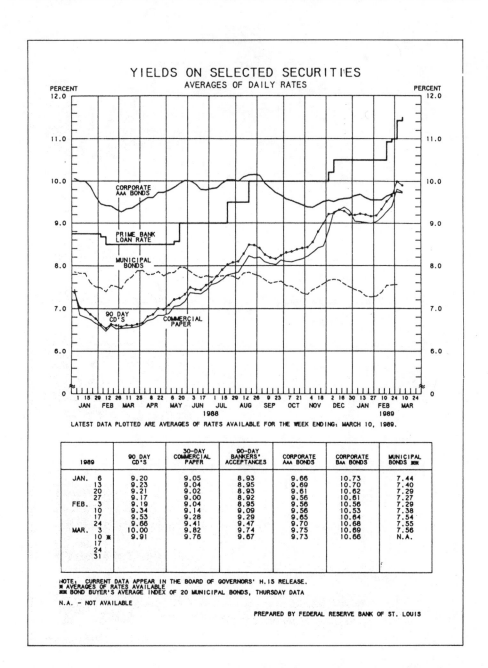

YIELDS ON SELECTED SECURITIES
AVERAGES OF DAILY RATES

LATEST DATA PLOTTED ARE AVERAGES OF RATES AVAILABLE FOR THE WEEK ENDING: MARCH 10, 1989.

1989	90 DAY CD'S	30-DAY COMMERCIAL PAPER	90-DAY BANKERS' ACCEPTANCES	CORPORATE AAA BONDS	CORPORATE BAA BONDS	MUNICIPAL BONDS ᵣᵣᵣ
JAN. 6	9.20	9.05	8.93	9.66	10.73	7.44
13	9.23	9.04	8.95	9.69	10.70	7.40
20	9.21	9.02	8.93	9.61	10.62	7.29
27	9.17	9.00	8.92	9.56	10.61	7.27
FEB. 3	9.19	9.04	8.95	9.56	10.56	7.29
10	9.34	9.14	9.09	9.56	10.53	7.38
17	9.53	9.28	9.29	9.65	10.64	7.54
24	9.66	9.41	9.47	9.70	10.68	7.55
MAR. 3	10.00	9.82	9.74	9.75	10.69	7.56
10 ᵣ	9.91	9.76	9.67	9.73	10.66	N.A.
17						
24						
31						

NOTE: CURRENT DATA APPEAR IN THE BOARD OF GOVERNORS' H.15 RELEASE.
ᵣ AVERAGES OF RATES AVAILABLE
ᵣᵣᵣ BOND BUYER'S AVERAGE INDEX OF 20 MUNICIPAL BONDS, THURSDAY DATA

N.A. - NOT AVAILABLE

PREPARED BY FEDERAL RESERVE BANK OF ST. LOUIS

Source: Federal Reserve Bank of St. Louis.

FIGURE 3-7: Selected Interest Rates Charted

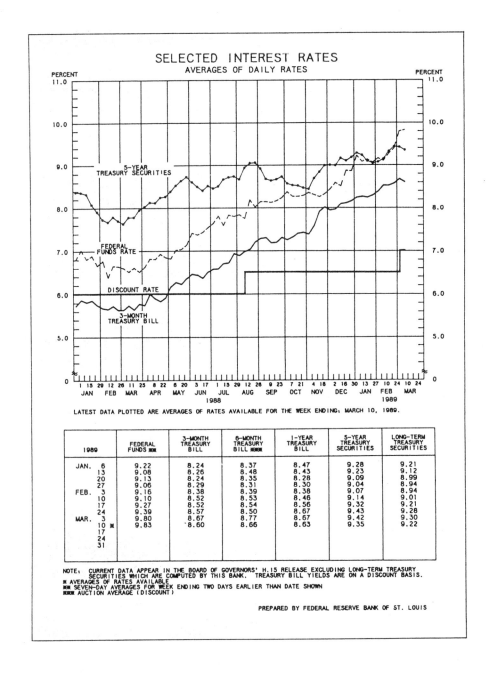

SELECTED INTEREST RATES
AVERAGES OF DAILY RATES

LATEST DATA PLOTTED ARE AVERAGES OF RATES AVAILABLE FOR THE WEEK ENDING: MARCH 10, 1989.

1989	FEDERAL FUNDS ✱	3-MONTH TREASURY BILL	6-MONTH TREASURY BILL ✱✱	1-YEAR TREASURY BILL	5-YEAR TREASURY SECURITIES	LONG-TERM TREASURY SECURITIES
JAN. 6	9.22	8.24	8.37	8.47	9.28	9.21
13	9.08	8.26	8.48	8.43	9.23	9.12
20	9.13	8.24	8.35	8.28	9.09	8.99
27	9.06	8.29	8.31	8.30	9.04	8.94
FEB. 3	9.16	8.38	8.39	8.38	9.07	8.94
10	9.10	8.52	8.53	8.46	9.14	9.01
17	9.27	8.52	8.54	8.56	9.32	9.21
24	9.39	8.57	8.50	8.67	9.43	9.28
MAR. 3	9.80	8.67	8.77	8.67	9.42	9.30
10 ✱	9.83	·8.60	8.66	8.63	9.35	9.22
17						
24						
31						

NOTE: CURRENT DATA APPEAR IN THE BOARD OF GOVERNORS' H.15 RELEASE EXCLUDING LONG-TERM TREASURY
       SECURITIES WHICH ARE COMPUTED BY THIS BANK.   TREASURY BILL YIELDS ARE ON A DISCOUNT BASIS.
✱ AVERAGES OF RATES AVAILABLE
✱✱ SEVEN-DAY AVERAGES FOR WEEK ENDING TWO DAYS EARLIER THAN DATE SHOWN
✱✱✱ AUCTION AVERAGE (DISCOUNT)

PREPARED BY FEDERAL RESERVE BANK OF ST. LOUIS

Source: Federal Reserve Bank of St. Louis.

Leading Economic Indicators are generally considered a sign of recession; two consecutive quarterly drops of GNP signal recession; or consecutive monthly drops of durable goods orders most likely result in less production and increasing layoffs in the factory sector. Recession tends to dampen consumer and investor spirit and thus depress prices of various investment vehicles, including securities and real estate.

Federal Deficit

The national debt is the sum of all money the government has borrowed to finance budget deficits. Another way of looking at it is as the accumulation of all past government decisions to borrow in order to pay debts rather than to raise tax revenues. The only way a government can reduce its debt is to run a budget surplus, that is, to obtain more money than it spends. The surplus must then be used to pay off maturing debts (bonds, notes, and so forth) rather than replacing them (rolling them over) with more debt. This federal deficit affects the economy as a whole.

The U.S. Balance of Payments

A balance of payments is a systematic record of a country's receipts from, or payments to, other countries. Balance of payments is somewhat similar to the balance sheets for businesses, only on a national level. Media reference to the "balance of trade" usually refers to goods within the *goods* and services category of the *current account*. It also refers to merchandise or "visible" trade, because it consists of tangibles like foodstuffs, manufactured goods, and raw materials. "Services," the other part of the category, is known as "invisible" trade, and consists of intangibles such as interest or dividends, technology transfers, services (insurance, tourism, financial), and investment flows.

If the net result of both the current account and the capital account yields more credits than debits, the country is said to have a surplus in its balance of payments. If there are more debits than credits, the country has a deficit in the balance of payments. *NOTE: Persistent deficits generally depress the value of the dollar and can boost inflation. The reason is that a weak dollar makes foreign goods relatively expensive, often allowing U.S. makers of similar products to raise prices as well. An investor must know the condition of a country's balance of payments, because its resulting inflation will affect the market.*

Strong Dollar or Weak Dollar

Which is better—a strong dollar or a weak dollar? Unfortunately, the answer is . . . it depends. A strong dollar makes American's cash go further overseas and reduces import prices, which is generally good for U.S. consumers and foreign manufacturers. If the dollar is overvalued, U.S. products are harder to sell abroad and at home, where they compete with low-cost imports. This aggravates the U.S. trade deficit.

A weak dollar can restore competitiveness to U.S. products by making foreign goods comparatively more expensive. Too weak a dollar can spawn inflation, first through higher import prices and then through spiraling prices for all goods. Even worse, a falling dollar can drive foreign investors away from U.S. securities, which lose value along with the dollar. A strong dollar can be induced by interest rates. Relatively higher domestic interest rates will attract many dollar-denominated investments, which will raise the dollar's value.

AGGREGATE ECONOMIC DATA SOURCES

Economic data are necessary for analyzing the past and forecasting future directions of the economy. The present and future economic environment will bear heavily on the types of investments selected when developing or managing an investment portfolio. Information on economic growth, inflation, employment, personal income, interest rate, money supply, and the like, are important economic data that will influence investor decisions. This information is available in many government and bank publications. A brief description follows of some major sources of economic data.

Federal Reserve Bulletin

The *Federal Reserve Bulletin* is published monthly by the Federal Reserve Board of Governors, Washington, D.C. The *Bulletin* contains the following:

- Monetary data such as money supply figures, interest rates, bank reserves.
- Various statistics on commercial banks.
- Fiscal variables such as U.S. budget receipts and outlays and federal debt figures.
- Data on foreign exchange rates and U.S. dealings with foreign and overseas banks.

Listed below is a partial *Bulletin* table of contents. Each heading may be divided into more detailed sections that provide information for the previous month, the current year (on a monthly basis), and several years of historical annual data.

Domestic Financial Statistics
Federal Reserve Banks
Monetary and Credit Aggregates
Commercial Banks
Financial Markets
Federal Finance
Securities Markets and Corporate Finance
Real Estate
Consumer Installment Credit
Domestic Nonfinancial Statistics
International Statistics

Securities Holdings and Transactions
Interest and Exchange Rates

Quarterly Chart Book and *Annual Chart Book*

These two books, also published by the Federal Reserve Board, graphically depict data in the **Federal Reserve Bulletin.**

The Report on Current Economic Conditions ("The Beige Book")

The *Report*, informally known as the **Beige Book,** is released about every six weeks by the Federal Reserve Board. It provides the most recent assessment of the nation's economy, with a *regional* emphasis. It is used to help the Fed decide on its monetary policy such as changes in interest rates.

Monthly Newsletters/Reviews Published by Federal Reserve Banks

Each of the 12 Federal Reserve banks publishes its own monthly letter or review, which includes economic data about its region and (sometimes) commentary on national issues or monetary policy. Bank addresses are listed in the Appendix to Chapter 13.

U.S. Financial Data, Monetary Trends, and *National Economic Trends*

The Federal Reserve Bank of St. Louis publishes some of the most comprehensive economic statistics on a weekly and monthly basis. Publications include *U.S. Financial Data, Monetary Trends,* and *National Economic Trends.*

 U.S. Financial Data, published weekly, includes data on the monetary base, bank reserves, money supply, a breakdown of time deposits and demand deposits, borrowing from the Federal Reserve Banks, and business loans from the large commercial banks. The publication also includes yields and interest rates on a weekly basis on selected short-term and long-term securities. Examples of these published interest rates appear in Figures 3-6 and 3-7.

 Monetary Trends, published monthly, includes charts and tables of monthly data. It covers a longer time period than *U.S. Financial Data.* The tables provide compound annual rates of change, whereas the graphs include the raw data with trend changes over time. Additional data are available on the federal government debt and its composition by type of holder and on the receipts and expenditures of the government.

 National Economic Trends presents monthly economic data on employment and unemployment rates, consumer and producer prices, industrial production, personal income, retail sales, productivity, compensation and labor costs, the GNP implicit price deflator, GNP and its components, disposable personal income, corporate profits, and inventories. This information is presented in graphic form and in tables showing the compounded annual rate of change on a monthly basis.

Survey of Current Business, Weekly Business Statistics, and Business Conditions Digest

The Bureau of Economic Analysis of the U.S. Department of Commerce publishes three major economic source books: *Survey of Current Business, Weekly Business Statistics,* and *Business Conditions Digest.*

The *Survey of Current Business* is published monthly and contains monthly and quarterly raw data. It presents a monthly update and evaluation of the business situation, analyzing such data as GNP, business inventories, personal consumption, fixed investment, exports, labor market statistics, financial data, and much more. For example, if personal consumption expenditures are broken down into subcategories, one would find expenditures on durable goods such as motor vehicles and parts and furniture and equipment; nondurables such as food, energy, clothing, and shoes; and services. *NOTE: The* Survey *can be extremely helpful for industry analysis in that it breaks down data into basic industries. For example, data on inventory, new plant and equipment, production, and more, can be found on such specific industries as coal, tobacco, chemicals, leather products, furniture, and paper. Even within industries (such as lumber), production statistics can be found on hardwoods and softwoods right down to Douglas firs, southern and western pine.*

Weekly Business Statistics, an update to the *Survey,* supplements the major series found in the *Survey of Current Business* and includes 27 weekly series and charts of selected series. To provide a more comprehensive view of what is available in the *Survey of Current Business* and *Weekly Business Statistics,* presented below is a list of the major series updates:

GNP
National Income
Personal Income
Industrial Production
Manufactures' Shipments, Inventories, and Orders
Consumer Price Index
Producer Price Index
Construction Put in Place
Housing Starts and Permits
Retail Trade
Labor Force, Employment, and Earnings
Banking
Consumer Installment Credit
Stock Prices
Value of Exports and Imports
Motor Vehicles

The ***Business Conditions Digest***, published monthly, provides the information that differs from the other publications previously discussed in that its primary emphasis is on cyclical indicators of economic activity. The National Bureau of Economic Research (NBER) analyzes and selects the time series data based on each series' ability to be identified as a leading, coincident, or lagging indicator over several decades of aggregate economic activity. Over the years, the NBER has identified the approximate dates when aggregate economic activity reached its cyclical high or low point. Each time series is related to the business cycle. Leading indicators move prior to the business cycle, coincident indicators move with the cycle, and lagging indicators follow directional changes in the business cycle. Figure 3-2 (on page 43) represents the composite index of 11 leading, 4 coincident, and 6 lagging indicators that have consistently performed well relative to the general swings in the economy. These 21 indicators were selected from several hundred found in the *Business Conditions Digest* and were time-tested by the NBER. *NOTE: The Digest can be very helpful in understanding past economic behavior and in forecasting future economic activity with a higher degree of success.*

Other Sources of Economic Data

In addition to those covered so far, other publications' data are summarized below:

• Many universities have bureaus of business research, that provide statistical data on a statewide or regional basis.
• Major banks (**Bank of America, Citicorp, Morgan Guaranty,** and **Manufacturer's Hanover**), publish monthly or weekly letters or economic reviews, including raw data and analyses.
• Several other government sources are available, such as *Economic Indicators* and the *Annual Economic Report of the President*, prepared by the Council of Economic Advisors.
• Moody's, Value Line's, and Standard & Poor's investment services all publish economic data along with much other market-related information.

4

Industry
Information

OVERVIEW

In their search for a security, investors who look for fundamentals begin by estimating the prospects for the industrial sector of which the firm is part. They consider factors such as operating costs, competition within the industry, import competition, future tax regulations, and deregulation. Then they assess specifics for the firm: future sales, strengths of the company's present products, market share, and profit growth potential. This chapter first discusses how well an industry fares within the context of the business cycle. Then it examines sources of industry information, including studies.

INDUSTRY GROUP PERFORMANCE IN THE BUSINESS CYCLE

Some industries do better than others, depending on the business cycle. In other words, certain industry groupings typically—but not always—attain earnings gains in periods when overall corporate profits decline. Soft drinks, utilities, tobacco, and office equipment stocks are the Standard & Poor's groups that historically perform well contrary to corporate downturns.

Typically, recession years and the beginning stages of an economic recovery have been good periods of stock market performance. Merrill Lynch has attempted to identify industry groups that are likely to outperform the broad market averages during the early stages of a new bull market (see Table 4-1). Major findings of the Merrill Lynch study led to these conclusions:

• Interest-sensitive stocks, excluding utilities, are good performers. They benefit from the anticipated decline in interest rates that is typical in the early phase of an economic recovery. Examples are bank, housing, and automobile stocks.

• Industries with high *betas* usually outperform the other groups or the market in the early stages of a bull market. (*Beta* will be discussed in detail in Chapters 7 and 9.)

Table 4-1: Group Performance in the Business Cycle

Master Group	Dominant Investment Characteristics	Best Relative Performance	Worst Relative Performance
Cyclical stocks:			
Credit cyclicals	Interest-rate sensitive— perform best when rates low. Most building-related.	Early and middle bull markets.	Early/middle bear— forest products excepted.
Consumer cyclicals	Consumer durables and non-durables. Profits vary with economic cycle.	Early and middle bull markets.	Early/middle bear— hotel/motel excepted.
Capital goods (cyclical only)	Many groups depend on capacity utilization.	Middle and late bull markets.	Late bear markets.
Energy (cyclical only)	Closely tied to economic cycle.	Early bull markets.	Early bear markets.
Basic industries	Profits depend on industry capacity utilization. Prices may benefit from short supplies at economic peaks.	Early and middle bear markets. Economic peaks.	Early or middle bull markets, depending on source of demand for products.
Financial	Banks, insurance, and gold mining.	Late bull and bear. Economic troughs.	Early bull markets.
Transportation	Surface transportation.	Early bull markets.	Early bear markets.
Defensive stocks:			
Defensive consumer staples	Nonvolatile consumer goods.	Late bear markets.	Early bull markets.
Energy (defensive only)	Major international and domestic oil. Volatility introduced by OPEC power.	Late bear markets.	Early bull markets.
Utilities	Large liquidity and operating stability.	Late bear markets.	Early bull markets.
Growth stocks:			
Consumer growth	Combination of growth and defensive. Several subgroups offer high yields.	Cosmetics, soft drinks, drugs: late bear. Other subgroups: early bull.	First groups have no variance in regular cyclical pattern. Others late bear.
Capital goods— technology Capital goods (growth only)	Linked to capital investment spending cycle, which tends to lag behind the economic cycle.	Early and middle bull markets.	Late bear markets.
Energy (growth only)	Linked to economic cycle and to OPEC.	Early bull markets but varies.	Varies.

Source: Merrill Lynch.

• Basic industries and industries classified as intermediate goods and services typically are poor performers in an early bull market.

SOURCES OF INDUSTRY INFORMATION

Industry information can be obtained primarily from government publications, private sources and advisory services, industry statistics and trade journals, reports of compilations, and industry studies.

Government Publications

• *Federal Reserve Quarterly Chart Book* (Board of Governors, Federal Reserve System, Publications Dept., MS 138, Washington, DC 20551, (202) 452-3000). Each industry may be affected differently by the business cycle. For example, the automobile and housing industries likely will be sensitive to short-term swings in the business cycle whereas food and pharmaceuticals tend not to depend on the economy. Figure 4-1 shows the automobile industry's sales relative to the real GNP's growth rate (1979-1987). Notice the similarity of the pattern.

• *U.S. Industrial Outlook* and *Current Industrial Reports* (U.S. Department of Commerce, Superintendent of Documents, U.S. Government Printing Office, Washington, DC 20402). Each of the above publications covers forecasts for some 350 specific industries.

Private Sources and Advisory Services

• *The Outlook* (Standard & Poor's Corporation). *The Outlook* highlights seven industries in each week's issue and carries analytical articles providing investment advice about the market and about specific industries and/or securities. Figure 4-2 is a sample article that highlights industries with superior potential.

• *Analyst's Handbook*. (Standard & Poor's Corporation). This handbook shows industry group trends. The data in Figure 4-3 present a broad overview of 40 key industries from Standard & Poor's list of 87 industry groups; each of these industry groups has its own market index that measures the performance of stocks within that group. Apparently, some industries have performed much better for investors than others.

• *Wall Street Journal* (Dow Jones, Inc.). The *Journal* (Figure 4-4) provides a list of industry groups leading and lagging and industry group performance in its "Dow Jones Industry Groups" section. This information is compiled jointly by Dow Jones, Inc., and Shearson Lehman Hutton, Inc.

• *Industry Surveys*. (Standard & Poor's Corporation). Perhaps most comprehensive of all surveys, it analyzes in detail major industries' operating statistics. Updated by quarterly supplements and completely revised every one to three years, it covers 22 industries. The Appendix at the end of this chapter reproduces parts of an industry analysis by S&P's Corporation. Titled *Health Care: Hospitals,*

FIGURE 4-1: Auto Sales Relative to Real GNP Growth Rate

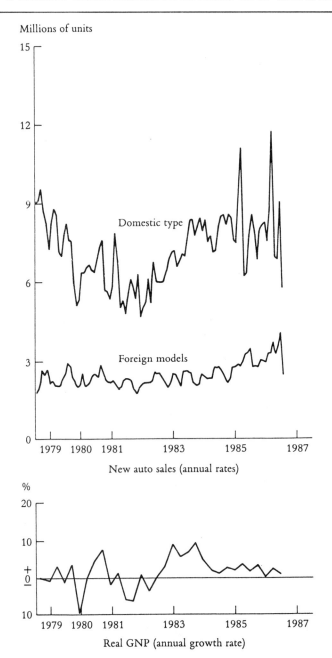

Source: Federal Reserve Quarterly Chart Book (Washington, D.C.: Board of Governors, Federal Reserve System).

FIGURE 4-2: One Private Source of Industry Information

BEST-SITUATED GROUPS

INDUSTRIES WITH SUPERIOR POTENTIAL

The industries highlighted on these two pages were chosen by
S&P's analysts for superior market performance. The chart on page 5 shows wide
variations in the action of stock groups thus far this year and demonstrates
clearly the value of investment selectivity. Each industry discussion
below includes stocks we cite for exceptional prospects.

APPAREL MAKERS
IN GOOD POSITION

Profits of apparel companies have varied widely this year. Despite sluggish consumer spending, LIZ CLAIBORNE, PHILLIPS-VAN HEUSEN, LESLIE FAY and V.F. CORP. have recorded good earnings gains from a year ago. Others, such as CRYSTAL BRANDS, HARTMARX, RUSS TOGS and TULTEX, either have reported year-to-year declines or losses. But the stocks of the industry as a whole have turned in an above-average performance; the S&P textile apparel manufacturers index has climbed more than 35% vs. the 15% gain of the S&P 500. The action is typical of these issues in an economic downturn. They are among the first of the cyclical groups to rise in anticipation of an earnings rebound. We estimate industry profits will surge about 25% in 1992 as consumers loosen their purse strings and retail inventories expand; only a slight earnings gain is expected for 1991. *We believe the following stocks will continue to outpace the market: KELLWOOD, V.F. CORP., LESLIE FAY, LIZ CLAIBORNE, OSHKOSH B'GOSH, OXFORD INDUSTRIES and PHILLIPS-VAN HEUSEN.*

DRUG STOCKS
TO REMAIN IN
MARKET FOREFRONT

The pharmaceutical industry should continue to enjoy uninterrupted above-average earnings growth over the foreseeable future, despite the sluggish economy, looming generic competition for a large number of top-selling products and recent restrictions on drug prices paid by the Medicaid program. We expect industry profits in 1992 will rise by at least 15%, which is what we estimate for this year. Profitability should benefit from new potential blockbuster products and mergers, restructurings and other corporate moves aimed at fattening bottom-lines, as well as from hefty common-share buyback programs. Although the group, as measured by the S&P drug stock index, is up 39%, or more than twice the gain of the S&P 500 this year, further gains appear in store in view of the outstanding fundamentals. Over the longer term, the industry should be aided by an increase in the number of elderly (for whom nearly one-third of all prescriptions are written) and continued ambitious research and development programs. *Favored for year-ahead above-average appreciation are: Master List ABBOTT LABORATORIES, BRISTOL-MYERS SQUIBB and MERCK & CO., as well as GLAXO HOLDINGS, LILLY (ELI), JOHNSON & JOHNSON and PFIZER.*

PROPERTY-CASUALTY
STOCKS HAVE
TURNAROUND POTENTIAL

The four-year property-casualty insurance underwriting downcycle appears ripe for a modest recovery by mid-1992. Record catastrophe losses endured by the industry this year, coupled with a drop in investment income because of lower interest rates, will reduce the industry's capital base and aid in firming rates. We don't, however, envision a wholesale upturn in insurance rates. Specialized lines of business are most likely to achieve price increases, while standard commercial lines (general liability) and most personal lines (auto and homeowners) will have a harder time posting gains due to regulatory and competitive pressures. With the S&P property-casualty group index lagging behind the market over the past two years, we believe that anticipation of a modest recovery in underwriting results will boost the better quality insurers (those with sound balance sheets and superior underwriting records). *Our favorites for total return are ST. PAUL COMPANIES, AMERICAN INTERNATIONAL GROUP and CHUBB CORP.*

RAILS TO GET BOOST
FROM RECOVERY

Rail issues have been among the market pace-setters in 1991, posting an average gain more than double that of the S&P 500. Despite a modest decline in freight tonnage, operating profits have held up well, thanks to labor productivity increases and an improving cost structure. With the economy expected to show more vigor in 1992, profits, excluding nonrecurring charges, should climb 18% to a record $4 billion. The industry's return on investment could also reach a record 7.3%, triple that of the late 1970s. We expect coal traffic, which accounts for about 40% of industry shipments, to advance more briskly in 1992 as export markets firm. Grain traffic, a significant factor for Midwest carriers, should improve with an upswing in exports to the Soviet Union. Long-

4   THE OUTLOOK   DECEMBER 11, 1991

FIGURE 4-3: Standard & Poor's Industry Information

Industry Group	Stock Price Index		Change in Index			1988 EPS	1988 P/E
	12/31/78	12/31/88	10 Year	5 Year	1 Year		
S&P 400 Industrials	$107.12	$321.26	199.9%	83.6%	12.3%	$26.02	12.3
Aerospace	$96.92	$312.90	222.8%	43.2%	21.3%	$36.29	3.1
Airlines	$106.32	$241.36	127.0%	55.6%	33.8%	$34.57	7.0
Automobiles	$76.16	$180.04	136.4%	100.8%	32.9%	$34.68	5.2
Beverages (Alcoholic)	$36.19	$217.14	500.0%	151.9%	2.6%	$18.52	11.7
Beverages	$113.09	$413.25	265.4%	183.8%	19.9%	$27.49	15.0
Broadcast media	$414.17	$3,588.12	766.3%	260.6%	16.6%	$124.17	28.9
Building materials	$56.85	$217.55	282.6%	141.0%	37.8%	$15.00	14.5
Chemicals	$52.84	$145.52	175.4%	108.3%	2.9%	$17.57	8.3
Comm. equip. mfgrs.	$10.19	$30.11	195.4%	−24.2%	−1.3%	$1.70	17.7
Computers/bus. equip.	$110.41	$201.06	82.1%	18.4%	−3.6%	$16.02	12.6
Computer services	$10.16	$64.50	534.8%	110.5%	−13.0%	$3.84	18.5
Conglomerates	$16.74	$50.60	202.2%	76.1%	12.3%	$4.25	11.9
Cosmetics	$65.65	$99.56	51.6%	82.7%	8.3%	$7.12	14.0
Drugs	$160.58	$662.74	312.7%	151.3%	13.1%	$40.19	16.5
Electric utils.	$33.45	$53.87	61.0%	38.5%	8.2%	$5.03	10.7
Electrical equip.	$21.89	$88.18	302.8%	10.5%	−4.7%	$5.32	16.6
Electronics (semicon.)	$19.02	$48.33	154.1%	−0.02%	−17.4%	$3.93	12.3
Entertainment	$146.50	$792.98	441.2%	172.4%	20.6%	$29.57	26.8
Foods	$74.13	$437.38	490.0%	263.3%	33.0%	$26.59	16.4
Homebuilding	$20.35	$43.84	115.4%	−19.6%	18.6%	$3.32	13.2
Hospital management	$10.48	$55.53	429.8%	−18.3%	24.0%	$4.73	11.7
Hospital supplies	$37.05	$112.99	204.9%	49.9%	−7.5%	$8.30	13.6
Hotel-motel	$52.00	$213.13	309.8%	105.5%	17.5%	$14.22	15.0
Household furnish.	$143.49	$423.50	195.1%	39.0%	8.9%	$29.08	14.6
Leisure	$28.84	$196.93	582.8%	102.1%	32.0%	$20.47	9.6
Natural gas	$132.76	$329.97	148.5%	61.4%	4.4%	$18.89	17.5
Oil: domestic	$162.34	$524.22	222.9%	62.2%	12.1%	$40.21	13.0
Oil: international	$75.07	$249.93	232.9%	124.4%	13.4%	$25.10	10.0
Pollution control	$27.80	$212.47	664.2%	218.1%	4.8%	$11.00	19.3
Publishing	$248.78	$1,661.45	567.8%	109.1%	15.8%	$67.84	24.5
Publishing newspapers	$23.10	$102.00	341.5%	64.2%	−5.4%	$7.22	14.1
Retail: dept. stores	$138.25	$737.00	433.0%	119.2%	59.7%	$62.29	11.8
Retail: drug chains	$22.20	$88.26	297.5%	55.6%	−1.5%	$6.42	13.7
Retail: food chains	$55.80	$303.70	444.2%	226.5%	61.1%	$13.36	22.7
Savings and loans	$25.96	$40.84	57.3%	9.8%	1.3%	$4.55	9.0
Telephone	$45.02	$53.32	18.4%	27.0%	20.9%	$8.83	6.0
Textiles apparel mfgrs.	$27.51	$152.93	455.9%	100.2%	10.8%	$12.35	12.4
Textile products	$49.07	$399.64	714.4%	276.4%	82.7%	$27.14	14.7
Tobacco	$73.28	$503.79	587.4%	247.9%	47.4%	$39.15	12.9
Toys	$10.52	$18.81	78.8%	−10.6%	17.7%	−$1.94	—

Reprinted from the *1988 Analyst's Handbook* by permission of Standard & Poor's Corporation. All rights reserved.

FIGURE 4-4: Dow Jones Industry Information

May 13, 1991, 4:30 p.m. Eastern Time

GROUPS LEADING (and strongest stocks in group)				**GROUPS LAGGING** (and weakest stocks in group)			
GROUP	CLOSE	CHG	%CHG	GROUP	CLOSE	CHG	%CHG
Retailers,apparel	**979.90**	**+ 24.75**	**+ 2.59**	**Oil drilling**	**103.67**	**– 3.00**	**– 2.81**
Nordstrom Inc	44	+ 2¾	+ 6.67	Global Marine	4⅝	– ⅜	– 7.50
Limited Inc	27⅜	+ ⅞	+ 3.30	Energy Svc	2⅝	– ⅛	– 4.55
U S Shoe Corp	12⅝	+ ⅜	+ 3.06	Parker Drilling	7	– ⅛	– 1.75
Commu-wo/AT&T	**238.68**	**+ 4.72**	**+ 2.02**	**Aluminum**	**319.26**	**– 7.28**	**– 2.23**
Motorola Inc	65⅜	+ 1⅝	+ 2.55	Alum Co Amer	69¼	– 2⅛	– 2.98
Comm Satell	29¾	+ ½	+ 1.71	Reynolds Mtls	59½	– 1⅛	– 1.86
Scientific-Atl	14⅜	+ ⅛	+ 0.88	Amax Inc	23⅝	– ¼	– 1.05
Comptrs-w/IBM	**201.76**	**+ 3.72**	**+ 1.88**	**Retailers,drug-based**	**425.17**	**– 9.39**	**– 2.16**
Seagate Tech	12⅝	+ ⅝	+ 5.21	Medco Contain	46¼	– 2½	– 5.13
Wang Labs B	3⅛	+ ⅛	+ 4.17	Walgreen Co	31½	– ¾	– 2.33
Apple Cmptr	52¾	+ 1½	+ 2.93	Rite Aid Corp	41⅞	– ⅛	– 0.30
Commu-w/AT&T	**348.72**	**+ 6.16**	**+ 1.80**	**Home construction**	**370.96**	**– 8.13**	**– 2.14**
Motorola Inc	65⅜	+ 1⅝	+ 2.55	Clayton Homes	17⅝	– 1⅛	– 6.00
AT&T	36½	+ ⅝	+ 1.74	Kaufman Hm	15¾	– ⅝	– 3.82
Comm Satell	29¾	+ ½	+ 1.71	Standard Pac	9⅝	– ¼	– 2.53
Retailers,broadline	**576.38**	**+ 9.11**	**+ 1.61**	**Securities brokers**	**350.80**	**– 6.28**	**– 1.76**
Dillard Dept St	123¼	+ 4⅞	+ 4.12	PaineWebber	22¼	– ⅝	– 2.73
Sears Roebuck	38½	+ 1	+ 2.67	Salomon Inc	32¼	– ⅞	– 2.64
Wal-Mart Str	40⅞	+ ⅞	+ 2.19	Quick & Reilly	18	– ⅜	– 2.04

INDUSTRY GROUP PERFORMANCE (June 30, 1982=100)

GROUP	CLOSE	CHG	% CHG	GROUP	CLOSE	CHG	% CHG
Basic Materials	344.90	+ 2.40	+ 0.70	Banks,regional	290.47	– 0.09	– 0.03
Aluminum	319.26	– 7.28	– 2.23	Banks-Central	461.76	+ 1.51	+ 0.33
Other non-ferrous	202.97	– 0.90	– 0.44	Banks-East	219.03	– 0.37	– 0.17
Chemicals	407.16	+ 5.23	+ 1.30	Banks-South	234.23	– 0.86	– 0.37
Forest products	244.31	+ 1.11	+ 0.46	Banks-West	337.92	– 0.10	– 0.03
Mining,diversified	277.95	+ 1.82	+ 0.66	Financial services	299.67	– 5.29	– 1.73
Paper products	437.65	+ 1.23	+ 0.28	Insurance,all	343.10	– 2.04	– 0.59
Precious metals	210.44	+ 3.22	+ 1.55	Ins-Full line	205.48	– 1.19	– 0.58
Steel	115.82	+ 0.16	+ 0.14	Ins-Life	468.79	– 4.42	– 0.93
Conglomerate	440.98	+ 1.18	+ 0.27	Property/Casualty	448.56	– 2.34	– 0.52
Consumer,Cyclical	406.87	+ 2.05	+ 0.51	Real estate	448.16	– 3.44	– 0.76
Advertising	479.89	+ 0.84	+ 0.18	Savings & loans	410.38	+ 3.49	+ 0.86
Airlines	344.43	– 0.46	– 0.13	Securities brokers	350.80	– 6.28	– 1.76
Auto manufacturers	257.35	– 0.67	– 0.26	**Industrial**	334.68	+ 0.17	+ 0.05
Auto parts & equip	219.72	– 1.21	– 0.55	Air freight	190.96	– 1.82	– 0.94
Casinos	506.64	+ 2.73	+ 0.54	Building materials	389.09	+ 2.80	+ 0.72
Home construction	370.96	– 8.13	– 2.14	Containers/pkging	566.42	– 3.59	– 0.63
Home furnishings	205.48	+ 0.22	+ 0.11	Elec comp/equip	345.26	+ 3.80	+ 1.11
Lodging	315.91	– 0.97	– 0.31	Factory equipment	272.99	+ 0.76	+ 0.28
Media	479.98	+ 2.70	+ 0.57	Heavy construction	315.69	+ 0.60	+ 0.19
Recreation products	273.93	+ 0.06	+ 0.02	Heavy machinery	159.61	– 1.69	– 1.05
Restaurants	486.73	– 0.14	– 0.03	Industrial services	344.87	– 0.09	– 0.03
Retailers,apparel	979.90	+ 24.75	+ 2.59	Industrial,divers	289.25	– 0.52	– 0.18
Retailers,broadline	576.38	+ 9.11	+ 1.61	Marine transport	426.24	– 1.49	– 0.35
Retailers,drug-based	425.17	– 9.39	– 2.16	Pollution control	881.29	+ 2.53	+ 0.29
Retailers,specialty	472.15	+ 1.55	+ 0.33	Railroads	354.10	– 1.08	– 0.30
Textiles and apparel	659.68	– 7.99	– 1.20	Transportation equip	217.22	– 1.21	– 0.55
Consumer,Non-Cycl	647.48	+ 1.04	+ 0.16	Trucking	246.78	– 2.44	– 0.98
Beverages	730.28	+ 0.64	+ 0.09	**Technology**	280.78	+ 2.73	+ 0.98
Consumer services	398.02	– 0.97	– 0.24	Aerospace/Defense	376.45	– 0.81	– 0.21
Cosmetics	501.97	+ 0.61	+ 0.12	Commu-w/AT&T	348.72	+ 6.16	+ 1.80
Food	782.05	+ 1.06	+ 0.14	Commu-wo/AT&T	238.68	+ 4.72	+ 2.02
Food retailers	706.48	– 2.12	– 0.30	Comptrs-w/IBM	201.76	+ 3.72	+ 1.88
Health care	400.12	+ 0.93	+ 0.23	Comptrs-wo/IBM	253.83	+ 3.03	+ 1.21
Household products	669.25	+ 0.84	+ 0.13	Diversified tech	263.62	+ 2.22	+ 0.85
Medical supplies	477.05	– 0.12	– 0.03	Industrial tech	312.00	+ 2.52	+ 0.81
Pharmaceuticals	608.33	+ 1.97	+ 0.32	Medical/Bio tech	613.79	– 8.23	– 1.32
Energy	280.86	– 1.51	– 0.53	Office equipment	249.79	– 0.20	– 0.08
Coal	234.56	– 0.51	– 0.22	Semiconductor	305.97	– 1.58	– 0.51
Oil drilling	103.67	– 3.00	– 2.81	Software	1565.50	+ 1.55	+ 0.10
Oil-majors	344.73	– 1.88	– 0.54	**Utilities**	246.78	+ 1.06	+ 0.43
Oil-secondary	202.92	– 1.99	– 0.97	Telephone	321.27	+ 3.05	+ 0.96
Oilfield equip/svcs	163.49	– 0.69	– 0.42	Electric	204.98	– 0.25	– 0.12
Pipelines	193.84	+ 1.12	+ 0.58	Gas	173.56	+ 1.80	+ 1.05
Financial	291.83	– 2.14	– 0.73	Water	399.72	+ 4.82	+ 1.22
Banks,money center	187.88	– 2.75	– 1.44	**DJ Equity Market**	351.78	+ 0.70	+ 0.20

History compiled by Dow Jones and Shearson Lehman Brothers.

FIGURE 4-5: Industry Information from *Forbes*

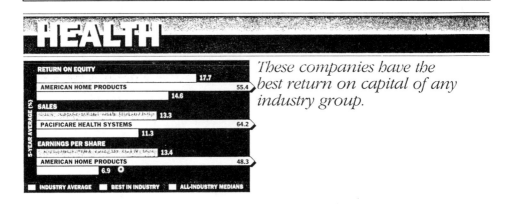

These companies have the best return on capital of any industry group.

OVER THE LAST 12 MONTHS, the median company in the health sector had a 16% increase in earnings per share. In contrast, the median company in the Forbes Industry survey of 1,150 corporations (excluding biotechnology firms) had a 2.6% decline in earnings. The magic bullets for the health companies are new drugs, an aging population, cost-cutting and consolidations.

Health care companies have bucked the downward trend in the Dow industrials. Through mid-November the health stocks followed by FORBES show an average gain of 0.8%, versus the Dow's 7% loss.

The outlook is particularly bullish for biotechnology com-

Health	Profitability				Growth				Sales	Net income	Profit margin
	Return on equity		Return on capital		Sales		Earnings per share				
Company	5-year average %	latest 12 mos %	latest 12 mos %	Debt/ capital %	5-year average %	latest 12 mos %	5-year average %	latest 12 mos %	latest 12 mos $mil	latest 12 mos $mil	latest 12 mos %
Drugs											
American Home Prods	55.4	61.1	33.5	34.1	5.8	2.4	48.3	13.8	6,802	1,207	17.7
Merck	44.6	48.9	39.3	2.7	14.7	16.0	29.5	20.2	7,333	1,707	23.3
Syntex	39.6	53.4	41.6	22.6	8.8	14.0	23.6	16.1	1,585	363	22.9
Marion Merrell Dow	35.8	42.5	36.9	3.6	30.2	103.8	20.7	88.8	2,169	396	18.3
Abbott Laboratories	34.4	34.7	28.7	4.2	12.3	12.9	18.6	15.7	5,904	939	15.9
Warner-Lambert	34.1	41.9	30.4	17.0	6.3	8.1	14.1b	19.8	4,485	472	10.5
Eli Lilly	24.8	26.9	25.0	6.6	6.2	20.2	13.4	21.6	4,894	1,097	22.4
Schering-Plough	23.9	27.9	24.4	7.5	12.2	5.7	20.1	19.6	3,300	546	16.5
Bristol-Myers Squibb	20.7b	19.0	18.1	4.1	11.7	10.6	NM	−30.8	9,924	970	9.8
Rhône-Poulenc Rorer	20.5	def	def	75.4	24.1	100.9	12.3	P-D	2,218	−117	def
Pfizer	18.8	15.9	14.8	3.4	8.6	10.3	6.9	0.2	6,115	734	12.0
Upjohn	16.8	11.0	9.4	10.7	7.3	2.1	5.5	−42.1	2,958	217	7.3
Cardinal Distribution	16.6	11.8	12.5	40.6	19.6	24.3	19.3	6.6	988	15	1.5
Bergen Brunswig	15.9	15.9	15.8	29.1	16.5	13.2	15.2	−1.5	4,442	63	1.4
Durr-Fillauer	13.8	14.7	14.4	2.1	14.3	17.3	12.8	1.2	791	16	2.1
McKesson	12.2	10.7	10.5	19.0	8.2	11.1	5.0	−10.4	8,165	99	1.2
Bindley Western Inds	8.1	9.1	7.6	49.8	24.2	28.0	−10.6	20.3	1,886	5	0.3
National Intergroup	def	def	def	29.1	NM	−4.6	NM	P-D	2,811	−266	def
Medians	20.6	17.5	16.9	13.9	11.9	13.1	13.8	10.2	3,871	380	10.1
Health care services											
FHP International	60.2b	22.8	20.3	18.7	41.2	40.6	31.2	6.9	1,064	30	2.9
PacifiCare Health	25.3	36.3	38.0	0.3	64.2	50.1	16.1	54.2	976	18	1.8
National Health Labs	20.0b	23.7	23.8	0.0	24.2	29.3	31.5	31.7	483	79	16.3
Humana	19.9	22.8	15.1	40.3	15.7	18.7	NM	20.3	4,852	318	6.6
US Healthcare	17.7	31.8	32.9	0.0	34.2	35.3	NM	169.0	1,222	54	4.4
Manor Care	14.5	13.4	7.6	58.0	9.5	13.8	NM	25.4	730	29	3.9
National Medical	12.9	20.4	10.1	45.2	10.7	0.4	NM	55.0	3,834	251	6.6
Lifetime	6.2	14.3	11.0	48.8	NM	55.8	NM	254.8	663	16	2.4
Universal Health	5.1	7.4	7.0	48.8	11.4	6.4	−14.0	48.2	615	12	1.9
United HealthCare	1.8	40.0	25.1	5.3	41.7	40.0	NM	115.4	534	28	5.3

D-D: Deficit to deficit.   D-P: Deficit to profit.   P-D: Profit to deficit.   def: Deficit.   NA: Not available.   NE: Negative equity.   NM: Not meaningful.   a: Four-year average.
b: Three-year average.   For further explanation, see page 95.

Sources: FORBES; Value Line Data Base Service via Lotus CD Investment.

Drugs and Cosmetics, it consists of several key sections: The Outlook; Basic Analysis (covering distribution, statistical analysis, and market action of the product); Industry References; Composite Industry Data; and Comparative Company Analysis.

• *United Business & Investment Report* (United Business Service). This report, published every two weeks, analyzes current business trends and specific industry factors.

• *Value Line Investment Survey* (Arnold Bernhard & Co., Inc.). The survey analyzes the current state and future prospects of four to six industries; published weekly.

• *Business Week* (McGraw-Hill, Inc.). The "Corporate Scorecard"issue summarizes recent performance data on some 24 industries on a recurring basis.

• *Forbes* (Forbes, Inc.). *Forbes* publishes an "Annual Report on American Industry" at the beginning of each calendar year. The report encompasses each of the major industries and, within the industry, rates firms based on two measures of performance: growth (five-year compounded rate for both sales and earnings) and profitability (five-year average for return on total assets and on equity). It further analyzes the past and prospective performance of major industries. Figure 4-5 presents easy-to-digest overviews of the health industry including outlook and vital industry statistics.

Services available to analysts and fund managers include the following:

• *Technical Analyses of Industry* (Merrill Lynch, Pierce, Fenner & Smith). This report is published by Merrill Lynch Capital Markets, Equity Research Department, and contains an overview of the apparel industry, its market performance, and vital industry statistics.

• *Crandall's Business Index* (Crandall, Pierce & Company, Chicago). This publication provides useful analyses along industry lines.

• *Institutional Investment Guides* (Brown Brothers Harriman & Co.). This guide provides institutional investors with useful industry analyses and guides.

Chase Econometrics, Evans & Associates, and Data Resources, Inc. (DRI/McGraw-Hill, Inc.) are private consulting firms that provide industry forecasts as well as economic forecasts based on their own econometric models.

Industry Statistics and Trade Journals

Trade association journals typically discuss current developments and topics of specific interest to the industry. Following is a list of such trade journals, copies of which are available in college and public libraries.

Airline Executive	*Automotive Industries*
American Banker	*Automotive News*
American Gas Association Monthly	*Baking Industry*
American Machinist	*Best's Insurance Report*
American Petroleum Institute Statistical Bulletin	*Brewers Digest*
	Broadcasting—Telecasting

Business Executive of America
Chemical Week
Coal Age
Coal Mining
Computer
Directory of National Trade
    Associations
Dodge Reports
Drug and Cosmetics Industry
Electrical World
Electronics
Engineering and Mining Journal
Engineering News—Record
Fibre Container and Paperboard Mills
Food Management
Implement and Tractor and *Farm*
    Implement News

Industrial and Engineering Chemistry
Iron Age
Leather and Shoes
Modern Plastics
Oil and Gas Journal
Paper Trade Journal
Petroleum Times
Polk's National New Car Sales
Printer's Ink
Public Utilities Fortnightly
Pulp, Paper, Board Packaging
Railway Age
Rock Products
Television Digest
Textile Organization
Textile World
Ward's Auto World

NOTE: The **Business Periodicals Index** *and the* **Applied Science and Technology Index** *list articles in all trade journals.*

Reports of Compilations

• *Encyclopedia of Associations,* Gale Research Company, Book Tower, Detroit, MI 48226-9990.
• *Encyclopedia of Business Information Services,* Gale Research Company, Dept 77748, Book Tower, Detroit, MI 48226-9990.

Both of the encyclopedias above list trade associations that issue annual reports of compilations.

Harvard Business School, Soldiers Field, Boston, MA 02163. Publishes minilists, including:

Basic U.S. Statistical Sources
Basic Investment Services
Lists of Largest Companies
Specific Industries and Businesses
Where to Find Information about Companies
Business Handbooks
Sources of Information for Industry Analysis
Business Dictionaries

Industry Studies

Studies of various industries are available from private consulting firms, such as:

> Business Trend Analysts—Commack, New York
> Arthur D. Little, Inc.—Cambridge, Massachusetts
> Stanford Research Institute—Menlo Park, California
> The Gale Research Co.—Detroit, Michigan (publishes *Statistical Sources* which is revised every three years with an annual supplement; *Trade Names Dictionary* revised in alternate years; and *The Dictionary of Directories*, revised in alternate years)
> Merrill Lynch Capital Markets, Equity Research Department, New York

Most notably, DRI/McGraw-Hill, Inc. (Lexington, Massachusetts), publishes the *DRI Economic Information System*, designed to facilitate industry analysis. It provides macroeconomic estimates and forecasts for some 79 industries, and its data bank includes nearly 7,000 economic and industry time series.

Appendix to Chapter 4

S&P's Industry Surveys: Health Care: Hospitals, Drugs, and Cosmetics*

STANDARD & POOR'S

industry surveys

*1991 Standard & Poor's Corporation   USPS No. 517-780.

AUGUST 22, 1990 (Vol. 159, No. 33, Sec. 1)   Replaces Basic Analysis dated August 2, 1990

health care hospitals, drugs and cosmetics BASIC ANALYSIS

*Sample sections. There are a total of 55 pages in the actual report.

THE OUTLOOK

New prescriptions for sick health care system

Congressional debates calling for reform of the U.S. health care system are likely to gain steam over the next year or so in anticipation of the national election in the fall of 1992. Although the quality of health care in this country ranks among the best in the world, its cost has escalated significantly in recent years, and the system as presently structured does not serve over 35 million Americans unable to afford health insurance. Underscoring the cost problem, federal budget director Richard Darman told Congress last April that if it continues at the present pace, health care will consume 17% of the nation's GNP by the turn of the century, compared with 12% in 1990, 9% in 1980, and about 6% in 1965.

Total national health care expenditures are projected to increase 11.9% in 1991, following increases of 11.9% in 1990, 11.0% in 1989, and 10.5% in 1988, based on estimates made by the Commerce Department and the Health Care Financing Administration (HCFA). These increases represent a reacceleration in medical costs, following a slowing period in the mid-1980s in response to the enactment of the government's more restrictive fixed-fee Prospective Payment System (PPS) for hospital inpatient reimbursement under Medicare.

Health care spending mushroomed from $42 billion in 1965 to an estimated $676 billion in 1990, a compound annual rate of increase of 11.8%. By comparison, GNP expanded at an 8.5% pace over the same period. Medical expenditures have risen faster than GNP in all but three years since 1960.

Medical cost inflation has also continued to surge ahead in recent years, despite relative price stabilization in most other sectors of the economy. Health care costs, as measured by the medical component of the consumer price index, increased at a compound annual rate of 9.2% over the 10 years through 1990, compared with CPI growth of 4.2% over the same period.

Third-party payment system cited

While expansion of government health care programs, demographics, and technology all played important roles, the principal factors behind spiraling health costs relate to

the vital nature of health-related goods and services and the third-party reimbursement structure of the U.S. health care system. Unlike other consumer purchases, the procurement of quality health care is considered a necessity—regardless of cost considerations.

Furthermore, since most consumers are insulated from paying directly for health care products and services, little consumer resistance exists to hold down the cost for these items. The bulk of U.S. medical expenditures is made by third-party payers such as large corporate employers, the government, and insurance companies. Thus, free-market competitive forces, which typically drive prices down in other markets, are not at work here. In addition, the fee-for-service basis of payment for physicians and certain health care professionals provides an incentive to expand instead of restrain all sorts of diagnostic tests, therapeutic procedures, and medications, many of which are believed to be unnecessary.

Rising U.S. medical expenditures are attributable to expansions of Medicare aid for the elderly and Medicaid

Herman B. Saftlas, Health Care Analyst

HEALTH CARE EXPENDITURES AS A % OF GNP
(In Billions of Dollars)

E–Estimated

Sources: Health Care Financing Administration

BASIC ANALYSIS

Industry faces new competitive pressures

Despite the recent implementation of price controls on drugs prescribed under the federal Medicaid program, looming generic competition on a large number of top-selling products, and the recessionary economy, the U.S. pharmaceutical industry should continue to enjoy uninterrupted above-average earnings growth over the foreseeable future. Industry profits are projected to rise about 15%–16% in 1991, with a comparable gain seen for 1992 as well. Earnings for the group of companies in the S&P Drug Stock Index advanced 18% in 1990.

The recession-resistant nature of the business relates to the fact that people get sick in good times and bad. Other positive industry fundamentals include Americans' insistence on quality health care regardless of cost; strong demographic trends among the elderly, who account for close to one-third of all prescriptions written; and continued ambitious research and development (R&D) programs. R&D efforts should spawn a steady stream of new pharmaceutical products, especially in the lucrative fields of cardiovascular, central nervous system, and gastrointestinal therapeutics.

Industry profitability is expected to benefit from a spate of recent mega-mergers and strategic alliances. In conjunction with these deals, there have been a number of restructurings and other corporate moves aimed at improving bottom-line results. Common share buyback programs, which have been running in the aggregate at some $1 billion per year, are also aiding year-to-year earnings per share comparisons of many leading drug firms.

Large U.S. firms dominate the market

Ethical drugs, prescription products available only through medical practitioners, accounted for about 72% of the total $37.9 billion pharmaceutical market last year, based on estimates made by the Commerce Department. (Nonprescription, or over-the-counter, medications represented the balance.) About 70% of the industry's prescription drug output is distributed through wholesalers to hospitals, health maintenance organizations (HMOs), and retail pharmacies, according to statistics provided by the Pharmaceutical Manufacturers Association (PMA). The remaining 30% is sold by the manufacturers directly to these end-user markets.

Although there are hundreds of companies operating in this industry, it is still fairly concentrated, with the four

largest players accounting for more than 25% of annual pharmaceutical sales in the U.S. Although industry concentration was in a declining mode during much of the past decade, a number of large mergers consummated over the past few years reversed that trend.

In addition, U.S. manufacturers dominate the world pharmaceutical market, although foreign producers have made significant inroads in many domestic and overseas markets in recent years. American drugmakers represent more than half of total worldwide pharmaceutical shipments. Of the world's top 20 drug producers, 11 were based in the U.S., three in Germany, three in Switzerland, and one each in the U.K., France, and Japan.

Higher prices fuel revenue growth

Total shipments of prescription pharmaceuticals are expected to rise about 8% in 1991, to about $29 billion, largely reflecting higher selling prices and greater penetration of foreign markets. According to the Department of Commerce, shipments of all pharmaceutical preparations (including both prescription and over-the-counter products) rose about 13% to $37.9 billion in 1990. In constant dollar terms, the gain was only 4.2%. Pharmaceutical sales in 1989, broken down by product classification, are as follows: drugs for the central nervous system and sense organs, 20%; preparations affecting parasitic and infective diseases, 16%; cardiovascular compounds, 15%; respiratory system drugs, 11%; pharmaceuticals affecting neoplasms, the endocrine system, and metabolic diseases, 7%; gastrointestinal and genito-urinary drugs, 14%; skin preparations, 5%; vitamins, nutrients, etc. 8%; and veterinary items, 4%.

Dealing with products affecting human health and well-being, the industry is highly regulated by governmental agencies, primarily the Food & Drug Administration (FDA). Yet pricing has not been regulated in the past. Although government and third-party payers fund more than half of the nation's drug costs, private funds still account for the largest single source of prescription drug funding. Based on a study done by the Purdue University Pharmaceutical Economics Research Center, out-of-pocket funds paid for about 44% of the nation's prescription drug bill in 1990, private insurance for 36%, and Medicaid for 20%.

With strong patents protecting a fair portion of the prescription market, drug makers have near monopolies in many key therapeutic areas, giving them wide latitude with respect to pricing. This fact, coupled with demand inelasticity due to third-party reimbursement, explains why drug prices have increased at superinflationary rates over the past decade. For the 12 months through July 1991, consumer prices for ethical pharmaceuticals increased 9.6%, year to year, compared with a gain of 4.5% for the overall CPI.

Competitive pressures, however, have helped to tone down inflationary tendencies at the manufacturers' level. Producer prices of prescription drugs for the 12 months through July 1991 increased 9.0%, and prices for nonprescription drugs increased 6.2%. According to data supplied by the Bureau of Labor Statistics, specific ethical drug categories showed the following year-to-year price increases through July 1991: analgesics, 5.1%; antiarthritics, 11.2%; systemic anti-infectives, 7.0%; bronchial dilators and antiasthmatics, 8.6%; cardiovasculars, 9.1%;

NATIONAL HEALTH EXPENDITURES
(In percent)

1960 — $27.1 Billion

1980 — $249.1 Billion

1991 — $756.3 Billion

Source: Health Care Financing Administration

Shipments of pharmaceutical preparations
(In millions of dollars)

Category	R1988 shipments	% of total	1989* shipments	% of total
Neoplasms, endocrine, metabolic diseases	2,081	7	2,396	7
Central nervous system	6,173	21	6,668	20
Cardiovascular system	4,450	15	4,826	15
Respiratory system	3,224	11	3,637	11
Digestive system	3,861	13	4,335	14
Dermatological	1,389	5	1,430	4
Vitamin, etc.	2,539	9	2,618	8
Parasitic and infective diseases	4,594	16	5,131	16
Veterinary	1,052	4	1,070	3
Total	29,361	100	31,909	100

R—Revised. *Latest available.
Source: Dept. of Commerce

AUGUST 22, 1991/INDUSTRY SURVEYS

INDUSTRY SURVEYS/AUGUST 22, 1991

H 16 HEALTH CARE

HEALTH CARE/H 15

Continued.

BASIC ANALYSIS (Continued)

cough and cold preparations, 10.3%; dermatologicals, 5.2%; and psychotherapeutics, 18.2%. Segments showing the largest percentage gains reflected the introduction of new therapeutics priced higher than the products they replaced, or areas where therapeutic demand was strong and product availability was limited.

Unlike many foreign countries where pharmaceutical prices are strictly regulated by government agencies, drug companies in the U.S. essentially have a free rein on product pricing, with price increases held in check largely by competitive forces and other marketplace conditions. Other factors at play in the determination of the price of a new drug include the need to recoup the heavy R&D costs incurred in the drug's development, its projected patent life, and the relative size of its market. Companies offering drugs with proven track records, brand recognition, and long patent lives are often able to obtain hefty yearly price increases.

Medicaid cuts: the first industry price controls

Marking the first imposition of price controls on the U.S. pharmaceutical industry, new legislation restricting prices on drugs paid for by the nation's Medicaid program went into effect at the start of 1991. The legislation, introduced by Senator David Pryor (D-Ark.) and passed despite intense lobbying efforts by pharmaceutical industry interests, is expected to save Medicaid about $1.9 billion over the 1991–95 period. These cuts were part of several budget reduction measures Congress enacted under the 1991 federal budget reconciliation package passed in the fall of 1990. Medicaid, the chief entitlements program paying for health care provided to the nation's poor, accounts for about 13% of all U.S. pharmaceutical sales.

Specifically, the new regulations mandate that manufacturers give state Medicaid administrations a rebate on their drug purchases equal to the greater of either: (1) the average market price (AMP) minus the manufacturer's "best price," defined as the lowest price offered to large purchasers, with the discount initially capped at 25%; or (2) a fixed discount from the average market price. This discount has been set at 13% for 1991–92 and will rise to 15% in 1993.

Other features of the new legislation include the indexing of increases in AMPs to the consumer price index, and mandated rebates on generic drugs, capped at 10% for the 1991–93 period, and at 11% thereafter. One concession granted to the industry was the striking of a proposal to establish a national formulary, which would have restricted reimbursement to a select list of "therapeutically equivalent" approved drugs. That proposal had aroused considerable opposition from the industry, since it would have disqualified a large number of drugs for coverage under the Medicaid program. However, state regulations requiring that physicians receive prior approval from state Medicaid agencies for drug reimbursement, often referred to as *de facto* formularies, were not barred.

The law, in many ways, was patterned after individual company initiatives. In early 1990, Merck, the leading U.S. prescription drug manufacturer, had proposed to reduce prices on drugs sold to state Medicaid programs until they equaled the discounted prices offered to such large-volume customers as the Veterans Administration (VA), as long as the state would allow Medicaid patients access to all patented Merck medications.

PRODUCER PRICE INDEXES - DRUGS
(1982=100)

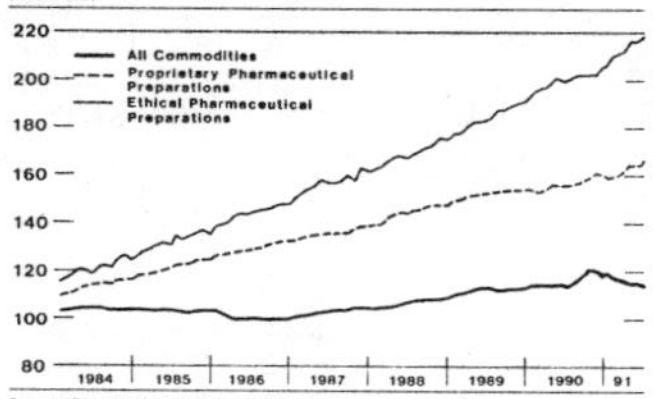

Source: Bureau of Labor Statistics

Producer price indexes for selected prescription drug products
(1982 = 100)

Product	1986	1987	1988	1989	P1990
Ethical preparations	143.6	156.6	169.0	184.4	200.8
Systemic anti-infectives	119.4	125.7	134.2	138.7	146.3
Anti-arthritics	111.1	119.6	125.3	130.4	136.5
Cardiovascular therapy	160.1	172.4	185.8	201.8	220.8
Hormones	120.1	126.9	126.6	143.4	161.5
Diuretics	140.3	151.2	161.0	176.7	192.4
Analgesics, internal	141.8	158.4	181.1	203.0	218.5

P—Preliminary.
Source: Department of Labor.

Costs shifted to private sector

With mandated Medicaid rebates required to match the deepest discounts offered to other large purchasers, many drugmakers have attempted to circumvent the law by eliminating discounts and increasing charges to hospital chains, HMOs, and other large buyers. Criticizing such practices, Senator Pryor pointed out in early 1991 that some drug companies were terminating contracts with HMOs and the VA, while others were trying to reduce rebates by developing schemes to make it difficult to determine actual prices being charged. In response to such actions, Pryor has threatened the industry with the elimination of several important benefits afforded pharmaceutical firms by federal and state government agencies.

Because Medicaid represents less than 5% of industry profits, the new legislation will probably have a relatively negligible impact on industry profitability at first. The fear, however, is that these cuts will set the stage for similar caps in the Medicare program—which represents about 30% of the market—and eventually in private insurance plans. One important outgrowth of the Medicaid legislation will be intensified emphasis on the development of new proprietary therapeutic drug products, since these would have no initial pricing restrictions.

While all demographic segments are affected by the high cost of pharmaceutical products, the elderly suffer a disproportionate hit because of their greater use of drugs. According to Ewe Rheinhardt, an economist at Princeton University, the average American over 65 uses five prescription drugs. The elderly are also more sensitive to high drug prices than other demographic sectors since, by and large, they must incur out-of-pocket costs for their drugs, while insurance companies and other third-party payers fund most employee drug costs. Under the Medicare program, pharmaceutical benefits are limited to hospital inpatient usage.

New drug filings with Food & Drug Administration

Year	Original INDs submitted	Original NDAs submitted	NDAs approved	New molecular entities
1990	1,530	98	64	23
1989	1,345	118	87	23
1988	1,337	126	67	20
1987	1,346	142	69	21
1986	1,623	120	98	20
1985	1,904	148	100	30
1984	2,112	217	142	22
1983	1,798	269	94	14
1982	1,467	202	116	28
1981	1,184	129	96	27
1980	1,087	162	114	12

IND—Investigational new drug. NDA—New drug application.
Source: Pharmaceutical Manufacturers Association.

Competitive pressures to intensify

Although the industry's overall prospects are good, there are several potential negatives that could restrain future profit growth. Besides the specter of increased government intervention to curb inflation in drug costs, makers of branded prescription drugs face a fair amount of sales erosion from generic manufacturers as many key ethicals go off patent. There will be intensified competition in many therapeutic areas heretofore dominated by a relatively few number of products. Increased competition will especially be noticed in the cardiovascular, cholesterol regulation, and antidepressant markets. Assuming a reactivation of generic approvals from the FDA, which have been crimped in recent years after the disclosure of foul play in the generic industry, generic inroads into several important branded markets could be substantial. Over the 1991–93 period, drugs which generated over $4 billion in sales last year are scheduled to lose patent protection.

Drug manufacturers are also facing significant increases in the length of time and expense required to bring a new drug to market, a trend which heightens the inherent risks of new product development. According to a recent PMA survey, it now takes close to 12 years and $230 million to move a drug from the test tube to the pharmacists' shelf, as compared with five years and $100 million five years ago. This exorbitant rate of increase in R&D costs is effectively closing the door to new drug development to all but a handful of the industry's largest players and is probably the main catalyst behind the spate of mega-mergers and consolidations seen in the worldwide drug industry over the past three years.

Research & development expenditures

Company	1988 Mil. $	1988 % of sales	1989 Mil. $	1989 % of sales	1990 Mil. $	1990 % of sales
Abbott	455	9	502	9	567	9
Bristol-Myers/Squibb	688	8	789	9	881	9
Johnson & Johnson	674	7	719	7	834	7
Eli Lilly	512	14	605	14	703	14
Merck	669	11	751	11	854	11
Pfizer	473	9	531	9	640	19
Schering-Plough	298	10	327	10	380	11
SmithKline	R639	9	R772	9	759	8
†Syntex	218	17	245	18	271	18
Upjohn	380	14	407	14	427	14
Warner-Lambert	259	7	309	7	379	8

R—Revised. †Fiscal year ending July 31.
Source: Annual reports.

Regulatory woes

On the regulatory front, the industry is contending with lengthy delays in new drug approvals by the FDA, reflecting underfunding and disarray at the agency in the wake of scandals in the generic drug division. Another possible pothole down the road may be the elimination of important tax credits afforded the industry from operations in Puerto Rico, if that territory is granted statehood. Eager to develop the area, the government has granted major tax breaks to companies investing in Puerto Rico. Taking advantage of the tax savings, pharmaceutical producers have invested heavily in manufacturing facilities in Puerto Rico over the past two decades. However, these important tax advantages would eventually be phased out once statehood is achieved.

Another important issue of concern to the industry is the possible elimination of the Orphan Drug benefit. Enacted by Congress in 1983 to foster the development of drugs for rare diseases (afflicting less than 200,000 patients), the Orphan Drug Act provides research grants, tax breaks, and exclusive rights to manufacturers of drugs aimed at relatively small patient markets that could otherwise be too small to justify commercial development. While the law has encouraged new drug development (45 "orphan drugs" were approved over the past seven years, versus only about 10 in the preceding 10 years) it has come under criticism recently because of large profits many firms are making from drugs which were initially classified as orphans, but have subsequently grown into blockbusters. Some of these include Burroughs Wellcome's *AZT* anti-AIDS drug, Amgen's *Epogen* anti-anemia medication, and Genentech's *Protropin* human growth hormone. Despite pressure to change the law, strong lobbying by patient groups and the Pharmaceutical Manufacturers Association is likely to block any material alteration of the present law.

The federal government is also attempting to defray part of the costs of operating the FDA, budgeted at $770 million for fiscal 1992, through the imposition of user fees to be paid directly by pharmaceutical companies submitting applications for new drug approvals. The Administration has proposed that some $197.5 million of the agency's fiscal 1992 budget be paid for by drugmakers via user fees. Understandably, pharmaceutical manufacturers are staunchly opposed to the levying of such fees, which may equal $764,000 per New Drug Application and more than $44,400 per Abbreviated New Drug Application (used for generics).

Research productivity declines

Although research expenditures have climbed steadily, R&D productivity has declined in recent years, a trend which is likely to continue as development costs continue to accelerate and new therapeutic breakthroughs become harder to come by. The approval rate of New Drug Applications has fallen steadily since the mid-1980s, and the number of approved new molecular entities (NMEs), defined by the FDA as holding "important therapeutic gains," totaled only 23 in 1990, versus 30 in 1985. According to the Pharmaceutical Manufacturers Association (PMA), the U.S. drug industry is expected to spend $9.2 billion on R&D in 1991, up 13.6% from the $8.1 billion spent in 1985 and more than double the amount spent in 1985.

The drug industry's ratio of research outlays to sales ranks among the highest of all major domestic industrial groups. According to the PMA, research outlays are projected to account for 16.9% of revenues in 1991, up from 16.5% in 1990 and about 11% ten years ago. While rising expenditures partly reflect intensified research on chronic and degenerative diseases, which is typically very expensive,

Continued.

INDUSTRY REFERENCES

Industry references

Publication	Frequency of publication	Publisher	Content
American Druggist	Monthly	The Hearst Corp. 959 Eighth Ave. New York, NY 10019 212-297-9680	Trends in prescription activities and general pharmacy and pharmaceutical topics
The BBI Newsletter	14 times a year	Biomedical Business International 1524 Brookhollow Dr. Santa Ana, CA 92705 714-755-5757	Analysis of health care markets and technologies
Drug Topics	Semi-monthly	Medical Economics Co. 680 Kinderkamack Road Oradell, NJ 07649 201-262-3030	Discussion of major issues affecting the pharmaceutical industry and pharmacies
Health Business	Weekly	Faulkner & Gray's Health Care Information Center 1133 Fifteenth St. NW, Suite 450 Washington, DC 20005	News, trends, and perspectives on health care issues
Health Care Financing Review	Quarterly	Superintendent of Documents Government Printing Office Washington, DC 20402 202-783-3238	Comprehensive compilation of national health statistics
Health U.S.	Annual	U.S. Dept. of Health & Human Svcs. Nat'l Center for Health Statistics 3700 East-West Hwy Hyattsville, MD 20782	Health statistics and industry trends
Hospitals	Semi-monthly	American Hospital Publishing, Inc. 211 E. Chicago Avenue Chicago, IL 60611 312-440-6800	General discussion on issues and trends in hospital management, plus government developments
Journal of the American Medical Association	Weekly	American Medical Association 535 N. Dearborn Street Chicago, IL 60610 312-280-7233	General forum for matters relating to medicine and health care
Market letter	Weekly	IMS World Publications Ltd. 800 Third Ave. New York, NY 10022	News on company and industry developments in worldwide pharmaceutical industry
MDDI Reports	Weekly	F-D-C Reports, Inc. 5550 Friendship Blvd. Chevy Chase, MD 20815	Covers the medical devices, diagnostics, and instrumentation industries
The Gray Sheet			Prescription and over-the-counter pharmaceutical industry news
The Pink Sheet			Reports on toiletries, fragrances, and skin care markets and on companies involved
The Rose Sheet			

COMPOSITE INDUSTRY DATA

Industry references, continued

Publication	Frequency of publication	Publisher	Content
Medical Advertising News	15 times a year	Engel Communications 820 BearTavern Rd. West Trenton, NJ 08628 609-530-0044	Advertising in health care industry
Medical Benefits	Semi-monthly	Kelly Communications 410 E. Water St. Charlottesville, VA 22901 804-296-5676	Specializes in health care costs, health policy, and employee benefits
Modern Healthcare	Weekly	Crain Communications Inc. 740 Rush St. Chicago, IL 60611	Issues concerning health care providers, including investor-owned chains
New England Journal of Medicine	Weekly	Massachusetts Medical Society 1440 Main Street Waltham, MA 02254 617-893-3800	Articles on medical treatment and health issues
PMA Newsletter	Weekly	Pharmaceutical Mfrs. Ass'n. 1100 Fifteenth Street, NW Washington, DC 20005 202-835-3400	News and information concerning pharmaceutical companies
Product Marketing	Monthly	U.S. Business Press 11 W. 19th Street New York, NY 10011 212-741-7210	Developments, trends, and articles about cosmetic, fragrance, and beauty markets
Review	Bimonthly	Federation of American Health Sys. 1405 N. Pierce Street, Suite 308 Little Rock, AR 72207	Trends in and perspectives on the investor-owned hospital industry

COMPOSITE INDUSTRY DATA

*Per-share data based on Standard & Poor's group stock price indexes

HOSPITAL MANAGEMENT

The companies used for this series of composite data are: American Medical International (deleted 10/25/89); Community Psychiatric Centers (added 06/24/87); Hospital Corp. of America (deleted 03/15/89); Humana Development; National Medical Enterprises.

	1982	1983	1984	1985	1986	R1987	R1988	1989
Sales	53.35	57.29	60.13	69.23	79.93	75.25	85.84	79.32
Operating Income	10.22	12.06	12.80	14.95	13.39	13.94	15.15	13.33
Profit Margin %	19.16	21.05	23.12	21.59	16.76	18.52	17.65	16.81
Depreciation	2.13	2.52	3.01	3.67	4.90	4.02	4.71	3.31
Taxes	2.42	3.10	3.53	3.30	3.15	3.15	3.03	3.03
Earnings	3.51	4.33	4.73	4.79	2.84	1.71	5.07	5.28
Dividends	0.71	0.88	1.09	1.30	1.44	1.40	1.49	1.82
Earnings as a % of Sales	6.58	7.56	7.87	6.92	2.14	3.51	5.91	6.66
Dividends as a % of Earnings	20.33	20.32	23.04	27.14	84.21	53.03	29.39	30.68
‡Price (1965 = 10) —High	64.96	81.90	68.21	76.59	82.06	85.86	58.33	91.06
—Low	29.26	52.65	49.73	45.20	38.74	42.40	56.48	56.48
Price-Earnings Ratios —High	18.51	18.92	14.42	15.99	35.32	25.33	11.50	18.23
—Low	8.33	12.48	11.13	10.38	24.52	14.87	8.40	10.70
Dividend Yield % —High	2.43	1.63	2.07	2.61	3.61	3.50	2.87	
—Low	1.09	1.07	1.60	1.70	2.22	2.09	2.55	1.78
	17.39	21.67	26.32	30.17	29.39	28.59	30.05	27.79
Book Value								
Return on Book Value %	20.18	19.98	17.97	15.88	9.69	9.23	16.87	19.00
‡Working Capital	4.85	4.51	5.74	6.35	8.78	8.79	7.07	7.22
Capital Expenditures	11.39	13.22	10.88	13.27	12.27	7.95	8.18	7.56

MEDICAL PRODUCTS & SUPPLIES

The companies used for this series of composite data are: Abbott Labs (deleted 01/14/87); American Hospital Supply (deleted 11/20/85); Bard (CR); Bausch & Lomb (added 01/14/87); Baxter Travenol; Becton, Dickinson; Biomet Inc. (added 08/27/90); Johnson & Johnson (deleted 01/14/87); Medtronic Inc. (added 10/22/86); St. Jude Medical (added 11/30/86).

	1982	1983	1984	1985	1986	R1987	R1988	1989
Sales	48.79	52.52	53.10	53.36	71.96	112.46	124.71	125.07
Operating Income	7.92	8.67	9.29	10.28	13.51	19.23	21.04	22.07
Profit Margin %	16.30	16.69	17.10	19.36	18.77	17.10	16.87	17.65
Depreciation	2.01	1.74	2.03	2.38	2.36	3.25	5.13	5.68
Taxes	2.09	2.13	1.87	2.38	2.10	3.66	3.78	4.47
Earnings	4.30	4.51	4.43	5.19	4.87	7.25	8.87	8.88
Dividends	1.36	1.57	8.00	1.91	2.21	2.08	2.48	2.49
Earnings as a % of Sales	8.81	8.59	40.63	9.77	8.77	6.46	7.11	7.10
Dividends as a % of Earnings	31.63	34.81	1.80	36.80	45.38	28.65	27.73	28.04
‡Price (1965 = 10) —High	74.69	82.20	72.50	89.02	130.19	150.44	141.08	151.83
—Low	50.25	66.50	53.05	56.71	80.20	107.08	107.19	114.16
Price-Earnings Ratios —High	17.37	18.23	16.37	17.15	26.73	20.72	15.81	17.10
—Low	11.69	15.18	11.98	10.93	16.47	14.75	12.06	12.86
Dividend Yield % —High	2.71	2.29	3.39	3.37	2.56	1.94	2.29	2.18
—Low	1.82	1.91	2.48	2.15	1.70	1.38	1.74	1.64
Book Value	23.50	25.99	27.07	27.50	22.50	22.21	61.52	60.06
Return on Book Value %	18.30	17.56	16.37	23.01	24.74	32.69	14.32	14.57
‡Working Capital	10.54	10.53	12.78	13.30	10.95	22.71	27.10	29.12
Capital Expenditures	3.92	3.86	3.79	3.71	5.32	7.84	10.96	9.08

Company Information

OVERVIEW

As indicated in Chapter 4, investors tend to look at the industry in terms of its prospects and then assess specifics for a particular company. This chapter discusses sources of company information, the importance of reading and analyzing annual and quarterly reports, what to know about financial statements, Securities and Exchange Commission (SEC) filings, and how to read a prospectus (with a case example).

SOURCES OF COMPANY INFORMATION

A number of publications and newsletters cover company information. Table 5-1 shows a selection of journals that provide data on individual corporations within each industry. Most are available through subscription; all can be found in public and college libraries.

WHY READ ANNUAL (10-K) AND QUARTERLY (10-Q) REPORTS?

A Securities and Exchange Commission (SEC) study of individual investors reported in the *Wall Street Journal* (10/7/80) revealed that only 17 percent relied on their broker's advice in reaching decisions; 86 percent found the corporate financial statement data extremely or moderately useful. Investors making their own investment decisions relied on four major sources of data: company-produced financial statements, forecast information, facts about management, and market-based information.

In *Financial Executive* (April, 1980) authors Phillip Reckers and A.J. Stagliano noted in "How Good are Investor's Data Services" that the failure of the 40 to 50 percent of those people who did not read the financial statement footnotes or the auditor's report "could easily lead to an erroneous overall appraisal." *NOTE: Many critical uncertainties need to be considered here. For example, footnotes des-*

TABLE 5-1: Information Sources for Individual Companies

Title	Publisher	Description
Business Week	McGraw-Hill, Inc.	"Corporate Scorecard" issue summarizes current performance/future prospects of over a thousand firms.
Forbes	Forbes, Inc.	The industry analysis issue, appearing early each year, covers the major firms within each industry; each biweekly issue discusses a number of firms.
United Business & Investment Report	United Business Service	Typically reviews individual firms within a selected industry; biweekly.
Moody's Manuals	Moody's Investor Service	In-depth historical sketch together with current data on all major firms; updated frequently.
The Outlook	Standard & Poor's Corporation	Reviews major current events that affect a specific stock; comparatively analyzes a major industry and its firms; weekly.
Stock Reports	Standard & Poor's Corporation	Detailed data on common and preferred stocks traded on NYSE, AMEX, and OTC markets; updated quarterly.
Corporation Records	Standard & Poor's Corporation	In-depth historical sketch and recent operating data on major firms; updated frequently.
Value Line Investment Survey	Arnold Bernhard & Co., Inc.	Comparative analysis of major firms within industries; each industry's review is updated every 13 weeks.

cribe the firm's accounting policies—information that is essential for interfirm companies. *Those who failed to read them or who said they lost interest also said the footnotes lacked clarity.*

The SEC study showed the following breakdown on investor use of annual report components: 52 percent, the income statement; 40 percent, the balance sheet; 23 percent, the statement of cash flows; 26 percent, the footnotes; and 19 percent, the auditor's report. These findings would indicate that these components are tools for the sophisticated individual investor, institutional investor, or securities analyst.

Research by Lucia Chang and K. Most ("The Importance of Financial Statements for Investment Decisions," A Center for the Study of Professional Accountancy, Florida International University) on investment objectives and news found that:

Another finding was that corporate annual reports were rated the most important sources of information for investment decisions by all these groups. Individual investors rated newspapers and magazines next, whereas institutional investors placed advisory services second. Financial analysts rated prospectuses second and communication with management third.

READING ANNUAL REPORTS

Before investing in a company's stocks or bonds, first read and analyze its annual report. If you already own stock in a particular company, you will automatically receive its annual report. The basic purpose of an **annual report** is to provide the company's financial statements so the reader can assess the company's financial health. Comparative balance sheets for the last two years and comparative income statements for the last three years are provided so as to identify trends.

A publicly held company must publish an annual report within 90 days of the end of the fiscal year. Because most companies operate on a calendar year basis (year ending December 31), they issue annual reports in March. Also, a company must file *Form 10-K* with the SEC within 90 days after year-end. *Form 10-K* is very often more detailed than the annual report; a company will send you a copy of theirs on request.

The financial position depicted in the annual report is **historical**, that is it does not present *prospective* financial information. Because an annual report is prepared by the company, the firm will try to present its financial position within the market in the most favorable light—subject to reporting and regulatory constraints.

All sections in the annual report must be read and evaluated to arrive at an informed judgment about the company's financial health. These sections, discussed below, include the highlights, letter to stockholders (or shareholders), review of operations, management's discussion and analysis, the financial statements (balance sheet, income statement, and statement of cash flows including related footnotes), supplementary schedules, auditor's report, and report by management.

Charts and graphs may be used to highlight or clarify information. For example, a chart showing dividends, earnings per share, and market price of stock history may be provided; or a chart showing the percentage of revenue derived by product line may be given.

Photographs provide a clear message for the reader, and they may convey a certain corporate image desired by the management. For example, glossy photographs of executives and products can be misleading if sales and profits do not corroborate a pictorial of corporate good health.

Highlights

The first section, "Highlights," presents an overview of the company and its financial standing. Comparative information may include at least the past two years' sales, net income, and earnings per share.

Management attempts to provide this information in an upbeat, positive manner. For it to be credible, however, one or two downturns should be presented along with upturns. In other words, a company might emphasize the positive aspects to give a favorable impression—for example, emphasizing an upward trend in dividends. Had dividends been cut back, however, an increase in research and development activity might be emphasized instead.

Figure 5-1 illustrates financial highlights appearing in the 1991 annual report for the Tandy Corporation.

Letter to Shareholders

The "Letter to Shareholders" (usually addressed "To Our Shareholders") is typically signed by the CEO and the president. Often, there is a picture of the two. (Although it opens the annual report, the letter is not a formal part of it.) *NOTE: Take care when reading the president's letter, which may be subjective and biased in an effort to make the company look good. The president wants to portray the company in a favorable light so as to create a positive image. Be cautious when the president sounds too optimistic. The president often writes that corporate growth is expected and there will be emerging products. He or she wants to come across as knowledgeable and honest.*

Even though the letter itself is not subject to audit, it does comment on the past year's financial results and their implications. An explanation is given of the company's performance, without regard to whether that performance is improving or deteriorating. Future plans, directions, and goals are also enumerated; such projections typically are not found elsewhere in the annual report. Reference to future possibilities may include mergers and acquisitions as well as product introductions. A comment may be made on social issues. *NOTE: Carefully evaluate future plans in light of industry conditions, the economy, political environment, and degree of competition.*

By being direct and forthright, the president will give the reader an impression of honesty. For example, in acknowledging "We had a difficult year because . . ." a president will create trust. If problems are stated, the president will likely indicate that he or she knows what the problems are and will take corrective actions. Negative financial results are explained and downplayed with optimistic statements about the future. The president may share a useful perspective about the company, for example by referring to an industry problem or foreign risk exposure.

Be wary of euphemisms; a "challenging" year is most likely an excuse for a *bad* year. An ambiguous statement such as "The company is positioned for growth in its product line" might mean that growth in the product line has yet to occur (had there *been* growth, it would have been reported). Learn to read between the lines.

Reliability of the president's letter may be inferred from past experience. That is, if the president consistently has been honest, that likely will be the case again. However, if previous assertions and predictions have proved to be exaggerations, then it's probable that current claims are "blown up" or just plain wrong.

FIGURE 5-1: Annual Report Financial Highlights Example

Year Ended June 30	1991	1990
Net sales and operating revenues	$4,561,782	$4,499,604
Income before cumulative effect of change in accounting principle	$ 206,063	$ 290,347
Net income	$ 195,444	$ 290,347
Income per share before cumulative effect of change in accounting principle	$2.58	$3.54
Net income per average common share	$2.44	$3.54
Total assets	$3,078,145	$3,239,980
Total debt	$ 607,685	$ 948,411
Stockholders' equity	$1,846,762	$1,723,496
Stockholders' equity per common share	$ 23.48	$ 21.78
Average common shares outstanding	78,258	81,943
Working capital	$1,550,848	$1,312,517
Current ratio	3.18 to 1	2.12 to 1
Total debt as a percent of total capitalization . . .	24.8%	35.5%

Dollar amounts in thousands, except per share figures.

If the company is a "penny stock firm," there is high risk and probability of failure because small companies usually have no track record; thus you should significantly discount the president's comments.

Review of Operations

Typically the longest section, "Review of Operations" is often public relations oriented, complete with nice pictures. This section provides key information about the company's products, services, facilities, and future directions. It also tries to direct the reader away from negative realities. For example, if the review emphasizes the future rather than the present, the current situation may not be that favorable. In a similar vein, if there is an emphasis on employee loyalty or the company's attempt to help build America, the intent may be to direct attention away from disappointing earnings.

Failure to discuss key areas may imply that the company is trying to hide something. If the company mentioned something last year but not this year, ask yourself why. For example, if in the previous year management stated that rapid growth and expansion is expected in a particular product line or business segment, but nothing is said about that prediction this year, perhaps expectations did not materialize. It is best for a company to be straightforward and forthright so as to gain reader respect and confidence.

Report of Independent Public Accountant

The independent auditor's report, which may be placed before or after the financial statement section, attests to the accuracy and validity of the financial statements. The auditor's opinion is heavily relied on because he or she is knowledgeable, objective, and independent. There are four types of audit opinions that may be rendered by the certified public accountant (CPA) in examining a company's financial statements: unqualified opinion, qualified opinion, disclaimer of opinion, and adverse opinion.

An *unqualified opinion* means that the CPA is satisfied that the financial statements present fairly the company's financial position. Such an opinion gives the reader confidence in the accuracy of the financial statements in portraying a company's financial health and operating performance.

Figure 5-2 shows the report of independent auditors appearing in the 1989 annual report of Maytag Corporation.

If a special situation or other uncertainty exists, a pending lawsuit for example, an unqualified opinion may still be given. However, an explanatory paragraph should describe the material uncertainty. The reader is well advised to note the contingency and its possible adverse financial effects on the company. For example, an adverse judgement arising from a lawsuit may result in significant damages; the loss of a tax case may result in additional taxes.

A *qualified opinion* may be issued if there is a limitation in scope of the CPA's work. A limitation in scope arises when an auditor is unable to do one or more of the following: gather enough evidence to support the expression of an unqualified opinion, apply a required auditing procedure, or apply one or more auditing procedures considered necessary under the circumstances.

If the limitation in scope is not severe enough to warrant the expression of a disclaimer of an opinion, an "except for" qualified opinion may be issued, in which case modifications to the report include:

- Adding the phase "except as discussed in the following paragraph" to the beginning or end of the second sentence of the scope paragraph.
- Adding a paragraph before the opinion paragraph that explains the nature of the scope limitations.
- Modifying the opinion paragraph for the possible effects of the scope limitation on the financial statements.

An example of an "except for" qualification is when the auditor is unable to confirm accounts receivable or observe inventory. *NOTE: A qualified opinion is a red flag that requires caution and more detailed evaluation.*

If a severe scope limitation exists and the auditor does not wish to express a qualified opinion, a *disclaimer of opinion* is given. A disclaimer indicates the auditor's inability to form an opinion on the fairness of the financial statements. If the

---

FIGURE 5-2: Example of an Independent Auditors Report

REPORT OF INDEPENDENT AUDITORS

SHAREOWNERS AND BOARD OF DIRECTORS
MAYTAG CORPORATION

We have audited the accompanying consolidated statements of financial condition of Maytag Corporation and subsidiaries as of December 31, 1989 and 1988, and the related consolidated statements of income and cash flows for each of the three years in the period ended December 31, 1989. These financial statements are the responsibility of the Company's management. Our responsibility is to express an opinion on these financial statements based on our audits.

We conducted our audits in accordance with generally accepted auditing standards. Those standards require that we plan and perform the audit to obtain reasonable assurance about whether the financial statements are free of material misstatement. An audit includes examining, on a test basis, evidence supporting the amounts and disclosures in the financial statements. An audit also includes assessing the accounting principles used and significant estimates made by management, as well as evaluating the overall financial statement presentation. We believe that our audits provide a reasonable basis for our opinion.

In our opinion, the financial statements referred to above present fairly, in all material respects, the consolidated financial position of Maytag Corporation and subsidiaries at December 31, 1989 and 1988, and the results of their operations and their cash flows for each of the three years in the period ended December 31, 1989, in conformity with generally accepted accounting principles.

Ernst + Young

Chicago, Illinois
January 30, 1990

---

auditor cannot come up with an opinion, what is the reader to think about the accuracy of the company's financial statements?

An *adverse opinion* is expressed when the financial statements do not present fairly, in conformity with generally accepted accounting principles, an entity's financial position, results of operations, retained earnings, and cash flows. The financial statements indeed may be misleading and should not be relied on by the reader.

NOTE: If a company fires an independent CPA over a disagreement in accounting policies, a red flag should go up. Failure to agree on an accounting policy could mean the company is resorting to an unrealistic policy to overstate earnings. Hence, the financial statement could be erroneous and misleading. Perhaps the company is hiding something?

Report by Management

In a "Report by Management," which typically accompanies the report of independent public accountants, management certifies it is responsible for the financial information under audit. This section states that the information is objective and reliable, that accounting estimates have been properly made, and that proper internal controls were in place. Management notes that its board of directors has oversight responsibility for the financial statements. The report further indicates that there is an audit committee including corporate directors. The report is usually signed by the chief financial officer and/or chief executive officer.

Figure 5-3 illustrates the report by management appearing in the 1990 annual report of the Procter and Gamble Company.

UNDERSTANDING FINANCIAL STATEMENTS

Understanding which basic financial statements present financial position and operating results and knowing how to analyze the statement of cash flows are central to evaluating a potential investment. You only want to invest in a company that has good financial health and future prospects. Is the company growing or declining? Will the company be around for a long time? How profitable is the firm? What are the company's financial resources and obligations? These questions and others can be answered only if you understand financial statements in the annual report.

The three required financial statements are the balance sheet, income statement, and statement of cash flows. Although their format may vary among different businesses or other economic units, their basic purpose is the same.

A Brief Look at the Financial Statements

The **balance sheet** portrays the financial position of the company at a particular point in time. It shows what is owned (assets), how much is owed (liabilities), and what is left over (assets minus liabilities, also known as stockholders' equity or net worth). The balance sheet is like a snapshot, a freeze-frame of the company's financial status as of a certain date.

The **income statement**, on the other hand, measures operating performance for a specified time period (for example, the year ended December 31, 19XX). It is a motion picture as can be seen in Figure 5-4. The income statement serves as a bridge between the two consecutive balance sheets. *NOTE: Simply put, with the balance sheet you are asking how wealthy or how poor the company is, whereas with the income statement you are asking how the company did last year—did it make money and if so, how much? Neither statement alone can tell you about the financial health of the company. For example, the fact that the company made a big profit does not necessarily mean it is wealthy; nor does a sharp downturn mean imminent failure. To get the total picture, you need both statements, because they complement each other.*

FIGURE 5-3: Example of a Report by Management

Responsibility For The Financial Statements

The financial statements of The Procter & Gamble Company and its subsidiaries are the responsibility of, and have been prepared by, the Company, in accordance with generally accepted accounting principles. To help insure the accuracy and integrity of its financial data, the Company has developed and maintains internal accounting controls which are designed to provide reasonable assurances that transactions are executed as authorized and accurately recorded, and that assets are properly safeguarded. These controls are monitored by an extensive program of internal audits.

The financial statements have been audited by the Company's independent public accountants, Deloitte & Touche. Their report is shown above.

The Board of Directors has an Audit Committee composed entirely of outside Directors. The Committee meets periodically with representatives of Deloitte & Touche and financial management to review accounting, control, auditing, and financial reporting matters. To help assure the independence of the public accountants, Deloitte & Touche regularly meets privately with the Audit Committee.

28

FIGURE 5-4: Balance Sheet/Income Statement Relationship

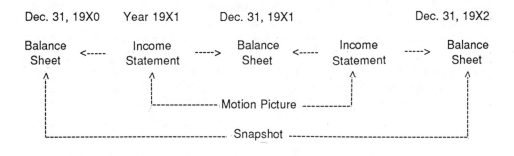

Unfortunately, neither the balance sheet nor the income statement provides information about a company's changes in cash position or flow of funds (cash) during a certain period. This is information you need to make a buy-or-sell decision.

The **statement of cash flows**, which provides this information, basically shows the sources and uses of cash, which is a basis for cash flow analysis for external investors. The statement aids you in answering vital questions like "Where was money obtained?" and "Where did money go and for what purpose?" Below is a list of more specific questions that can be answered by the statement of cash flows and cash flow analysis.

- Is the company growing or just maintaining its competitive position?
- Can the company meet its financial obligations?
- Where did the company obtain funds?
- What use was made of net income?
- How much of the required capital was generated internally?
- How was the expansion in plant and equipment financed?
- Is the business expanding faster than it can generate funds?
- Is the company's dividend policy in balance with its operating policy?
- Is the company's cash position sound, and what effect will it have on the market price of stock?

NOTE: You might want to know the cash flow per share, *which equals net cash flow divided by the number of shares outstanding. A high ratio is desirable because it indicates a liquid position.*

Footnotes

The annual report often contains this statement: "The accompanying footnotes are an integral part of the financial statements." This is because the financial statements themselves are concise and condensed. Hence, any explanatory information that cannot be abbreviated readily is explained in greater detail in the footnotes.

Footnotes, which appear at the end of the financial statements and *explain* the figures in those statements, provide detailed information regarding financial statement figures, accounting policies, and explanatory data (such as mergers and stock options). They also furnish any necessary additional disclosure, examples of which include accounting methods and estimates (such as inventory pricing, pension fund and profit-sharing arrangements, terms or characteristics of long-term debt, particulars of lease agreements, contingencies, and tax matters). *NOTE: Footnote information may be both* quantitative *and* qualitative. *An example of quantitative information is the fair market value of pension plan assets. An example of a qualitative disclosure is a lawsuit against the company. It is essential that the investor carefully evaluate footnote information to arrive at an informed opinion about the company's financial health and operating performance.*

Supplementary Schedules

Supplementary schedules enhance reader comprehension of the company's financial health. Some of the more common schedules are the five-year summary of operations, two-year quarterly data, and segmental information.

Five-Year Summary of Operations

This supplement provides income statement information for five years including dividends on preferred stock and common stock. It also reveals operating trends. Some companies provide ten-year comparative data. Figure 5-5 illustrates a five-year summary of operations and year-end position for Tandy Corporation.

Two-Year Quarterly Data

This schedule furnishes a quarterly breakdown of sales, profit, the high and low stock price, and the common stock dividend. The operating information is particularly useful on a quarterly basis for a seasonal business. The quarterly market price reveals the fluctuation in the market price of stock whereas the dividend quarterly information depicts the regularity with which the company pays dividends. Figure 5-6 presents quarterly results of operations for Maytag Corporation.

Segmental Disclosure

This schedule presents financial statistics for each segment of the business. Segmental reporting provides investors with useful information to evaluate a segment's profit potential and risk. Data may be by industry, foreign area, major customer, and government contract. A segment is reportable if revenue is 10 percent or more of combined revenue, operating profit is 10 percent or more of total operating profit, *or* identifiable assets are 10 percent or more of total assets. Figure 5-7 presents segmental disclosure for the Maytag Corporation.

A company must also disclose if foreign operations, sales to a major customer, or domestic contract revenues are 10 percent or more of the total. The percentage derived and the source must be stated. *NOTE: Segment information useful to investors may include sales, operating profit, total assets, fixed assets, intangible assets, inventory, cost of sales, depreciation, and amortization.*

Management's Discussion and Analysis of the Financial Condition and Results of Operations

This section is a narrative presentation giving management's comments on the results of operations, capital resources, and liquidity. Management interprets and analyzes past and prospective financial developments. Any significant developments in these areas, whether favorable or unfavorable, must be discussed. In presenting operating results, companies provide operating details and unusual events. Also, uncertainties and trends are mentioned along with their potential future effects.

With regard to capital resources, management discusses its acquisitions of property, plant, and equipment. The financing of such acquisitions in terms of equity or debt financing is given. Lease arrangements may also be discussed.

FIGURE 5-5: Example of Five-Year Summary of Operations

Tandy Corporation and Subsidiaries
Dollars and shares in thousands,
except per share amounts.

	1991	1990	1989	1988	1987
Operations					
Net sales and operating revenues	$4,561,782	$4,499,604	$4,180,703	$3,793,767	$3,452,178
Income before income taxes, cumulative effect of accounting change and equity in operations spun off	$ 338,890	$ 473,939	$ 527,399	$ 514,680	$ 458,791
Provision for income taxes	132,827	183,592	203,895	198,326	213,625
Income before cumulative effect of accounting change and equity in operations spun off	206,063	290,347	323,504	316,354	245,166
Equity in net loss of operations spun off	—	—	—	—	(2,837)
Cumulative effect on prior years of change in accounting principle	(10,619)	—	—	—	—
Net income	$ 195,444	$ 290,347	$ 323,504	$ 316,354	$ 242,329
Net income per average common share	$ 2.44	$ 3.54	$ 3.64	$ 3.54	$ 2.70
Average common shares outstanding	78,258	81,943	88,849	89,466	89,899
Dividends declared per common share[1]	$ .60	$ .60	$ .60	$ .575	$ .375
Net interest (income) expense	$ (11,218)	$ 5,939	$ (12,217)	$ (588)	$ 21,937
Ratio of earnings to fixed charges	3.11	4.34	5.94	6.10	6.43
Year-End Financial Position					
Inventories	$1,301,854	$1,452,065	$1,285,373	$1,287,854	$1,128,435
Total assets	$3,078,145	$3,239,980	$2,574,310	$2,530,092	$1,965,389
Working capital	$1,550,848	$1,312,517	$1,373,311	$1,336,812	$1,141,763
Current ratio	3.18 to 1	2.12 to 1	3.41 to 1	3.06 to 1	4.76 to 1
Capital structure:					
Current debt	$ 179,818	$ 695,871	$ 192,096	$ 306,475	$ 31,304
Long-term debt	$ 427,867	$ 252,540	$ 141,124	$ 180,598	$ 194,608
Total debt	$ 607,685	$ 948,411	$ 333,220	$ 487,073	$ 225,912
Total debt, net of cash and short-term investments	$ 421,392	$ 813,214	$ 274,822	$ 298,849	$ 147,798
Stockholders' equity	$1,846,762	$1,723,496	$1,782,838	$1,603,112	$1,380,039
Total capitalization	$2,454,447	$2,671,907	$2,116,058	$2,090,185	$1,605,951
Long-term debt as a % of total capitalization	17.4%	9.5%	6.7%	8.6%	12.1%
Total debt as a % of total capitalization	24.8%	35.5%	15.7%	23.3%	14.1%
Stockholders' equity per common share	$23.48	$21.78	$20.65	$18.10	$15.38
Financial Ratios					
Return on average stockholders' equity [2]	11.5%	16.6%	19.1%	21.2%	18.0%
Percent of sales:					
Income before income taxes, cumulative effect of accounting change and equity in operations spun off	7.4%	10.6%	12.6%	13.6%	13.3%
Income before cumulative effect of change in accounting principle	4.5%	6.5%	7.7%	8.3%	7.1%

[1] A quarterly dividend of $.125 was instituted in December 1986. The dividend rate was increased to $.15 in December 1987.
[2] Computed using income before cumulative effect of accounting change.

Liquidity is mentioned, including the status of working capital and liquidity ratios. Such ratios include the current ratio, quick (acid-test) ratio, inventory turnover, and accounts receivable turnover. (These ratios will be discussed in detail in Chapter 7.) Lines of credit with banks are also cited in management's discussion.

Investor's Information

This section provides useful investor information including the exchanges on which the stock is traded, the date and place of the annual meeting, when proxy materials

FIGURE 5-6: Example of Two-Year Quarterly Data Report

QUARTERLY RESULTS OF OPERATIONS (Unaudited)

The following is a summary of unaudited quarterly results of operations for the years ended December 31, 1989 and 1988:

In thousands except per share data	December 31	September 30	June 30	March 31
1989				
Net sales	$800,176	$796,459	$813,545	$678,573
Gross profit	200,783	198,444	201,567	175,314
Net income	39,816	29,304	28,239	34,113
Net income per average share	.38	.28	.27	.35
1988				
Net sales	$477,408	$490,682	$480,823	$436,728
Gross profit	115,379	122,361	119,100	115,174
Income from continuing operations	33,116	35,907	35,179	31,320
Net income	52,597	37,586	35,843	32,536
Income from continuing operations per average share	.43	.47	.46	.41
Net income per average share	.69	.49	.47	.43

The quarter ended December 31, 1989 includes tax benefits of approximately $9 million ($.08 per share) resulting from overseas reorganizations.

will be mailed, the names of addresses of the registrar and transfer agent, and the names of the trustees. It also gives the number of common and preferred shareholders and the particulars and terms of a dividend reinvestment plan, if any. *NOTE: Also read SEC **Form 10-K** because it contains additional information such as historical background, experience and compensation of senior executives, management holdings of securities, names of principal security holders, detailed financial schedules, properties held, product and service information, markets, distribution channels, employment history, number of employees, competition, backlogs, patents and licenses, franchises, and governmental regulations (e.g., environmental safety).*

Directors and Officers

This section lists members of the board of directors and their affiliations, along with names and titles of senior executives. Names of board members who serve on various committees (e.g., finance and audit) are also provided. *NOTE: Ask how many members on the board are outside the company and whether they are more concerned with outside interests (such as banks and suppliers) than with stockholders.*

FIGURE 5-7: Segmental Data

INDUSTRY SEGMENT AND GEOGRAPHIC INFORMATION

Principal financial data by industry segment is as follows:

In thousands	1989	1988	1987
Net Sales			
Home appliances	$2,855,383	$1,663,951	$1,634,078
Vending equipment	233,370	221,690	188,028
Total	$3,088,753	$1,885,641	$1,822,106
Income Before Taxes			
Home appliances	$ 262,418	$ 182,901	$ 218,542
Vending equipment	50,311	53,438	44,863
Corporate (including interest expense)	(105,757)	(21,117)	(10,427)
Total	$ 206,972	$ 215,222	$ 252,978
Capital Expenditures–net			
Home appliances	$ 101,013	$ 93,580	$ 39,224
Vending equipment	10,631	4,549	1,200
Corporate	(1,081)	14	(19)
Total	$ 110,563	$ 98,143	$ 40,405
Depreciation and Amortization			
Home appliances	$ 74,617	$ 32,295	$ 33,438
Vending equipment	1,555	1,457	1,366
Corporate	822	702	473
Total	$ 76,994	$ 34,454	$ 35,277
Identifiable Assets			
Home appliances	$2,217,576	$ 785,693	$ 666,802
Vending equipment	112,937	74,883	59,321
Corporate	105,806	469,493	128,802
Total	$2,436,319	$1,330,069	$ 854,925

Information about the Company's operations in different geographic regions for 1989 is as follows:

In thousands	Net Sales	Income Before Taxes	Identifiable Assets
North America	$2,545,230	$311,595	$1,633,585
Other	543,523	1,134	696,928
Corporate		(105,757)	105,806
Total	$3,088,753	$206,972	$2,436,319

Sales between affiliates of different geographic regions are not significant. Operations outside of North America were not material in 1988 and 1987. The amount of exchange loss included in operations in 1989 was not significant.

TABLE 5-2: ABC Common Stock High/Low Bid Prices, 19X1

	High	*Low*
First quarter	$30	$26
Second quarter	28	25
Third quarter	34	31
Fourth quarter	32	27

History of Market Price

This is an optional section, but some companies choose to provide a brief history of the market prices of its stock. For example, the highs and lows for each quarter may be presented, thus revealing the variability and direction in a stock's market price (see Table 5-2 above).

READING QUARTERLY REPORTS

Besides the annual report, publicly held companies issue **quarterly reports**, which provide updated information regarding sales and earnings. If any material changes have occurred in the business or operations, these will be stated in the quarterly report. Quarterly reports may provide *unaudited* financial statements or updates on operating highlights, changes in outstanding shares, compliance with debt restrictions, and other relevant matters affecting stockholders.

The minimum financial information that must be contained in the quarterly reports are sales, net income, taxes, nonrecurring revenue and expenses, accounting changes, contingencies (such as lawsuits), additions or deletions of business segments, and material changes in financial position.

A company may provide financial figures for the quarter itself (e.g., third quarter comprising July 1–September 30) or cumulatively from the beginning of the year (e.g., cumulative up to the third quarter comprising January 1–September 30). However, prior year's data must be provided on a comparative basis. *NOTE: Read quarterly reports in conjunction with the annual report.*

SECURITIES AND EXCHANGE COMMISSION FILINGS

The **Securities and Exchange Commission (SEC)**, established by the Securities Exchange Act of 1934, is empowered to regulate trading on the exchanges and to re-quire corporate disclosure of information relevant to the stockholders of publicly traded companies. The SEC also dictates accounting conventions.

Information available through the SEC consists primarily of corporate income statements, balance sheets, detailed support of accounting information, and internal data not always found in a company's annual report. There are specific reports that companies are required to file with the SEC, as discussed below.

Annual 10-K Report

The 10-K is perhaps the most widely known and can usually be obtained free directly from the company rather than paying the SEC a copying charge. This report should be read in combination with the firm's annual report because it contains the same type of information but in greater detail, as was discussed in the previous section.

8-K Report

The 8-K report must be filed when the corporation undergoes an important event that stockholders would be interested in knowing about, such as changes in control, bankruptcy, resignation of officers or directors, and other material events.

Quarterly 10-Q Report

The 10-Q is a quarterly update to the 10-K report. It must be filed no later than 45 days after the end of a quarter. The 10-Q provides information about outstanding securities, debt compliance arrangements, changes in stockholdings, legal proceedings, and stockholder voting matters (e.g., electing board of directors). It also contains quarterly financial statements.

Other SEC Reports

Other SEC reports include *proxy statements*, which disclose information relevant to stockholders' votes, and the *prospectus*, which must be issued whenever a new offering of securities is made to the public. The Securities Act of 1933 requires issues of most new corporate underwritings to file a registration statement prior to offering. In this statement, the issuer is required to make *full disclosure* of relevant financial statements, which are summarized in the prospectus.

READING A PROSPECTUS

Few investments are more alluring than new stock in a promising growth company. For example, Tetra Technologies of Texas went public, and the stock soared 22 percent in the first day of trading. But the risks can be tremendous. In February 1990, I-Flow Corp. of Irvine, California, went public, selling three shares of common stock and one warrant at $6; two months later, the unit sold for $3.125.

How do you separate the winners from the losers among companies making their initial public offerings? Often, the key to buying stock as a company goes public lies in the prospectus, which companies are required to prepare before offering shares to the public.

A **prospectus**—available from the company or stockbroker—is a lengthy and, ostensibly, a boring document. But, according to stock analysts, few pieces of paper can help investors better understand a company. A prospectus is a circular, required by the Securities Act of 1933, that describes securities offered for sale. Its purpose is full disclosure, especially of adverse prospects for the issuing company. It covers facts regarding the issuer's financial status, operations, management, any anticipated legal matters that could affect the company, and potential risks of investing in the company. The key is knowing how to decipher the clues that a prospectus holds.

The 10 Key Questions Test

An investor should ask 10 questions before jumping into a new issue.

1. Who's Selling What?

Experts say they can often tell a book by its cover. Basically, there are two key facts on the first sheet of the prospectus: what's being sold and who's doing the selling. Investment pros like their offerings "straight." Warrants, units, or bundles of preferred shares are a dead giveaway that something's amiss, they say. Another signal to the pros is the underwriters—the stock brokerages hired to market these newly minted shares. If they haven't heard of the underwriter, investors don't buy.

2. Is This a Real Business?

You do not want to invest in someone's dream of success or a slow-starting industrial giant of the future. You want to see results—now. Therefore, look for fundamentals, starting right there on page 3 ("Prospectus Summary"), where the company's business lines and need for new funds are quickly outlined. The summary also serves as a financial snapshot of the company.

This is where you start your calculators, hoping to find a company with rapidly expanding sales figures supported by a corresponding growth in profits.

3. Who's the Competition?

Some businesses actually invite profit—by selling the cure for cancer or AIDS or owning half the U.S. market in a particular commodity. For others, it can be success today, bankruptcy tomorrow.

A key to determining where a company might fit is determining how much competition it has. This information is often contained in "The Company" or "Management's Discussion of Business" section of a prospectus. You might ask whether the firm has patented products. Can it control pricing? Or is it just another name in an already crowded field?

4. Will the Business Grow?

Bigger sales means bigger profits, which means bigger stock prices. But numbers don't tell the whole story. You also should scour the prospectus for hints about the company's growth prospects. You want to know who buys the products and who distributes them. You also want to know where the raw materials come from and how plentiful future supplies of those cherished goods will be. Key information can be found in the "Risk Factors" section, as well as "The Company" or "Management's Discussion of Business."

5. Will Profits Continue?

Anyone reviewing a prospectus should be aware that businesses planning to go public have nasty habits of having very good financial results just before the stock sale. That's why it's important to ask "Will the good fortune continue once the public has been brought in as partners?"

The "Management's Discussion of Operations" section is a favorite hunting ground for profit information. You want to know what makes the company profitable. How does gross profit margin shrink down to net income?   Are the margins consistent, or do they vary seasonally or after sales promotions?

6. What's the Real Price?

One way to figure what newly issued shares of a company are worth on paper is to look at the "Dilution" section. *Dilution*, as its name implies, means how much less a share is actually worth after accounting for expenses, proceeds from the sale that do not go to the company, and a readjustment of the books after the offerings. Another measure of value is the *price/earnings (P/E) ratio*. But there's a catch: do you use the last complete year's earnings figures or perhaps extrapolate a current year number from other figures provided?

7. What Are the Risks?

Everyone checks out the "Risk Factors" section. By definition, this part of a prospectus should scare off some investors, for it is there to warn the public about past, present, or potential company problems.

Some of the risks listed are *boilerplate* (i.e., standardized). For example, noting that the company is relatively new and can give no promise that its results will be good in the future, or that the company is heavily dependent on managers "who could leave tomorrow," or that no market has ever existed for the shares.

8. Who's Running the Place?

Review the "Management" and "Principal and Selling Stockholders" sections for the background check on top executives and major shareholders. Although the one-paragraph summaries of key player business backgrounds is by no means a definite test of management skills, the list often highlights specialties or experience gained at other firms.

9. What Are They Getting Out of It?

Prospectuses contain some of the most intimate details about a company, especially when it comes to rewards reaped by top managers and large stockholders. Parts of "Management," "Certain Transactions," and "Principal and Selling Stockholders" can say a lot about a firm.

10. Any Surprises Left?

You don't want surprises. That's why you should *not* forget to read footnotes, small type, and "Notes to Financial Statements."

Case Study: Advanced Logic Research (ALR)

As a case study, the prospectus of Advanced Logic Research, an Irvine, California-based computer company that went public in April 1990, will be put through the 10 key questions test. Figure 5-8 reproduces the first 9 of the prospectus's 42 pages plus 16 pages of the independent auditors report.

The section headings of the table of contents show the topics covered in pages 10–42 and the financials beginning on page F1. ALR could not comment because of SEC rules that prohibit stock-selling companies from commenting on their offering documents. Here is how ALR fared on the 10 key questions test:

Who's selling what? ALR's underwriters are PaineWebber and Prudential-Bache, two of Wall Street's biggest. The company has top-flight underwriters, lawyers, and accountants—which says a lot.

Is this a real business? ALR's financial results show sales growing from $950,000 in 1985 to $73 million in fiscal 1989 to $39 million for the first quarter of fiscal 1990. Profits in that span jumped from $23,000 in 1985 to $2.8 million last year and $3 million in 1990's first three months.

The first thing we want to find out is, is this a *real* company? There is every indication that, not only is it real, but it's going to be phenomenal!

Who's the competition? In the case of ALR, the computer manufacturing industry is one of the stiffest marketing and sales battlegrounds.

Despite the company's mention that its products have won prestigious awards, we noted that ALR was no different from a host of others in the arena. Even ALR's prospectus gave homage to its competition, stating that 11 companies it listed "have significantly greater financial, marketing and technological resources than the company."

Will the business grow? ALR's current growth rate looks great. Sales were up 98 percent in 1989 and 1990's first quarter was equal to 54 percent of last year's total. The trends are good, but the predictability is questionable.

That's because from reading the "Risk Factors" section, we noted that the company has one main supplier of its machine's key component, the computer chip. Also, a large chunk of sales—49 percent—went through only three distributors; one twist could damage sales growth.

Additionally, ALR stated that after 1990's second quarter, which it expects to be as good as the first three months, "sequential revenue growth rate in the next few quarters will be lower than that achieved over the last three quarters."

You see something like that and you hold your breath.

Will profits continue? By checking tables of results expressed as a percentage of sales, we should note that ALR was operating on thin (and somewhat erratic) profit margins.

In 1989, ALR's gross profit margin was 3.8 percent, narrow for personal computers. Its ratio of operating income to sales fell in 1989 to 7.7 percent from 12.2 percent the previous year, which is scary.

What's the real price? At ALR, new shareholders will pay $32 million for 31 percent of the company at the estimated price of $12 per share. The current owners will have paid $312,000 (or $0.05 a share) for their 69 percent stake. That means a share that sold for $12 has a book value of $4.34.

But we saw the small amount of capital invested by insiders as a positive sign. It shows that the business is self-financing.

Using 1989 figures and a $12 offering price, ALR's P/E ratio is about 30. The stock of an ALR's competitor, AST Research of Irvine, is trading at a price/earnings multiple of 10. However, by analyzing 1990's strong first-quarter performance, this multiple comes down to a modest 7. It appears that pricing is hefty.

What are the risks? Among the risks listed are obvious ones for a computer maker, such as the industry's cutthroat competition. But another caught our eye.

ALR states that it must improve its management of its manufacturing or "its inability to successfully produce, test, and deliver sufficient products in time to meet demand would adversely affect the company's operating results." It's a red flag!

Who's running the place? The management headed by CEO Eugene Lu is what analysts called a typical blend of people with technology backgrounds and requisite sales and accounting expertise.

More notable was that ALR's Singapore-based manufacturing partner, Wearnes Technology, would control 62.4 percent of the shares after the offering. That's because Lu gave Wearnes, which makes the major internal parts for ALR's computers, voting control of 1.4 million (or 16 percent of all stock) of the 1.6 million shares he owns.

The prospectus contained no financial information on Wearnes, which is owed $10.9 million for parts it made for ALR and has guaranteed a $15 million line of credit for the company.

It would be very helpful to know a little bit more about Wearnes Technology. Although you're not *actually* buying stock in Wearnes, you are, *sort of.*

What are they getting out of it? ALR plans to take in $25.1 million if stock is sold at $12. Chief Executive Eugene Lu will get $2 million for his shares, and ALR plans to repay $6.5 million of the debt it owes to Wearnes, its largest shareholder. As an investor, you'd rather see the money stay in the company.

Any surprises left? ALR's notes contained nuggets such as $2.3 million listed as expenses last year followed by a $1.1 million promotion cost in 1990's first quarter, which were generally unassuming.

NOTE: As of December 10, 1991, the ALR stock was selling for $9 1/2 a share on the OTC market.

FIGURE 5-8: ALR (Advanced Logic Research, Inc.) Prospectus for 10 Key Question Analysis

3,000,000 Shares

Common Stock

Of the 3,000,000 shares of Common Stock offered hereby, 2,650,000 shares are being sold by Advanced Logic Research, Inc. ("ALR" or the "Company") and 350,000 shares are being sold by the Selling Stockholders. See "Principal and Selling Stockholders." The Company will not receive any of the proceeds from the sale of the shares by the Selling Stockholders. Prior to this offering, there has been no public market for the Common Stock of the Company. See "Underwriting" for information relating to the factors considered in determining the initial public offering price.

These securities involve a high degree of risk. See "Risk Factors" for information that should be considered by prospective investors.

THESE SECURITIES HAVE NOT BEEN APPROVED OR DISAPPROVED BY THE SECURITIES AND EXCHANGE COMMISSION OR ANY STATE SECURITIES COMMISSION NOR HAS THE SECURITIES AND EXCHANGE COMMISSION OR ANY STATE SECURITIES COMMISSION PASSED UPON THE ACCURACY OR ADEQUACY OF THIS PROSPECTUS. ANY REPRESENTATION TO THE CONTRARY IS A CRIMINAL OFFENSE.

	Price to Public	Underwriting Discounts and Commissions(1)	Proceeds to Company(2)	Proceeds to Selling Stockholders(2)
Per Share	$13.00	$0.91	$12.09	$12.09
Total	$39,000,000	$2,730,000	$32,038,500	$4,231,500
Total Assuming Full Exercise of Over-Allotment Option(3)	$44,850,000	$3,139,500	$37,479,000	$4,231,500

(1) See "Underwriting."

(2) Before deducting expenses estimated at $769,500, of which $677,000 are payable by the Company and $92,500 are payable by the Selling Stockholders.

(3) Assuming exercise in full of the 45-day option granted by the Company to the Underwriters to purchase up to 450,000 additional shares, on the same terms, solely to cover over-allotments. See "Underwriting."

The shares of Common Stock are offered by the Underwriters, subject to prior sale, when, as and if delivered to and accepted by the Underwriters, and subject to their right to reject orders in whole or in part. It is expected that delivery of the Common Stock will be made in New York City on or about April 19, 1990.

PaineWebber Incorporated   Prudential-Bache Capital Funding

The date of this Prospectus is April 11, 1990

3,000,000 Shares

Common Stock

PROSPECTUS

PaineWebber Incorporated

Prudential-Bache Capital Funding

April 11, 1990

TABLE OF CONTENTS

FIGURE 5-8: *continued*

**ALR's Products:
Recognized for High Performance**

"In a field of powerhouse machines there can only be one winner, and ALR's FlexCache is it."

The PowerFlex "represents a price-to-performance breakthrough...."
BYTE
January 1990

"The PowerCache 4 has the best overall performance...and is a reasonably priced high-end system...."
MIPS
November 1989

"With the FlexCache 25386, "ALR has delivered a machine that earns the crown as the king of speed."
Personal Computing
September 1988

The Company intends to furnish stockholders with annual reports containing audited consolidated financial statements, with an opinion thereon expressed by an independent public accounting firm, and quarterly reports containing unaudited consolidated financial information for each of the first three quarters of each fiscal year.

IN CONNECTION WITH THIS OFFERING, THE UNDERWRITERS MAY OVER-ALLOT OR EFFECT TRANSACTIONS WHICH STABILIZE OR MAINTAIN THE MARKET PRICE OF THE COMMON STOCK OF THE COMPANY AT A LEVEL ABOVE THAT WHICH MIGHT OTHERWISE PREVAIL IN THE OPEN MARKET. SUCH STABILIZING, IF COMMENCED, MAY BE DISCONTINUED AT ANY TIME.

2

PROSPECTUS SUMMARY

The following summary is qualified in its entirety by the more detailed information and consolidated financial statements appearing elsewhere in this Prospectus. The shares of Common Stock offered hereby involve a high degree of risk. Investors should carefully consider the information set forth under the heading "Risk Factors."

The Company

Advanced Logic Research designs, manufactures and markets microcomputer systems that offer leading edge performance and value. The Company's 14 basic products, all of which are based on Intel's 80286, 386SX, 1386 or i486 microprocessors, target a broad range of performance and functionality for each of the high-end, midrange and entry-level segments of the microcomputer market. The Company has incorporated into its products a number of innovative technological enhancements, including advanced memory management architectures, which greatly enhance the speed of its systems. To achieve maximum compatibility and broad market acceptance for its products, the Company supports all three industry bus architecture standards, MCA, EISA, and ISA; the three major industry standard operating systems, MS-DOS, UNIX and OS/2; and the current leading network protocol, NetWare. The Company is strongly committed to offering a full range of MCA-compatible products and, with the introduction of the Company's PowerCache 4 and MicroFlex systems last year, has demonstrated leadership in this emerging market. The Company markets its products through a worldwide network of distributors and resellers to provide extensive marketing presence for its systems and local sales support and service to end-users.

The Offering

Common Stock offered by the Company	2,650,000 shares(1)
Common Stock offered by the Selling Stockholders	350,000 shares
Common Stock to be outstanding after the Offering	8,886,790 shares(1)(2)
NASDAQ symbol	AALR
Use of proceeds	General corporate purposes, including working capital and payment of certain trade indebtedness.

Summary Consolidated Financial Data
(in thousands, except per share amounts)

	Fiscal Year Ended September 30,					Three Months Ended December 31,	
	1985	1986	1987	1988	1989	1988	1989
Income Statement Data:							
Net sales	$ 950	$5,689	$15,093	$37,082	$73,083	$12,877	$39,522
Gross profit	191	1,220	3,693	9,394	17,807	3,451	11,365
Operating income (loss)	(6)	251	1,468	4,527	5,619	1,635	5,819
Net income	23	163	753	2,479	2,790	848	3,020
Net income per share	$ —	$ .03	$ .11	$ .36	$ .41	$ .12	$ .44
Shares used in per share calculation	6,476	6,476	6,883	6,963	6,885	6,848	6,917

	September 30, 1989	December 31, 1989	
		Actual	As Adjusted(1)(3)
Balance Sheet Data:			
Working capital	$14,647	$18,590	$49,952
Total assets	39,471	62,464	93,826
Long-term debt, excluding current portion	10,000	10,000	10,000
Stockholders' equity	6,433	9,456	40,818

(1) Assumes the Underwriters' over-allotment option is not exercised. See "Underwriting."
(2) Excludes, as of March 31, 1990, 699,720 shares of Common Stock subject to outstanding options at such date.
(3) Adjusted to reflect the sale of shares offered by the Company hereby.

Except as otherwise noted, all information in this Prospectus has been adjusted to give effect to the April 1990 reincorporation of the Company from California to Delaware including a 7.14-for-1 stock split.

3

FIGURE 5-8: continued

THE COMPANY

ALR designs, manufactures and markets microcomputer systems that offer leading edge performance and value. The microcomputer, or personal computer, industry has grown substantially since its inception, as technological breakthroughs and continued performance improvements have expanded the applications for personal computers. Increased functionality combined with lower pricing have made high-end, midrange and entry-level personal computers essential tools for business use.

The Company's strategy is to be early-to-market with products that achieve new levels of performance and price/performance. ALR believes that this strategy enables it to obtain industry recognition, which is an important competitive advantage. The Company's products incorporate a number of innovative technological enhancements, including advanced memory management architectures which greatly enhance the speed of its i386- and i486-based systems. These enhancements have been developed with a view to their being transferable to other Company products that may still be early in their design cycle. The Company believes that its strategy of early introduction of technically advanced products, followed by a migration of its technology into midrange and entry-level products shortens new product design cycles while facilitating technical feasibility.

A number of the Company's products have gained industry recognition for their performance, technical design and early introduction. For example, in July 1986, ALR shipped the industry's first i386-based microcomputer, its Access 386. In the fall of 1989, the Company became the first manufacturer to offer systems based on Intel's i486 microprocessor utilizing each of the MCA, EISA and ISA bus architectures. In addition, the Company received *PC Magazine*'s 1988 "Technical Excellence Award" for its 25 MHz i386 system, an award previously given in its five-year history only to microcomputers manufactured by IBM and Compaq. ALR also received *BYTE* magazine's 1989 "Award of Distinction" for its upgradeable PowerFlex system.

The Company's products target a broad range of performance and functionality for each of the high-end, midrange and entry-level segments of the microcomputer market. The Company currently offers 14 basic microcomputer products, all of which are based on Intel's 80286, 386SX, i386 or i486 microprocessors. To achieve maximum compatibility and broad market acceptance, the Company supports all three industry bus architecture standards, MCA, EISA and ISA; the three major industry standard operating systems, MS-DOS, UNIX and OS/2; and the current leading networking protocol, NetWare. The Company intends to maintain compatibility with other major standards as they evolve. The Company is strongly committed to offering a full range of MCA-compatible products and, with the introduction of its PowerCache 4 and MicroFlex systems last year, the Company has demonstrated leadership in this emerging market.

To protect its customers' original hardware investments, the Company's PowerFlex system, based on an ISA bus, enables its customers to upgrade easily from 80286 to 386SX to 486 performance, while its new PowerVEISA system, based on the 32-bit EISA bus, allows its customers to upgrade from an i386 to an i486 CPU. To upgrade, customers simply insert one of the Company's proprietary modules containing a higher performance microprocessor. This innovation results in significant cost savings over the purchase of a new system offering a similar level of performance.

The Company markets its products through a worldwide network of distributors and resellers to provide extensive market presence for its systems and local sales support and service to end-users. In the Pacific Rim, Middle East and Southern Europe, ALR markets its products through its 51%-owned subsidiary, ALR International (Pte) Ltd ("ALR International"). By not selling directly to its end-users, the Company minimizes competition with its distributors and resellers. ALR believes that distribution strength and local service and support are key competitive factors. The Company is continuing to expand its distribution network in the United States and internationally.

Wearne Brothers, Ltd. ("Wearnes"), a diversified industrial and financial concern based in Singapore, through its affiliate, Wearnes Technology (Private) Limited ("Wearnes Technology"), was an early financial investor in the Company. Wearnes Technology will retain a significant ownership interest in the Company following the Offering. Another affiliate of Wearnes, Wearnes Automation Pte Ltd ("Wearnes Automation")

4

manufactures certain of the Company's system requirements under license from the Company. This relationship provides ALR with substantial benefits, including access to low cost manufacturing capacity, additional flexibility to respond to market demand and reduced capital costs for manufacturing and inventory. See "Business — Manufacturing" and "— Relationship with Wearnes and its Affiliates."

The Company's predecessor was incorporated in California in September 1984 and was merged into its Delaware successor, the Company, in April 1990. Unless the context otherwise requires, references in this Prospectus to the "Company" shall refer to ALR and its subsidiaries. The Company's executive offices are located at 9401 Jeronimo, Irvine, California 92718, and its phone number at that location is (714) 581-6770.

The following information is supplied pursuant to California law: The Company does not do business in, and does not do business with any person or group located in, South Africa. However, this information is only accurate as of the date of this Prospectus. Current information may be obtained from the California Secretary of State at the following address: South Africa Business Notice, Office of the Secretary of State, 1230 J Street, Room 100, Sacramento, California 95814 (telephone (916) 327-6427).

ADVANCED LOGIC RESEARCH, INC. and FLEXCACHE are registered trademarks of the Company. ALR, MICROFLEX, POWERFLEX, POWERVEISA and POWERCACHE are also trademarks of the Company. This Prospectus includes registered trademarks and trademarks of companies other than ALR.

RISK FACTORS

An investment in the securities being offered by this Prospectus involves a high degree of risk. The following factors, in addition to those discussed elsewhere in this Prospectus, should be carefully considered in evaluating the Company and its business before purchasing the shares of Common Stock offered hereby.

Competition

The personal computer industry is intensely competitive and is characterized by constant pricing pressures. The Company competes with a large number of manufacturers, including Apple Computer, AST Research, Compaq Computer, Dell Computer, Epson America, Everex Systems, IBM, NCR, NEC Information Systems, Wyse Technology and Zenith Electronics, as well as private label products manufactured by companies such as Intel. Most of these companies have significantly greater financial, marketing and technological resources than the Company. The Company also competes with a number of manufacturers that market products principally on the basis of price. There can be no assurance that ALR will be able to continue to compete effectively. See "Business — Competition."

Rapid Technological Change and Dependence on New Products

The microcomputer market is characterized by rapid technological change and product obsolescence. Although the Company's immediate success will depend primarily on the continued market acceptance of its existing products, its future success will depend on its ability to introduce new products. There can be no assurance that ALR will successfully develop new products or that the new products it develops will be introduced in a timely manner and receive substantial market acceptance. There also can be no assurance that new products will be introduced in a way that will not adversely affect sales of the Company's existing product lines. Because new products may partially or fully displace certain other ALR products, resulting in a risk of excess component or finished goods inventory, the Company's operating results could be adversely affected if ALR is unable to manage its product transitions successfully. See "Business — Technology," "— Products" and "— Research and Product Development."

Dependence on Suppliers

The Company's manufacturing process requires a high volume of quality components provided by various suppliers. Certain components, including Intel's 386SX, i386 and i486 microprocessors, are currently available

5

FIGURE 5-8: *continued*

only from single suppliers. The Company and the microcomputer industry, from time to time, have experienced shortages of supply of these components and certain other components, including dynamic random access memories ("DRAMs"). Supply shortages may cause component price increases, which could result in pressure on the Company's operating results. In certain circumstances, supply shortages could result in production delays which also could adversely affect the Company's operating results. Intel recently announced that the 386SX and i386 microprocessors are in relatively short supply. Although ALR believes that it will receive adequate supplies of this product to meet its anticipated needs, a prolonged shortage could adversely affect the Company's operating results. See "Business — Manufacturing."

Continued Revenue Growth and Profitability

The Company was incorporated in September 1984. Although ALR has been profitable and experienced revenue growth each fiscal year since its inception, there can be no assurance that the Company's revenue growth or profitability will continue on a quarterly or annual basis in the future. ALR's future success is dependent on several factors, including increased acceptance of the Company's current products, the Company's ability to develop and introduce new products which compete effectively on the basis of price and performance, increased penetration of domestic and international markets and its ability to provide customers with satisfactory service and support. See "Management's Discussion and Analysis of Financial Condition and Results of Operations."

Fluctuations in Quarterly Performance

The Company's customers generally order products on an as-needed basis. Therefore, virtually all of the Company's net sales in each quarter result from orders received in that quarter. The Company anticipates that the rate of new orders will vary significantly from month to month. Since ALR operates with a limited backlog, the Company's manufacturing plans and expenditure levels are based primarily on sales forecasts. The Company's operating expenditures are increasing as ALR expands its operations. Consequently, if anticipated sales and shipments in any quarter do not occur when expected, expenditure and inventory levels could be disproportionately high and the Company's operating results for that quarter, and potentially future quarters, would be adversely affected. See "Management's Discussion and Analysis of Financial Condition and Results of Operations — Quarterly Results of Operations" and "Business — Backlog."

Dependence on Distributors

Continued access to distribution channels is critical to the Company's future success. In the first fiscal quarter of 1990, the Company derived approximately 49% of its net sales from shipments to its distributors, including Ingram Micro D, Gates/FA and Softsel Computer Products. The Company expects to continue to derive a significant percentage of its net sales from shipments to distributors. In conformance with industry practice, the Company generally provides its distributors with "stock balancing" and "price protection" rights which permit its distributors to return slow-moving products to the Company for credit and which also provide for price adjustments for inventories of the Company's products held by distributors if the Company subsequently lowers the price of those products. To date, the Company has not experienced any significant stock balancing returns or granted any significant price protection adjustments; however, there can be no assurance that the Company will not experience significant returns or price protection adjustments in the future. The Company's customers are not contractually committed to future purchases of the Company's products and may discontinue carrying the Company's products in favor of a competitor's products or for other reasons. The loss of any of the Company's major distributors could have a significant adverse effect on the Company's results of operations until alternative distribution channels could be established. See "Business — Sales, Marketing and Support."

International Operations

The Company's international sales represented 21% and 30% of total sales in fiscal 1989 and the three months ended December 31, 1989, respectively. A portion of international sales is priced in local currencies and is subject to currency exchange fluctuations. Foreign sales are also generally subject to the risk of

compliance with additional laws, import/export restrictions, and tariff regulations. See "Business — Sales, Marketing and Support."

Manufacturing and Inventory Control

The Company significantly increased its manufacturing volume during calendar year 1989 and expects to further increase its manufacturing volume in calendar year 1990. The Company has also increased the number and diversity of products offered to customers. As a result, the Company must continue the improvement of its inventory controls and the implementation of more sophisticated management information systems. The improvements to date in inventory controls include a more structured part numbering system, more clearly defined inventory locations and standard costing procedures. The Company has also installed more sophisticated management information software and has implemented regular data back-up procedures. The inability of the Company to continue to expand its manufacturing capability and to enhance its inventory controls and other management information systems, or its inability to successfully produce, test and deliver sufficient products in time to meet demand, would adversely affect the Company's operating results. See "Business — Manufacturing."

License Agreement With IBM

ALR licenses from IBM the right to use certain technology covered under patents issued to IBM, including patents that may be issued on IBM's PS/2 computers and MCA. Currently, ALR expects to pay royalties to IBM on sales of a substantial number of existing and future personal computer products manufactured by the Company. In the event certain additional patents are issued to IBM for its PS/2 computers, ALR expects to pay additional royalties on sales of its products covered by those additional patents. IBM has previously licensed certain of its patent rights to other personal computer manufacturers for lower royalty fees than the Company expects to pay. In addition, IBM has announced that it will offer lower royalties to prospective licensees that possess patent rights of interest to IBM. ALR could be at a disadvantage to the extent that its competitors avoid the payment of royalties or obtain more favorable royalty payment terms from IBM. See "Business — License Agreement with IBM" and "Management's Discussion and Analysis of Financial Condition and Results of Operations."

Infringement of Intellectual Property Rights

From time to time, certain companies have asserted exclusive patent, copyright and other intellectual property rights to technologies which are important to the industry. ALR evaluates each claim relating to its products and, if appropriate, seeks a license to use the protected technology. There can be no assurance that the Company would be able to obtain licenses to use such technology or obtain such licenses on terms which would not have a material adverse effect on the Company. If the Company or its suppliers are unable to license protected technology used in the Company's products, ALR could be prohibited from marketing such products. The Company could also incur substantial costs to redesign its products or obtain any legal action taken against it. If the Company's products should be found to infringe protected technology, it could be required to pay damages to the infringed party. See "Business — Patents, Trademarks and Licenses."

Patents and Proprietary Information

The Company relies upon trade secrets, proprietary information and possibly, in the future, patents to maintain and enhance its competitive position. Although it has filed applications in the United States and Taiwan for a patent relating to certain of its technology, to date the Company has not been granted patent protection in either country. There can be no assurance that these patents will be granted, or if granted, that these patents will provide adequate protection. There also can be no assurance that the confidentiality agreements upon which ALR relies to protect its trade secrets will be adequate or that the Company's competitors will not independently develop or patent technologies that are substantially equivalent or superior to the Company's technology. The Company licenses certain of its technology to other manufacturers, which may permit them to compete directly with the Company's own products. See "Business — Patents, Trademarks and Licenses."

7

6

FIGURE 5-8: continued

FCC Approvals

The Federal Communications Commission (the "FCC") has adopted regulations setting radio frequency emission standards for computing equipment. All of the Company's current products meet the FCC's Class A requirements and certain of the Company's products qualify for the more stringent Class B approval. From time to time, however, the Company has experienced delays in securing FCC Class B approvals. To the extent the Company's present and future products may be required to meet the more stringent Class B requirements, there can be no assurance that similar delays will not occur in the future.

Dependence on Key Management

Eugene Lu, the founder of the Company and its President and Chief Executive Officer, participates in significant operating decisions concerning the strategic direction of the Company and serves a central role in the product development efforts of the Company. The loss of the services of Mr. Lu could have a material adverse effect upon the Company. The Company's success also depends, in part, upon a small number of key managerial personnel and technical employees as well as its ability to continue to attract and retain additional highly talented managerial and technical personnel. There can be no assurance that the Company can retain its key managerial and technical employees or that it can attract similar additional employees in the future. See "Business — Employees" and "Management — Directors and Executive Officers."

Voting Control of the Company

Following the completion of this offering, without giving effect to the exercise of the Underwriters' over-allotment option, Mr. Lu and Wearnes Technology and its affiliates will own, in the aggregate, approximately 64% of the Company's outstanding Common Stock. Mr. Lu has agreed to grant Wearnes Technology a three-year irrevocable proxy, effective upon the closing of the Offering, with respect to 1,400,000 of Mr. Lu's shares to enable Wearnes Technology to have voting control of a majority of the Company's outstanding shares following the Offering. As a result, Wearnes Technology will have controlling influence over all matters requiring approval by the stockholders of the Company, including the ability to elect all of the directors. Pursuant to the proxy arrangement, Mr. Lu holds a right of first refusal on transfer of Wearnes Technology's shares of the Company's Common Stock and Wearnes Technology has a right of first refusal on transfer of Mr. Lu's shares that are covered by the proxy. In addition, in connection with future financings, ALR has granted to Wearnes Technology a right to purchase additional voting securities of the Company to maintain its percentage ownership interest in ALR. There may in the future develop conflicts of interest between Wearnes or its affiliates and the Company relating to their vendor/customer relationship, their creditor/debtor relationship, their potential competitor relationship arising out of Wearnes' manufacture and sale of microcomputer products, and Wearnes Technology's controlling stockholder position. The Company intends, following this Offering, to nominate two independent directors to replace two of the four Wearnes representatives on the Company's Board of Directors as soon as qualified candidates can be identified and appointed. The Company believes that its contractual arrangements with Wearnes have been entered into on a basis such that the terms of such arrangements are no less favorable to the Company than could otherwise have been obtained from unaffiliated third parties. See "Business — Relationship with Wearnes and its Affiliates," "Certain Transactions" and "Principal and Selling Stockholders."

No Prior Market, Possible Volatility of Stock Price and Dilution

There has been no prior market for the Company's Common Stock and there is no assurance that a viable public market will develop or be sustained after the Offering. The initial public offering price will be determined by negotiations between the Company and the Representatives of the Underwriters. ALR believes that factors such as announcements of new products by the Company or its competitors and quarter-to-quarter variances in financial results could cause the market price of the Common Stock to fluctuate substantially. In addition, the stock market has recently experienced significant price and volume fluctuations. These fluctuations have often been unrelated to the operating performance of the specific companies whose stocks are traded. Broad market fluctuations, as well as general economic conditions such as a recessionary period or a high interest rate environment, may adversely affect the market price of the Company's Common Stock.

Also, investors participating in the Offering will incur immediate, substantial book value dilution. See "Dilution" and "Underwriting."

Shares Eligible for Future Sale

Sales of substantial amounts of Common Stock of the Company in the public market following the Offering made hereby could adversely affect prevailing market prices. In addition to the 3,000,000 shares offered hereby (assuming no exercise of the Underwriters' over-allotment option), approximately 215,000 shares of Common Stock held for more than three years by stockholders who are not affiliates of the Company and who are not subject to lock-up agreements will, on June 17, 1990, be eligible for sale in the public market without restriction. Approximately 40,000 additional shares not subject to lock-up agreements will become eligible for sale beginning 90 days from the date of this Prospectus, subject to compliance with the restrictions of Rule 144 under the Securities Act of 1933 (the "Securities Act"). In addition, approximately 1,803,000 shares will become eligible for sale under Rule 144 beginning 180 days from the date of this Prospectus, upon expiration of lock-up agreements between the Underwriters and all officers and directors and certain other stockholders of the Company. An additional 3,927,000 shares will become eligible for sale under Rule 144 beginning 365 days from the date of this Prospectus, upon expiration of a lock-up agreement between the Underwriters and Wearnes Technology. The Company intends to register approximately 1,332,500 shares issued or reserved for issuance under the Company's informal stock option program and the Flexible Stock Incentive Plan approximately 90 days after the date of this Prospectus. Beginning 90 days after the date of this Prospectus, approximately 90,000 option shares will be eligible for sale upon the exercise of outstanding options. Beginning 180 days after the date of this Prospectus (or earlier with the consent of the Underwriters), approximately 492,000 additional option shares will be eligible for sale upon the exercise of outstanding options following the expiration of lock-up agreements between the Underwriters and the holders of such options. See "Principal and Selling Stockholders" and "Shares Eligible for Future Sale."

USE OF PROCEEDS

The net proceeds to be received by the Company from the sale of the Common Stock offered hereby are estimated to be $31,361,500 ($36,802,000 if the Underwriters' over-allotment option is exercised in full). Wearnes Technology and Wearnes Automation have provided ALR with access to low cost manufacturing capacity and extended payment terms for inventory. Approximately $6.5 million of the net proceeds will be used in April 1990 to repay a portion of the extended accounts payable owed to Wearnes Automation. The balance of the net proceeds will be used for working capital, primarily to finance higher levels of inventory and accounts receivable. Pending such uses, the Company will invest the proceeds in deposits with banks, investment grade securities and short-term, interest-bearing securities including government obligations and other money market instruments. See "Management's Discussion and Analysis of Financial Condition and Results of Operations — Liquidity and Capital Resources."

The Company will not receive any proceeds from the sale of shares by the Selling Stockholders. See "Principal and Selling Stockholders."

8   9

FIGURE 5-8: *continued*

INDEX TO CONSOLIDATED FINANCIAL STATEMENTS

F-1

INDEPENDENT AUDITORS' REPORT

The Board of Directors
Advanced Logic Research, Inc.:

We have audited the accompanying consolidated balance sheets of Advanced Logic Research, Inc. and subsidiaries as of September 30, 1988 and 1989, and the related consolidated statements of income and stockholders' equity for each of the years in the three-year period ended September 30, 1989, the consolidated statement of changes in financial position for the year ended September 30, 1987 and the consolidated statements of cash flows for each of the years in the two-year period ended September 30, 1989. These consolidated financial statements are the responsibility of the Company's management. Our responsibility is to express an opinion on these consolidated financial statements based on our audits.

We conducted our audits in accordance with generally accepted auditing standards. Those standards require that we plan and perform the audit to obtain reasonable assurance about whether the financial statements are free of material misstatement. An audit includes examining, on a test basis, evidence supporting the amounts and disclosures in the financial statements. An audit also includes assessing the accounting principles used and significant estimates made by management, as well as evaluating the overall financial statement presentation. We believe that our audits provide a reasonable basis for our opinion.

In our opinion, the consolidated financial statements referred to above present fairly, in all material respects, the financial position of Advanced Logic Research, Inc. and subsidiaries at September 30, 1988 and 1989, the results of their operations for each of the years in the three-year period ended September 30, 1989, the changes in their financial position for the year ended September 30, 1987 and their cash flows for each of the years in the two-year period ended September 30, 1989 in conformity with generally accepted accounting principles.

As discussed in Note 1 to the consolidated financial statements, the Company adopted Statement of Financial Accounting Standards No. 95, "Statement of Cash Flows," on a prospective basis in 1988.

KPMG PEAT MARWICK

Orange County, California
November 29, 1989, except as
to note 13 which is as of
March 1, 1990

F-2

FIGURE 5-8: *continued*

ADVANCED LOGIC RESEARCH, INC. AND SUBSIDIARIES

CONSOLIDATED BALANCE SHEETS
(in thousands, except share data)

ASSETS
(note 6)

	September 30, 1988	September 30, 1989	December 31, 1989 (unaudited)
Current assets:			
Cash	$ 353	$ 636	$ 2,391
Trade accounts receivable, less allowance of $156 and $324 at September 30, 1988 and 1989, respectively, and $792 at December 31, 1989	4,238	12,885	21,987
Inventories (note 2)	11,444	21,930	33,339
Prepaid expenses and other assets	498	899	1,063
Deferred income taxes (note 8)	555	1,086	1,452
Total current assets	17,088	37,436	60,232
Equipment, furniture and fixtures, net (note 3)	814	1,696	1,815
Other assets (note 4)	217	339	417
	$18,119	$39,471	$62,464

LIABILITIES AND STOCKHOLDERS' EQUITY

	September 30, 1988	September 30, 1989	December 31, 1989 (unaudited)
Current liabilities:			
Current portion of long-term debt (note 7)	$ —	$ 3,000	$ 3,000
Notes payable to banks (note 6)	1,767	1,500	2,221
Payable to parent and affiliate (note 4)	8,124	10,020	23,962
Accounts payable	3,855	4,602	4,999
Accrued expenses (note 9)	733	2,871	4,726
Income taxes (note 8)	—	796	2,734
Total current liabilities	14,479	22,789	41,642
Long-term debt, excluding current portion (note 7)	—	10,000	10,000
Total liabilities	14,479	32,789	51,642
Commitments (note 12)			
Minority interest in subsidiary	—	249	1,366
Stockholders' equity (notes 5 and 13):			
Preferred stock, $.01 par value; 5,000,000 shares authorized; none issued or outstanding	—	—	—
Common stock, $.01 par value; 50,000,000 shares authorized; 6,211,800 and 6,229,650 shares issued and outstanding at September 30, 1988 and 1989, respectively, and 6,236,790 at December 31, 1989	62	62	62
Additional paid in capital	244	247	250
Retained earnings	3,334	6,124	9,144
Total stockholders' equity	3,640	6,433	9,456
Subsequent events (notes 5 and 13)			
	$18,119	$39,471	$62,464

See accompanying notes to consolidated financial statements.

F-3

ADVANCED LOGIC RESEARCH, INC. AND SUBSIDIARIES

CONSOLIDATED STATEMENTS OF INCOME
(in thousands, except per share data)

	Year Ended September 30,			Three Months Ended December 31, (unaudited)	
	1987	1988	1989	1988	1989
Net sales (note 11)	$ 15,093	$ 37,082	$ 73,083	$ 12,877	$ 39,522
Cost of sales (note 4)	11,400	27,688	55,276	9,426	28,157
Gross profit	3,693	9,394	17,807	3,451	11,365
Operating expenses:					
Selling, general and administrative (note 9)	1,825	3,677	8,508	1,210	3,792
Research and development	400	1,190	1,911	359	661
Royalty expense (note 9)	—	—	1,769	247	1,093
Total operating expenses	2,225	4,867	12,188	1,816	5,546
Operating income	1,468	4,527	5,619	1,635	5,819
Interest expense (note 4)	150	540	1,060	218	321
Income before minority interest and income taxes	1,318	3,987	4,559	1,417	5,498
Minority interest	—	—	—	—	308
Income before income taxes	1,318	3,987	4,559	1,417	5,190
Income taxes (note 8)	565	1,508	1,769	569	2,170
Net income	$ 753	$ 2,479	$ 2,790	$ 848	$ 3,020
Net income per common and common equivalent share (note 13)	$ .11	$ .36	$ .41	$ .12	$ .44
Common and common equivalent shares used in per share calculation (note 13)	6,883	6,963	6,885	6,848	6,917

See accompanying notes to consolidated financial statements.

F-4

FIGURE 5-8: *continued*

ADVANCED LOGIC RESEARCH, INC. AND SUBSIDIARIES

CONSOLIDATED STATEMENTS OF STOCKHOLDERS' EQUITY

(in thousands, except share data)

	Common Stock (note 13)		Additional Paid-in Capital	Retained Earnings	Total Stockholders' Equity
	Shares	Amount			
Balance, September 30, 1986	6,426,000	$64	$248	$186	$498
Net income	—	—	—	753	753
Balance, September 30, 1987	6,426,000	64	248	939	1,251
Purchase of common stock	(214,200)	(2)	(4)	(84)	(90)
Net income	—	—	—	2,479	2,479
Balance, September 30, 1988	6,211,800	62	244	3,334	3,640
Issuance of common shares under stock option plan	17,850	—	3	—	3
Net income	—	—	—	2,790	2,790
Balance, September 30, 1989	6,229,650	62	247	6,124	6,433
Issuance of common shares under stock option plan (unaudited)	7,140	—	3	—	3
Net income (unaudited)	—	—	—	3,020	3,020
Balance, December 31, 1989 (unaudited)	6,236,790	$62	$250	$9,144	$9,456

See accompanying notes to consolidated financial statements.

F-5

ADVANCED LOGIC RESEARCH, INC. AND SUBSIDIARIES

CONSOLIDATED STATEMENTS OF CASH FLOWS

(in thousands)

	Year Ended September 30,		Three Months Ended December 31,	
			(unaudited)	
	1988	1989	1988	1989
Cash flows from operating activities:				
Net income	$ 2,479	$ 2,790	$ 848	$ 3,020
Adjustments to reconcile net income to net cash provided by operating activities:				
Depreciation and amortization	100	277	48	111
Loss on sale of equipment, furniture and fixtures	10	27	—	—
Provision for losses on accounts receivable	96	246	23	492
Deferred income tax expense (benefit)	(367)	(468)	5	(348)
Minority interest in income of subsidiary	—	—	—	308
Changes in assets and liabilities:				
Trade accounts receivable	(1,794)	(8,893)	(171)	(9,594)
Inventories	(6,380)	(10,486)	80	(11,409)
Prepaid expenses	(429)	(401)	105	(182)
Other assets	(190)	(122)	2	(78)
Accounts payable	2,125	747	(770)	397
Accrued expenses	455	2,138	420	1,855
Income taxes	(607)	733	357	1,938
Total adjustments	(6,981)	(16,202)	99	(16,510)
Net cash provided by (used in) operating activities	(4,502)	(13,412)	947	(13,490)
Cash flows from investing activities:				
Purchase of equipment, furniture and fixtures	(624)	(1,284)	(110)	(230)
Proceeds from sale of equipment, furniture and fixtures	35	98	—	—
Net cash used in investing activities	(589)	(1,186)	(110)	(230)
Cash flows from financing activities:				
Net borrowings under notes payable	1,057	12,733	(417)	721
Net borrowings from parent and affiliates	4,055	1,896	(749)	13,942
Issuance of stock under stock option plan	—	3	—	3
Purchase of common stock	(90)	—	—	—
Minority interest	—	249	—	809
Net cash provided by (used in) financing activities	5,022	14,881	(1,166)	15,475
Net increase (decrease) in cash	(69)	283	(329)	1,755
Cash at beginning of period	422	353	353	636
Cash at end of period	$ 353	$ 636	$ 24	$ 2,391
Supplemental disclosure of cash flow information:				
Cash paid during the period for:				
Interest	$ 64	$ 1,379	$ 33	$ 102
Income taxes	$ 2,659	$ 1,268	—	$ 538

—See accompanying notes to consolidated financial statements.

F-6

FIGURE 5-8: *continued*

ADVANCED LOGIC RESEARCH, INC. AND SUBSIDIARIES

CONSOLIDATED STATEMENT OF CHANGES IN FINANCIAL POSITION
(in thousands)

	Year Ended September 30, 1997
Sources of working capital:	
Net income	$ 753
Add depreciation which did not require working capital	39
Working capital provided by operations	792
Uses of working capital:	
Purchase of equipment, furniture and fixtures, net	310
Increase in deposits	18
Total uses of working capital	328
Increase in working capital	$ 464
Changes in components of working capital:	
Increase in current assets:	
Cash	$ 163
Trade accounts receivable	1,618
Inventories	3,885
Prepaid expenses	27
	5,693
Increase in current liabilities:	
Notes payable to bank	704
Payable to parent and affiliate	2,781
Accounts payable	1,273
Accrued expenses	100
Income taxes	371
	5,229
Increase in working capital	$ 464

See accompanying notes to consolidated financial statements.

F-7

ADVANCED LOGIC RESEARCH, INC. AND SUBSIDIARIES

NOTES TO CONSOLIDATED FINANCIAL STATEMENTS

Years ended September 30, 1987, 1988 and 1989 and the three months ended December 31, 1988 (unaudited) and 1989 (unaudited)

(1) Summary of Significant Accounting Policies

Organization

Advanced Logic Research, Inc. (the "Company") was incorporated on September 20, 1984 and is engaged in the business of designing, manufacturing and marketing microcomputer systems. A majority of the Company's outstanding common stock is owned by Wearnes Technology (Private) Limited ("Wearnes").

During 1988, the Company incorporated a wholly owned subsidiary, Advanced Logic Research International, Inc. The Company has elected to treat the subsidiary as a foreign sales corporation under Section 922 of the Internal Revenue Code to receive certain tax benefits.

During 1989, the Company formed two wholly-owned subsidiaries, Advanced Logic Research (U.K.) Limited and Advanced Logic Research, Inc. (Canada), as foreign sales offices in England and Canada, and ALR International (Pte) Ltd a manufacturing and sales office located in Singapore. During September 1989, the Company's interest in ALR International (Pte) Ltd was reduced to 51% when Wearnes acquired a 49% minority interest. During December 1989, the Company and Wearnes made additional investments in ALR International (Pte) Ltd at their respective ownership percentages.

Principles of Consolidation

The accompanying consolidated financial statements include the accounts of Advanced Logic Research, Inc. and its subsidiaries. All intercompany balances and transactions have been eliminated in consolidation.

Interim Financial Statements

The financial statements for the three months ended December 31, 1988 and 1989 are unaudited. In the opinion of management, all adjustments (consisting only of normal recurring accruals) considered necessary for a fair presentation have been included. The results of operations for the three months ended December 31, 1989 are not necessarily indicative of the results that may be expected for the year ending September 30, 1990.

Inventories

Inventories are valued at the lower of cost (first-in, first-out) or market (net realizable value).

Depreciation

Depreciation of equipment, furniture and fixtures is computed using the straight-line method over the estimated useful lives of the individual assets, ranging from three to five years.

Revenue Recognition and Warranty Policy

Revenue is recognized upon product shipment. The Company grants certain distributors limited rights to exchange products and price protection on unsold merchandise. The Company also has financing agreements with credit corporations which provide for extended payment terms to pre-approved dealers. These financing agreements generally require the Company to repurchase inventory which has been repossessed by the credit corporations from these dealers. The Company establishes an estimated allowance based on experience for future product returns by charges to current operations. An allowance is also provided for price protection at the time of the price adjustment. Estimated warranty costs are accrued as revenue is recognized.

F-8

FIGURE 5-8: *continued*

ADVANCED LOGIC RESEARCH, INC. AND SUBSIDIARIES

NOTES TO CONSOLIDATED FINANCIAL STATEMENTS (Continued)

Years ended September 30, 1987, 1988 and 1989 and the three months ended December 31, 1988 (unaudited) and 1989 (unaudited)

Statement of Cash Flows

The Company adopted Statement of Financial Accounting Standards No. 95 ("SFAS 95"), "Statement of Cash Flows," on a prospective basis in 1988. SFAS 95 reports annual cash receipts and payments according to operating, investing and financing activities.

Foreign Currency Translation

The Company uses the foreign currencies as the functional currencies of its international operations. Accordingly, assets and liabilities outside the United States were translated into dollars at the rate of exchange in effect at the balance sheet date. Income and expense items are translated at the weighted average exchange rates prevailing during the year. Net foreign currency translation adjustments or exchange gains or losses were not significant to the Company's consolidated results of operations or financial position.

Income Taxes

Amounts provided for income taxes are based on income reported for financial statement purposes at current tax rates. Such amounts include taxes deferred to future periods resulting from timing differences in the recognition of income and expenses in different accounting periods for tax and financial reporting purposes.

Statement of Financial Accounting Standards No. 96 ("SFAS 96"), "Accounting for Income Taxes," was issued by the Financial Accounting Standards Board in December 1987. SFAS 96 requires a change from the deferred method to the liability method of accounting for income taxes. Under the liability method, deferred income taxes are recognized for the tax consequences of "temporary differences" by applying enacted statutory tax rates applicable to future years to differences between the financial statement carrying amounts and the tax bases of existing assets and liabilities. Under SFAS 96, the effect on deferred taxes of a change in tax rates is recognized in income in the period that includes the enactment date.

SFAS 96 is effective for years beginning after December 15, 1991. Upon adoption, the provisions of SFAS 96 may be applied without restating prior years' financial statements or may be applied retroactively by restating any number of consecutive prior years' financial statements. Management has not yet determined when or by what method the Company will adopt SFAS 96, however, it believes that the adoption of SFAS 96 will have an insignificant impact on the Company's consolidated financial position and results of operations.

Net Income Per Share

Net income per share is computed using the weighted average number of shares and dilutive common stock options (at the average market price for the period) which are considered common stock equivalents. Fully dilutive earnings per share amounts are not presented because they approximate primary income per share.

F-9

ADVANCED LOGIC RESEARCH, INC. AND SUBSIDIARIES

NOTES TO CONSOLIDATED FINANCIAL STATEMENTS (Continued)

Years ended September 30, 1987, 1988 and 1989 and the three months ended December 31, 1988 (unaudited) and 1989 (unaudited)

(2) Inventories

A summary of the components of inventories follows (in thousands):

	September 30,		December 31, 1989
	1988	1989	(unaudited)
Raw materials and component parts	$ 7,695	$10,465	$19,913
Work in process	3,097	6,127	7,000
Finished goods	652	5,338	6,426
	$11,444	$21,930	$33,339

(3) Equipment, Furniture and Fixtures

Equipment, furniture and fixtures, at cost, consist of the following (in thousands):

	September 30,		December 31, 1989
	1988	1989	(unaudited)
Machinery and equipment	$ 595	$ 1,505	$ 1,637
Vehicles	166	294	329
Furniture and fixtures	171	232	279
Leasehold improvements	37	64	80
	969	2,095	2,325
Less accumulated depreciation and amortization	(155)	(399)	(510)
	$ 814	$ 1,696	$ 1,815

(4) Transactions with Related Parties

The payable to Wearnes bears interest at 7% per annum beginning 90 days from the date of inventory shipment. Total inventory purchases from Wearnes during fiscal years 1987, 1988 and 1989 were $4,137,000, $8,490,000 and $18,559,000, respectively, and $26,619,000 during the three months ended December 31, 1989 (unaudited).

Pursuant to a Manufacturing Agreement ("Agreement") with the Company, Wearnes Automation, a wholly owned subsidiary of Wearnes, manufactures printed circuit boards for the Company which are used in certain of the Company's products. Wearnes Automation has the nonexclusive, royalty-free right to manufacture and sell circuit boards covered by the Agreement along with certain derivative products. The territory covered by this Agreement, however, excludes the United States, Canada, and Latin America. The Company is required under the Agreement to purchase, under certain conditions, at least 50% for those products covered by the Agreement from Wearnes Automation.

All amounts are due and payable ninety days from shipment date. A summary of the payable to (receivable from) Wearnes and affiliate follows (in thousands):

	September 30,		December 31, 1989
	1988	1989	(unaudited)
Wearnes	$8,124	$10,020	$(1,725)
Wearnes Automation	—	—	25,687
	$8,124	$10,020	$23,962

F-10

FIGURE 5-8: *continued*

ADVANCED LOGIC RESEARCH, INC. AND SUBSIDIARIES

NOTES TO CONSOLIDATED FINANCIAL STATEMENTS (Continued)

Years ended September 30, 1987, 1988 and 1989 and the three months ended December 31, 1988 (unaudited) and 1989 (unaudited)

During June 1989 the Company assumed a $123,000 loan to its president from an affiliate of Wearnes. The loan bears interest at 6% per annum and the amount has been included in other assets in the accompanying consolidated financial statements.

(5) Stockholders' Equity

During fiscal 1986, the Board of Directors authorized the granting of up to 714,000 shares of common stock for issuance to key individuals or directors under an informal stock option program ("1986 Plan"). The options become exercisable at varying periods relative to the date of employment or the grant of the option. The options generally expire 2½ years after the date the options become exercisable or upon termination of employment.

The following is a summary of transactions under the 1986 Plan:

	Number of Shares	Price Per Share
Options outstanding at September 30, 1987	574,770	$.07–$ .14
Granted	7,140	.42
Options outstanding at September 30, 1988	581,910	.07– .42
Granted	85,680	.42
Exercised	(17,850)	.14
Options outstanding at September 30, 1989	649,740	.07– .42
Granted (unaudited)	57,120	.42– 1.68
Exercised (unaudited)	(7,140)	.42
Options outstanding at December 31, 1989 (unaudited)	699,720	$.07–$1.68

As a result of the difference between the grant prices and the deemed fair market prices of 57,120 options granted to certain employees by the Company during the quarter ended December 31, 1989, compensation expense of approximately $75,000 was recorded during the three months ended December 31, 1989 with the remaining amount of $310,000 to be expensed over the related option vesting period (next five quarters).

On January 24, 1990, the Board of Directors of the Company adopted the Flexible Stock Incentive Plan (the "Plan"), which is subject to approval by the Company's stockholders. The Plan contains three components: a stock option component, a stock bonus/stock purchase component and a stock appreciation rights component. The purpose of the Plan is to provide incentives to selected individuals for increased efforts and successful achievements on behalf of the Company and its affiliates.

The Plan provides for the granting of stock options, stock bonuses, stock appreciation rights or rights to purchase stock for up to an aggregate of not more than the greater of (i) 5% of the authorized shares of the Company's common stock or (ii) 15% of the shares of common stock outstanding as of the close of business on the last day of the Company's prior fiscal year. The Company's Board of Directors has determined that it will not grant options under the Plan if, at the time of any such grant, the total number of then outstanding options to purchase common stock would exceed 15% of the then outstanding shares of common stock (8,886,790 shares at March 31, 1990, after giving effect to the proposed reincorporation and the issuance of 2,650,000 additional shares of the Company's common stock as part of its initial public offering). Giving effect to this public offering, as of March 31, 1990, 633,298 shares were available for issuance pursuant to the Plan. Awards under the Plan can be granted to directors, officers, employees and other individuals as determined by the committee of the Board of Directors which administers the Plan (the "Committee"). However, a person

F-11

ADVANCED LOGIC RESEARCH, INC. AND SUBSIDIARIES

NOTES TO CONSOLIDATED FINANCIAL STATEMENTS (Continued)

Years ended September 30, 1987, 1988 and 1989 and the three months ended December 31, 1988 (unaudited) and 1989 (unaudited)

who holds 10% or more of the Company's outstanding common stock, any affiliate of such 10% stockholder and members of the Committee are not eligible to participate in the Plan.

Options granted under the Plan may be either "incentive" stock options or options that do not qualify as Incentive Options ("Nonqualified Options"). The exercise price of shares of common stock covered by each Incentive Option cannot be less than the per-share fair market value of the Company's common stock on the date the option is granted. The exercise price in the case of Nonqualified Options granted under the Plan is set by the Committee on the date the option is granted. No stock options, stock bonuses, stock appreciation rights or rights to purchase stock have been made under the Plan.

(6) Notes Payable

The Company has a $5,000,000 line of credit from a bank which expires May 31, 1990. The line of credit originated during fiscal 1988. Borrowings under the line of credit at September 30, 1988 and 1989 were $1,750,000 and $1,500,000, respectively, and bear interest at the bank's prime rate plus 1%. The weighted average interest rate during fiscal years 1988 and 1989 was 10.06% and 11.86%, respectively. The maximum and average amount outstanding during fiscal 1988 was $1,750,000 and $624,000, respectively, and for fiscal 1989 $3,750,000 and $1,592,000, respectively. Borrowings are secured by all assets of the Company. As a condition of the credit line, Wearnes has subordinated $1,000,000 of its trade receivables from the Company to the bank.

At December 31, 1989 (unaudited), $1,600,000 was outstanding under the same line of credit. The maximum and average amounts outstanding during the three-month period were $1,600,000 and $867,000, respectively, with a weighted average interest rate of 11.50%.

Additionally, ALR International (Pte) Ltd has lines of credit, bearing interest at the lending bank's prime rate, of $4,736,000, of which $607,000 was outstanding as of December 31, 1989. The maximum and average amounts outstanding during the three month period ended December 31, 1989 were $607,000 and $202,000, respectively. The weighted average interest rate for both lines during the three month period was 6.75%.

(7) Long-Term Debt

On January 26, 1989, the Company entered into a $15,000,000 term loan agreement from Singapore International Merchant Bankers Limited which is available through July 26, 1990. Payment on the loan is due in semiannual principal installments of $1,500,000 through January 26, 1994. Borrowings under the agreement at September 30, 1989 and December 31, 1989 (unaudited) were $13,000,000 and bear interest at the Singapore Inter-Bank Offer Rate for the U.S. dollar plus 0.3125–0.5%. Additionally, borrowings are secured by a full guarantee from Wearnes.

The maturities of long-term debt are as follows (in thousands):

Year Ending September 30,	
1990	$ 3,000
1991	3,000
1992	3,000
1993	3,000
1994	1,000
	$13,000

F-12

FIGURE 5-8: *continued*

ADVANCED LOGIC RESEARCH, INC. AND SUBSIDIARIES

NOTES TO CONSOLIDATED FINANCIAL STATEMENTS (Continued)

Years ended September 30, 1987, 1988 and 1989 and the three months ended December 31, 1988 (unaudited) and 1989 (unaudited)

(8) Income Taxes

Income tax expense consists of the following (in thousands):

| | Year Ended September 30, | | | Three Months Ended December 31, | |
	1987	1988	1989	1988	1989
				(unaudited)	
Current:					
Federal	$449	$1,442	$1,600	$414	$1,717
State	123	433	454	150	506
Foreign	—	—	183	—	295
	572	1,875	2,237	564	2,518
Deferred:					
Federal	(11)	(305)	(364)	23	(277)
State	4	(62)	(104)	(18)	(71)
Foreign	—	—	—	—	—
	(7)	(367)	(468)	5	(348)
	$565	$1,508	$1,769	$569	$2,170

Total income tax expense differs from the amount computed by applying the Federal corporate income tax rate of 43% for 1987 and 34% for 1988 and 1989 to income before income taxes as follows (in thousands):

| | Year Ended September 30, | | | Three Months Ended December 31, | |
	1987	1988	1989	1988	1989
				(unaudited)	
Computed "expected" income taxes	$567	$1,356	$1,550	$482	$1,765
State franchise taxes, net of Federal income tax benefit	72	246	231	87	* 287
Incremental research and development expense credit	(40)	(94)	(153)	—	—
Other	(34)	—	63	—	75
●Loss of U.K. subsidiary	—	—	78	—	43
	$565	$1,508	$1,769	$569	$2,170

ADVANCED LOGIC RESEARCH, INC. AND SUBSIDIARIES

NOTES TO CONSOLIDATED FINANCIAL STATEMENTS (Continued)

Years ended September 30, 1987, 1988 and 1989 and the three months ended December 31, 1988 (unaudited) and 1989 (unaudited)

Total taxes on income differs from taxes currently payable as a result of differences in the recognition of revenue and expense for tax and financial statement purposes. The sources of these differences and the tax expense (benefit) of each are as follows (in thousands):

| | Year Ended September 30, | | Three Months Ended December 31, | |
	1988	1989	1988	1989
			(unaudited)	
State income taxes not currently deductible	$ (78)	$ 15	$ 89	$ —
Losses of unconsolidated affiliate not currently deductible	(65)	—	—	(20)
Employee compensation not currently deductible	(48)	7	39	(41)
Inventory reserve recorded for financial statement purposes greater than amount recognized for tax purposes	(43)	(325)	(81)	(151)
Overhead costs capitalized as inventory for tax purposes greater than amount capitalized for financial statement purposes	(43)	(48)	(12)	(40)
Other	(90)	(117)	(30)	(94)
	$(367)	$(468)	$ 5	$(348)

(9) Operating Expenses

Selling expenses include advertising costs of $549,000, $796,000 and $2,318,000 for the years ended September 30, 1987, 1988 and 1989, respectively, and $150,000 and $1,123,000 for the three months ended December 31, 1988 (unaudited) and 1989 (unaudited), respectively.

On October 1, 1988, the Company entered into a nonexclusive licensing agreement with International Business Machines Corporation ("IBM") which enables the Company to make, use, lease, sell, manufacture or have manufactured certain products under patent with IBM. Under this agreement, the Company will pay a royalty to IBM for products sold that utilize the IBM technology. Royalty expense for the year ended September 30, 1989 was $1,769,000 and for the three months ended December 31, 1988 (unaudited) and 1989 (unaudited) was $247,000, and $1,093,000, respectively. Included in accrued expenses at September 30, 1989 and December 31, 1989 (unaudited) are accrued royalties of $690,000 and $1,785,000, respectively.

(10) Profit Sharing Plan

In September 1988, the Company established a pretax savings and profit sharing plan under Section 401(k) of the Internal Revenue Code. Under the plan, eligible employees are able to contribute from 1% to 10% of their compensation. The Company makes a matching contribution of 50% of the first 5% contributed by the employee and may, in its discretion make additional contributions to the plan, up to a maximum of 15% of the employee's compensation. The Company's matching contribution was approximately $61,000 and $57,000 for 1988 and 1989, respectively, and $13,000 for the three months ended December 31, 1989 (unaudited).

FIGURE 5-8: *continued*

ADVANCED LOGIC RESEARCH, INC. AND SUBSIDIARIES

NOTES TO CONSOLIDATED FINANCIAL STATEMENTS (Continued)

Years ended September 30, 1987, 1988 and 1989 and the three months ended December 31, 1988 (unaudited) and 1989 (unaudited)

(11) International Operations and Export Sales

The following table reflects information with respect to the Company's domestic and foreign operations for the year ended September 30, 1989 and the three months ended December 31, 1989 (unaudited). Earlier years are not presented as the Company's two wholly-owned subsidiaries were formed during fiscal 1989.

	North America	Asia	Elimination	Total
Year ended September 30, 1989				
Sales to unaffiliated customers	$61,867	$ 9,707	$ —	$71,574
Intercompany sales	2,798		(2,798)	—
Sales to affiliated customers	59	1,450		1,509
Net sales	$64,724	$11,157	$(2,798)	$73,083
Net income	$ 2,678	$ 137	$ (25)	$ 2,790
Identifiable assets	$32,602	$ 7,242	$ (373)	$39,471
Three months ended December 31, 1989 (unaudited)				
Sales to unaffiliated customers	$32,504	$ 6,591	—	$39,095
Intercompany sales	1,197		(1,197)	—
Sales to affiliated customers	41	386		427
Net sales	$33,742	$ 6,977	$(1,197)	$39,522
Net income	$ 2,835	$ 223	$ (38)	$ 3,020
Identifiable assets	$53,374	$10,304	$(1,214)	$62,464

The Company had export sales to unaffiliated customers of $1,189,000, $3,360,000 and $4,475,000 for 1987, 1988 and 1989, respectively, and $683,000 and $4,728,000 for the three months ended December 31, 1988 (unaudited) and 1989 (unaudited), respectively.

No customer accounted for more than 10% of net sales during fiscal years 1987, 1988, or 1989, or during the three months ended December 31, 1988 (unaudited). During the three months ended December 31, 1989 (unaudited), sales to two distributors accounted for 27% and 13%, respectively, of net sales.

(12) Commitments

The Company leases its corporate manufacturing warehouses and office facilities under noncancellable operating leases which expire in 1994 and are renewable at the Company's option, for an additional five-year period. Additionally, an office facility lease for Advanced Logic Research (U.K.) Limited expires in 2010. Rental expense during the years ended September 30, 1987, 1988 and 1989 amounted to $103,000, $272,000 and $694,000, respectively, and $158,000 and $289,000 for the three months ended December 31, 1988 (unaudited) and 1989 (unaudited).

ADVANCED LOGIC RESEARCH, INC. AND SUBSIDIARIES

NOTES TO CONSOLIDATED FINANCIAL STATEMENTS (Continued)

Years ended September 30, 1987, 1988 and 1989 and the three months ended December 31, 1988 (unaudited) and 1989 (unaudited)

At September 30, 1989, future minimum rental payments under all noncancellable operating leases with terms in excess of one year are as follows (in thousands):

Year Ending September 30,	
1990	$ 919
1991	1,347
1992	1,394
1993	1,405
1994	784
Thereafter	444
	$6,293

During December 1989 ALR International (Pte) Ltd entered into two operating leases which expire in November 1992. Combined annual rental payments for these operating leases approximate $120,000 (unaudited).

(13) Subsequent Events

On March 1, 1990, subject to stockholder approval, which is assured, the Board of Directors of the Company authorized a 7.14-for-1 split of common stock. Data related to shares and per share amounts for all periods presented have been adjusted to reflect the effect of the stock split.

In addition, the Board of Directors of the Company adopted a resolution to reincorporate in the State of Delaware. Accordingly, the consolidated financial statements have been prepared to give effect to the reincorporation and resulting change in capital structure. The components of stockholders' equity prior to reincorporation (but after giving effect to the stock split, including an increase in the number of shares of common stock) are as follows (in thousands except share data):

	September 30, 1988	September 30, 1989	December 31, 1989 (unaudited)
Common stock, no par value, 50,000,000 shares authorized; 6,211,800 and 6,229,650 shares issued and outstanding at September 30, 1988 and 1989, respectively, and 6,236,790 at December 31, 1989	$ 306	$ 309	$ 312
Retained earnings	3,334	6,124	9,144
Net stockholders' equity	$3,640	$6,433	$9,456

Source: ALR Prospectus, April, 1990.

6

How To Analyze
Financial Statements

OVERVIEW

Analysis of financial statements reveals important information to present and prospective investors. Financial statement analysis attempts to answer the following basic questions:

- How well is the business doing?
- What are its strengths?
- What are its weaknesses?
- How does it fare in the industry?
- Is the business improving or deteriorating?

This chapter will discuss financial statement analysis and its importance to investors, basic components of ratio analysis, how to distinguish between trend analysis and industry comparison, how to calculate and interpret various ratios, and limitations of ratio analysis.

FINANCIAL STATEMENT ANALYSIS: WHAT AND WHY

An investor is interested in the present and future level of return (earnings) and risk (liquidity, debt, and activity). Evaluation of a stock is based on examining the firm's financial statements, which consider industrywide financial health, nationwide economic and political conditions, and companywide future outlook. The analysis attempts to ascertain whether the stock is overpriced, underpriced, or priced in proportion to its market value and, thus, whether the stock is of value for a particular investor. Financial statement analysis uncovers much of the data needed to forecast earnings and dividends.

Horizontal and Vertical Analysis

Horizontal analysis, also called *trend analysis,* is a time series analysis of financial statements covering more than one accounting period. It looks at the percentage change

FIGURE 6-1: TLC Inc. Comparative Balance Sheet

TLC Inc. :   Comparative Balance Sheet (in Thousands of Dollars)
For Years Ended December 31, 19X2, 19X1, 19X0

	19X2	19X1	19X0	Incr.or Decr. 19X2-X1	19X1-X0	% Incr. or Decr. 19x2-X	19X1-X0
ASSETS							
Current Assets:							
Cash	$28	$36	$36	-8	0	-22.2%	0.0%
Marketable Securities	$22	$15	$7	7	8	46.7%	114.3%
Accounts Receivable	$21	$16	$10	5	6	31.3%	60.0%
Inventory	$53	$46	$49	7	-3	15.2%	-6.1%
Total Current Assets	$124	$113	$102	11	11	9.7%	10.8%
Plant & Equip.	$103	$91	$83	12	8	13.2%	9.6%
Total Assets	$227	$204	$185	23	19	11.3%	10.3%
LIABILITIES							
Current Liabilities	$56	$50	$51	6	-1	12.0%	-2.0%
Long-term debt	$83	$74	$69	9	5	12.2%	7.2%
Total Liabilities	$139	$124	$120	15	4	12.1%	3.3%
STOCKHOLDERS' EQUITY							
Common Stock*	$46	$46	$46	0	0	0.0%	0.0%
Retained Earnings	$42	$34	$19	8	15	23.5%	78.9%
Total Stockholders' Equity	$88	$80	$65	8	15	10.0%	23.1%
Total Liab.&Stkhldrs' Equity	$227	$204	$185	23	19	11.3%	10.3%

*$10 par, 4,600 shares

in an account over time. The percentage change equals the change over the prior year. For example, if sales in 19X1 are $100,000 and in 19X2 are $300,000, there is a 200% increase ($200,000 ÷ $100,000). By examining the magnitude of direction of a financial statement item over time, the investor can evaluate its reasonableness. Horizontal analysis typically is presented in comparative financial statements. (See TLC Inc. financial data in Figures 6-1 and 6-2.) In annual reports, comparative financial data are usually shown for five-year periods.

Horizontal analysis helps you pinpoint areas of wide divergence requiring investigation. For example, in Figure 6-2, the significant rise in sales returns taken with the reduction in sales for 19X1-19X2 should lead you to compare these results with those of competitors.

It is essential to present both the dollar amount of change and the percentage of change because using one without the other may result in erroneous conclusions. For example, the interest expense from 19X0–19X1 went up by 100.0 percent, but this percentage change represented a *dollar* change of only $1,000 and may not need

---

FIGURE 6-2: Comparative Income Statement

TLC Inc.: Comparative Income Statement (in Thousands of Dollars)
For Years Ended December 31, 19X2, 19X1, 19X0

	19X2	19X1	19X0	Incr. or Decr. 19X2-X1	Incr. or Decr. 19X1-X0	% Incr. or Decr. 19X2-X1	% Incr. or Decr. 19X1-X0
Sales	$98.3	$120.0	$56.6	($21.7)	$63.4	-18.1%	112.0%
Returns& Allowances	$18.0	$10.0	$4.0	$8.0	$6.0	80.0%	150.0%
Net Sales	$80.3	$110.0	$52.6	($29.7)	$57.4	-27.0%	109.1%
Cost of Goods Sold	$52.0	$63.0	$28.0	($11.0)	$35.0	-17.5%	125.0%
Gross Profit	$28.3	$47.0	$24.6	($18.7)	$22.4	-39.8%	91.1%
Operating Expenses							
-Selling	$12.0	$13.0	$11.0	($1.0)	$2.0	-7.7%	18.2%
-General	$5.0	$8.0	$3.0	($3.0)	$5.0	-37.5%	166.7%
Total Operating Exp.	$17.0	$21.0	$14.0	($4.0)	$7.0	-19.0%	50.0%
Inc. from Operations	$11.3	$26.0	$10.6	($14.7)	$15.4	-56.5%	145.3%
Nonoperating Income	$4.0	$1.0	$2.0	$3.0	($1.0)	300.0%	-50.0%
Inc. before Int.&Tax	$15.3	$27.0	$12.6	($11.7)	$14.4	-43.3%	114.3%
Interest Expense	$2.0	$2.0	$1.0	$0.0	$1.0	0.0%	100.0%
Income before Taxes	$13.3	$25.0	$11.6	($11.7)	$13.4	-46.8%	115.5%
Income Taxes (40%)	$5.3	$10.0	$4.6	($4.7)	$5.4	-46.8%	115.5%
Net Income	$8.0	$15.0	$7.0	($7.0)	$8.0	-46.8%	115.5%

---

further investigation. Conversely, a large dollar change might cause a small percentage change and thus may be negligible.

Key changes and trends can also be highlighted by the use of **common-size statements**, those in which items appear separately in percentage terms whose preparation is known as **vertical analysis**. In vertical analysis, a material financial statement item is used as a base value, and all other accounts on the financial statement are compared to it. In the balance sheet, for example, total assets equal 100 percent, and each asset is stated as a percentage of total assets. Similarly, total liabilities and stockholders' equity is assigned 100 percent, with a given liability or equity account stated as a percentage of the total liabilities and stockholders' equity.

Placing all assets in common-size form clearly shows the relative importance of the current assets as compared to the noncurrent assets. It also shows that significant changes have taken place over the past year in the composition of the current assets. Notice (in Figure 6-1) that receivables have increased in relative importance and that cash has declined in relative importance. Deterioration in the cash position may be a result of inability to collect from customers.

For the income statement, 100 percent is assigned to net sales, with all other revenue and expense accounts related to it. It is possible to see at a glance how each dollar of sales is distributed between the various costs, expenses, and profits. For ex-

FIGURE 6-3: TLC Inc. Income Statement and Common-Size

TLC Inc.: Income Statement & Common Size Analysis (in Thousands of Dollars)
For Years Ended December 31, 19X2 & 19X1

	19X2 Amount	%	19X1 Amount	%
Sales	$98.3	122.4%	$120.0	109.1%
Sales Return & Allowances	$18.0	22.4%	$10.0	9.1%
Net Sales	$80.3	100.0%	$110.0	100.0%
Cost of Goods Sold	$52.0	64.8%	$63.0	57.3%
Gross Profit	$28.3	35.2%	$47.0	42.7%
Operating Expenses				
- Selling	$12.0	14.9%	$13.0	11.8%
-General	$5.0	6.2%	$8.0	7.3%
Total Operating Expenses	$17.0	21.2%	$21.0	19.1%
		0.0%		0.0%
Income from Operations	$11.3	14.1%	$26.0	23.6%
Nonoperating Income	$4.0	5.0%	$1.0	0.9%
Income before Interest & Taxes	$15.3	19.1%	$27.0	24.5%
Interest Expense	$2.0	2.5%	$2.0	1.8%
Income before Taxes	$13.3	16.6%	$25.0	22.7%
Income Taxes (40%)	$5.3	6.6%	$10.0	9.1%
Net Income	$8.0	9.9%	$15.0	13.6%

ample, notice in Figure 6-3 that 64.8 cents of every dollar of sales was needed to cover cost of goods sold in 19X2, as compared to only 57.3 cents in the prior year; also notice that only 9.9 cents out of every dollar of sales (net income) remained for profits in 19X2—down from 13.6 cents in the prior year. Also compare the vertical percentages of the business to those of the competition and to the industry norms. Then you can determine how the company fares in the industry.

The common-size income statement in Figure 6-3 is based on the data provided in Figure 6-2.

Working with Financial Ratios

Horizontal and vertical analyses compare one figure to another within the same category. It is also vital to compare two figures applicable to different categories; this is accomplished by ratio analysis. In this section, you will learn how to calculate and interpret the various financial ratios. The results of ratio analysis will allow you to:

- Appraise the position of a business,
- Identify trouble spots that need attention, and

- Provide the basis for making projections and forecasts about the course of future operations.

Think of ratios as measures of the relative health or sickness of a business. Just as a doctor takes readings of a patient's temperature, blood pressure, heart rate, and the like, you will take readings of a company's liquidity, profitability, leverage, efficiency in using assets, and market value. Just as the doctor compares a patient's readings to generally accepted norms (such as a temperature of 98.6 degrees) you compare ratios to established norms.

To obtain useful conclusions from the ratios, you must make two comparisons: an industry comparison and a trend analysis. An **industry comparison** allows you to answer " How does a business fare in the industry?" by comparing the company's ratios to those of competing companies in the industry or with industry standards (averages). You can obtain industry norms from financial services such as Value Line, Dun & Bradstreet, Standard & Poor's, and Robert Morris Associates. A **trend analysis** indicates how the business does over time. You make a trend analysis by comparing a given ratio for one company over several years to see the direction of financial health or operational performance.

FINANCIAL RATIOS: CONCEPTS

Financial ratios can be grouped according to several concepts: liquidity, asset utilization, solvency, profitability, and market value.

Liquidity

Liquidity is a firm's ability to satisfy maturing short-term debt. Liquidity, which is crucial to carrying out business operations—especially during periods of adversity—relates to the short term, typically a period of one year or less. Poor liquidity might lead to higher cost of financing and inability to pay bills and dividends. The three basic measures of liquidity are net working capital, the current ratio, and the quick (acid-test) ratio. Throughout this discussion, refer to Figures 6-1 through 6-4 so as to understand where the numbers come from.

Net Working Capital

Net working capital equals current assets minus current liabilities. Referring to Figure 6-1, net working capital for 19X2 is:

$$\text{Net working capital} = \text{Current assets} - \text{Current liabilities}$$

$$= \$124 - \$56 = \$68$$

In 19X1, net working capital was $63 (Figure 6-4). The rise over the year is favorable.

FIGURE 6-4: Summary of Financial Ratios

Trend & Industry Comparisons
TLC Inc. 19X2 and 19X1

Ratios	Definitions	19X1	19X2	(a) 19X2 Ind. Ave.	Evaluation (b) 19X2 Ind. Comp.	Trend 19X1-19X2	Overall
LIQUIDITY							
Net working capital	Current assets - current liabilities	63	68	56	good	good	good
Current Ratio	Current assets/current liabilities	2.26	2.21	2.05	OK	OK	OK
Quick (Acid-test) ratio	(Cash + marketable securities + accounts receivable)/current liabilities	1.34	1.27	1.11	OK	OK	OK
ASSET UTILIZATION							
Accounts receivable turnover	Net credit sales/average accounts receivable	8.46	4.34	5.5	OK	poor	poor
Average collection period	365 days/accounts receivable turnover	43.1 days	84.1 days	66.4 days	OK	poor	poor
Inventory turnover	Cost of goods sold/average inventory	1.33	1.05	1.2	OK	poor	poor
Average age of inventory	365 days/inventory turnover	274.4 days	347.6 days	N/A	N/A	poor	poor
Operating cycle	Average collection period + average age of inventory	317.5 days	431.7 days	N/A	N/A	poor	poor
Total asset turnover	Net sales/average total assets	0.57	0.37	0.44	OK	poor	poor
SOLVENCY							
Debt ratio	Total liabilities/total assets	0.61	0.61	N/A	N/A	OK	OK

FIGURE 6-4: continued

Ratio	Formula						
Debt-equity ratio	Total liabilities/stockholders' equity	1.55	1.58	1.3	poor	poor	poor
Times interest earned	Income before interest and taxes/ interest expense	13.5 times	7.65 times	10 times	OK	poor	poor
PROFITABILITY							
Gross profit margin	Gross profit/net sales	0.43	0.35	0.48	poor	poor	poor
Profit margin	Net income/net sales	0.14	0.1	0.15	poor	poor	poor
Return on total assets	Net income/average total assets	0.077	0.037	0.1	poor	poor	poor
Return on equity (ROE)	Earnings available to common stockholders/ average stockholders' equity	0.207	0.095	0.27	poor	poor	poor
MARKET VALUE							
Earnings per share (EPS)	(Net income -preferred dividend)/ common shares outstanding	3.26	1.74	4.51	poor	poor	poor
Price/earnings (P/E) ratio	Market price per share/EPS	7.98	6.9	7.12	OK	poor	poor
Book value per share	(Total stockholders' equity - preferred stock)/ common shares outstanding	17.39	19.13	N/A	N/A	good	good
Price/book value ratio	Market price per share/book value per share	1.5	0.63	N/A	N/A	poor	poor
Dividend yield	Dividends per share/market price per share	-	(c) -	N/A	N/A	-	-
Dividend payout	Dividends per share/EPS	-	-	N/A	N/A	-	-

(a) From sources not included in this Chapter.   (b) Represents subjective evaluation.   (c) Not calculated here.

Current Ratio

Reflects the company's ability to satisfy current debt from current assets. Expressed arithmetically, current ratio equals current assets divided by current liabilities:

$$\text{Current ratio} = \frac{\text{Current assets}}{\text{Current liabilities}}$$

For 19X2, the current ratio is:

$$\frac{\$124}{\$56} = 2.2143$$

In 19X1, the current ratio was 2.26; the decline over the year points to a slight reduction in liquidity.

Quick (Acid-Test) Ratio

A more stringent liquidity test can be found in the quick (acid-test) ratio. Inventory and prepaid expenses are excluded from the total of current assets, leaving only the more liquid (or quick) assets to be divided by current liabilities. Thus:

$$\text{Acid-test ratio} = \frac{\text{Cash + Marketable securities + Accounts receivable}}{\text{Current liabilites}}$$

The quick ratio for 19X2 is:

$$\frac{\$28 + \$22 + 21}{\$56} = 1.2679$$

In 19X1, the ratio was 1.34; the small reduction in the ratio over the period points to less liquidity.

The overall liquidity trend shows a slight deterioration as reflected in the lower current and quick ratios, although it is better than the industry norms (see Figure 6-4 for industry averages). But a mitigating factor is the increase in net working capital.

Asset Utilization

Asset utilization (also called activity, turnover) ratios reflect the way in which a company uses its assets to obtain revenue and profit. One example is how well receivables turn into cash; the higher the ratio, the more efficiently the business manages its assets.

Accounts Receivable Ratios

These comprise the accounts receivable turnover and the average collection period. The *accounts receivable turnover* describes the number of times accounts receivable are collected in the year. It is derived by dividing net credit sales by average accounts receivable. Calculate *average* accounts receivable by adding the beginning balance and the ending balance and dividing by two.

For 19X2, the average accounts receivable is:

$$\frac{\$16 + \$21}{2} = \$18.50$$

$$\text{Accounts receivable turnover} = \frac{\text{Net credit sales}}{\text{Average accounts receivable}}$$

The accounts receivable turnover for 19X2 is:

$$\frac{\$80.30}{\$18.50} = 4.34$$

In 19X1, the turnover was 8.46; there is a sharp reduction in the turnover rate, pointing to a collection problem.

The *average collection period* is the length of time it takes to collect receivables and represents the number of days receivables are held. Thus:

$$\text{Average collection period} = \frac{365 \text{ days}}{\text{Accounts receivable turnover}}$$

In 19X2, the average collection period is:

$$\frac{365}{4.34} = 84.1 \text{ days}$$

It takes this firm about 84 days to convert receivables to cash. In 19X1, the collection period was 43.1 days. The significant lengthening of the collection period may be a cause for some concern, as it may be a result of doubtful accounts or poor credit management.

Inventory Ratios

Inventory ratios are useful especially when a buildup in inventory exists. Inventory ties up cash. Holding large amounts of inventory can result in lost opportunities for profit as well as increased storage costs. Before extending credit or lending money, a creditor should examine the firm's *inventory turnover* and *average age of inventory.* Calculate *average* inventory by adding beginning and ending inventories and dividing by two.

The average inventory for 19X2 is:

$$\frac{\$46 + \$53}{2} = \$49.50$$

$$\text{Inventory turnover} = \frac{\text{Costs of goods sold}}{\text{Average inventory}}$$

The inventory turnover for 19X2 is:

$$\frac{\$52}{\$49.50} = 1.05$$

For 19X1, the turnover was 1.33.

$$\text{Average age of inventory} = \frac{365 \text{ days}}{\text{Inventory turnover}}$$

In 19X2, the average age is:

$$\frac{365}{1.05} = 347.6 \text{ days}$$

In the previous year, the average age was 274.4 days.

The reduction in turnover and increase in inventory age point to a longer inventory holding period. Ask why the inventory is not selling as quickly.

The *operating cycle* is the number of days it takes to convert inventory and receivables to cash. To calculate:

Operating cycle = Average collection period + Average age of inventory

In 19X2, the operating cycle is:

84.1 days + 347.6 days = 431.7 days

In the previous year, the operating cycle was 317.5 days. An unfavorable direction is indicated because additional funds are tied up in noncash assets, and cash collection is sluggish.

By calculating the *total asset turnover*, you can find out whether the company is efficiently employing its total assets to obtain sales revenue. A low ratio may indicate too much investment in assets compared to the sales revenue generated:

$$\text{Total asset turnover} = \frac{\text{Net sales}}{\text{Average total assets}}$$

In 19X2, the ratio is:

$$\frac{\dfrac{\$80.30}{(\$204 + \$227)}}{2} = \frac{\$80.30}{\$215.50} = 0.37$$

In 19X1, the ratio was 0.57 ($110 ÷ $194.50). There has been a sharp reduction in asset utilization.

TLC Inc. has suffered a sharp deterioration in activity ratios, pointing to a need for improved credit and inventory management. However, the 19X2 ratios are not far out of line with the industry averages (see Figure 6-4). It appears that problems are inefficient collection and obsolescence of inventory.

Solvency

Solvency (leverage and debt service) is the company's ability to satisfy long-term debt as it becomes due. Be concerned about the long-term financial and operating structure of any firm in which you are interested. Another important consideration is the size of debt in the firm's capital structure, referred to as *financial leverage*. (Capital structure is the mix of the *long-term* sources of funds used by the firm.)

Solvency also depends on earning power; in the long run, a company will not satisfy its debts unless it earns a profit. A leveraged capital structure subjects the company to fixed interest charges, which contributes to earnings instability. Excessive debt may also make it difficult for the firm to borrow funds at reasonable rates during tight money markets.

Debt Ratio

The debt ratio reveals the amount of money a company owes to its creditors. Excessive debt means greater risk to the investor. *NOTE: Equity holders come after creditors in bankruptcy. The debt ratio is calculated by dividing total liabilities by total assets:*

$$\text{Debt} = \frac{\text{Total liabilities}}{\text{Total assets}}$$

In 19X2, the ratio is:

$$\frac{\$139}{\$227} = 0.61$$

Debt/Equity Ratio

This will show whether the firm has a large amount of debt in its capital structure. Large debts mean that the borrower has to pay significant periodic interest and principal. Also, a heavily debted firm has a higher risk of running out of cash in difficult times. Interpretation of this ratio depends on several variables, including the ratios of other firms in the industry, the degree of access to additional debt financing, and stability of operations. So, then:

$$\text{Debt to equity} = \frac{\text{Total liabilities}}{\text{Stockholders' equity}}$$

In 19X2, the ratio is:

$$\frac{\$139}{\$88} = 1.58$$

In the previous year, the ratio was 1.55; the trend is relatively static.

Times Interest Earned (Interest Coverage) Ratio

Tells how many times the firm's before-tax earnings would cover interest. It is a safety margin indicator in that it reflects how much of a reduction in earnings a company can tolerate. To calculate:

$$\text{Interest coverage} = \frac{\text{Income before interest and taxes}}{\text{Interest expense}}$$

For 19X2, the ratio is:

$$\frac{\$15.30}{\$2.00} = 7.65$$

In 19X1, interest was covered 13.5 times. The coverage reduction during the period is a bad sign—it means that less earnings are available to satisfy interest charges.

Also note liabilities not yet accounted for in the balance sheet by closely examining footnote disclosures—for example, lawsuits, noncapitalized leases, and future guarantees.

As shown in Figure 6-4, although it remained fairly constant, the company's overall solvency is poor, relative to industry averages. There has been no marked change in its ability to satisfy long-term debt, and significantly less profit is available to cover interest payments.

Profitability

A company's ability to earn a good profit and return on investment is an indicator of its financial well-being and the efficiency with which it is managed. Poor earnings have detrimental effects on market price of stock and dividends. Total dollar net income has little meaning unless it is compared to the input in getting that profit.

Gross Profit Margin

The *gross profit margin* shows the percentage of each dollar remaining once the company has paid for goods acquired. A high margin reflects good earning potential. Thus, the relationship between gross profit and net sales is expressed as:

$$\text{Gross profit margin} = \frac{\text{Gross profit}}{\text{Net sales}}$$

In 19X2, the ratio is:

$$\frac{\$28.30}{\$80.30} = 0.35$$

The ratio was 0.43 in 19X1. The reduction shows that the company now receives less profit on each dollar sale. Perhaps higher relative cost of merchandise sold is at fault.

Profit Margin

This shows the earnings generated from revenue and is a key indicator of operating performance. It indicates the firm's pricing, cost structure, and production efficiency. This relationship is expressed as follows:

$$\text{Profit margin} = \frac{\text{Net income}}{\text{Net sales}}$$

The ratio in 19X2 is:

$$\frac{\$8}{\$80.30} = 0.10$$

For the previous year, profit margin was 0.14. The decline in the ratio shows a downward trend in earning power. (These percentages are shown in the common-size income statement in Figure 6-3.)

Return on Investment

A prime indicator: it allows you to evaluate the profit you will earn if you invest in the business. Two key ratios are the *return on total assets* and the *return on equity*.

Return on total assets ratio shows whether management is efficient in using available resources to get profit:

$$\text{Return on total assets} = \frac{\text{Net income}}{\text{Average total assets}}$$

In 19X2, the return is:

$$\frac{\dfrac{\$8}{\dfrac{(\$227 + \$204)}{2}}} = 0.037$$

In 19X1, the return was 0.077. There has been a deterioration in the productivity of assets in generating earnings.

Return on equity (ROE) ratio reflects the rate of return earned on the stockholders' investment.

$$\text{Return on common equity} = \frac{\text{Net income available to stockholders}}{\text{Average stockholders' equity}}$$

The return in 19X2 is:

$$\frac{\dfrac{\$8}{\dfrac{(\$88 + \$80)}{2}}} = 0.095$$

In 19X1, the return was 0.207; there was a significant drop in return to the owners.

Overall profitability of the company has decreased considerably, causing a decline in both the return on assets and return on equity. Perhaps lower earnings were due in part to higher costs of short-term financing arising from the decline in liquidity and activity ratios. Moreover, as asset turnover rates go down, so will profits decline because of lack of sales and higher costs of carrying higher current asset balances. Industry comparisons (Figure 6-4) reveal that the company is faring very poorly industrywide.

Table 6-1 lists industries with return on equity (ROE) in excess of 20 percent.

Market Value Ratios

Market value ratios relate the company's stock price to its earnings (or book value) per share. Also included are dividend-related ratios.

Earnings Per Share (EPS)

The EPS is the ratio most widely watched by investors. EPS reflects the net income per share owned. For preferred stock, reduce net income by the preferred dividends

---

TABLE 6-1: Industries with High Return on Equity (ROE)

Rates (in excess of 20%)

Drugs and research	31.9
Personal care	28.1
Tobacco	21.3
Pollution control	20.2
Food processing	21.6
Beverages	23.7

Source: *Corporate Scorecard, Business Week*, McGraw-Hill, March 18, 1991, pp. 52-93.

to obtain the net income available to common stockholders. If preferred stock is not in the capital structure, determine EPS by dividing net income by common shares outstanding. EPS is a gauge of corporate operating performance and of expected future dividends.

$$\text{EPS} = \frac{\text{Net Income} - \text{Preferred dividend}}{\text{Common shares outstanding}}$$

EPS in 19X2 is:

$$\frac{\$8,000}{4,600 \text{ shares}} = \$1.74$$

For 19X1, EPS was $3.26. The sharp reduction over the year should cause alarm among investors. As shown in Figure 6-4, the industry average EPS in 19X2 is much higher than that of TLC Inc. ($4.51 per share versus $1.74 per share).

Table 6-2 displays EPS of some highly profitable companies.

Price/Earnings (P/E) Ratio

Also called *earnings multiple,* the P/E ratio reflects the company's relationship to its stockholders. The P/E ratio represents the amount investors are willing to pay for each dollar of the firm's earnings. A high multiple is favorable in that it shows that investors view the firm positively. On the other hand, investors looking for value would prefer a relatively low multiple compared with companies of similar risk and return. Assume a market price per share of $12 on December 31, 19X2, and $26 on December 31, 19X1. The P/E ratios are:

$$\text{Price/earnings ratio} = \frac{\text{Market price per share}}{\text{Earnings per share}} \text{ , } or$$

TABLE 6-2: Highly Profitable Companies (in terms of EPS)

Wells Fargo	$13.39
Ralston Purina	6.73
Atlantic Richfield	10.21
Geico	13.64
Capital Cities/ABC	27.71
Grey Advertising	10.97
IBM	10.51

Source: *Corporate Scorecard, Business Week,* McGraw-Hill, March 18, 1991, pp. 52-93.

$$19X2: \frac{\$12}{\$1.74} = 6.90$$

$$19X1: \frac{\$26}{\$3.26} = 7.98$$

From the lower P/E multiple, you can infer that stockholders now have a lower opinion of the business. However, some investors argue that a low P/E ratio can also mean that the stock is undervalued. Nevertheless, the decline over the year in stock price was 54 percent ($14 ÷ $26), which should cause deep investor concern. *NOTE: What does it mean when a firm's stock sells on a high or low P/E ratio?* **Gordon's dividend growth model** can be helpful in answering this question. If a company's dividends are expected to grow at a constant rate, then

$$P_o = \frac{D_1}{r - g}$$

where P_o = the current price of stock, D_1 = the expected dividend next year, r = the return required by investors from similar investments, and g = the expected growth in dividends. To find the P/E ratio:

$$\frac{P_o}{EPS} = \frac{D_1}{EPS} \times \frac{1}{r - g}$$

Thus, a high P/E ratio may indicate that:

  • Investors expect high dividend growth (g), *or*
  • The stock has low risk and, therefore, investors are content with a low prospective return (r), *or*
  • The company is expected to achieve average growth while paying out a high proportion of earnings:

TABLE 6-3: P/E (Price/Earnings) Ratios—1990

Company	Industry	1990
Amax	Metals & Mining	10
Reynolds & Reynolds	Office Equipment	9
Adolph Coors	Beverages	19
Carolina Freight	Trucking	45
Scana	Utilities	8

Source: *Corporate Scorecard, Business Week,* McGraw-Hill, March 18, 1991, pp. 52-93.

$$\frac{D_1}{EPS}$$

(The Gordon model will be taken up again in Chapter 7.) Table 6-3 shows price/earnings ratios of certain companies.

Book Value Per Share

Book value per share equals the net assets available to common stockholders divided by shares outstanding. By comparing it to market price per share, you can get another view of how investors feel about the business.

$$\text{Book value per share} = \frac{\text{Total stockholers' equity} - \text{Preferred stock}}{\text{Common shares outstanding}}$$

The book value per share in 19X2 is:

$$\frac{\$88,000 - 0}{\$4,600} = \$19.13$$

In 19X1, book value per share was $17.39. The increased book value per share is a favorable sign, because it indicates that each share now has a higher book value. However, in 19X2, market price is much less than book value, which means that the stock market does not value the security highly. In 19X1, market price did exceed book value, but there is now some stockholder doubt concerning the company. However, some analysts may argue that the stock is underpriced.

Price/Book Value Ratio

This shows the market value of the company in comparison to its historical accounting value. A company with old assets may have a high ratio, whereas one with new assets may have a low ratio. Hence, in appraising corporate assets you should note the changes in the ratio.

$$\text{Price/book value ratio} = \frac{\text{Market price per share}}{\text{Book value per share}}$$

In 19X2, the ratio is:

$$\frac{\$12}{\$19.13} = 0.63$$

In 19X1, the ratio was 1.5. The significant drop may indicate a lower opinion of the company in the eyes of investors. Market price of stock may have dropped because of a deterioration in liquidity, activity, and profitability ratios. The major indicators of a company's performance are intertwined (i.e., one affects the other), so that problems in one area may spill over into another. This appears to have happened to the company in this example.

Dividend Ratios

Dividend ratios help you determine current income from an investment. Two relevant ratios are *dividend yield* and *dividend payout*:

$$\text{Dividend yield} = \frac{\text{Dividend per share}}{\text{Market price per share}}$$

The stock's dividend yield is simply the expected dividend as a percentage of the stock price. Remember, it is helpful to consider a concern with a constant expected dividend growth. In this case:

$$\text{Dividend yield} = \frac{D_1}{P_o} = r - g$$

Thus a high yield may indicate that investors expect low dividend growth *(g)* or that the stock's risk merits a high expected return *(r)*.

$$\text{Dividend payout} = \frac{\text{Dividend per share}}{\text{Earnings per share}}$$

There is no such thing as a "right" payout ratio. Stockholders look unfavorably upon reduced dividends because it is a sign of possible deterioration of financial health. However, companies with ample opportunities for growth at high rates of return on assets tend to have low payout ratios.

Table 6-4 shows the dividend payout ratios of certain companies.

TABLE 6-4: Dividend Payout Ratios—1987

Chevron	82%
Bell Atlantic	0%
Capital Cities/ABC	1%

Source: "Corporate Scorecard," *Business Week,* McGraw Hill, April 15, 1988, pp. 174-240

Summary of Financial Ratios

As indicated throughout this chapter, a single ratio or a single group of ratios is inadequate for assessing all aspects of a firm's financial condition. Figure 6-4 (page 114) summarizes the 19X1 and 19X2 ratios calculated in the previous sections, along with the industry average ratios for 19X2. It also shows the formula used to calculate each ratio. The last three columns contain subjective assessments of TLC's financial condition, based on trend analysis and 19X2 comparisons to industry norms. (In general, five-year ratios are needed for trend analysis to be more meaningful.)

By appraising the trend in the company's ratios from 19X1 to 19X2, we see from the drop in the current and quick ratios that there has been a slight detraction in short-term liquidity, although ratios have been above industry averages. On the other hand, working capital has improved. A material deterioration in the activity ratios has occurred, indicating that improved credit and inventory policies are required. This is not terribly alarming, however, because these ratios are not way out of line with industry averages. Also, total utilization of assets, as indicated by the total asset turnover, shows a deteriorating trend.

Leverage (amount of debt) has been constant. However, there is less profit available to satisfy interest charges. TLC's profitability has deteriorated over the year. In 19X2, it is consistently below the industry average in every measure of profitability. Consequently, the return on the shareholders' investment and the return on total assets have gone down. The earnings decrease may be partly due to the firm's high cost of short-term financing and partly due to operating inefficiency.

The higher costs may be due to receivables and inventory difficulties that forced a decline in the liquidity and activity ratios. Furthermore, as receivables and inventory turn over less, profit will fall off from lack of sales and the costs of carrying more in current asset balances.

The firm's market value, as measured by the price/earnings (P/E) ratio, is respectable compared with the industry, although it does show a declining trend.

It appears, then, that, in many categories the company is doing satisfactorily in the industry. The 19X1-19X2 period, however, seems to indicate that the company is heading for financial trouble in terms of earnings, activity, and short-term liquidity. TLC needs to concentrate on increasing operating efficiency and asset utilization.

Is Ratio Analysis a Panacea?

Ratio analysis is an effective tool for assessing a business's financial condition, but you also must recognize the following limitations:

• Accounting policies vary among companies and can inhibit useful comparisons. For example, the use of different depreciation methods (straight-line versus double declining balance) will affect profitability and return ratios.

• Management may "fool around with" ("window-dress") the figures. For example, it can reduce needed research expense just to bolster net income. This practice, however, will almost always hurt the company in the long run.

• A ratio is static and does not reveal future flows. For example, it will not answer questions such as "How much cash do you have in your pocket now?" or "Is that sufficient, considering your expenses and income over the next month?"

• A ratio does not indicate the quality of its components. For example, a high quick ratio may contain receivables of bad debt risk.

• Reported liabilities may be undervalued, for example failure to properly account for a lawsuit.

• The company may have multiple lines of business, making it difficult to identify the industry group of which the company is a part.

• Industry averages cited by financial advisory services are only approximations; you may have to compare a company's ratios to those of competing companies.

SOURCES OF INDUSTRY FINANCIAL RATIOS

There are six major sources of industry financial ratios you can use to compare the ones of the company you are analyzing.

Key Business Ratios, published by Dun & Bradstreet, is a compilation of 14 significant ratios on 800 different lines of business listed by SIC (standard industrial classification) code. Included are current assets to current debt, net profits on net sales, and total debt to tangible net worth.

Annual Statement Studies (published annually) by Robert Morris Associates, a banking industry group, provides common-size statements and financial ratios on over 375 industry classifications (see Figure 6-5).

Almanac of Business and Industrial Financial Ratios is an exhaustive source published annually by Prentice-Hall, Inc. This comprehensive volume provides comparative financial ratios in 181 fields of business and industry. It ranks small, medium, and large companies by 22 key financial ratios. It also contains a complete collection of bar chart graphs for all 22 ratios (see Figure 6-6).

Down Jones-Irwin Business and Investment Almanac is published annually by Dow Jones-Irwin. This comprehensive source contains mostly industry financial ratios and common-size income statements. Some information is given on very large companies.

Standard & Poor's Industry Survey is published annually and contains various statistics, including some financial ratios, provided by industry and on leading companies within each industry grouping.

Business Week, "**The Top 1,000,**" published annually in March or April, is a special issue with many financial ratios on the 1,000 largest U.S. companies.

FIGURE 6-5: Annual Statement Studies

186 MANUFACTURERS - FARM MACHINERY & EQUIPMENT SIC# 3523

Type of Statement distribution (Current Data Sorted By Assets)

	0-500M	500M-2MM	2-10MM	10-50MM	50-100MM	100-250MM	Type of Statement	Comparative Historical Data ALL 6/30/86-3/31/87	ALL 6/30/87-3/31/88
		1	21	14	3	3	Unqualified	50	47
		1	1	1	1		Qualified	5	4
	3	10	6	2			Reviewed	18	17
	7	10	4	1			Compiled	20	23
	1						Tax Returns		
	3	6	9	3			Other	13	11
		46(4/1-9/30/90)		65(10/1/90-3/31/91)					
	0-500M	500M-2MM	2-10MM	10-50MM	50-100MM	100-250MM		ALL 106	ALL 102
	14	28	41	21	4	3	NUMBER OF STATEMENTS		

ASSETS

%	%	%	%	%	%		%	%
8.5	6.0	4.4	6.4			Cash & Equivalents	7.5	7.8
22.5	17.4	19.0	30.3			Trade Receivables - (net)	20.2	22.0
44.4	48.2	44.4	34.9			Inventory	43.7	41.7
.2	2.1	1.6	1.6			All Other Current	1.8	1.6
75.5	73.7	69.4	73.2			Total Current	73.2	73.1
22.9	21.3	22.9	17.7			Fixed Assets (net)	19.8	19.9
.9	.5	.7	1.0			Intangibles (net)	1.2	1.1
.7	4.5	7.0	8.1			All Other Non-Current	5.8	5.9
100.0	100.0	100.0	100.0			Total	100.0	100.0

LIABILITIES

11.1	14.0	14.5	13.8			Notes Payable-Short Term	18.3	14.6
2.8	4.0	3.3	3.0			Cur. Mat.-L/T/D	4.1	3.0
20.7	14.7	11.5	9.1			Trade Payables	11.4	11.2
1.0	.5	1.0	.4			Income Taxes Payable	1.3	.7
8.2	8.9	8.2	10.6			All Other Current	8.3	8.6
44.0	42.2	38.4	36.9			Total Current	43.4	37.9
17.8	15.4	17.9	14.4			Long Term Debt	13.4	14.9
.0	.1	.9	.8			Deferred Taxes	.5	.5
4.8	3.0	2.1	2.8			All Other Non-Current	2.0	2.0
33.4	39.3	40.7	45.1			Net Worth	40.7	44.7
100.0	100.0	100.0	100.0			Total Liabilities & Net Worth	100.0	100.0

INCOME DATA

100.0	100.0	100.0	100.0			Net Sales	100.0	100.0
29.2	31.1	28.9	26.7			Gross Profit	30.0	29.6
24.7	24.8	22.0	17.9			Operating Expenses	27.5	25.3
4.5	6.3	6.9	8.9			Operating Profit	2.5	4.3
1.6	2.7	2.6	2.0			All Other Expenses (net)	2.2	1.5
2.9	3.6	4.3	6.9			Profit Before Taxes	.3	2.9

RATIOS

2.3	2.8	2.5	3.2			Current	2.7	3.4
1.7	2.0	1.8	2.0				1.8	2.1
1.6	1.1	1.4	1.7				1.4	1.4
.9	1.0	1.1	1.6			Quick	1.1	1.7
.6	.5	.5	1.1				.6	.9
.4	.3	.4	.6				.4	.4
13 27.2	12 30.3	24 15.1	41 8.8			Sales/Receivables	22 16.3	24 14.9
26 13.9	22 16.4	37 10.0	63 5.8				42 8.7	41 9.0
35 10.5	43 8.5	49 7.5	111 3.3				62 5.9	61 6.0
47 7.7	73 5.0	76 4.8	69 5.3			Cost of Sales/Inventory	94 3.9	86 4.3
61 6.0	126 2.9	126 2.9	101 3.6				135 2.7	122 3.0
96 3.8	174 2.1	183 2.0	159 2.3				215 1.7	192 1.9
6 56.5	11 33.2	17 21.7	20 18.5			Cost of Sales/Payables	18 20.0	17 21.7
27 13.3	24 15.3	26 13.9	28 12.9				29 12.5	25 14.6
62 5.9	51 7.1	46 7.9	37 10.0				49 7.5	42 8.7
5.4	4.5	3.7	2.4			Sales/Working Capital	2.9	2.6
9.6	7.6	6.1	4.6				4.6	4.6
6.2	67.4	9.6	7.0				9.0	9.9
7.5	5.0	4.3	9.5			EBIT/Interest	3.8	5.2
(13) 3.8	(26) 3.0	(40) 2.3	(20) 2.4				(102) 1.6	(91) 2.4
1.4	1.5	1.3	1.7				.3	1.2
	5.1	3.6	49.0			Net Profit + Depr., Dep., Amort./Cur. Mat. L/T/D	4.5	7.4
	(16) 1.9	(34) 2.5	(13) 4.4				(66) 1.4	(63) 2.8
	.7	1.0	1.8				.0	1.4
.3	.2	.3	.2			Fixed/Worth	.2	.2
.5	.6	.6	.3				.4	.4
1.5	1.1	.9	.6				.9	.9
1.0	.7	.8	.7			Debt/Worth	.7	.5
1.7	1.8	1.5	1.0				1.6	1.2
3.5	4.0	2.8	3.6				3.4	3.2
55.6	50.7	30.7	34.5			% Profit Before Taxes/Tangible Net Worth	31.2	32.5
(13) 33.1	(27) 21.2	(40) 17.5	21.0				(100) 8.3	(94) 14.8
8.1	8.3	3.6	10.5				-4.9	3.0
22.4	15.3	11.7	15.3			% Profit Before Taxes/Total Assets	10.7	12.7
7.2	9.2	7.7	8.7				2.4	5.8
3.3	1.9	1.4	3.9				-2.7	1.1
43.2	28.4	16.0	19.6			Sales/Net Fixed Assets	16.4	22.2
14.1	10.7	9.4	9.8				8.7	10.1
6.9	6.6	5.0	7.1				5.3	5.8
4.4	2.7	2.4	2.0			Sales/Total Assets	2.1	2.2
3.4	2.2	1.6	1.4				1.6	1.7
1.8	1.6	1.3	1.1				1.1	1.2
1.1	.9	.9	1.0			% Depr., Dep., Amort./Sales	1.1	1.3
(12) 1.6	(26) 1.3	(40) 1.7	(20) 1.8				(96) 2.0	(93) 2.0
3.1	3.1	2.6	2.6				3.6	3.3
	1.3					% Officers', Directors', Owners' Comp/Sales	2.0	2.6
	(13) 5.9						(34) 3.9	(32) 5.0
	11.9						5.7	10.3
12032M	66780M	347880M	809740M	439290M	551867M	Net Sales ($)	1208495M	1069690M
4236M	30715M	189788M	517151M	269982M	534206M	Total Assets ($)	852896M	678890M

©Robert Morris Associates 1991

M = $thousand   MM = $million
See Pages 1 through 15 for Explanation of Ratios and Data

Continued.

FIGURE 6-5: *continued*

MANUFACTURERS - FARM MACHINERY & EQUIPMENT SIC# 3523   187

Comparative Historical Data			Type of Statement	Current Data Sorted By Sales					
61	59	42	Unqualified	5	4	8	9		16
2	3	4	Qualified		2			2	
23	22	21	Reviewed	4	7	4	3	2	1
22	20	22	Compiled	6	10	2	1	2	1
		1	Tax Returns						
17	22	21	Other	2	5	3	4	4	3
6/30/88-3/31/89 ALL	6/30/89-3/31/90 ALL	4/1/90-3/31/91 ALL		46(4/1-9/30/90)			65(10/1/90-3/31/91)		
125	126	111	NUMBER OF STATEMENTS	0-1MM 13	1-3MM 27	3-5MM 15	5-10MM 16	10-25MM 17	25MM & OVER 23
%	%	%	**ASSETS**	%	%	%	%	%	%
6.8	6.7	5.8	Cash & Equivalents	7.4	6.9	4.6	4.0	4.5	6.7
20.4	24.4	21.9	Trade Receivables - (net)	25.0	16.9	13.1	22.3	25.1	29.0
45.1	41.2	42.2	Inventory	43.3	46.0	52.4	35.9	46.0	32.2
2.4	1.9	1.8	All Other Current	.6	1.6	2.0	2.3	.7	2.1
74.7	74.3	71.5	Total Current	76.3	71.5	72.1	64.5	76.3	70.0
18.8	19.9	21.2	Fixed Assets (net)	22.0	23.1	20.1	25.9	17.6	18.4
.9	1.0	.9	Intangibles (net)	1.3	.3	1.0	.8	.4	1.9
5.6	4.8	6.4	All Other Non-Current	.4	5.1	6.8	8.7	5.7	9.7
100.0	100.0	100.0	Total	100.0	100.0	100.0	100.0	100.0	100.0
			LIABILITIES						
15.1	15.3	13.1	Notes Payable-Short Term	13.1	14.0	16.4	9.0	17.9	9.4
4.1	3.5	3.2	Cur. Mat.-L/T/D	3.0	4.2	3.7	2.0	4.0	2.1
11.7	13.4	12.8	Trade Payables	20.9	13.1	12.0	10.1	13.7	9.7
.7	.7	.8	Income Taxes Payable	1.1	.2	1.0	.9	1.3	.6
8.4	8.9	9.2	All Other Current	6.2	8.4	9.7	9.6	8.2	11.9
40.0	41.8	39.1	Total Current	44.2	39.8	42.9	31.5	45.1	33.7
15.9	16.9	16.2	Long Term Debt	22.3	15.9	17.8	17.3	11.6	14.7
.6	.5	.5	Deferred Taxes	.0	.1	.3	.9	1.5	.5
3.3	1.7	2.8	All Other Non-Current	5.2	3.4	2.9	1.9	1.8	1.9
40.2	39.2	41.4	Net Worth	28.2	40.8	36.1	48.4	40.0	49.0
100.0	100.0	100.0	Total Liabilities & Net Worth	100.0	100.0	100.0	100.0	100.0	100.0
			INCOME DATA						
100.0	100.0	100.0	Net Sales	100.0	100.0	100.0	100.0	100.0	100.0
28.6	28.1	29.1	Gross Profit	31.9	31.5	29.3	28.6	26.5	26.8
23.8	21.9	22.4	Operating Expenses	28.9	24.1	23.8	21.9	17.7	19.8
4.9	6.2	6.7	Operating Profit	3.0	7.4	5.5	6.7	8.8	7.0
1.5	2.4	2.2	All Other Expenses (net)	2.0	3.3	2.2	2.0	2.0	1.3
3.4	3.8	4.4	Profit Before Taxes	1.0	4.1	3.3	4.7	6.8	5.7
			RATIOS						
3.4	3.0	2.6	Current	2.3	2.8	2.4	3.8	3.3	2.9
2.0	1.9	1.8		1.7	2.1	1.7	2.0	1.8	2.0
1.4	1.3	1.5		1.5	1.2	1.5	1.5	1.1	1.7
1.3	1.3	1.2	Quick	1.0	1.0	.6	1.5	1.3	1.7
.7	.7	.6		.6	.4	.5	1.0	.4	1.1
.4	.4	.4		.5	.3	.4	.5	.4	.6
22 16.9	24 15.0	22 16.4	Sales/Receivables	20 18.0	12 31.5	14 26.6	34 10.8	22 16.3	36 10.2
39 9.4	43 8.5	36 10.2		33 11.2	24 15.1	24 15.2	38 9.7	42 8.6	63 5.8
57 6.4	70 5.2	63 5.8		63 5.8	38 9.7	39 9.3	51 7.2	61 6.0	94 3.9
81 4.5	74 4.9	69 5.3	Cost of Sales/Inventory	45 8.2	66 5.5	104 3.5	65 5.6	76 4.8	61 6.0
122 3.0	111 3.3	107 3.4		64 5.7	126 2.9	169 2.3	89 4.1	94 3.9	101 3.6
183 2.0	152 2.4	169 2.3		228 1.6	192 1.9	228 1.6	146 2.5	152 2.4	146 2.5
16 23.1	17 21.2	16 22.4	Cost of Sales/Payables	17 21.6	12 30.5	15 24.7	12 30.3	18 20.5	21 17.4
28 13.0	28 13.1	27 13.5		37 10.0	24 15.2	26 13.9	27 13.4	24 15.3	28 12.9
43 8.4	44 8.3	45 8.2		69 5.3	54 6.7	45 8.2	52 7.0	42 8.7	35 10.3
2.7	3.3	3.4	Sales/Working Capital	4.1	4.2	4.2	3.5	3.4	2.7
5.1	6.1	6.1		8.2	7.6	6.3	6.0	9.3	4.8
10.0	11.8	11.1		17.4	14.6	8.2	7.9	21.6	6.9
5.1	5.0	4.8	EBIT/Interest	4.7	5.5	4.9	4.3	4.5	8.4
(108) 2.7	(118) 2.4	(106) 2.5		(12) 2.0	(25) 2.5	2.4	(15) 2.4	2.4	(22) 3.3
1.3	1.4	1.6		-.5	1.4	1.3	1.3	2.0	1.7
9.1	7.5	7.5	Net Profit + Depr., Dep., Amort./Cur. Mat. L/T/D		5.2	4.8	8.8	3.8	20.2
(73) 2.5	(76) 3.1	(73) 2.8			(15) 1.1	(11) 1.9	(14) 3.5	(13) 2.7	(16) 8.0
1.1	1.1	1.2			.5		2.5	1.8	3.7
.2	.2	.2	Fixed/Worth	.2	.2	.2	.3	.2	.2
.4	.4	.4		.5	.7	.5	.4	.4	.4
1.1	1.0	1.0		1.5	1.1	1.0	.9	.7	.8
.7	.9	.8	Debt/Worth	1.6	.7	.9	.6	.7	.5
1.5	1.7	1.5		2.2	1.4	1.9	1.0	1.8	1.0
3.4	3.4	2.8		4.4	4.3	4.3	2.2	3.3	2.1
32.4	33.5	35.4	% Profit Before Taxes/Tangible Net Worth	48.2	52.6	30.3	23.5	37.1	33.9
(115) 16.7	(122) 17.0	(108) 20.4		(12) 27.8	20.6	(13) 16.7	13.2	28.0	16.0
4.6	7.0	6.9		-11.4	5.5	7.4	4.9	21.2	6.6
12.6	12.8	14.4	% Profit Before Taxes/Total Assets	19.1	15.4	14.1	13.8	11.7	17.1
6.5	6.1	7.2		7.1	6.5	3.7	6.2	9.5	8.7
1.0	2.3	2.0		-6.2	1.8	1.5	1.7	6.9	2.0
23.8	20.5	20.0	Sales/Net Fixed Assets	44.1	19.1	27.4	14.7	21.6	16.1
11.6	10.6	10.0		12.6	9.7	10.4	7.2	12.0	9.6
7.0	6.6	6.5		6.7	5.5	5.4	5.0	8.8	8.4
2.4	2.4	2.6	Sales/Total Assets	4.6	3.0	2.5	2.2	2.9	2.1
1.8	1.8	1.8		2.2	2.2	1.8	1.6	2.2	1.7
1.3	1.4	1.3		1.4	1.4	1.4	1.3	1.3	1.2
1.1	.9	1.0	% Depr., Dep., Amort./Sales	1.5	1.1	.6	1.2	.8	1.2
(107) 1.7	(111) 1.5	(104) 1.6		(12) 1.6	(24) 1.6	(14) 1.1	2.3	1.2	(21) 1.8
2.8	2.7	2.6		3.1	3.3	2.3	3.0	2.2	2.2
1.7	2.2	1.6	% Officers', Directors', Owners' Comp/Sales			1.7			
(31) 2.8	(35) 4.7	(29) 2.6				(11) 3.8			
6.5	9.3	10.2				13.0			
2153072M	2490851M	2227589M	Net Sales ($)	8671M	57229M	60654M	118941M	247898M	1734196M
1288250M	1560107M	1546077M	Total Assets ($)	4176M	33834M	39609M	77192M	149742M	1241524M

©Robert Morris Associates 1991   M = $thousand   MM = $million
See Pages 1 through 15 for Explanation of Ratios and Data

Interpretation of Statement Studies Figures: RMA cautions that the Studies be regarded only as a general guideline and not as an absolute industry norm. This is due to limited samples within categories, the categorization of companies by their primary Standard Industrial Classification (SIC) number only, and different methods of operations by companies within the same industry. For these reasons, RMA recommends that the figures be used only as general guidelines in addition to other methods of financial analysis.

FIGURE 6-6: Comparative Ratio Reports (2500 Manufacturing: Furniture & Fixtures)

Item Description For Accounting Period 7/87 Through 6/88	A Total	B Zero Assets	SIZE OF ASSETS IN THOUSANDS OF DOLLARS (000 OMITTED)										
			C Under 100	D 100 to 250	E 251 to 500	F 501 to 1,000	G 1,001 to 5,000	H 5,001 to 10,000	I 10,001 to 25,000	J 25,001 to 50,000	K 50,001 to 100,000	L 100,001 to 250,000	M 250,001 and over
1. Number of Enterprises	4649	62	1206	1162	529	566	826	107	103	45	20	-	-
2. Total receipts (in millions of dollars)	28251.5	314.6	92.6	1156.2	741.6	1224.6	4279.3	1842.1	2988.0	2729.7	2826.8	-	-
Selected Operating Factors in Percent of Net Sales													
3. Cost of operations	69.1	68.8	15.7	75.8	73.4	68.7	68.3	72.0	69.7	73.1	71.1	-	-
4. Compensation of officers	2.0	2.2	24.4	6.0	3.7	4.7	3.5	2.1	1.9	1.2	0.7	-	-
5. Repairs	0.4	0.3	0.7	0.3	0.2	0.4	0.4	0.1	0.4	0.1	0.5	-	-
6. Bad debts	0.3	0.1	-	0.4	0.5	0.3	0.3	0.1	0.3	0.3	0.3	-	-
7. Rent on business property	1.0	1.3	8.6	1.2	2.0	2.4	0.8	0.5	0.6	0.6	0.7	-	-
8. Taxes (excl Federal tax)	2.5	3.2	4.5	3.2	2.4	2.4	2.6	2.2	2.5	2.2	2.4	-	-
9. Interest	1.1	1.3	3.7	0.4	0.8	1.2	0.9	1.4	1.2	1.2	1.4	-	-
10. Deprec/Deplet/Amortiz†	2.4	1.5	5.7	1.4	1.4	1.8	1.8	1.8	2.5	2.2	2.6	-	-
11. Advertising	1.3	1.3	-	0.3	0.6	0.6	1.4	1.2	1.1	1.3	2.4	-	-
12. Pensions & other benef plans	1.6	1.7	1.3	0.4	0.3	0.4	1.4	1.3	1.6	1.6	1.1	-	-
13. Other expenses	13.5	11.3	27.0	7.3	12.8	12.7	15.2	13.9	12.6	12.6	11.6	-	-
14. Net profit before tax	4.8	7.0	8.4	3.3	1.9	4.4	3.4	3.4	5.6	3.6	5.2	-	-
Selected Financial Ratios (number of times ratio is to one)													
15. Current ratio	2.3	-	1.5	2.4	2.1	2.0	2.0	2.0	2.6	2.4	2.5	-	-
16. Quick ratio	1.2	-	1.3	1.9	0.9	0.9	1.0	1.0	1.4	1.2	1.3	-	-
17. Net sls to net wkg capital	5.8	-	23.6	12.2	8.8	8.3	6.5	7.1	4.5	4.6	5.1	-	-
18. Coverage ratio	7.3	-	3.3	-	3.7	5.0	5.6	4.5	6.9	5.2	6.4	-	-
19. Asset turnover	1.9	-	-	-	-	-	2.4	2.3	1.7	1.8	1.8	-	-
20. Total liab to net worth	0.8	-	1.1	1.1	0.9	1.4	1.1	1.5	0.7	1.1	1.0	-	-
Selected Financial Factors in Percentages													
21. Debt ratio	45.5	-	51.9	52.0	48.2	58.4	51.8	59.4	41.5	51.6	50.2	-	-
22. Return on assets	15.6	-	-	-	11.6	17.8	12.2	14.0	14.4	11.4	15.9	-	-
23. Return on equity	17.0	-	42.4	-	14.3	32.0	16.0	16.8	14.7	14.7	18.8	-	-
24. Return on net worth	28.7	-	66.3	74.5	22.4	42.7	25.3	34.5	24.6	23.6	32.0	-	-

†Depreciation largest factor

From the book, *Almanac of Business and Industrial Financial Ratios*, 1991 edition, by Leo Troy Ph.D., ©1991. Used by permission of the publisher, Prentice Hall/a division of Simon & Schuster, Englewood Cliffs, NJ.

Common Stocks
and Preferred Stocks

OVERVIEW

Securities cover a broad range of investment instruments, including common stocks, preferred stocks, bonds, and options. Two broad categories of securities are available to investors: equity securities (such as common stocks), which represent ownership in a company, and debt securities (such as bonds), which represent a loan from the investor to a company or government. Each type of security has distinct characteristics, as well as advantages and disadvantages that vary depending on investor objectives. This chapter discusses: characteristics of various types of common and preferred stock, how to calculate the yield on stock and forecast stock price, and how to read stock quotations.

UNDERSTANDING COMMON STOCK

Common stock is an equity investment that represents ownership in a corporation. It corresponds to the capital account for a sole proprietorship or capital contributed by each partner for a partnership. Corporate stockholders have certain rights and privileges. First, they exercise *control of the firm* by electing directors who in turn select officers to manage the business. They also enjoy *preemptive rights*, that is, the right to purchase new stock. A **preemptive right** entitles a common stockholder to maintain his or her proportional ownership by offering the stockholder an opportunity to purchase, on a pro rata basis, any new stock being offered or any securities convertible into common stock.

Types of Common Stock

Stocks are classified according to their special characteristics, as described below.

Blue Chip Stocks

Blue chips are high-quality common stocks that have a long and proven record of earnings and dividend payments. Often viewed as long-term investment instruments, these stocks carry low risk and provide modest but dependable return. Examples include AT&T, Exxon, and Du Pont.

Growth Stocks

Growth stocks are issues that have a long record of higher-than-average earnings and dividends than the economy as a whole and the industry of which they are a part. Examples include high-tech stocks such as Robotics.

Income Stocks

Income issues are characterized by a higher dividends per share ratio and dividend payout ratio. These stocks are ideal for investors who desire high current income (rather than future capital gains) with little risk. Examples are utility stocks such as Southern California Gas and Consolidated Edison.

Cyclical Stocks

Cyclical stocks earnings and prices move with the business cycle. Stocks of the construction, building materials, airlines, and steel industries fall into this category.

Defensive Stocks

These stocks tend to be less affected than the average issue by downswings in the business cycles. In other words, they are recession-resistant. Utilities, soft drink, and consumer product stocks are examples.

Speculative Stocks

These stocks generally lack a track record of high earnings and dividends. Despite uncertain earnings, they have the chance to hit it big in the market. Many of the new issues of oil and gas stocks and cancer-related pharmaceutical stocks, although ''gambles'', are ideal for investors who are risk oriented, hoping for a big return.

Why Buy Common Stock?

Common stock is attractive as an investment alternative because it:

   • Provides an ownership feature, in contrast to fixed-income securities such as bonds.
   • Provides income potential, not only in terms of current income in the form of dividends but also future capital gains (or losses).
   • Offers shareholders the opportunity to participate in the firm's earnings and lay claim to all the residual profits of the entity.

• Can be a good inflation hedge, if the total return from investment in common stock exceeds the rate of inflation.

• Offers a variety of stocks so that an investor can choose from a broad spectrum of risk-return combinations.

Common Stock Yield

What is the yield on your stock investment? It is the return for a common stock at its initial cost or present market value. So,

$$\text{Yield} = \frac{\text{Dividend per share}}{\text{Market price per share}}$$

EXAMPLE 1

Assume you paid $80 for a stock currently worth $100. The dividend per share is $4. Thus, yield on your investment is calculated as follows:

$$\frac{\$4}{\$80} = .05 = 5\% \text{ or } \frac{\$4}{\$100} = .04 = 4\%$$

You can use the yield as an indication of how reasonably priced the stock is, particularly when dividends are stable (as with utilities, for example). Knowing stock yield is also helpful for an income-oriented investor who wishes to compare equity dividend returns with those of fixed-income securities. Yield for a single period can be calculated more accurately using a formula derived from the Gordon model introduced in Chapter 6. Then:

$$r = \frac{D_1}{P_0} + \frac{(P_1 - P_0)}{P_0}$$

where r = expected return for a single period, D_1 = dividend at the end of the period, P_1 = price per share at the end of the period, and P_0 = price per share at the beginning of the period. Stated in words,

$$r = \frac{\text{Dividends}}{\text{Beginning price}} + \frac{\text{Capital gain}}{\text{Beginning price}} = \text{Dividend yield} + \text{Capital gain yield}$$

If a company's dividends are expected to grow at a constant rate, then:

$$P_0 = \frac{D_1}{(r - g)}$$

Solving for r gives:

$$r = \frac{D_1}{P_o} + g, \text{ where } g = \frac{(P_1 - P_o)}{P_o} \text{ for a single period.}$$

EXAMPLE 2

Assume a stock sells for $50. The company is expected to pay a $3 cash dividend at the end of the year, at which time the stock's market price is expected to be $55 a share. Thus, the expected return would be:

$$r = \frac{D_1}{P_o} + \frac{(P_1 - P_o)}{P_o} = \frac{\$3}{\$50} + \frac{(\$55 - \$50)}{\$50} = \frac{(\$3 + \$5)}{\$50} = 6\% + 10\% = 16\%$$

Or,

$$\text{Dividend yield} = \frac{\$3}{\$50} = 6\%$$

$$\text{Capital gain yield} = \frac{\$5}{\$50} = 10\%$$

$$\text{Total yield} = \text{Dividend yield} + \text{Capital gain yield} = 6\% + 10\% = 16\%$$

A PRAGMATIC APPROACH TO FORECASTING STOCK PRICE

Many common stock analysts use the simple formula:

Forecasted price at end of year =

Estimated EPS of the year t × Estimated P/E ratio

Of course, for this method to be effective in forecasting the future value of a stock, earnings need to be correctly projected and the appropriate P/E multiple applied.

Forecasting EPS is not an easy task. Some analysts use a simple forecasting method: sales forecast combined with an after-tax profit margin, as follows:

Estimated after-tax earnings in year t =

Estimated sales year t × After-tax profit margin expected year t

$$\text{Estimated EPS year t} = \frac{\text{Estimated after-tax earnings year t}}{\text{Number of common shares oustanding year t}}$$

EXAMPLE 3 _____

Assume a company reported sales of $100 million, and its estimated sales will grow at an annual rate of 6%, whereas the profit margin is about 8%. The company had 2 million shares outstanding. Its P/E ratio was 15 times earnings and is expected to continue for the next year. Projected sales next year will be $106 million ($100 million × 1.06).

Estimated after-tax earnings next year is:

$$\$106 \text{ million} \times 8\% = \$8.48 \text{ million}$$

$$\text{Estimated EPS next year} = \frac{\$8.48 \text{ million}}{2 \text{ million}} = \$4.24$$

Then the company's stock should be trading at a price of $63.60 by the end of next year:

$$\text{Estimated share price next year} = \$4.24 \times 15 = \$63.60$$

_____

NOTE: *If you are looking for an advisory service's estimate of a company's EPS for the next year, you can obtain it from publications such as* Value Line Investment Survey.

Determining Price/Earnings Ratio

Determining the P/E multiple is a very complex process. Empirical evidence seems to suggest that the following factors contribute to this determination:

- Historical growth rate in earnings
- Forecasted earnings
- Average dividend payout ratio
- Beta—the company's systematic (uncontrollable) risk
- Earnings instability
- Financial leverage
- Other factors such as competitive position, management ability, and economic conditions

Reading Beta Measures

Beta measures a security's volatility relative to an average security. Put another way, beta is a measure of a security's return over time to that of the overall market. For example, if ABC's beta is 2.0, it means that if the stock market goes up 10 percent, ABC's common stock goes up 20 percent; if the market goes down 10 percent, ABC goes down 20 percent. *NOTE: Generally, the higher a security's beta, the greater the return expected (or demanded) by the investor and, therefore, the more risky the investment.*

TABLE 7-1: What Beta Means

Beta	What It Means
0.0	The security's return is independent of the market. An example is a risk-free security such as a T-bill.
0.5	The security is only half as responsive as the market.
1.0	The security has the same responsiveness or risk as the market (i.e., average risk). This is the beta value of the market portfolio such as Standard & Poor's 500 or Dow Jones 30 Industrials.
2.0	The security is twice as responsive, or twice as risky, as the market.

Table 7-1 above is a guide for reading betas. *NOTE: Beta of a particular stock is useful in predicting how much the security will go up or down, provided investors know which way the market will go. Beta helps to figure out risk and expected return.*

Betas for stocks are available in many investment newsletters and directories. Here are a few betas for selected companies as reported in *Value Line Investment Survey* on March 8, 1991: Apple Computer 1.25; Bristol-Myers, 1.00; IBM, 0.95; Nieman-Marcus, 1.65; Mead Corporation, 1.45; Mobil Corporation 0.85.

READING STOCK QUOTATIONS

Financial dailies such as *Investor's Business Daily* and the *Wall Street Journal* are key sources of securities price quotations.

Investor's Business Daily: NYSE and AMEX Stocks

Table 7-2 is a typical listing of a common stock in *Investor's Business Daily* followed by explanations for key columns.

Investor's Business Daily listings are very similar to *Wall Street Journal* listings except that *Investor's Business Daily* are in what is called "smarter numbers," which analysts believe will help investors make better investment decisions. Proponents believe you must look well beyond P/E ratios, dividend yields, and a company's last earnings report to the smarter numbers—labeled here as columns (1) EPS Rnk, (2) Rel Str, and (3) 52-Week High Low.

Wall Street Journal: NYSE and AMEX Stocks

Shown in Figure 7-1 are typical common stock listings in the *Wall Street Journal*. Each numbered column is explained in the annotations. Additional details are listed in the "Explanatory Note" section following the stock quotations in Figure 7-1.

TABLE 7-2: *Investor's Business Daily* NYSE and AMEX Stock Listings

EPS Rnk	Rel. Str	52-Week High-Low	Stock Name	Closing Price	Chng	Vol. % Change	Vol. 100s	Grp Str.	Day's High	Price Low
80	52	47 5/8 34 7/8	Amer Brands	42 3/8	3/8	-42	1555	B	42 1/2	42 1/4
(1)	(2)					(3)				

(1) **EPS Rnk (earnings per share ranking)**, according to *Investor's Business Daily*, is based on belief that a percentage increase in a company's EPS is a better barometer of stock price performance than P/E ratios or dividend yields. This column tracks a company's per share earnings growth over the last five years and ranks that earnings performance against all other publicly traded issues. A ranking of 80, for example, means that the company's earnings record outperformed 80 percent of the companies measured.

(2) **Rel Str (relative price strength)**, ranked on a scale of 0 to 99, measures each stock's price movement over the past year and compares its performance with 6,000 other stocks on the NYSE, AMEX, and OTC/NASDAQ markets. A ranking of 52, for example, means that the stock performed in the top 48 percent of all publicly traded issues.

(3) **Vol. % Change. (changes in trading volume)** shows how that day's volume compares with the stock's average trading volume during the past 50 days—up or down. For example, listing of -42 means the stock traded 42 percent below its normal trading volume for the day.

Source: *Investor's Business Daily, America's Business Daily*, (October 14, 1991), ©Investor's Business Daily Inc. 1991.

FIGURE 7-1: *Wall Street Journal* Sample Stock Quotations and Explanatory Notes

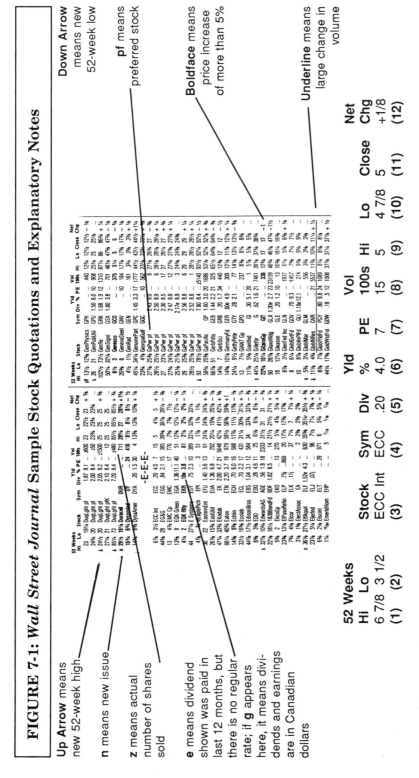

Up Arrow means new 52-week high

n means new issue

z means actual number of shares sold

e means dividend shown was paid in last 12 months, but there is no regular rate; if **g** appears here, it means dividends and earnings are in Canadian dollars

Down Arrow means new 52-week low

pf means preferred stock

Boldface means price increase of more than 5%

Underline means large change in volume

| 52 Weeks | | Stock | Sym | Div | Yld % | PE | Vol 100s | Hi | Lo | Close | Net Chg |
Hi	Lo										
6 7/8	3 1/2	ECC Int	ECC	.20	4.0	7	15	5	4 7/8	5	+1/8
(1)	(2)	(3)	(4)	(5)	(6)	(7)	(8)	(9)	(10)	(11)	(12)

(1)   **52 Weeks Hi:** The highest price per share at which the stock sold during the latest 52-week period, excluding the latest day's trading; prices are quoted in dollarsand one-eighths of dollars, so a price of 6 7/8 = $6.875 a share. Thus, ECC Int's highest price was $6.875.

(2)   **52 Weeks Lo:** The lowest price per share at which the stock sold during the latest 52-week period. ECC Int's lowest price was $3.50.

NOTE: Highs and lows for split stocks are adjusted to reflect the split. High and lows for new issues begin at the date of issue. Where a split or stock dividend amounting to 25 percent or more has been paid, the high-low range and dividends are shown for the new stock only.

(3)   Stock: The company name, which may be abbreviated. It uses no spaces. If you see a space, it is to set aside a footnote. *NOTE: If no qualifier follows the company name, the issue is a common stock. A name followed by "pf" indicates the listing is for preferred stock. Other qualifiers will be explained later in the chapter.*

(4)   Sym: Exchange ticker symbol. *NOTE: This symbol is used to identify the stock when looking it up on a variety of computer data bases. ECC Int is ECC.*

(5)   Div: The expected regular dividend in the current year based on what the company paid in the last quarter or six months. Some companies also pay extra dividends in good earning years, but these are not shown in a quotation. ECC's regular dividend was estimated at $0.20 a share. *NOTE: Special or extra dividends or payments are identified in qualifier footnotes.*

(6)   Yld %: The **current yield**, which is found by dividing the current year regular dividend by the closing price of the stock. ECC's current yield is 4.0 percent, which is calculated by dividing the expected dividend ($0.20) by the closing share price [5, col. **(11)**] and rounding the answer to the nearest tenth of a percent. *NOTE: The yield represents the return an investor can expect on each share of stock owned. This yield measure needs to be compared with those of other stocks or with the interest paid on debt securities. This yield measure is based on cash dividends only; although stock dividends are paid by some companies, these are not included unless a company pays only stock dividends or has a history of paying any stock dividend regularly.*

(7)   P/E: The price/earnings (P/E) ratio, often called **P/E multiple** or **earnings multiple**, is computed by dividing the stock's selling price by the company's per share earnings for the most recent four quarters. *NOTE: There is no entry if earnings are negative. The P/E ratio is used as a barometer of relative stock performance. High P/E ratios indicate a stock price that represents a high multiple of a company's earnings and suggest that investors are more optimistic about the stock's prospects. Low P/E figures, on the other hand, often represent lower investor favor. Unfortunately, there is no such thing as "ideal" or "best" ratio. Reasons for high or low P/E ratios include the company's riskiness, earnings stability, growth outlook, or the industry of which the company is part.*

(8)   Vol 100s: For common stocks, sales are reported in lots of 100 shares. So 1,500 shares (15 x 100) were traded on that day. *NOTE: If a "z" precedes the volume number, the figure that follows represents the actual number of shares traded. For example, z35 means 35—not 3,500—shares were traded.*

(9)   Hi: The highest price paid for the stock that day. ECC's was 5 ($5.00).

(10)   Lo: The lowest price paid for the stock that day. ECC's was 4 7/8 ($4.875).

(11)   Close: The last (or closing) price paid that day. ECC's was 5 ($5.00).

(12)   Net Chg: The difference between the closing price that day and the closing price of the previous trading day. The closing price for ECC was 1/8 ($0.125) higher than its closing price on the preceding business day.

Over-the-Counter Stock Quotations

Over-the-counter (OTC) stocks are *not* listed on either national exchange. These stocks are traded by telephone, one broker to another, which is different from the exchanges, where specialists execute transactions on an exchange floor.

At one time, newspaper quotations for OTC stocks were, of necessity, less comprehensive than quotations for stocks on the national exchanges. Although this is still true in some listings, those quotations for what is called the National Market now cover OTC issues as thoroughly as exchange issues. Individual papers, of course, may omit certain components like yield, P/E ratio, or the 52-week high and low, but many major papers have adopted this new comprehensive format. The quotations usually appear under some version of the following headings: "NASDAQ National Market" or "National Market Issues."

National Market quotations can be interpreted the same as quotations for exchange issues; however, many papers carry one or more lists that are not in the National Market format. Traditionally, OTC quotations have differed from exchange quotations in two important ways: OTC quotations provide less information, and an OTC daily quotation lists two prices, called *Bid* and *Asked*. Both prices are current, but they are not necessarily the amounts of actual transactions.

Bid price is the price a dealer is willing to *pay* for a stock. Bid prices quoted in the newspaper are always the highest available.

Asked price is the price at which a dealer is willing to *sell* a stock. Asked prices quoted in the newspaper are always the lowest available.

OTC stock quotations that are in addition to the National Market list appear in newspapers under many headings, including "Over-the-Counter Quotations," "Over-the-Counter Market," "NASDAQ Bid and Asked Quotations," "NASDAQ Over-the-Counter," or "OTC." Many papers also carry an additional OTC list entitled "Additional OTC Quotes" or "NASDAQ Supplementary OTC."

The agency that initially reports OTC stock price data from the market makers is **NASDAQ (National Association of Securities Dealers Automated Quotations service)**. NASDAQ is wholly owned by the National Association of Securities Dealers (NASD), the regulatory agency for the over-the-counter market.

Quotations for over-the-counter stocks are reported slightly differently from those in the national exchange. For example, see the quotation explanations for Apple in Table 7-3.

The Fifth Letter of OTC Ticker Symbols

OTC stocks are easily distinguished from exchange issues by their ticker symbols, which contain four or five letters (exchange issues contain one to three). The fifth letter, if present, is a qualifier appended by NASDAQ. Table 7-4 briefly defines these letters.

TABLE 7-3: OTC Stock Listing

Stock & Div	Sales 100s	Bid	Asked	Net Chg.
AppleC .60	2999	47 5/8	47 3/4	+1/8
(1)	(2)	(3)	(4)	(5)

(1) Stock & Div: The name of the company and its annual dividend, if any, based on the latest quarterly payment. The regular dividend for Apple Computers is $0.60 per share.

(2) Sales 100s: Apple had 299,900 shares (2999 x 100) traded. The "z" notation used in the NYSE and AMEX lists applies also to the OTC quotation table. Thus, *z15* means just 15 shares changed hands, not 1,500.

(3) and **(4) Bid** and **Asked:** The Bid and Asked prices are the highest prices the stock can be sold for and the lowest price the stock can be purchased for, respectively, at the close of that day's trading. *NOTE: The bid price of 47 5/8 means you would have received $47.625 if you wanted to sell a share, and the 47 3/4 asked price means you would have paid $ 47.75 to buy a share. The spread between the bid and the asked prices is part of the broker's commission (or profit) for making a market in the stock.*

(5) Net Chg.: is the change in the bid price from the previous day's trading. The net change of +1/8 indicates an increase of 12.5 cents a share from the bid price on the reported day versus the bid price of the previous trading day.

Qualifiers: Stocks

A number of alphabetic qualifiers appear throughout stock quotations. The particular qualifiers used and their definitions depend on which news service supplies the quotations.

Most newspapers in this country receive their financial quotations from the Associated Press (AP); other quotations come from United Press International (UPI). *Some* of the qualifiers used by UPI are the same as those used by AP. Because AP supplies the majority of papers, their definitions are listed first. If UPI definitions are the same, or if there is no UPI definition, no further comment is made. If the UPI definition is different, or it is the sole definition, this information is marked in brackets, e.g., [UPI . . .].

Newspapers usually provide a table of symbols. Most newspapers use the same qualifiers for OTC quotations as for the national exchange. However, verify this in your own newspapers before assuming that the following definitions (Table 7-5) are also applicable to the OTC quotations.

NOTE: The Wall Street Journal uses UPI quotations for OTC stocks and AP Quotations for the NYSE and AMEX listings.

TABLE 7-4: NASDAQ Qualifiers

A	Class A, common or preferred stock
B	Class B, common or preferred stock
C	The security has been temporarily exempted from listing qualifications by NASDAQ
D	New issue, within past 52 weeks
E	NASD has found the company to be delinquent in filing required SEC documents
F	Foreign security
G	The company's first convertible bond
H	The company's second convertible bond
I	The company's third convertible bond
J	Voting issue
K	Nonvoting issue
L	Miscellaneous (e.g., second class units, third class warrants, or sixth class of preferred stock)
M	Fourth preferred stock issued by this company
N	Third preferred stock issued by this company
O	Second preferred stock issued by this company
P	First preferred stock issued by this company
Q	In bankruptcy
R	Rights
S	Shares of beneficial interest
T	Issue, usually units, that contains warrants or rights
U	Units
V	When issued and when distributed
W	Warrants
Y	American Depository Receipts (ADRs) of foreign security
Z	Miscellaneous (e.g., second class of warrants, fifth class of preferred stock, and unit or certificate representing a limited partnership interest)

Foreign Stock Quotations

The *Wall Street Journal* and *Investor's Business Daily* provides two listings associated with foreign securities: (1) foreign securities in U.S. dollars (Figure 7-2), which shows two closing prices for each foreign stock and (2) foreign exchange rates (Figure 7-3), which gives currencies of the respective countries and lists a current closing price and a closing price for the previous trading day.

Capsule Earnings Report

Figure 7-4 shows earnings reports on two corporations. The second one, for Cucos Inc., provides only the most basic information. Even so, data are given for two years so that current performance can be compared with last year's. *Investor's Business Daily* seperates earnings reports into those that are up and those that are down letting you know who's producing results and who isn't. *NOTE: The amount a company earns can influence the price of its stock, and many investors attempt to forecast the*

TABLE 7-5: Qualifiers and Definitions—National Exchange

a   Amount in "dividend" column includes one or more amounts in addition to the usual dividend.

b   Amount in "dividend" column is the annual cash dividend plus a stock divided.

c   Amount in "dividend" column completely liquidates the stock (as in the final dividend from income shares of a dual-purpose fund or the final payment from a bankrupt company).

cld   Called. A company is calling in (and paying off or perhaps substituting new stock for) a particular issue of preferred stock.

d   Price indicated (usually in the "low" column) is a new 52-week low; for example, "high-low-close (or last)." Sometimes applies to the closing price only.

e   Amount in the "dividend" column was declared or paid within the preceding 12 months, but there is no regular rate.

g   Following the stock name, "g" means dividends and earnings are in Canadian currency. Trading is in U.S. dollars. No yield or P/E ratio is shown unless stated in U.S. dollars. Dividends for U.S. citizens may be subject to Canadian withholding.

h   A temporary exception to NASD qualifications has been made for this security.

i   The dividend indicated was declared or paid after an earlier stock dividend or split.

j   The dividend amount indicated has been paid so far this year, but the current dividend has been omitted or deferred, or no action was taken on dividends at the last board meeting.

k   The dividend indicated has been declared or paid so far this year on a cumulative issue of preferred stock with dividends in arrears.

n   This is a new stock issued within the past 52 weeks. The listed 52-week high and low are as of the inception of trading. Because of its effect on the 52-week high and low price, the "n" is retained in the quotation for 52 weeks.

nd   Next Day delivery of stock certificates. Settlement (payment) is also required on that day.

pf   Preferred stock.

pp   Holder still owes one (in some quotations, more than one) installment on the purchase price.

r   The amount indicated was declared or paid in dividends during the preceding 12 months, plus a stock dividend.

rt   The quotation is for *rights*, not stock. Rights are like warrants, except they are shorter term. Some stocks, particularly new issues, first appear in units that can include rights. After rights are exercised or expire, the stock will trade without them. Rights can be traded separately from stocks.

s   Following the stock name, "s" means that either a stock split or a stock dividend within the past 52 weeks has increased the number of shares outstanding by 25% or more. *NOTE: A **split** is a division of shares into a larger number of shares. For instance, a two-for-one split of a stock selling at $10 per share means that the shareholders, by virtue of the split, now own twice as many shares at $5 per share. However, a split is usually interpreted as a sign of strength and often stimulates market interest, which results in higher relative prices for the new stock. After a stock split, the 52-week high and low are changed to correspond to the new price. For example, in a two-for-one split, the 52-week high and low are both halved in order to be in line with the new price of the stock. A **reverse split** results in fewer shares than before. Because of its effect on the 52-week high and low, the "s" is retained in the quotation for 52 weeks.*

Continued.

TABLE 7-5: *continued*

---

t	The amount paid in stock dividends during the preceding 12 months. Estimated cash value is of stock on ex-dividend or ex-distribution date (see "x-dis" below).
u	The amount indicated (usually in the "high" column) is a new 52-week high. Sometimes this applies to the closing price only.
v	Trading of this issue has been halted on the primary market on which it is listed.
vj or **vi**	(The correct symbol is *vj.*) Preceding the company name, it means that the company is in bankruptcy or receivership or that it is being reorganized under the 1978 Bankruptcy Act and/or the SEC is in control of such companies. *NOTE: Bankruptcy does not necessarily mean a company ceases to exist or that the stockholders lose their entire investment. After emerging from bankruptcy some companies have appreciated considerably. However, if the company is liquidated, common stockholders will be paid in proportion to the number of shares they hold but only after major creditors, bondholders, and preferred stockholders have been paid.*
	The term "vj" comprises two letters (usually adjacent to each other) as a guarantee against a typographical error mistakenly indicating that a company is bankrupt. This could happen if the tail of the "j" does not print, causing it to look like an *i.*
wd	When distributed. Legally the stock has been issued, but the certificates are not yet available (for example, not yet been printed). If the security trades at this time, the purchaser will not receive a certificate of ownership until certificates are distributed.
wi	Short for "when, as, and if issued." The stock is trading before it has cleared all legal requirements for issuance. Should the stock not be issued, all trades will be canceled.
wt	The quotation is for warrants, not stock.
ww	With warrants. Sometimes new issues of stock appear in units that include a number of warrants. These may be detached and traded separately or remain with the stock certificates as they are specified here. You must determine from your broker or a stock guide how long the warrants remain valid.
x	Ex-dividend or ex-rights. The security trades the day after dividends and rights were awarded. Often appears in the "sales" or "volume" column. Ex-dividend, "without dividend," means the immediately preceding dividend was paid to the previous owner on the previous day, and the purchaser of stock from this issue will not receive a dividend until the next payment is declared.
x-dis	Ex-distribution. Indicates the day after the distribution of stock dividends was made. Ex-distribution, "without distribution," means the immediately preceding stock dividend was declared to the previous owner on the previous day, and the purchaser of this stock will not receive it.
xr	Ex-rights. Indicates that the stock is now trading without the rights formerly attached to it.
xw	Ex-warrant. Indicates that the stock is now trading without the warrant formerly attached to it (see "ww").
y	Ex-dividend (see "x") and sales in full—i.e., the actual number of shares traded is shown.
z	Sales in full. The actual number of shares is quoted, not the number of round lots. It is done to accommodate those stocks that are normally traded in lots other than 100 shares (i.e., 10-, 25-, or 50-share lots).

FIGURE 7-2: Foreign Securities Quotations

TOKYO (Japanese Yen)

	Cur.	Prev.
Ajinomto	1520	1500
Alps	1270	1290
Amada	941	955
Anitsu	1270	1270
Asahi Chem	747	728
Asahi Glas	1180	1180
Bank of Tokyo	1540	1500
Banyu	1390	1420
Brigestone	1140	1120
Brother	551	546
Canon Cam	1370	1380
C. Itoh	623	640
Calpis	1230	1210
Casio	1320	1320
Dai Nippon	1420	1420
Daiei	1160	1220
Dai–Ichi Kan	2540	2490
Daiwa House	2010	1960
Daiwa Sec	1220	1190
Descente	700	695
Eisai	1760	1770
Fanuc	4090	4080
Fuji Bank	2680	2650
Fuji Elec	755	761
Fuji Photo	2860	2910
Fujisawa	1520	1530
Fujitsu	838	843
Green Cross	1180	1160
Hattori	1900	1880
Nissan	660	655
Nittsuko	796	804
Nomura Sec	1680	1680
NTN Toyo	590	589
NTT	770000	770000
Oki Elec	579	590
Okuma	1100	1060
Olympus	1430	1440
Omron Corp	1670	1690
Pioneer	3290	3190
Renown	648	648
Ricoh	600	605
Sankyo	2620	2590
Sanwa Bank	2350	2360
Sanyo	512	513
Seikisui	1430	1430
Sharp	1320	1340
Shionogi	1010	1010
Shiseido	1720	1720
Skylark	2480	2500
Sony	4500	4580
Stanley	766	790
Sumitomo Bnk	2510	2350
Sumitomo Chm	466	462
Sumitomo Cp	1030	1040
Sumitomo Elc	1220	1210
Sumitomo Tst	1530	1530
Taisei Cp	860	851
Takeda	1460	1440
Tanabe Sei	1230	1270
TDK	4610	4700
Teijin	500	505

	Cur.	Prev.
CN Gold	0.33	0.31
Coal All	10.10	10.20
Coles Myer	12.06	12.00
Comalco	3.56	3.57
CRA	12.16	12.34
Crusader Oil	1.54	1.50
CSR	4.66	4.72
ERA	1.20	1.25
FAI	0.65	0.68
Foster's	1.79	1.78
GM Kalg	0.77	0.70
Goodman	1.66	1.69
Hardie J	3.02	3.08
Jennings	1.05	1.00
L Lease	17.80	17.72
Leighton	1.33	1.35
Magellan	2.25	2.28
Mayne N	8.18	8.20
MIM	2.19	2.21
Nat Aust	7.98	8.00
News Corp	15.40	15.08
North BH	2.36	2.35
Oakbridge	1.15	1.18
Pan Cont	0.83	0.80
Pac Dunlop	5.65	5.73
Pioneer C	3.20	3.26
Placr Pac	2.83	2.68
RGC	5.00	4.90
South Pac	0.48	0.48
Santos	3.12	3.06
TNT	1.41	1.45
Westpac	4.55	4.88

	Cur.	Prev.
Eng China	455.50	474.00
Eurotunnel	390.00	390.00
Fisons	399.00	400.00
Forte	258.00	261.00
Freegold	$9.09	$8.16
GEC	182.00	186.00
Gen Accid	437.00	429.00
Glaxo	780.00	770.00
GKN	298.00	300.00
Gold Fields	$24.75	$23.25
Granada	187.00	192.00
Grand Met	836.00	836.00
Groot	$1.50	$1.35
Guardian	135.00	136.00
Guiness	509.00	504.00
Gus A	1298	1333
Hanson	201.00	201.50
Harmony	$6.75	$6.35
Harties	$5.25	$4.80
Hawker	675.00	719.00
Hillsdown	176.00	184.00
Hong Kong	68.00	67.00
H.K. Bank	251.00	250.00
Hutchison	103.00	104.00
ICI	1192.00	1201.00
Inchcape	387.00	385.00
Jardine	272.00	275.00
Johnson	322.50	325.00
Kingfisher	505.00	526.00
Kinross	$14.62	$14.12
Kleinwort	299.00	299.00
Kloof Gld	$11.00	$10.50
Stilfontn	$1.20	$1.05
Storehouse	94.00	99.00
Sun Alliance	304.00	303.00
Tarmac	139.00	142.00
Tate & Lyle	351.00	351.00
Tesco	213.00	213.00
Thomson Cp	745.00	725.00
Thorn EMI	760.00	765.00
Ti Group	561.00	560.00
Trafalgar	214.00	215.00
TSB	130.00	126.00
Unilever	839.00	829.00
Unisel	$2.75	$2.75
United Bis	380.00	382.00
Ultramar	335.00	330.00
Vaal Reefs	$71.00	$66.25
Warburg	537.00	540.00
Welkom	$5.41	$4.97
Wellcome	859.00	860.00
West Areas	$1.55	$1.40
Whitbread	442.00	442.00
Winkels	$13.50	$11.75
WPP	63.00	63.00

JOHANNESBURG (So African Rand)

	Cur.	Prev.
Anglo Amer	124.75	119.50
De Beers	94.25	93.40
Kloof	33.25	31.75
Messina	6.00	5.50
Rust Plat	71.50	70.00
Samanco	31.25	31.25

Reprinted by permission of *Investor's Business Daily, America's Business Newspaper* (November 25, 1991), ©Investor's Business Daily Inc. 1991.

earnings before they are released. However, a major determinant of stock prices is earnings per share (EPS), rather than total earnings. Key elements of Figure 7-4 are annotated.

Dividend Report

Dividends also affect stock price movements. Figure 7-5 shows a sample dividend report from *Investor's Business Daily*. Key elements are annotated. *Moody's Dividend Record*, an annual publication, presents quarterly dividends and the date of declaration, date of record, date payable, and ex-dividend date.

FIGURE 7-3: Foreign Exchange Rates

Currency	Fgn. Currency In Dollars 11/22	11/21	Dollar In Fgn.Currency 11/22	11/21
60-day fwd	.6274	.6207	1.5940	1.6112
90-day fwd	.6249	.6183	1.6003	1.6173
Greece	.005511	.005511	181.45	181.45
Hong Kong	.1290	.1290	7.7533	7.7533
y-India	.0386	.0386	25.907	25.907
Indonesia	.000506	.000506	1978.00	1978.00
Ireland	1.6750	1.6750	.5970	.5970
Israel	.4389	.4389	2.2784	2.2784
Italy	.000836	.000824	1196.50	1213.25
Japan	.007740	.007719	129.20	129.55
30-dy fwd	.007730	.007710	129.36	129.71
60-dy fwd	.007724	.007703	129.47	129.82
90-dy fwd	.007716	.007696	129.60	129.94
Jordan	1.4500	1.4500	.68970	.68970
Lebanon	.001134	.001134	881.50	881.50
Malaysia	.3655	.3655	2.7360	2.7360
z-Mexico	.000325	.000325	3073.01	3073.01
Netherlands	.5552	.5543	1.8012	1.8040
N. Zealand	.5670	.5666	1.7637	1.7649
Norway	.1599	.1585	6.2550	6.3100

Fgn. Currency in Dollars: Number of U.S dollars per unit of foreign currency.

Dollars in Fgn. Currency Units of foreign currency per one U.S. dollar.

NOTE: These rates, however, are interbank rates. As a rule of thumb, add 2% to the interbank rate to determine the rate for stock transactions. To determine a rough price for foreign securities in U.S. dollars, multiply the price by the applicable exchange rate. For example, in the case of Alps closing at 1,270 yen (Figure 7-4), note that for the Japanese yen, the latest exchange rate is $0.007740, as shown in Figure 7-5. Two percent added to this gives an estimated exchange rate of $0.007895. Multiplying the price of the stock in foreign currency (here the Japanese yen) by the approximate U.S. equivalent of yen gives a rough per share price of the stock in U.S. dollars. Thus:

1,270 Yen (price of stock) × $0.007895 U.S. $
(rough exchange value of $1) =
$10.03 U.S. $ (price of stock in U.S. dollars)

Art reprinted by permission of Investor's Business Daily, America's Business Newspaper (November 25, 1991), ©Investor's Business Daily Inc. 1991.

Short Interest

Knowing the size of short positions for a stock can be helpful for investors. The short interest is the number of shares of selected stocks that have been sold by investors hoping to profit from a fall in the stock market. *NOTE: A large short interest in a stock can mean that the stock is bearish because many investors expect the price of the stock to fall. The* Wall Street Journal *reports three short interest reports each month—for NYSE, AMEX, and NASDAQ—under the heading ''Short Interest Highlights''. An example is shown in Figure 7-6.*

HOW STOCKS ARE SOLD THROUGH THE STOCK EXCHANGE

Figure 7-7 is a sample announcement of a new stock issue (a ''tombstone'' ad). Components of the offering prospectus cover are keyed and explained in the notes.

UNDERSTANDING PREFERRED STOCK (NONCONVERTIBLE)

Preferred stock carries a fixed dividend that is paid quarterly. The dividend is stated in dollars per share, or as a percentage of par (stated) value of the stock. Preferred stock is considered a hybrid security because it possesses features of both common stock and corporate bonds. It is like common stock in that it represents equity ownership and is issued without stated maturity dates, and it pays dividends. Preferred stock is also like a corporate bond in that it provides for prior claims on earnings and assets, its dividend is fixed for the life of the issue, and it can carry call and convertible features and sinking fund provisions.

Because preferred stocks are traded on the basis of the yield offered to investors, they are viewed as fixed-income securities and, as a result, are in competition with bonds in the marketplace. Corporate bonds, however, occupy a position senior to preferred stocks.

Advantages of owning preferred stocks include the following:

- They offer high current income, which is highly predictable.
- They are safe.
- They have a lower unit cost ($10 to $25 per share).

Disadvantages are:

- They are susceptible to inflation and high interest rates.
- They lack substantial capital gains potential.

Most preferred stock is cumulative, that is, it requires any dividends in arrears to be paid before common stockholders can receive their dividends.

TYPES OF PREFERRED STOCKS

Like common stock, preferred stock is categorized according to special features.

Convertible preferred. Convertible into common shares and thus offering growth potential plus fixed income. Convertible preferreds tends to behave differently in the marketplace than does straight preferred.

Noncumulative preferred. This class of preferreds is a carryover from the heyday of the railroads and is a rarity today. Unpaid dividends do not accumulate.

Cumulative preferred. This is the most common type of preferreds. Skipped dividends accrue, and common dividends cannot be paid until arrearages are paid.

Participating preferred. Typically issued by firms desperate for capital, these shares allow holders to share in profits with common holders. This is done by way of extra dividends declared after regular dividends are paid. Preferred shareholders may have voting rights.

Adjustable-rate preferred. Also called floating-rate or variable-rate preferred, these stocks adjust the dividend rate quarterly (usually based on three-month U.S. Treasury bill rate) to reflect money market rates. This category of preferreds is aimed at corporate investors seeking after-tax yield combined with secondary market price stability. Dividends can go down as well as up.

Prior preferred stock (or **preference shares**). This type has a priority claim on assets and earnings over other preferred shares.

FIGURE 7-4: Earnings Report

CATHERINES STORES CORP	CATH 11
Retail-Apparel/Shoe	Eps 94 Rel 56
Quar Nov 02: h1991	h1990
Sales $31,895,637	$29,939,976
Net Income 967,741	62,748
Avg shares 7,086,493	3,029,105
Share earns:	(OTC)
Net Income 0.14	0.01
% Change +1,300% ★	
39 weeks:	
Sales 97,941,900	87,082,675
Net Income 3,646,167	314,267
Avg shares 4,507,359	3,035,273
Share earns:	
Net Income 0.79	0.08
% Change +888%	
h−Per share figures after preferred	
dividend requirements.	
CUCOS INC	CUCO 1¼
Retail-Food&Restaurants	Eps 68 Rel 88
Quar Oct 20: 1991	1990
Sales $5,332,619	$4,586,182
Net Income 110,472	102,056
Avg shares 2,113,747	2,083,747
Share earns:	(OTC)
Net Income 0.05	0.05

Name of the company, usually shortened, and closing price. The *Wall Street Journal* reports the primary market on which common shares are traded here. Catherines Stores Corp. shares are traded on the OTC. Exchange abbreviations used by *Wall Street Journal* include: A, AMEX, O, OTC; Pa, Pacific; M, Midwest; P, Philadelphia; B, Boston, T, Toronto, Mo, Montreal; F, Foreign.

Time period of the report, cumulative for the year, so a third- quarter report is, in effect, a nine-month report. Footnotes are explained at the end of the company's earnings report.

Years for which figures are given; those for the previous year are always for the same period of time (number of months) as the present report.

Sales figures in dollars, or revenue, is always net, allowances having been made for discounts and returns.

Net income in dollars represents the profit after payment of all obligations except dividends for the common stock. A minus sign preceeding a number signifies a loss. The *Wall Street Journal* reports losses in parenthesis.

Share earnings is the net income divided by the number of shares outstanding. It shows how much the earnings is represented by each share of stock issued.

% change for the latest quarter is boldfaced. An asterisk signifies the change for the latest report is 20% or more.

Art reprinted by permission of *Investor's Business Daily, America's Business Newspaper,* (December 5, 1991), ©Investor's Business Daily Inc. 1991.

FIGURE 7-5: Dividend Report

REGULAR:	Period	Amt.	Payment Date	Record Date
Air Products	Q	.39	02-10-92	01-03-92
Amcore Fincl	Q	.14	12-10-91	11-30-91
Am Mutual Fund	Q	.22	12-09-91	12-06-91
BEI Electronics	Q	.02	12-20-91	12-06-91
CentralJersey Fn	Q	.09	12-31-91	12-10-91
Champion Intl	Q	.05	01-07-92	12-20-91
Community BkSyst	Q	.19	01-10-92	12-16-91
Comstock Ptnrs	M	.0666	11-29-91	11-20-91
Continentl Cp	Q	.65	12-15-91	12-04-91
Dial Corp	Q	.35	01-02-92	12-02-91
Dresser Indus	Q	.15	12-20-91	12-02-91
E Town	Q	.50	12-21-91	12-07-91
Eastern Bncp	Q	.02	12-12-91	12-02-91
Elco Indust	Q	.13	12-13-91	11-29-91
Farm & Home	U	.075	12-31-91	12-10-91
Filtertek	Q	.05	02-14-92	01-31-92
Fst Boston Inco	M	.075	12-16-91	12-02-91
FstBoston Strat	M	.10	12-16-91	12-02-91
Fst Indiana	Q	.07	12-19-91	12-13-91
Global Ocean	U	.07	12-27-91	12-16-91

Company name.

Period: Most dividends are declared quarterly (designated by Q). Other designations include: A, annually; S, semiannually; H, monthly; U, undetermined; I, initial; Y, year-end; G, Canadian funds.

Amount: How much, usually in dollars per share.

Payment date: The day this amount is payable.

Record date: The day on which a shareholder must be listed as the holder of record to qualify for the dividend.

For the first company, Air Products, the regular dividend is paid quarterly, the dividend is $0.39 per share, the dividend will be paid to shareholders of record January 3, 1992 and the actual payment will be made on February 10, 1992. *NOTE: On the day after the record date, the stock trades ex-dividend and usually falls a little in price to compensate for the fact that it no longer is eligible for the latest dividend.*

Art reprinted by permission of *Investor's Business Daily, America's Business Newspaper,* (November 25, 1991), ©Investor's Business Daily Inc. 1991.

FIGURE 7-6: Largest Short Positions

Rank	Sep. 13	Aug. 15	Change	
	NYSE			**Rank and name** of the stock.
1 AT&T	39,280,084	22,069,477	17,210,608	**Sep.13:** Short position at mid-month.
2 Blockbust Entn	14,512,617	15,991,015	−1,478,398	**Aug 15:** Short position for the previous month.
3 Citicorp	12,298,177	13,002,263	−704,086	**Change** in short positions.
4 NCNB	9,856,120	6,438,726	3,417,394	

Art reprinted from the *Wall Street Journal* by permission. ©1991 Dow Jones & Company, Inc. All rights reserved worldwide.

Calculating Preferred Stock Return

The expected return from preferred stock is calculated in the same way as the expected return on bonds (to be discussed in Chapter 8). Because preferred stock usually has no maturity date when the company redeems it, you cannot calculate a yield to maturity, only a current yield as follows:

$$\text{Current yield} = \frac{D}{P}$$

where D = annual dividend, and P = market price of the preferred stock.

EXAMPLE 4 _____

What is the current yield on a preferred stock paying $4.00 a year in dividends and having a market price of $25?

$$\text{Current yield} = \frac{\$4}{\$25} = 16\%$$

READING PREFERRED STOCK QUOTATIONS

Preferred stocks listed on organized exchanges are reported in the same newspaper sections as common stocks. The symbol "pf" appearing after the name of the corporation indicates the issue is preferred. Preferred stock quotations are read the same way as common stock quotations. The issues are listed in *Moody's Bond Record*. Key elements and explanations of preferred stock listings are as follows:

High	Low	Stock	Div	Yld %	PE	Sales 100s	High	Low	Close	Net Chg.
1/8	52 1/8	Aetna pf	4.97e	9.3	–	10	53 1/4	43 1/8	43 1/4	-1/8
119 1/8	110 1/2	A Can pf	13.75	11.8	–	5	117	117	117	-7/8
100	59	Anheuspf	3.60	3.8	–	36	96	94 1/2	94 1/2	+1
33 5/8	20 3/8	Lil pf	–		–	24	27 3/4	27 1/4	27 5/8	+1/4

The symbol "**e**" after the dividend indicates a varying dividend payment; this issue is probably adjustable rate preferred. **High yield** of 11.8 percent suggests

FIGURE 7-7: Announcement of a New Common Stock Issue

(1) *This advertisement is neither an offer to sell nor a solicitation of an offer to buy these securities. The offering is made only by the Prospectus.*

(2) **2,850,000 Shares**

Chambers Development Company, Inc.

(3) *Class A Common Stock*

(4)

Price $25 Per Share

(5) *Copies of the Prospectus may be obtained from any of the several Underwriters. only in states in which such Underwriters are qualified to act as dealers in securities and in which the Prospectus may be legally distributed.*

(6)   *Dean Witter Reynolds Inc.*

Kidder, Peabody & Co.
Incorporated

First Analysis Securities Corporation

Bear, Stearns & Co. Inc.	*The First Boston Corporation*	*Alex. Brown & Sons* Incorporated
Dillon, Read & Co. Inc.	*Donaldson, Lufkin & Jenrette* Securities Corporation	*Drexel Burnham Lambert* Incorporated
Goldman, Sachs & Co.	*Lazard Frères & Co.*	*Merrill Lynch Capital Markets*

PaineWebber Incorporated

Prudential-Bache Capital Funding

Salomon Brothers Inc

Shearson Lehman Hutton Inc.

Smith Barney, Harris Upham & Co.
Incorporated

Wertheim Schroder & Co.
Incorporated

Bateman Eichler, Hill Richards
Incorporated

Sutro & Co.
Incorporated

April 25, 1989

FIGURE 7-7: *continued*

(1) Standard disclaimer stating that this is not an offer to sell stock. Such offers can legally be made only through a **prospectus** (discussed in Chapter 5). Tombstones are for information purposes only; often the stock has already been sold. (A *tombstone ad,* seen on the facing page, is a newspaper advertisement placed by investment bankers in a public offering of securities.)

(2) This is the total number of shares *offered for sale*. There may have been many more authorized by the corporation's charter, but the board of directors has not decided to issue them.

(3) Preferred shares and bonds are also offered in tombstone announcements. Sometimes you will see units offered that consist of, for example, 1 share and 2 warrants. (The warrant is like an option and can be used in the future to buy more shares at a specified price after a given date.)

(4) This is the price at which the security will sell (or has been sold) in advance of its issuance. Demand for these issues on the secondary market will determine the price, as is the case for all outstanding securities. If there are more offers to buy than there are shares to go around in the initial offering, the stock is regarded as a "hot issue," and the market price will rise as soon as the shares begin trading on the secondary market. Incidentally, shares of a new issue cannot be purchased *on margin,* a type of credit you can get from your broker using other shares you own as collateral. The shares must be paid for in full by the purchaser.

(5) Legal sale of a new issue cannot be made unless a prospective buyer receives a prospectus in advance of the transaction. As a buyer, if you don't receive a prospectus before you receive a confirming notice of trade, you have a legal right to cancel the transaction without penalty within a reasonable time. Because new issues are generally more speculative than securities already trading on the open market, the prospectus requirement prevents a broker from "strongarming" you into buying a security about which you may know very little. *NOTE: There are two prospectuses. The preliminary prospectus is called a "red herring," because of a statement printed on the cover in red to the effect that the registration has not been declared effective by the SEC. The purpose of the preliminary prospectus is to stimulate sales when the registration is first filed with the SEC. The SEC may or may not require revision or amendment. After the SEC has accepted the preliminary prospectus, a new prospectus—without the red herring—is printed and used to offer the shares. The reference in the tombstone advertisement is to the second (or final) prospectus.*

(6) This is the list of investment bankers, or underwriters, that make up the syndicate bringing out the issue. Those with the largest number of shares to sell are listed first (in more prominent type). If you wish to acquire the security at the initial price, before it starts trading on the secondary market, you must get the shares through one of these firms or a firm specifically contracted by one of them to sell the securities. Some will be retail brokers selling to the general public, but others may only handle sales to large institutional buyers.

Source of art: *Wall Street Journal,* April 25, 1989.

a straight preferred. **Low yield** of 3.8 precent is good indication of a convertible issue. The lack of a yield figure indicates that dividends are not being paid.

HOW TO USE COMMON/PREFERRED STOCK INFORMATION

Standard & Poor's *Stock Guide*

Standard & Poor's Stock Guide, a monthly publication, enables you to take a preliminary look at the common and preferred stock of several thousand companies (and over 400 mutual funds). Figure 7-8 reproduces two pages from the *Stock Guide*.

Standard & Poor's *Corporation Records*

One of the S&P's more popular publication series, the reports are often mailed from brokerage houses to customers who want basic information on a company. Figure 7-9 shows an example of what to expect to find in such reports. Information is more detailed than the *Stock Guide*, is similar to *Moody's Manuals* but is organized alphabetically rather than by trade categories. *Corporation Records* are published monthly, and the six volumes are updated by daily supplements. Information found in the volumes includes historical company background, financial statements, news announcements, earnings updates, and other news of general interest. Companies found in the *Corporation Records* are listed, and their subsidiary companies are cross-listed. *NOTE: The statistical section found in the T–Z volume includes a mutual fund summary, an address list of many no-load mutual funds, and foreign bond statistics. Special tables contained in the T–Z volume list new stock and bond offerings on a monthly basis. This volume also presents a classified index of industrial companies listed by standard industrial classification code (SIC) numbers. For example, if you want to find out about cereal breakfast food companies, you would first find the corresponding SIC number for cereal breakfast foods, which is listed in alphabetical order. The number, 2043, then leads you to the cross-listing of companies.* The corporate reports are compiled in three separate multiple-volume sets—the NYSE Stocks, AMEX Stocks, and OTC and Regional Stocks. Each company is updated quarterly with new earnings, dividends, and recent developments. About 1,020 NYSE stocks are selected and bound in an annual publication called the *Standard & Poor's Stock Market Encyclopedia*, which contains end-of-the-year corporate reports.

Moody's *Manuals*

Moody's Manuals are used widely and present historical financial data on the companies listed, their officers, and their general corporate condition. The manuals are divided into several categories (Banks and Finance, Industrial, Municipals and Government, OTC Industrial, Public Utility, and Transportation). Each manual has a biweekly news supplement that updates quarterly earnings, dividend announcements, mergers, and other news of interest. *Moody's Manuals* are comprehensive, with each category taking up one or two volumes and several thousand pages.

Moody's *Handbook of Common Stocks*

This handbook is a quarterly reference guide to common stocks (see Figure 7-10). Historical data and analytical comments provide the answers to five basic questions.

1. What does the company do?
2. How has it done in the past?
3. How is it doing now?
4. How will it fare in the future?
5. For what type of investor is the stock suitable (investment quality)?

Each summary begins with capsule stock information including short-term price scores (STPS) and long-term price scores (LTPS) and an evaluation of the grade (quality) of its common stock: high grade, 1; investment grade, 2; medium grade, 3; and speculative grade, 4. In addition, the handbook provides a discussion of corporate background, recent developments, and prospects. Approximately 1,000 companies are listed. (Refer to the "How To Use This Book" section of the Handbook.)

Moody's *Stock Survey*

Moody's Stock Survey is a weekly that discusses the weekly investment climate and market performance. This publication also presents some selected stocks for purchase.

The *Value Line Investment Survey,* Ratings, and Reports

Published by Arnold Bernhard & Company, the *Value Line Investment Survey* is one of the most widely used investment services by individuals, stockbrokers, and small bank trust departments. The survey tracks 1,700 companies, and each common stock is covered in a one-page summary. Figures 7-11 shows a sample page from the survey and how to use it. Figure 7-12 shows additional information provided by *Value Line Investment Survey.*

Value Line is noted for its comprehensive coverage: Raw financial data are available as well as trendline growth rates, price history patterns in graphic form, quarterly sales, earnings and dividends, and a breakdown of sales and profit margins by line of business. The survey has 13 sections divided into several industries. The first few pages begin with an industry classification and an overview of the industry, with the company summaries following. Each section is revised on a 13-week cycle.

This report contains both descriptive and analytical information. Examples of descriptive information are "company's capital structure" and "monthly price ranges—past 15 years"; examples of analytical information are "rank for timeliness" and "estimated average price range—3 to 5 years ahead." *NOTE: Value Line has a unique evaluation system that is primarily dependent on historical relationships and regression analysis. From the valuation model, each company is rated 1 through 5, with 1 being the highest positive rating and 5 the lowest. Each company is rated on timeliness and safety. It should be noted that Value Line minimizes the potential for errors of human judgment.*

FIGURE 7-8: Reprentative Pages from *Standard & Poor's Stock Guide*

(1) (2) (3) (4) (5) (6) (7) (8) (9) (10) (11) (12)

202 TJI-TRA

Standard & Poor's Corporation

¶ S&P 500 # MidCap 400 • Options

Index	Ticker Symbol	Name of Issue (Call Price of Pfd. Stocks)	Market	Com. Rank. & Pfd. Rating	Par Val.	Inst. Hold Cos	Inst. Hold Shs. (000)	Principal Business	Price Range 1971-89 High	1971-89 Low	1990 High	1990 Low	1991 High	1991 Low	Nov. Sales in 100s	November, 1991 Last Sale Or Bid High	Low	Last	%Div Yield	P-E Ratio
1	TJCO	T J International	OTC	B+	1	43	2535	Prefab joists for constrn	36¼	1¼	26½	14⅛	30	15½	1995	24½	22	22½B	1.9	39
¶2•[1]	TJX	TJX Companies	NY,B,M,P,Ph	B+	1	222	57453	Off-price specialty stores	43⅞	⅜	17¾	8¾	20⅜	9⅝	47159	16⅜	13⅞	14½	3.2	12
3	TLMT	TLM Corp	OTC,B	NR	1¢	7	56	Seeking acquisitions	4¾	1 3/16	2¾	¼	½	⅛	53	⅛	⅛	⅛B	...	d
4	TMCI	TM Century	OTC	NR	1¢	1	4	Broadcast consulting svcs	4⅛	⅛	5/16	⅛	⅜	⅛	174	⅛	⅛	⅛B	...	d
5	TNP	TNP Enterprises	NY,M,Ph	A	No	42	2291	Electric sv:Texas & New Mex	24	6¾	22½	14½	21	15⅞	8905	19⅜	17	17¾	9.2	8
6	TOD	Todd Shipyards	NY,M	B−	1¢	25	2340	Major shipbldg & repair co	41¾	1⅝	6⅜	2⅞	6⅝	4	5761	5⅜	4½	4⅝	...	3
7	TOF	Tofutti Brands	AS	NR	1¢	8	165	Non-dairy frozen desserts	18	1¼	2	3/16	9/16	3/16	684	7/16	3/16	5/16B	...	d
8	TOK	Tokheim Corp	NY,B,M,Ph	B−	No	42	3864	Design/mfr gas station equip	35¼	⅞	25⅞	9¾	15⅞	8⅝	2175	9¾	8⅝	8⅞	...	d
9	TKIOY	Tokio Marine/Fire ADR[54]	OTC	NR	[54] . .	21	1982	Japan's lgst non-life insurer	93¾	3	72⅜	34½	56½	40½	4545	51⅝	47	47B	0.5	28
10•[2]	TKOS	Tokos Medical Corp	OTC	NR	.001	102	8694	Special home hlth care svcs	....	....	16½	7½	38½	10½	46115	38	28½	33⅛B	...	83
11	TOL	Toll Brothers	NY,M,Ph	B	1¢	39	9862	Luxury single family homes	16½	2⅞	4	2¼	8⅝	2⅜	17806	7⅜	6	7¼	...	..
12	TBK	Tolland Bank	AS	NR	1	..	...	Savings bank, Connecticut	18	6¾	9¼	3⅞	4⅞	2¾	104	3¼	2⅞	3¼	...	d
13	TOMKY	Tomkins plc ADS[55]	OTC	NR	[55] . .	..	...	Industrial investment/mgmt co	19	14⅜	23¼	15⅜	30	16¾	537	30	27¼	27⅝B	2.8	13
14	TR	Tootsie Roll Indus	NY,M,Ph	A	694/9¢	71	2363	'Tootsie' line of candies	36¼	⅞	48½	30⅛	64⅛	35⅝	859	64⅛	61⅛	64⅛	s0.4	25
#15•[3]	TOPP	Topps Co	OTC	NR	1¢	82	12572	Mkts collectible picture prod	12½	2⅞	17¼	8½	19	12	25507	15½	13¾	14¼B	1.7	13
¶16•[4]	TMK	Torchmark Corp	NY,B,M,P	A+	1	269	24862	Insurance:fin'l services	58¾	3⅞	57⅜	38	58½	46⅜	11872	55⅜	51	52½	3.0	11
17	TRGL	Toreador Royalty	OTC	NR	15⅝¢	13	668	Oil & gas explor & devel	14¾	9/16	4⅛	2¼	3¾	2¼	796	3¼	2¾	2¾B	...	..
18	TTC	Toro Co	NY,M,Ph	B	1	67	6110	Power mowers, sprinklers, etc	26	2 5/16	30	11	20½	13¼	4751	16	13¾	15⅜	3.1	20
19•[5]	TD	Toronto-Dominion Bk	To,Mo,Vc	A−	No	64	34729	General Banking,Canada	23⅛	1 9/16	20¾	14½	19¾	16⅜	63546	19¼	17⅜	17½	4.3	12
20	TTL	Torotel, Inc	AS	B−	50¢	5	135	Mfr magnetic components	16⅞	1/16	2¼	1	3⅞	1	765	2⅜	1⅞	2⅛B	...	9
#21•[6]	TOS	Tosco Corp	NY,B,M,P,Ph	B−	75¢	117	11221	Refining & dstr petroleum prod	225⅝	5	24⅝	14½	25⅞	14⅝	16264	25	22⅛	22¾	2.6	17
22	Pr F	$4.375 cm Cv F Pfd([58]53.0625)	NY	BB−	1	18	1535		....	....	....	....	63	52½	526	61½	59	59	7.4	..
23	TOT	TOTAL 'B' ADS[59]	NY	NR	[59] . .	..	...	Intl o&g explor,dev,prod'n	....	....	....	....	25⅝	20½	230458	25⅝	21⅝	24¾	...	9
24	TOG	Total Canada Oil & Gas	AS,Ph	NR	No	29	2608	Oil&gas explor,dev,prod'n	....	....	....	....	6⅜	4⅜	781	6⅜	5½	5⅞B	...	16
25•[7]	TPN	Total Petrol'm NA	AS,B,M,P,Ph,Mo,To	B−	No	49	3829	Petroleum refining/mktg	31⅞	3⅝	29⅛	19¼	25⅝	12¼	1514	14⅛	12¼	12½	6.4	d
26	Pr	$2.88 cm Cv Pfd(50)vtg	AS,To,Ph	NR	No	2	84		53½	15¼	43¾	31½	42¼	31⅝	2	37⅝	37⅝	36½B	♦7.0	..
27	TPCA	Total Pharmaceutical Care	OTC	NR	No	23	1584	Home infusion/therapy svcs	....	....	....	....	19¾	11½	11379	19¾	16	19B	...	35
28	TSS	Total Systems Svcs	NY,M,Ph	NR	10¢	16	509	Bankcard data process'g svc	34	3⅛	35½	26⅞	32¾	25	295	28	25½	26	1.1	29
29	TNC	Town & Country Cl'A'	AS,M	B	1¢	31	3565	Mfr/wholesaler of jewelry	11¾	4¼	7½	1¼	5½	1⅜	4155	3¼	2	2⅜	...	2
30	TOYOY	Toyota Motor Corp ADR[63]	OTC	NR	[63] . .	11	623	Autos,forklifts,prefab homes	35⅜	13/16	29½	21¾	25⅞	21½	2562	24¾	22¼	22¼B	1.0	12
¶31•[8]	TOY	Toys R Us	NY,B,M,P,Ph	B+	10¢	592	176194	Disc toy supermarts:dept str	26⅞	5/16	35	19⅞	36	22	180798	29⅞	26	28	...	21
32	TPIE	TPI Enterprises	OTC	C	1¢	45	9554	Restaurants/movie theatres	16	3/16	7½	4	7½	3½	31830	7	5½	5¾B	...	18
33	TRKA	Trak Auto	OTC	B−	1¢	14	892	Retail auto parts stores	48¾	7	11	5½	10¼	5	613	10¼	8½	9¼B	...	d
34	TCR	Trammell Crow RE Inv[65]	NY,M	NR	10¢	14	564	REIT:self-liquid'g 12-31-97	15⅜	4¼	5	2	4⅜	2	2391	2½	2	2⅛	15.1	d
35	TAU	Transalta Util	To,Mo	B+	No	28	13172	Electric service in Alberta	15¾	2¾	14⅜	11⅛	13¾	11⅞	55721	13¾	13	13½	7.3	31
¶36•[3]	TA	Transamerica Corp	NY,B,C,M,P,Ph	B	1	259	49161	Insurance/financial svcs	51½	5⅜	44⅝	23¼	40	29⅝	34566	40	35⅞	38⅜	5.2	11
37	TAI	Transamerica Inc Shrs	NY,M,P	NR	1	6	246	Closed end invest co-debt	26⅝	14	24¼	20	26½	21½	586	25⅝	24	24¼	8.9	..
#38	TRH	Transatlantic Holdings	NY,M,Ph	NR	1	87	10443	Reinsur: property/casualty	....	....	29⅛	18⅞	39⅜	25	4803	36	33½	34	0.6	11
39•[9]	TRP	TransCanada P.L.	NY,Mo,To,M,Ph	B	No	99	27307	Nat gas pipeline/o&g explr	29	3¾	15⅜	12⅜	15⅞	14	72853	15⅞	15	15⅜	♦4.1	11
40	TFC	Transcapital Fin'l	NY,M	C	1	15	1062	Savings & loan, Ohio	19⅛	3⅜	4⅞	1	5	1½	1086	2⅛	1½	1⅞	...	d
41	QTNI.A	Transcisco Cl'A'[69]	AS	D	1¢	9	373	Railcare maintenance & repair	9	4	6½	1⅞	4¼	⅛	1729	⅝	⅛	3/16	...	d
42	QTNI.B	Cv Class'B'[70]	AS	D	1¢	8	209	dvlp elec cogeneration proj	9	2⅜	6⅜	2¼	4	1/16	299	⅜	1/16	⅛	...	d
¶43•[10]	E	Transco Energy	NY,B,C,M,P	B	50¢	176	14817	Nat'l gas PL:coal prod'n	64¼	4¾	48⅜	31	36⅜	16¾	33817	23¼	19⅛	20⅛	3.0	d
44	Pr A	$4.75 cm Cv Pfd([72]51.90)	NY,M	↓BB−	No	40	1463	Oil & gas explor, develop	59	37¾	54¼	47½	52	39⅞	2209	48½	45	45¼	10.5	..
45	EXP	Transco Expl Ptnrs[73]	NY,M,P	LIQ	No	28	2258	Selling assets&liquidating	25¾	3¼	4	2⅜	3⅜	⅞	6805	1⅜	⅞	1⅛	...	..

Uniform Footnote Explanations-See Page 1. Other: [1]CBOE:Cycle 1. [2]Ph:Cycle 3. [3]Ph:Cycle 2. [4]ASE:Cycle 2. [5]To:Cycle 3. [6]ASE:Cycle 1. [7]To:Cycle 1. [8]CBOE:Cycle 3. [9]Vc:Cycle 2. [10]NY:Cycle 2. [51]Fiscal Dec'89 & prior. [52]11 Mo Sep'90. [53]Excl $29M reclassified as current. [54]ADR represents 5 shrs,par 50 yen. [55]Each ADS rep 4 ord, 5p. [56]Stk of Southland Royalty. [57]®$3.94,'90. [58]Fr 8-15-94,scale to $50 in 2001. [59]Each ADS rep 0.125 ord'B'FF50. [60]Excl subsid pfd. [61]Stk dstr of Total Canada Oil & Gas. [62]Fiscal May'88 & prior. [63]Each ADR rep 2 ord, y50. [64]Approx. [65]Shrs Ben Int. [66]Est return of capital. [67]100% non-taxable,'90. [68]Special divd. [69]1/10 vtg. [70]Cv into 1 Cl'A' shr. [71]Excl $111M subsid Pfd. [72]Thru 11-1-92,scale to $50 in'95. [73]Depositary unit. [74]Liq divd.

FIGURE 7-8: *continued*

(1) **Index:** The numbers are a visual guide to the columnar data. Stocks with options are indicated by * ; stocks in the S&P 500 are flagged with ¶.

(2) **Ticker symbols** are those of the exchange listed first in the "market" column. OTC stocks carry NASDAQ trading system symbols. Supplementary symbols as would appear on the ticker tape following symbol, such as "Pr" for preferred stocks, etc., are indented.

(3) **A stock's name of issue** as shown in this column is not necessarily the same as the corporate title. Also, because of space limitations, the occasional use of abbreviations has been necessary. Where the name of the company is not followed by the designation of a particular issue of its stock, it is the common or capital stock that are referred to. The *call price of preferred stock* is shown in parentheses following the name of the issue: the footnoted data indicate the year in which the call price declines. Unit of trading for stocks on the NYSE and Amex indicated as follows: 10, 10 shares; 25, 25 shares; 50, 50 shares; all others, 100 shares.

(4) **Common stock ranking and preferred stock rating** (see the Appendix at end of this chapter, the sections titled "S&P's Earnings and Dividend Rankings for Common Stock," and "S&P's Preferred Stock Ratings").

(5) **Par Value:** assigned to the stock; in determining transfer taxes, no par issues are figured the same as $100 par.

(6) **Inst. hold cos shs (000)** represents the number of financial institutions—banks, insurance companies, endowments funds, and "13F" money managers—that hold this stock and the number of shares (000 omitted) held.

(7) **Principal business** refers to the company's primary business. For a company engaged in several lines of business, every effort is made to list that line from which it obtains the bulk of its revenue. In addition, an indication of the company's rank in industry is given where possible.

(8) **The price range** is shown for two measures. *Historical high & low* price ranges are for the calendar years indicated. *Last year's high & low* price ranges are not exclusive for the exchange on which the stock is currently traded but are based on the best available data covering the period shown in the column head. Price ranges of over-the-counter stocks are based on the best available high and low bid prices during the period and should be viewed as reasonable approximations.

(9) **Month sales in 100s** describes trading for the month indicated, in hundreds of shares. NYSE and AMEX companies are based on composite tape; all others are for primary exchanges shown.

(10) **Last (month) sale or bid price** reports last sales on principal exchanges at closing quotations for the preceding month. For Canadian issues, prices are quoted in Canadian dollars provided the first exchange listed in the "market" column is a Canadian exchange. For NASDAQ and OTC stocks, the latest available bid price is shown under the "last" column.

(11) **Percentage (%) dividend yield:** Yields derived by dividing total indicated dividend rates by the stock price. Such rate is based on latest dividend paid including (+), or excluding (e) extras as shown by footnote. Additional symbols used: (s), including stock; (++), extras and stock.

(12) **P/E ratio.** Price/earnings ratio.

Continued

FIGURE 7-8: *continued*

(13) (14) (15) (16) (17) (18) (19) (20) (21)

Common and Convertible Preferred Stocks

TJI-TRA 203

Splits ◆ Index	Cash Divs. Ea. Yr. Since	Dividends: Latest Payment Period $	Date	Ex. Div.	Total $ So Far 1991	Ind. Rate	Paid 1990	Financial Position Mil-$ Cash& Equiv.	Curr. Assets	Curr. Liab.	Balance Sheet Date	Capitalization Lg Trm Debt Mil-$	Shs. 000 Pfd.	Com.	Earnings $ Per Shr. Years End	1987	1988	1989	1990	1991	Last 12 Mos.	Interim Earnings Period	$ per Shr. 1990	1991	Index
1◆	1977	Q0.10½	10-16-91	9-16	0.42	0.42	0.41½	1.50	72.9	39.3	9-28-91	26.5	634	6461	Dc	1.90	2.51	2.12	1.65	....	0.58	9 Mo Sep	1.58	0.51	1
2◆	1980	Q0.11½	11-27-91	11-1	0.46	0.46	0.44½	27.2	662	427	7-27-91	305	...	69781	Ja	△2.10	d2.97	d1.10	1.06	E1.20	1.02	9 Mo Sep	0.84	0.80	2
3	....	None Since Public			...	Nil	....	1.31	1.88	0.41	9-30-91	....	...	4228	Dc	0.09	d0.06	0.37	d0.89	....	d0.86	9 Mo Sep	d0.10	d0.07	3
4	....	None Since Public			...	Nil	....	0.24	3.15	0.67	6-30-91	0.98	...	22284	Sp	□d0.15	d0.19	[51]d0.13	[52]0.04	....	Ed0.02	6 Mo Mar	0.05	d0.01	4
5	1936	Q0.40¾	12-15-91	11-21	1.63	1.63	1.63	8.72	52.8	184	6-30-91	362	123	8282	Dc	2.41	5.19	1.90	1.84	....	2.22	12 Mo Sep	2.02	2.22	5
6	....	0.33	2-1-87	1-9	...	Nil	....	27.3	74.7	33.0	6-30-91	0.72	...	11956	Mr	d5.75	d21.06	*6.97	△□2.65	....	1.55	6 Mo Sep	△□2.10	*1.00	6
7	....	None Since Public			...	Nil	....	0.08	1.07	0.91	6-30-91	....	...	5439	Dc	d0.38	d0.12	d0.22	d0.01	....	d0.01	9 Mo Sep	Nil	Nil	7
8	1920	0.14	8-30-91	8-5	0.42	Nil	0.56	10.8	114	86.7	8-31-91	[53]11.7	954	6307	Nv	1.68	△1.36	1.15	d0.27	....	d2.03	9 Mo Aug	0.33	d1.43	8
9◆	1951	0.24½	7-16-91	3-22	0.24½	0.25	0.222	....	...	...		824	...	1544793	Mr	1.57	2.25	1.68	1.69	....	1.69	No interim report			9
10	....	None Since Public			...	Nil	....	11.1	51.8	12.2	6-30-91	2.07	...	14818	Dc	0.11	0.17	0.06	d0.20	....	0.40	9 Mo Sep	d0.05	0.55	10
11◆	....	None Paid			...	Nil	....	Equity per shr $3.51			7-31-91	151	...	32788	Oc	0.57	0.80	0.44	△0.30	....	0.05	9 Mo Jul	△0.29	△0.04	11
12	1987	0.04	11-13-90	10-25	...	Nil	0.40	Book Value $13.16			3-31-91	5.58	...	1150	Dc	0.99	0.93	0.83	d0.59	....	d1.60	9 Mo Sep	0.31	d0.70	12
13	1988	0.557	10-22-91	8-2	0.781	0.78	†2.225	252	1156	642	5-04-91	81.9	141300	273137	Ap	1.03	1.66	2.00	2.35	2.17	2.17				13
14◆	1943	Q0.06½	10-10-91	9-20	s0.24½	0.26	s0.218	31.1	83.8	18.6	6-29-91	0.13	...	±9933	Dc	1.46	1.67	2.04	2.27	....	2.53	9 Mo Sep	1.90	2.16	14
15◆	1987	Q0.06	11-1-91	10-11	0.23	0.24	0.18	3.02	72.6	64.8	8-31-91	25.0	...	47302	Fb	0.56	0.59	0.80	1.15	....	1.13	6 Mo Aug	0.60	0.58	15
16	1933	Q0.40	2-3-92	1-6	1.50	1.60	1.40	Book Value $16.19			12-31-90	p682	869	p51074	Dc	□2.98	3.11	3.88	4.28	E4.85	4.37	9 Mo Sep	3.39	3.48	16
17	....	h[56]....	11-16-81	10-8	...	Nil	....	1.50	1.68	0.08	6-30-91	....	...	4534	Dc	0.04	d0.02	d0.05	0.01	....	0.02	9 Mo Sep	Nil	0.01	17
18◆	1984	Q0.12	10-12-91	9-19	0.48	0.48	0.48	17.0	319	108	7-31-91	145	...	11913	Jl	1.52	1.84	2.10	1.55	0.81	0.77	3 Mo Oct	d0.47	d0.51	18
19◆	1857	gQ0.19	10-31-91	9-13	g0.76	0.76	g0.76	Book Value $13.82			j10-31-90	853	17666	301090	Oc	□1.68	2.14	2.20	1.80	....	1.51	9 Mo Jun	1.43	1.14	19
20	....	5%Stk	5-15-85	4-24	...	Nil	....	0.05	5.18	1.50	7-31-91	2.09	...	2614	Ap	d0.76	*0.19	0.12	0.13	△0.11	0.24	6 Mo Oct	△0.03	0.16	20
21◆	1989	Q0.15	9-30-91	9-17	0.45	0.60	0.60	12.3	262	167	6-30-91	367	★2000	29886	Dc	*0.65	*3.25	1.71	[57]5.37	....	1.36	9 Mo Sep	5.37	1.36	21
22	1991	Q1.093	11-15-91	10-29	1.093	4.375	....	Cv into 2.0833 com,$24				....	2000	...	Dc	...	...	...	....	....	....				22
23	....	Plan annual div			...	....	....	2496	8884	6209	6-30-91	2978	[60]...	±★41517	Dc	±0.84	±0.82	±1.30	±2.18	E2.70	3.07	6 Mo Jun	±0.63	±1.52	23
24	....	None Since Public			...	Nil	....	3.00	14.6	10.6	j3-31-91	40.0	...	35251	Dc	...	...	...	p0.42	....	0.37	9 Mo Sep	p0.21	0.16	24
25◆	1978	tQ0.20	12-20-91	11-22	t[61]0.80	0.80	t0.80	16.8	404	380	6-30-91	159	314	35608	Dc	d1.35	2.55	1.51	1.16	....	d0.18	9 Mo Sep	1.21	d0.13	25
26	1980	gQ0.72	12-20-91	11-22	g2.88	2.88	g2.88	Cv into 2.0 common,$25				....	314	...	Dc	n/a	b2.54	b2.45	b2.62	....	....				26
27	....	None Since Public			...	Nil	....	28.9	37.5	3.27	6-30-91	0.13	...	±5427	Dc	0.13	[62]d1.16	*0.12	*0.36	....	0.54	9 Mo Sep	*0.23	0.41	27
28	1990	Q0.07	10-1-91	9-17	0.28	0.28	0.28	4.91	33.7	10.5	6-30-91	20.5	...	15891	Dc	0.45	0.60	0.71	0.80	....	0.89	9 Mo Sep	0.56	0.65	28
29◆	....	None Since Public			...	Nil	....	109	299	87.3	8-31-91	205	...	±12030	Fb	0.79	0.65	0.56	±△d0.05	....	1.37	6 Mo Aug	±d0.25	△±1.17	29
30◆	1970	[64]0.107		12-23	0.229	0.22	0.177	14409	33772	17590	6-30-90	7982	...	3367425	Je	1.05	1.34	1.32	1.65	P1.85	1.85				30
31◆	....	None since reorg.			...	Nil	....	105	1920	1887	8-03-91	★394	...	288772	Ja	0.69	0.91	1.09	1.11	E1.35	1.07	9 Mo Oct	0.30	0.26	31
32	....	None Paid			...	Nil	....	15.3	104	86.4	6-30-91	119	...	18052	Dc	d0.34	d0.10	d0.20	0.07	....	0.32	9 Mo Sep	d0.26	d0.01	32
33	....	None Since Public			...	Nil	....	13.8	101	56.8	7-31-91	26.0	...	5780	Ja	0.78	0.47	0.44	d0.72	....	d1.24	6 Mo Jul	0.36	d0.16	33
34	1986	[66]0.08	11-25-91	11-7	[66]0.41½	0.32	[67]0.70	Equity per shr $7.55			6-30-91	83.2	...	9075	Dc	0.04	d0.10	d0.30	d0.29	....	d0.33	6 Mo Jun	d0.23	△d0.27	34
35◆	1956	gQ0.24½	1-1-92	11-26	g0.98	0.98	g0.98	....	228	345	j12-31-90	1470	★27022	137300	Dc	1.33	0.88	1.01	0.26	....	0.44	9 Mo Sep	0.62	0.80	35
36	1934	Q0.50	10-31-91	9-30	1.97	2.00	1.93	Equity per shr $30.84			9-30-91	7216	2	76885	Dc	5.47	4.42	4.18	3.29	E3.40	2.54	9 Mo Sep	2.97	2.22	36
37	1973	0.18	12-15-91	11-22	2.16	2.16	2.16	Net Asset Val $24.10			11-22-91	....	...	5266	Mr	§22.37	§22.05	§22.30	§23.13	....	....				37
38	1990	0.05	12-16-91	11-22	0.20	0.20	0.05	Equity per shr $20.89			9-30-91	....	...	22861	Dc	*1.74	*1.97	2.44	2.71	....	3.02	9 Mo Sep	1.95	2.26	38
39	1964	gQ0.18	10-31-91	9-24	g0.72	0.72	g0.68	856	1271	743	j9-30-91	3416	3786	170953	Dc	0.96	d0.31	1.09	1.23	jE1.35	j1.31	9 Mo Sep	0.92	1.00	39
40	1989	[68]0.25	4-24-90	4-16	...	Nil	[68]0.25	Book Value $11.36			6-30-91	994	...	9806	Dc	1.25	1.86	d2.04	□d4.47	....	d4.38	9 Mo Sep	□d2.80	□d2.71	40
41◆	1986	0.075	1-22-91	12-21	0.075	Nil	0.30	File bankruptcy Chapt 11				0.11	...	±4407	Dc	±0.81	±1.51	±0.67	±d0.46	....	d4.57	6 Mo Jun	±0.06	±d4.05	41
42◆	1984	0.02½	1-22-91	12-21	0.02½	Nil	0.10	Cv into 1 Cl'A' shr				....	...	1306	Dc	±0.81	±1.51	±0.67	±d0.46	....	d4.57	6 Mo Jun	±0.06	±d4.05	42
43	1952	Q0.15	12-3-91	11-5	1.17	0.60	1.36	20.5	881	1471	9-30-91	1634	[71]6010	30650	Dc	△d3.52	d3.18	3.10	0.53	Ed1.00↓	d2.01	9 Mo Sep	0.93	■d1.61	43
44	1986	Q1.18¾	11-1-91	10-9	4.75	4.75	4.75	Cv into 0.894 com				....	2980	...	Dc	b0.37	b0.32	b0.80	b1.08	....	....				44
45	....	[74]0.35	12-29-89	12-11	...	Nil	....	Net Asset Val per Unit $2.24			6-30-91	....	...	77170	Dc	d0.18	d0.62	n/a	n/a	....	....				45

◆**Stock Splits & Divs By Line Reference Index** [1]2-for-1,'87. [2]No adj for dstr of Waban, Inc,'89. [9]10-for-1,'87:Adj for 5%,'90. [11]3-for-2,'87:2-for-1,'87. [14]2-for-1 in Cl'B','87:Adj to 3%,'91. [15]3-for-2 twice,'89,once'90. [18]3-for-2,'87. [19]2-for-1,'89. [21]1-for-5 REVERSE,'89. [25]No adj for stk dstr,'91. [29]2-for-1 in Cl'A','87. [30]Adj to 5%,'89:10%,'90,'91. [31]3-for-2,'89,'90. [35]2-for-1,'88. [41]10%,'87. [42]10%,'87.

FIGURE 7-8: continued

(13) Index: Details of stock dividends and stock splits, effected during the past five years, are reported by symbol ♦ and footnotes, which carry numerals corresponding to those in the "index" column. Adjustments have been made for all stock dividends.

(14) Cash dividend each year since: One or more cash dividends were paid each calendar year to date, without interruption, beginning with year listed.

(15) Dividends: *Latest payment* is latest dividend payment. If dividends as paid at a regular established rate, it is so noted by M— Monthly, Q—Quarterly, S—Semiannually, or A—Annually. *Date* refers to the date of disbursement of the latest payment. If an extra or stock dividend also is being paid, it is so indicated by footnote. The date shown under *Ex. Div.* is that on which the stock sells "ex-dividend", that is, the date on which it sells without the right to receive the latest declared dividend.

(16) Total $: *This year* refers to payments made or declared payable thus far in the current calendar year, including both regular and extras, if any. *Ind. rate:* Indicated rates are usually based on most recent quarterly or semiannual payments, or on dividends paid during the past 12 months. *Last year:* Total dividend payments, including extras if any, made in the preceding calendar year. For preferred dividend accumulations to latest payment due date, see "financial position" column.

(17) Financial position: *Cash & Equivalent*, *Current Assets*, (includes cash/equiv), and *Current Liabilities* are given in millions of dollars (000,000 omitted), as 17.0—$17,000,000; 1.75—$1,750,000; 0.18—$175,000. Where current balance sheet items are not of analytical significance, special calculations pertinent to the industry in which the company operates are presented, as tangible "Book Value per Share" for Banks, "Net Asset Value per Share" for Investment Trusts, and tangible "Equity per Share" (stockholders) for Insurance and Finance Companies. Intangibles such as goodwill, debt discount, or preferred liquidating value have been deducted.

(18) Capitalization. *Long-Term Debt* is in millions of dollars, as 25.0—$25,000,000; 2.58—$2,580,000; 0.20—$200,000. It includes funded debt, long-term bank loans, etc. Preferred and common stocks are in shares to the nearest thousands (000 omitted), as 150—150,000; 30—30,000; 2—1,500 (due to rounding). Outstanding shares exclude Treasury stock. The figure shown under the "preferred shares" (Pf.) column on the company (Com.) name line represents the combined number of preferred shares outstanding.

(19) Annual Earnings. *Year ends. Year ends.* Earnings are in general on a "primary" basis as reported by company including discontinued operations but excluding extraordinary items. *Per Share Latest Five Years.* Earnings for fiscal years ending March 31 or earlier are shown under the column of the preceding calendar year. **S&P Earnings Estimates** are the final product of careful analysis by industry specialists of available relevant information. They are unofficial and responsibility for their accuracy cannot be assumed. An arrow denotes changes in current estimates. *Last 12 Months* indicates 12-month earnings through the period shown in the *interim earnings* column, when available, or annual, if not.

(20) Interim Earnings for Remarks: Interim earnings are shown, when available, for the longest accounting interval since the last fiscal year-end. Also published in this column from time to time are references to sinking fund provisions and dividend arrears of preferred stock. See also "Financial Position" column for such notations.

(21) Index numbers are a visual guide to the columnar data.

FIGURE 7-9: *Standard and Poor's Corporate Reports,* Sample Pages

Texas Instruments 2208

NYSE Symbol TXN Options on CBOE (Jan-Apr-Jul-Oct) In S&P 500

Price	Range	P-E Ratio	Dividend	Yield	S&P Ranking	Beta
Oct. 11'88 40½	1988 60-37½	12	0.72	1.8%	B+	1.49

Summary

Texas Instruments is one of the world's largest producers of semiconductors. It also derives over half of its revenues from defense electronics, computers, terminals and calculators. A 40% interest is held in a seismic services company. Despite sharply lower royalty income, which totaled $191 million in 1987, earnings are projected to rise sharply in 1988 due largely to strong sales of semiconductors. Further progress is likely in 1989 as well.

Current Outlook

Earnings for 1989 should approximate $5.00 a share, up from the $4.25 estimated for 1988.

The $0.18 quarterly dividend is likely to be increased in 1988.

Sales for 1989 are likely to increase close to 10%. The gain should be led by defense electronics operations, which are experiencing an increase in orders and backlog despite the slowing of defense spending generally. Components are also expected to have higher sales, although the rate of growth will be far below the extremely strong increase projected for 1988 due to a slowing of the industry's expansion. Digital products should benefit from new product introductions. Margins are expected to continue to benefit from the higher volume, aggressive cost reductions and reduced losses at the digital products segment. Somewhat restraining will be a decline in royalty income.

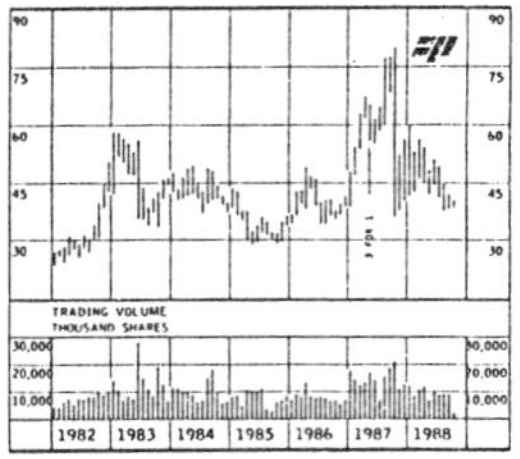

Net Sales (Million $)

Quarter:	1988	1987	1986	1985
Mar.	1,467	1,272	1,145	1,288
Jun.	1,558	1,372	1,244	1,237
Sep.	---	1,416	1,249	1,191
Dec.	---	1,535	1,336	1,209
	---	5,595	4,974	4,924

Sales for the six months ended June 30, 1988 rose 14%, year to year, primarily because of major increases in semiconductors and defense electronics. Margins widened substantially, and operating income rose 125%. Following a 40% decline in other income, pretax income advanced 21%. After taxes at 28.8%, versus 24.0%, net income increased 13%, to $1.97 a share from $1.90 (restated).

Common Share Earnings ($)

Quarter:	1988	1987	1986	1985
Mar.	0.95	0.92	d0.18	0.12
Jun.	1.02	0.56	0.12	d0.05
Sep.	E1.00	0.63	0.14	d1.10
Dec.	E1.28	0.85	0.30	d0.55
	E4.25	2.96	0.38	d1.59

Important Developments

Jul. '88—TXN said that its higher margins in the first half principally resulted from improvement in the components segment. Profits in the defense electronics segment remained essentially unchanged despite a $14 million charge. Digital products operated at a loss.

Next earnings report expected in late October.

Per Share Data ($)

Yr. End Dec. 31[1]	1987	1986	1985	1984	1983	1982	1981	1980	1979	1978
Book Value	21.95	18.60	18.91	20.86	16.69	19.18	17.81	16.69	13.92	12.37
Earnings[1]	2.96	0.38	d1.59	4.35	d2.03	2.03	1.54	3.07	2.53	2.05
Dividends	0.70⅔	0.66⅔	0.66⅔	0.66⅔	0.66⅔	0.66⅔	0.66⅔	0.66⅔	0.66⅔	0.58⅓
Payout Ratio	23%	180%	NM	16%	NM	33%	43%	22%	26%	29%
Prices—High	80¼	49½	43⅞	49⅞	58¾	50⅞	42⅝	50¼	33¾	30⅞
Low	36¼	34¼	28¾	37¼	33¾	23½	25	26¼	26	20½
P/E Ratio—	27-12	NM	NM	11-9	NM	25-12	27-16	16-9	13-10	15-10

Data as orig. reptd. Adj. for stk. div(s). of 200% Jun. 1987. 1. Bef. spec. item(s) of +0.83 in 1987, -0.14 in 1986. NM-Not Meaningful. d-Deficit. E-Estimated.

Standard NYSE Stock Reports
Vol. 55/No. 202/Sec. 17

October 19, 1988

Standard & Poor's Corp.
25 Broadway, NY, NY 10004

2208 Texas Instruments Incorporate

Income Data (Million $)

Year Ended Dec. 31	Revs.	Oper. Inc.	% Oper. Inc. of Revs.	Cap. Exp.	Depr.	Int. Exp.	Net Bef. Taxes	Eff. Tax Rate	[2]Net Inc.	% Ne Inc. c Revs
1987	5,594	597	10.7%	[1]463	380	33.4	415	38.1%	257	4.6
1986	4,974	528	10.6%	447	426	38.2	99	59.6%	40	0.8
1985	4,924	488	9.9%	515	516	55.0	d115	NM	d119	NM
1984	5,742	948	16.5%	722	423	48.9	487	35.0%	316	5.5
1983	4,580	63	1.4%	479	351	36.0	d323	NM	d145	NM
1982	4,327	574	13.3%	342	339	33.1	213	32.4%	144	3.3
1981	4,206	586	13.9%	350	333	41.3	175	38.0%	109	2.6
1980	4,075	676	16.6%	548	257	44.3	379	44.0%	212	5.2
1979	3,224	507	15.7%	435	187	19.5	309	44.0%	173	5.4
1978	2,550	385	15.1%	311	131	8.4	257	45.5%	140	5.5

Balance Sheet Data (Million $)

Dec. 31	Cash	Current Assets	Current Liab.	Current Ratio	Total Assets	Ret. on Assets	Long Term Debt	Common Equity	Total Cap.	% LT Debt of Cap.	Ret. on Equi
1987	663	2,563	1,247	2.1	4,256	6.7%	487	1,726	2,733	17.8%	14.8
1986	214	1,781	1,113	1.6	3,337	1.2%	191	1,727	1,919	10.0%	1.8
1985	159	1,531	1,129	1.4	3,076	NM	382	1,428	1,810	21.1%	NM
1984	274	1,858	1,412	1.3	3,423	10.2%	381	1,541	1,921	19.8%	22.8
1983	185	1,452	1,231	1.2	2,713	NM	225	1,203	1,428	15.8%	NM
1982	420	1,527	959	1.6	2,631	5.8%	214	1,361	1,575	13.6%	11.0
1981	150	1,197	765	1.6	2,311	4.6%	212	1,260	1,472	14.4%	8.9
1980	140	1,299	971	1.3	2,414	9.7%	212	1,165	1,376	15.4%	19.9
1979	117	1,083	882	1.2	1,908	10.1%	18	953	970	1.8%	19.2
1978	115	915	637	1.4	1,518	10.1%	19	845	864	2.2%	17.7

Data as orig. reptd. 1. Net of curr. yr. retirement and disposals. 2. Bef. spec. item(s) in 1986. NM-Not Meaningful. d-Deficit.

Business Summary

Texas Instruments produces a variety of electrical and electronics products for industrial, consumer and government markets. Contributions (profits in million $) by industry segment in 1987:

	Sales	Profits
Components	42%	$346
Defense electronics	35%	212
Digital products	16%	-28
Metallurgical materials	3%	10
Services	4%	-10

Foreign sales accounted for 40% of revenues and 35% of operating income in 1987. Sales to the U.S. Government were 25% of the total.

Components include semiconductor integrated circuits, semiconductor discrete devices, assembled modules, and electrical and electronic control devices.

Defense electronics products include radar infrared surveillance systems and missile guidance and control systems.

Digital products include minicomputers, electronic data terminals and peripherals, geophysical and scientific equipment, electronic calculators, learning aids and other products.

Metallurgical materials primarily involve clad metals which are used in variety of application

Services (40%-owned since February, 1988) ar petroleum-exploration related.

Dividend Data

Dividends have been paid since 1962. A "pois pill" stock purchase right was adopted in 198

Amt. of Divd. $	Date Decl.	Ex-divd. Date	Stock of Record	Payme Date
0.18	Nov. 20	Dec. 24	Dec. 31	Jan. 25
0.18	Mar. 18	Mar. 23	Mar. 29	Apr. 25
0.18	Jun. 17	Jun. 24	Jun. 30	Jul. 25
0.18	Sep. 16	Sep. 21	Sep. 27	Oct. 24

Next dividend meeting: late Nov. '88.

Capitalization

Long Term Debt: $630,400,000.

Market Auction Pref. Stk.: 3,000 shs.

Conv. Money Market Cum. Pfd. Stk.: 2,208 sh 3 series.

Common Stock: 79,760,187 shs. ($1 par). Institutions hold approximately 74%. Shareholders of record: 32,914.

Office—13500 North Central Expressway, Dallas, Texas 75265. Tel—(214) 995-3773. Pres & Chrmn—J. R. Junkins. VP-Secy—R. J. Agnich CFO & Treas—W. A. Aylesworth. Investor Contact—M. Post. Dirs—B. M. Farber, G. W. Fronterhouse, D. C. Garrett, Jr., J. R. Junkins, E. R. I D. M. Roderick, M. Shepherd, Jr., J. C. Toomay, J. M. Voss, W. P. Weber. Transfer Agents & Registrars—First RepublicBank Dallas; Morgan Shareholder Services Trust Co., NYC. Incorporated in Delaware in 1938. Empl—75,347.

Information has been obtained from sources believed to be reliable, but its accuracy and completeness are not guaranteed. Paul H. Valentin

FIGURE 7-10: Sample, *Moody's Handbook of Common Stock*

TEXAS INSTRUMENTS INCORPORATED

LISTED	SYM.	LTPS♦	STPS♦	IND. DIV.	REC. PRICE	RANGE (52-WKS.)	YLD.
NYSE	TXN	68.0	93.0	$0.72	33	48 - 23	2.2%

MEDIUM GRADE. THIS LEADING PRODUCER OF SEMICONDUCTORS HAS A GOOD EARNINGS RECORD SUBJECT TO CYCLICAL SWINGS.

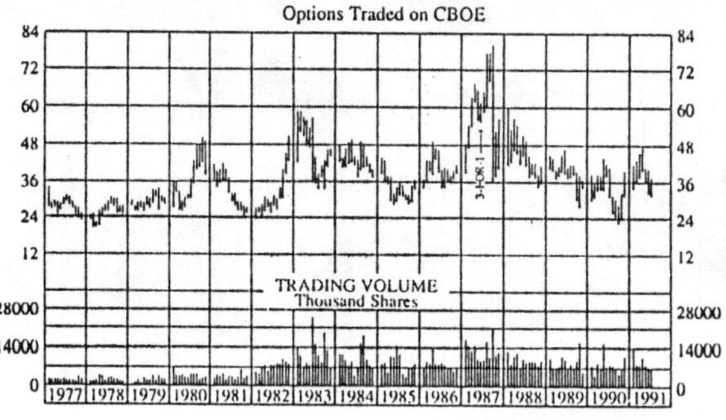

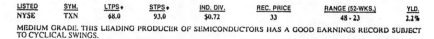

CAPITALIZATION: (12/31/90)

	(000)	(%)
Long-Term Debt	$ 715,000	23.2
Pref. Stk.	521,000	17.0
Com. & Surp.	1,837,000	59.8
Total	$3,073,000	100.0

Shs. ($1)-81,778,219

INTERIM EARNINGS:

Qtr.	3/31	6/30	9/30	12/31
1987ce	0.92	0.56	0.63	0.85
1988c	0.95	1.02	1.03	1.04
1989	0.90	1.14	0.67	0.33
1990	0.05	0.02	d0.19	d0.80
1991	d0.77	d1.99	...	...

INTERIM DIVIDENDS:

Amt.	Dec.	Ex.	Rec.	Pay.
0.18Q	6/15/90	6/20/90	6/26/90	7/23/90
0.18Q	9/21	9/26	10/2	10/29
0.18Q	11/16	11/12	12/31	1/28/91
0.18Q	3/15/91	3/20/91	3/26/91	4/22
0.18Q	6/21	6/27	7/3	7/22

BACKGROUND:

Texas Instruments develops, manufactures and sells products in the electrical and electronics industry for industrial, government and consumer markets. These products consist of semiconductors, such as integrated circuits, discrete devices and subassemblies, and electrical and electronic control devices; defense electronics such as radar, infrared surveillance systems, missile guidance and control systems, and electronic warfare systems; and digital products such as multiuser minicomputers, personal computers and workstations, software development tools, electronic data terminals and printers, industrial automation and control systems, electronic calculators and learning aids.

RECENT DEVELOPMENTS:

For the quarter ended 6/30/91, net loss totaled $157 million compared with net income of $11 million a year ago. Revenues increased 6% to $1.69 billion. The loss included a pretax charge of $130 million related to job attributions and an early retirment program. Poor results were attributed to weak demand for semiconductors and digital products as well as lower memory prices. Also, the drop in defense spending and lower demand for metallurgical materials contributed to the losses. Meanwhile, higher patent royalties benefited margins in the components segment.

PROSPECTS:

Despite the difficult enviroment for semiconductors, TI has invested heavily on the development of submicron CMOS wafer fabrication facilities in order to exploit market opportunities when conditions become favorable. Also, the shift in product mix towards the more profitable differentiated semiconductor products such as application specific integrated circuits will benefit results. TI's aggressive pursuit of patent royalties and lucrative agreements for patent cross licenses will help improve profits. However, further pricing pressures in the semiconductor industry combined with lower demand from the defense and automotive industry will severely hamper near-term earnings.

STATISTICS:

YEAR	GROSS REVS. ($mill.)	OPER. PROFIT MARGIN %	RET. ON EQUITY %	NET INCOME ($mill.)	WORK CAP. ($mill.)	SENIOR CAPITAL ($mill.)	SHARES (000)	EARN. PER SH.$	DIV. PER SH.$	DIV. PAY. %	PRICE RANGE	P/E RATIO	AVG. YIELD %
81	4,206.0	6.0	8.6	108.5	432.1	211.7	70,740	1.54	0.67	43	42⅛ - 25	21.8	2.0
82	4,326.6	5.4	10.6	144.0	422.4	214.0	70,956	2.03	0.67	33	50⅛ - 23½	18.3	1.8
83	4,579.8	d	—	d145.4	221.2	225.1	72,084	d2.03	0.67	—	58⅝ - 33⅝	—	1.4
84	5,741.6	9.2	20.5	316.0	446.2	380.7	73,848	4.35	0.67	15	49⅞ - 37¼	10.0	1.5
a85	4,924.5	d	d	ad118.7	401.8	381.9	75,504	ad1.59	0.67	—	43⅞ - 28¾	—	1.8
86	4,974.0	2.0	2.3	b39.9	668.3	191.4	76,722	b0.38	0.67	—	49⅜ - 34¼	N.M.	1.6
87	5,594.5	3.9	13.7	ce256.9	1,316.1	486.5	78,618	ce2.96	0.693	23	80¼ - 36¼	19.7	1.2
88	6,294.8	5.8	16.3	c366.3	1,349.2	1,144.6	80,646	c4.05	0.72	18	60 - 34½	11.7	1.5
89	6,521.9	4.9	11.7	291.7	1,143.6	1,138.3	81,504	3.04	0.72	24	46¾ - 28⅛	12.3	1.9
90	**6,567.0**	**d**	**d**	**d39.0**	**826.0**	**1,236.0**	**81,778**	**d0.92**	**0.72**	**—**	**44 - 22½**	**—**	**2.2**

♦Long-Term Price Score — Short-Term Price Score; see page 4a. STATISTICS ARE AS ORIGINALLY REPORTED. Adjusted for a 3-for-1 stock split, 6/87. a-Includes charge of $63.8 million for plant closing. b-Excludes loss from the redemption of debentures of $10.8 million ($0.14 a share). c-Includes gain of $191 million from settlement of litigation; 1987; and $124 million, 1988. e-Before extraordinary credit $51.0 million ($0.63 a share).

INCORPORATED:
Dec. 23, 1938 — DE

PRINCIPAL OFFICE:
P.O. Box 655474
Dallas TX 75265
Tel.: (214) 995-2011

ANNUAL MEETING:
Third Thursday in April

NUMBER OF STOCKHOLDERS:
36,268

TRANSFER AGENT(S):
Harris Trust and Savings Bank
Chicago, IL

REGISTRAR(S):
Harris Trust and Savings Bank
Chicago, Il

INSTITUTIONAL HOLDINGS:
No. of Institutions: 369
Shares Held: 54,996,776

OFFICERS:
Chmn., Pres. & C.E.O.
J. R. Junkins
Exec. Vice Presidents
W. I. George
W. B. Mitchell
W. P. Weber
Sr. V.P., Treas. & C.F.O.
W. A. Aylesworth
Sr. V.P., Sec. & Gen. Counsel
R. J. Agnich

FIGURE 7-11: Sample Page from *Value Line Investment Survey*

The Value Line— reported earnings plus depreciation (cash flow) multiplied by a number selected to correlate the stock's 3- to 5-year projected target price with cash flow projected to 1993-95.

Highest & lowest price of year.

Relative strength—past price performance relative to the Value Line Composite Average of 1700 stocks. Timeliness Rank usually predicts line's future direction.

Recent price—nine days prior to delivery date.

P/E ratio—the most recent price divided by the latest six months' earnings per share plus earnings estimated for the next six months.

P/E median—a rounded average of four middle values of the range of average annual price-earnings ratios over the past 10 years.

Relative P/E ratio—current P/E divided by the median P/E for all stocks under Value Line review.

Dividend yield—cash dividends estimated to be declared in the next 12 months by recent price.

The 3- to 5-year target price range, estimated. The range is placed in proper position on the price chart and is shown numerically in the "1993-95 Projections" box on the left side of price chart.

Monthly price ranges of the stock–plotted on a ratio (logarithmic) grid to show percentage changes in true proportion.

Options patch—indicates listed options are available on the stock and on what exchange they are most actively traded.

Number of shares traded monthly as a percentage of the total outstanding.

Statistical milestones that reveal significant long term trends presented in two ways: 1) upper series records results on a per-share basis; 2) lower records results on a company basis.

The Core of Value Line's advice—rank for Safety; Beta.

Projected average annual return based on estimated 3- to 5-year price appreciation plus dividend income.

Record of insider decisions by officers and directors to buy or sell as reported to the SEC a month or more after execution.

Record of decisions taken by the biggest institutions (over $70 million in equity holdings) to buy or sell during the past three quarters, how many shares were involved, and total number of shares they hold.

CATERPILLAR NYSE-CAT

TIMELINESS 3 Average (Relative Price Performance Next 12 Mos.)	
SAFETY 3 Average (Scale: 1 Highest to 5 Lowest)	
BETA 1.15 (1.00 = Market)	

1993-95 PROJECTIONS

	Price	Gain	Ann'l Total Return
High	135	(+185%)	32%
Low	90	(+90%)	20%

Insider Decisions

	N	D	J	F	M	A	M	J	J
to Buy	0	0	0	0	0	0	0	0	0
Options	0	0	0	0	1	0	1	4	2
to Sell	0	0	0	0	2	1	1	0	

Institutional Decisions

	3Q89	4Q89	1Q90
to Buy	99	104	143
to Sell	115	112	90
Hld'000	652284	679451	671411

RECENT PRICE	P/E RATIO	RELATIVE P/E RATIO	DIV'D YLD	VALUE LINE
47	17.1 (Trailing: 13.2 / Median: 18.0)	1.42	3.0%	1348

Target Price Range 1993 | 1994 | 1995

Options: ASE

Relative Price Strength

© VALUE LINE PUB., INC. 93-95

	1974	1975	1976	1977	1978	1979	1980	1981	1982	1983	1984	1985	1986	1987	1988	1989	1990	1991	93-95
Sales per sh A																		*127.75*	*161.80*
"Cash Flow" per sh	4.13	6.46	6.59	7.60	9.53	9.30	10.81	11.73	3.68	2.31	2.52	6.21	7.40	10.35	9.54	7.45		*9.80*	*14.80*
Earnings per sh B	2.67	4.65	4.45	5.16	6.56	5.69	6.53	6.64	d2.04	d3.12	d2.60	1.80	2.11	3.49	6.07	4.90		*5.10*	*12.10*
Div'ds Decl'd per sh C ■	1.10	1.23	1.46	1.58	1.88	2.10	2.33	2.40	2.40	1.50	.50	.50	.50	.75	1.20	1.20		*1.60*	*2.60*
Cap'l Spending per sh	4.08	5.19	5.75	5.99	6.29	7.82	8.66	8.14	6.05	3.41	2.42	2.97	4.60	7.82	10.74	9.35		*9.80*	*9.25*
Book Value per sh D	17.06	20.49	23.54	27.16	31.87	35.46	39.68	44.03	39.61	35.07	29.46	31.19	31.86	35.15	40.56	44.11	45.55	*49.00*	*92.20*
Common Shs Outst'g E	85.81	85.93	86.13	86.26	86.36	86.43	86.49	87.59	88.27	95.15	96.80	98.38	98.83	101.42	101.41	101.42	101.75	*102.00*	*102.75*
Avg Ann'l P/E Ratio																			*11.0*
Relative P/E Ratio	1.92	1.24	1.64	1.36	1.16	1.42	4.13												*.90*
Avg Ann'l Div'd Yield	3.0%	2.8%	2.6%	2.9%	3.4%	3.8%	4.0%												*2.3%*
Sales ($mill) F							8597.8	9154.5	6469.0	5424.0	6576.0	6725.0	7321.0	8180.0	10435	11126	11800	*10000*	*16625*
Operating Margin							14.0%	14.8%	3.9%	3.6%	6.4%	11.6%	9.4%	10.9%	13.7%	11.7%	9.0%	*11.0%*	*14.5%*
Depreciation ($mill)							370.2	448.4	505.0	286.0	492.0	436.0	403.0	348.0	434.0	471.0	480	*485*	*485*
Net Profit ($mill)							564.8	578.9	d180.0	d286.0	d248.0	207.0	178.0	348.0	616.0	497.0	290	*520*	*1035*
Income Tax Rate							30.1%	28.5%	NMF	NMF	NMF	12.0%	15.6%	27.7%	31.1%	26.1%	20.0%	*34.0%*	*26.0%*
Net Profit Margin							6.6%	6.3%	NMF	NMF	NMF	3.1%	2.4%	4.3%	5.9%	4.5%	2.4%	*4.0%*	*6.2%*
Working Cap'l ($mill)							1221.4	1174.9	2236.0	1807.0	976.0	1240.0	1183.0	1421.0	1882.0	1804.0	1680	*1745*	*2455*
Long-Term Debt ($mill) A							931.6	960.9	2389.0	1894.0	963.0	1177.0	963.0	1421.0	1953.0	2288.0	2270	*2365*	*2560*
Net Worth ($mill)							3432.0	3856.8	3496.0	3337.0	2852.0	3068.0	3149.0	3565.0	4113.0	4474.0	4605	*5000*	*7120*
% Earned Total Cap'l							13.7%	12.8%	NMF	NMF	NMF	6.4%	5.5%	8.9%	11.8%	8.8%	5.5%	*5.5%*	*12.0%*
% Earned Net Worth							16.5%	15.0%	NMF	NMF	NMF	6.7%	5.7%	9.8%	15.0%	11.1%	6.0%	*10.5%*	*14.5%*
% Retained to Comm Eq							10.6%	9.6%	NMF	NMF	NMF	5.2%	4.1%	8.4%	13.1%	8.4%	3.5%	*3.5%*	*11.0%*
% All Div'ds to Net Prof							36%	36%	NMF	NMF	NMF	24%	28%	14%	13%	24%	44%	*31%*	*26%*

Bold figures are Value Line estimates

Capital structure as of recent date showing percentage of capital in long-term debt (33%) and in common stock (67%); number of times that total interest charges were earned (2.8 in 1990).

Current position—assets, liabilities, and other components of working capital.

Annual rates of change (on a per-share basis). Actual past, estimated future.

Quarterly earnings shown on a per-share basis (estimates in bold type), quarterly sales on a gross basis.

Quarterly dividends paid are actual payments. Total of dividends paid in four quarters may not equal the figure shown in the annual series on dividends declared. (Sometimes a dividend declared at the end of the year will be paid in the first quarter of the following year.)

Footnotes explain a number of things: the way earnings are reported, whether "fully diluted," on a "primary" or on an "average share outstanding" basis.

CAPITAL STRUCTURE as of 3/31/90 A
Total Debt $4155 mill. Due in 5 Yrs $2882 mill.
LT Debt $2249 mill. LT Interest $198.0 mill.
(LT interest earned: 4.3x; total interest
coverage: 2.8x) (33% of Cap'l)

Pension Liability None

Pfd Stock None

Common Stock 101,422,807 shs. (67% of Cap'l)

CURRENT POSITION^A ($MILL)	1988	1989	3/31/90
Cash Assets	74.0	148.0	91.0
Receivables	2669.0	2813.0	3028.0
Inventory (LIFO)	1986.0	2120.0	2072.0
Other	588.0	627.0	636.0
Current Assets	5317.0	5708.0	5827.0
Accts Payable	1495.0	1550.0	1500.0
Debt Due	1307.0	1706.0	1906.0
Other	633.0	648.0	655.0
Current Liab.	3435.0	3904.0	4061.0

ANNUAL RATES of change (per sh)	Past 10 Yrs.	Past 5 Yrs.	Est'd '87-'89 to '93-'95
Sales	2.0%	8.0%	9.0%
"Cash Flow"	-2.5%	26.0%	8.5%
Earnings	--	--	13.0%
Dividends	-8.0%	-14.0%	21.0%
Book Value	2.5%	3.0%	9.5%

Cal-endar	QUARTERLY SALES ($ mill) A				Full Year
	Mar.31	Jun.30	Sep.30	Dec.31	
1987	1647	2042	2250	2241	8180.0
1988	2382	2602	2789	2662	10435
1989	2680	3041	2643	2762	11126
1990	2937	2947	*2900*	*3096*	*11880*
1991	*3200*	*3200*	*3400*	*3200*	*13000*

Cal-endar	EARNINGS PER SHARE B				Full Year
	Mar.31	Jun.30	Sep.30	Dec.31	
1987	d.36	1.15	1.45	1.25	3.49
1988	1.16	1.44	1.87	1.60	6.07
1989	1.39	1.39	1.07	1.05	4.90
1990	.97	.46	*.45*	*.87*	*2.75*
1991	*1.10*	*1.20*	*1.65*	*1.15*	*5.10*

Cal-endar	QUARTERLY DIVIDENDS PAID C ■				Full Year
	Mar.31	Jun.30	Sep.30	Dec.31	
1986	.125	.125	.125	.125	.50
1987	.125	.125	.125	.125	.50
1988	.187	.187	.187	.187	.75
1989	.30	.30	.30	.30	1.20
1990	.30				

(A) Includes Finance subsidiary from 1/88.
(B) Primary earnings. Excludes nonrecurring charges, net: '83, 62¢; '84, $1.87; '85, 9¢; '86, $1.03; '87, 90¢. Next earnings report due mid-

Factual material is obtained from sources

BUSINESS: Caterpillar Inc. is the world's largest producer of earthmoving equipment. Major markets include road building, mining, logging, agriculture, petroleum, and general construction. Products include tractors, scrapers, graders, compactors, loaders, off-highway trucks, and pipelayers. Also makes diesel & turbine engines and lift trucks. Has 30 plants, more than 1,000 dealers worldwide. International business accounts for over 50% of sales; R&D: 2.1%. 1989 depreciation rate: 6.6%. Estimated plant age: 9 years. Has about 60,785 employees, 34,755 stockholders. Insiders control .6% of stock. Chairman: G.A. Schaefer; President: Donald Fites. Incorporated: Delaware. Address: 100 N.E. Adams Street, Peoria, Illinois 61629. Telephone: 309-675-1000.

Caterpillar's shareholders are licking their wounds. Following Cat's June 25th revision of its economic outlook for the year, the price of these shares plunged by about 17%. On that date, the company revealed that profit for 1990 would be "substantially," below that generated in 1989. This would in large part reflect heavy losses in Brazil caused by a government-sponsored program there to stop runaway inflation. Since Cat maintains that detailed reporting on geographic segments is inappropriate and misleading, investors were unaware of the importance of Brazil to the company's profits. To its great surprise, Wall Street learned that although Brazil only accounted for about 5% of the company's sales last year, it contributed roughly $1 of the $4.90 that the company earned in 1989.

We've sharply reduced our earnings estimate for both 1990 and 1991. Under Brazilian accounting rules, inventories there are valued in dollars at historical costs and exchange rates. As a result of the rapid devaluation of the local currency (down about 50% vs. the dollar in the June quarter alone), inventory costs are far higher than current costs when translated into dollars at current exchange rates. Thus, until older, higher-dollar-value inventory is sold, continued losses are in prospect there. Moreover, as that country attempts to restructure its economy, it's not clear that Cat will continue to receive such favorable tax treatment—it paid no Brazilian tax at all in '89. Still, Brazil was not the only problem in the June quarter. The company's Plant With A Future program is behind schedule, delaying the "crossover point"(when its benefits exceed its costs) at least until the second quarter of 1991. And the company continues to suffer from weak sales to the domestic construction industry, and an unfavorable yen-dollar relationship which enhances the competitive position of its Asian rival. In all, we now look for earnings of $2.75 a share in 1990, and tentatively estimate a partial earnings recovery to $5.10 a share in 1991.

There's no urgent reason to buy Cat shares at this point, although patient investors are likely to be amply rewarded over the 3- to 5-year pull.

Mark Leach   *August 17, 1990*

Oct. (C) Next dividend meeting about Sept. 12. Goes ex about Oct. 23. Approximate dividend payment dates: 20th of Feb, May, Aug, Nov. ■ Dividend reinvestment plan available. (D) Incl.

intangibles. In '89 $147.7 mill. $12.87/sh. (E) In millions. (F) Depreciation on accelerated basis.

believed to be reliable, but the publisher is not responsible for any errors or omissions contained herein.

Condensed summary of the business.

A 400-word report on recent developments and prospects issued once every three months on preset schedule.

Date of delivery—aims for delivery to every subscriber on Friday afternoon.

Value indexes of financial strength, price stability, price growth persistence, & earnings predictability.

Company's Financial Strength	A
Stock's Price Stability	55
Price Growth Persistence	20
Earnings Predictability	15

FIGURE 7-12: Additional Information from *Value Line Investment Survey*

Building Your Portfolio		Maintaining Your Portfolio
What Value Line Does	**What You Do**	

By Industry—Timeliness ™

Value Line ranks groups in order of their Timeliness (Relative Performance in the Next 12 Months). You will find them listed on page 24 of the *Summary & Index*.	Read the latest Value Line reports on the 25 top-ranked industries. Select eight or more industry groups from among the 25 that Value Line ranks the most timely. See page 1 of the *Summary & Index* for the page numbers of these industry reports.	

By Stock—Timeliness ™

Value Line ranks 1700 (plus) stocks in five categories according to their Timeliness. The top 100 stocks are ranked 1 (Highest) for performance in the next 12 months; 300 are ranked 2 (Above Average); about 900, 3 (Average); 300, 4 (Below Average); and 100, 5 (Lowest).	Make up a list of those stocks included in your eight or more most timely industry groups that are also ranked 1 (Highest) or 2 (Above Average) for Performance in the Next 12 Months. You will find the latest full-page report on each stock in *Ratings & Reports*.	When and if a stock in your portfolio is found to be no longer a relatively timely investment—that is to say, it has fallen in rank to 4 or 5 for Timeliness—make that stock a candidate for sale. (See Post Script and Note at the bottom of this page.)

By Stock—Safety ™

Value Line also ranks 1700 (plus) stocks according to their Safety in five categories with 1 (Highest) expected to be least volatile and financially most strong, and 5 (Lowest) most volatile and least strong financially.	Eliminate from this list of timely stocks in timely industries those that fall short of your Safety standard.	These safety ranks are significant and should not be ignored. (If you wish to rely on the Beta count please see page 49 of the "Subscriber's Guide.")

By Stock—Income

Value Line estimates the next 12 months' dividend yield of each stock at its most recent price. The expected yield is updated in the weekly *Summary & Index*. Value Line also shows, for comparative purposes, the median yield of all dividend-paying stocks on the first page of the weekly *Summary & Index*.	Eliminate from your list of timely stocks in timely industries, which also have met your Safety standard or your Beta constraint, those that fall short of your current-income standard. For example, if your standard is 4%, eliminate stocks that yield less that 4%. Or if you accept a stock that yields less than 4%, see to it that other stocks you select yield enough more to bring the average up to 4%.	When a stock is sold, replace it with another stock ranked 1 or 2 for Timeliness that also meets your standards for Safety and current income. It would be best in the long run to maintain diversification through 15 or more stocks in more than eight different industries. (See Note below.)

Value Line Reports

Value Line reports on each stock and each industry once every three months, on a preset schedule, in the *Ratings & Reports* section. The page numbers on which the reports appear are shown in the weekly *Summary & Index*. When new evidence requires, a "Supplementary Report" is published as often as weekly. The "Supplementary Reports" appear in the final pages of the *Ratings & Reports* section.

Read the latest Value Line reports on the industry groups and stocks that have qualified according to all your standards.

Make your final selection of 15 or more stocks from the list that has been refined through the above procedures. See to it that you have stock representation in at least eight different industry groups.

Selection & Opinion

Value Line's *Selection & Opinion* section provides a current appraisal of the economy and of the stock market. It recommends how much of one's capital should be invested in common stocks and how much set aside temporarily in cash reserves. Value Line will recommend the types of bonds or other safe haven for cash-reserve investment when such a cash reserve seems timely. Value Line will also recommend, as a general strategy, investment in stocks with lower Beta counts if we believe that stocks in general are overvalued in the marketplace.

When the Value Line service in its *Selection & Opinion* section recommends building cash reserves because the general market seems temporarily to be too high, sell stocks and invest instead in short-term government bonds or other safe instruments, which will be recommended in the *Selection & Opinion* section. In selling, dispose of stocks ranked 5 or 4 or 3, in that order.

Post Script: Aggressive accounts may follow a policy of switching out of stocks when they fall to rank 3 for Timeliness and replacing them with others ranked 1. This strategy, of course, will result in a higher turnover rate. Tests have shown that, if followed consistently year in and year out, such a strategy will give an even higher return than the less aggressive policy of switching only when stocks have fallen to ranks 4 and 5.

Note: There can be no assurance that every one of the 1700-odd stocks will always perform in accordance with its rank for Timeliness. But it can be said that such a high percentage have done so in the past that you place the odds strongly in your favor if you keep your portfolio lined up with the Timeliness Ranks. Note that diversification is essential to this strategy.

Of the Safety Ranks it can be said that stocks ranked high for Safety have held up better than average during significant market declines in the past. In strongly rising markets, however, Safety could prove to be a restraining influence upon performance. For example, in the case of two stocks, both ranked 1 (Highest) for Timeliness, the stock ranked 1 for Safety will tend to go up less than another ranked 5 for Safety during a rising phase in the market. Conversely, in a down market, a high Safety Rank would help the stock ranked 1 (Highest) for Timeliness hold up better than another stock ranked 1 for Timeliness that rated low for Safety.

In the case of well diversified portfolios—those consisting of 15 or more stocks in more than eight different industries—we recommend that risk be controlled by applying Beta counts instead of the Safety ranks. (See page 48 of the "Subscriber's Guide.")

Explanation: In a widely diversified portfolio, the variations in individual stock prices in response to their individual characteristic risks tend to cancel each other out, leaving the general market fluctuation as the main influence. The Beta measures the individual stock's sensitivity to the general market. The Safety Rank, on the other hand, is a measure of the stock's total risk, i.e., sensitivity to the market plus restraining influence to all other factors affecting the individual stock's price.

Stock Rating Systems

STANDARD & POOR'S COMMON STOCK EARNINGS AND DIVIDEND RANKINGS

The investment process involves assessment of various factors—such as product and industry position, corporate resources, and financial policy—resulting in some common stocks being more highly esteemed than others. In this assessment, Standard & Poor's believes that earnings and dividend performance is the end result of the interplay of these factors and that, over the long run, the record of this performance has a considerable bearing on relative quality. The rankings, however, do not pretend to reflect all of the factors, tangible or intangible, that bear on stock quality.

Relative quality of bonds or other debt, that is, degrees of protection for principal and interest (called creditworthiness), cannot be applied to common stocks, and therefore rankings are not to be confused with bond quality ratings, which necessarily are arrived at by a different approach.

Growth and stability of earnings and dividends are deemed key elements in establishing S&P's earnings and dividend rankings for common stocks, which are designed to capsulize the nature of this record in a single symbol. It should be noted, however, that the process also takes into consideration certain adjustments and modifications deemed desirable in establishing such rankings.

The point of departure in arriving at these rankings is a computerized scoring system based on per share earnings and dividend records of the most recent 10 years—a period deemed long enough to measure significant time segments of secular growth, to capture indications of basic change in trend as they develop, and to encompass the full peak-to-peak range of the business cycle. Basic scores are computed for earnings and dividends, then adjusted as indicated by a set of predetermined modifiers for growth, stability within long-term trend, and cyclicality. Adjusted scores for earnings and dividends are then combined to yield a final score.

Further, the ranking system makes allowance for the fact that, in general, corporate size imparts certain recognized advantages from an investment standpoint. Conversely, minimum size limits (in terms of corporate sales volume) are set for the various rankings; but the system provides for making exceptions where the score reflects an outstanding earnings-dividend record.

The final score for each stock is measured against a scoring matrix determined by analyzing the scores of a large and representative sample of stocks. The range of scores in this sample has been aligned with the following ladder of rankings:

A+ Highest	B+ Average	C Lowest
A High	B Below Average	D In Reorganization
A- Above Average	B- Lower	

NR signifies no ranking because of insufficient data or because the stock is not amenable to the ranking process. The positions as determined above may be modified in some instances by special considerations, such as natural disasters, massive strikes, and nonrecurring accounting adjustments.

A ranking is not a forecast of future market price performance, but is basically an appraisal of past performance of earnings and dividends, and relative current standing. These rankings must not be used as market recommendations; a high-score stock may at times be so overpriced as to justify its sale, whereas a low-score stock may be attractively priced for purchase. Rankings based on earnings and dividend records are no substitute for complete analysis. They cannot take into account potential effects of management changes, internal company policies not yet fully reflected in the earnings and dividend record, public relations standing, recent competitive shifts, and a host of other factors that may be relevant to investment status and decision making.

STANDARD & POOR'S PREFERRED STOCK RATINGS

A Standard and Poor's preferred stock rating is an assessment of the capacity and willingness of an issuer to pay preferred stock dividends and any applicable sinking fund obligations. A preferred stock rating differs from a bond rating inasmuch as it is assigned to an equity issue, which is intrinsically different from and subordinate to, a debt issue. Therefore, to reflect this difference, the preferred stock rating symbol will normally not be higher than the bond rating symbol assigned to, or that would be assigned to, the senior debt of the same issuer. See Table 7-6 for a list of symbols and explanation of what they mean.

The preferred stock ratings are based on the following three considerations:

1. Likelihood of payment. Capacity and willingness of the issuer to meet the timely payment of preferred stock dividends and any applicable sinking fund requirements in accordance with the terms of the obligation.

2. Nature and provisions of the issue (e.g., cumulative, participative, or convertible.)

3. Relative position of the issue in the event of bankruptcy, reorganization, or other arrangements affecting creditors' rights, in terms of its seniority on claims of earnings over other securities.

TABLE 7-6:   Standard & Poor's Rating Guide—Preferred Stock

AAA   The highest rating they may be assigned to a preferred stock issue; indicates an extremely strong capacity to pay the preferred stock obligations.

AA   Also qualifies as a high-quality, fixed-income security. The capacity to pay obligations is very strong, although not as strong as for issues rated AAA.

A   Issue is backed by a sound capacity to pay obligations, although it is somewhat more susceptible to the adverse effects of changes in circumstances and economic conditions.

BBB   Issue is backed by an adequate capacity to pay obligations. Whereas BBB-rated issues normally exhibit adequate protection parameters, adverse economic conditions or changing circumstances are more likely to lead to a weakened capacity to make payments for a preferred stock in this category than for A-rated issues.

BB, B,   Regarded, on balance, as predominately speculative issues with respect to the
CCC   issuer's capacity to pay obligations. BB indicates the lowest degree of speculation and CCC the highest degree of speculation within this category. Whereas such issues will likely have some quality of protection, safety is outweighed by marked uncertainty or major risk exposure to adverse conditions.

CC   The rating reserved for an issue in arrears on dividends or sinking fund payments but one that is currently paying.

C   The rating reserved for a nonpaying issue.

D   The rating reserved for a nonpaying issue with the issuer in default on debt instruments.

NR   Indicates that no rating has been requested, that there is insufficient information on which to base a rating, or that S&P does not rate the type of obligation in question as a matter of policy.

(+) or (-)   The ratings from AA to CCC may be further modified by the addition of a plus (+) or minus (-) sign to show relative standing within a major rating category.

Source: *Security Owner's Stock Guide,* June, 1991. Standard & Poor's Corporation, 25 Broadway, New York, NY 10014.

The strategy is to find a preferred issue with dividends in arrears and selling at a very low price relative to what its value should be if the arrearage were paid and regular dividend payments resumed. To accomplish this, first look for a company in a turnaround situation with respect to its earnings. Earnings improvement is the key to resuming preferred dividends, particularly if the company has a history of paying dividends on the common stock and hopes to resume these payments. Second, you might consider companies that are likely to be taken over. Part of the takeover agreement might stipulate that preferred stock be retired at its face value and any arrearages paid.

MOODY'S PREFERRED STOCK RATING SYSTEM

Moody's uses a slightly different system, seen in Table 7-7, than Standard & Poor's. These ratings are intended to indicate the quality of the issue and are based largely on an assessment of the firm's ability to pay preferred dividends in a prompt and timely fashion. *NOTE: Preferred stock ratings should not be compared with bond ratings, as they are not equivalent.*

FITCH PREFERRED STOCK RATING SYMBOLS

Ratings of preferred stock should be viewed within the framework of preferred stocks and in relationship to bonds. Preferred stocks, by definition, are junior to debt obligations. Preferred capital is basically permanent capital although sinking funds that provide for repayment of capital give investors added protection. Preferred dividends are payable only when declared; they are not contractually guaranteed. See Figure 7-8.

TABLE 7-7: Moody's Preferred Stock Rating System

aaa	Top quality
aa	High grade
a	Upper medium grade
baa	Lower medium grade
ba	Speculative type
b	Little assurance of future dividends
caa	Likely already to be in arrears

TABLE 7-8: Fitch Rating Guide—Preferred Stock

AAA The highest quality rating in the universe of preferred and preference stocks. Strong asset protection, conservative balance sheet ratios, and positive indications of continued protection of preferred dividend requirements are prerequisites for an AAA rating.

AA Very high quality. Maintenance of asset protection and dividend-paying ability appear assured but not quite to the extent of AAA issues.

A Good quality. Asset protection and coverage of preferred dividend are considered adequate and are expected to be maintained.

BBB Reasonably safe, but issues lack the more protective assurances of the A to AAA ratings. Current results should be watched for signs of possible deterioration.

BB Considered speculative. The margin of protection is slim or subject to wide fluctuations. The longer-term financial capacities of the enterprises cannot be predicted with assurance.

B Highly speculative. Whereas earnings should normally cover dividends, directors may reduce or omit payment due to unfavorable developments, inability to finance, or wide fluctuations in earnings.

CCC The issue is hazardous and should be assessed on its prospects in a possible reorganization.

Fixed-Income
Securities

OVERVIEW

Fixed-income securities generally stress current fixed income and offer little or no opportunity for appreciation in value. They are usually liquid and bear less market risk than other types of investments. Fixed-income investments perform well during stable economic conditions and lower inflation. As interest rates drop, the price of fixed-income investments increases. Examples of fixed-income securities include corporate bonds, convertible bonds, government bonds, tax-exempt bonds, and short-term debt securities.

This chapter covers basics of corporate and government bonds and the types of bonds issued, how to calculate bond yields and read bond quotations, selecting the right bond for you, other short-term, fixed-income securities, and sources of information on fixed-income securities.

UNDERSTANDING BONDS

A **bond** is a certificate or security showing that you loaned funds to a company or to a government in return for fixed future interest and repayment of principal. Bonds offer the following advantages:

- Annual fixed-interest income
- Safety over equity securities (e.g., common stock) because bondholders have senior priority over common stockholders in the distribution of earnings and in the event of corporate bankruptcy.

Bondholders suffer the following disadvantages:

- They do not participate in incremental profitability.
- They have no voting right.

Terms and Features of Bonds

The terms and features that apply specifically to bonds are discussed in the following sections.

Par Value

The par value of a bond is the face value, usually $1,000.

Coupon Rate

The coupon rate is the nominal interest rate that determines the actual interest to be received on a bond. It is an annual interest per par value. For example, if you own a $1,000 bond with a coupon rate of 6 percent, the annual interest payment is

$$\$1,000 \times 6\% = \$60$$

Maturity Date

This is the final date on which repayment of the bond principal is due.

Indenture

A bond indenture is the lengthy legal agreement detailing the issuer's obligations pertaining to a bond issue. It contains the terms of the bond issue as well as any restrictive provisions placed on the firm, known as **restrictive covenants**. A restrictive covenant may include maintenance of required levels of working capital, a particular current ratio, and a specified debt ratio. The indenture is administered by an independent trustee.

Trustee

The trustee is the third party with whom the indenture is made. The trustee's job is to see that the terms of the indenture are carried out.

Yield

The yield, different from the coupon interest rate, is the effective interest rate earned on a bond investment. If a bond is bought below its face value (i.e., purchased at a discount), the yield is higher than the coupon rate. If a bond is acquired above face value (i.e., bought at a premium), the yield is below the coupon rate.

Calculations of various yield measures on a bond are given later in this chapter.

Call Provision

A call provision entitles the corporation to repurchase, or "call," the bond from their holders at stated prices over specified periods.

Sinking Fund

In a sinking fund bond, money is put aside by the company periodically for the repayment of debt, thus reducing the total amount of debt outstanding. This particular provision may be included in the bond indenture so as to protect investors.

Types of Bonds

There are many types of bonds, each type noted by different criteria.

Mortgage Bonds

Mortgage bonds are secured by physical property. In case of default, the bondholders may foreclose on the secured property and sell it to satisfy their claims.

Debentures

Debentures are unsecured bonds. They are protected by the general credit of the issuing corporation. Credit ratings are very important for this type of bond. Federal, state, and municipal government issues are debentures. Subordinated debentures are junior issues ranking after other unsecured debt as a result of explicit provisions in the indenture. Finance companies have made extensive use of these types of bonds.

Convertible Bonds

Convertible bonds are subordinated debentures that may be converted, at your option, into a specified amount of other securities (usually common stock) at a fixed price. They are hybrid securities in that they have characteristics of both bonds and common stock and provide fixed-interest income and potential appreciation through participation in future price increases of the underlying common stock.

Income Bonds

Income bonds pay interest only if it's earned. They are often called reorganization bonds.

Tax-Exempt Bonds

Tax-exempt bonds are usually municipal bonds where interest income is not subject to federal tax, although the Tax Reform Act (TRA) of 1986 imposed restrictions on the issuance of tax-exempt municipal bonds. Municipal bonds may carry a lower interest than taxable bonds of similar quality and safety. However, after-tax yield from these bonds is usually more than that from a bond with a higher rate of taxable interest. *NOTE: Municipal bonds are subject to two major risks—interest rate and default.*

U.S. Government Securities

Government securities include bills, notes, bonds, and mortgages such as Ginnie Maes (GNMAs) or Fannie Maes (FNMAs). Treasury bills represent short-term government financing and mature in 12 months or less. U.S. Treasury notes mature in 1 to 10 years, whereas Treasury bonds mature in 10 to 25 years and can be purchased in denominations as low as $1,000. All of these U.S. government securities are subject to federal income taxes but not state and local taxes. Ginnie Maes represent pools of 25- to 30-year Federal Housing Administration (FHA) or Veterans Administration (VA) mortgages guaranteed by the Government National Mortgage Association.

Zero-Coupon Bonds

Instead of being paid out directly, zero-coupon bond interest is added to the principal semiannually and both the principal and accumulated interest are paid at maturity. The effect of this compounding factor is that, at maturity, a zero-coupon bondholder receives higher returns on the original investment. Zero-coupon bonds are not fixed-income securities in the historical sense because they provide no periodic income; interest is paid at maturity. However, accrued interest, though not received, is taxable yearly as ordinary income. Zero-coupon bonds have two basic advantages over regular coupon-bearing bonds: A relatively small investment is required to buy these bonds and you are assured a specific yield throughout the term of the investment.

Junk Bonds

Junk bonds are bonds with a speculative credit rating of BB or lower by Moody's and Standard & Poor's rating systems. Junk bonds are issued by companies with no track records of sales and earnings and therefore considered risky for conservative investors. Because junk bonds are known for their high yields, many risk-oriented investors specialize in trading them.

Serial Bonds

Serial bonds mature in installments over time rather than at one maturity date.

SELECTING A BOND

When selecting a bond, five factors should be taken into consideration:

1. Investment quality (bond rating)
2. Length of maturity (short term, 0–5 years; medium term, 6–15 years; long term, more than 15 years)
3. Bond features (call or conversion)
4. Tax status
5. Yield to maturity

TABLE 8-1: Description of Bond Ratings

Moody's	Standard & Poor's	Quality Indication
Aaa	AAA	Highest quality
Aa	AA	High quality
A	A	Upper medium grade
Baa	BBB	Medium grade
Ba	BB	Contains speculative elements
B	B	Outright speculative
Caa	CCC and CC	Default definitely possible
Ca	C	Default, partial recovery likely
C	D	Default, little recovery likely

NOTE: Ratings may also include a + or - sign to show relative standings in class.

Quality

The investment quality of a bond is measured by its bond rating, which reflects the degree of probability that a bond issue will go into default. The rating should influence your perception of risk and therefore dictate the interest rate you are willing to accept, the price you are willing to pay, and the maturity period you are willing to agree to.

Bond investors tend to place more emphasis on independent analyses of quality than do common stock investors. Bond analyses and ratings are done by Standard & Poor's and Moody's, among others. Table 8-1 lists the designations used by these well-known independent agencies, along with brief summaries of each ranking. For original descriptions, see Moody's **Bond Record** and Standard & Poor's **Bond Guide**.

Pay careful attention to ratings—they can affect not only potential market behavior but relative yields as well. The higher the rating, the lower the yield of a bond, other things being equal. *NOTE: Because ratings change over time, the rating agencies have "credit watch lists" of various types. See if you can select only those bonds rated Baa or above by Moody's or BBB or above by Standard & Poor's, even though doing so means giving up about 3/4 of a percentage point in yield.*

Maturity

In addition to watching the ratings, you can control the risk element through the maturities you select. The maturity indicates how much you stand to lose if interest rates rise. The longer a bond's maturity, the more volatile its price. The trade-off? Shorter maturities usually mean lower yields. If you are a conservative investor, select bonds with maturities of no more than 10 years. The longer a bond's maturity, the greater its price susceptibility to changing interest rates.

Features

Check to see if a bond has a call provision, which gives the issuing company the option of redeeming bonds after a certain date, rather than at maturity. If an issue is called, you are generally paid a small premium over par but not as much had you held the bond until maturity. Bonds are usually called only if their interest rates are higher than the going market rate. *NOTE: Try to avoid bonds of companies that have a call provision and may be involved in event risk (e.g., mergers and acquisitions or leveraged buyouts).*

Also check to see if a bond is convertible, that is, can it be converted into common stock at a later date? Convertibles provide fixed income in the form of interest. You also can benefit from the appreciation value of common stock. *NOTE: If you have only a small amount to invest or would like to have someone else make the selection, you can buy shares in one of the bond (income) mutual funds.*

Tax Status

If you are in a high tax bracket, you may want to consider tax-exempt bonds. Most municipal bonds are rated A or above, making them a good grade risk. They can also be bought in mutual funds.

Yield to Maturity

Yield has a lot to do with the rating of a bond. Calculation of yield is taken up in the next section. *NOTE: A bond may be bought at a discount (below face value) when there is a long maturity period, it is issued by a risky company, or its interest rate is less than the current market interest rate. Conversely, a bond may be bought at a premium (above face value) when the aforementioned circumstances are opposite.*

CALCULATING BOND YIELD (EFFECTIVE RATE OF RETURN)

Bonds are evaluated based on many different types of returns including current yield, yield to maturity, yield to call, realized yield, and before-tax yield.

Current Yield

Current yield is the annual interest payment divided by the current price of the bond. Current yield of bonds is reported in the *Wall Street Journal*, among other places. The formula for current yield is:

$$\text{Current yield} = \frac{\text{Annual interest payment}}{\text{Current price}}$$

EXAMPLE 1

A 12% coupon rate $1,000 par value bond is selling for $960. The annual interest payment is $1,000 x 0.12 = $120. What is the current yield?

$$\frac{\$120}{\$960} = 12.5\%$$

The problem with current yield is that it does not take into account the bond's maturity date. A bond with 1 year to run and another with 15 years to run would have the same current yield quote if interest payments were $120 and the price were $960. Clearly, the one-year bond would be preferable under this circumstance because you would get not only $120 in interest, but a gain of $40 ($1,000 – $960) with a one-year time period, and this amount could be reinvested.

Yield to Maturity (YTM)

The yield to maturity takes into account the maturity date of the bond. It is the real return you would receive from interest income plus capital gain, assuming the bond is held to maturity. Exact calculation of this measure is a little complicated and is not presented here. But the approximate method is as follows:

$$YTM = I + \frac{\dfrac{(\$1,000 - V)}{n}}{\dfrac{(\$1,000 + V)}{2}}$$

where I = dollars of interest paid per year, V = the market value of the bond, and n = number of years to maturity.

EXAMPLE 2

Assume you were offered a 10-year, 8% coupon, $1,000 par value bond at a price of $877.70. What is the rate of return (yield) you could earn if you bought the bond and held it to maturity? Is the yield greater or lower than the coupon rate?

$$YTM = \$80 + \frac{\dfrac{(\$1,000 - \$877.70)}{10}}{\dfrac{\$1,000 + \$877.70)}{2}}$$

$$= \frac{\$80 + \$12.23}{\$938.85} = \frac{\$92.23}{\$938.85} = 9.82\%$$

Because the bond was bought at a discount, the yield (9.82%) came to more than the coupon rate of 8%.

Yield to Call

Not all bonds are held to maturity. If the bond is callable prior to maturity, the yield to maturity formula will have the call price in place of the par value of $1,000.

EXAMPLE 3 _____

A 20-year bond was initially issued at a 13.5% coupon rate. After two years, rates have dropped. The bond is currently selling for $1,180, the yield to maturity on the bond is 11.15%, and the bond can be called in five years after issue at $1,090. Thus if you buy the bond two years after issue, your bond may be called back after three more years at $1,090. To compute the yield to call:

$$\dfrac{\$135 + \dfrac{(\$1,090 - \$1,180)}{3}}{\dfrac{(\$1,090 + \$1,180)}{2}}$$

$$= \dfrac{\$135 + \dfrac{(-\$90)}{3}}{\$1,135} = \dfrac{\$105}{\$1,135} = 9.25\%$$

NOTE: The yield to call of 9.25% is 190 basis points less than the yield to maturity of 11.15%. You must be aware of the differential because a lower return is earned.

Realized Yield

You may trade in and out of a bond long before it matures. You obviously need a measure of return to evaluate the investment appeal of any bonds you intend to buy and sell. Realized yield is used for this purpose. This measure is simply a variation of yield to maturity, as only two variables are changed in the yield to maturity formula to provide this measure. Future price is used in place of par value ($1,000), and the length of holding period is substituted for the number of years to maturity.

EXAMPLE 4 _____

Referring to Example 2, assume that you anticipate holding the bond for only three years and that you estimate interest rates will change in the future so that the price of the bond will move to about $925 from its present level of $877.70. Thus, you will

TABLE 8-2: Bond Value Table Sample

Yield to Maturity (Percent)	Coupon Rate (10 Percent)				Coupon Rate (12 Percent)				Yield to Maturity (Percent)
	1 Year	5 Years	10 Years	20 Years	1 Year	5 Years	10 Years	20 Years	
8%	101.89%	108.11%	113.50%	119.79%	103.77%	116.22%	127.18%	139.59%	8%
9	100.94	103.96	106.50	109.20	102.81	111.87	119.51	127.60	9
10	100.00	100.00	100.00	100.00	101.86	107.72	112.46	117.16	10
11	99.08	96.23	94.02	91.98	100.92	103.77	105.98	108.02	11
12	98.17	92.64	88.53	84.93	100.00	100.00	100.00	100.00	12
13	97.27	89.22	83.47	78.78	99.09	96.41	94.49	92.93	13
14	96.38	85.95	78.81	73.34	98.19	92.98	89.41	86.67	14

Reprinted from the *Thorndike Encyclopedia of Banking and Financial Tables.* ©Warren Gorham and Lamont. All rights reserved.

buy the bond today at a market price of $877.70 and sell the issue three years later at a price of $925. Compute the realized yield.

$$\text{Realized yield} = \frac{\$80 + \dfrac{(\$925 - \$877.70)}{3}}{\dfrac{(\$925 + \$877.70)}{2}}$$

$$= \frac{\$80 + \$15.77}{\$901.35} = \frac{\$95.77}{\$901.35} = 10.63\%$$

NOTE: You can use a bond table to find the value for various yield measures. One source is Thorndike Encyclopedia of Banking and Financial Tables *(see Table 8-2).*

Equivalent Before-Tax Yield

Yield on a municipal bond needs to be looked at on an equivalent before-tax yield basis, because the interest received is not subject to federal income taxes. The formula used to equate interest on municipals to other investments is:

$$\text{Tax equivalent yield} = \frac{\text{Tax - exempt yield}}{(1 - \text{tax rate})}$$

EXAMPLE 5

Assume you have a marginal tax rate of 28% and are evaluating a municipal bond paying 10% interest. What is the equivalent before-tax yield on a taxable investment?

$$\frac{10\%}{(1 - .28)} = 13.9\%$$

Thus you could choose between a taxable investment paying 13.9% and a tax-exempt bond paying 10% and be indifferent between the two.

FIXED-INCOME SECURITIES: SHORT-TERM "PARKING LOTS"

Besides bonds and preferred stock, you may choose other significant forms of debt instruments; they are primarily short-term in nature. You may treat them as "parking lots" until you decide what your next investment should be.

Certificates of Deposit (CDs)

These safe instruments are issued by commercial banks and thrift institutions and traditionally have been in amounts of $10,000 or $100,000 (jumbo CDs). You can invest in a CD for much less (e.g., $2,000 or $5,000). CDs have a fixed maturity period varying from several months to many years. However, a penalty exists for cashing in a certificate prior to its maturity date.

Commercial Paper

Commercial paper is issued to the public by large corporations. It usually comes in minimum denominations of $25,000. Commercial paper represents an unsecured promissory note and usually has higher yield than small CDs. The maturity is usually 30, 60, and 90 days. The degree of risk depends on the company's credit rating.

Treasury Bills

Treasury bills have a maximum maturity of one year, common maturities of 91 and 182 days. T-bills trade in minimum units of $10,000. They do not pay interest in the traditional sense; they are sold at a discount and redeemed at face value when the maturity date comes around. T-bills are extremely liquid in that there is an active secondary or resale market for them. T-bills carry extremely low risk because they are backed by the U.S. government. Yields on discount securities such as T-bills are calculated using the formula:

$$\frac{\$10,000 - P}{P} \times \frac{365}{\text{Days to maturity}}$$

where P = purchase price. The formula states the yield on the discount security is equal to the gain on the bill relative to its face of $10,000, ($10,000 – P) divided by P, multiplied by a factor that annualizes this gain, 365 divided by days to maturity.

EXAMPLE 6

Assume that P = $9,800. What is the T-bill yield?

$$\frac{\$10,000 - \$9,800}{\$9,800} \times \frac{365}{90} = \frac{\$200}{\$9,800} \times 4.05 = 8.27\%$$

Money Market Funds

Money market funds are special forms of mutual funds. You can own a portfolio of high-yielding CDs, T-bills, and other similar short-term securities, with a small amount. There is a great deal of liquidity and flexibility in withdrawing funds through check-writing privileges (the usual minimum withdrawal is $500). Money market funds are considered conservative, because most securities purchased by the funds are quite safe. (For more about money market funds, refer to Chapter 9, Mutual Funds.)

READING BOND QUOTATIONS

Corporate Bond Quotations

Corporate bond prices appear in the financial pages of many newspapers. A typical listing, as reported by the *Wall Street Journal,* and explanations are shown below. Figure 8-1 reproduces typical *Investor's Business Daily* bond quotations.

Bonds	Cur Yld	Vol	Close	Net Chg
IBM 7.7s 04	8.3	7	92 1/4	+1 5/8
NWA 71/2 10	cv.	24	104	-1/2
(1) (2)	(3)	(4)	(5)	(6)

(1) Name of issuer: IBM is an abbreviation for International Business Machines.
(2) Coupon rate of interest and the year of maturity: 7.7s denotes the bond pays $77 a year interest, which is 0.077 x $1,000 (the face value of the bond). The last two digits of the year is the year in which the bond's principal will be paid off. The "s" is used for ease of pronunciation. Thus, 7.7s04 means "seven-point.sevenths of oh-four,"—7.7 percent bonds due in year 2004. This is the fixed interest rate the borrowing company will pay you for this bond issue.
(3) Current yield: Here IBM's current yield of 8.3% is determined by dividing the annual interest of $77 by the bond's closing price of $922.50. *NOTE: This figure represents the effective, or real, rate of return on the current market price represented by the bond's interest earnings. It tells what investors will actually earn from a bond.* **The symbol "cv."** tells us the NWA bond is a convertible, and current yields are not calculated for convertibles. *NOTE: As in stock quotations, a number of alphabetic qualifiers appear throughout bond quotations, as shown in Table 8-3.*

(4) Vol means the number of bonds traded: seven IBM bonds traded on that day.
(5) Close is the price of the day: IBM's closing price is 92 1/4. But this price is one-tenth the actual price; to get the actual price, multiply the reported price by 10.

Actual price = 10 × Reported price = 10 × 92 1/4 = 10 × 92.25 = $922.50

(6) Net Chg is the difference between today's closing price and the previous trading day's closing price. IBM's price increased (+) by 1 5/8, i.e., the price was up $16.25 (10 × 1 5/8) for the day. The NWA bond was down $5.00 (10 × 0.5) for the day. *NOTE: Bond market price is usually expressed as a percent of its par (face) value customarily $1,000. Corporate bonds are quoted to the nearest one-eighth of a percent; a quote of 92 1/4 above means a price of $922.50, or 92 1/4% of $1,000.*

Treasury Bonds/Notes Quotations (*Investor's Business Daily*)

Figure 8-2 reproduces a typical *Investor's Business Daily* government bond and note quotation. Explanatory notes follow.

FNMA Quotations (*Investor's Business Daily*)

Figure 8-3 reproduces an *Investor's Business Daily* quotation. Explanations follow.

Tax-Exempt Bond Quotations (*Wall Street Journal*)

Figure 8-4 illustrates another *Wall Street Journal* quotation, for tax-exempt bonds.

Stripped Treasuries Quotation (*Investor's Business Daily*)

Figure 8-5 is an example of U.S. Treasury strips. Stripped Treasuries are zero-coupon bonds sold by the U.S. Treasury and created by "stripping" the coupons from a Treasury bond and selling them separately from the principal.

Treasury Bill Quotations (*Investor's Business Daily*)

Figure 8-6 is a sample T-bill quotation.

BOND OFFERINGS

New Issues Bond

Figure 8-7 is an example of an ad for a new bond issue.

Convertible Debenture Offerings

Figure 8-8 is an example of an ad for a new issue of convertible bonds.

TABLE 8-3: Qualifiers: Bonds

ct/cf   Certificate. This bond has matured, but the certificate is still of value and still being traded.

cv   Convertible bond. Convertible into stock under certain conditions.

d   Deep discounts.

f   Flat. The bond is traded without the accrued interest (i.e., it won't be added to the price). Once an interest payment has been missed, the bond trades flat. After an extended period in which interest payments are met, it is possible to restore a bond to a normal trading.

m   Matured bonds. These bonds have already matured; they are no longer drawing interest, and their negotiability has been impaired. They should be redeemed.

na/nc   Nonaccrual bond. There is no obligation to pay back interest owed.

r   Registered. The bondholder's name is registered with the company or its agent, and interest payments are automatically mailed (as opposed to bonds with coupons). Most listed corporate bonds are either registered or available in either registered or coupon form. They are not marked "r" unless a distinction is necessary. For example, the registered form and bearer form may be trading at slightly different prices.

vj   (Sometimes misprints "vi"). The company is in bankruptcy or receivership or is being reorganized under the 1978 Bankruptcy Act. Claims of the bondholders are senior to those of common or preferred stockholders in case of liquidation. However, when corporations have more than one bond issue, some may take precedence over others.

wd   When distributed. The bond certificate has not been printed and will be available at a later date.

ww   With warrants. The purchaser of these bonds will also receive warrants for the purchase of a specified price. The warrants are usually attached to the bond certificate.

x   Ex-interest. This is a day on which a new purchaser of a bond that normally trades flat will not qualify for the current interest payment.

xw   Ex-warrants. The purchaser of the bond will not receive warrants. Applies to bonds that once had warrants that presumably, have expired, been sold, or exercised by a previous owner.

zr   Zero coupon.

USING BOND INFORMATION SOURCES

Typical sources of bond information are: Moody's *Bond Record* or *Bond Survey* and Standard & Poor's *Bond Guide*. They are discussed below.

Moody's *Bond Record*

This is a monthly publication of Moody's Investors Service that contains data on corporates, convertibles, governments, municipals, and ratings on commercial paper

Continued on page 193.

FIGURE 8-1: Sample Corporate Bond Quotations

S&P Rates	Bond	Ex	Coupon Rate	Mat-ures	Yld. Cur.	Yld.to Mat.	Vol.	Bond Close	Chg
AA	AetnaLif	NY	8.125	10/07	8.5	8.6	20	96	...
A	AlbmaPwr	NY	8.750	07/07	8.6	8.6	5	101½	− ⅜
A	AlbmaPwr	NY	9.750	06/04	9.5	9.3	5	103⅛	− ⅞
A	AlbmaPwr	NY	9.250	10/07	8.9	8.8	2	104	+ ¾
A	AlbmaPwr	NY	9.000	11/00	8.8	8.6	30	102¼	+ ¼
A	AlbmaPwr	NY	7.875	04/02	8.0	8.1	4	98⅜	+ 1⅛
A	AlbmaPwr	NY	8.875	08/03	8.7	8.7	9	101⅝	− ⅛
A−	AldCorp	NY	ZrCpn	10/92	...	5.7	36	95.10	+ .18
A−	AldCorp	NY	ZrCpn	08/09	...	9.1	70	20¾	− ⅛
A−	AldCorp	NY	ZrCpn	08/00	...	8.9	7	46⅞	− ⅝

NOTE: In addition to price and volume information, Investor's Business Daily *includes S&P ratings, exchange, year to maturity, and yield to maturity.*

Art reprinted by permission of *Investor's Business Daily, America's Business Newspaper,* (November 25, 1991), ©Investor's Business Daily Inc. 1991.

FIGURE 8-2: Government Bond and Note Quotations

GOVT. BONDS & NOTES

Rate	Maturity Mo/Yr		Bid	Asked	Chg.	Ask Yld.
7¾s	11-91	p	100.00	100.4	..	1.96
7⅝s	12-91	p	100.8	100.12	− .1	3.67
8¼s	12-91	p	100.11	100.15	..	3.33
8⅛s	1-92	p	100.20	100.24	− .1	3.88
11⅝s	1-92	p	100.31	101.3	..	3.55
6⅝s	2-92	p	100.11	100.15	− .1	4.42
8½s	2-92	p	100.30	101.2	− .1	4.34
9⅛s	2-92	p	100.29	101.1	− .1	4.34
14⅝s	2-92	n	102.2	102.8	− .2	4.26
7⅞s	3-92	p	101.2	101.6	..	4.35
8½s	3-92	p	101.9	101.13	− .1	4.33
8⅞s	4-92	p	101.24	101.28	..	4.42
11¾s	4-92	k	102.20	102.24	− .2	4.48
6⅝s	5-92	p	100.29	101.1	..	4.39
9 s	5-92	p	101.30	102.2	− .1	4.53
13¾s	5-92	n	104.4	104.8	− .2	4.55
8½s	5-92	p	101.27	101.31	..	4.58
8¼s	6-92	p	102.00	102.4	..	4.59
8⅜s	6-92	p	102.2	102.6	..	4.61
10⅜s	7-92	p	103.14	103.18	..	4.63
8 s	7-92	p	102.2	102.6	− .1	4.69
4¼s	8-87−92		98.14	99.16	..	4.95
7¼s	8-92		101.20	101.26	+ .2	4.66
8⅛s	8-92	p	102.12	102.16	..	4.74
8¼s	8-92	p	102.11	102.15	+ .1	4.72
7⅞s	8-92	p	102.1	102.5	..	4.79
8⅛s	9-92	p	102.19	102.23	− .1	4.80

Rate refers to the coupon rate. The last bond (checkmarked) has a coupon rate of 8 1/8 percent (8.125%).

Maturity Mo/Yr refers to the month and year in which the bond matures. The last bond doesn't mature until September, 1992. The symbol "n" indicates the instrument is a Treasury *note* rather than a bond; a "k" indicates that non-resident aliens are exempt from a withholding tax; a "p" means both "n" and "k". It is common practice to refer to both bonds and notes as *bonds*; the *Wall Street Journal* uses *only* an "n" to designate the difference between a note and a bond.

Bid is the highest price bond dealers were offering to buy the bond. Fractional prices are quoted in 32nds of $10; thus, the last bond's fractional price of 19 means 19/32 of $10, or $.5938. To find the price per $1,000 of par value, multiply the whole number by 10 and add the fractional part. Thus, 10 x $100 = $1,000; $1,000 + $5.938 = $1,005.938.

Asked is the lowest price dealers were accepting. The last bond's asked price was 102.23, or $1,007.188.

Chg. shows the difference between today's price and the previous trading day's price. So, the last bond was down -.1, that is, $-0.3125 (1/32 x $10).

Ask Yld. means yield to maturity (YTM) based on the asked price. The *current* yield is obtained by dividing the annual interest by the current (asked) price. For the last bond, the current yield is 8.07%:

$$\frac{\text{Annual interest}}{\text{Current (asked) price}} = \frac{8.125\% \times \$1{,}000}{\$1{,}007.188} = \frac{\$81.25}{\$1{,}007.188} = 8.07\%$$

The last note has a yield to maturity (YTM) of 4.80%.

NOTE: Prices are quoted in percent of par. U.S. government bonds are highly marketable and deal in keenly competitive markets, so they are quoted in thirty-seconds or sixty-fourths rather than one-eighths. Moreover, decimals are used, rather than fractions, in quoting prices. For example, a quotation of 106.17 for a Treasury bond indicates a price of $1,065.31 [$1,060 + (17/32 x $10)]. When a plus sign follows the quotation, the Treasury bond is being quoted in a sixty-fourth. Therefore, double the number following the decimal point and add 1 to determine what fraction of $10 is represented in the quote. For example, a quote of 95.16+ indicates a price of $955.16 [$950 + (33/64 x $10)]. (See Table 8-4 for the value of fraction.) Accrued interest must be added.

Art reprinted from *Investor's Business Daily, America's Business Newspaper*, (November 25, 1991), ©Investor's Business Daily Inc. 1991.

Table 8-4: Fraction Equivalents

1/32				.03125
2/32	1/16			.06250
3/32				.09375
4/32	2/16	1/8		.12500
5/32				.15625
6/32	3/16			.18750
7/32				.21875
8/32	4/16	2/8	1/4	.25000
9/32				.28125
10/32	5/16			.31250
11/32				.34375
12/32	6/16	3/8		.37500
13/32				.40625
14/32	7/16			.43750
15/32				.46875
16/32	8/16	4/8	1/2	.50000
17/32				.53125
18/32	9/16			.56250
19/32				.59375
20/32	10/16	5/8		.62500
21/32				.65625
22/32	11/16			.68750
23/32				.71875
24/32	12/16	6/8	3/4	.75000
25/32				.78125
26/32	13/16			.81250
27/32				.84375
28/32	14/16	7/8		.87500
29/32				.90625
30/32	15/16			.93750
31/32				.96875

FIGURE 8-3: FNMA Quotations

Rate	Mat. Date	Bid	Ask	Bid Chg	Yld
FNMA ISSUES					
11.75	12-91	100.14	100.18	....	
8.50	1-92	100.14	100.18	....	3.86
7.00	3-92	100.20	100.23	....	4.44
12.00	4-92	102.20	102.23	....	4.56
8.45	5-92	101.21	101.24	....	4.56
8.50	5-92	101.22	101.25	....	4.54
7.05	6-92	101.6	101.9	+ .1	4.62
10.12	6-92	102.25	102.28	+ .1	4.68
8.45	7-92	102.5	102.8	....	4.74
7.75	8-92	101.30	102.2	+ .1	4.74
9.15	9-92	103.6	103.9	....	4.86
10.60	10-92	104.22	104.28	....	4.86
8.20	11-92	103.00	103.4	....	4.82
9.87	12-92	104.26	104.29	....	4.98
10.90	1-93	106.8	106.11	....	5.03
7.95	2-93	103.3	103.6	....	5.18
7.90	3-93	103.7	103.13	....	5.13
10.95	3-93	106.31	107.2	....	5.21

Rate refers to coupon rate. The FNMA bond checkmarked has a coupon rate of 10.95%.

Mat. Date refers to the month and year of the bond's maturity. This bond doesn't mature until March 1993.

Bid (and asked) prices are in percent of par. Bid is the highest price bond dealers were offering to buy the bond. Fractional prices are quoted in 32nds of $10; thus, the last bond's fractional price of 31 means 31/32 of $10, or $9.688. To find the price per $1,000 of par value, multiply the whole number by 10 and add the fractional part. Thus, 10 x $106 = $1,060; $1,060 + $9.688 = $1,069.68. Remember accrued interest must also be added.

Bid Chg. shows the difference between today's price and the previous trading day's price. There was no price change on the last bond.

Asked is the lowest price dealers were accepting. The last bond's ask price was 107.2 or 107.0625

Yld. means yield to maturity (YTM) based on the asked price. The last bond has a yield to maturity of 5.21%.

Art reprinted by permission of *Investor's Daily, America's Business Newspaper,* (November 25, 1991), ©Investor's Business Daily Inc. 1991.

FIGURE 8-4: Tax-Exempt Bond Quotations

ISSUE	COUPON	MAT	PRICE	CHG	BID YLD
Beaver Co. IDA Pa.	7.000	06-01-21	99	...	7.08
Bristol Hlth & Ed	7.000	09-01-21	99⅛	...	7.07
Burlington Kans.	7.000	06-01-31	99	– ⅛	7.07
Calif Dept Wtr	6.600	12-01-19	95⅝	...	6.95
Calif. Health Fac.	7.125	06-01-21	99⅝	...	7.16
Charlte NC Part Conv	6.750	12-01-21	97¾	...	6.92
Chicago O'Hare	7.875	11-01-25	100⅝	...	7.82
Conn. Ser 91A	6.750	06-01-11	97½	...	6.98
Fla Dept Natrl Res	6.750	07-01-13	98¼	...	6.91
Fla. Dept Transp	7.125	07-01-18	101	...	7.05
Hawaii Airport Sys	7.000	07-01-20	98½	...	7.12
Ill. Ser N Build	7.000	06-15-20	98¼	...	7.14
Inglewood Calif.	6.750	05-01-13	96⅞	...	7.03
Jasper Ind PCR Refnd	7.100	07-01-17	99⅝	– ⅛	7.13
Knox Co. Tenn.	7.000	01-01-15	99⅛	– ⅛	7.08
L.A. Calif Wastewtr	7.100	06-01-18	99⅞	...	7.11
L.A. Calif.	6.500	09-01-13	95⅜	...	6.91
L.A. Co. Transp	6.750	07-01-18	97⅞	...	6.93
L.A. Co. Transp	6.900	07-01-21	98	...	7.06
Lee Fla Waste 91A-B	7.000	10-01-11	99½	...	7.05

Issue refers to the issuing agency.

Coupon refers to coupon rate. Bristol Hlth & Ed has a coupon rate of 7%.

Mat refers to the month, date, and year of the bond's maturity. The Bristol Hlth & Ed bond matures on September 1, 2021.

Price the bond is traded for. Price quotations are in percent of par. Bristol Hlth & Ed's price was 991/8, which is $99.125. Again, accrued interest must be added to the price.

Chg shows the difference in the bid price between today's quotation and the previous trading day's quotation. So, Bristol had no change.

Bid Yld means yield to maturity (YTM). The current yield is not given in most quotations but can be calculated easily. For Bristol, the coupon rate of 7% yields $70.00 per $1,000 bond. This is a 7.06% yield on the current price, $99.125.

$$\frac{\$70.00}{\$99.125} = 7.06\%$$

The bond, however, also showed a yield to maturity of 7.07%.

NOTE: Yield on a tax-exempt bond, such as a municipal bond, needs to be looked at on an equivalent before-tax yield basis, because the interest received is not subject to federal income taxes. The formula used to equate interest on municipals to other investments is:

$$\text{Tax-equivalent yield} = \frac{\text{Tax-exempt yield}}{(1 - \text{Tax rate})}$$

For example, if you have a marginal tax rate of 28% and are evaluating a municipal bond that currently yields 7.72 percent, the equivalent before-tax yield on a taxable bond is

$$\frac{7.72\%}{(1 - .28)} = 10.72\%$$

which means your municipal bond yields the equivalent of a 10.72% corporate bond. Thus, you could choose between a taxable investment that pays 10.72% and a tax-exempt bond that pays 7.72% without concern for the difference.

FIGURE 8-5: Stripped U.S. Treasury Quotations

STRIPPED SECURITIES

Mat. Date	Bid	Asked	Bid Chg.	Yield
2-92 a	98.31	99.00	+ .1	4.53
5-92 a	97.27	97.28	+ .2	4.59
8-92 a	96.20	96.22	+ .1	4.72
11-92 a	95.13	95.17	..	4.76
2-93 a	93.29	94.1	+ .1	5.10
5-93 a	92.20	92.25	+ .1	5.15
8-93 a	91.7	91.12	+ .1	5.30
11-93 a	89.29	90.4	+ .1	5.34
2-94 a	88.7	88.14	+ .1	5.60
5-94 a	86.26	87.3	− .1	5.67
8-94 a	85.13	85.21	..	5.77
11-94 a	83.28	84.5	− .1	5.89
2-95 a	82.5	82.14	− .1	6.08
5-95 a	80.22	80.31	..	6.17

Maturity (first column) refers to the month and year of the strip's maturity. The last stripped Treasury doesn't mature until August 1995.

Type refers to qualifiers associated with stripped Treasuries: "a" means "stripped *coupon* interest," which is a security that represents the interest-bearing or "coupon" portion of a Treasury bond that has been separated from the bond itself (represented by a "ci" in the *Wall Street Journal*); "b" (not shown here) means "Treasury *bond*, stripped principal ('bp' in the *Wall Street Journal*"; "c" means "Treasury *note*, stripped principal ('np' in the *Wall Stret Journal*."

Bid (third column) is the highest price dealers were offering to buy the strip.

Asked is the lowest price dealers were accepting.

Chg shows the difference between today's price and the previous day's price.

Yld means yield to maturity (YTM) based on the bid price. The last bond has a YTM of 6.17 %.

NOTE: Because this is a stripped Treasury, the coupon rate is all zero.

FIGURE 8-6: Sample Treasury Bill Quotations

T-BILLS

Mat. Date	Bid	Asked	Bid Chg.	Yield
11-29 91	4.14	3.63	– .10	3.69
12-05 91	4.11	4.03	+ .07	4.10
12-12 91	4.16	4.06	– .02	4.14
12-19 91	4.04	4.00	+ .02	4.08
12-26 91 ✔	4.21	4.19	– .01	4.27
1-02 92	4.21	4.19	– .03	4.28
1-09 92	4.30	4.28	– .01	4.38
1-16 92	4.35	4.31	..	4.41
1-23 92	4.38	4.34	+ .02	4.45
1-30 92	4.39	4.38	– .01	4.48
2-06 92	4.42	4.38	– .02	4.49

Mat. Date refers to the month, date, and year of the bill's maturity. The fifth bill matures on December 26, 1991.

Days to Mat. (not shown here but included in *Wall Street Journal* quotations) refers to the number of days to maturity, For the fifth bill it was 30 days.

Bid is the highest price dealers were offering to buy the bill. The fifth bill's bid price was 4.21%.

Asked is the lowest price dealers were accepting. The fifth bill's ask price was 4.19%.

Bid Chg. is the difference between today's price and the previous day's price.

Yield means yield to maturity (YTM). The fifth bill has a yield to maturity of 4.27%. The yield on the T-bills is calculated using the formula:

$$\frac{\$10,000 - P}{P} \times \frac{365}{\text{Days to maturity}}$$

where P = purchase price (the asked price). For example, if a T-bill maturing in 30 days sells for $9,900, its yield is 12.29%, as calculated below.

$$\frac{\$10,000 - \$9,900}{\$9,900} \times \frac{365}{30} \times \frac{\$100}{\$9,900} \times 12.17 = 12.29\%$$

NOTE: T-bills are quoted in discount yields, so we would like to calculate the price. Solving for P,

$$P = \$10,000 - \frac{\$10,000 \ (\text{yield}) \ (\text{days to maturity})}{365}$$

With 30 days to maturity, and the asked price bill, quoted at 5.69%,

$$P = \$10,000 - \frac{\$10,000 \ (.0569) \ (30 \ \text{days})}{365} = \$9,953.23$$

Art reprinted by permission of *Investor's Business Daily, America's Business Newspaper,* (November 25, 1991), ©Investor's Business Daily Inc. 1991.

FIGURE 8-7: New Issue Bond Example

This announcement is not an offer to sell or a solicitation of an offer to buy any of these securities. The offering is made only by the Prospectus and the related Prospectus Supplement, copies of which may be obtained in any State in which this announcement is circulated only from underwriters qualified to act as dealers in securities in such State.

NEW ISSUE

April 27, 1989

(1)

$300,000,000

(2)

GTE Corporation   GTE

(3)   10¼% Debentures Due 2019

Price 99.45%
Plus accrued interest from May 1, 1989

(4)   PaineWebber Incorporated

Goldman, Sachs & Co.

Salomon Brothers Inc

The First Boston Corporation	Merrill Lynch Capital Markets	Morgan Stanley & Co. Incorporated
Shearson Lehman Hutton Inc.		UBS Securities Inc.
Bear, Stearns & Co. Inc.	Daiwa Securities America Inc.	Deutsche Bank Capital Corporation
Dillon, Read & Co. Inc.	Donaldson, Lufkin & Jenrette Securities Corporation	Drexel Burnham Lambert Incorporated
Grigsby Brandford Powell Inc.	Kidder, Peabody & Co. Incorporated	Lazard Frères & Co.
The Nikko Securities Co. International, Inc.		Nomura Securities International, Inc.
Paribas Corporation		Prudential–Bache Capital Funding
Smith Barney, Harris Upham & Co. Incorporated		Sogen Securities Corporation
SBCI Swiss Bank Corporation Investment banking		Wertheim Schroder & Co. Incorporated
Dean Witter Reynolds Inc.		Yamaichi International (America), Inc.

(1) Total amount of borrowing. If the bonds are all in denominations of $1,000, this issue is 300,000 bonds. (300,000 x $1,000 = $300,000,000).
(2) Name of company issuing the bonds.
(3) Coupon rate and **maturity date.**
(4) Underwriters conducting initial marketing of the bonds.

Source of art: *Wall Street Journal,* April 27, 1989.

FIGURE 8-8: Convertible Debenture Offering Announcement

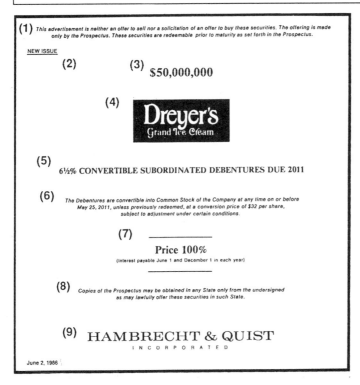

(1) This advertisement is neither an offer to sell nor a solicitation of an offer to buy these securities. The offering is made only by the Prospectus. These securities are redeemable prior to maturity as set forth in the Prospectus.

NEW ISSUE

(2)　　　　　**(3)** $50,000,000

(4) Dreyer's Grand Ice Cream

(5) 6½% CONVERTIBLE SUBORDINATED DEBENTURES DUE 2011

(6) The Debentures are convertible into Common Stock of the Company at any time on or before May 25, 2011, unless previously redeemed, at a conversion price of $32 per share, subject to adjustment under certain conditions.

(7) ———————
Price 100%
(Interest payable June 1 and December 1 in each year)

(8) Copies of the Prospectus may be obtained in any State only from the undersigned as may lawfully offer these securities in such State.

(9) HAMBRECHT & QUIST
INCORPORATED

June 2, 1986

(1) Standard disclaimer states this is not an offer to sell bonds. Offers can legally be made only through prospectus (see Chapter 5). Tombstones are for information only; often the bond has already been sold.
(2) New issue—first-time offering.
(3) The **amount** of borrowing.
(4) Issuing company.
(5) 6 1/2% **coupon** rate convertible debenture maturing in 2011.
(6) Statement says this debenture is a convertible bond.
(7) Price at which the security will sell (or sold) in advance of its issuance. "Price 100%" means $1,000 (100% x $1,000). Demand on the secondary market will determine the price, as is the case for all outstanding securities. If there are more offers to buy than there are bonds in the initial offering, the bond is deemed a "hot issue," and the market price will rise as soon as the bond begins trading on the secondary market. Interest is paid semiannually.

(8) **A legal sale** of a new issue cannot be made unless a prospective buyer receives a prospectus in advance of the transaction. If you don't receive a prospectus before you receive a confirmation of trade, you have a legal right to cancel the transaction without penalty within a reasonable time. Because new issues are generally more speculative than securities already trading on the open market, the prospectus requirement prevents a broker from "strongarming" you into buying a security about which you may know very little. Remember, as noted in Chapter 7, there are two prospectuses: the preliminary, or "red herring", prospectus is called a "red herring," because of a statement printed on the cover in red to the effect that the registration has not been declared effective by the SEC. The purpose of the preliminary prospectus is to stimulate sales when the registration is first filed with the SEC. The SEC may or may not require revision or amendments. After the SEC has accepted the preliminary prospectus a new prospectus, without the red lettering, is printed and used for offering the shares. The ad reference is to the second, or final, prospectus.

(9) The **investment banker** or **underwriter** (there may be more than one) bringing out the issue. Those with the largest number of bond shares to sell are listed first, and in bolder type than those with a relatively minor stake.

Source of art: *Wall Street Journal,* June 22, 1986.

and preferred stock. Corporate bond information includes the interest coupon, payment dates, call price, Moody's rating, and yield to maturity. The current price as well as the yearly and historical high and low prices are presented. The total amount of the bond issue outstanding is given with a designation for a sinking fund and the original issue date. Data on convertible bonds also include the conversion price, conversion value, and conversion period. Information on industrial revenue and municipal bonds is usually limited to the Moody's rating. Moody's *Bond Record* also contains historical yield graphs for various types of bonds over at least 30 years. Figure 8-9 provides an example of what an investor would expect to find in such a report. Moody's bond rating system (the column marked with a **(1)** in Figure 8-9) is discussed in the Appendix at the end of this chapter.

Moody's *Bond Survey*

Moody's *Bond Survey* reviews weekly activity in the bond market—rating changes, new issues, and bonds called for redemption.

Standard & Poor's *Bond Guide*

The S&P's *Bond Guide* has the same format as the *Stock Guide*. Published monthly in booklet form, it presents data on corporate and convertible bonds. Figure 8-10 shows one page of **convertible** bonds from the *Bond Guide*. Looking at Figure 8-10, you will see convertible bonds having different coupons, interest payment dates, and maturities. The S&P rating is given. All conversion data are given with bond prices and common stock prices. Figure 8-11 shows a page on **corporate** bonds with explanatory notes. The S&P rating is presented along with the bond form (coupon or registered), call prices, sinking funds, yields, prices, and other information.

Components for **convertible** bonds differing from other listings are explained in Figure 8-10. Components for **foreign** bonds differing from other listings are explained in Figure 8-12.

YIELDS ON SHORT-TERM DEBT SECURITIES

The *Wall Street Journal* provides information on short-term debt securities, examples of which are shown in Figures 8-13, 8-14, 8-15.

Figure 8-13 ("Key Interest Rates") provides interest rates (or yields) on 90-day T-bills, 90-day commercial paper, and 90-day CDs, for example. It also shows rates on some other key interest rates.

Figure 8-14 ("Consumer Savings Rates") provides average rates paid by 100 large banks and thrifts in 10 large metropolitan areas as compiled by *Bank Rate Monitor*.

Figure 8-15 ("Banxquote Money Markets") compiled by **BANXQUOTE**, a registered trademark and service mark of **MASTERFUND INC.** (800-325-3242), provides average yields on money market investments and CDs of major banks.

FIGURE 8-9: Example of Bond Rating Report

8 AAR—Alli — MOODY'S BOND RECORD — January 1992

U.S. Corporate Bonds

(Where an issue is printed in **bold face type** such company also has convertible debt securities outstanding. See U.S. Convertible Bonds and/or International Bonds Section.)

CUSIP	ISSUE	(1)* MOODY'S RATING	INTEREST DATES	CURRENT CALL PRICE	CALL DATE	SINK FUND PROV	CURRENT PRICE	YIELD TO MAT.	1991 HIGH	1991 LOW	AMT. OUTST. MIL. $	ISSUED	PRICE	YLD.
000361AA	AAR Corp. nts. 9.50 2001	Baa2 r	M&N 1	[1] N.C.	----	No	111¾ bid	7.75	111¾	98¼	65.0	10-24-89	100.00	9.50
847809AA	♦Aaron Spelling Prod. sub.nts. 12.25 1993[2]	B2 r	F&A 1	101.80	to 7-31-92	Yes	100½ sale	11.89	101½	81	19.8	8-1-86	100.00	12.25
002824AA	•Abbott Laboratories s.f.deb. 6.25 1993	Aa1 r	J&J 15	100.00	to 1-14-93	Yes	100 bid	6.25	100	95⅝	1.035	1-9-68	99.50	6.29
002824AB	• s.f.deb. 7.625 1996	Aa1 r	M&S 1	100.00	to 2-28-92	Yes	100½ bid	7.48	101½	96½	11.05	3-3-71	99.50	7.67
002824AC	• s.f.deb. 9.20 1999	Aa1 r	A&O 15	101.38	to 10-14-92	Yes	104¼ sale	8.44	105	100⅛	17.39	10-16-74	100.00	9.20
000800AY	ACF Industries eq.tr. 14.875 M 1992	Ba3 r	F&A 1	N.C.	----	Yes	----	----	----	----	44.0	7-20-82	99.87	14.90
000800AX	s.f.cert. 14.50 L 1996	Ba3 r	J&D 1	N.C.	----	Yes	----	----	----	----	24.0	11-19-81	100.00	14.50
000800BA	sr.deb. 15.25 1996	B2 r	J&D 15	104.20	to 12-14-92	Yes	96½ bid	16.30	101	74	456	12-14-84	98.65	15.50
000800AR	s.f.cert. 11.60 J 2000	Ba3 r	M&N 15	N.C.	----	Yes	----	----	----	----	40.0	5-28-80	100.00	11.60
066356AA	Adams-Russell Co., Inc. sr.sub.nts. 1997[3]	Caa r	[4]N.P.	100.00	to 12-30-97	No	----	----	----	----	273	5-5-88	49.29	
006516AA	Addington Resources, Inc. sr.nts. 12.00 1995	Ba2 r	J&J 1	103.43	fr 7-1-93	No	103¾ bid	10.68	104½	98	125	6-30-88	100.00	12.00
006848AA	Adelphia Comm. Corp. sr.sub.nts. 13.00 1996	B3 r	F&A 15	103.71	to 8-15-96	No	95 bid	14.52	95	37	98.8	8-12-86	98.63	13.18
006848AB	sr.nts. 16.50 1999[5]	B2 r	M&S 15	104.00	fr 3-15-92	No	98 bid	16.99	98½	29¾	250	12-19-88	60.05	
006875AA	•Adience Equities Inc. sr.sub.nts. 15.00 1999[6]	Caa r	J&D 15	103.00	fr 6-15-94	Yes	75 sale	----	90	58	75.0	6-12-89	98.73	
872883AA	Advanta Corp. sr.sub.deb. 12.75 1998[7]	B2 r	J&D 1	105.00	to 11-30-92	Yes	----	----	----	----	50.0	11-26-86	100.00	12.75
008140AD	Aetna Life & Cas. Co. nts. 8.625 1998	Aa3 r	M&S 1	N.C.	----	No	108¼ bid	6.94	108¼	97½	100	2-24-88	99.50	8.70
008140AA	• sr.nts. 8.125 2007	Aa3 r	A&O 15	103.36	to 10-14-92	Yes	101 sale	8.01	101	88¼	238	10-13-77	99.50	8.17
008140AB	deb. 8.00 2017	Aa3 r	J&J 15	104.00	fr 1-15-97	Yes	93⅜ bid	8.65	93⅜	83¼	200	1-8-87	97.75	8.20
008182AB	Affiliated Bankshares nts. 11.625 1993	Ba2 r	A&O 1	100.00	to 4-1-93	No	100⅞ bid	10.78	100⅞	96¾	50.0	4-5-83	100.00	11.63
008677AA	Ahmanson (H.F.) & Co. sub.nts. 9.875 1999	Baa3 r	M&N 15	N.C.	----	No	103⅝ bid	9.21	103⅝	86¼	250	11-9-89	99.88	9.90
----	AIG Matched Funding Corp. flt.rt.nts. 0.00 2005[8]	Aaa	J&D 1	N.C.	----	No	----	----	----	----	1.000	12-21-90	00.00	
----	AIG World Finance Corp flt.rt.nts. 0.00 2005[8]	Aaa	J&D 1	N.C.	----	No	----	----	----	----	1.000	12-21-90	00.00	
009158AE	•Air Prod. & Chem.Inc. nts. 11.50 1995	A1 r	M&N 1	N.C.	----	No	114 bid	6.73	108	107	100	4-18-85	100.00	11.50
009158AH	nts. 8.875 2001	A1 r	F&A 1	N.C.	----	No	109 bid	7.53	109	96⅛	100	8-3-89	99.60	8.93
009158AG	deb. 8.50 2006	A1 r	A&O 1	100.00	to 4-1-06	No	106¾ bid	7.70	106¾	90½	100	4-2-86	99.43	8.56
009158AF	• deb. 11.375 2015	A1 r	M&N 1	§107.75	to 10-31-92	Yes	104⅜ bid	10.85	----	----	100	Ref. fr. 11-1-95 @ 105.54		
009158AJ	deb. 8.75 2021	A1 r	A&O 15	N.C.	----	No	98 bid	8.94	----	----	100	4-17-91	97.71	8.97
045659AA	Aircoa Hospitality Svs. sr.nts. 14.00 1996[9]	N.R. r	M&S 15	103.63	to 3-14-92	Yes	37⅜ bid	----	37⅜	15	34.5	3-11-86	98.69	14.25
010202AB	Akzona, Inc. deb. 7.50 1997	A3 r	F&A 15	100.38	to 2-14-92	Yes	----	----	----	----	43.9	2-17-72	100.00	7.50
010284AD	Alabama Gas Corp. 1st 8.00 F 1994[10]	A1 r	F&A 1	100.86	to 1-31-92	Yes	100⅞ bid	7.52	100⅞	98¼	5.540	2-20-69	98.64	7.37
010284AE	1st 9.50 G 1996[11]	A1 r	J&J 1	101.15	to 12-31-92	Yes	101⅞ bid	8.92	104½	101¾	10.03	1-7-71	101.00	8.66
010284AG	deb. 9.00 2014	A2	M&N 1	105.00	fr 11-1-94	No	107 bid	8.30	107	98⅞	30.0	10-18-89	100.00	9.00
010392AQ	Alabama Power 1st 4.375 1992	A1	J&D 1	100.00	to 5-31-92	Yes	99⅞ bid	4.44	99⅞	95	14.36	6-1-62	99.88	4.38
010392AR	1st 4.375 1993	A1	M&N 1	100.16	to 4-30-92	Yes	99⅝ bid	4.60	99⅝	91⅝	13.8	5-10-63	100.08	4.37
010392AS	1st 4.625 1994	A1	M&N 1	100.41	to 4-30-92	Yes	98¾ bid	5.18	98¾	89	24.1	5-16-64	101.22	4.55
010392AT	1st 4.875 1995	A1	M&S 1	100.59	to 8-31-92	Yes	96⅞ bid	5.82	96⅞	85⅞	33.28	9-10-65	100.75	4.82
010392AU	1st 6.25 1996	A1	A&O 1	101.05	to 9-30-92	Yes	98⅞ bid	6.51	98⅞	88¾	29.37	10-14-66	101.36	6.15
010392AV	1st 6.50 1997	A1	A&O 1	101.13	to 9-30-92	Yes	98¼ bid	6.86	98¼	87⅞	28.0	10-3-67	100.00	6.50
010392AW	1st 7.00 1998	A1	M&N 1	101.45	to 10-31-92	Yes	99 bid	7.17	99	88⅝	25.0	10-29-68	100.00	7.00
010392AX	1st 8.625 1999	A1	M&N 1	102.28	to 10-31-92	Yes	102⅜ bid	8.20	102⅜	96½	35.0	10-29-69	100.81	8.55
010392AY	• 1st 9.00 2000	A1 r	M&N 1	102.49	to 10-31-92	Yes	102⅛ sale	8.65	102⅞	98⅜	44.92	11-17-70	100.00	9.00
010392AZ	• 1st 8.50 2001	A1 r	J&J 1	102.95	to 6-30-92	Yes	101⅜ sale	8.28	102	94⅛	85.0	7-21-71	101.00	8.41
010392BC	• 1st 7.75 2002	A1 r	M&S 1	103.02	to 8-31-92	Yes	99¾ bid	7.78	100½	90	65.0	9-12-72	101.00	7.66
010392BA	1st 7.50 2002	A1 r	J&J 1	102.07	to 12-31-92	Yes	99¼ bid	7.59	99¼	88	25.5	12-15-71	100.00	7.50
010392BB	• 1st 7.875 2002	A1 r	A&O 1	102.82	to 3-31-92	Yes	98½ sale	8.09	98½	90⅛	98.0	4-19-72	100.29	7.78
010392BD	• 1st 8.875 2003	A1 r	F&A 1	103.67	to 7-31-92	Yes	103 sale	8.46	103	96¾	100	8-7-73	100.79	8.80
010392BE	• 1st 8.25 2003	A1 r	J&D 1	103.51	to 11-30-92	Yes	102¼ sale	7.95	102¼	91¾	75.0	12-5-73	101.00	8.16
010392BF	• 1st 9.75 2004	A1 r	J&D 1	104.24	to 5-31-92	Yes	103½ bid	9.26	105	100	100	6-12-74	100.49	9.75
010392BG	• 1st 10.875 2005	A1 r	A&O 1	105.38	to 9-30-92	Yes	106½ bid	9.99	110	102⅛	4.008	9-23-75	101.11	10.75
010392BJ	• 1st 8.875 2006	A1 r	M&S 1	103.67	to 2-28-92	Yes	101¼ sale	8.72	101⅝	95¼	50.0	3-24-76	98.71	9.00

**For a complete explanation of Moody's rating system, see the Appendix at the end of this chapter.*

Art reprinted by permission from Moody's *Bond Record*. ©Moody's Investor's Services, Inc. All rights reserved.

Yields on money market mutual funds appear in local newspapers and financial dailies, explained in detail in Chapter 9, Mutual Funds.

CREDIT MARKETS

The "Credit Markets" column appears daily in the *Wall Street Journal* and *Investor's Business Daily* (Figure 8-16) and provides a capsule view of current conditions and future prospects in the bond market. *NOTE: On this particular day, this column (shown only in part) was devoted to the gain in T-Bills and bond yields. The "Key Corporate Rates" table appears daily in this column.*

FIGURE 8-10: Standard & Poor's *Bond Guide*, Convertibles

224 Convertible Bonds

Exchange ↓ Issue, Rate, Interest Dates and Maturity	S&P Debt Rating	(1) Bond Form	Outstdg. Mil-$	(2) Conv. Ex-pires	Shares per $1,000 Bond	Price per Share	(3) Div. Income per Bond	1991 Price Range High	1991 Price Range Low	Curr Bid Sale(s) Ask(A)	Curr. Yield	Yield to Mat	(4) Stock Value of Bond	(5) Conv Parity	Stock Data Month End	Stock Data P/E Ratio	Earnings Per Share Yr. End	1990	1991	(6) Last 12 Mos
• Western Co No Amer[1] 7¼s Jj15 2015	B −	R	90.0	2015	58.82	17.00	....	104	54	56	12.95	13.49	35⅜	9⅝	•6	d	Dc	△0.19	....	[9]d0.19
• Western Digital[2] .... 9s Jd 2014	CCC	R	59.0	2014	69.20	14.45	....	66	28	s39	23.08	23.33	16½	5¾	•2⅜	d	Je	0.82	d4.59	[9]d5.95
◆West'n Invt R.E. Tr[3](Sr) .... 8s [4]Qjan 2008	BBB	R	74.9	2008	44.98	22.23	50.38	93	82	86½	9.25	9.65	50⅛	19¼	◆11⅛	11	Dc	1.15	....	[9]0.99
• [5]Western Union[6] .... 5¼s §fA 1997	D	R	27.7	1997	15.15	66.00	....	32	10¾	s11⅝	....	Flat	⅜	7¾	•3/16	..	Dc	△d0.70	....	[9]0.23
• Westinghouse Elec 9s fA15 2009	A −	R	61.0	2009	64.52	15.50	90.33	198⅜	115	s116	7.76	7.37	101⅝	18	•15¾	d	Dc	0.91	Ed3.50	[9]d5.64
Weston(Roy F.),Inc 7s Ao15 2002	B +	R	31.4	2002	[7]47.33	21.13	....	76⅞	45	72½	9.66	11.63	47⅜	15⅜	10	20	Dc	±0.27	....	[9]0.49
Westwood One[8] 9s aO15 2002	CCC +	R	33.2	2002	285.71	3.50	....	85¾	60	71	12.68	14.34	53⅝	2½	1⅞	d	Nv	d1.25	....	[8]d1.28
Westwood One 6¾s aO15 2011	CCC +	R	15.5	2011	40.68	24.583	....	35	18½	35	19.29	20.11	7¾	8⅝	1⅞	d	Nv	d1.25	....	[8]d1.28
Wetterau Inc[9] 7s jD15 2000	BBB	R	108	2000	30.303	33.00	20.61	110	95½	95½	7.33	7.70	69	31⅝	22¾	9	Mr	2.23	....	[9]2.30
• Weyerhaeuser Co 5¼s Jd15 2017	NR	R	193	2017	20.83	48.00	25.00	80¼	61	s71	7.39	7.91	49	34⅛	•23½	27	Dc	1.87	E0.85	[9]1.16
◆Wherehouse[10]Entmt[11] .... 6¼s jJ 2006	NR	R	19.5	2006	Conv into $507.22			51	48⅛	50¾	12.32	14.42	....	....	....	..		....	....	....
• Whirlpool Corp[12](Zero)[13] .... [14] 2011	A	R	[15]675	2011	7.237	....	7.96	31	25¼	27¾	....	6.70	24⅜	38⅜	•33⅝	12	Dc	1.04	E2.60	[9]1.09
• Willcox & Gibbs[16] .... 7s fA 2014	B +	R	50.0	2004	41.15	24.30	4.12	68	50	62	11.29	11.86	29⅞	15⅛	•7¼	65	Dc	0.40	....	[9]0.11
[17]Winners Corp .... 8¼s Jd 2003	NR	R	22.4	2003	56.34	17.75	....	67	45	67	12.31	14.14	14⅞	12	•2⅝	13	Dc	△0.16	....	[9]0.19
• Witco Corp[18] 4½s jD15 1993	A −	R	1.20	1993	67.52	14.81	124.24	No Sale		260	1.73	....	260	38⅝	•38½	12	Dc	2.95	E3.00	[9]2.85
• Witco Corp 5½s Ms15 2012	A −	R	150	2012	18.33	54.55	33.73	93	69	82	6.71	7.20	70⅝	44¾	•38½	12	Dc	2.95	E3.00	[9]2.85
• WMS Industries[19] .... 12¾s mN 1996	CALL	R	14.8	12-19-91	49.58	20.17	....	140	61	s110	11.59	Call	112¼	22¼	•22⅝	17	Je	d1.24	*0.94	[9]1.32
• Xerox Corp .... 6s mN 1995	A −	R	65.0	1995	10.87	92.00	32.61	99	87¼	s98½	6.09	6.44	67½	90⅝	•62	12	Dc	1.66	E5.00	[9]5.45
[20]Zehntel, Inc 9¼s Ms15 2012	NR	R	14.2	2012	42.55	23.50	....	91	52	89½	10.34	10.51	57	21⅛	•13⅜	24	Dc	d0.71	E0.55	[9]0.29
• Zenith Electronics .... 6¼s Ao 2011	CCC	R	115	2011	32.00	31.25	....	48¼	36	s44⅞	13.93	15.10	20⅞	14⅛	•6½	d	Dc	d2.36	Ed2.00	[9]d2.76
• Zurn Indus .... 5¾s mN 1994	NR	R	2.38	1994	70.18	14.25	61.76	No Sale		243	2.37	....	243	34¾	•34⅝	13	Mr	2.46	E2.50	[9]2.45

Uniform Footnote Explanations-See Page 1. Other: [1] (HRO)On Chge of Ctrl at 101. [2] (HRO)For Fundamental Chge at 100. [3] (HRO)On any Jun 30 at 100. [4] Due 6-30-08. [5] Now New Valley Corp. [6] Default 8-1-91 int. [7] Into Cl A com. [8] (HRO)On Chge of Ctrl at 100. [9] (HRO)At 100 for a Risk Event. [10] Subsid of WEI Hldgs. [11] (HRO)On Chge in Ctrl,as defined. [12] (HRO)On5-14-96(01&06)at$356.27($502.56&$708.91). [13] (HRO)To 5-14-96 on Chge in Ctrl. [14] Due 5-14-11. [15] Incl disc. [16] (HRO)At 100 for a Risk Event bef 8-1-99. [17] Now Volunteer Capital. [18] Was Witco Chemical. [19] Was Williams Electronics. [20] Asmd by & data of Teradyne Inc.

(1) **Bond Form.** C—Coupon only; CR-Coupon or Registered (interchangeable); R—Registered only.

(2) **Conv. Expires.** The year in which the conversion expires.

(3) **Div. Income per Bond.** If a $1,000 bond were converted, the annual amount of dividends expected to be paid by the company on the stock, based on most recent indication of annual rate of payment.

(4) **Stock Value of Bond.** Price at which bond must sell to equal price of stock, i.e., number of shares received on conversion times price of stock.

(5) **Conv. Parity.** Price at which stock must sell to equal bond price, i.e., price of bond divided by number shares received on conversion.

(6) **Last 12 Mos.** Indicates earnings through period indicated by superior number preceding figure: 1 for Jan., 2 for Feb., etc. Figure without superior number indicates fiscal year-end. The letter "d" means dilution, indicating earnings on a fully diluted basis.

FIGURE 8-11: Standard & Poor's Bond Guide, Corporates

BAR-BEL   37

Corporate Bonds

(1) **Title-Industry Code & Co. Finances** (in Italics). Name of issuer and pertinent control information (e.g., name change, subsidiary, etc.), footnoted to reference on respective pages.

(2) **Ind** (for **Industry**) Company's principal business is numerically coded to directory.

(3) **Fixed Charge Coverage—19xx/19xx/19xx Year End.** Represents number of times available earnings (*before income taxes and extraordinary charges or credits*) cover fixed charges. Charges include interest on funded debt, other interest, amortization of debt discount and expense, and similar charges. **Year End** represents month in which fiscal year ends. For fiscal years ending March 31 or earlier, figures are shown under columns of preceding calendar year.

(4) **Million $—Cash & Equiv./Curr. Assets/Curr. Liab./Bal. Sheet Date.** Figures are reported in millions of dollars (000,000 omitted): 1275—$1,275,200,000; 17.5—$17,500,000, for example. Data are updated from annual and interim reports. Utilities with a reasonable debt to property ratio may often report current liabilities in excess of current assets. In many instances this is of no real significance, as utilities have constant tax deferrals, high current debt maturity, and the ability to forecast revenues.

(5) **L. Term Debt (Mil $).** Debts and certain obligations due after one year, including bonds, debentures, mortgages, and capitalized lease obligations. Increased debt resulting from new financing and offered subsequent to latest balance sheet date is indicated by symbol "**".

(6) **Capitalization (Mil $).** Sum of stated values of common shareholders' equity, preferred and preference stock, total debt, and minority interest.

(7) **Total Debt % Capital.** Company's total debt (including short-term debt) divided by total capital. Indicates a company's measure of leverage.

(8) **Exchange.** "•" designates the New York Stock Exchange; "♦" designates the American Stock Exchange.

(9) **Individual Issue Statistics.** Description of individual issues. For example, Senior Nts 81/8s '96 means these are 8 1/8 Senior Notes due in 1996. Abbreviations are found on page 2 of the *Bond Guide.*

(10) **Interest Dates.** Interest dates are indicated by the first letter of alternate six months in which interest is payable. An "A"or "Q" preceding dates means interest is payable either annually or quarterly. Unless otherwise noted, dates are the first day of the month. Month of maturity is indicated by a capital letter. Symbols following interest dates (none shown here) note foreign issues payable in U.S. funds, currency of issuing country, or issues in default. These symbols are explained on page 1 of the *Bond Guide.*

(11) **S&P Debt Rating.** Debt rating definitions appear in the front section of the *Bond Guide* and in the Appendix to this chapter.

(12) **Eligible.** Eligible for bank purchase (explained on page 1 of the *Bond Guide*).

(13) **Bond Form.** C—Coupon only; CR—Coupon or Registered (interchangeable); R—Registered only.

(14) **Redemption Provisions—Regular/Price/(Begins) Thru.** Regular call price with beginning or ending date. Additional information on page 1 of *Bond Guide.* **Sinking Fund/Price/(Begins) Thru.** Sinking fund, if any, is reported together with applicable price and beginning or ending date. **Refund/Other Restriction/Price/(Begins) Thru.** Refund restrictions are denoted by the symbol "®", giving date at which restriction expires. Redemption provision may include the symbol "NC", which means noncallable, and others (‡, Z, *), explained on page 1 of the guide.

(15) **Outst' 0 (Mil $).** Amount of issue outstanding, in millions of dollars, as of the latest available complete balance sheet.

(16) **Underwriting—Firm/Price/Year.** Keyed to "Directory of Underwriters" in Table of Contents of the *Bond Guide.* Indicates the original underwriter (usually the head of the syndicate), the price, and the year the issue was originally offered.

(17) **Price Range—19xx/High/Low.** Price ranges for current calendar year to date. An explanation of price methodology for listed and over-the-counter bonds appears on page 1 of the guide.

(18) **Mo. End Price Sale(s) or Bid.** Last sale price is shown for listed issues, and latest bid price or S&P valuation for over-the-counter issues or listed issues not traded last day of the month. "Flat" (or "f") indicates issues traded "without accrued interest." A—Ask price (none shown here).

(19) **Curr. Yield—Yield to Mat.** Yields (current and to maturity) are computed on month-end price shown in preceding column.

FIGURE 8-12: Standard & Poor's *Bond Guide*, Foreign

Foreign Bonds | AFR-BRI 195

(1) Exchange	(2) BONDS Description	Interest Rate	Due	Interest Dates	S&P Debt Rating	Redemption Provisions: Regular	Redemption Provisions: For Sinking Fund	Redemption Provisions: Refund Earliest/Other	Underwriting: Firm	Underwriting: Price	Underwriting: Year	Out-standing Mil-$ This Issue	Price Range 1972-1990: High	Price Range 1972-1990: Low	1991: High	1991: Low	Month End Price Sale(s) or Bid	Yield to Maturity
•	African Development Bank .... Notes	10½s	1995	$mN	AAA	NC	....	....	K2	99.63	'85	100	99⅝	99⅝	No Sale		105	8.96
•	African Development Bank .... Notes	10s	1997	$mN	AAA	NC	....	....	K2	100	'87	200	104	99⅜	110½	110½	104	9.11
•	African Development Bank .... Sub Notes ('88)	9½s	1995	$jD15	AA	NC	....	....	K2	99.87	'88	100	104⅞	97¾	101	98¼	104	8.31
•	African Development Bank .... Sub Notes ('88)	9¾s	2003	$jD15	AA	NC	....	....	K2	100	'88	100	100	99¼	No Sale		100	9.75
	African Development Bank .... Sub Notes ('90)[1]	9.30s	2000	$jJ	AA	NC	....	....	K2	99.55	'90	300	101½	95¼	108¼	100⅞	107⅝	8.05
	Alberta(Province of) .... Notes	9¼s	1994	$mN23	AA	NC	....	....	F2	99.88	'87	400	103⅝	96⅛	105¼	101⅞	104⅞	7.40
	Alberta(Province of) .... Notes	9.20s	1997	$mN	AA	NC	....	....	M3	99	'90	300	102½	99	109¾	102¼	109¾	7.15
	Alberta(Province of) .... Notes	9¼s	2000	$Ao	AA	NC	....	....	M6	99⅞	'90	500	102¾	97⅝	108¾	102	108⅝	7.82
	Alberta Gvt Tel Com .... SF[2]Deb	6¼s	1992	$aO	AA	100	....	....	H1	98¾	'67	35.0	97⅛	50¼	100	97	99⅞	6.39
	Alcan Aluminium Ltd .... Deb	9.40s	1995	$Jd	A	NC	....	....	F2	100	'90	150	102½	99¾	107⅝	102⅜	107⅝	6.91
	Alcan Aluminium Ltd .... Deb	9.70s	1996	$aO15	A	NC	....	....	M6	99.82	'90	125	102⅞	99⅞	109¾	102¾	109¾	7.29
	Alcan Aluminium[3]Ltd[4] .... [5]Deb	9½s	2010	$Jj15	A	[6]103.494	....	Z103	M6	98.99	'89	100	99½	92⅝	106¾	98½	105½	8.88
	Alcan Aluminium Ltd[4] .... [7]SF[3]Deb[8]	9⅝s	2019	$jJ15	A	[9]104.64	[10]100	Z103	F2	99.65	'89	150	100¾	92	105⅝	97¼	104⅞	9.14
•	Aluminum Co Canada .... Deb	9⅞s	1998	$Jj15	A	[11]102	....	....	M6	99⅜	'86	100	104	96	No Sale		106¼	8.54
•	Amoco Canada Petroleum .... Jr[12]Notes[13]		2003	$mS	AA –	100	[14]100	....	Plan	....	'88	340	140⅜	110	163	142⅞	155	Flat
•	Asian Development Bank .... Bonds	10¾s	1997	$Jd	AAA	NC	....	....	S5	99.73	'85	100	105¾	99⅝	No Sale		115⅛	7.36
•	Asian Development Bank .... Bonds	11⅛s	1998	$Mn	AAA	NC	....	....	F2	99.45	'83	76.2	100	99⅜	No Sale		118⅜	7.47
•	Asian Development Bank .... Bonds	8s	2001	$Ao31	AAA	NC	....	....	M3	99.55	'86	56.2	100½	97½	No Sale		99⅞	8.02
•	Asian Development Bank .... Notes Zero Cpn		1992	[15]	AAA	100	....	....	L4	25	'82	[16]400	77½	25	No Sale		95¾	7.04
•	Asian Development Bank .... Notes	9⅜s	1995	$Jd8	AAA	NC	....	....	S1	....	'88	100	No U.S. Sale		No Sale		107	7.09
	Asian Development Bank .... Notes[17]	9⅛s	2000	$Jd	AAA	NC	....	....	S5	99.20	'90	300	102⅛	96¾	108¼	101¾	108⅛	7.80
•	Australia(Commonwealth) .... Bonds	12¾s	1992	$mS15	AA	NC	....	....	M6	100	'82	200	124	97½	106¾	103.28	103⅜	8.23
•	Australia(Commonwealth) .... Bonds	11⅜s	1993	$fA	AA	NC	....	....	M6	99¼	'83	98.6	117¼	90½	108⅞	104¼	105	8.10
•	Australia(Commonwealth) .... Bonds	9¼s	1996	$fA	AA	NC	....	....	M6	99.55	'86	65.0	107⅝	98	102½	100½	105⅛	7.91
	Australia(Commonwealth) .... Bonds	7⅝s	1997	$mS15	AA	NC	....	....	M6	99¼	'87	99.8	99¼	84⅝	101¼	95½	101¼	7.35
•	Australia(Commonwealth) .... Bonds	9⅝s	2006	$Fa	AA	NC	....	....	M6	99.20	'86	114	107⅜	99⅛	100	100	101	9.49
•	Australia(Commonwealth) .... SF Bonds	13⅜s	2007	$mS15	AA	[18]106.19	100	....	M6	99¾	'82	[19]44.8	121½	96	112	103	107	12.35
•	Australia(Commonwealth) .... SF Bonds	12⅛s	2008	$fA	AA	[20]105.06	100	....	M6	99	'83	45.1	117½	91	108	102	105¼	11.41
	Australia(Commonwealth) .... Bonds	8⅜s	2017	$Ms15	AA	NC	....	....	M6	99.87	'87	68.0	99⅞	79⅞	101	94¼	99⅜	8.43
	Austria (Republic of) .... Bonds	9⅛s	1999	$Ao25	AAA	NC	....	....	S1	99.27	'88	100	105	94⅝	109⅛	100⅝	109⅛	7.49
•	Barclays N. Amer Capital .... [21]Gtd Cap Notes	11⅝s	2003	$Mn	AA	[22]100	....	Z100	G2	99½	'83	400	117¾	80	111½	106	113⅝	9.63
	Barclays N. Amer Capital .... [21]Gtd Cap Notes	10½s	2017	$jD15	AA	[23]104.929	....	Z100	S5	99.35	'87	400	113⅝	96¾	112½	101	111¾	9.29
	Bell Tel Canada[24] .... 1st AV	8s	1994	©mN15	AA	100	....	....		....	'71	65.0	100¾	50	99	93¾	‡98⅞	8.43
•	Bell Tel Canada[24] .... Deb DA	8¾s	2006	$Ao	AA	±103.20	....	....	S1	99¼	'76	200	104⅜	55	101⅞	94¾	103	8.38
•	Bell Tel Canada[24] .... Deb DE	9s	2008	$Jj15	AA	[25]103.60	....	....	S1	100	'78	200	104⅞	54	100¾	97	105¾	8.34
•	Bell Tel Canada[24] .... Deb DJ	13⅜s	2010	$aO15	AA	[26]105.35	....	....	S1	100	'80	200	130½	82	121⅞	117½	123¾	10.46
	BET Icecalm B.V. .... Gtd[27]Notes[28]	8⅝s	2001	$aO15	A +	NC	....	....	M3	99.60	'91	200	....	....	100	99½	100	8.62

(1) **Exchange.** • New York Stock Exchange; ♦ American Stock Exchange

(2) **Individual Issue Statistics.** Description of individual issues; abbreviations are found on page 2 of the *Bond Guide.*

FIGURE 8-13: Key Interest Rates

Key Interest Rates

Annualized interest rates on certain investments as reported by the Federal Reserve Board on a weekly-average basis:

	Week Ended:	
	Oct. 25, 1991	Oct. 18, 1991
Treasury bills (90 day)-a	5.01	5.00
Commrcl paper (Dealer, 90 day)-a	5.34	5.33
Certfs of Deposit (Resale, 90 day)	5.33	5.31
Federal funds (Overnight)-b	5.24	5.28
Eurodollars (90 day)-b	5.35	5.33
Treasury bills (one year)-c	5.39	5.33
Treasury notes (three year)-c	6.30	6.21
Treasury notes (five year)-c	·6.96	6.85
Treasury notes (ten year)-c	7.66	7.50
Treasury bonds (30 year)-c	8.07	7.93

a-Discounted rates. b-Week ended Wednesday, October 23, 1991 and Wednesday October 16, 1991. c-Yields, adjusted for constant maturity.

FIGURE 8-14: Consumer Savings Interest Rates

Consumer Savings Rates

Money Market Deposits-a	4.89%
Super-NOW Accounts-a	4.42%
Six-month Certificates-a	5.19%
One-year Certificates-a	5.43%
Thirty-month Accounts-a	5.91%
Five-Year Certificates-a	6.53%
U.S. Savings Bonds-b	6.57%

a-Average rate paid yesterday by 100 large banks and thrifts in the 10 largest metropolitan areas as compiled by Bank Rate Monitor.
b-Current annual yield. Guaranteed minimum 6%.

FIGURE 8-15: *Banxquote®* Money Markets

BANXQUOTE® MONEY MARKETS

Survey ended Thursday, September 12, 1991
AVERAGE YIELDS OF MAJOR BANKS

	MMI*	One Month	Two Months	Three Months	Six Months	One Year	Two Years	Five Years
NEW YORK								
Savings	4.86%	z	z	5.19%	5.31%	5.41%	5.89%	7.01%
Jumbos	4.92%	5.30%	5.30%	5.30%	5.37%	5.55%	5.88%	6.39%
CALIFORNIA								
Savings	5.20%	z	z	5.31%	5.36%	5.55%	6.18%	7.25%
Jumbos	5.40%	5.33%	5.39%	5.42%	5.51%	5.63%	6.32%	7.54%
PENNSYLVANIA								
Savings	5.00%	z	z	5.02%	5.27%	5.49%	5.71%	6.87%
Jumbos	5.33%	5.11%	5.11%	5.13%	5.20%	5.36%	5.87%	6.69%
ILLINOIS								
Savings	5.12%	z	z	5.27%	5.41%	5.61%	6.32%	7.16%
Jumbos	5.36%	5.25%	5.27%	5.32%	5.44%	5.66%	6.38%	7.27%
TEXAS								
Savings	5.45%	z	z	5.19%	5.38%	5.53%	5.98%	7.00%
Jumbos	5.45%	5.23%	5.23%	5.25%	5.45%	5.60%	6.09%	7.05%
FLORIDA								
Savings	4.86%	z	z	4.83%	5.10%	5.42%	6.15%	7.08%
Jumbos	5.00%	4.84%	4.84%	4.94%	5.11%	5.52%	6.07%	7.05%
BANK AVERAGE								
Savings	5.09%	z	z	5.14%	5.31%	5.50%	6.05%	7.06%
Jumbos	5.24%	5.18%	5.19%	5.23%	5.35%	5.55%	6.13%	7.13%
WEEKLY CHANGE (in percentage point)								
Savings	−0.01	z	z	−0.01	−0.02	−0.04	−0.03	−0.04
Jumbos	−0.03	−0.05	−0.06	−0.05	−0.08	−0.10	−0.08	−0.07

SAVINGS CD YIELDS OFFERED THROUGH LEADING BROKERS

	Three Months	Six Months	One Year	Two Years	Five Years
BROKER AVERAGE	5.68%	5.50%	5.50%	6.08%	7.30%
WEEKLY CHANGE	+0.04	−0.07	−0.15	−0.42	−0.08

*Money Market investments include MMDA, NOW, savings deposits, passbook and other liquid accounts.
    Each depositor is insured by the Federal Deposit Insurance Corp. (FDIC) up to $100,000 per insured institution.
    COMPOUND METHODS: c-Continuously, d-Daily, w-Weekly, m-Monthly, q-Quarterly, s-Semi-annually, a-Annually, si-Simple interest.
    F-Floating rate, P-Prime CD, T-T-Bill CD.

YIELD BASIS: A-365/365, B-360/360, C-365/360.

The information included in this table has been obtained directly from broker-dealers, banks and savings institutions, but the accuracy and validity cannot be guaranteed. Rates are subject to change. Yields, terms and creditworthiness should be verified before investing.

z-Unavailable.

HIGH YIELD SAVINGS

Small minimum balance, generally $500 to $25,000

Money Market Investments*	Rate		Yield
Standard Pac, Newport Beach Ca	6.25%	dC	6.54%
Hamilton Svgs, San Francisco Ca	6.25%	dA	6.45%
Columbia First, Arlington Va	6.15%	dC	6.43%
Perpetual Savings, Vienna Va	6.20%	dA	6.40%
Beverly Hills, Laguna Hills Ca	6.10%	dA	6.29%

Six Months CDs	Rate		Yield
First NY Bank, New York NY	6.75%	FP	6.96%
Chevy Chase, Laurel Md	6.20%	qA	6.35%
Potomac Svgs, Silver Spring Md	6.15%	dA	6.34%
Bankeast, Manchester NH	6.15%	mA	6.33%
Chittenden Bank, Burlington Vt	6.11%	dA	6.30%

One Month CDs	Rate		Yield
Merchants Bank, Kansas City Mo	5.90%	dA	6.08%
San Joaquin Bank, Bakersfield Ca	5.90%	siA	5.90%
Dartmouth Bank, Manchester NH	5.74%	mA	5.89%
First NY Bank, New York NY	5.60%	dA	5.76%
Chevy Chase, Laurel Md	5.60%	dA	5.76%

One Year CDs	Rate		Yield
First NY Bank, New York NY	6.75%	FP	6.96%
Home Fed Bank, San Diego Ca	6.53%	dA	6.75%
Great American, Phoenix Az	6.54%	qA	6.70%
Credit-International, Wash DC	6.50%	dA	6.66%
MBNA, Newark De	6.45%	dA	6.66%

Two Months CDs	Rate		Yield
Merchants Bank, Kansas City Mo	5.90%	dA	6.08%
Dartmouth Bank, Manchester NH	5.74%	mA	5.89%
San Joaquin Bank, Bakersfield Ca	5.85%	siA	5.85%
Gateway Bank, San Francisco Ca	5.65%	mA	5.80%
Standard Pac, Newport Beach Ca	5.55%	dC	5.79%

Two Years CDs	Rate		Yield
Hamilton Svgs, San Francisco Ca	7.00%	dA	7.25%
Sthern Cal Svgs, Beverly Hills Ca	6.85%	dA	7.09%
Pioneer Savings, Rocky Mount NC	6.90%	dA	7.08%
Continental Svgs, San Fran Ca	6.77%	dA	7.00%
California Thrift, Snta Barbara Ca	6.78%	mA	6.99%

Three Months CDs	Rate		Yield
Washington Mutual, Seattle Wa	6.00%	mA	6.17%
Beverly Hills, Laguna Hills Ca	5.95%	dA	6.13%
Meritor Savings, Arlington Va	5.90%	dA	6.08%
Merchants Bank, Kansas City Mo	5.90%	dA	6.08%
First Deposit, Tilton NH	5.87%	dA	6.05%

Five Years CDs	Rate		Yield
United Savings, San Francisco Ca	7.70%	dA	8.00%
Merchants Bank, Kansas City Mo	7.70%	dA	8.00%
Hamilton Svgs, San Francisco Ca	7.70%	dA	8.00%
Continental Svgs, San Fran Ca	7.70%	dA	8.00%
Eastern Savings, Baltimore Md	7.67%	mA	7.95%

HIGH YIELD JUMBOS

Large minimum balance, generally $95,000 to $100,000

Money Market Investments*	Rate		Yield
Standard Pac, Newport Beach Ca	6.25%	dC	6.54%
Hamilton Svgs, San Francisco Ca	6.25%	dA	6.45%
Beverly Hills, Laguna Hills Ca	6.25%	dA	6.45%
Columbia First, Arlington Va	6.15%	dC	6.43%
Perpetual Savings, Vienna Va	6.20%	dA	6.40%

Six Months Jumbo CDs	Rate		Yield
First Deposit NCCB, Concord NH	6.18%	dA	6.37%
Washington Mutual, Seattle Wa	6.15%	mA	6.33%
Bankeast, Manchester NH	6.15%	mA	6.33%
Chittenden Bank, Burlington Vt	6.11%	dA	6.30%
MBNA, Newark De	6.10%	dA	6.29%

One Month Jumbo CDs	Rate		Yield
San Joaquin Bank, Bakersfield Ca	6.00%	siA	6.00%
Merchants Bank, Kansas City Mo	5.85%	siC	5.93%
Chevy Chase, Laurel Md	5.90%	siA	5.90%
Poughkeepsie SB, Poughkpsie NY	5.80%	siC	5.88%
Washington Fed, Washington DC	5.85%	siA	5.85%

One Year Jumbo CDs	Rate		Yield
First American, Atlanta Ga	6.80%	siA	6.80%
MBNA, Newark De	6.55%	dA	6.77%
Home Fed Bank, San Diego Ca	6.53%	dA	6.75%
First Deposit NCCB, Concord NH	6.39%	dA	6.60%
Credit International, Wash DC	6.50%	siA	6.50%

Two Months Jumbo CDs	Rate		Yield
First Deposit NCCB, Concord NH	5.83%	dA	6.00%
Poughkeepsie SB, Poughkpsie NY	5.90%	siC	5.98%
San Joaquin Bank, Bakersfield Ca	5.95%	siA	5.95%
Washington Fed, Washington DC	5.95%	siA	5.95%
Merchants Bank, Kansas City Mo	5.85%	siC	5.93%

Two Years Jumbo CDs	Rate		Yield
Hamilton Svgs, San Francisco Ca	7.10%	siA	7.10%
First Deposit NCCB, Concord NH	6.81%	dA	7.05%
California Thrift, Snta Barbara Ca	6.82%	mA	7.04%
Pioneer Savings, Rocky Mount NC	6.95%	siA	6.95%
Key Bank USA, Albany NY	6.70%	mA	6.91%

Three Months Jumbo CDs	Rate		Yield
First Deposit NCCB, Concord NH	5.98%	dA	6.16%
Merchants Bank, Kansas City Mo	6.05%	siC	6.13%
Poughkeepsie SB, Poughkpsie NY	6.00%	siC	6.08%
Pioneer Savings, Rocky Mount NC	6.05%	siA	6.05%
First Deposit, Tilton NH	5.87%	dA	6.05%

Five Years Jumbo CDs	Rate		Yield
Eastern Savings, Baltimore Md	7.67%	mA	7.95%
First Deposit NCCB, Concord NH	7.65%	dA	7.95%
Hamilton Svgs, San Francisco Ca	7.80%	siA	7.80%
Citibank SD, Sioux Falls SD	7.38%	dC	7.77%
Metropolitan Bank, Arlington Va	7.50%	mA	7.76%

For more information call MASTERFUND at (800) 325-3242.

Source: BANXQUOTE, Wilmington, De.
BANXQUOTE is a registered trademark and service mark of MASTERFUND INC.

FIGURE 8-16: "Credit Markets," *Investor's Business Daily*

Stocks' Losses Are T-Bills' Gain; Bond Yields Return To 8% Level

By Phil Hawkins
Investor's Business Daily

NEW YORK — Market participants will be served a hearty $43 billion of new Treasury bills and notes before the Thanksgiving feast on Thursday.

A weekly auction is scheduled on Monday by the department of $20.4 billion in equal portions of new three-month and six-month bills. Both new bills require a purchase of at least $10,000.

Two large notes sales also are slated. They comprise $13.5 billion of two-year notes in minimum denominations of $5,000 on Monday and $9 billion of five-year notes in minimums of $1,000

Credit Markets

on Tuesday. Their yields have been projected at about 5.46% and 6.54%, respectively.

Seasoned fixed-income securities turned in another eventful session last Friday.

Treasury bills again attracted investors who were fleeing from common stocks, which dropped about 30 points. They have skyrocketed to their best levels in nearly 15 years on the flight to safety as well as anticipation of another imminent official reduction in nearby short-term interest rates.

Key Corporate Rates

Issue			Moody's Rating	Bid	Ask	Chg	Yield %
JP Morgan	7⅝	1998	Aa-2	100	100¼	Unch	7.58
Avco Fin	7½	1996	A-1	100¼	100½	Unch	7.39
AMR	8.10	1998	Baa-1	99⅝	99⅞	Unch	8.12
Caesars	13½	1997	B-1	103½	104	Unch	12.47
Ft How	12⅜	1997	B-2	103	103½	Unch	11.46
Safeway	10	2001	Ba-3	101	101½	Unch	9.79
Wheel-Pitt	12¼	2000	Ba-3	100½	101	Unch	11.92
Fr-McMor	6.55	2001	Ba-3	91	93	Unch	Conv
Home Dep	6	1997	A-2	189	192	Unch	Conv
Mead	6¾	2012	Baa-1	88½	89½	Unch	Conv
Br-Ferr	6¼	2012	A-3	78½	79½	Unch	Conv
IBM	7⅞	2004	Aa-1	101½	102	Unch	Conv

Conv-Convertible.

Nevertheless, the MCM official said, "we remain constructive about bonds over several months" immediately ahead. "Bonds typically move in tandem when stocks drop sharply; simultaneous flights into Treasury bills cause the yield curve to steepen. When stocks stabilize and the Fed doesn't ease (official policy), bills come under pressure, bonds rally and the yield curve returns to its earlier shape.

"Inflation fears stemming from stock market weakness are overblown," the MCM analysts contended. "Although there have been four stock market breaks of more than 3% in as many years, the Fed eased (policy) aggressively only once (in 1987) to reliquify the financial system.

Bond Rating Systems

MOODY'S

Aaa Judged to be of the best quality and least investment risk; generally referred to as "gilt edge." Interest payments are protected by a large or exceptionally stable margin, and principal is secure. Although various protective elements may change, such foreseeable changes are least likely to impair the fundamentally strong position of such issues.

Aa Judged to be of high quality by all standards. Together with the Aaa group they comprise what are generally known as high-grade bonds. Aa bonds are rated lower because margins of protection may not be as large as in Aaa securities, fluctuation of protective elements may be of greater amplitude, or other elements might make the long-term risks appear somewhat larger than in Aaa securities.

A Deemed to possess many favorable investment attributes as upper-medium-grade obligations. Factors securing principal and interest are considered adequate, but elements may be present that suggest a susceptibility to future impairment.

Baa Considered medium-grade obligations, neither highly protected nor poorly secure. Principal and interest appear adequate for the present, but certain protective elements may be lacking or have speculative characteristics.

Ba Judged to have speculative elements; their future cannot be considered well assured. Often the protection of interest and principal may be very moderate and thus inadequately safeguarded during future good and bad times. Uncertainty characterizes bonds in this class.

B Generally lack characteristics of a desirable investment. Assurance of interest and principal payments or of maintenance of other contractual terms over a long period of time may be small.

Caa Judged to have poor standing, such issues may risk default or have elements of danger with respect to principal or interest.

Ca Represent obligations that are highly speculative. Such issues are often in default or have other marked shortcomings.

Continued.

C   Can be regarded as having extremely poor prospects of ever attaining any real investment standing.

NOTE: Moody's applies numerical modifiers—1, 2, and 3—in each generic rating classification from Aa through B in its corporate bond rating system. The modifier 1 indicates that the security ranks in the higher end of its generic rating category; the modifier 2 indicates a mid-range ranking; and the modifier 3 indicates that the issue ranks in the lower end of its generic rating category.

Source: *Moody's Bond Record: Corporates, Convertibles, Governments, and Municipals*, June, 1991, Moody's Investors Services.

STANDARD & POOR'S CORPORATE AND MUNICIPAL RATINGS

A Standard & Poor's corporate or municipal debt rating is a current assessment of the creditworthiness of an obligor with respect to a specific obligation. This assessment may take into consideration obligors such as guarantors, insurers, or lessees.

The debt rating is not a recommendation to purchase, sell, or hold a security inasmuch as it does not comment on market price or suitability for a particular investor.

The ratings are based on current information furnished by the issuer or obtained by Standard & Poor's from other sources it considers reliable. Standard & Poor's does not perform an audit in connection with any rating and may, on occasion, rely on unaudited financial information. The ratings may be changed, suspended, or withdrawn as a result of changes in, or unavailability of, such information, or of other circumstances.

The ratings are based, in varying degrees, on the following three considerations:

1. Likelihood of default that is, capacity and willingness of the obligor to make timely payment of interest and repayment of principal in accordance with the terms of the obligation;

2. Nature and provisions of the obligation;

3. Protection afforded by, and relative position of, the obligation in the event of bankruptcy, reorganization, or other arrangements under the laws of bankruptcy and other laws affecting creditors' rights.

Standard & Poor's Rates

AAA   The highest rating; capacity to pay interest and repay principal is extremely strong.

AA   Very strong capacity to pay interest and repay principal; different from the higher-rated issues only in small degree.

A   Strong capacity to pay interest and repay principal, although this category is
        more susceptible to adverse effects of changes in circumstances and
        economic conditions.

BBB Adequate capacity to pay interest and repay principal. Whereas BBB bonds
        normally exhibit adequate protective parameters, adverse economic
        conditions or changing circumstances are more likely to lead to a weakened
        capacity to pay interest and repay principal.

BB, B, Regarded, on balance, as predominantly speculative with respect to capacity
CCC, to pay interest and repay principal payments in accordance with the terms of
CC   the obligation. BB indicates the lowest degree of speculation and CC the
        highest degree of speculation within this category. Although bonds with
        either of these ratings will likely carry some protection, they are outweighed
        by significant uncertainty or major risk exposure to adverse conditions.

C   Reserved for income bonds on which no interest is paid.

D   Bonds in default; payment of interest and/or repayment of principal is in
        arrears.

(+) or The ratings from AA to B may be further modified by the addition of a plus
(-) (+) or a minus sign (-) to show relative standing within the major rating
        categories.

Provisional Ratings

The letter **"p"** indicates that the rating is provisional. A provisional rating assumes
the successful completion of the project being financed by the debt being rated and
indicates that payment of debt service requirements is largely or entirely dependent
on the successful and timely completion of the project. This rating, however, while
addressing credit quality subsequent to completion of the project, makes no comment
on the likelihood or risk of default upon failure of such completion. The investor
should exercise his own judgment with respect to such likelihood and risk.

The letter **"L"** indicates that the rating pertains to the principal amount of
those bonds where the underlying deposit collateral is fully insured by the Federal
Savings and Loan Insurance Corporation (FSLIC) or the Federal Deposit Insurance
Corporation (FDIC). Continuation of the rating is contingent upon S&P's receipt of
an executed copy of the escrow agreement or closing documentation confirming
investments and cash flows.

"NR" indicates that no rating has been requested, that there is insufficient
information on which to base a rating, or that S&P does not rate a particular type of
obligation as a matter of policy.

Debt obligations of issuers outside the United States and its territories are
rated on the same basis as domestic, corporate, and municipal issues. The ratings
measure the creditworthiness of the obligor but do not take into account currency
exchange rates and related uncertainties.

Bond Investment Quality Standards

Under present commercial bank regulation issued by the Comptroller of the Currency, bonds rated in the top four S&P categories (AAA, AA, A, BBB, commonly known as "investment-grade" ratings) are generally regarded as eligible for bank investment. In addition, the Legal Investment Laws of various states may impose certain ratings or other standards for obligations eligible for investment by savings banks, trust companies, insurance companies, and fiduciaries.

Source: Standard & Poor's *Debt Ratings Criteria: Industrial Overview*, 1986.

FITCH'S

AAA	Considered to be investment grade and of the highest quality. The obligor has an extraordinary ability to pay interest and repay principal, which is unlikely to be affected by reasonably foreseeable events.
AA	Considered to be investment grade and of high quality. The obligor's ability to pay interest and repay principal, while very strong, is somewhat less than the AAA-rated securities.
A	Considered to be investment grade and of good quality. The obligor's ability to pay interest and repay principal is deemed strong but may be more vulnerable to adverse changes in economic conditions and circumstances than higher-rated bonds.
BBB	Considered to be investment grade and of satisfactory quality. The obligor's ability to pay interest and repay principal is deemed adequate. Adverse changes in economic conditions and circumstances, however, are more likely to weaken this ability than bonds with higher ratings.
BB	Considered speculative and of low investment grade. The obligor's ability to pay interest and repay principal is not strong and is vulnerable to adverse changes in economic conditions.
B	Considered speculative. Bonds in this class are thinly protected as to the obligor's ability to pay interest over the life of the issue and repay principal when due.
CCC	These issues may have certain characteristics that, with the passage of time, could lead to default on principal or interest payments.
CC	These bonds are minimally protected. Default in payment of interest and/or principal seems probable.
C	Bonds in actual or imminent default in payment of interest or principal.
DDD, DD, D	Bonds in default and in arrears in interest and/or principal payments. Such bonds are extremely speculative and should be valued only on the basis of their value in liquidation or reorganization of the obligor.
(+) or (-)	The ratings from AA to BB within a rating category indicate refinements more closely reflecting strengths and weaknesses and are not to be used as trend indicators.

Key to Fitch's Rating Process

Fitch's rating process begins with a request to Fitch by an issuer or its authorized representative, or an institutional investor. After all pertinent financial and operating data relating to the issuer and the security are submitted, the rating request is assigned to an analyst specializing in the issuer's industry.

The entire process takes approximately two weeks, depending on the complexity of the issue. Once the relevant data have been examined, analysts review their findings and their rating recommendations with the Fitch Rating Committee. Before a rating is approved, it must have the support of a majority of the committee's members.

If a rating is contested, appeal procedures go into effect. During an appeal, additional information and/or a more detailed explanation of previously submitted information will be considered. Once the appeal is completed, the final decision is made by the Rating Committee.

Fitch ratings are widely accepted by regulatory agencies in states that require ratings on investments by banks, pension funds, and savings and loan institutions.

Key to Fitch's Rating Symbols

Fitch's ratings guide investors in determining the investment risk attached to a security. A rating represents Fitch's assessment of the issuer's ability to meet its obligations on a specific debt issue.

Fitch's ratings are not recommendations to buy, sell, or hold securities, for the ratings incorporate no information on market price or a yield relative to other debt instruments. A rating takes into consideration special features of the issue, its relationship to other obligations of the issuer, the issuer's record, any guarantor's record, and the political and economic environment that might affect the issuer's future financial strength.

Securities with the same rating are of similar, but not necessarily identical, investment quality due to the limited number of rating categories, which cannot fully reflect small differences in the degree of risk. Moreover, the risk factor varies among industries and among corporate, health care, and municipal obligations.

Fitch's Demand Bond or Note Ratings

Certain demand securities empower the holder, at the holder's option, to require the issuer (usually through a remarketing agent) to repurchase the security with notice (customarily 7 to 30 days with accrued interest at par). This is also referred to as a put option. The ratings of the long-term and the demand provision may be changed or withdrawn at any time if, in Fitch's sole judgement, changing circumstances warrant such action.

Fitch's demand-provision ratings carry the same symbols and related definitions as those for commercial paper and long-term bonds, for example AA/F-1.

Fitch Investment Note Rating Symbols

Fitch investment note ratings are grouped into four categories, as described below. Ratings on notes with maturities generally from one to three years reflect Fitch's current appraisal of assurance of timely payment, whatever the source.

FIN-1 +   Notes are regarded as having the strongest degree of assurance for timely payment.

FIN-1   Notes reflect an assurance of timely payment only slightly less than the strongest issues.

FIN-2   Notes have a degree of assurance for timely payment but with a lesser margin of safety than the prior two categories.

FIN-3   Notes have speculative characteristics, which suggest that the degree of assurance for timely payment is minimal.

Source: *Fitch Ratings Monthly*, Fitch Investors Services, Inc., One State Street Plaza, New York, NY 10004.

MOODY'S SHORT-TERM DEBT RATINGS

Moody's short-term debt ratings represent its opinions of issuers' ability to repay punctually senior debt obligations with an original maturity not exceeding one year.

Among the obligations covered are commercial paper, Eurocommercial paper, bank deposits, bankers' acceptances, obligations to deliver foreign exchange, and insurance company senior policyholder and claims obligations. Obligations relying on support mechanisms—such as letters of credit and bonds of indemnity—are excluded unless explicitly rated.

Moody's employs the following three designations, all judged to be investment grade, to rate the relative repayment ability of issuers:

1. **Issuers rated Prime-1** (or supporting institutions) show superior ability to repay senior short-term debt obligations. Prime-1 repayment ability often will be evidenced by the following characteristics:

- Leading market positions in well-established industries
- High rates of return of funds employed
- Conservative capitalization structure with moderate reliance on debt and ample asset protection
- Broad margins in earnings coverage of fixed financial charges and high internal cash generation
- Well-established access to a range of financial markets and assured sources of alternate liquidity

2. **Issuers rated Prime-2** (or supporting institutions) show strong ability to repay senior short-term debt obligations. This will normally be evidenced by many

of the characteristics cited above, but to a lesser degree. Earnings trends and coverage ratios, although sound, may be more subject to variation. Capitalization characteristics, albeit still appropriate, may be more affected by external conditions. Ample alternate liquidity is maintained.

3. **Issuers rated Prime-3** (or supporting institutions) show acceptable ability to repay senior short-term debt obligations. The effect of industry characteristics and market compositions may be more pronounced. Variability in earnings and profitability may result in changes in the level of debt protection measurements and may require relatively high financial leverage. Adequate alternate liquidity is maintained.

Therefore, issuers rated **NOT prime** do not fall within any of the Prime rating categories.

Obligations of a bank branch are considered to be domiciled in the country where the branch is located. Unless noted as an exception, Moody's rating on a bank's ability to repay senior obligations extends only to branches located in countries that carry a Moody's sovereign rating. Such branch obligations are rated at the lower of the bank's rating or Moody's sovereign rating for bank deposits for the country in which the bank is located.

If the currency in which an obligation is denominated is different from the currency of the country in which the obligation is domiciled, Moody's ratings do not incorporate an opinion as to whether payment of the obligation will be affected by actions of the government controlling the currency of denomination. In addition, risks associated with bilateral conflicts between an investor's home country and either the issuer's home country or the country where an issuer's branch is located are not incorporated into Moody's short-term debt ratings.

Moody's makes no representation that rated bank or insurance company obligations are exempt from the registration under the U.S. Securities Act of 1933 or issued in conformity with any other applicable law or regulation. Nor does Moody's represent that any specific bank or insurance company obligation is legally enforceable or a valid senior obligation of a rated issuer. If an issuer represents to Moody's that its short-term debt obligations are supported by the credit of another entity (or entities), then the name (or names) of such supporting entity (or entities) is (are) listed within the parentheses beneath the name of the issuer; or a footnote refers the reader to another page for the name (or names) of the supporting entity or (entities). In assigning ratings to such issuers, Moody's evaluates the financial strength of the affiliated corporations, commercial banks, insurance companies, foreign governments, or other entities—but only as one factor in the total rating assessment. Moody's makes no representation and gives no opinion on the legal validity or enforceability of any support arrangement.

Moody's ratings are opinions, not recommendations to buy or sell, and their accuracy is not guaranteed. A rating should be weighted solely as one factor in an investment decision, and you should make your own study and evaluation on any issuer whose securities or debt obligations you consider buying or selling.

NOTE: Moody's ratings are subject to change. Because of the possible time lapse between Moody's assignment or change of a rating and use of this publication, verify the current rating of any security or issuer before acting.

Source: *Moody's Bond Record: Corporates, Convertibles, Governments, and Municipals*, June, 1991, Moody's Investor Services.

Standard Abbreviations

The following abbreviations are commonly used throughout the investment world.

–	Deficit, loss
NA or N	Not Available
NR	Not Rated by Moody's
CP E-O-Q	Commercial Paper outstanding at End Of Quarter
QT	Fiscal quarter
CTNs	Collateral Trust Notes

MOODY'S MUNICIPAL RATINGS

Note and Demand Feature Ratings

Moody's short-term ratings are designated Moody's Investment Grade (MIG) 1 through 4 (or VMIG) 1 through 4. This is a rating given on an issue having a demand feature—Variable Rate Demand Obligation (VRDO). When Moody's assigns a MIG or Variable Moody's Investment Grade (VMIG) rating, all categories define an investment grade situation. The purpose of the MIG or VMIG ratings is to provide investors with a simple system by which the relative investment qualities of short-term obligations may be evaluated.

Such ratings recognize the differences between short-term credit risk and long-term risk. Factors affecting the liquidity of the borrower and short-term cyclical elements are critical in short-term ratings, whereas other factors of major importance in bond risk—long-term secular trends for example—may be less important over the short run.

A short-term rating may also be assigned on an issue having a demand feature generally as a variable rate demand obligation (VRDO). Such ratings will be designated as VMIG or, if the demand feature is not rated, as NR. Short-term ratings on issues with demand features are differentiated by the use of the VMIG symbol to reflect such characteristics as payment upon periodic demand rather than fixed maturity dates and payment relying on external liquidity. Additionally, investors should be alert to the fact that the source of payment may be limited to the external liquidity with no (or limited) legal recourse to the issuer in the event the demand is not met. A VMIG rating may also be assigned to commercial paper programs. Such programs are characterized as having variable short-term maturities but having neither a variable rate nor demand feature.

In the case of VRDOs, two ratings are assigned: one represents an evaluation of the degree of risk associated with scheduled principal and interest payments; the other represents an evaluation of the degree of risk associated with the demand feature. The short-term rating assigned to the demand feature of VRDOs is designated as VMIG. If no rating is applied to the long- or short-term aspect of a VRDO, it will be designated NR.

Short-Term Loan Ratings: Definitions

MIG 1/ This designation denotes best quality, with current strong protec-
VMIG 1 tion—established cash flows, superior liquidity support, or demonstrated broad-based access to the market for refinancing.
MIG 2/ This designation denotes high quality. Margins of protection are ample
VMIG 2 although not so wide as MIG 1/VMIG 1.
MIG 3/ This designation denotes favorable quality. All security elements are
VMIG 3 accounted for but not to the extent of preceding ratings. Liquidity and cash flow protection may be narrow and market access for refinancing is likely to be less well established.
MIG 4/ This designation denotes adequate quality. Protection commonly required
VMIG 4 of an investment security is present and, although not distinctly or predominantly speculative, there is specific risk.

Issues or features associated with MIG or VMIG ratings are identified by date of issue, date of maturity or maturities, rating expiration date, and description to distinguish each rating from other ratings. Thus each rating designation is unique, even for similar issues from the same obligor. MIG ratings terminate at the retirement of the obligation, but VMIG expirations will be a function of each issue's specific structural or credit features.

Source: *Moody's Bond Record: Corporates, Convertibles, Governments, and Municipals*, June, 1991, Moody's Investors Services, p. 476.

COMMERCIAL PAPER RATINGS

Standard & Poor's Ratings: Definitions

A Standard & Poor's commercial paper rating is a current assessment of the likelihood of timely payment of debt having an original maturity of no more than 365 days. Ratings are graded into four categories from A (highest quality) to D (lowest):

A Regarded as having the greatest capacity for timely payment, issues in this category are designated 1, 2, or 3 to indicate their relative degree of safety.
A-1 The degree of safety regarding timely payment is either overwhelming or very strong. Issues with overwhelmingly safe characteristics are indicated by a plus (+) sign.

A-2   Capacity for timely payment is strong. However, the relative degree of safety is not as high as for issues designated A-1.

A-3   Issues have a satisfactory capacity for timely payment. They are, however, somewhat more vulnerable to adverse changes in circumstances than obligations carrying higher designations.

B   Issues regarded as having adequate capacity for timely payment. However, such capacity may be damaged by changing conditions or short-term adversities.

C   Short-term debt obligations with a doubtful capacity for payment.

D   The issue is either in default or expected to be in default upon maturity.

The commercial paper rating is not a recommendation to purchase or sell a security. The ratings are based on current information furnished to Standard & Poor's by the issuer or obtained from other sources it considers reliable. The ratings may be changed, suspended, or withdrawn as a result of changes in, or unavailability of, such information.

Source: Standard and Poor's *Debt Rating Criteria: Industrial Overview*, 1986.

Fitch Ratings: Definitions

Fitch Commercial Paper Ratings are assigned at the request of an issuer of debt obligations that have an original maturity not in excess of 270 days. The ratings reflect Fitch's current appraisal of the degree of assurance of timely payments of such debt. The name *Fitch* in commercial paper rating symbols may be abbreviated, for example F-1.

Fitch commercial paper ratings are graded into four categories from 1 (highest grade) to 4 (lowest), as defined below:

Fitch-1.   The highest-Grade commercial paper has the strongest assurance for timely payments.

Fitch-2.   Issues are graded very good, reflecting an assurance of timely payment that is only slightly less than F-1 issues.

Fitch-3.   Good-grade commercial paper has satisfactory assurance for timely payment, but the margin of safety is not as great as F-1 and F-2 issues.

Fitch-4.   Poor-grade issues have characteristics suggesting that assurance for timely payment is minimal, susceptible to near-term adverse change due to less favorable financial or economic conditions.

STANDARD & POOR'S MUNICIPAL NOTES RATINGS

A Standard & Poor's note rating reflects the liquidity concerns and market access risks unique to notes. Notes due in three years or less will likely receive a note rating. Notes maturing beyond three years will most likely receive a long-term debt rating. The rating received further depends on two factors:

1. Amortization schedule. The larger the final maturity relative to other maturities, the more likely it will be treated as a note.
2. Source of payment. The more dependent the issue is on the market for its refinancing, the more likely it will be treated as a note.

S&P's note ratings are described briefly.

SP-1   This designation denotes very strong or strong capacity to pay principal and interest. Issues in this group that are determined to possess overwhelming safety characteristics will be given a plus (+) designation.
SP-2   This designation denotes satisfactory capacity to pay principal and interest.
SP-3   This designation denotes speculative capacity to pay principal and interest.

S&P's Tax-Exempt Demand Bonds

Standard & Poor's assigns "dual" ratings to all long-term debt issues that have as part of their provisions a demand or double feature.

The first rating addresses the likelihood of repayment of principal and interest as due, and the second rating addresses only the demand feature. The long-term debt rating symbols are used for bonds to denote long-term maturity, and the commercial paper rating symbols are used to denote put options (for example, AAA/A-1+). For newer "demand notes," S&P's note rating symbols are used in combination with the commercial paper symbols (for example, SP-1+/A-1+).

Source: *Debt Ratings Criteria: Industrial Review*, 1986, Standard & Poor's Corporation.

THOMPSON DOMESTIC AND FOREIGN BANK RATINGS

Thompson BankWatch ratings are based on a quantitative analysis of all segments of an organization including, where applicable, holding company, member banks or associations, and other subsidiaries. Thompson BankWatch assigns only one rating to each company, based on consolidated financials. Although the ratings are intended to apply equally to all operating entities of the organization, certain cases may show one segment to be more liquid (or less creditworthy) than another (i.e., a holding company versus a bank).

Thompson BankWatch ratings are not merely an assessment of the likelihood of timely principal and interest payment. Also incorporated is Thompson's opinion on the company's vulnerability to adverse developments, which may impact the market's perception of the company and thereby affect marketability of its securities.

Thompson BankWatch ratings do not constitute recommendations to buy or sell; nor do they suggest specific investment criteria for individual clients.

If, in Thompson's opinion, disclosure is incomplete and/or untimely, a qualified rating (QR) is assigned to the institution. QRs are derived exclusively from a quantitative analysis of publicly available information; qualitative judgments have not been incorporated.

Generally, banks with assets of less than $500 million are assigned a numerical "score" based exclusively on a statistical model developed by BankWatch. These scores, which are compiled from regulatory reports, represent a performance evaluation of each company relative to a nationwide composite of similar-size banks. The score indicates the bank's percentile ranking, i.e., a score of 75 suggests that the company has outperformed 75 percent of its peer group. If a bank of this size is associated with a holding company that is not rated by BankWatch, an asterisk (*) may precede the holding company name. The asterisk indicates that the analysis/score on that company has been done on a "bank only" basis and does not reflect the consolidated company's financial performance.

IMPORTANT: Be advised as to the proprietary nature of the Thompson BankWatch Service. Under no circumstances should ratings be disseminated to parties other than officers or employees of the client.

Thompson Ratings: Definitions

A   Company shows an exceptionally strong balance sheet and earnings record, translating into an excellent reputation and unquestioned access to its natural money markets. If weakness or vulnerability exists in any aspect of the company's business, it is entirely mitigated by the strengths of the organization.

A/B   Company is financially very solid, with a favorable track record and no apparent weakness. Its overall risk profile, while low, is not quite as favorable as for companies rated A-.

B   Company is strong with a solid financial record and is well received by its natural money markets. Some minor weaknesses may exist, but any deviation from the company's historical performance levels should be both limited and of short duration. The likelihood of a problem developing is small yet slightly greater than for a higher-rated company.

B/C   Company is clearly viewed as good credit. Some shortcomings are apparent, but they are not serious and are quite manageable in the short term.

C   Company is inherently a sound credit with no serious deficiencies, but financials reveal at least one fundamental area of concern that prevents a higher rating. The company may recently have experienced a period of difficulty, but those pressures should not last long. The company's ability to absorb a surprise, however, is less than that for organizations with better operating records.

C/D Although still considered an acceptable credit, the company has some meaningful deficiencies. Its ability to deal with further deterioration is less than that for better-rated companies.

D The company's financials suggest obvious weaknesses, most likely created by asset quality considerations and/or a poorly structured balance sheet. Meaningful uncertainty and vulnerability resists going forward. The ability to address further unexpected problems must be questioned.

D/E The company has areas of major weakness, which may signal funding and/or liquidity difficulties. A high degree of uncertainty exists as to the company's ability to absorb incremental problems.

E Very serious problems exist for the company, creating doubt as to its continued viability without some form of outside assistance—regulatory or otherwise.

Qualified Ratings

QR-A Exceptionally strong company as evidenced by recent financial statements and historical record.

QR-B Statistically a very sound institution. Financials reveal no abnormal lending or funding practices, and profitability, capital adequacy, and asset quality indicators consistently rank above peer group standards.

QR-C Statistical credentials should be viewed as average relative to peer group norms. A sound credit with one or more concerns preventing a higher rating.

QR-D The company's financial performance has typically fallen below average parameters established by its peers. Existing earnings weakness, exposure to margin contraction, asset quality concerns, and/or aggressive management of loan growth raise serious questions.

QR-E Several serious problems exist. Key financial indicators and/or abnormal growth patterns suggest significant uncertainty over the near term. The institution may well be under special regulatory supervision, and its continued viability with outside assistance may be at issue.

Country Rating

A Thompson country rating is an assessment of overall political and economic stability of a country in which a bank is domiciled. Ratings are graded from:

I This characterizes an industrialized country with a long history of political stability complemented by an overall sound financial condition. The country must have demonstrated ability to access world capital markets on favorable terms.

II This grades an industrialized country with a history of political and economic stability that is experiencing some current political unrest or significant economic difficulties. It enjoys continued ability to access capital markets worldwide but at increasingly higher margins. In the short run, the risk of default is minimal.

III   This rating refers to an industrialized or developing country that, despite a wealth of resources may have difficulty servicing its external debt as a result of political and/or economic problems. Although it has access to capital markets worldwide, this cannot be assured in the future.

IV   This marks a developing country currently facing extreme difficulty in raising external capital at all maturity levels.

V   This is a country that has defaulted on its external debt payments or is in a position where a default is highly probable.

Source: *Data Book*, quarterly, Thompson BankWatch, Inc., 61 Broadway, New York, NY 10006.

Mutual Funds

OVERVIEW

If you are an investor interested in receiving the benefit of professional portfolio management but do not have sufficient funds and/or time to purchase a diversified mix of securities, you will find the purchase of mutual fund shares attractive. Topics in this chapter include special features of mutual fund investment, performance criteria, how to choose a mutual fund and read mutual fund quotations, money market funds and quotations, and reading mutual fund statements and prospectuses.

SPECIAL FEATURES OF MUTUAL FUND INVESTMENT

A **mutual fund** is an investment company run by professional managers who pool the money of a number of investors so as to purchase a diverse portfolio. Participation is characterized by ownership of fund shares, each unit of ownership representing a pro rata interest in each of the fund's investments. For example, assume that ABC Mutual Fund owns 100 shares of IBM, 200 shares of Xerox, and 50 shares of GM. If an investor made a 2 percent investment in ABC Fund, the investor would own 2 shares of IBM (100 shares × 2%), 4 shares of Xerox (200 shares × 2%), and 1 share of GM (50 shares × 2%).

There are six major **advantages** of investing in mutual funds:

    1. **Diversification.** Each fund share gives you an interest in a cross section of stocks, bonds, or other investments. The variety and large number of holdings also help reduce risk. *NOTE: Spreading money among many investments increases the chance of picking some that will do well.*

    2. **Small minimum investment.** You can achieve diversification with a small amount of money ($250 or less) because of the large number of securities in the portfolio. A handful of funds have no minimums.

    3. **Automatic dividend reinvestment.** Most funds allow you to automatically reinvest dividends and any capital gains that may arise from the fund's buying and

selling activities. Funds typically do not charge a sales fee on automatic reinvestments.

   4. **Automatic withdrawals.** Most funds will allow you to withdraw money on a regular basis.

   5. **Liquidity.** You can redeem the shares owned.

   6. **Switching.** Although your long-term goals may remain the same, the investment climate does not. Therefore, you may want to make changes in your investments. To facilitate switching among funds, companies such as Fidelity and Vanguard have introduced "families" of funds. You may move among these families with relative freedom, usually at no fee.

   There are some **disadvantages** in mutual fund ownership: tracking a fund's record is not simple and often confusing; a fund's performance record only measures the past and does not guarantee its future performance; and some funds charge high management fees.

What is Net Asset Value

The price of a mutual fund is measured by net asset value (NAV):

$$\text{NAV} = \frac{\text{Fund's total assets} - \text{Liabilities}}{\text{Number of shares outstanding in the fund}}$$

EXAMPLE 1 _____

Looking again at ABC Mutual Fund, the market values below existed. ABC has total liabilities of $15,000. It has 1,000 shares outstanding. The NAV of the fund is calculated as follows:

	Market Value
IBM — $100 per share × 200 shares	$20,000
Xerox — $50 per share × 25 shares	10,000
GM — $75 per share × 100 shares	7,500
Value of the fund's portfolio	$37,500
Less: Total liabilities	15,000
Net value	$22,500
Numbers of the fund's shares outstanding	1,000
NAV per share ($22,500 ÷ 1,000)	$22.50

If you own 5% of the fund's outstanding shares, what is the value of your investment?

   You own 50 shares (5% × 1,000 shares). The value of your investment is $1,125 ($22.50 × 50 shares).

Most investors grew up on stocks and they are used to just looking at a price (NAV) in the paper. Keep in mind that this is perfectly acceptable for evaluating stock performance but not mutual fund performance. The NAV only indicates the current market value of the underlying portfolio. You must know how many shares you have in order to figure out the total value of your holdings.

To get a good feel for how many shares are owned, look at the most recent statement from the fund company. By multiplying the number of shares by the net asset value per share, you can come up with a more accurate picture of how much money you have actually made.

For example, in a six-year investment in T. Rowe Price's International Fund, $10,000 invested in 1982 was worth at the end of 1988 more than $32,000 for a 220 percent ($22,000/$10,000) total return. But nearly half of those gains came from capital gains and dividends. Looking only at net asset value would have suggested a 120 percent return.

Distribution

Chances are, after several months in a fund an investor will have more shares than when he or she started. This is because most funds pay dividends and capital gains distributions, which usually are reinvested automatically in the form of additional shares.

Dividends

Mutual funds are closely regulated by federal and state laws. In order to retain their tax-exempt status, mutual funds ordinarily must distribute at least 90 percent of their income each year. The amount of income depends largely on the types of investments in the fund. Dividends from mutual funds are taxable and must be reported as ordinary dividends on your tax return.

Capital Gains Distribution

When a mutual fund sells securities at a higher price than it paid for them, this gain will be distributed to the shareholders as a capital gain distribution. Some funds invest in small, fast-growing companies and other speculative stocks in an attempt to achieve high returns from capital gains.

Investment Programs

Not only are there many different types of mutual funds, there are many diverse ways of buying into them. The investment method should be based on your financial position and your ultimate investment goal (extra income, retirement fund, education fund, and the like). Some of the more common investment programs are described briefly in the next sections.

Withdrawal Plan

You can receive monthly or quarterly payments of a specified amount.

Accumulation Plan

An investor generally invests on a monthly basis, usually between $25 and $50. This plan is an excellent choice for a long-term investor.

Automatic Dividend Reinvestment

Under this plan, all proceeds from the fund (dividends and capital gains) are automatically reinvested.

Individual Retirement Account (IRA)

IRAs allows you to set aside up to $2,000 before-tax income annually. Withdrawals are made after retirement, when it is assumed you will be in a lower tax bracket.

403(B) Plan

Employees of nonprofit organizations, hospitals, school districts, or municipalities can shelter before-tax income in plans of this type.

Payroll Deduction Plans

Investment through payroll deduction allows companies to purchase low-load or no-load mutual fund shares for employees.

Life Insurance and Mutual Fund Plans

Funds of this type combine life insurance with shares of a particular mutual fund. If the fund does well it will pay your life insurance premiums. If, however, the fund's share value drops significantly you may be required to pay the premium yourself.

Fees

All mutual funds charge a fee. It is important that you know what the associated fees are to judge whether your investment is worth paying them. Mutual fund fees can be categorized in the following ways: loads, management and expense fees, 12b-1 fees, redemption or exit fees, and deferred sales charges or back-end loads.

Load

For many mutual funds, brokers or other members of a sales force charge a sales commission—called a load—for the purchase of fund shares. Typically the charge ranges from 2 percent to 8.5 percent of the initial investment. The charge is added to the net asset value per share when determining the offer price. Although not all mutual funds have a load, it is important to note that the absence of a sales charge in no way affects the performance of the fund's management and, ultimately, the return on investment.

Management and Expense Fees

All funds, whether "no load" or "load," have management and expense fees—paid by the fund to the fund's adviser for managing its investments. These fees represent computer costs, salaries, and office expenses and range from 0.25 to 1.5 percent of the fund's annual assets. An unusually high fee might indicate poor management of fund costs.

12b-1 Fees

12b-1 fees cover advertising and marketing costs, but do nothing to improve fund performance. Their main purpose is to bring in new customers and ultimately more money for the fund's management to invest.

Redemption (or Exit) Fees

When you sell your share of a fund, some funds charge a fee. These fees can range from a flat $5 to 2 percent of the amount withdrawn.

Deferred Sales Charges or Back-End Loads

Similar to exit fees, deferred charges are assessed when you withdraw money from the fund. These charges are intended to discourage frequent trading in the fund. Deferred sales charges are usually on a scale, which reduces them each year until it disappears after a predetermined period of time. An example of a mutual fund having a back-end load is Prudential-Bache.

Types of Mutual Funds

Mutual funds may be classified into different types, according to organization, the fees charged, methods of trading funds, and their investment objectives.

In **open-end funds**, you buy from and sell shares back to the fund. This type of fund offers to sell and redeem shares on a continual basis for an indefinite time period. Shares are purchased at NAV plus commission, and redeemed at NAV less a service charge if there is one. On the other hand, **closed-end funds** operate with a fixed number of shares outstanding, which trade among individuals in secondary markets like common stocks. That is, if you wish to invest in a closed-end fund, you must purchase shares from someone willing to sell them. In the same manner, in order to sell shares you must locate a buyer. Transactions involving closed-end mutual funds are easy to arrange, however, because most are traded on the New York Stock Exchange, American Stock Exchange, or the over-the-counter market. All open- and closed-end funds charge management fees. A major consideration with closed-end funds is the size of discount or premium, which is the difference between their market prices and their NAVs. Many funds of this type sell at discounts, which enhances their investment appeal.

Unlike load funds, *no-load* funds charge no sales commissions. Sales strategy includes advertisements and (800) toll-free telephone orders. Load funds perform no better than no-loads. Many believe you should buy only no-load or low-load funds. You should have no trouble finding funds that meet your investment requirements.

Depending on their investment philosophies, mutual funds generally fall into ten major categories:

Money Market Funds

Money market funds are mutual funds that invest exclusively in debt securities maturing within one year, such as government securities, commercial paper, and certificates of deposit. These funds provide a safety valve because the price never changes. They are known as dollar funds, which means you always buy and sell shares at $1.00 each. Money market funds are a good choice if you are looking for high interest income with no risk of losing your principal.

Growth Funds

Growth funds seek to maximize their return through capital gains. They typically invest in established companies whose stocks are expected to rise in value faster than inflation. These stocks are best if you desire steady growth over a long term.

Aggressive Growth Funds

Aggressive growth funds are willing to take greater risk in order to yield maximum appreciation (instead of current dividend income). They invest in the stocks of upstart and high-tech-oriented companies. Return can be great, but so can risk. *NOTE: These funds are suitable only if you are not particularly concerned with short-term fluctuations in return but with long-term gains.* Aggressive investment strategies include leverage purchases, options, short sales, and even the purchase of junk stock. Aggressive growth funds are also called maximum capital gain, capital appreciation, and small-company growth funds.

Income Funds

Income funds are suitable if you seek a high level of interest and dividend income. Income funds usually invest in high-quality bonds and blue chip stocks with consistently high dividends.

Growth and Income Funds

Growth and income funds seek both current dividend income and capital gains. The goal of these funds is to provide long-term growth without much variation in share value.

Balanced Funds

Balanced funds combine investments in common stock and bonds, and often, preferred stock; they attempt to provide income and some capital appreciation. Balanced funds tend to underperform all-stock funds in strong bull markets.

Bond and Preferred Stock Funds

These funds invest in bonds and preferred stock, with the emphasis on income rather than growth. The funds that invest exclusively in bonds are called bond funds, of which there are two types: bond funds that invest in corporate bonds, and municipal bond funds that provide tax-free income and a diversified portfolio of municipal securities. If you are in a high tax bracket, consider investing in tax-free municipal bond funds. In periods of volatile interest rates, bond funds are subject to price fluctuations. The value of the shares will fall when interest rates rise. Some municipal bond funds provide insurance on the amount invested.

Index Funds

Index funds invest in a portfolio of corporate stocks, the composition of which is determined by Standard and Poor's 500 or some other market index. Vanguard Index Trust invests exclusively in all the companies comprising the Standard & Poor's 500 Stock Index.

Sector Funds

Sector funds invest in one or two fields or industries. These funds are risky in that they rise and fall depending on how the individual fields or industries do. They are also called specialized funds.

International Funds

International funds invest in the stocks and bonds of corporations traded on foreign exchanges. Some international funds invest exclusively in one region, such as Fidelity Europe Fund and Vanguard Trustees Commingled International Portfolio. These funds make significant gains when the dollar is falling and when foreign stock prices are rising.

Evaluating Bond (Income) Funds

Before investing in a bond fund, investigate five key indicators, which you can evaluate from the fund's annual report or prospectus or directly from the fund.

First determine the *quality* of the fund. Check the credit rating of the typical bond in the fund. Ratings by Standard & Poor's and Moody's show the relative likelihood that an issuer will default on interest or principal payments. AAA is the best grade; a rating of BB or lower signifies a junk bond.

Second, the average *maturity* of the fund's bonds indicates how much you stand to lose if interest rates rise. The longer the term of the bonds, the more volatile the price. For example, a 20-year bond may fluctuate in price four times as much as a four-year issue. *NOTE: Short-term bonds offer protection from such movements while paying a yield better than money markets.*

Third, *premium* and *discount* are important indicators. Some funds with high current yields hold bonds that trade for more than their face value (at a premium). Such funds are less vulnerable to losses if rates go up. Funds that hold bonds trading at a discount can lose most.

Fourth, *total return* tells which bonds generate more than interest payouts. Capital gains or losses can make a huge difference in performance. Total return reflects both interest and price changes.

Fifth, check *commissions, loads*, or *fees*. The difference between yields on the best and worst bond funds is often slight. Fees can be more important to total return than to the money manager.

Guidelines for Selecting a Bond Fund

Rising interest rates drive down the value of all bond funds. For this reason, rather than focusing only on current yield, look primarily at total return (yield plus capital gains from falling interest rates or minus capital losses if rates climb).

Bond funds do not benefit equally from tumbling interest rates. If you think interest rates will decline and you want to increase your total return, buy funds that invest in U.S. Treasuries, or top-rated corporate bonds. Consider high-yield corporate bonds (junk bonds) if you believe rates are stabilizing.

Unlike bonds, bond funds do not allow you to lock in a yield. A mutual fund with a constantly changing portfolio is not like an individual bond, which you can keep to maturity. If you want steady, secure income over several years or more, consider, as alternatives to funds, buying individual top-quality bonds or investing in a municipal bond unit trust, which maintains a fixed portfolio.

Bond funds vary greatly. Some are aggressively managed and carry high risks; others buy only government issues and are best suited for conservative investors. *Read the prospectus.*

International bond funds frequently generate handsome returns, not because of higher interest abroad but because of a fall in the U.S. dollar value. So check out the exchange rate.

NOTE: Bond funds are rated on the basis of SEC standardized yield.

Unit Investment Trusts

Like a mutual fund, a unit investment trust offers small investors the advantages of a large professionally selected and diversified portfolio. Unlike a mutual fund, however, its portfolio is fixed; once structured, it is not actively managed. Several varieties of unit investment trusts are available: tax-exempt bonds, money market securities, corporate bonds of different grades, mortgage-backed securities, preferred stocks, and utility common stocks. Unit trusts are most suitable for people who need a fixed income and a guaranteed return of capital. These trusts disband and pay off investors after the majority of their investments have been redeemed.

MUTUAL FUND'S PERFORMANCE

Mutual funds, like other investments, are evaluated on the basis of return and risk.

Calculating Annual Rate of Return

The annual rate of return, or the holding period return (HPR), in a mutual fund is calculated by incorporating dividends, capital gains, and price appreciation:

$$HPR = \frac{[Dividend + Capital\ gain\ distribution + (Ending\ NAV - Beginning\ NAV)]}{Beginning\ NAV}$$

where (ending NAV – beginning NAV) = price appreciation.

EXAMPLE 2 _____

Assume your mutual fund paid dividends of $0.50 per share, had capital gain distributions of $0.35 per share over the course of the year, and had a price (NAV) at the beginning of the year of $6.50 that rose to $7.50 per share by the end of the year. What is the holding period return?

$$HPR = \frac{[(\$0.50 + 0.35 + (\$7.50 - \$6.50)]}{\$6.50} = \frac{\$1.85}{\$6.50} = 28.46\%$$

See Figure 9-1 for a more accurate way of calculating personal rate of return.

_____

As discussed previously, mutual funds provide returns in the form of dividend income, capital gain distribution, and change in capital (or NAV) of the fund. *Remember:* To calculate your personal rate of return, do not just look at the net asset value in the newspaper. To calculate your personal rate of return, use the information provided on the statement you receive from the fund company and fill

---

FIGURE 9-1: Figuring Your Personal Rate of Return

	Example	Your Fund
1. The number of months for which your fund's performance is being measured.	8	_____
2. Your investment at the beginning of the period (multiply the total number of shares owned by the NAV). [(32.501 + 2.667) x $18.75]	$659.40	_____
3. The ending value of your investment (multiply the number of shares you currently own by the current NAV, or 57.508 x $20.15).	$1,158.79	_____
4. Total dividends and capital gains received in cash. ($10.40 + $13.60)	$24.00	_____
5. All additional investments (any redemptions subtracted). ($100 + $100 + $150 + $50)	$400.00	_____
6. Computation of your gain or loss: Step a: Add line 2 to 1/2 of the total on line 5 [$659.40 + 1/2($400)]	$859.40	_____
Step b: Add line 3 and line 4, then subtract 1/2 of the total on line 5 [($1,158.79 + $24) - 1/2($400)]	$982.79	_____
Step c: Divide the step b sum by the step a sum ($982.79/$859.40)	1.144	_____
Step d: Subtract 1 from the result of step c, then multiply by 100 [(1.144 - 1) x 100]	14.4	_____
7. Computation of your annualized return (divide the number of months on line 1 into 12; multiply the result by the step d %). [(12/8) x 14.4]	21.6%	_____

---

out the form given in Figure 9-1. As an example, Figure 9-1 uses the data provided in Figure 9-2 for the hypothetical ABC Mutual Fund.

Risk, Stability, and Performance of a Mutual Fund

In assessing performance, you must also refer to the published measures of risk or volatility of funds to determine the amount of risk. There are four popular measures of risk: beta, alpha, R-squared, and standard deviation.

Beta shows how volatile a mutual fund is compared with the market as a whole, as measured by Standard & Poor's 500 Stock Index. For example, if the S&P goes up 10 percent and your fund goes up in the same period, the fund has a beta of 1. But if the fund goes up 20 percent it has a beta of 2, meaning it is twice as volatile as the market. The higher the beta, the greater the risk.

A beta of 1.0 means the fund moves up and down just as much as (or moves with) the market. A beta greater than 1.0 (>1.0) means the fund tends to climb higher

FIGURE 9-2: Statement of ABC Mutual Fund, Inc.

Date	Transaction	Dollar Amount	Share Price	Shares
	Beginning balance			32.501
07/01/19x1	Investment	$50.00	$18.75	2.667
09/07	Investment	100.00	20.63	4.847
09/25	Cash dividend at 0.26	10.40 **(1)**	-	-
10/02	Investment	100.00	21.53	4.645
11/30	Investment	150.00	19.55	7.673
12/31	Cash dividend at 0.26	13.60 **(2)**	-	-
12/31	Capital gain reinvestment at 1.03	53.90 **(3)**	20.01	2.694
02/27/19x2	Investment	50.00	20.15	2.481
	Total shares			57.508

(1) (32.501 + 2.667 + 4.847) shares × $0.26 per share = 40.015 × 0.26 = $10.40
(2) (32.501 + 2.667 + 4.847 + 4.645 + 7.673) shares × $0.26 per share
= 52.333 × 0.26 = $13.60
(3) (32.501 + 2.667 + 4.847 + 4.645 + 7.673) shares x $1.03 per share
= 52.333 × 1.03 = $53.90

in bull markets and dip lower in bear markets than the S&P index. A beta less than 1.0 (<1.0) means the fund is less volatile (risky) than the market. Betas for individual funds are available in many investment newsletters and directories, such as **Value Line Investment Survey.**

The adequacy of a fund's performance can be measured against the market line. The difference between a fund's performance and the market line is viewed as a measure of performance. This value, called *alpha* or *average differential return*, is the excess return that would be expected on the fund if the excess return on the market portfolio were zero. For a mutual fund, an alpha value represents the difference between the return on a fund and a point on the market line that corresponds to a beta equal to the fund, where the market line describes the relationship between excess returns and the portfolio beta. Use the following formula to compute alpha:

Alpha = Actual excess return − Expected (required) excess return

NOTE: A positive alpha (differential return) indicates superior performance, whereas a negative value leads to the opposite conclusion.

EXAMPLE 3 _____

If the market return (r_m) is 8% and risk-free rate (r_f) is 5% the market excess return $(r_m - r_f)$ equals 3%. A fund with a *beta* of 1 should expect to earn the market rate of excess returns $(r_m - r_f)$ equal to 3% $(1 \times 3\%)$. A fund with a beta of 1.5 should provide excess returns of 4.5 $(1.5 \times 3\%)$.

_____

EXAMPLE 4 _____

The fund in Example 3 has a beta of 1.5, which indicates an expected excess return of 4.5% along the market line, and an actual excess return of only 4.1%. That means the fund has a negative alpha of .4%, as shown below.

Alpha = Actual excess return − Expected (required) excess return

= 4.1% − 4.5% = −0.4%

The fund's performance is therefore inferior to that of the market.

NOTE: "Keep your alpha high and your beta low" is a basic strategy for those who wish to generate good mutual fund investment performance. Always ask: Can a fund consistently perform at positive alpha levels? Can it generate returns better than those available along the market line?

_____

Some analysts prefer to use R-squared, whereas others use standard deviation—"R²" or "Std. Dev." in mutual fund tables such as those in ***Mutual Fund Values*** published by **Morningstar**. *R-squared* is the percentage of a fund's movement that can be explained by changes in the S&P. *Standard deviation* says that in 95 cases out of 100, the fund's period-ending price will be plus or minus a certain percentage of its price at the beginning of the period, usually one month. In general, the higher the standard deviation, the greater the volatility or risk.

*NOTE: If alpha, beta, R^2, and/or standard deviation are used to help pick a fund, these measures should cover at least **three years** to give the most accurate picture about the risk and instability of the fund. All these numbers, of course, should be weighted against other indicators, including total return over at least five years, performance in the up or down market, and fund management expertise.*

CHOOSING A MUTUAL FUND

Choosing a mutual fund is neither easy nor to be taken lightly. The following six steps are recommended:

1. Develop a list of funds that appear to meet your investment goals.

2. Obtain and study the prospectus closely to select a fund meeting your investment goals and tolerance for risk. The prospectus discloses the fund's investment objective, method of selecting securities, performance figures, sales charges, and other expenses. Note risk factors and investment limitations. Also request the Statement of Additional Information, which includes details on fees and lists the investments; a copy of the annual report; and the most recent quarterly report.

3. Analyze the fund's past performance in view of its objectives—in good and bad markets. The quarterly and annual statements will show results for the previous year and probably a comparison with the S&P 500 stock average. Look at historical performance over a five- or ten-year period. Look for risk measures (such as beta figures) in investment newsletters and directories. Also, read the prospectus summary section of per share and capital changes. *NOTE: **Money, Forbes,** and other magazines publish semiannual or annual performance data on mutual funds.*

4. Study the prospectus for clues as to management's ability to accomplish the fund's investment objectives. Emphasize the record, experience, and capability of the management company.

5. Note what securities comprise the fund's portfolio; not all mutual funds are fully diversified, and not all mutual funds invest in high-quality companies.

6. Compare various fees (such as management and redemption fees), sales charges, if any, and various shareholder services (such as the right of accumulation, switch privileges within fund families, available investment plans, and a systematic withdrawal plan).

Risk-Reducing Investment Strategies

In a bearish market, minimizing or spreading risk is particularly important. Here are five proven risk-reducing strategies for making money in mutual funds.

1. Shoot for low-cost funds. Especially in difficult times, fees and expenses will loom larger, deepening losses and prolonging subsequent recoveries.

2. Build a well-balanced, diversified portfolio. Sensible diversification will spread (or minimize) risks.

3. Use dollar-cost averaging or value averaging strategies. Investing a fixed amount at regular intervals keeps you from committing your entire savings at a market peak. This is how the *dollar-cost averaging* technique works: If your fund's NAV drops, your next payment automatically picks up more of the low-priced shares, cuts your average cost per share, and raises your ultimate gain. *Value Averaging*, developed by Professor Michael E. Edleson in 1988, is an alternative formula strategy. Instead of a fixed dollar rule as with dollar cost averaging, the rule under value averaging is to make the value of your stock holdings go up by some fixed amount (e.g., $100 or more) each month. It is a bit more complex than dollar cost averaging. But it has a lower average per share purchase price than dollar cost averaging and usually provides higher returns. Note, however, that like dollar cost

averaging this strategy works best with very diversified investments, such as a broad-based mutual fund or, preferably, an index fund. (For details, refer to Edleson, Michael E., *Value Averaging*, International Publishing Corporation, Chicago, 1991).

4. Divide your money among fund managers with different styles and philosophies. Funds with differing styles will take turns outperforming, and being outperformed by, the other. In sum, *diversify* across mutual funds or family of funds.

5. Concentrate on short- or intermediate-term bond funds. Typically, the longer the maturity of the bonds in a fund's portfolio, the greater the fund's return—but also the deeper its losses as interest rates rise.

READING MUTUAL FUND QUOTATIONS

Two major types of mutual fund quotations appear regularly in newspapers under the headings "**Mutual Funds**" or "**Money Market Funds.**" Figure 9-3 is a mutual fund quotation abstracted from the *Wall Street Journal* with explanatory notes.

Closed-End Funds

Figure 9-4 is a typical *Wall Street Journal* listing for a closed-end fund.

INFORMATION AND RATINGS

With 3,000-plus mutual funds in existence today, no one source will satisfy your information needs completely. You can, however, refer to specific sources for information.

• *Mutual Fund Fact Book* and *A Guide to Mutual Funds* (Investment Company Institute, 1775 K Street N.W., Suite 600, Washington, DC 20006). These list most mutual funds broken down by investment objective, statistics on specific funds, background on trends in the mutual fund industry, and brief mutual fund term definitions.

• *The Individual Investor's Guide to No-Load Mutual Funds*. (American Association of Individual Investors, 625 North Michigan Ave., Chicago, IL 60611. 312/280-0170). This classic annual guide provides investment objective, operating statistics, and various performance measures, covering all the no-load and low-load mutual funds listed in newspapers.

• *Investor's Directory* and *No-Load Mutual Fund Resource List*. (Mutual Fund Education Alliance, 1900 Erie St., Suite 120, Kansas City, KS 64116).

These publications offer a bibliography of newsletters, magazines, books, other publications and organizations, including advisory services. You can get help in selecting mutual funds from a number of othersources, including investment advisory services that charge fees. More readily available sources, however, include

---

FIGURE 9-3: Example of a Mutual Fund Quotation

Fund	NAV	Offer Price	NAV Change
ABT Midwest Funds:			
Emerg Gr	10.00	10.93	-0.04
Growth	13.62	14.89	-0.10
Int Gov't	10.63	NL	+0.04
(1)	**(2)**	**(3)**	**(4)**

(1) The fund's name abbreviated. Several names under one heading indicates a fund family. Emerg Gr and Growth are load funds. *NOTE: In a load fund, the price you pay for a share is called the offer price, and it is higher than net asset value (NAV)—the difference being the commission.*

(2) The net asset value of a share at the close of the preceding business day. The NAV column may also be called "sell" or "bid." This is the price you would have received (less any end-load fee or redemption charge) had you sold your shares back to the mutual fund on that business day. Compute the most recent value of your holdings by multiplying the NAV by the number of shares you own.

(3) The offer price, also called "buy" or "asked," is the price you would have paid to buy shares at the close of the preceding business day. NL indicates a no-load fund, where the price you pay is NAV. Its offer price is the same as the NAV.

NOTE: The difference between NAV and the offer price is the front-end load. It should be viewed in percentage terms. It is 9.3% for the two load funds:

	NAV	*Offer Price*	*Load*	*Load %*
Emerg Gr	10.00	10.93	0.93	0.93/10.00 = 0.093 (9.3%)
Growth	13.62	14.89	1.27	1.27/13.62 = 0.093 (9.3%)

(4) Change from the previous day; Emerg Gr was down 4 cents per share.

Qualifiers: Mutual Funds

Qualifier	Definition
e	Ex-capital gain distribution
f	Previous day's quotation
p	Fund assets are used to pay distribution costs; 12b-1 plan.
r	Redemption charge or contingent sales fee may apply.
s	Stock dividend or split
t	Both p and r apply
x	Ex-dividend
NL	No-load fund

FIGURE 9-4: Example of a Closed-End Fund Quotation

Fund Name	Stock Exch.	N.A. Value	Stock Price	% Diff.
Diversified Common Stock Funds				
Adams Express	NYSE	19.49	17 3/8	– 10.85
Baker Fentress	NYSE	20.78	17 7/8	– 13.98
Blue Chip Value	NYSE	7.88	7 1/2	– 4.82
Clemente Global Gro	NYSE	b11.04	9 1/4	– 16.21
Gemini II Capital	NYSE	16.09	13	– 19.20
Gemini II Income	NYSE	9.32	12 1/2	+ 34.12
General Amer Invest	NYSE	25.84	22 5/8	– 12.44
Growth Stock Outlook	NYSE	10.45	9 7/8	– 5.50
Liberty All-Star Eqty	NYSE	10.27	9 3/8	– 8.71
Niagara Share Corp.	NYSE	16.02	13 5/8	– 14.95
Nicholas-Applegate	NYSE	12.44	12 1/4	– 1.53
Quest For Value Cap	NYSE	20.02	13 7/8	– 30.69
Quest For Value Inco	NYSE	11.62	13 1/2	+ 16.18
Royce Value Trust	NYSE	10.70	10 1/2	– 1.87
Salomon Fd	NYSE	15.30	12 7/8	– 15.85
Source Capital	NYSE	40.77	41 5/8	+ 2.10
Tri-Continental Corp.	NYSE	27.86	24 3/4	– 11.16
Worldwide Value	NYSE	16.61	14 1/4	– 14.21
Zweig Fund	NYSE	11.43	13	+ 13.74

% Diff.: A negative difference means the shares sell at a discount; positive difference means they sell at a premium.

Money, Forbes, Barron's, and the ***Kiplinger's Personal Finance Magazine. Money*** features a "Fund Watch" column in each issue. In addition, it ranks 450 funds twice a year, reporting each fund's 1-, 5-, and 10-year performances along with a risk rating. *Kiplinger's Personal Finance Magazine* publishes a review of mutual funds in October.

Forbes' annual report covers each fund's performance both in up and down markets. An excerpt from a *Forbes* survey is presented in Figure 9-5. The left-hand margin lists performance ratings for the funds in up and down markets. For example, Acorn Fund is shown (in Figure 9-5) as having a B rating in an up market and a C rating in a down market. In terms of grading, the top 12.5 percent get an A+; the next 12.5 percent, an A; the next 25 percent, a B; and so on.

Value Line Investment Survey shows the make-up of the fund's portfolio beta values. Remember: do not choose a fund only on the basis of its performance rating; consider performance *and* risk.

In addition to various newspapers, including the *Wall Street Journal*, college and public libraries are stocked with publications and books on mutual funds.

Figures 9-6 and 9-7 are samples of mutual fund information and mutual fund ratings from *Money* and *Business Week* respectively.

The *Money* Rankings

Money's risk-adjusted grades compare funds by five-year, risk-adjusted return, a measure developed by William Sharpe. The Sharpe measure is as follows:

$$\text{Sharpe measure} = \frac{\text{Excess returns}}{\text{Fund standard deviation}}$$

$$= \frac{\text{Total fund return} - \text{Risk-free rate}}{\text{Fund standard deviation}}$$

The fund manager is thus able to view excess returns per unit of risk. For example, if a fund has a return of 10 percent, the risk-free rate is 6 percent, and the fund standard deviation is 18 percent, then the Sharpe measure is .22, as shown below.

$$\text{Sharpe measure} = \frac{10\% - 6\%}{18\%} = \frac{4\%}{18\%} = .22$$

This measure is compared with other funds or to the market in general to assess performance.

Lipper Rankings

The **Lipper** Market-Phase Ratings compare each fund's return with others in its category during three periods: the current market phase (a bearish one for stocks but bullish for bonds), the previous up phase, and the prior downturn. *NOTE: In both the* Money *and* Lipper *systems, As go to the top 20 percent, Bs to the next 20 percent, and so on.*

The **five-year projection** states what you would pay in sales charges and other expenses on a $1,000, five-year investment if it were to grow at a 5 percent annual rate. *NOTE: You should go for lower expenses.*

Most funds have toll-free telephone services that can get you detailed information on each family of funds. Toll-free numbers can easily be obtained by calling the toll-free directory service (800) 555-1212.

For more resources, see Chapter 13, Investment Advisories and Newsletters.

Standard & Poor's Stock Guide **for Mutual Funds**

The *Standard & Poor's Stock Guide* includes a Mutual Fund Summary, designed to provide comprehensive statistical alphabetic reference list of mutual funds. Covering a broad cross-section of the industry, it features data necessary for making systematic approach to investing in mutual funds. Figures 9-8 and 9-9 depicts representative pages of this summary.

Data for each fund should be evaluated individually and a decision to invest in a fund should be made only after reading the prospectus. Percentage return, or change in net asset value, represent results for past periods and are based on calculations which are explained at end of the alphabetic section.

FIGURE 9-5: Example of Annual Fund Ratings from *Forbes*

Stock funds

This table covers funds that have at least $25 million in assets and at least 12 months of performance history. FORBES grades stock funds against the three market cycles of the S&P 500. To be graded, a fund must have been in existence for at least two of the market cycles—that is, since June 30, 1983. Balanced funds, global stock funds and foreign stock funds are graded separately against different benchmarks (see pages 252, 256 and 258). The fund's name is followed by that of its distributor; the table of distributors at the end of the fund survey has phone numbers. Closed-end funds have no distributor; they can be bought and sold in the secondary market and are traded just like common stock. A table of closed-ends trading at discounts to net asset value appears on page 250.

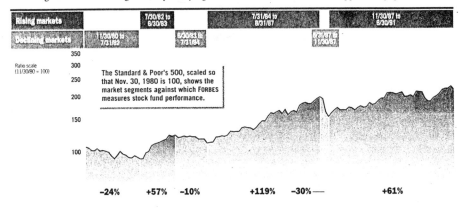

Performance UP markets	DOWN markets	Fund/distributor	Total return Annual average 11/80 to 6/91	Total return Last 12 months	Yield	Assets 6/30/91 ($mil)	Assets % change 91 vs 90	Maximum sales charge	Annual expenses per $100
		Standard & Poor's 500 stock average	14.2%	7.4%	3.3%				
		Forbes stock fund composite	12.2%	6.0%	2.6%				$1.29
		AAL Capital Growth Fund/AAL	— *	10.0%	2.2%	$223	56%	4.75%	*1.41*
		AARP Growth–Capital Growth/Scudder	— *	-0.5	2.2	214	-2	none	1.11p
		AARP Growth–Growth & Income/Scudder	— *	7.6	4.8	334	24	none	1.03
C	D	ABT Growth & Income Trust/ABT	9.1%	0.7	3.3	88	-8	4.75	*1.29*
F	A	ABT Utility Income Fund/ABT	10.6	2.0	5.6	141	-2	4.75	*1.25*
B	C	Acorn Fund/Acorn	12.9	-1.4	1.6	969	2	†	0.82
C	B	Adams Express/closed-end	12.4	10.6	3.5	597	5	NA	0.60
		Addison Capital Fund/Addison	— *	5.4	1.2	29	-1	3.00	*2.38*
		Advantage Growth Fund/Advest	— *	6.6	0.8	32	7	4.00b	*2.33*
D	A	Aegon USA Growth¹/Aegon	12.2	5.2	2.4	38	3	4.75	*0.99p*

■ Fund rated for two periods only; maximum allowable grade A.   * Fund not in operation for full period.   † Closed to new investors.   § Distributor may impose redemption fee, which proceeds revert to the fund.   *Expense ratio is in italics if the fund has a shareholder-paid 12b-1 plan exceeding 0.1% (hidden load) pending or in force.*   b: Includes back-end load that reverts to distributor.   p: Net of absorption of expenses by fund sponsor.   NA: Not applicable or not available.   ¹Formerly MidAmerica Mutual Fund.

Distributor table, page 294. Rules, page 210.

FIGURE 9-6: Example of Mutual Fund Ratings from *Money*

OVERSEAS

Ranked by five-year performance	Type	MONEY risk-adjusted grade	% compounded annual gain (or loss) to Jan. 1, 1992				Value of $10,000 invested five years ago (net of sales charge)	% gain (or loss) during recent up and down markets/Lipper grade			Telephone
			One year	Three years	Five years	10 years		Oct. 11, 1990 to Dec. 26, 1991	July 25, 1990 to Oct. 11, 1990	Dec. 4, 1987 to July 25, 1990	
▲CATEGORY AVERAGE			14.8	7.6	9.4	15.0					
1. Templeton Foreign	Intl	A	18.3	14.4	17.9	—	$20,843	14.4 / B	(12.5) / A	93.0 / A	800-237-0738
2. First Investors Global	Glo	A	16.9	12.2	16.1	15.3	19,653	13.0 / D	(19.5) / D	90.6 / A	800-423-4026
3. G.T. Global–Japan Growth	Intl	A	(2.8)	3.7	15.6	—	19,663	(11.2) / E	(24.9) / E	116.9 / A	800-824-1580
4. Oppenheimer Global	Glo	A	27.4	19.6	15.2	17.4	19,118	24.2 / B	(16.5) / C	107.6 / A	800-525-7048
5. Ivy International	Intl	A	16.9	9.3	15.1	—	19,067	10.5 / C	(16.9) / D	96.4 / A	800-235-3322
6. G.T. Global–Pacific Growth	Intl	A	13.0	14.2	14.2	15.7	18,491	9.7 / C	(15.9) / B	117.5 / A	800-824-1580
7. EuroPacific Growth	Intl	A	18.6	13.7	13.9	—	18,027	18.2 / A	(12.6) / B	85.1 / A	800-421-0180

	Portfolio analysis						Expense analysis			Minimum initial investment
Net assets (millions)	% yield	P/E ratio	% cash	Largest sector (% of assets)	Senior fund manager, age (years managing fund)	% turnover	% maximum initial sales charge	Annual expenses (% of assets)	Five-year projection	
▲CATEGORY AVERAGE	1.4								$124	$500
$1,252.9	2.9	N.A.	19.4	Europe (60.0)	John Templeton, 79 (9)	11	8.5	0.80	$124	$500
223.8	0.0	N.A.	0.0	United States (35.0)	Jerry Mitchell, 53 (1)	116	6.9	1.95	167	2,000
80.3	0.0	N.A.	0.7	Japan (100.0)	Committee management	138	4.5	2.20	162	500
1,105.1	0.3	N.A.	6.0	Europe (64.0)	Kenneth Oberman, 61 (21)	27	5.75	1.68	168	1,000
96.4	1.3	N.A.	6.4	Europe (67.0)	Hakan Castegren, 57 (5)	29	5.75	1.66	90	1,000
360.6	3.6	N.A.	3.6	Japan (34.0)	Committee management	75	4.5	2.10	157	500
1,575.7	1.8	N.A.	14.6	Europe (58.0)	Multiple portfolio counselors	7	5.75	1.28	124	250

Art reprinted by permission of *Money* magazine.

FIGURE 9-7: Sample of *Business Week's* Mutual Fund Scoreboard

FUND	RATING	OBJECTIVE	SIZE ASSETS $ MIL	SIZE % CHG. 1990-91	FEES SALES CHARGE (%)	FEES EXPENSE RATIO (%)	CURRENT RESULTS 1991 TOTAL RET. (%)	CURRENT RESULTS YIELD (%)	RANK WITHIN OBJECTIVE
AAL CAPITAL GROWTH		Growth	330.0	95	4.75	1.30†	30.2	2.1	158/245
AARP CAPITAL GROWTH	AVG	Growth	284.6	64	No load	1.17	40.5	0.7	83/245
AARP GROWTH & INCOME	AVG	Growth/income	458.4	73	No load	0.96	26.5	3.5	80/116
ABT GROWTH & INCOME	↓	Growth/income	94.7	16	4.75	1.32†	29.5	2.2	54/116
ABT UTILITY INCOME	AVG	Utilities	150.2	8	4.75	1.24†	18.0	5.0	16/20
ACORN ↓	AVG	Small company	1150.3	49	2.00†‡	0.73	47.3	1.1	38/65
ADDISON CAPITAL SHARES	↓	Growth/income	32.3	24	3.00	2.34†	30.6	1.3	39/116
ADVANTAGE GROWTH	AVG	Growth	40.9	64	4.00**	2.27†	38.1	0.5	94/245
ADVANTAGE INCOME	AVG	Income	49.4	10	4.00**	2.07†	21.2	4.9	9/11
ADVISORS		Maximum growth	158.6	13	5.50	3.80†	37.5	0.0	26/35
AEGON USA GROWTH	AVG	Growth	44.5	31	4.75	0.99†	34.6	0.0	123/245
AFFILIATED ↓	↓	Growth/income	3605.2	12	6.75	0.58†	21.8	3.8	100/116

FUND	HISTORIC RESULTS AVG. ANN'L TOTAL RET. (%) 3 YEARS	5 YEARS	10 YEARS	TREND BW 10-YEAR ANALYSIS	PORTFOLIO DATA TURNOVER	% CASH	P/E RATIO	LARGEST HOLDING COMPANY	% ASSETS	RISK
AAL CAPITAL GROWTH	19.4				Very low	4	20.4	American Home Products	4	
AARP CAPITAL GROWTH	16.5	15.1			High	8	21.1	Time Warner	3	High
AARP GROWTH & INCOME	16.2	11.9			Average	11	16.9	Union Camp	2	Low
ABT GROWTH & INCOME	10.9	11.1	13.6		Low	13	19.6	Merck	3	Average
ABT UTILITY INCOME	14.0	10.5	12.4		Low	5	13.8	Commonwealth Edison	5	Very low
ACORN	14.9	14.6	16.7		Low	4	24.7	Harley-Davidson	4	Average
ADDISON CAPITAL SHARES	16.0	11.9			Average	1	15.1	General Electric	2	Average
ADVANTAGE GROWTH	17.6	13.7			Average	11	20.9	Mobil	4	Average
ADVANTAGE INCOME	12.9	9.1			Average	3	17.5	Meditrust	3	Very low
ADVISORS	New fund, not rated				Very high	22	22.2	Telefonos de Mexico	3	
AEGON USA GROWTH	14.4	11.9	14.3		Average	7	19.4	FNMA	3	Low
AFFILIATED	12.6	10.6	15.7		Average	6	16.5	Mobil	5	Average

FUND	TELEPHONE TOLL FREE (800)	IN-STATE
AAL CAPITAL GROWTH	553-6319	WI 414-734-7633
AARP CAPITAL GROWTH	253-2277	MA 617-330-5400
AARP GROWTH & INCOME	253-2277	MA 617-330-5400
ABT GROWTH & INCOME	289-2281	FL 407-655-7255
ABT UTILITY INCOME	289-2281	FL 407-655-7255
ACORN	922-6769	IL 312-621-0630
ADDISON CAPITAL SHARES	526-6397	PA 215-665-6000
ADVANTAGE GROWTH	243-8115	MA 617-742-9858
ADVANTAGE INCOME	243-8115	MA 617-742-9858
ADVISORS	451-2010	NY 212-464-8068
AEGON USA GROWTH	624-4339	FL 813-585-6565
AFFILIATED	874-3733	NY 212-848-1800

Art reprinted from the February 17, 1992 issue of *Business Week* by special permission. ©1992 McGraw-Hill, Inc.

Standard & Poor's Mutual Bond Fund Ratings

A Standard & Poor's rating on the shares of a mutual bond fund is a current assessment of the creditworthiness of the investments held. The assessment does not take into account the extent to which fund activities might affect the yield to investors or the effect of interest rate fluctuations on the market price of fund shares. S&P's Corporate and Municipal rating definitions can be found in Chapter 8.

Funds rated **AAAf** are composed exclusively of investments rated AAA by Standard & Poor's, and/or short-term investments issued by entities whose long-term, unsecured debt is rated AAA.

Standard & Poor's qualifies its ratings by stating the following:

Preferred stock and mutual bond fund ratings are not a recommendation to purchase or sell a security, inasmuch as market price is not considered in arriving at the rating. Preferred stock ratings are wholly unrelated to Standard & Poor's earnings and dividend rankings for common stocks.

The ratings are based on current information furnished to Standard & Poor's by the issuer and obtained by Standard & Poor's from other sources it considers reliable. The ratings may be changed, suspended, or withdrawn as a result of changes in, or unavailability of, such information.

Standard & Poor's Corporation receives compensation for rating securities. Such compensation is based on the work done and is paid either by issuers of such securities or by the underwriters from $1,500 to $20,000 for corporate securities .

Wiesenberger Investment Companies Service Reports

Wiesenberger Reports, published annually with quarterly updates (Warren, Gorham and Lamont in Boston), provide more comprehensive information to use in screening a mutual fund. This hardback, oversized book provides background, management policy, and financial records for all leading U.S. and Canadian mutual funds. It can be found in most college and public libraries. A sample page is shown on page 240 in Figure 9-10.

Wiesenberger also provides a service entitled *Mutual Fund Performance Monthly.* It includes an alphabetical listing of mutual funds and gives ranked *alpha* and *beta* values for 10 years, 5 years, and the latest 12 months. Net asset values for the past 2 years, the year to date, and the most recent month are also provided.

Lipper Mutual Fund Investment Performance Averages

Lipper Analytical Services compiles the Lipper Mutual Fund Investment Performance Averages. The performance of all mutual funds is ranked quarterly and annually, by type of fund. Lipper publishes three basic indexes for growth funds, growth-income funds, and balanced funds. Mutual fund managers attempt to outperform the average as well as all other funds in their category. A sample page from the Lipper analytical series is shown in Figure 9-11.

FIGURE 9-8: Example of Standard & Poor's Mutual Fund Summary

(1) Fund / Year Offered	(2) Prin. Obj.	(3) Type	(4) Sept.30,1991 Total Net Assets (MIL.$)	(5) Cash & Equiv (MIL.$)	(6) See Foot-notes	(7) At 1987	Dec.31 1988	1989	1990	Nov.30 1991	(8) Min. Unit	(9) Max. Sales Chg.%	(10) Inc. 1990	Inc. 1991	Sec. 1990	Sec. 1991	(11) $10,000 Invested 12-31-85 Now Worth	(12) 1991 High	Low	NAV Per Shr.	Offer Price	(13) % Yield From Inv. Inc.
Putnam Florida Tax Exempt Inc. *90	I	TF	128.7	(1.2)	1/†				+3.6	+9.4	$500	4.75	0.199	0.562				8.90	8.54	8.86	9.30	2.1
Putnam Mass.Tax Exempt Inc.II. *89	I	TF	47.8	1.9	†				+6.8	+10.9	$500	4.75	0.623	0.571				8.93	8.50	8.89	9.33	6.7
Putnam Mich.Tax Exempt Inc.II. *89	I	TF	23.9	(1.9)	†				+5.4	+9.5	$500	4.75	0.591	0.516				8.74	8.34	8.68	9.11	6.5
Putnam Minn.Tax Exempt Inc.II. *89	I	TF	19.3	0.3	†				+5.6	+7.8	$500	4.75	0.604	0.514				8.67	8.44	8.62	9.05	6.7
Putnam N.J.Tax Exempt Inc. *90	I	TF	115.9	1.6	2†				+6.8	+9.5	$500	4.75	0.509	0.556				8.88	8.53	8.83	9.27	5.5
Putnam N.Y.Tax Exempt Income *83	I	TF	1618.5	(21.8)	3/†	+0.3	+11.1	+8.6	+3.7	+11.9	$500	4.75	0.577	0.552			16,542	8.81	8.27	8.75	9.19	6.3
Putnam Ohio Tax Exempt Inc.II. *89	I	TF	27.2	0.5	†				+6.1	+8.1	$500	4.75	0.602	0.479				8.70	8.39	8.70	9.10	6.6
Putnam Option Inc.Tr II *85	R	O	706.6	133.5	†	-3.7	+17.5	+18.2	+6.2	+13.4	$500	6.75	0.50	0.22	0.35		15,436	8.92	7.43	7.91	8.39	6.0
Putnam OTC Emerg.Gwth *82	G	O	239.6	11.0	5	+5.5	+16.1	+28.9	-10.0	+24.5	$500	5.75				0.74	20,875	8.70	6.40	8.54	9.06	
Putnam Penn.Tax Exempt Income *89	I	TF	73.8	2.6	†				+7.2	+10.0	$500	4.75	0.628	0.56				8.70	8.35	8.66	9.09	6.9
Putnam Strategic Income Trust *77	O	O	436.4	34.9	6	-4.2	+21.8	+15.1	-7.0	+14.8	$500	6.75	0.93	0.24	0.18	0.06	15,873	7.82	6.30	7.29	7.73	12.0
Putnam Tax Exempt Inc. *76	I	TF	1512.9	(35.3)	7/†	-1.3	+12.6	+10.6	+4.5	+9.3	$500	4.75	0.566	0.49		0.02	16,964	8.88	8.47	8.83	9.27	6.1
Putnam Tax Free High Income *89	I	TF	285.9	4.9	†	+0.2	+10.9	+8.4	+3.6	+9.9	$500	4.75	0.687	0.627				8.64	8.34	8.59	9.02	7.6
Putnam Tax Free High Yield *85	I	TF	763.9	15.2	8†	+0.5	+10.7	+9.5	+5.0	+9.4	$500	ERF	1.016	0.907			16,178	14.01	13.51	13.94	13.94	7.3
Putnam Tax Free Inc.Insured *85	I	TF	371.6	7.3	2†*					+8.1	$500	ERF	0.82	0.721			15,976	14.69	14.08	14.60	14.60	5.6
Putnam U.S.Govt.Income Fund *84	I	GB	2531.7	(164.3)	9*	+4.3	+7.3	+12.9	+9.0	+9.0	$500	4.75	1.323	1.199			16,604	13.94	13.54	13.86	14.55	9.1
Putnam Vista Basic Val. *68	G	C	289.2	24.0	9*	+7.4	+14.7	+25.1	-6.9	+24.7	$500	5.75	0.145	0.05	0.26		21,183	7.51	5.39	7.07	7.50	1.9
Putnam Voyager *69	G	C	1100.2	64.5	10	+13.7	+11.6	+34.4	-2.9	+31.5	$500	5.75	0.07			0.63	25,913	9.81	6.60	9.30	9.87	0.7
Quest for Value Fund *80	G	C	73.6	5.8	10	-1.5	+22.5	+19.9	-6.9	+21.4	$1,000	5.5	0.163		0.26		18,723	10.85	7.67	10.29	10.89	1.5
Quest for Value:U.S.Govt.Inc. *88	G	GB	74.7	14.8	6				+11.5	+8.8	$1,000	4.75	0.928	0.678	0.087	0.085		11.84	11.00	11.82	12.41	7.5

Uniform Footnote Explanations-See page 232. **Stock Splits & Divs.** (figures adjusted): 1 1990 % change fr 8/90. 11 1990 % change fr 2/90. 2 1990 % change fr 2/90. 3 2-for-1 split,Oct.89. 4 5-for-1 split,Oct.89. 5 Incl.ret.of cap. Was Option Inc.Trust. 3 3-for-1 split,Oct.89. 8 5% ERF reducing over 7 yrs. 9 'Gtd'dropped fr name(1/91). 11 2% E.R.F before 6 yrs. Incl.Tot.Return & Inc.Funds(6/28/91). 12 1% E.R.F.within 5 yrs. 13 Was Lehman Capital(5/90). 14 Was One William Street. Was Lehman Investors(5/90). 15 Incl.Scudder Special: Each Special hldr.rec'd 4.5785 Cap.Growth shs. 16 Sec.Action is on contractual basis. 17 Was Union Capital. 18 Was Natl. Investors.

(1) **Fund-Year Formed:** Name and the year formed. An * indicates IPO.

(2) **Principal Objective:** Each letter defines the fund's principal objective: G, Growth; I, Income; R, Return on Capital; S, Stability; E, All objectives are equal; P, Preservation of Capital in order of importance. If there is more than one letter listed, the one listed first is the fund's primary objective (e.g., GI means the fund's primary objective is Growth, and Income is second).

(3) **Type:** Fund abbreviations include B, Balanced; BD, Bond; C, Com; CV, Bond and Preferred; FL, Flexible; GB, Long term government, GNMA, etc.; GL, Global; H, Hedge; INTL, Int'l; L, Leverage; P, Preferred; PM, Precious Metals; O, Options; SP, Specialized; TF, Tax Free; ST, Short Term Investments.

(4) **Total Net Assets** at market value less current liabilities. Cash and equivalents are included.

(5) **Cash & Equivalents** reports cash and receivables including U.S. Government securities, short-term municipal and corporate bonds and notes, less current liabilities.

(6) **IRA and Keogh** plans available in all funds except where noted: ∫ = no IRA plan; † = No Keogh plan. Footnotes are referenced at the bottom of the page.

(7) **Net Asset Value per Share** presents NAV at end of period including capital gains and dividends distributed during the period less NAV at beginning of period; divided by NAV at beginning of period. Sales charges excluded.

(8) **Minimum Unit** is the minimum initial purchase of shares.

(9) **Maximum Sales Charge:** A charge coverering costs and commissions. This is added to net asset value in computing the offering price.

(10) Reports dividends from net investment income and distributions in years indicated.

(11) **Shows results** of a $10,000 investment assuming that all dividends and capital gains are reinvested at year end. Calculations are based on NAV and do not include any sales charges.

(12) **Price Record** ranges are based on net asset value per share.

(13) **Dividends** from investment income divided by current offering price.

Art reprinted from Standard & Poor's *Mutual Fund Summary* by permission of Standard & Poor's Corporation. All rights reserved.

FIGURE 9-9: Five-Year Performance of the S&P "500"

Five-year performance statistics for the S&P 500 with dividends reinvested at annual rates, prorated monthly. Page reference where explanations for similar calculations for mutual funds can be found here.

| | % Change From Previous Dec. 31 | | | | | | Dividends paid | so far | $10,000 Invested 12-31-85 | 1991 Range | | Close |
| | | At Dec. 31 | | | | Nov 29 | 1990 | 1991 | Now Worth | High | Low | 11-29-91 |
	1986	1987	1988	1989	1990	1991						
S&P 500	+18.6	+5.1	+16.6	+31.7	−3.1	+17.1	12.10	11.23	21,708	397.41	311.49	375.22
MIDCAP 400	+16.2	−2.0	+20.9	+35.5	−5.1	+34.2	3.16	2.71	23,754	139.07	95.11	131.34

Art reprinted from Standard & Poor's *Mutual Fund Summary* by permission of Standard & Poor's Corporation. All rights reserved.

FIGURE 9-10: Sample of *Wiesenberger Reports*

T. ROWE PRICE NEW ERA FUND, INC.

The investment objective of the fund is long-term growth of capital. It may seek this in any industry, but its current portfolio consists largely of securities of companies in the energy sources area, forest products, precious metals and other metals and minerals; other basic commodities, and companies which own or develop land. Investments in companies which provide consumer products and services are included, as well as companies operating in technological areas, such as the manufacture of labor-saving machinery and instruments.

At the 1986 year-end, the fund had 85.1% of its assets

in common stocks, of which the major portion was in five industry groups: science & technology (14.6% of assets), diversified resources (10.5%), integrated petroleum (10.4%), diversified metals (8.5%) and precious metals (7.6%). The five largest common stock holdings were Salomon (4.6% of assets), IBM (4.4%), Newmont Mining (4.1%), Dow Chemical (3.5%) and Digital Equipment (3.4%). The rate of portfolio turnover during the latest fiscal year was 32.4% of average assets. Unrealized appreciation amounted to 25.7% of year-end total net assets.

Statistical History

Year	Total Net Assets ($)	Number of Shareholders	Net Asset Value Per Share ($)	Yield (%)	Cash & Equiv- alent	Bonds & Pre- ferreds	Com- mon Stocks	Income Div- idends ($)	Capital Gains Distribu- tion ($)	Expense Ratio (%)	Offering Price ($) High	Low
1986	496,242,331	39,248	17.76	2.4	15	—	85	0.50	3.25	0.73	20.84	17.45
1985	529,469,479	42,102	18.67	3.4	8	—	92	0.68	1.41†	0.72	18.87	15.67
1984	471,995,371	45,828	17.13	3.3	10	—	90	0.61	1.29†	0.68	18.94	15.14
1983	485,072,775	47,214	18.44	4.4	12	6	82	0.81	0.072	0.68	18.60	14.97
1982	411,506,259	46,422	15.53	4.6	11	—	89	0.863	3.045	0.71	19.35	11.38
1981	436,197,041	44,712	19.34	3.4	20	—	80	0.672	1.489	0.64	25.53	17.87
1980	571,568,790	41,463	25.27	1.9	10	1*	89	0.47	0.362	0.63	27.23	14.58
1979	330,817,793	30,172	17.45	2.3	15	—	85	0.38	0.388	0.67	17.45	11.15
1978	189,827,658	28,600	11.66	2.7	7	—	93	0.316	0.254	0.73	12.79	9.66
1977	198,186,550	32,680	11.00	2.2	8	—	92	0.244	0.03	0.67	11.66	10.25
1976	245,158,364	35,574	11.74	2.4	6	3*	91	0.279	—	0.68	11.74	10.00

AT YEAR-ENDS / *ANNUAL DATA* / — % of Assets in —

* Includes a substantial proportion in convertible issues.
† Includes short-term capital gains of $0.45 in 1984; $0.67 in 1985.

An assumed investment of $10,000 in this fund, with capital gains accepted in shares and income dividends reinvested, is illustrated below. The explanation in the introduction to this section must be read in conjunction with this illustration.

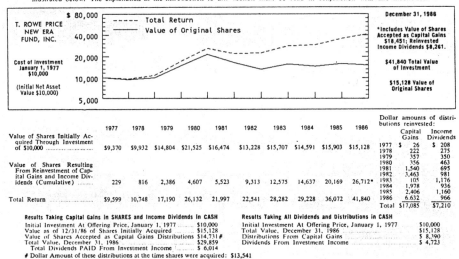

	1977	1978	1979	1980	1981	1982	1983	1984	1985	1986
Value of Shares Initially Acquired Through Investment of $10,000	$9,370	$9,932	$14,804	$21,525	$16,474	$13,228	$15,707	$14,591	$15,903	$15,128
Value of Shares Resulting From Reinvestment of Capital Gains and Income Dividends (Cumulative)	229	816	2,386	4,607	5,523	9,313	12,575	14,637	20,169	26,712*
Total Return	$9,599	10,748	17,190	26,132	21,997	22,541	28,282	29,228	36,072	41,840

Dollar amounts of distributions reinvested:

	Capital Gains	Income Dividends
1977	$ 26	$ 208
1978	222	275
1979	357	350
1980	356	463
1981	1,540	695
1982	3,463	981
1983	105	1,176
1984	1,978	936
1985	2,406	1,160
1986	6,632	966
Total	$17,085	$7,210

Results Taking Capital Gains in SHARES and Income Dividends in CASH

Initial Investment At Offering Price, January 1, 1977	$10,000
Value as of 12/31/86 of Shares Initially Acquired	$15,128
Value of Shares Accepted as Capital Gains Distributions $14,731 #	
Total Value, December 31, 1986	$29,859
Total Dividends PAID From Investment Income	$ 6,014

Dollar Amount of these distributions at the time shares were acquired: $13,541

Results Taking All Dividends and Distributions in CASH

Initial Investment At Offering Price, January 1, 1977	$10,000
Total Value, December 31, 1986	$15,128
Distributions From Capital Gains	$ 8,390
Dividends From Investment Income	$ 4,723

FIGURE 9-11: Lipper Mutual Fund Ratings Example

Mutual Fund Scorecard/A-Rated Bond

INVESTMENT OBJECTIVE: Generally holds at least 65% of issues in corporate bonds with A or better credit rating and may hold governments

(Ranked by 12-month return)	NET ASSET VALUE AUG. 31	TOTAL RETURN[1] IN PERIOD ENDING AUG. 31				ASSETS JUNE 30 (In millions)[2]
		4 WEEKS	SINCE 12/31	12 MONTHS	5 YEARS	
TOP 15 PERFORMERS						
SEI Instl: Bond[3,5]	$10.22	3.47%	7.16%	18.03%	**%	$33.3
Vanguard Fi: Inv Grade[3]	8.31	2.69	10.24	17.83	54.89	1458.4
Transam Bd: Invest Qual	8.94	2.51	8.86	17.18	42.90	83.3
MAS Pooled: Fxd Inc II[3,5]	27.51	2.92	8.22	17.11	**	36.1
Shearson Inv: Inv Grade[3]	11.03	3.01	11.79	17.09	40.89	389.5
IAI Bond Fund[3]	10.32	2.99	7.40	16.91	47.01	113.6
RSI Tr: Actvly Mgd Bd[3,5]	21.22	2.96	8.10	15.58	40.17	182.4
Dodge & Cox Income[3]	11.15	2.29	9.07	15.56	**	64.9
Bond Port Fr Endwmts[3,5]	18.21	2.53	11.56	15.43	51.33	44.5
Twentieth Cent: LgTmBd[3]	93.26	2.58	7.23	15.33	**	85.3
Dreyfus A Bonds Plus[3]	13.99	2.81	9.15	15.16	46.67	367.6
Lutheran Bro Income	8.58	2.13	9.33	14.63	53.29	750.6
Sentinel: Bond	6.29	2.46	9.40	14.62	49.01	37.9
Portico Fds: BndImmdex[4]	26.10	2.51	8.20	14.60	**	65.7
Scudder Income[3]	13.39	2.29	8.33	14.59	48.68	325.9
AVG. FOR CATEGORY		2.35%	8.25%	14.09%	45.80%	
NUMBER OF FUNDS		55	53	49	28	
BOTTOM 10 PERFORMERS						
Comstock Prtnrs Strtgy[3]	$9.58	1.87%	6.37%	8.30%	**%	$1199.9
Crowley: Income[4]	10.88	1.87	6.35	10.37	**	2.5
Newton Inc: Income Fund	8.37	1.95	6.66	11.99	42.51	19.0
Assoc Planrs: Inv Qual Bd	9.07	1.78	7.82	12.05	**	9.1
Babson Bond: Portfolio L[3]	1.56	1.97	7.15	12.51	46.82	101.8
Aso Outlook: Bond Fund[4]	10.60	2.35	6.68	12.68	**	25.5
Merrill Corp: Hi Qual[3]	11.40	2.35	7.62	12.72	**	182.1
Keystone B-1[3]	15.68	2.09	7.05	12.72	35.85	433.3
United: Bond	5.94	2.73	8.12	12.76	45.47	437.0
FS/Pacifica: Income[4]	10.31	2.03	7.74	12.85	**	63.3

[1]Change in net asset value with reinvested dividends and capital gains
[2]Some funds may not qualify for daily quotation of net asset values
[3]No initial load
[4]Low initial load of 4.5% or less
[5]Fund may not be open to all investors

*Fund existed only part of period
**Fund didn't exist in period
N.A.=Not available

Source: Lipper Analytical Services Inc.

Art reprinted by permission of the *Wall Street Journal*. ©1991 Dow Jones & Company, Inc. All rights reserved worldwide. Also reprinted by permission of Lipper Analytic Services.

Morningstar's *Mutual Fund Values*

Mutual Fund Values, a biweekly publication, provides thorough, in-depth information about the operating characteristics, investment holdings, and market behavior of almost 1,000 mutual funds. Some of the key elements included are:

- Risk-adjusted ratings computed over 3, 5, 10 years
- Beta, alpha, R-squared (R^2), and standard deviation
- Annual total return for past 10 years
- Total return for past 3 months, 6 months, 1 year, 3 years, 5 years, and 10 years
- Portfolio composition
- Annual net assets, annual expense ratio, annual income ratio, annual turnover ratio for past 10 years
- Weighted average P/E ratio
- And much more (see Figure 9-12)

MONEY MARKET FUNDS AND QUOTATIONS

Money market mutual funds invest in short-term government securities, commercial paper, and certificates of deposits. They provide more safety of principal than other mutual funds in that net asset value never fluctuates. Each share has a net asset value of $1. The yield, however, fluctuates daily. Several advantages are that:

- Money market funds are no-load.
- A minimum deposit in these funds can be as little as $1,000. If you want to buy short-term securities, a minimum purchase is at least $10,000.
- The fund is a form of checking account, allowing you to write checks against your balance in the account. The usual minimum withdrawal is $500.
- You earn interest daily.
- You can use these funds as a "parking place" in which to put money while waiting to make another investment.

The one disadvantage is that your deposit in these funds is not insured as it is in a money market account or other federally insured bank deposits.

Figures 9-13 and 9-14 show examples from money market fund quotations. The first is from *Barron's* and the second is from *Donoghue's Money Letter*.

Wall Street Journal

Figure 9-15 is the *Wall Street Journal* Money Market Fund published each Thursday.

UNDERSTANDING MUTUAL FUND STATEMENTS*

An advantage of mutual fund investing is the wealth of information that the fund must provide current fund investors and prospective investors. Taken together, the various reports provide vital information concerning fund financial matters and how it is managed, both of which are key to the selection process. In fact, mutual fund prospectuses, along with performance statistics, are the only sources most investors will need to select a mutual fund.

Though the information may seem overwhelming at first, regulations governing the industry have standardized the report format. So, once you're familiar with the reporting format, information will be easy to locate. Mutual funds produce five basic statements: the prospectus; the statement of additional information; annual, semiannual, and quarterly reports; marketing brochures; and account statements. The statement of additional information is part of the prospectus. However, the SEC has allowed mutual funds to simplify the prospectus and, if they choose, the fund may divide the prospectus into two parts: part A, what is typically refered to as the prospectus which all prospective investors must receive; and part B, the Statement of Additional Information, which the fund sends only to investors who specifically request it.

The Prospectus

This is the most important document produced by the mutual fund, and it is *must* reading, by law, for prospective investors. Prospective investors must receive and read a prospectus before the fund can accept initial share purchases. Existing shareholders receive new prospectuses as they are updated.

The prospectus is usually organized into sections. The cover usually gives an overview and may state, briefly, the fund's investment objective, sales or redemption charges, minimum investment, available retirement plans, address, and telephone number. Detailed sections are in the body of the prospectus including a fee table, condensed financial information, a full description of the investment objective and policy, fund management background and fee schedule, and other information. See Figure 9-16 for highlights of policies included in one prospectus.

Fee Table

Under a recent SEC ruling, all mutual fund prospectuses must include a table near the front that thoroughly describes all fees and charges. The table has three sections:

Continued on page 248.

---

*This section has been adapted from Chapter 2 of the American Association of Individual Investor's *Guide to No-Load Mutual Funds,* 10th ed. (Chicago, International Publishing Corporation, 1991).

FIGURE 9-12: Sample Morningstar Mutual Fund Report

MORNINGSTAR, INC. **MUTUAL FUND VALUES**

(1) **Delaware Group Decatur I**

OBJECTIVE	LOAD %	YIELD %	ASSETS($MIL)	N.A.V.
Equity-Inc.	8.50	4.8	1701.5	16.44

(2) Delaware Group Decatur Fund Decatur I Series seeks a high level of current income without undue risk to principal.

The fund studies and may invest in all types of securities. Generally, the fund chooses to invest in common stocks that management believes have better income and appreciation potential than available fixed-income securities. As a rule, a security must provide a yield of at least 3.3% for the fund to purchase it. Similarly, if a security's yield drops below 2.8%, the issue will be removed from the portfolio.

The fund was formerly named Decatur Income Fund.

TOP LINE: Adjusted NAV
BOTTOM LINE: Relative Strength

(3) RETURN / RISK — Average / Below Avg — RATING ★★★ — Neutral

(4) **TOTAL RETURN %**

	1st Qtr.	2nd Qtr.	3rd Qtr.	4th Qtr.	TOTAL
1987	16.53	5.16	3.95	-18.94	3.25
1988	7.37	6.73	1.42	3.14	19.89
1989	8.59	5.26	8.09	-1.66	21.50
1990	-3.78	0.82	-15.08	6.41	-12.35
1991	10.53	---	---	---	---

INCOME

					TOTAL
1989	0.20	0.20	0.20	0.45	1.05
1990	0.20	0.20	0.20	0.20	0.80
1991	0.20	0.20	---	---	0.40

CAPITAL GAINS

					TOTAL
1989	0.00	0.00	0.00	1.49	1.49
1990	0.00	0.00	0.00	0.17	0.17
1991	0.00	0.00	---	---	0.00

(6) **PERFORMANCE/RISK** 05/31/91

	TOTAL RETURN %	+/- S&P 500	PERCENTILE RANK ALL	PERCENTILE RANK OBJ.
3 MONTH	5.76	-1.29	47	68
6 MONTH	17.51	-5.53	53	65
1 YEAR	2.52	-9.30	84	97
3 YEAR AVG.	10.29	-7.93	59	74
5 YEAR AVG.	10.01	-3.32	35	43
10 YEAR AVG.	14.73	-1.23	23	38
15 YEAR AVG.	14.71	0.44	36	50

	ALPHA	BETA	R²	STD. DEV.
	-6.0	0.91	94	3.89
PERCENTILE RANK { ALL	80	49	12	66
OBJ.	90	10	17	14

Percentile Ranks 1 = highest, 100 = Lowest
Except MFV Risk 1 = Lowest, 100 = Highest

HISTORY

	1979	1980	1981	1982	1983	1984	1985	1986	1987	1988	1989	1990	05/91
N.A.V.	13.28	14.46	12.93	14.36	15.27	14.74	16.16	16.86	14.73	16.55	17.51	14.42	16.44
TOTAL RETURN %	25.70	24.39	5.37	25.65	23.14	9.43	26.31	21.40	3.25	19.89	21.50	-12.35	15.44
+/- S&P 500 INDEX	7.40	-7.83	10.45	4.19	0.68	3.30	-5.33	2.77	-1.97	3.38	-10.17	-9.25	-4.25
TOT. RTN/ALL FUNDS	39	55	29	59	30	28	44	17	39	17	44	82	53
% RANK/OBJECTIVE	24	36	59	53	53	50	50	20	31	34	49	85	57
INCOME	0.76	0.93	1.14	1.20	0.80	0.90	0.91	0.80	0.93	0.81	1.05	0.80	0.20
CAPITAL GAIN	0.17	1.02	1.13	0.51	1.54	1.00	1.56	2.00	1.75	0.26	1.49	0.17	0.00
EXPENSE %	0.79	0.69	0.66	0.68	0.67	0.67	0.65	0.63	0.69	0.73	0.67	0.70	---
INCOME %	6.47	7.08	7.98	9.13	6.10	6.08	6.21	4.84	4.37	4.80	5.48	5.78	---
TURNOVER %	61	101	91	98	73	56	75	72	56	39	38	44	---
NET ASSETS ($MIL)	250.8	350.6	376.9	432.0	525.9	628.4	850.4	1214.2	1365.5	1515.5	1892.3	1575.4	1701.5

	MFV RISK % RANK	MFV RETURN	MFV RISK	MFV RISK-ADJUSTED RATING
	ALL	OBJ.	100 = EQUITY AVG	
3 YEAR	63	94	0.57	0.89 → ★★
5 YEAR	54	85	0.90	0.83 → ★★★
10 YEAR	45	69	1.16	0.73 → ★★★★
WEIGHTED AVG.			0.96	0.79 ★★★

NET ASSETS: 200 / 1000 / 0 ($MIL)

PORTFOLIO TOTAL # STOCKS 82   TOP 30 EQUITY HOLDINGS AS OF 05/31/91

SHARE CHANGE	AMOUNT	STOCK	VALUE $000	% NET ASSETS
-62200	891700	IBM	63825	3.75
0	827200	AMERICAN HOME PRODUCTS	48908	2.87
-75000	1000000	K MART	48500	2.85
359900	1132000	EASTMAN KODAK	47969	2.82
-44000	730000	TEXACO	47085	2.77
-26700	975000	EI DUPONT DE NEMOURS	46191	2.71
-21000	700200	MOBIL	46126	2.71
403800	920000	SEARS ROEBUCK	37375	2.20
-12000	625000	EXXON	36484	2.14
-50000	700000	CIGNA	36400	2.14
241700	891700	AT & T	33104	1.95
-20000	700000	TENNECO	32200	1.89→
1225200	1225200	MARATHON OIL	31396	1.85
-517800	973900	WEYERHAEUSER	29582	1.74
-347000	950000	GTE	28500	1.67
973900	973900	UNITED TELECOMMUNICATIONS	28365	1.67
0	806100	WR GRACE	28113	1.65
25000	250000	FHLMC	27770	1.63
-90000	500000	JP MORGAN	27500	1.62
500000	500000	BANKERS TRUST NEW YORK	26875	1.58
-26000	475300	DOW CHEMICAL	26379	1.55
-170200	500000	SOUTHWESTERN BELL	25875	1.52
0	650200	AMERICAN GENERAL	25683	1.51
-377000	1023000	LYONDELL PETROCHEMICAL	24936	1.47
19800	19800	SLMA	23735	1.39
0	702700	SUN	23101	1.36
-38800	460000	DUN & BRADSTREET	22540	1.32
-12700	750000	ALLIED-SIGNAL	22406	1.32
-109700	450000	UNION CAMP	21038	1.24
-125000	600000	TRANSAMERICA	20700	1.22

PORTFOLIO STATISTICS 05/31/91

	PORT-FOLIO AVG.	% OF STOCKS	REL. S&P 500
PRICE/EARNINGS RATIO	14.2	92	0.83
PRICE/BOOK RATIO	2.1	93	0.62
5 YR. EARN. GR. %	7.6	62	0.57
RETURN ON ASSETS	5.9	71	0.74
DEBT % TOTAL CAP.	41.1	92	1.28
MED. MKT. CAP. ($MIL)	7695	95	0.65

SECTOR WEIGHTINGS

	PORT-FOLIO %	REL. S&P 500
NATURAL RESOURCES	28.6	1.44
INDUSTRIAL PRODUCTS	10.1	0.79
CONSUMER DURABLES	2.5	0.46
NON-DURABLES	5.2	0.24
RETAIL TRADE	6.4	1.04
SERVICES	4.3	0.51
UTILITIES	17.8	1.21
TRANSPORTATION	1.3	0.76
FINANCE	16.5	2.42
MULTI-INDUSTRY	7.3	2.68

COMPOSITION % 03/31/91

CASH	0.3	PREFERREDS	0.0
STOCKS	87.5	CONVERTIBLES	0.4
BONDS	11.8	OTHER	0.0

(13) **ANALYSIS** Josh Charlson 06/28/91

Delaware Group Decatur Fund Series I is turning over its system to new hands.

This managerial change shouldn't be of too much concern to shareholders. To some extent, how the fund is run is circumscribed by the Decatur system, which produces an acceptable list of stocks based on dividend yields and valuations. Over long time horizons, this system has worked out well, producing total returns in the upper half of the equity-income group, but at risk levels still well below equity-fund average.

Moreover, the new manager, Marion Dixon, is quite familiar with this system, having managed the Decatur II fund since 1988. And he has proved to be quite adept at selecting stocks within his required parameters; in each of his first three years at Decatur II, the fund outperformed this one by a fairly significant margin.

Last year was tough for both funds, as their yield-oriented approach tends to favor value-type stocks, especially financials, which were pounded in 1990. The fund's rebound has been reasonably brisk in 1991, with its 15.4% gain placing near the group's middle. Utilities, one of the main drags on fund returns along with oil stocks, have been reduced from 22% to 15% of assets. These monies have gone primarily into credit-cyclicals, including such banks as Bankers Trust and NCNB. Dixon has also increased basic industry and capital goods holdings. John Deere was a recent pickup.

Dixon also took the opportunity during the first half of the year to purchase some "attractively priced government paper" that has boosted the fund's yield, but also contributed to its defensiveness. RBOCs, which have been major underperformers, are now looking attractive to Dixon again.

This fund doesn't provide much excitement, but it makes for a dependable core holding.

(12) **OPERATIONS**

ADDRESS	Ten Penn Center Plaza, Philadelphia, PA 19103
ADVISOR	Delaware Management
DISTRIBUTOR	Delaware Distributors
PORTFOLIO MANAGER	Marion M. Dixon (1991)
MANAGEMENT FEE	0.60% max./0.47% min.
FEES	8.50%L
TICKER	DELDX
TELEPHONE NUMBER	215-988-1333 / 800-523-4640
PHONE SWITCH	Yes
# OF SHAREHOLDERS	124392
MINIMUM INITIAL PURCHASE	250
MINIMUM SUBSEQUENT PURCHASE	25
DATE OF INCEPTION	03/18/57
SHAREHOLDER REPORT RATING	C-

© 1991 Morningstar, Inc. • 53 West Jackson Boulevard • Chicago, IL 60604 • (312) 427-1985
Although gathered from reliable sources, data accuracy and completeness cannot be guaranteed.

85

(1) **Banner:** Official mutual fund name, objective, percent load fee, percent yield, assets, and NAV.

(2) **Investment Criteria:** Description of the fund's primary objective and policies. Any events that could bear on performance are also mentioned here.

(3) **Rating Box:** Includes fund's historical total **returns** calculated net of expenses and sales charges and compared to other funds in the same category, **risk** level relative to others in its class, and **rating** representing the fund's historical risk/reward ratio relative to others in its class.

(4) **Quarterly Information:** Total return by quarter and year-end for five years (not adjusted for loads). Income distributions (dividends and interest) for three calendar years. Short- and long-term capital gains distributions for three calendar years.

(5) **Graphs:** The first line, plotted on an a logarithmic scale, displays a fund's monthly adjusted NAV for 13 years. The numbers on the vertical axis refer to NAV in per-share dollar amounts. The second line shows fund performance relative to a general index—S&P 500 Index for equity and Lehman Brothers Government/Corporate Bond Index for bonds. The bar graph displays the fund's year-end total net assets for the trailing 12 years and current year through the most recent quarter.

(6) **Performance/Risk Analysis:** List the fund's total returns from the past three months to the past 15 years and compares them with the S&P 500 Index (equity funds) and the Shearson Lehman Government/Corporate Bond Index (fixed-income funds). The fund's total returns are also compared to all other funds, and other funds in the same objective group. The exclusive risk measure assesses downside risk, compares risk with other funds, and rates the fund's 3-, 5-, and 10-year performance versus risk.

(7) **History:** For each of the past 13 years and most recent month-end price listed, provides the fund's totat return, the return compared to the S&P 500 Index (equity funds) and Shearson Lehman Government/Corporate Bond Index (fixed-income funds), the return compared to all other funds, and the return compared to all other funds with the same objective; plus expense ratio, turnover ratio, income ratio, and net assets.

(8) **Portfolio:** The 30 largest equity holdings (12 largest for bond funds) are listed in descending order by size of the holding. Includes number of shares held, change in shares since last reported portfolio, market value, and percent of fund's net assets. Plus, total number of stocks held.

(9) **Portfolio Statistics:** Provides the weighted average P/E ratio, price-to-book ratio, and 5-year earnings growth rate.

(10) **Composition:** Lists the portion of the fund's net assets in cash, stocks, bonds, convertible securities, and preferreds.

(11) **Sector Weightings:** Shows the percentage of the fund's net assets invested in 10 major industry classifications and how the fund compares to the S&P 500 Index's current weighting of the same sector.

(12) **Operations:** Shows information needed to assess the operations and other provisions of the fund including portfolio manager and length of time with the fund, a table listing loads and fees including redemption, management, performance, and 12b-1 fees as well as address and toll-free phone numbers.

(13) **Analysis:** *A Mutual Fund Values Report* analyst's candid assessment of the fund's performance and risk, portfolio, and recent developments. The analyst listed has final sign-off responsibilities on the fund page.

FIGURE 9-13: Excerpt from *Barron's* Money Market Funds

(1) 52 Weeks High	52 Weeks Low	(2)	(3) Asset Values ($Mil)	(4) Days Avg Mat	(5) Avg 7-day Yld	(6) Comp 7-day Yld
6.32	2.78	DWSrNY	68	45	3.37	3.43
6.52	3.25	DWSears	870	38	3.66	3.73
5.83	3.08	DWSrCal	351	75	3.52	3.58
5.83	3.27	DelaTax	57	69	3.55	3.61
6.40	2.89	DreyCalTx	327	72	3.69	3.76
6.02	3.57	DryCTMu	195	60	4.33	4.42
4.72	4.22	DyrMAMun	39	74	4.24	4.33
7.65	4.03	DrMI Mun	109	39	4.14	4.23
6.78	3.71	DrNJMun	866	59	4.10	4.18
4.39	4.13	DryOHMu	27	44	4.41	4.51
7.50	4.06	DRPA Mun	110	39	4.52	4.62
6.03	3.12	DrNYTE	449	55	3.68	3.75
6.74	3.43	DreyTxEx c	1583	62	3.92	4.00
6.40	3.48	EatnVn	35	21	3.55	3.62
6.65	3.37	Emblem	127	38	3.77	3.84
6.02	3.79	EvgrnCal	40	68	4.14	4.23
7.32	4.17	EvgrnTE	516	48	4.42	4.52
6.15	3.41	FFB TF	105	54	4.02	4.10
6.95	3.05	FN Netwk	58	56	3.63	3.70
5.87	3.02	FMCTSvc	141	44	3.47	3.53
6.56	3.59	FMMASv	81	56	4.00	4.07
4.37	3.65	FMMNCsh	69	28	3.74	3.81
7.06	3.86	FMMNIn	125	28	4.14	4.23
4.69	3.96	FMOHIns	45	52	4.13	4.21
6.80	3.66	FMPASvc	321	48	4.00	4.08
4.24	3.53	FMPACsh	19	48	3.60	3.66
4.40	3.66	FdOHMull	95	52	3.83	3.90
6.41	3.65	FedTxF c	1700	52	4.03	4.11
6.17	3.10	FidCA	543	73	3.69	3.76
6.39	3.79	FidCT	403	70	4.09	4.17
6.51	3.29	FidDlyTE	298	64	3.99	4.07

(7) MONEY FUND REPORT

October 29, 1991

TAX-EXEMPT FUNDS

	Last Week	Prev. Week	Year Ago
Asset Levels, Bil $	89.5	89.6	82.7
Avg. maturity, days	60	61	55
Avg. 7-day compound yield	3.94	3.83	5.41

MONEY MARKET FUNDS

Asset Levels, Bil $	462.2	462.3	407.6
Avg. maturity, days	63	63	47
Avg. 7-day compound yield	5.10	5.15	7.70
Avg. 7-day simple yield	4.97	5.02	7.42
Avg. 30-day compound yield	5.16	5.21	7.73
Avg. 30-day simple yield	5.03	5.08	7.45

Source: IBC/Donoghue's Money Fund Report, Holliston, Mass. 01746 800-343-5413.

(1) 52-Week High and Low

(2) Fund Name

(3) Assets, the value of the fund's assets (in million of dollars to the nearest $100,000).

(4) Average maturity, in days, for the entire investments of the fund. Because money market funds invest exclusively in short-term debt securities, the average maturity is short. Generally, the shorter the maturity, the faster the fund responds to changing interest rates. *NOTE: This is advantageous when rates are on the rise, and vice versa. The change in the average maturity figure is construed as an excellent predictor of the direction of short-term interest rates.*

(5) 7-day average yield %, also called current or 7-day simple yield, is the fund's total return (minus management fees and expenses) for a particular week, expressed on an annualized basis. It is expressed as a percentage of the average share price. This yield measure does not reflect compounded earnings.

(6) 7-day compound yield (%), also called compound effective yield. This represents the current yields after compounding interest over a 12-month period.

(7) Money Fund Report, reported by IBC/Donoghue, represents average maturity, 7-day average yield, and 7-day compound yield for 400 taxable money funds and 30-day yield, the yield average for the previous 30 days. This is considered more reliable than 7-day yields for projecting the longer-term performance of the fund. *NOTE: Past yields are not necessarily indicative of future yields.*

FIGURE 9-14: Donoghue's Money Market Fund Report

Net Assets ($mil)	TAXABLE FUNDS	7-Day	30-Day	Compound 7-Day	Ave. Mat. (days)	Treas.	Other	Repos	Time Deposits	Domestic Bank Oblig	Foreign Bank Oblig	First Tier	Second Tier	FRNs	Total Second Tier
	100% U.S. TREASURY														
687.2	Alex Brown Cash Res/Treas Ser k	5.07	5.10	5.20	50	100	-	-	-	-	-	-	-	-	-
954.8	CMA Treasury Fund	5.38	5.47	5.52	83	100	-	-	-	-	-	-	-	-	-
23.1	Calvert Money Mgt Plus/Govt	4.66	4.71	4.77	66	100	-	-	-	-	-	-	-	-	-
3,415.3	Capital Preservation Fund	5.26	5.24	5.40	50	100	-	-	-	-	-	-	-	-	-
3,686.3	Dreyfus 100% US Treas MMF LP k	5.68	5.73	5.84	76	100	-	-	-	-	-	-	-	-	-
2,695.0	Fidelity Spartan US Treas MMF k	5.67	5.71	5.83	71	100	-	-	-	-	-	-	-	-	-
101.9	First Cash Funds Treas Port k r	5.25	5.29	5.39	46	100	-	-	-	-	-	-	-	-	-
50.4	First Funds of America Treas k r	5.05	5.09	5.18	46	100	-	-	-	-	-	-	-	-	-
310.5	Freedom Govt Sec Fund	4.94	4.90	5.06	63	100	-	-	-	-	-	-	-	-	-
779.5	Fund for Govt Investors	4.97	5.00	5.09	55	100	-	-	-	-	-	-	-	-	-
102.1	Hanover Treasury Secs MMF k r	5.16	5.21	5.29	69	100	-	-	-	-	-	-	-	-	-
16.5	HighMark 100% US Treas Cl A	5.14	5.24	5.27	64	100	-	-	-	-	-	-	-	-	-
225.1	HighMark 100% US Treas Cl B k r	5.14	5.25	5.27	64	100	-	-	-	-	-	-	-	-	-
25.7	Liquid Green Government Trust k	5.45	5.49	5.60	41	100	-	-	-	-	-	-	-	-	-
49.9	Merrill Lynch US Treasury MF	5.51	5.45	5.66	67	100	-	-	-	-	-	-	-	-	-
252.0	Neuberger & Berman Govt MF	5.08	5.09	5.21	74	100	-	-	-	-	-	-	-	-	-
358.5	Prime Value Treasury Fund k	5.38	5.41	5.52	89	100	-	-	-	-	-	-	-	-	-
279.4	Prudential Govt Sec/US Treas k	5.12	5.17	5.25	78	100	-	-	-	-	-	-	-	-	-
8.7	Prudential Special US Treas k r	5.09	5.03	5.22	75	100	-	-	-	-	-	-	-	-	-
18.4	Strong US Treasury MF k	5.13	5.16	5.26	78	100	-	-	-	-	-	-	-	-	-
561.8	T Rowe Price US Treas MF	5.03	5.08	5.16	65	100	-	-	-	-	-	-	-	-	-
24.1	The US Treasury Trust k	5.28	5.34	5.42	65	100	-	-	-	-	-	-	-	-	-
55.0	US Treasury MF of America k	4.99	5.22	5.11	79	100	-	-	-	-	-	-	-	-	-
12.9	USAA Treasury MM Trust k	5.15	5.21	5.28	81	100	-	-	-	-	-	-	-	-	-
2,040.9	Vanguard US Treasury	5.30	5.36	5.44	57	100	-	-	-	-	-	-	-	-	-
$ 16,735.0	SUBTOTAL														
	AVERAGE YIELD & MATURITY	5.20	5.24	5.33	65										
	U.S. TREASURY & REPO														
18.7	AMA Money Fund/Treasury Port	3.94	4.07	4.02	89	85	-	15m	-	-	-	-	-	-	-
356.7	ASO Outlook Group Treas MMF	5.06	5.07	5.19	52	29	-	71m	-	-	-	-	-	-	-
87.6	Ambassador US Treas Fund k r	5.14	5.18	5.27	33	68	-	32m	-	-	-	-	-	-	-
102.3	American Performance US Treas k	5.05	5.05	5.18	51	26	-	74m	-	-	-	-	-	-	-
246.1	Bayshore US Treasury k	5.24	5.25	5.38	69	36	-	64m	-	-	-	-	-	-	-
428.5	Bison MMF/Treasury MMP k r	5.54	5.58	5.69	25	20	-	80m	-	-	-	-	-	-	-
33.0	Blanchard Govt MMF k	4.63	4.69	4.74	68	54	-	46m	-	-	-	-	-	-	-
106.9	Boston Company Govt MF	5.11	5.15	5.24	61	72	-	28m	-	-	-	-	-	-	-
495.5	CBC Cornerstone US Treas MMF k	5.26	5.27	5.40	44	36	-	64m	-	-	-	-	-	-	-
486.4	Capital Preservation Fund II	5.02	4.98	5.15	1	-	-	100m	-	-	-	-	-	-	-
108.1	Capital Reserves US Govt Port k	5.18	5.20	5.31	42	17	-	83m	-	-	-	-	-	-	-
2.3	Capitol Treasury Port Class A k r	5.45	5.28	5.60	57	30	-	70m	-	-	-	-	-	-	-
2.7	Capitol Treasury Port Class B k r	5.10	5.11	5.23	57	30	-	70m	-	-	-	-	-	-	-
787.8	Compass Cap US Treas Fund	5.27	5.30	5.41	52	46	-	54m	-	-	-	-	-	-	-
300.2	Conestoga US Treas Sec Fund k	5.12	5.14	5.25	36	65	-	35m	-	-	-	-	-	-	-
714.1	Dreyfus MM Instruments Govt	5.31	5.36	5.45	74	40	-	60m	-	-	-	-	-	-	-
434.9	Emblem Government Port	5.30	5.30	5.44	56	46	-	54m	-	-	-	-	-	-	-
684.2	Emerald Treasury Fund k r	5.42	5.46	5.57	47	38	-	62m	-	-	-	-	-	-	-
186.5	Emerald Treasury Trust Fund r	5.45	5.48	5.60	56	46	-	54m	-	-	-	-	-	-	-
290.8	FFB US Treasury Fund	5.22	5.26	5.36	42	27	-	73m	-	-	-	-	-	-	-
955.6	First Prairie MM/Govt Series	4.85	4.82	4.97	3	9	-	91m	-	-	-	-	-	-	-
223.8	Fountain Square US Treas Oblig k	5.45	5.43	5.60	36	24	-	76m	-	-	-	-	-	-	-
185.8	Franklin Federal MF	4.81	4.85	4.93	1	-	-	100m	-	-	-	-	-	-	-
655.6	Gradison Cash Reserves	5.05	5.06	5.18	63	33	-	67m	-	-	-	-	-	-	-
36.1	Gradison US Govt Trust	4.91	4.93	5.03	61	32	-	68m	-	-	-	-	-	-	-
85.2	Hatteras Treasury Port k	5.18	5.20	5.31	49	31	-	69m	-	-	-	-	-	-	-
322.9	Helmsman Treasury Oblig Port k	5.24	5.24	5.38	51	54	-	46m	-	-	-	-	-	-	-
122.7	Independence One US Treas MMF k	5.26	5.23	5.40	49	32	-	68m	-	-	-	-	-	-	-
386.4	Landmark U.S. Treasury Reserves k	5.46	5.39	5.61	56	94	-	6m	-	-	-	-	-	-	-
46.4	Laurel US Treasury MM I Port k	5.27	5.28	5.41	53	35	-	65m	-	-	-	-	-	-	-
322.2	Losantiville Treasury Fund	5.16	5.16	5.29	41	24	-	76m	-	-	-	-	-	-	-
178.9	Mariner US Treasury	5.44	5.45	5.59	37	28	-	72m	-	-	-	-	-	-	-
4,491.5	Merrill Lynch CMA Govt	5.50	5.40	5.65	65	18	-	82m	-	-	-	-	-	-	-
674.4	Merrill Lynch USA Govt Res	5.02	5.03	5.15	63	41	-	59m	-	-	-	-	-	-	-
100.9	Midwest Income ST Govt	4.94	4.98	5.06	85	72	-	28m	-	-	-	-	-	-	-
143.5	Monitor US Treasury MMF r	5.30	5.31	5.44	56	48	-	52m	-	-	-	-	-	-	-
92.7	NE Cash Mgt Tr/US Govt	5.27	5.33	5.41	89	53	-	47m	-	-	-	-	-	-	-
213.2	Pacific American US Treas Port k r	5.24	5.24	5.38	32	33	-	67m	-	-	-	-	-	-	-
1,688.3	Pacific Horizon Treas	5.28	5.30	5.42	53	41	-	59m	-	-	-	-	-	-	-
932.4	PaineWebber RMA MF/US Govt	5.17	5.19	5.30	57	56	-	44m	-	-	-	-	-	-	-

(1) Annualized yields. This is often presumed to be the most accurate representation of actual return because it is based on a period that is longer than one year. It represents total return assuming reinvestment of dividends for up to one year.

(2) Donoghue's compound average follows the calculation method of the following formula:

$$\text{Compound average} = \left[1 + \frac{7\text{–day average yield}}{(100 \times 52.142857)} \right]^{52.142857} - 1$$

FIGURE 9-15: *Wall Street Journal* **Money Market Fund**

Avg. Mat. Average Maturity represents the average maturity time, in days, for the entire investment of the fund. Due to the fact that money market funds invest exclusively in short-term debt securities, the average maturity is short. Generally, the shorter the maturity, the swifter the fund responds to changing interest rates. *NOTE: (a) This is advantageous when rates are on the rise, but disadvantageous when rates are falling. The change in the average maturity figure is construed as an excellent predictor of the direction of short-term interest rates. The fact that a fund's average maturity increases by several days for several weeks indicates that its managers expect short-term interest rates to drop; and vice versa. (b) The information about the weekly change in the fund's average maturity is given in* **Money Fund Table Commentary.**

Fund	Avg. Mat.	7Day Yld.	e7Day Yld.	Assets
AALMny	70	5.58	5.73	228
AARP	59	5.68	5.84	377
AIM MM	36	5.28	5.42	88
AMA TrP	101	5.03	5.16	19
AMA PrP	75	5.04	5.16	125
AMEV	37	5.52	5.67	134
ASO Pr	39	5.90	6.07	371
ASO US	37	5.57	5.73	328
ActAsGv	64	5.58	5.74	594
ActAsMny	65	5.74	5.90	3697
AlexBwn	39	5.73	5.89	1268
AlxBTr	51	5.62	5.78	677
AlgerMM	81	6.28	6.48	161
AlllaCpRs	69	5.64	5.80	1981
AllaGvR	61	5.48	5.63	1059
AlllMny	71	5.62	5.78	1277
AlturaPr	46	5.88	6.05	222
AlturUS	52	5.57	5.73	77
AmAAdMM	113	7.19	7.45	610
AmCRes	41	5.52	5.68	426

7 Day Yld. (7 Day Yield). The average annual yields based on the market fo the last 7 days.
e 7 Day Yld. (7 Day Effective Yield). The effective, compounded, yield for the same 7 days.
Assets represents the value of the fund's assets (in millions of dollars to the nearest $100,000).

Art reprinted by permission of the *Wall Street Journal*. ©1991 Dow Jones & Compnay, Inc. All rights reserved worldwide.

The first section of the fee table, Shareholder Transaction Expenses, lists all transaction charges to the investor, including all front- and back-end loads on purchases and reinvested dividends, and redemption fees; the second section, Annual Fund Operating Expenses, includes management fees, any 12b-1 charges, and any other expenses including the fund's total operating expenses. *NOTE: Footnotes to the first two sections appear close to the applicable section; make sure to read these carefully.* The third section is an example of the total cost of these fees and charges to an investor assuming an initial investment of $1,000 and a 5 percent growth rate for the fund, and includes the total dollar cost to an investor who redeems shares at the end of one, three, five, and ten years. (See Figure 9-17).

Condensed Financial Information

This is one of the most important sections of the prospectus. This section provides statistics on income and capital changes per share of the fund (an example is shown in Figure 9-18). The per share figures are given for the life of the fund or 10 years, whichever is less. Occasionally these financial statements are referred to in the prospectus but are actually contained in the annual report.

The per share section summarizes the financial activity over the year to arrive at the end-of-year net asset value for the fund. The summarized financial activity includes increases in net asset value due to dividend and interest payments received and capital gains from investment activity. Decreases in net asset value are due to

FIGURE 9-16: Example of Fund Policies—Highlights

OBJECTIVE AND POLICIES	Vanguard Specialized Portfolios, Inc. (the "Fund") is a no-load, open-end diversified investment company that consists of five Portfolios: Energy, Gold and Precious Metals, Health Care, Service Economy and Technology. The objective of the Fund is to provide long-term capital appreciation. Each Portfolio invests primarily in equity securities, including common stocks and securities convertible into common stocks, and concentrates its holdings in a particular industry or group of related industries. **Page 7**
RISK CHARACTERISTICS	Each Portfolio of the Fund is subject to market risk and industry risk. Market risk is the possibility that stock prices will decline over short or even extended periods. The stock market tends to be cyclical, with periods when stock prices generally rise and periods when stock prices generally decline. Each Portfolio is expected to be strongly influenced by these broad fluctuations in stock prices.
	In addition, unlike more widely diversified mutual funds, the Portfolios are subject to industry risk, the possibility that a particular group of related stocks will decline in price due to industry-specific developments. Securities held by the Energy Portfolio will be influenced by cyclical fluctuations in the supply and demand for oil, as well as tax and regulatory policies, conservation trends, and international oil politics. The Gold and Precious Metals Portfolio will be subject to the highly volatile and often erratic markets for gold and precious metals and for the common stocks of mining companies. Investments relating to gold and precious metals or minerals are considered speculative, and are affected by a host of world-wide economic, financial and political factors.
	Stocks held by the Health Care Portfolio will be affected by government policies on health care reimbursements, regulatory approval for new drugs and medical instruments, and similar matters. The Service Economy Portfolio will be influenced by the relative growth and profitability of selected service businesses — including financial, information, media, business and consumer services. Finally, investors in the Technology Portfolio will be exposed to the substantial risks associated with new technology ventures and the high degree of price volatility characteristic of technology stocks. **Page 10**
THE VANGUARD GROUP	The Fund is a member of The Vanguard Group of Investment Companies, a group of 31 investment companies with 64 distinct investment portfolios and total assets in excess of $64 billion. The Vanguard Group, Inc. ("Vanguard"), a subsidiary jointly owned by the Vanguard Funds, provides on an at-cost basis all corporate management, administrative, distribution, marketing and shareholder accounting services to the Funds in the Group. **Page 14**
INVESTMENT ADVISERS	Wellington Management Company serves as investment adviser to the Energy, Health Care, Service Economy and Technology Portfolios. M&G Investment Management Limited serves as investment adviser to the Gold and Precious Metals Portfolio. **Page 15**
DIVIDENDS, CAPITAL GAINS AND TAXES	Each Portfolio is expected to distribute its net investment income, if any, in the form of an annual dividend. Any net realized capital gains will also be distributed annually. Dividend and capital gains distributions are generally subject to federal, state and local income taxes. Also, a sale of shares — whether by outright redemption or telephone exchange — is a taxable event and may result in a capital gain or loss. **Page 17**
PURCHASING SHARES	You may purchase shares by mail, wire, or exchange from another Vanguard Fund. The minimum initial investment is $3,000 per Portfolio; the minimum for subsequent investments is $100. There are no sales commissions or 12b-1 fees. **Page 20**

Continued.

FIGURE 9-16: *continued*

SELLING SHARES	You may redeem shares of each Portfolio by mail or by telephone. **Each redemption of shares is subject to a 1% redemption fee, deducted from the redemption proceeds and payable to the Fund.** Each Portfolio's share price is expected to fluctuate, and at the time of redemption may be more or less than at the time of initial purchase, resulting in a gain or loss. Page 23
EXCHANGING SHARES	You may exchange a Portfolio's shares for those of another Portfolio of the Fund or other Vanguard Funds. **An exchange from a Portfolio of the Fund to another Vanguard Fund will be subject to a 1% redemption fee, deducted from the exchange proceeds.** However, for defensive moves out of a Portfolio, the 1% redemption fee can be temporarily avoided by making an exchange to a special money market account. **Page 24**
SPECIAL CONSIDERATIONS	(1) Under normal circumstances, at least 80% of the assets of each Portfolio will be invested in equity securities concentrated in a particular industry or group of industries. As a result, a Portfolio of the Fund may be subject to greater fluctuations in market value than a mutual fund which invests in a more widely diversified group of stocks. Due to the specialized focus of the individual Portfolios, an investment in a Portfolio should not be considered a complete investment program. **Page 8**
	(2) The Gold and Precious Metals Portfolio may invest all of its assets in foreign securities, and each of the other Portfolios of the Fund may invest a portion of its assets in foreign securities. Each Portfolio may enter into forward foreign exchange contracts in order to protect against uncertainty in the level of future foreign exchange rates but not for speculative purposes. **Page 12**
	(3) Each Portfolio may lend its securities. **Page 13**

Sample of "Special Considerations," Page 8

INVESTMENT POLICIES: **Each Portfolio invests in industry-specific common stocks**	Under normal circumstances, at least 80% of a Portfolio's assets will be invested in the equity securities (common stocks and securities convertible into common stocks) of companies in a particular industry or group of related industries and, in the case of the Gold and Precious Metals Portfolio, in gold or other precious metal bullion and coins. A common stock or other equity security will generally be considered appropriate for a given Portfolio if, as determined by the investment adviser, at least 50% of the company's assets, revenues or net income are related to or derived from the industry or industries designated for a Portfolio.

The Portfolios of the Fund will invest primarily in equity securities that trade in U.S. markets. However, the Gold and Precious Metals Portfolio may invest up to 100% of its assets in foreign securities, and each other Portfolio may invest up to 20% of its assets in foreign securities. In order to protect against fluctuations in foreign exchange rates, each Portfolio may invest in forward foreign currency exchange contracts.

Besides investing primarily in equity securities, each Portfolio may hold certain short-term fixed income securities as cash reserves. Each Portfolio may also invest in stock futures contracts and options to a limited extent. See "Implementation of Policies" for a description of these and other investment practices of the Fund.

The specific investment policies of the five Portfolios are as follows.

The **Energy Portfolio** invests in the equity securities of companies engaged in the following energy-related activities: the production, transmission, marketing, control or measurement of energy or energy fuels; the making of component products for such activities; energy research or experimentation; and activities related to energy conserva-

---

Source: Vanguard Specialized Portfolio prospectus, May 21, 1991.

FIGURE 9-17: Example of a Prospectus Fee Table

FUND EXPENSES   The following table illustrates all expenses and fees that you would incur as a shareholder of the Fund. The expenses and fees set forth in the table are for the fiscal year ended January 31, 1991.

Shareholder Transaction Expenses	Energy Portfolio	Gold Portfolio	Health Care Portfolio	Service Economy Portfolio	Technology Portfolio
Sales Load Imposed on Purchases	None	None	None	None	None
Sales Load Imposed on Reinvested Dividends	None	None	None	None	None
Redemption Fees*	1%	1%	1%	1%	1%
Exchange Fees	None	None	None	None	None

* *The 1% fee withheld from redemption proceeds is paid to the Fund*

Annual Fund Operating Expenses	Energy Portfolio	Gold Portfolio	Health Care Portfolio	Service Economy Portfolio	Technology Portfolio
Management Expenses	None	None	None	0.13%	None
Investment Advisory Fees	0.27%	0.27%	0.28%	0.27	0.27%
Shareholder Accounting Costs	None	None	None	None	None
12b-1 Fees	None	None	None	None	None
Distribution Costs	None	None	None	None	None
Other Expenses	0.08	0.15	0.08	0.19	0.21
Total Operating Expenses	**0.35%**	**0.42%**	**0.36%**	**0.59%**	**0.48%**

The purpose of this table is to assist you in understanding the various costs and expenses that you would bear directly or indirectly as an investor in the Fund.

As noted, each Portfolio assesses a 1% redemption fee. This 1% charge applies to redemptions from a Portfolio or exchanges from a Portfolio to another Vanguard Fund; however, the fee does not apply to exchanges among the five Vanguard Specialized Portfolios. The 1% fee is deducted from your redemption or exchange proceeds and is paid to the Fund to help offset the brokerage and other trading costs associated with trading in portfolio securities.

When making a temporary defensive move out of a Portfolio, you can avoid the 1% fee by establishing a special money market account at Vanguard. The 1% fee will not be assessed for exchanges among the Portfolios of the Fund and the special money market account. However, redemptions from the special money market account, or exchanges from the special money market account to another Vanguard Fund, will be charged the 1% fee. See "Establishing a Special Money Market Account" (page 22).

The following example illustrates the expenses that you would incur on a $1,000 investment over various periods, assuming (1) a 5% annual rate of return and (2) redemption at the end of each period.

	1 year	3 years	5 years	10 years
Energy Portfolio	$14	$23	$32	$60
Gold & Precious Metals Portfolio	$15	$25	$36	$69
Health Care Portfolio	$14	$23	$33	$61
Service Economy Portfolio	$17	$30	$45	$89
Technology Portfolio	$15	$27	$39	$76

This example should not be considered a representation of past or future expenses or performance. Actual expenses may be higher or lower than those shown.

Source: Vanguard Specialized Portfolio prospectus, May 21, 1991.

FIGURE 9-18: Past Performance of a Fund

	1988	1989	1990
Investment income (1)	$.81	$.84	$.98
Less expenses (2)	.11	.10	.14
Net investment income (3)	.70	.74	.84
Dividends from net investment income (4)	(.72)	(.71)	(.84)
Net realized and unrealized gain (loss) on security transactions (5)	3.33	(.70)	2.96
Distribution from realized gain (6)	(.05)	(4.40)	(1.97)
Net increase (decrease) in net asset value (NAV) (7)	3.26	(5.07)	.99

Net asset value:

	1988	1989	1990
Beginning of year (8)	14.82	19.89	18.90
End of year (9)	$18.08	$14.82	$19.89
Ratio of operating expenses to average net assets (10)	.66%	.66%	.71%
Ratio of net investment income average net assets (11)	4.25%	5.06%	4.34%
Portfolio turnover rate (12)	215%	200%	210%
Shares outstanding at end of year (000 omitted) (13)	42,116	41,671	33,629

(1)   **Investment income:** The dividends and interest the fund earned during its fiscal year. An increase in investment income increases NAV.

(2)   **Expenses:** Fund costs such as the management fee, legal fees, transfer agent fees, and the like. These expenses are detailed in the *statement of operations* section of the annual report.

(3)   **Net investment income:** Investment income (1) less expenses (2). *NOTE: This item is important because it reflects the level and stability of net income over the time period. Funds whose chosen objective is income rather than growth would most likely have a high net investment income. Net investment income is distributed to shareholders so the fund avoids direct taxation. A high net investment income, therefore, has the potential of translating into a high tax liability for the investor.*

(4)   **Dividends from net investment income:** Dividend income.

(5)   **Net realized and unrealized gain (loss) on security transactions:** The change in the value of investments that have been sold or continue to be held by the fund during the year. Net gains increase NAV and net losses decrease NAV.

(6)   **Distributions from realized gain:** Capital gains distributions to fund investors include dividends from net investment income from the current fiscal year and any realized capital gains. The new tax law requires that all income earned must be distributed in the calendar year earned.

(7)   **Net increase (decrease) in net asset value (NAV):** The change in NAV. It is calculated as: line 7 = line 3 − line 4 + line 5 − line 6. For example, the 1988 net increase in NAV was found as $.70 − (.72) + 3.33 − (.05) = $3.26.

Continued.

(8) Beginning of year: The NAV of one share of the fund at the beginning of the year.

(9) End of year: The NAV of one share of the fund at the end of the year. It is calculated by determining the total assets and dividing by the number of fund shares outstanding. The figure will change for a variety of reasons, including changes in investment income, expenses, gains, losses and distributions. *NOTE: Consider changes in net asset value carefully to determine return—a decline may not necessarily indicate a negative return rate.*

(10) Ratio of operating expenses to average net assets: An indicator of fund performance and strategy. The *expense ratio* relates operating expenses incurred by the fund to average net assets. Net assets are totaled for the year and divided by 2 to find the average. Operating expenses include the investment advisory fee, legal and accounting fees, and 12b-1 charges; they do not include brokerage fees, loads, or redemption fees. A high expense ratio detracts from investment return. The average expense ratio for common stock funds is 1.4 percent, and for bond funds about 1.1 percent. Ratios above 1.5 percent are high; funds with ratios above 2.0 percent should be carefully evaluated.

(11) Ratio of net investment income to average net assets: This is a comparison between earnings and average net assets and should reflect the fund's investment objective. Bond funds normally have ratios more than twice those of common stocks funds.

(12) Portfolio turnover rate: Relates the number of shares bought and sold by the fund to the total number of shares held in the fund's portfolio. A high turnover rate would indicate a lot of trading. It is the lower of purchases or sales divided by average net assets. This does not mean a fund replaces its holdings entirely. *NOTE: It tells how much volatility the fund experiences. Take note of high portfolio turnover rates because the higher the turnover, the greater the brokerage costs incurred by the fund—brokerage costs are directly reflected in a decrease in NAV, and high turnover rates generally have higher capital gains distributions.* A 100 percent portfolio turnover rate indicates that securities in the portfolio have been held for one year on average; 200 percent indicates that securities on average have been traded every six months. The average mutual fund has a turnover rate around 100 percent.

(13) Shares outstanding at end of year (000s omitted): The number of the fund's shares outstanding at the end of the year.

---

capital losses from investment activity, investment expenses, and payouts to fund shareholders in the form of distributions.

Investment Objective/Policy

A full descriptions of the type of investments the fund will make—bonds, stocks, convertible securities, or options—along with guidelines as to the proportions of these securities within the fund's portfolio and may state the allowable proportions in certain investment categories. In common stock funds, a statement usually indicates whether it will be oriented toward capital gains or income. Management will also briefly discuss approaches to market timing, risk assumption, anticipated level of portfolio turnover, and any investment restrictions they have placed on the fund. The restrictions section is usually given in more detail in the Statement of Additional Information (see Figure 9-19.)

FIGURE 9-19: Investment Objectives and Policies

INVESTMENT OBJECTIVE:	Vanguard Specialized Portfolios, Inc. (the "Fund") is a no-load, open-end diversified investment company with five Portfolios: Energy, Gold and Precious Metals, Health Care, Service Economy and Technology. The objective of the Fund is to provide long-term capital growth. Although a Portfolio may provide dividend income to a limited extent, current income will be secondary to the Fund's primary objective of achieving capital appreciation. There is no assurance that the Fund will achieve its stated objective.
The Fund seeks to provide long-term capital growth	The investment objective of the Fund is fundamental and so cannot be changed without the approval of a majority of the Fund's shareholders.

INVESTMENT POLICIES:	Under normal circumstances, at least 80% of a Portfolio's assets will be invested in the equity securities (common stocks and securities convertible into common stocks) of companies in a particular industry or group of related industries and, in the case of the Gold and Precious Metals Portfolio, in gold or other precious metal bullion and coins. A common stock or other equity security will generally be considered appropriate for a given Portfolio if, as determined by the investment adviser, at least 50% of the company's assets, revenues or net income are related to or derived from the industry or industries designated for a Portfolio.
Each Portfolio invests in industry-specific common stocks	

Source: Vanguard Specialized Portfolio prospectus, May 21, 1991.

Fund Management

Lists the directors and executive officers of the fund and may include the background information including age, address, positions held with the fund, number of shares held, and principal occupations during the past five years. The adviser and the advisory fee schedule may appear under management or as a separate section. Most advisers charge a management fee on a sliding scale, which decreases as assets under management increase. Occasionally, some portion of the fund adviser's fees are subject to the fund's performance relative to the market.

For most funds this information is provided in more detail in the Statement of Additional Information. Fund shareholders elect the board of directors who select the fund adviser. The adviser is usually a firm operated by or affiliated with officers of the fund. Rarely mentioned is the portfolio manager for the fund who is responsible for the day-to-day investment decisions of the fund and is employed by the fund adviser. To find out who the portfolio manager is and length of time in the position usually requires a telephone call to the fund.

Other Important Sections

Several other sections in a mutual fund prospectus appear under various headings, depending on the prospectus, but they are not difficult to find.

Mutual funds that have 12b-1 plans, also known as distribution plans, must be prominently placed in the prospectus. The distribution plan details the marketing aspects of the fund and how it relates to fund expenses. Sometimes the adviser pays for these expenses. The actual cost to the fund of a 12b-1 plan will also be listed at the front of the prospectus in the fee table.

The purchase and redemption of capital stock, or fund share characteristics, section provides shareholders with a summary of where shares may be purchased, their voting rights, participation in dividends and distributions, and the number of authorized and issued shares of the fund. A separate section may discuss the tax treatment that will apply to fund distributions, which may include dividends, interest, and capital gains.

A how-to-buy-shares section will give you the minimum initial investment and any subsequent minimums; load charges or fees; information on mail, wire, and telephone purchases; distribution reinvestment options; and any automatic withdrawal or retirement options.

The how-to-redeem-shares section discusses telephone, written, and wire redemption options, with a special section on signature guarantees and other documents that may be needed; details any fees for reinvestment or redemption; shareholder services with emphasis on switching among funds in a family of funds including any fees for switching and any limits on the number of switches allowed.

Statement of Additional Information

This section elaborates on the prospectus. The investment objectives section is more in-depth, with a list and description of investment restrictions. The management section may expand or include brief biographies of directors and officers and provides the number of fund shares owned beneficially by the officers and directors named. The investment adviser section gives all the expense items and contract provisions of the agreement between the adviser and the fund. If the fund has a 12b-1 plan, further details will likely be in the Statement of Additional Information.

Many times, the Statement of Additional Information will include much more information on the tax consequences of mutual fund distributions and investment. Conditions under which withholding for federal income tax will take place are also provided. The fund's financial statements are incorporated by reference to the annual report to shareholders, and generally do not appear in the Statement of Additional Information. Finally, the independent auditors give their opinion on the representativeness of the fund's financial statements.

Annual, Semiannual, and Quarterly Reports

All funds must send shareholders audited annual and semiannual reports. Funds are allowed to combine their prospectus and annual report; some do, but many do not.

The annual report describes fund activities over the past year and provides a listing of all investments of the fund at market value as of the end of the fiscal year. Sometimes, the cost basis of the investment is also given for each. In-depth reviews of individual securities held by the fund is probably not a good use of your time. However, you should be aware of the overall investment categories. For instance, investors should look at the percentage invested in common stocks, bonds, convertible bonds, and any other holdings. In addition, a look at the types of common stocks held and the percentage of fund assets by industry classification gives you some indication of how the portfolio will fare in various market environments. The annual report will also have a balance sheet, which lists all fund assets and liabilities by general category.

The statement of operations itemizes fund expenses. For most funds, the management fee is by far the largest expense; the expense ratio in the prospectus conveys much more useful information. The statement of changes in net assets is very close to the financial information in the prospectus, however, per share information frequently will be detailed in the annual report in a separate section. Footnotes to the financial statements elaborate on the entries.

Quarterly or semiannual reports are current accounts of the investment portfolio and provide more timely views of the fund's investments than does the annual report.

Marketing Brochures and Advertisements

Promotional materials provide a brief description of the fund, including the telephone number to call to receive the fund prospectus and annual report.

A new SEC ruling requires all mutual funds that use performance figures in their ads to include 1-, 3-, 5- and 10-year total return figures. Bond funds that quote yields must use a standardized method for computing yield, and they must include total return figures, as well. Finally, any applicable sales commissions must be mentioned in the advertisement.

Account Statements

Account statements detail reinvestment of dividend and capital gains distributions, new purchases or redemptions, and any other account activity such as service fees. This statement provides a running account balance by date with share accumulations, account value to date, and a total of distributions made to date. These statements are handy for tax purposes and should be saved. In January, the fund also sends out a Form 1099-Div for any distributions made the previous year, and a Form 1099-B for any mutual fund shares sold during the previous year.

READING THE MUTUAL FUND PROSPECTUS

Too often, mutual fund prospectuses are confusing and hard to read. The SEC goes under the impression that everyone reads them, because their purpose is to help investors analyze a fund. In reality, few individual investors ever read their prospectuses because they are still beyond their comprehension.

Why Read the Prospectus?

Reading the prospectus helps you avoid problems by knowing:

- The fund's minimum initial investment so you avoid selecting a fund you cannot afford;
- How mutual fund switching generates taxable transactions, which can help avoid problems with the IRS;
- Your mutual fund investment will be made at the end of the day you invest rather than the previous day's close, so you avoid confusing surprises;
- You have to fill out the proper form to gain the telephone redemption privilege, which can help avoid the frustrating experience of needing your money and not being able to get it in time;
- You can file a letter of intent and qualify for multiple investment amounts in the same fund for a quantity discount on broker's commissions.

Other things you need to read in a prospectus are:

- The date. Make sure you have the latest information. Prospectuses are updated at least annually.
- The minimum. Make sure you have enough capital to qualify for investment.
- The investment objective. Is this the right fund for you? All mutual funds are not alike, and you need to know that the fund's investment objectives match yours.
- Performance. How has the fund done in the past? How does the fund do in good and bad markets? What is the variability in the fund's return?
- Risk. The fund should disclose the kinds of risks you could face. Don't panic reading these frightening lists, but understand which risks you are exposed to and discuss them with your accounting, tax, and financial advisers. Risk analysis and evaluation is crucial and should adhere to your risk preferences.
- Services. Know what services you are entitled to, and use them effectively—especially those that are free. You never know when you might need them.
- Fees. A lot of people bought "no-load" funds only to discover that it was a back-end loaded fund (you pay when you redeem the shares). Determine what normal or average fees are, then decide whether they are worth it.
- Quality. Is your fund at least an average performer among similar funds?

An excellent guide to reading the mutual fund prospectus is available from the Investment Company Institute (ICI), 1600 M Street, N.W., Suite 600, Washington, DC 20036, (202) 293-7700. Single copies are free. Figure 9-20 shows you what the 27-page booklet covers. Each category is discussed using an actual legal example followed by an explanation in everyday language (see Figure 9-21).

FIGURE 9-20: Table of Contents from *An Investor's Guide to Reading the Mutual Fund Prospectus*

CHECKLIST

Source: Investment Company Institute (ICI), *An Investor's Guide To Reading the Mutual Fund Prospectus.*

FIGURE 9-21: Sample Page from *An Investor's Guide to Reading the Mutual Fund Prospectus*

STATEMENT OF INVESTMENT OBJECTIVES

Examples

From a typical money market fund: "The investment objective of the fund is to provide maximum current income consistent with the preservation of capital and the maintenance of liquidity."

From a typical aggressive growth fund: "The investment objective of the fund is long-term capital appreciation. The generation of current income is only a secondary objective."

From a typical global equity fund: "The fund's investment objective is to earn a high level of total return through investments in the various capital markets of the world."

From a typical balanced fund: "The fund strives for the balanced accomplishment of three investment objectives—income, capital growth, and stability."

From a typical government securities fund: "The investment objective of the fund is to realize high current income consistent with reasonable safety of principal by investing in obligations issued or guaranteed by the U.S. Treasury or by various agencies of the U.S. government."

From a typical long-term municipal bond fund: "The fund's investment objective is to seek as high a level of interest income exempt from federal income tax as is consistent with the preservation of capital."

Explanation

The examples given above represent only six out of 22 different investment objectives recognized by the Investment Company Institute, the national association of mutual funds. However, as these examples illustrate, all investment objectives focus on achieving one or more of three main goals:

1. **stability:** protecting your principal—the amount you invest—from the risk of loss (also known as preservation of capital),
2. **growth:** increasing the value of your principal through capital gains (reflected in share price appreciation),
3. **income:** generating a steady stream of income payments (and for some funds, tax-free income) through dividends.

In general, when you make an informed decision to assume some risk, you create the opportunity for greater reward. Because of this tradeoff, no fund can maximize all three goals simultaneously. Some funds emphasize only one goal; others try to assign priorities among two or three; still others try to balance two or three by aiming for lower than maximum results.

Frequently, following the statement of objectives, you'll see a sentence like, "There are market risks in all securities transactions," or "There is no assurance the fund will achieve its objectives." These statements are not meant to alarm you but to remind you that there are no guarantees. The value of your shares may go up or down; your dividend payments may be more or less than you expected. If you are disappointed by one of your investments, the questions to ask yourself are: "What are my alternatives? Could I do better elsewhere?"

As the economic climate and your own financial needs change, so too may your investment objectives. You'll want to review your investment objectives periodically, to make sure they match your current circumstances.

Investment Company Institute (ICI), *An Investor's Guide to Reading the Mutual Fund Prospectus.*

10

Warrants, Options, and Futures

OVERVIEW

Warrants, stock rights, options, and futures are called leveraged investments because you can participate in these investment vehicles with a small sum of money. Their value is derived from the value of their underlying securities. This chapter will examine the different types of options, performance, how to read option quotations, stock warrants, and futures.

UNDERSTANDING OPTIONS

Options convey the right to purchase a security at a specified price for a stated period of time. Options possess their own inherent value and are traded in *secondary markets*. You may want to acquire an option to take advantage of an expected rise in the price of the underlying stock. Option prices are directly related to the prices of the common stock to which they apply. The types of options include stock rights, warrants, and calls and puts. Investing in options is very risky and requires specialized knowledge.

Stock Rights

In a **stock rights** offering, current stockholders have first right to buy new shares and thus maintain their present ownership interest. This is known as a **preemptive right**.

EXAMPLE 1

Assume you own 3% of XYZ Company. If the company issues 5,000 additional shares, you may receive a stock rights offering—a chance to buy 3%, or 150 shares, of the new issue.

This right enables you to purchase new common stock at a **subscription price** (sometimes called an **exercise price**) for a short time, usually no more than several weeks. This subscription (exercise) price is *lower* than the current market price of the stock.

EXAMPLE 2 _____

If a company has 2 million shares outstanding and wants to issue another 100,000 shares, each existing stockholder will receive one right per share owned. Thus, a stockholder would need 20 rights to buy one new share.

In addition to enjoying the lower exercise price, stockholders do not have to pay a brokerage fee when they buy the additional stock. *NOTE: Stockholders who do not want to buy additional stock can sell their rights in the secondary market. (Of course, if a right is not used before the expiration date, it no longer has value.)*

The Value of a Right

The value of a right depends on whether the stock is traded **rights-on** or **rights-off**. In a rights-on trade the stock is traded with rights attached so the investor who purchases a share receives the attached stock right. In a rights-off, or ex-rights, trade the stock and its rights are separate from each other and are traded in different markets. Regardless of the form of the rights, the value of the right equals

$$\frac{\text{Market price of current stock} - \text{Subscription price of new stock}}{\text{Number of rights to purchase one share}}$$

EXAMPLE 3 _____

If a stock's current market price is $30 a share and the new share has an exercise price of $26, an investor needs two rights to obtain one new share. The right equals:

$$\frac{\$30 - \$26}{2} = \frac{\$4}{2} = \$2, \text{ provided the stock price holds at around \$30 a share}$$

Right Quotation

The stock rights quotation is not reported separately but as part of the regular stock quotation. In Figure 10-1, the company "Brooke" has stock rights, as indicated with the qualifier **"rt"** following the company name.

FIGURE 10-1: Stock Warrants and Rights

	EPS Rnk	Rel. Str.	52-Week High	52-Week Low	Stock Name	Closing Price	Chg.	Vol.% Change	Vol. 100s	PE	Day's Price High	Day's Price Low	
	39	71	39½	24½	BritishAirway	35⅞	+ ⅛	−7	1044	..	36¼	35¾	o
	57	34	51⅜	39	British Gas	43⅛	+ ⅜	+6	346	9	43⅜	43	
✓	..	..	9⅜	1⅞	BritP wt	2¼	− ¼		1825	..	2½	2⅛	
	61	27	79⅝	63⅞	British Pete	65⅛	+ ¼	−41	1200	11	65⅛	64⅝	o
	7	5	27¾	**N L**	British Steel	13⅛	....	+20	1517	8	13¾	13	o
	70	41	74	51¼	Brit Telecom	62⅝	− ¼	−56	331	10	62⅞	62⅜	
	72	93	18⅛	4½	Broad Inc	15¼	− ¼	−46	887	12	15½	15¼	o
	47	70	**47½**	29	Broken Hill	43¾	+ ⅛	**+171**	114	15	43¾	43½	k
	6	14	9⅝	4¾	Brooke Grp	6¼	+ ⅛	+401	1282	..	6¼	6⅛	
✓	..	..	6¼	½	Brooke rt	5⅝	....		1075	..	5¾	5½	
	55	52	**30⅝**	27	Brklyn Union	29½	− ⅛	−66	92	14	29⅝	29⅜	
	42	14	12⅝	7⅛	Brown Sharp	7⅛	− ⅛	−71	15	..	7¼	7⅛	

Art reprinted by permission of *Investor's Business Daily, America's Business Nespaper,* December 5, 1991, ©Investor's Business Daily Inc. 1991.

Stock Warrants

A **warrant** is an option to purchase a certain number of shares at a stated price for a specified time period at a subscription price that is *higher* than the current market price. A warrant may or may not come in a one-to-one ratio with stock already owned. Unlike an option, a warrant is usually good for several years; some, in fact, have no maturity date.

Warrants are often given as "sweeteners" for a bond issue. This allows the firm to float the debt or issue the bond at a lower interest rate. Warrants included with a bond may also occur in a merger when the acquiring company offers cash plus warrants in exchange for the voting common stock of the acquired business. Generally, warrants are detachable from the bond once it has been issued. Detachable warrants have their own market price. So even though warrants are exercised, the debt with which they were first issued still exists. Also, stock warrants may be issued with preferred stock. Most warrants are traded on the AMEX, but some are traded on the NYSE.

Warrants are not issued frequently and are not available for all securities. They pay no dividends and carry no voting privileges. The warrant enables the holder to take part indirectly in price appreciation of common stock and to obtain a capital gain. One warrant usually equals one share, but in some cases more than one warrant is needed to get one share.

Warrants can be bought from a broker. The price of a warrant is listed along with that of the common stock of the company. Brokerage fees for warrants are the same as those for stocks and depend on the market price of the security.

If the price per common share goes up, the holder of the warrant may either sell it (since the warrant also increases in value) or exercise the warrant and get the stock. Trading in warrants is speculative; there is potential for high return, but high risk exists because of the possibility of variability in return.

EXAMPLE 4 _____

Assume a warrant of XYZ Company stock enables you to purchase one share at $25. If the stock increases past $25 before the expiration date, the warrant increases in value. If the stock goes below $25, the warrant loses its value.

_____

The exercise price for a warrant is usually constant over the warrant's life. However, the price of some warrants may rise as the expiration date approaches. Exercise price is adjusted for stock splits and large stock dividends.

Return on a Warrant

To calculate the return on a warrant for a holding period of no more than one year, use the following formula:

$$\frac{\text{Selling price} - \text{Acquisition price}}{\text{Acquisition price}}$$

EXAMPLE 5 _____

Assume that you sell a warrant at $21. That same warrant cost you only $12. The return is:

$$\frac{\$21 - \$12}{\$12} = \frac{\$9}{\$12} = 75\%$$

_____

The return on a warrant for a holding period exceeding one year equals:

$$\frac{\dfrac{\text{Selling price} - \text{Acquisition price}}{\text{Years}}}{\text{Average investment}}$$

NOTE: Warrants are speculative because their value depends on the price of the common stock for which they can be exchanged. If stock prices fluctuate widely, the value of warrants will sharply vacillate.

The Value of a Warrant

A warrant's value is greatest when the market price of the related stock is equal to or greater than the exercise price of the warrant. Thus, the value of a warrant equals:

(Market price of common stock – Exercise price of warrant)

× Number of common stock shares bought for one warrant

EXAMPLE 6 _____

Suppose that a warrant has an exercise price of $25. Two warrants equal one share. The market price of the stock is $30. The warrant has a value of:

$$(\$30 - \$25) \times 0.5 = \$2.50$$

Usually the market value of a warrant is greater than its intrinsic value, or premium, because of the speculative nature of warrants. Typically, as the value of a warrant goes up, the premium goes down. Premium equals the market price of the warrant minus its intrinsic value.

EXAMPLE 7 _____

If the warrant in example 6 has a market price of $4.00, the premium is $1.50.

EXAMPLE 8 _____

Assume that $100,000 in bonds are issued; there are, therefore, 100 bonds. If each bond has eight warrants attached, each warrant permits the investor to purchase one share of stock at $12 until one year from the date of the bond. The warrant will have no value at the issue date if the stock is selling below $12. If the stock increases in value to $25 a share, the warrant will be worth about $13 ($25 - $12). The eight warrants will thus be worth approximately $104 ($13 × 8).

EXAMPLE 9 _____

Assume XYZ common stock is $40 per share. One warrant can be used to buy one share at $34 in the next three years. The intrinsic (minimum) value per warrant is $6 ($40 – $34) × 1. Because the warrant has three years left and can be used for speculation, it may be traded at an amount higher than $6. Assuming the warrant was selling at $8, it has a premium of $6. The premium is the $2 difference between the warrant price and intrinsic value.

Even though the stock is selling for less than $34 a share, there might be a market value for the warrant because speculators may wish to buy it on the expectation of an attractive increase in common stock price in the future.

EXAMPLE 10 ———————————————————————————————

If the common stock was at $30, the warrant has a negative intrinsic (minimum) value of $4, but the warrant might have a dollar value of, say, $1 because of an expected rise in common stock value.

Leverage Effect of a Warrant

You may use the leveraging effect to boost your dollar returns.

EXAMPLE 11 ———————————————————————————————

Assume you have $7,000 to invest. If you purchase common stock when the market price is $35 a share, you can buy 200 shares. If the price increases to $41 a share, you will have a capital gain of $1,200. But if you invest the $7,000 in warrants priced at only $7 a share, you can acquire 1,000 of them (one warrant equals one share). If the price of the warrants increases by $6, your profit will be $6,000. In this instance you earn a return of only 17.1% on the common stock investment, whereas on the warrants you get a return of 85.7%.

On the other hand, assume the price of the stock drops by $6. If you invest in the common stock you will lose $1,200 for a remaining equity of $5,800. However, if you invest in the warrant you will lose everything (assuming no warrant premium exists).

NOTE: If an investor is to get maximum price potential from a warrant, the market price of the common stock must equal or exceed the warrant's exercise price. Also, lower-priced issues offer greater leverage opportunity. Finally, a warrant with a low unit price generates higher price volatility and less downside risk, and thus is preferable to a warrant with a high unit price.

Warrants can be used to protect a speculative transaction. For example, if an investor sells a stock short and the price rises, the speculator cannot keep the short position continually open, and it may be too costly to wait till the stock goes down. To protect the short sale the investor may purchase a warrant, fixing the purchase price and limiting the potential loss on the trade.

EXAMPLE 12 ———————————————————————————————

Assume you sell short 100 shares at $15 each and then buy warrants for 100 shares at $13 a share. The cost of the option is $3, or 3 points a share—a total of $300. In effect, you are buying the stock at $16 a share. Thus, if the stock rises above $15, your loss is limited to $1 a share.

Here are some **advantages** of warrants:

• The price change in a warrant follows that of the related common stock, making a capital gain possible.
• The low unit cost allows the investor to obtain a leverage opportunity in the form of lowering the capital investment without damaging the investment's capital appreciation. This increases the potential return.
• Lower downside risk potential exists because of the lower unit price.

These are **disadvantages** of warrants:

• If no price appreciation occurs before the expiration date, the warrant loses its value.
• The warrant holder receives no dividends.
• Investment in warrants requires extensive study and experience.

Warrant Quotation

The warrant quotation is not reported separately but as part of regular stock quotation (see Figure 10-1). The company ''BritP'' has its warrant, as indicated with the qualifier ''**wt**'' following the company name.

Warrant Offering

Figure 10-2 shows an announcement of a stock issue with detachable warrants. Components of the announcement are explained.

Calls and Puts

Calls and **puts** can be bought or sold in round lots, usually 100 shares. When you purchase a call, you are buying the right to purchase stock at a fixed price because you expect the price of that stock to rise. In buying a call you stand a chance of making a significant gain from a small investment, but you also risk losing your full investment if the stock does not rise in price. Calls come in bearer negotiable form and have a life of one to nine months.

Purchasing a put gives you the right to sell stock at a fixed price. You might buy a put if you expect a stock price to fall. By purchasing a put you get an opportunity to make a considerable gain from a small investment, but you will lose the entire investment if the stock price does not fall. Like calls, puts come in bearer negotiable form and have a life of one to nine months.

Calls and puts are typically written for widely held and actively traded stock on organized exchanges. Figure 10-3 shows a partial page (and Footnotes) from the *Directory of Exchange Listed Options* published by The Options Exchange. The *Directory* is a list of options available on companies' common stock.

FIGURE 10-2: Example of a Warrant Offering

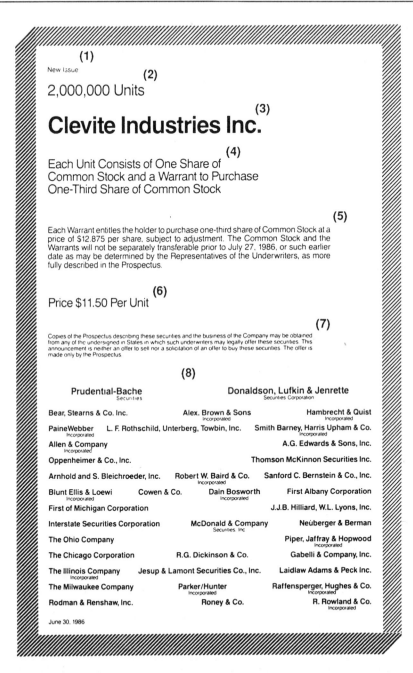

(1)   **New issue** means this is an initial offering. The security is being sold by the company through the underwriters (investment bankers) listed at the bottom of the tombstone ad. The company will receive only the net proceeds of the sale.

(2) Units are the total number of warrants being offered for sale.

(3) The **name** of the company.

(4) Statement defining the equivalent value of each unit.

(5) A detailed **explanation** of what unit of common stock shares each warrant is exchangeable for and at what price the stock is offered.

(6) The **price** at which the security will sell. The issue demand on the secondary market will determine the price. If there are more offers to buy than there are shares to go around in the initial offering, the stock is called a "hot issue," and the market price will rise as soon as the shares begin trading on the secondary market. Incidentally, shares of a new issue cannot be purchased "on margin," a type of credit you can get from your broker using other shares you own as collateral. The shares must be paid for in full by the purchaser.

(7) No legal sale of a new issue can be made unless a prospective buyer receives a prospectus in advance of the transaction. As a buyer, if you don't receive a prospectus before you receive a confirming notice of trade, you have a legal right to cancel the transaction without penalty within a reasonable amount of time. Because new issues are generally more speculative than securities already trading on the open market, the prospectus requirement prevents a broker from "strongarming" you into buying a security about which you may know very little. Again, there are two prospectuses: the preliminary "red herring," because of a statement printed on the cover in red to the effect that the registration has not been declared effective by the SEC. The purpose of the preliminary prospectus is to stimulate sales when the registration is first filed with the SEC. The SEC may or may not require revision or amendments. After the SEC has accepted the preliminary prospectus, a new prospectus—without the red lettering—is used for offering the shares. The reference in the tombstone ad is to the *second prospectus*.

(8) The **list of investment bankers** or underwriters that make up the syndicate bringing out the issue. Those with the largest number of shares to sell are listed first and in more prominent type. If you wish to acquire the security at the initial price, before it starts trading on the secondary market, you must get the shares through one of these firms or a firm specifically contracted by one of them to sell the securities. Some will be retail brokers, selling to the general public, but some may only handle sales to large institutional buyers.

Source of art: *Wall Street Journal,* January 30, 1986.

Calls carry no voting privileges, ownership interest, or dividend income. However, option contracts are adjusted for stock splits and stock dividends. *NOTE: The life of calls and puts is shorter than that of warrants but longer than that of rights. They are similar to warrants in that they are an alternative investment to common stock, leverage opportunity, and speculative investment.*

Calls and puts are not issued by the company with the common stock but rather by option makers or option writers. The maker of the option receives the price paid for the call or put minus commission costs. The option trades on the open market. Calls and puts are written and can be acquired through brokers and dealers. The writer is required to purchase or deliver the stock when requested.

Holders of calls and puts do not necessarily have to exercise them to earn a return. They can trade them in the secondary market for whatever their value is. The value of a call increases as the underlying common stock goes up in price. The call can be sold on the market before its expiration date.

FIGURE 10-3: Common Stock Equity Options List

EQUITY OPTIONS[1]

symbol[2]	name[3]	cycle[4]	exchange[5]	industry group	position limit
AIR	AAR Corporation	1	X	Wholesale Trade/Durable Goods	3000
ABT	Abbott Laboratories	2	X	Drugs	8000
ZBT	**Abbott Laboratories (Jan-93)**	**1**	**X**	**Drugs**	**8000**
WBT	**Abbott Laboratories (Jan-94)**	**1**	**X**	**Drugs**	**8000**
ACN	Acuson Corp.	1	P	Medical Instruments & Supplies	3000
AEQ/ADBE	Adobe Systems, Inc.	1	P	Computer/Data Processing Services	8000
AMD	Advanced Micro Devices, Inc.	1	P	Electronic Components/Accessories	8000
AET	Aetna Life & Casualty Company	1	A	Insurance Carriers	8000
ARQ/AGNC	Agency Rent-A-Car, Inc.	1	A	Auto Repair/Services/Parking	3000
AHM	Ahmanson (H.F.) & Company	1	A	Depository Institutions	8000
ABF	Airborne Freight Corporation	2	C,X	Air Transportation	3000
APD	Air Products & Chemicals, Inc.	3	X	Chemicals & Allied Products	5500
ALK	Alaska Air Group, Inc.	1	A	Air Transportation	3000
ABS	Albertson's Inc.	3	X	Food Stores	5500
AL	Alcan Aluminium Limited	3	A	Primary Metal Industries	8000
ASN	Alco Standard Corporation	3	N	Wholesale Trade/Nondurable Goods	3000
AA	ALCOA (Alum. Co. of America)	1	C	Primary Metal Industries	8000
AUQ/ALDC	Aldus Corporation	1	P	Computer/Data Processing Services	5500
AAL	Alexander & Alexander Services, Inc.	2	C	Insurance Agents/Brokers/Service	8000
ALQ/ALEX	Alexander & Baldwin, Inc.	1	A	Water Transportation/Cruises	3000
AGN	Allergan Inc.	1	X	Drugs	5500
ATK	Alliant Techsystems	2	C,N,X	Fabricated Metal Products	3000
ALD	Allied Signal, Inc.	3	X	Transportation Equipment	8000
ZAL	**Allied Signal, Inc. (Jan-93)**	**1**	**X**	**Transportation Equipment**	**8000**
WAD	**Allied Signal, Inc. (Jan-94)**	**1**	**X**	**Transportation Equipment**	**8000**
AT	Alltel Corporation	1	P	Telephone Communications	3000
AWQ/ALWS	Allwaste, Inc.	2	A,X	Electric/Gas/Sanitary Services	5500
AZA	ALZA Corporation	1	P	Engineering/Management Services	3000
AMX	AMAX Inc.	3	A	Primary Metal Industries	5500
AMH	Amdahl Corporation	2	C	Computer/Office Equipment	8000
AHC	Amerada Hess Corporation	2	X	Petroleum/Coal Products	5500
ABX	American Barrick Resources Corp.	1	A	Metal Mining	8000
AMB	American Brands, Inc.	3	A	Tobacco Products	8000
ACY	American Cyanamid Company	1	A	Chemicals/Allied Products	8000
AEP	American Electric Power Company, Inc.	2	C	Electric/Gas/Sanitary Services	8000
AXP	American Express Company	1	A,C	Security Brokers/Dealers	8000
LAX	American Express Co. (July-92)	1	A	Security Brokers/Dealers	8000
ZAX	American Express Co. (Dec-93)	1	A	Security Brokers/Dealers	8000

FOOTNOTES

1. All options added since the last Directory (4/91) are indicated by bold face type.

2. Over-the-Counter stocks are listed with two symbols. The first symbol represents the Option code and the second symbol represents the National Association of Securities Dealers (NASD) code.

3. Long-Term Equity Options are noted by expiration month and year.

4. Expiration cycles
    1 = January Sequential
    2 = February Sequential
    3 = March Sequential

5. A = American Stock Exchange
    C = Chicago Board Options Exchange
    N = New York Stock Exchange
    P = Pacific Stock Exchange
    X = Philadelphia Stock Exchange

6. Options on Indexes, Foreign Currencies and Treasuries have various expiration specifications. For further information please see the following section or contact the appropriate exchange.

Note: Refer to the exchange bulletins or information circulars for non-standard position limits.

Trading Calls and Puts

Calls and puts are traded on listed option exchanges, which are secondary markets like the Chicago Board Options Exchange, American Stock Exchange, Philadelphia Stock Exchange, and Pacific Stock Exchange. They are also traded in the OTC markets. Option exchanges deal only in the purchase and sale of call and put options. Listed options are options traded on organized exchanges. Conventional options are those options traded in the OTC market.

The **Options Clearing Corporation** issues calls listed on the options exchanges. Orders are placed with this corporation, which then issues the calls or closes the position. No certificates are issued for options, so the investor must have a brokerage account. A holder exercising a call must go through the clearing corporation, which picks at random a writer from member accounts. A call writer is required to sell 100 shares of the common stock at the exercise price.

Exchanges permit general order (i.e., limit) and orders applicable only to option (i.e., spread order).

The price per share for 100 shares, at which the purchaser may buy (call), is referred to as the **striking price (exercise price)**. For a put, the strike price is the price at which the stock may be sold. The purchase or sale of the stock is to the writer of the option. The striking price is set for the life of the option on the options exchange. When stock price changes, new exercise prices are introduced for trading purposes, reflecting the new value.

With conventional calls, no restrictions exist as to the striking price. However, it is usually close to the market price of the related stock. In the case of listed calls, stocks priced lower than $50 a share must have striking prices in $5 increments. Stocks between $50 and $100 have striking prices in $20 increments. Striking prices are adjusted for material stock splits and stock dividends.

The expiration date of an option is the last day it can be exercised. For conventional options, the expiration date can be any business day; for a listed option there is a standardized expiration date.

The cost of an option is referred to as a **premium**, the price the purchaser of the call or put has to pay the writer. (With other securities, the premium is the excess of the purchase price over a determined theoretical value.)

The premium for a call depends on:

- The dividend trend of the related security
- The volume of trading in the option
- The exchange on which the option is listed
- The variability in price of the related security (a higher variability means a higher premium because of the greater speculative appeal of the option)
- Prevailing interest rates
- The market price of the related stock
- The range of the stock's price spread relative to the option's exercise price (a wider spread means a higher price)
- The amount of time remaining before the option's expiration date (the longer the period, the greater the premium's value).

In-the-Money and Out-of-the-Money Call Options

When the market price exceeds the strike price, the call is said to be **in-the-money**. But when the market price is less than the strike price, the call is **out-of-the-money**.

Call options in-the-money have an intrinsic value equal to the difference between the market price and the strike price. Thus:

Value of call = (Market price of stock – Exercise price of call) × 100

EXAMPLE 13 _____

Assume the market price of a stock is $45, with a strike price of $40. The call has a value of $500.

_____

NOTE: Out-of-the-money call options have no intrinsic value.

If the total premium (option price) of an option is $7 and the intrinsic value is $3, there is an additional premium of $4 arising from other considerations. In effect, the total premium consists of the intrinsic value plus speculative premium (time value) based on factors such as risk, variability, forecasted future prices, expiration date, leverage, and dividend. Thus:

Total premium = Intrinsic value + Speculative premium

In-the-Money and Out-of-the-Money Put Options

The definition of in-the-money and out-of-the-money are different for puts because puts permit the owner to sell stock at the strike price. When strike price exceeds market price of stock, we have an in-the-money put option. Its value is determined as follows:

Value of put = (Exercise price of put – Market price of stock) × 100

EXAMPLE 14 _____

Assume the market price of a stock is $53 and the strike price of the put is $60. The value of the put is $700.

_____

When market price of stock exceeds strike price, there is an out-of-the money put. Because a stock owner can sell it for more in the market than by exercising the put, there is no intrinsic value of the out-of-money put.

For a summary of in-, at-, and out-of-the-money call and put strike prices see Table 10-1.

TABLE 10-1: Call and Put Strike Price Summary

	XYZ Calls at 50 Strike Price	XYZ Puts at 50 Strike Price
	Stock Price	Stock Price
In-the-money	Over 50	Under 50
At-the-money	50	50
Out-of-the-money	Under 50	Over 50

The theoretical value for calls and puts indicates the price at which the options should be traded. Typically, however, if options have a long period to go, they are traded at prices higher than true value. This difference is referred to as investment premium, and is determined as follows:

$$\text{Investment premium} = \frac{\text{Option premium} - \text{Option value}}{\text{Option value}}$$

EXAMPLE 15

If a put has a theoretical value of $1,500 and a price of $1,750, it is traded at an investment premium of 16.67%.

$$\frac{(\$1,750 - \$1,500)}{\$1,500} = \frac{\$250}{\$1,500} = 16.67\%$$

Calls. The call purchaser takes the risk of losing the entire price he or she paid for the option if a price increase does not occur.

EXAMPLE 16

If a two-month call option allows you to acquire 500 shares of XYZ Company at $20 per share and within that time you exercise the option when the market price is $38, you gain $9,000 $38 – $20 = $18 × 500 shares) before paying the brokerage commission. If the market price had declined from $20 you would not have exercised the call option, and you would have lost the cost of the option.

By buying a call you can own common stock for a fraction of the cost of regular shares. Calls cost less than common stock. Leverage is obtained because a little change in common stock price can result in a major change in the call option's price. An element of the percentage gain in the price of the call is the speculative premium attributable to the remaining time left on the call. Calls can also be viewed as a means of controlling 100 shares of stock without a large dollar investment.

Significant percentage gains on call options are possible from the low investment compared to the price of the related common stock.

EXAMPLE 17 _____

Assume a stock has a present market price of $35. A call can be purchased for $300 allowing an acquisition of 100 shares at $35 each. If the price of the stock increases, the call will also be worth more. Assuming that the stock is at $55 at the call's expiration date, the profit is $20 ($55 - $35) on each of the 100 shares of stock in the call, or a total of $2,000 on an investment of $300—a return of 667% ($200 ÷ $300). In effect, when the holder exercises the call for 100 shares at $35 each, he or she can immediately sell them at $55 per share. *NOTE: The investor could have earned the same amount by investing directly in the common stock, but the investment would have been $3,500, so the rate of return would have been significantly lower.*

EXAMPLE 18   _____

You can buy ABC Company stock at $30 a share, or $3,000 for 100 shares. You can acquire a $33 three-month call for $400. Thus, you could invest $2,600 cash and have the opportunity to buy 100 shares at $33. Assume, however, that you decide to invest your $2,600 in a three-month CD earning 14 percent interest. The CD will return $91 (14% × $2,600 X 3/12). If the ABC Company stock goes to $16, the option will be worthless, but the significant loss on the stock of $14 a share did not occur. Rather, the loss is limited to $309 ($400 – $91). However, note that by not buying a stock you may have forgone a dividend. If the stock went up to $43, the call would be exercised at $33, resulting in a sizable gain with little investment.

Here is another example of call trading: Assume that a call gives you the right to acquire 100 shares of $30 stock at $27. The call will trade at a price of about $3 a share. Call options may also be used when you believe the stock price will increase in the future but you have a cash flow problem and are unable to buy the stock. However, you will have sufficient cash to do so later. In this situation, you can buy a call so as not to lose a good investment opportunity.

EXAMPLE 19 _____

On February 6 you purchase a $32 June call option for $3 a share. If the stock has a market price of $34 1/2, the speculative premium is $0.50. In June you exercise the call option when the stock price is $37. The cost of the 100 shares of stock, for tax reporting purposes, is the strike price ($32) plus the option premium ($3), or $35.

Puts. The put holder may sell 100 shares at the strike price for a given period to a put writer. A put is purchased when there is an anticipation of a price decline. The maximum loss is the premium cost (investment), which will be lost if the price of the stock does not drop.

EXAMPLE 20   _____

Suppose a stock has a market price of $35. You acquire a put to sell 100 shares of stock at $35 per share. The cost of the put is $300. At the exercise date of the put, the price of the stock goes to $15 a share. You then realize a profit of $20 per share, or $2,000. As the holder of the put, you simply buy on the market 100 shares at $15 each and then sell them to the writer of the put for $35 each. The net gain is $1,700.

EXAMPLE 21   _____

A stock's price was $55 on March 2. You buy a $56 June put for $4. The speculative premium is therefore $3. On June 7, the stock price falls to $47 and the price of the June $56 put to $8. The intrinsic value is $9 ($56 - $47) and the speculative premium is $1 ($9 - $8). As the put holder, you now have a gain of $4 ($8 - $4).

Call and Put Investment Strategies

Investment approaches with calls and puts include hedging, speculation, straddles, and spreads. Owners of call and put options can **hedge** by holding on to two or more securities to lower risk and at the same time make some profit. Hedging may involve buying a stock and later purchasing an option on it. For example, a stock may be bought along with writing a call on it. Also, a holder of stock that has risen in price may buy a put to furnish downside risk protection.

EXAMPLE 22   _____

Assume you buy 100 shares of XYZ at $26 each and a put for $200 on the 100 shares at an exercise price of $26. If the stock remains static, you will lose $200 on the put. If the price decreases, your loss on the stock will be offset by your gain on the put. If stock price rises, you'll earn a capital gain on the stock and lose your investment in the put. Thus, to get the benefit of a hedge, you have to incur a loss on the put. (Also, at expiration of the put, you incur a loss with no further hedge.)

EXAMPLE 23   _____

You can also buy a put to hedge your position after making a profit on the stock—for example if you hold 100 shares of XYZ stock purchased at $60 a share. That stock increased to $80, earning a profit of $20 a share. To guarantee your profit you buy a put with an $80 exercise price at a cost of $300. No matter what happens later, you will have a minimum gain of $1,700. If the stock falls, your minimum profit will be $1,700, but if the stock price rises, you'll realize an additional profit. Some other time you might buy a call to protect a short sale from the risk of increasing stock price. By doing this, you hedge your position as follows: When you use a call, you as a short lowered your profit by the cost of the call.

Calls and puts may also be used for speculation as an alternative to investment in the related stocks. The idea is buy low and sell high. You would acquire options if you think you will earn a higher return than by investing in the underlying stock. In general, you can obtain a higher return rate at lower risk with out-of-the-money options. The problem with out-of-money options is that price consists only of the investment premium, which you can lose if the stock does not rise.

EXAMPLE 24

A speculator purchases an option contract to buy 100 shares at $25 a share. The option costs $150. Assume a rise in stock price to $33 a share. The speculator exercises the option and sells the shares in the market, realizing a gain of $650 ($33 − $25 − $1.50 = $6.50 × 100 shares). Now the speculator can sell the option in the market and make a profit because of its increased value. However, if there is a decline in stock price, the loss to the holder is limited to $150 (the option's cost). Of course, brokerage fees are also involved. In effect, this call option permitted the speculator to purchase 100 shares worth $2,500 for $150, for a short period.

Straddling integrates a put and call on the same stock with the identical strike price and exercise date. It is used by a speculator who, in trading on both sides of the market, hopes for significant movement in stock price in one direction so as to make a gain that exceeds the cost of both options. If the price movement does not go as expected, however, the loss will equal the cost of the options. Straddle holders may widen risk and profit potential by closing one option before closing the other.

EXAMPLE 25

You buy a call and put for $4 each on September 30, when the stock price is $42. The expiration period is four months. The investment is $8, or $800 total. Assume the stock increases to $60 at expiration of the options. The call earns a profit of $14 ($18 − $4), and the loss on the put is $4. Your net gain is $10, or $1,000 altogether.

A **spread** is the purchase of an option (long position) and the writing of an option (short position) in the same security, using call options. Sophisticated investors may write many spreads to gain from the differences in option premiums. Return potential is significant, but the risk is very high. There are different types of spreads: A **vertical** spread is the purchase and writing of two contracts at different striking prices with the same expiration date. A **horizontal** spread is the purchase and writing of two options with the same strike price but for different periods. A **diagonal** spread combines the features of horizontal and vertical spreads.

Spreads require you to buy one call and sell another call. The gain or loss from a spread position depends on the change between two option prices as the price increases or decreases. The difference between two option prices is the price spread.

The speculator who uses a vertical bull spread anticipates an increase in price of stock, but this strategy reduces the risk. Here there is a ceiling on the gain or loss.

A speculator using a vertical bear spread expects the stock price to decline. This investor sells short the call with the lower strike price and places a cap on upside risk by buying a call with a higher strike price.

Puts, straddles, and spreads may be bought either to maximize return or to minimize risk. Not traded on listed exchanges, they must be acquired through brokerage houses and members of the **Put and Call Brokers and Dealers Association**.

Users of straddles, spreads, and similar strategies often use extensive computer analysis. Leave these investment approaches to very sophisticated investors.

Option Writing

The writer of a call agrees to sell shares at the strike price for the price paid for the call option. Call option writers do the opposite of what buyers do. Investors write options because they believe that a price increase in the stock will be less than what the call purchaser expects. They may even expect the price of the stock to remain static or to decrease. Option writers receive the option premium minus related transaction costs. If the option is not exercised, the writer earns the price paid for it. But, if an option is exercised, the writer suffers a loss—sometimes a significant one.

When the writer of an option decides to sell, he or she must come up with the stock at the agreed-on price if the option is exercised. In either case, the option writer receives income from the premium. (Shares are sold in lots of 100.) An investor usually sells an option when he or she expects it not to be exercised. The risk of option writing is that the writer, if uncovered, must buy stock or, if covered, loses the gain. As the writer, you can buy back an option to terminate your exposure.

EXAMPLE 26

The strike price is $40 and the premium for the call option is $5. If the stock is at less than $40, the call would not be exercised, and you would earn the premium of $5. If the stock exceeds $40, the call may be exercised, and you must provide 100 shares at $40. The call writer would lose money only if the stock price exceeded $45.

Naked or Covered Options

Options may be naked (uncovered) or covered. **Naked** options are options on stock a writer does not own. The investor writes the call or put for the premium and keeps it if the price change is in his favor or is negligible. But the writer's loss exposure is unlimited. **Covered** options are written against stocks the writer owns and are not quite as risky. For example, a call can be written for stock the writer owns, or a put can be written for stock sold short. This is a conservative mechanism to obtain positive returns. The goal is to write an out-of-the-money option, keep the premium paid, and have the market price of the stock equal but not exceed the option exercise price. The writing of a covered call option is similar to hedging a position because if stock price falls, the writer's loss on the stock is partly netted against the option premium.

READING OPTION QUOTATIONS

Figure 10-4 is a sample listing of option quotations, along with explanatory notes. The market value of an option equals 100 × quoted price. *NOTE: For example, the S&P 100 Index (June maturity) costs $1,200.00 (12 × 100) for the 355 call.*

Standard & Poor's 100 and 500 Stock Index Option

See Figure 10-5 for sample price quotations on the S&P 100 and S&P 500 Indexes.

FUTURES CONTRACTS

In the futures market, investors trade in commodities and financial instruments. A **future** is a contract to purchase or sell a given amount of an item for a given price by a certain date in the future—thus the name "futures market"). The seller of a futures contract agrees to deliver the item to the buyer of the contract, who agrees to purchase the item. The contract specifies the amount, valuation, method, quality, month and means of delivery, and exchange to be traded on. The month of delivery is the expiration date—in other words, the date on which the commodity or financial instrument must be delivered. Commodity contracts are guarantees by a seller to deliver a commodity (e.g., cocoa or cotton). Financial contracts are a commitment by the seller to deliver a financial instrument (e.g., a Treasury bill) or a specific amount of foreign currency. Futures can by risky; to invest in them, you will need specialized knowledge and great caution. Tables 10-2 and 10-3 show the available commodity and financial futures. Table 10-4 presents various futures contract dimensions (sizes).

The Long and Short of It

A **long position** is the acquisition of a contract in the hope that its price will rise; a **short position** is selling it in anticipation of a price drop. The position may be termi-

FIGURE 10-4: Sample Stock Option Quotations

(1) Shows **calls (C)** or **puts (P)**.

(2) **Name** of the company. All options listed alphabetically. Options are listed by exchage in the *WSJ*.

(3) **Exchange** where traded: A, American; C, Chicago; N, New York; P, Pacific; X, Philadelphia.

(4) **Stock Price Close:** Closing price for the previous day of the underlying company's stock on the NYSE.

(5) **Strike Price:** Prices or premiums of options (in points). It shows various striking prices, or prices at which options confer the right to buy or sell. Quoted price is per share of the underlying stock.

(6) **Volume, Last Price** All options have the same first two expiration months. The third expiration month in boldface in the far right column. Also shows the daily trading **volume** for each option; **no trade** means an option was not offered for sale as of the reporting date, and **no option** means a given option was not traded during the period reported. In the *WSJ* **"s"** means no trade, **"r"** means no option. *NOTE: Because the standard contract requires delivery of 100 shares, multiply by 100 to determine a contract's total value.* **(1) (2) (3) (4) (5) (6)**

The quotation table (labeled with callouts (1) Call (C)/Put (P); (2) Name; (3) Exchange; (4) Stock Price Close; (5) Strike; (6) Volume, Last Price):

Put(P) C	X Strike Price	Dec Vol.	Dec Last Price	Jan Vol.	Jan Last Price	Vol.	Last Price
ADT Limited						Stk Close 5¼	**Mar**
C C	7½	no trade		no trade		8	¼
AMP Inc						Stk Close 53½	**Feb**
C C	45	no trade		no trade		43	8½
C C	50	no trade		9	3¾	16	4¼
C C	55	10	¾	2	1	29	1½
P C	45	no trade		no trade		2	¾
P C	55	no trade		1	2¾	28	3¾
AMR Corp						Stk Close 60¼	**Feb**
C A	60	82	1½	12	2¼	5	3½
C A	65	10	5/16	17	1	49	1½
P A	55	30	¼	no option		11	1½
P A	60	103	1¾	15	2¼	10	3
P A	65	60	5	no trade		no trade	
AST Research						Stk Close 17¾	**Feb**
C A	15	112	3	no trade		14	3¾
C A	17½	335	1	30	1¼	52	2¼
C A	20	82	5/16	209	¾	40	1 1/16
C A	22½	no trade		10	5/16	no trade	
C A	25	no trade		no option		10	5/16

nated by reversing the transaction. The long buyer can later take a short position of the same amount of the commodity or financial instrument. Almost all futures are offset (canceled out) before delivery. Delivery rarely settles a futures contract.

Trading in futures is conducted by hedgers and speculators. Hedgers protect themselves with futures contracts in the commodity they produce or in the financial instrument they hold. For instance, a producer of wheat who anticipates a decline in wheat prices can sell a futures contract to guarantee a higher current price. When future delivery is made, the producer will receive the higher price. Speculators use futures contracts to obtain capital gains on price rises of the commodity, currency, or financial instrument. Commodity futures trading is done by open outcry auction.

A futures contract can be traded in the futures market through specialized brokers; certain commodities firms deal only in futures. The fees for futures contracts are based on the amount of the contract and the price of the item. The commissions vary according to the amount and nature of the contract. Trading futures is basically the same as dealing in stocks, except that the investor must establish a commodity trading account; the margin buying and kinds of orders are the same, however. The investor can purchase or sell contracts with desired terms. Futures trading can help an investor cope with inflation. However, as we said earlier, futures contracts are a specialized, high-risk area because of the numerous variables involved, one of which is the international economic situation. Futures contract prices can be quite volatile.

FIGURE 10-5: Sample S&P 100 and S&P 500 Indexes

Friday, May 3, 1991

OPTIONS

(1) **CHICAGO BOARD**

(2) **S&P 100 INDEX-$100 times index**

(3) Strike Price	Calls—Last May	Calls—Last Jun (4)	Calls—Last Jul	Puts—Last May	Puts—Last Jun (5)	Puts—Last Jul
300	....	..	....	1/16	..	....
305	....	....	....	1/16	....	....
310	50	....	....	⅛	....	....
315	....	....	....	⅛	....	....
320	40½	....	....	3/16	⅞	....
325	....	....	....	3/16	1⅛	....
330	....	....	....	5/16	1½	2¾
335	25⅝	....	....	7/16	1⅞	3⅜
340	21¼	....	....	9/16	2½	4¼
345	16⅜	....	....	⅞	3⅜	4⅞
350	11⅞	14¾	....	1 7/16	4⅜	6⅜
355	7¾	12	....	2⅜	6	8
360	4⅜	9	11½	4⅛	7¾	9¾
365	2 7/16	6⅝	8¾	7¼	10⅜	....
370	1¼	4½	7⅛	10¾	14¾	....
375	9/16	2⅞	5¼	17½	....	....
380	¼	1⅞	3¾	....	21½	22⅛
385	⅛	1⅛	2½	....	....	....

(6) Total call volume 82,994 Total call open int. 344,995
Total put volume 73,737 Total put open int. 383,683
(7) The index: High 361.28; Low 358.54; Close 360.54, −0.06

S&P 500 INDEX-$100 times index

(8) Strike Price	Calls—Last May	Calls—Last Jun	Calls—Last Sep	Puts—Last May	Puts—Last Jun	Puts—Last Sep
320	....	....	....	....	⅜	....
330	....	....	....	....	9/16	....
340	....	....	....	....	1	....
345	....	....	....	....	....	4¼
350	....	....	....	....	1⅜	4¾
355	....	....	....	....	1 13/16	6⅛
360	....	....	....	⅝	2⅝	7¼
365	....	....	....	1	3⅛	....
370	10⅛	15¾	....	1⅜	4⅞	10⅛
375	7½	12½	....	2 5/16	5⅞	11⅜
380	4⅞	9⅛	....	4⅛	7¾	12⅞
385	2½	6½	14¼	6⅝	9⅞	....
390	1 1/16	4⅛	11⅛	10½	13	....
395	¾	2 15/16	....	15	....	....
400	¼	1¾	7	....	20⅞	....
425	....	¼	....	....	....	....

Total call volume 2,218 Total call open int. 447,721
Total put volume 9,673 Total put open int. 493,680
The index: High 381.00; Low 378.82; Close 380.80, +0.28

(1) Name of the exchange: Chicago Board Option Exchange (CBOE)

(2) Name of the S&P Index.

(3) Prices or premiums of options (in points). For example, the S&P 100 Index (June maturity) would cost $1,200.00 ($12 x 100) for the 355 call.

(4) Calls-Last are the closing prices, or premiums, for calls. Index options expire in about three months at most. You were paying 7 3/4, or $775.00 per contract, for the expensive, deep in-the-money May 355 calls. This is because the index closed at 360.54 [as shown in number (8)] making its monetary value $36,054.00. The call holder with a strike price of 355, or $35,500, has an option with an intrinsic value of $554.00 and hopes that the value will rise even higher so the option can be sold or exercised at a profit after commission. In the meantime, the 380 strike price call options have no intrinsic value because they are **out-of-the-money** and thus cheap. A May 380 cost only 1/4, or $25, per contract, and gives the buyer the right to pay $38,000 for an investment worth $36,054.

(5) Puts-Last are the closing prices, or premiums, for puts. Premiums on puts move in the opposite direction of calls. The June puts with a 370 strike price are expensive ($1,475.00 per contract) because they are deep in-the-money; they give the holder the right to demand $37,000.00 for an index that is worth only $36,054.00.

(6) The number of call contracts traded during the session and the number of contracts still open (open interest). *NOTE: These figures reflect investment optimism, in that calls are gambles that the market will rise.*

(7) The same type of information given in (6) except that it deals with puts. *NOTE: These figures measure investment pessimism, in that puts are gambles that the market will fall.*

(8) The highest, lowest, and closing values of the index, and change from its previous close. The index lost 0.06 points, which indicates that the value of the index fell $6.00.

Commodities Futures

In a commodities contract, the seller promises to deliver a given commodity by a certain date at a predetermined price. The contract specifies the item, price, expiration date, and standardized unit to be traded (e.g., 50,000 pounds). Commodities contracts

TABLE 10-2: Categories of Commodities Futures

Grains & Oilseeds	Livestock & Meat	Food & Fiber	Metals & Petroleum	Wood
Corn	Cattle-feeder	Cocoa	Copper	Lumber
Oats	Cattle-live	Coffee	Gold	Plywood
Soybeans	Hogs-live	Cotton	Platinum	
Wheat	Pork bellies	Orange juice	Silver	
Barley	Turkeys	Potatoes	Mercury	
Rye	Broilers	Sugar	Heating	
		Rice	oil #2	
		Butter		

TABLE 10-3: Financial Futures Contracts Available

Financial Group	Specific Financial Instruments
Currencies	British pound, Canadian dollar, Japanese yen, Swiss franc, W. German mark, and U.S. dollar index
Interest-rate	Eurodollars, Treasury bonds, Treasury bills, Treasury notes
Securities	GNMA passthroughs, bank CDs, and stripped Treasuries
Indexes	Municipal bond index, S&P 500 index, NYSE composite index, KC Value Line index, major market index, and the CRB index

TABLE 10-4: Futures Contract Dimensions

Contract	Size of a Contract*
Corn	5,000 bushels
Wheat	5,000 bushels
Live cattle	40,000 pounds
Pork bellies	40,000 pounds
Coffee	37,500 pounds
Cotton	50,000 pounds
Gold	100 troy ounce
Copper	25,000 pounds
Japanese yen	12.5 million yen
Treasury bills	$1 million
Treasury bonds	$100,000
S&P 500 Stock Index	500 times the index

*The size of some contracts may vary by exchange.

may run up to one year. Investors must continually evaluate the effect of market activity on the value of the contract.

Let's say that you buy a futures contract for the delivery of 1,000 units of a commodity five months from now at $4 per unit. The seller of the contract does not have to have physical possession of the item, and you (as the contract buyer), need not take custody of the commodity at the "deliver" date. Typically, commodity contracts are reversed, or terminated, prior to their consummation. For instance, as the initial buyer of 1,000 bushels of corn, you may enter into a similar contract to sell the same quantity, in effect closing out your position. *NOTE: A person can invest directly or indirectly in a commodity through a mutual fund or buy into a limited partnership involved in commodity investments. Mutual fund and partnership strategies are more conservative: Risk is spread and management know-how is provided.*

Investors may engage in commodities trading in the hope of high return rates and inflation hedges. In inflation, commodities move favorably because they are tied into economic trends. But high risk and uncertainty exist because commodities prices vacillate and because there is much low-margin investing. Investors must have plenty of cash available in the event of margin calls and to cover their losses. To reduce risk, commodities investors should hold a diversified portfolio and determine the integrity and reliability of the salesperson.

The buyer of a commodity always has the option terminate the contract or let it run to gain possible higher profits. On the other hand, he or she may utilize the earnings to put up margin on another futures contracts. This strategy is referred to as an *inverse pyramid* in a futures contract.

Commodity futures exchanges enable buyers and sellers to negotiate cash (spot) prices. Cash is paid "on the spot" for immediately receiving physical possession of a commodity. Prices in the cash market rely to some degree on prices in the futures market. There may be higher prices for the commodity over time, incorporating holding costs and anticipated inflation.

Commodities and financial futures are traded in the **Chicago Board of Trade (CBT),** the largest exchange. Other exchanges specialize in certain commodities. Examples of commodity exchanges are the **New York Cotton Exchange, Chicago Mercantile Exchange**, and **Amex Commodities Exchange**. Because there is a chance of significant gains and losses in commodities, exchanges have restrictions on the highest daily price movements for a commodity. Commodities exchanges are regulated by the **Federal Commodity Futures Trading Commission**.

Return on a Futures Contract

Return on a futures contract comes from capital gain (selling price minus purchase price) in that no current income is involved. High capital gain is possible due to commodity price volatility and the effect of leverage from the low margin requirement. However, if things go sour, the entire investment in the form of margin could be lost quickly. When dealing in commodities (whether a long or short position), the return on investment (ROI) is determined as follows:

$$\text{ROI} = \frac{\text{Selling price} - \text{Purchase price}}{\text{Margin deposit}}$$

EXAMPLE 27　　　　_____

Assume you purchase a commodity contract for $60,000, putting up an initial deposit of $5,000. You later sell the contract for $64,000. The return is:

$$\frac{\$64,000 - \$60,000}{\$5,000} = 80\%$$

Margin requirements for commodity contracts are relatively low, usually ranging from 5 percent to 10 percent of the contract's value. (For stocks, you will remember, the margin requirement is 50 percent of the cost of the security.) In commodities trading, no money is really lended, so no interest is paid.

An **initial margin** is required as deposit on a futures contract. The purpose of the deposit is to cover a market value decline on the contract. The amount of the deposit depends on the nature of the contract and the commodities exchange involved.

Investors also have to put up a **maintenance deposit**, which is lower than the initial deposit and provides the minimum margin that must always by maintained in the account. The maintenance deposit is usually about 80 percent of the initial margin.

EXAMPLE 28　　　　_____

On July 1, you enter into a contract to buy 37,500 pounds of coffee at $5.00 a pound, to be delivered by October. The value of the total contract is $187,500. Assume the initial margin requirement is 10%, or $18,750. The margin maintenance requirement is 70%, or $13,125. If there is a contract loss of $1,500, you must put up the $1,500 to cover the margin position; otherwise, the contract will be terminated with the resulting loss.

EXAMPLE 29　　　　_____

Assume you make an initial deposit of $10,000 on a contract and a maintenance deposit of $7,500. If the market value of the contract does not decrease by more than $2,500, you'll have no problem. However, if the market value declines by $4,500, the margin on deposit will go to $5,500, and you will have to deposit another $5,500 to keep the sum at the initial deposit level. If you don't come up with the additional $5,500, the contract will be canceled.

Commodities trading may be in the form of hedging, speculating, or spreading. Investors hedge to protect their position in a commodity. For instance, a citrus grower (the seller) will hedge to get a higher price, whereas a processor (or buyer) of the item will hedge to obtain a lower price. By hedging an investor minimizes the risk of loss but loses the prospect of sizable profit.

EXAMPLE 30 _____

Assume that a commodity is currently selling at $120 a pound, but the potential buyer (for example, a manufacturer) expects the price to rise in the future. To guard against higher prices, the buyer acquires a futures contract selling at $135 a pound. Six months later, the price of the commodity moves to $180. The futures contract price will similarly increase to, say, $210. The buyer's profit is $75 a pound. With 5,000 pounds, total profit is $375,000. At the same time, the cost on the market rose by only $60 a pound, or $300,000. In effect, the manufacturer has hedged, coming out with a profit of $75,000, and has kept the rising costs of the commodity under control.

_____

Some people invest in commodities for speculative purposes.

EXAMPLE 31 _____

Suppose you purchase an October futures contract for 37,500 pounds of coffee at $5.00 a pound. If the price rises to $5.40, you'll gain $0.40 a pound for a total gain of $15,000. The percent gain, considering the initial margin requirement—say, 10%, is 80% ($0.40 ÷ $0.50). If the transactions occurred over a two-month period, your annual gain would be 480% (80% × 12 months ÷ 2 months). This resulted from a mere 8% ($0.40 ÷ $5.00) gain in the price of a pound of coffee.

_____

Similar to stock option trading, *spreading* attempts to take advantage of wide swings in price and at the same time puts a cap on loss exposure. The investor, entering into at least two contracts to obtain some profit while limiting loss potential, purchases one contract and sells the other in the hope of achieving a minimal but reasonable profit. If the worst happens, the spread helps minimize the investor's loss.

EXAMPLE 32 _____

Suppose you acquire contract 1 for 10,000 pounds of commodity Z at $500 a pound. At the same time, you sell short contract 2 for 10,000 pounds of the same commodity at $535 a pound. Subsequently you sell contract 1 for $520 a pound and buy contract 2 for $543 a pound. Contract 1 yields a profit of $20 a pound, but contract 2 takes a loss of $8.00 a pound. On net, however, you earn a profit of $12.00 a pound, so your total gain is $120,000.

_____

Financial Futures

The basic types of financial futures are interest rate futures, foreign currency futures, and stock-index futures. Financial futures trading is similar in many ways to commodities trading and now constitutes about two-thirds of all contracts. Because of the instability in interest and exchange rates, financial futures can be used to hedge. They can also be utilized as speculative investments because of the potential for significant price variability. Also, financial futures have a *lower* margin requirement than commodities. The margin on a U.S. Treasury bill, for example, may be a low as 2 percent.

Financial futures are traded in the **New York Futures Exchange, Amex Commodities Exchange, International Monetary Market** (part of **Chicago Mercantile Exchange**), and the **Chicago Board of Trade**. Primarily, financial futures are for fixed-income debt securities to hedge or speculate on interest rate changes and foreign currency.

An interest rate futures contract provides the holder with the right to a given amount of the related debt security at a later date (usually no more than three years). The contract may be in Treasury bills and notes, certificates of deposit, commercial paper, or Ginnie Mae (GNMA) certificates, among others.

Interest rate futures are stated as a percentage of the par value of the applicable debt security. The value of interest rate futures contracts is directly tied into interest rates. For example, as interest rates decrease, the value of the contract increases. As the price or quote of the contract goes up, the purchaser of the contract gains while the seller loses. A change of one basis point in interest rates causes a price change (a basis point is 1/100 of 1 percent).

Those who trade in interest rate futures do not usually take possession of the financial instrument. In essence, the contract is used to hedge or to speculate on future interest rates and security prices. For example, a banker might use interest rate futures to hedge his or her position. For example, assume a company will issue bonds in 90 days, and the underwriters are now working on the terms and conditions. Interest rates are expected to rise in the next three months. Thus, investors can hedge by selling short their Treasury bills. A rise in interest rates will result in a lower price to repurchase the interest rate future with the resulting profit. This will net against the increased interest cost of the debt issuance.

Speculators find financial futures attractive because of their potentially large returns on a small investment. With large contracts (say, a $1 million Treasury bill), even a small change in the contract price can provide significant gain. But, significant risk also exists in that interest futures may involve volatile securities with great gain or loss potential. If you are a speculator hoping for increasing interest rates, you will want to sell an interest rate future, because soon it will decline in value.

A **currency futures contract** gives you a right to a specified amount of foreign currency at a future date. The contracts are standardized, and secondary markets do exist. Currency futures are expressed in dollars or cents per unit of the related foreign currency. Currency futures typically have a delivery period of no more than one year.

Currency futures can be used for either hedging or speculation. The purpose of hedging in a currency is to lock in the best money exchange possible. For example, a manager enters into an agreement to get francs in four months. If the franc decreases compared to the dollar, the manager obtains less value. To hedge his exposure, the manager can sell a futures contract in francs by going short. If the franc declines in value, the futures contract will make a profit, thus offsetting the manager's loss when he receives the francs.

EXAMPLE 33 _____

Assume a standardized contract of 100,000 pounds. In February you buy a currency futures contract for delivery in June. The contract price is $1, which equals 2 pounds. The total value of the contract is $50,000, and the margin requirement is $6,000. The pound strengthens until it equals 1.8 pounds, to $1. Hence, the value of your contract increases to $55,556 ($50,000 × 2 ÷ 1.8), giving you a return of 92.6 percent ($5,556 ÷ £6,000). If the pound had weakened, you would have taken a loss on the contract.

A **stock-index futures contract** is tied into a broad stock market index. Introduced in 1982, futures contracts currently can apply to the **S&P 500 Stock Index, New York Stock Exchange Composite Stock Index**, and **Value Line Composite Stock Index**. However, smaller investors can avail themselves of the **S&P 100 futures contract**, which involves a smaller margin deposit. Stock-index futures allow you to participate in the general change in the entire stock market. You can buy and sell the "market as a whole" rather than a specific security. If you anticipate a bull market but are unsure which particular stock will rise, you should buy (long position) a stock-index future. Because of the risks involved, you should trade in stock-index futures for the purposes of hedging or speculation only. Table 10-5 displays specifications for stock index futures contracts.

How to Get into Futures

There are at least four ways an investor gets into futures:

   • Through full-service brokers, who keep their eye on the markets and call their clients when they think they see a good trade.
   • Through discount brokers, most of whom will not call you with trades—you must manage your own account.
   • Through commodity pools; these multimillion-dollar pools are managed by professional traders and are to futures what mutual funds are to stocks. Their disclosure documents are filed with the *Commodity Futures Trading Commission* (CFTC). *NOTE:* **Management Account Reports,** *a monthly newsletter (Maryland), tracks funds and provides data about their fees and track records.*
   • Through opening an individually managed account; you put up the money and select a commodities trading adviser (CTA) to trade it for you.

TABLE 10-5: Stock Index Futures Contracts Specifications

Index and Exchange	Trading Hours	Index	Contract Size and Value	Contract Months
S&P 500 Index				
Index and Options Market (IOM) of the Chicago Mercantile Exchange (CME)	10:00 am to 4:15 pm (NYT)*	Value of 500 selected stocks Traded on NYSE, AMEX, and OTC, weighted to reflect market value of issues	$500 × the S&P 500 Index	March, June, September, December
NYSE Composite Index				
New York Futures Exchange (NYFE) of the New York Stock Exchange	10:00 am to 4:15 pm (NYT)*	Total value of NYSE Market: 1550 listed common stocks, weighted to reflect market value of issues	$500 × the NYSE Composite Index	March, June, September, December
Value Line Index				
Kansas City Board of Trade (KCBT)	10:00 am to 4:15 pm (NYT)*	Equally-weighted average of 1700 NYSE, AMEX, OTC, and regional stock prices expressed in index form	$500 × the Value Line Index	March, June. September, December
Major Market Index				
Chicago Board of Trade (CBT)	10:00 am to 4:15 pm (NYT)*	Price-weighted average of 20 blue-chip companies	$250 × MMI Index	March, June, September, December
*New York Time				

READING FUTURES CONTRACT QUOTATIONS

Commodities Futures Quotations

The financial pages of some newspapers, such as the **Wall Street Journal**, provide the beginning, high, low, and ending (settle) prices for each day, along with the daily change for the commodity. In addition, the all-time high and low are provided. Open interest is the number of outstanding futures contracts for the commodity and the expiration dates.

To determine the price of each contract, multiply the unit price by the contract size. The contract size usually following the name of the commodity. In Figure 10-6, you see first the name of the contract (Corn) followed by the contract size (5,000 bushels). Table 10-6 reproduces commodity futures prices quoted on the PBS program, "**Nightly Business Report.**"

Financial Futures Quotations

There is little difference between financial futures and commodity futures. In financial futures, there are hedgers and speculators just as in physical commodities. In this case, hedgers need the financial instruments, or they need to lock in specific interest rates. Financial futures are written on fixed-rate instruments such as Treasury bonds, certificates of deposit, or fixed amounts of foreign currencies. It is the fixed-rate component with which hedgers seek to protect themselves from the loss and with which speculators seek to make profits.

Table 10-7 shows financial futures prices quoted on the PBS program, "Nightly Business Report."

Figure 10-7 is a *Wall Street Journal* currency futures quotation.

Figure 10-8 is a Treasury bond futures quotation in the *Wall Street Journal*.

Figure 10-9 is a Treasury bill futures quotation in the *Wall Street Journal*.

Figure 10-10 is a *Wall Street Journal* Index Futures Contract quotation.

INFORMATION ON WARRANTS, OPTIONS, AND FUTURES

Several guides explain the uses and risks of warrants, options, and futures.

Value Line Options and Convertibles

This book, published by Arnold Bernhard and Company, Inc., 711 Third Avenue, New York, 10017, has basic price and maturity information on warrants, options, and convertibles. It computes such performance measures as price volatility (in the case of a warrant) and payback years and current yield (in the case of convertible issues).

Understanding the Risks and Uses of Listed Options

A 46-page booklet based on the premise that options are not for everyone. It provides a plain-language explanation of the risk-reward arithmetic of some of the most common options trading strategies. Prepared jointly by the American Stock Exchange, Inc.; Chicago Board Options Exchange; New York Stock Exchange, Inc.; Pacific Stock Exchange, Inc.; Philadelphia Stock Exchange, Inc.; and Options Clearing Corporation, it is available from the Consumer Information Center, Pueblo, CO 81009.

FIGURE 10-6: Commodities Futures Quotations

	(4)	(5)	(6)	(7) Lifetime	(10) Open
	Open	High	Low	Settle	Change	High	Low	Interest

-GRAINS AND OILSEEDS-

CORN (CBT) 5,000 bu.; cents per bu.

	Open	High	Low	Settle	Change	Lifetime High	Low	Open Interest
Sept	250¾	253¾	249¾	250	− 1¾	287½	218½	20,779
Dec	255½	258¼	254	254½	− 1	275	220	130,920
Mr92	262	265¼	261¼	261½	− 1	275¼	228½	34,501
May	266¾	269¼	265½	265¾	− 1¾	279½	234¾	12,407
July	269	271¼	267¾	268	− 2	282	239½	9,112
Sept	256½	257	254	254	− 2	265	236½	920
Dec	251¾	253½	250½	250¾	− 2	262½	236½	3,350

Est vol 56,000; vol Tues 38,707; open Int 211,989, −2,210.

OATS (CBT) 5,000 bu.; cents per bu.

	Open	High	Low	Settle	Change	High	Low	Int
Sept	122	124¼	122	122¾	....	153	109½	2,669
Dec	130¾	133¼	130¾	131¼	− ¼	151½	118½	7,032
Mr92	138	140	138	138½	+ ¼	157	126½	760

Est vol 2,000; vol Tues 2,105; open Int 10,585, −146.

SOYBEANS (CBT) 5,000 bu.; cents per bu.

	Open	High	Low	Settle	Change	High	Low	Int
Sept	574	585½	570	570½	− 4¼	670	513½	8,304
Nov	587	598	582	583	− 3¾	675	517	51,400
Ja92	597	608½	593½	594½	− 3¼	649½	527½	9,378
Mar	608	618	604	602¼	− 3¾	660	538	6,470
May	615	625	612	612¼	− 3¾	662½	547	3,733
July	621	629½	618	618	− 3	666	554	2,983
Aug	622½	623	615	615	− 6	660	565	164
Sept	599	606	599	598	− 2	628	557	207
Nov	596	601½	596	596	− 2½	620¾	552	1,828

Est vol 46,000; vol Tues 32,285; open Int 84,468, +845.

SOYBEAN MEAL (CBT) 100 tons; $ per ton.

	Open	High	Low	Settle	Change	High	Low	Int
Sept	184.70	188.60	184.50	185.90	+ .90	195.20	160.00	12,308
Oct	182.80	187.40	182.80	184.30	+ .70	195.00	159.90	10,299
Dec	182.20	187.00	181.80	183.30	+ .90	196.50	160.00	22,907
Ja92	181.50	186.30	181.50	182.60	+ .10	197.00	161.30	5,166
Mar	181.50	185.90	181.50	182.60	− .10	197.00	163.50	5,535
May	182.20	184.50	181.00	181.20	− 1.30	194.00	164.50	1,258
July	182.00	184.00	180.00	180.50	− .50	196.00	166.00	673

Est vol 24,000; vol Tues 23,710; open Int 58,187, +1,310.

SOYBEAN OIL (CBT) 60,000 lbs.; cents per lb.

	Open	High	Low	Settle	Change	High	Low	Int
Sept	19.95	20.28	19.85	19.86	− .10	25.10	18.37	12,996
Oct	20.16	20.43	20.01	20.04	− .08	24.90	18.50	14,860
Dec	20.51	20.83	20.40	20.41	− .05	24.75	18.81	24,867
Ja92	20.71	20.96	20.58	20.60	− .08	24.15	19.00	9,749
Mar	21.05	21.35	20.92	20.93	− .08	24.10	19.31	6,074
May	21.58	21.60	21.58	21.11	− .09	23.90	19.60	2,436
July	21.55	21.55	21.55	21.36	− .15	24.30	19.88	900
Aug	21.75	21.75	21.75	21.40	− .11	22.10	20.05	399

Est vol 19,000; vol Tues 18,003; open Int 72,296, +1,200.

WHEAT (CBT) 5,000 bu.; cents per bu.

	Open	High	Low	Settle	Change	High	Low	Int
Sept	302	309	302	305¼	+ 2½	326	258½	7,041
Dec	316¼	322	315½	317½	+ 1¼	325	272½	29,128
Mr92	322	326½	321½	322¼	+ ½	332½	279	8,398
May	317	320½	315½	315½	+ 2	331	280½	2,234
July	307½	310½	304½	304¾	+ 2¼	312¾	279	3,944
Sept	314½	315½	314½	313	+ 1½	319	292	153

Est vol 17,000; vol Tues 11,029; open Int 50,898, −905.

(1) **Name of commodity**

(2) **Trading exchange:** (CBT), Chicago Board of Trade.

(3) **Quantity** of commodity to be delivered.

(4) **High and low** prices for reported day.

(5) **Last price of day;** used for daily resettlement of investors margin account.

(6) **Difference** (change) between settle prices on reported day and previous day. The 1 loss for December corn signifies a $500.00 (.10 cents x 5,000).

(7) **Lifetime,** life of the contract.

(8) **Delivery months;** they differentiate one contract from another.

(9) **Prices** are in cents per bushel; 254 1/2 = $2.0545. At $2.0545, the close in the December future made the contract worth $10,272.50 ($2.0545 per bushel x 5,000 bushels).

(10) **"Open interest"** means the number of open positions reported by the clearing house.

(11) **Estimates** of the number of contracts that changed hands during the last session (56,000); volume of the previous session (38,707); the total open interest of the two previous days (211,989), and the change in the number of open contracts (−2,210).

Art reprinted by permission of the *Wall Street Journal.* ©1991 Dow Jones & Company, Inc. All rights reserved worldwide.

Before Trading Commodities—Get the Facts

This is an easy-to-read 9-page guide to commodity futures investing. Commodity Futures Trading Commission, 2033 K Street, N.W., Washington DC, 20581.

Understanding Opportunities and Risks in Futures Trading

This 45-page booklet provides a plain-language explanation on opportunities and risks associated with futures investing. Published by National Futures Association, 200 W.

TABLE 10-6: Commodity Futures Price Quotations

Settlement Prices

(1)	Copper: (June)	7640	– 10
(2)	Sugar: (June)	1188	+ 12
(3)	Cotton: (June)	6358	+ 33

(1) June copper futures at 7640. The price 7640 means $0.764 per pound, because it's quoted to 1/100 of a cent—7640 ÷ 10,000 = $0.764. The notation -10 means that the price is down $0.0100 from the previous day's settlement price.

(2) June sugar futures at 1188, which means $0.1188 per pound. This price is up $.012 from the previous day's settlement price.

(3) June cotton futures at 6358, which means $0.6358 per pound. This price is up $0.033 from the previous day's settlement price.

TABLE 10-7: Financial Futures Price Quotations

Settlement Prices

(1)	GNMA: (July)	6116	– 7/32
(2)	T-bonds: (July)	6226	– 5/32
(3)	T-bills: (July)	8475	UNCH.

(1) July Ginnie Mae (GNMA) futures at 6116. The first two digits are percent of par value (61%) and the second two are thirty-seconds of a percent (16/32%, which equal 0.5%). The settlement price is therefore 60.5% of par. This price is down 7/32nds from the previous day's settlement price.

(2) July T-bond futures at 6226. The first two numbers are percent of par value (62%) and the second two are thirty-seconds of a percent (26/32%, which equal 0.8125%). The settlement price is therefore 62.8125% of par value, down 5/32nds.

(3) July T-bill futures at 8475. Figure is a straight percent of par value carried to 1/100 of a percent. The price is 84.75%, unchanged from the previous day's settlement price.

Madison Street, Suite 1600, Chicago, IL 60606, it is available from the Consumer Information Center, Pueblo, CO 81009.

Commodity Yearbook

The *Commodity Yearbook* runs several feature articles of business interest, covering commodities or situations that are currently in the forefront of commodities trading.

FIGURE 10-7: Currency Futures Quotations

FUTURES

(1) Price is in dollars per yen, mark, pound, etc. .7320 means each yen costs $0.7320.

	Open	High	Low	Settle	Change	Lifetime High	Low	Open Interest
JAPAN YEN (IMM)—12.5 million yen; $ per yen (.00)								
Sept	.7322	.7360	.7320	.7358 +	.0053	.7995	.7003	44,213
Dec	.7300	.7336	.7294	.7334 +	.0055	.7770	.6997	8,440
Mr92	.7289	.7328	.7289	.7324 +	.0057	.7540	.7000	1,214
June	....	....		.7323 +	.0058	.7281	.7015	1,140
Sept	....	....		.7326 +	.0060	.7300	.7300	1,100
Est vol 17,031; vol Fri 12,560; open int 56,107, +970.								
DEUTSCHEMARK (IMM)—125,000 marks; $ per mark								
Sept	.5739	.5758	.5726	.5749 +	.0031	.6810	.5401	65,847
Dec	.5689	.5707	.5675	.5698 +	.0031	.6770	.5365	7,173
Mr92	.5635	.5647	.5635	.5651 +	.0031	.5840	.5353	1,208
Est vol 30,136; vol Fri 33,948; open int 74,242, +556.								
CANADIAN DOLLAR (IMM)—100,000 dlrs.; $ per Can $								
Sept	.8762	.8765	.8751	.8751 +	.0001	.8765	.7985	21,489
Dec	.8697	.8705	.8691	.8691 +	.0001	.8705	.8175	5,640
Mr92	.8638	.8640	.8638	.8637 +	.0001	.8649	.8253	1,737
June	....	....		.8583 +	.0001	.8600	.8330	254
Est vol 3,978; vol Fri 3,689; open int 29,129, +179.								
BRITISH POUND (IMM)—62,500 pds.; $ per pound								
Sept	1.6882	1.6928	1.6840	1.6912 +	.0142	1.9360	1.5824	18,171
Dec	1.6690	1.6730	1.6640	1.6718 +	.0148	1.7900	1.5670	2,561
Mr92	1.6570	1.6570	1.6570	1.6558 +	.0152	1.6700	1.5560	113
Est vol 11,759; vol Fri 13,178; open int 20,845, +126.								
SWISS FRANC (IMM)—125,000 francs; $ per franc								
Sept	.6538	.6572	.6519	.6560 +	.0017	.8055	.6254	31,469
Dec	.6500	.6534	.6482	.6521 +	.0015	.8090	.6235	3,204
Mr92	....	....		.6492 +	.0014	.6995	.6225	102
Est vol 15,659; vol Fri 16,550; open int 34,775, +177.								
AUSTRALIAN DOLLAR (IMM)—100,000 dlrs.; $ per A.$								
Sept	.7755	.7814	.7749	.7801 −	.0036	.7862	.7415	1,836
Est vol 729; vol Fri 59; open int 1,899, +4.								
U.S. DOLLAR INDEX (FINEX)—500 times USDX								
Sept	93.35	93.50	93.06	93.16 −	.49	98.23	83.17	4,254
Dec	94.54	94.55	94.15	94.26 −	.59	98.96	92.05	964
Mr92	....	....	....	95.31 −	.59	98.90	97.27	541
Est vol 1,680; vol Mon 1,414; open int 5,764, −231.								
The Index: High 93.31; Low 92.91; Close 92.97 −.52								

—OTHER CURRENCY FUTURES—

Settlement prices of selected contracts. Volume and open interest of all contract months.

British Pound (MCE) 12,500 pounds; $ per pound
Sep 1.6912 +.0142; Est. vol. 140; Open int. 186
Japanese Yen (MCE) 6.25 million yen; $ per yen (.00)
Sep .7358 +.0053; Est. vol. 216; Open int. 403
Swiss Franc (MCE) 62,500 francs; $ per franc
Sep .6560 +.0017; Est. vol. 200; Open int. 473
Deutschemark (MCE) 62,500 marks; $ per mark
Sep .5749 +.0031; Est. vol. 110; Open int. 748

Art reprinted by permission of the *Wall Street Journal.* ©1991 Dow Jones & Company, Inc. All rights reserved worldwide.

It also covers each traded commodity from alcohol to zinc. For example, corn is covered in six pages: The first page is a description of the corn crop and occurrences for the current year. The next five pages cover much data in tabular form for the past 13 years. The book is supplemented three times a year by the *Commodity Yearbook Statistical Abstract*.

Other publications about commodities come from mainline brokerage houses and specialty commodities brokers. In addition, the commodities exchanges publish educational booklets and newsletters. The **International Monetary Market (IMM)** publishes the *IMM Weekly Report*, which discusses the interest rate markets, gold, and selected cash market information such as the federal funds rate and the prime rate. The **Chicago Board of Trade (CBT)** publishes an interest rate futures newsletter (see list in Chapter 12).

FIGURE 10-8: Treasury Bond Futures Quotations

	Open	High	Low	Settle	Chg	Yield Settle	Chg	Open Interest
TREASURY BONDS (CBT)—$100,000; pts. 32nds of 100%								
June	96-17	96-24	96-06	96-18	5	8.357 −	.016	249,029
Sept	95-25	95-29	95-14	96-25	5	8.440 −	.017	32,734
Dec	94-26	95-07	94-24	95-02 +	5	8.518 −	.017	8,273
Mr92	94-09	94-18	94-06	94-14 +	5	8.587 −	.017	1,508
June	93-18	93-29	93-18	93-28 +	5	8.649 −	.017	1,031
Sept	93-13	93-13	93-10	93-12 +	5	8.705 −	.017	254
Dec	92-30	92-30	92-27	92-29 +	5	8.758 −	.017	136

Est vol 300,000; vol Tues 415,144; op Int 292,965, +3,693.

(labels above table): (1) (3) (4) (5) Yield / Open (2)

(1) Face value of bonds to deliver if they were 9% coupon, 20-year maturity.

(2) Prices are in thousands and thirty-seconds of a thousand; so 96–18 = 96,000 + 18/32 (1,000) = 96,563.

(3) Change in settlement price between reported trading day and previous day. Contract's value was up $156.25 (5/32 x $1,000).

(4) Yield to maturity (YTM). The contract is based on a bond with a 9% coupon rate (payable semiannually) and a maturity of 20 years. At a settlement price of $96,563.00, YTM = 0.0876 = 8.76%.

(5) Change in yield between the reported trading day and the previous day.

FIGURE 10-9: Treasury Bill Futures Quotations

	Open	High	Low	Settle	Chg	Discount Settle	Chg	Open Interest
TREASURY BILLS (IMM)—$1 mil.; pts. of 100%								
June	94.54	94.57	94.50	94.52 −	.01	5.48 +	.01	33,229
Sept	94.45	94.46	94.42	94.43 +	.02	5.57 −	.02	10,541
Dec	94.05	94.07	94.02	94.02 +	.03	5.98 −	.03	1,426
Mr92	....	....	....	93.84 +	.05	6.16 −	.05	123

Est vol 7,462; vol Tues 12,673; open Int 45,390, +1,160.

(labels above table): (1) / (2) / (3) Discount / Open

(1) Face value of bills to be delivered.

(2) Settlement price plus yield always equal 100.00 (94.52 + 5.48 = 100.00).

(3) This is an **index number**, not a price (value). To determine price, you must use the formula below. Price equals:

$$\$1,000,000 - \frac{(\text{Yield} \times \$1,000,000 \times 90)}{360} = \$1,000,000 - \frac{(.0548 \times \$1,000,000 \times 90)}{360}$$

$$= \$1,000,000 - \$13,700 = \$986,300 \text{ (where we assume delivery of 90–day bills)}$$

FIGURE 10-10: Stock Index Futures Quotations

	Open	High	Low	Settle	Chg	High	Low	Open Interest
S&P 500 INDEX (CME) 500 times index								
June	376.25	381.90	376.25	381.60 +	5.70	393.50	300.90	143,042
Sept	378.60	384.03	378.60	384.20 +	5.75	396.20	304.00	7,939
Dec	383.00	387.30	382.80	387.00 +	5.70	399.30	316.50	3,267

Est vol 51,152; vol Tues 60,936; open Int 154,272, +457.
Indx prelim High 380.46; Low 375.27; Close 380.29 +4.95

(labels above table): (2) / (1) / Open

(1) Settlement is always in cash.

(2) Value of a contract = 500 x Index. Thus, Value = 500 × $381.60 = $190,800.

11

Tangibles:
Real Estate and
Other Real Assets

OVERVIEW

Investing in tangibles such as real estate, precious metals, and collectibles is considered an inflation hedge. Collectibles include coins, stamps, baseball cards, and antiques, among others. Despite TRA'86, real estate investing still provides some tax shelters to investors. This chapter discussess the advantages and pitfalls of real estate investing, REITs, limited partnerships, and mortgage-backed securities, and basics about precious metals and collectibles.

INVESTING IN REAL ESTATE IS AN "IDEAL" SITUATION

It has often been said that real estate is the IDEAL investment. Each letter in the acronym stands for an advantage to real estate as an investment.

Advantages of Real Estate Investment

 • **I,** *interest deduction* (or it could mean inflation hedge or income tax benefits). The mortgage interest paid on both the first and second residential homes is tax deductible. On the average, real estate is a good hedge against inflation because property values and the income from properties rise to keep pace with inflation.
 • **D,** *depreciation.* The building on your land depreciates in book value each year, and you can deduct this depreciation from your taxable gross income. This is true only for investment property, not residential property.
 • **E,** *equity buildup.* This buildup of a capital asset is like money in the bank. As you amortize a mortgage, the value of your equity investment will steadily rise. In the case of income-producing property, this amortization could mean that your tenants help you build your estate.
 • **A,** *appreciation.* Your property value goes up every year, hopefully. Be careful because this is not guaranteed.
 • **L,** *leverage.* When you buy a house you make a down payment—say 10 percent—and you borrow the balance—say 90 percent. You get the benefit of all 100

percent even though you put up only 10 percent of your own money. You can maximize return with other people's money (OPM). Using a mortgage and OPM means that you can use small amounts of cash to gain control of large investments and earn large returns on the cash invested. Besides IDEAL, you could add the following advantages of investing in real estate:

> —*Tax-free refinancing*. Mortgage proceeds even from refinancing are not taxable income to you. Therefore, refinancing is a way to recover your cash investment and, in some cases, you profit tax free.
> —*Pride of ownership*. You may find greater personal satisfaction in owning property than stock certificates.
> —*Investment and consumption*. Certain types of real estate, such as land and vacation homes, can serve both as investments and as sources of pleasure.

Some Disadvantages with Real Estate Investment

Real estate investing is not free from problems. Watch out for the following:

• High transaction costs, such as brokerage commissions and closing expenses. These costs eat up short-term profits. *NOTE: If you might need to take your money out in a hurry, do not invest in real estate.*

• Negative cash flow with little down (too much leverage); in industry jargon, an alligator.

• Balloon payment due; the unpaid balance of a mortgage loan that is paid off in a lump sum at the end of the loan term. Typically this is a large amount, which if you cannot pay may cause you to lose your property.

• Limited marketability; lack of a central market or exchange to make real estate investments more liquid.

• Management headaches—unreliable tenants or otherwise high professional management fees.

ENHANCING THE VALUE OF REAL ESTATE

You can enhance the value of real estate by buying below market, making cosmetic improvements, benefiting from zoning changes, making financing available, increasing rent in multifamily units, and subdividing property. However, watch out for get-rich schemes that lack economic reality. A *beginning* investor in real estate should:

• Buy a property you can easily manage
• Buy a property at a price you can afford
• Select a good location, particularly an emerging attractive area
• Buy a residential property containing from one to four units (a single unit, such as a single-family house, is generally preferable)

• Make sure that, if you buy a property needing work, it has "curable" problems that can be solved at a cost below the increment in value
• Try to buy a property that will generate revenue to cover your annual cash outlay
• Buy a property that is in good condition

NOTE: Because real estate typically is not a liquid investment, try to maintain at least three months' income or three months' living expenses in liquid funds against an emergency.

TYPES OF REAL ESTATE INVESTMENTS

The kinds of real estate to invest in include undeveloped land, residential rental property (e.g., single-family houses and multiunit apartments), commercial property (e.g., office buildings, shopping centers, and industrial property), and real estate investment trusts (REITs).

Factors to consider before investing in real estate include location, method of financing the property purchase, before-tax cash flow, after-tax cash flow, vacancy rate for rental property, gain or loss for tax purposes, and management problems.

Indirect Ways of Investing in Real Estate

In some situations, a direct investment in real estate may be impractical but still hold some appeal for an investment portfolio. Three ways of investing in real estate *indirectly* are through pooled real estate investment arrangements—real estate investment trusts, limited partnerships, and mortgage-backed investments.

Real Estate Investment Trusts (REITs)

REITs are corporations that operate much like closed-end mutual funds, investing shareholders' money in diversified real estate or mortgage portfolios instead of stocks or bonds. REIT shares trade on the major stock exchanges or over the counter.

By law, REITs must distribute 95 percent of their net earnings to shareholders, and in turn they are exempt from corporate taxes on income or gains.

Because REIT earnings are not taxed before they are distributed, you get a larger percentage of the profits than with stocks; thus REIT yields are high.

There are three types of REITs: **Equity** REITs invest primarily in income-producing properties; **mortgage** REITs lend funds to developers or builders; and **hybrid** REITs do both. Equity REITs are considered the safest; however, their total returns are the lowest of the three. Table 11-1 provides a brief synopsis of what you should know about REITs.

TABLE 11-1: What Should You Know about REITs?

Where to Buy	Stockbrokers
Pluses	Dividend income with competitive yields
	Potential appreciation in price
	A liquid investment in an illiquid area
	Means of portfolio diversification and participation in a variety of real estate with minimal cash outlay
Minuses	Possible glut in real estate or weakening demand
	Market risk: possible decline in share price
Safety	Low
Liquidity	Very high: shares traded on major exchanges or over-the-counter and therefore sold at any time
Taxes	Income subject to tax upon sale.

Before buying any REIT, be sure to read the latest annual report, *The Value Line Investment Survey, Audit Investment's Newsletter*, or *Realty Stock Review*. Be sure to check the following points:

- Track record: How long in business as well as solid dividend record.
- Debt level: Make sure the unsecured debt level is low.
- Cash flow: Make sure the operating cash flow covers the dividend.
- Adequate diversification: Beware of REITs investing in only one type of property.
- Property location: Beware of geographically depressed areas.
- Type of property: Nursing homes, some apartment buildings, shopping centers presently favored; "seasoned" properties preferred.
- Aggressive management: Avoid REITs that do not upgrade properties.
- Earnings: Monitor earnings regularly; be prepared to sell when the market of property location weakens.

Sources of REIT Information

There are more than 200 REITs from which to choose. Further information may be obtained from the following publications.

REIT Fact Book. An annual published by the National Association of Real Estate Investment Trusts, 1129 20th Street, N.W., Suite 705, Washington, DC 20036,

(202) 785-8717), this book provides an overview of 25 years of the REIT industry: who, when, and how. It contains historical and year-end statistics and current industry information.

The Value Line Investment Survey, Ratings & Report. From Value Line Services, Arnold Bernhard Co., 5 E. 44th St., New York, NY 10017, this weekly report covers many REITs and includes ratings on timeliness, safety, and financial strength for each. Figure 11-1 has *Value Line Investment Survey* data for MGI Properties.

Limited Partnerships (Syndicates)

A limited partnership (syndicate) is another form of indirect investment in real estate that enables investors to buy into properties that are too large for a single investor. A group of investors form a partnership, each putting up a specified amount to purchase a large project, such as an apartment complex or a shopping mall.

Syndicates have both general and limited partners. The *general manager* usually originates and manages the project for a fee, whereas the *limited partners* invest funds and are liable only for the amount of their investment.

Here are some **advantages** of limited partnerships:

- They enable you to invest in a large project with professional management.
- They offer possible price appreciation.
- They help you obtain a tax-sheltered cash flow.

The **disadvantages,** or risks, include the following:

- Illiquidity can be a problem, since there is no active secondary market, unlike REITs.
- High management fees and expenses typically are assessed against initial investments and also as part of the profit expected from activities in the program. *NOTE: Review the "Use of Proceeds" section in a prospectus before investing. As a rule, the total of all fees should not exceed 15 percent. Also carefully read the sharing arrangement disclosed in the prospectus. In some cases, the general partner is entitled to a substantial share of capital gains and other income, although you and the other limited partners put up all or most of the money.*
- Sometimes it is difficult for average investors to understand the fine print of syndicates in terms of the complex risks and rewards associated with them.
- Adverse tax rulings can destroy the widely publicized tax benefits of syndicates.

Figure 11-2 is a **limited partnership announcement**.

FIGURE 11-1: *Value Line Investment Survey* REIT data

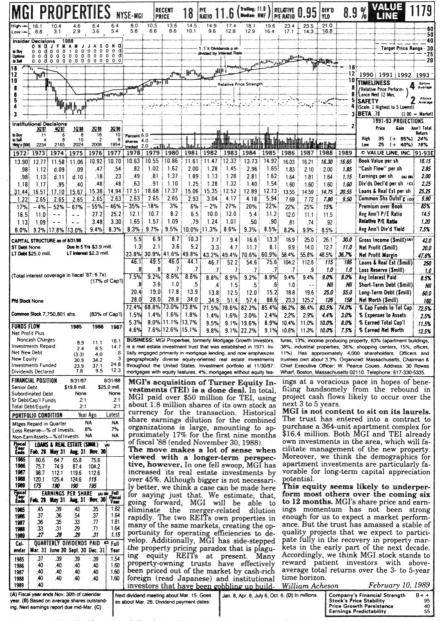

FIGURE 11-2: Announcement of a Limited Partnership

This announcement constitutes neither an offer to sell nor a solicitation of an offer to buy these securities. The offering is made only by the Prospectus, copies of which may be obtained in any State from such of the undersigned and others as may lawfully offer these securities in such State.

(1)

December 5, 1986

2,600,000 Units **(2)**

Boston Celtics (3)

Limited Partnership

Price $18.50 per Unit **(4)**

Smith Barney, Harris Upham & Co. **(5)**
Incorporated

Bear, Stearns & Co. Inc.	The First Boston Corporation	Alex. Brown & Sons
		Incorporated
Donaldson, Lufkin & Jenrette	Drexel Burnham Lambert	Goldman, Sachs & Co.
Securities Corporation	Incorporated	
Hambrecht & Quist	Kidder, Peabody & Co.	Lazard Frères & Co.
Incorporated	Incorporated	
Merrill Lynch Capital Markets	Montgomery Securities	PaineWebber
		Incorporated

Prudential-Bache   Robertson, Colman & Stephens   L. F. Rothschild, Unterberg, Towbin, Inc.
Securities

Salomon Brothers Inc	Shearson Lehman Brothers Inc.	Dean Witter Reynolds Inc.
A. G. Edwards & Sons, Inc.	Robert W. Baird & Co.	Blunt Ellis & Loewi
	Incorporated	Incorporated
J. C. Bradford & Co. Dain Bosworth McDonald & Company		The Ohio Company
Incorporated Incorporated Securities, Inc.		
Piper, Jaffray & Hopwood Stifel, Nicolaus & Company		George K. Baum & Company
Incorporated Incorporated		
The Chicago Corporation	R. G. Dickinson & Co.	Parker/Hunter
		Incorporated

(1) Standard disclaimer stating that this is not an offer to sell stock. Such offers can legally be made only through a prospectus. In principle, tombstones are only for information purposes; often the stock has already been sold out.

(2) Total number of units being offered for sale.

(3) Name of the limited partnership: Boston Celtics (basketball team).

(4) The **price** at which one unit of the partnership will sell (or has been sold) in advance of its issuance. Demand on the secondary market will determine the price, as is the case for all outstanding issues. If there are more offers to buy than there are units to go around in the initial offering, the security is called a "hot issue," and the market price will rise as soon as the units begin trading on the secondary market.

(5) List of investment bankers or underwriters that make up the syndicate bringing out the issue. Again, those with the largest number of units to sell are listed first, and in more prominent type. If you wish to acquire the security at initial price, before it starts trading on the secondary market, you must get the units through one of these firms or a firm specifically contracted by one of them to sell the securities. Some will be retail brokers, selling to the general public, but some may handle only sales to large institutional buyers.

Source of art: *Wall Street Journal*, December 5, 1986.

Mortgage-Backed Investments

A third way to get into the real estate market is through mortgage-backed (pass-through) securities. A mortgage-backed security is a share in an organized pool of residential mortgages, the principal and interest payments on which are "passed through" to shareholders, usually monthly. There are several kinds of mortgage-backed securities, as discussed below.

Ginnie Maes. The Government National Mortgage Association (GNMA) is the largest pass-through security issuer. It packages and sells pools of mortgages issued by the Federal Housing Administration (FHA) and Veterans Administration (VA), now called the Department of Veteran Affairs..

Freddie Macs. The Federal Home Loan Mortgage Corporation (FHLMC) is the major issuer of participation certificates (PCs). Freddie Mac offers pools containing conventional mortgages. It is government-sponsored but gives *no* government guarantees.

Fannie Maes. The Federal National Mortgage Association (FNMA) offers a pass-through security similar to the PC. It is a privately owned corporation with government sponsorship but provides *no* government guarantees.

Collaterized mortgage obligations (CMOs). CMOs are mortgage-backed securities that separate mortgage pools into short-, medium-, and long-term portions.

Mortgage-backed securities enjoy liquidity and a high degree of safety because they are either government-sponsored or otherwise insured. Most are sold, in minimum amounts of $25,000, which is out of reach for most small investors.

INVESTING IN PRECIOUS METALS

Investments in tangible assets such as gold, silver, and other precious metals have gained popularity in the past decade, offering: a hedge against inflation, an opportunity to diversify holdings, and psychic pleasure. It should be noted, however, that this type of defensive investment does not produce current income. Further, precious metals are not easily converted into cash. Appreciation may take years and resale may not be easy.

Gold and silver are two highly volatile forms of tangible assets in which price movements often run counter to events in the economy and the world. Bad news is good news (and vice versa) for precious metal investors. Gold and silver may be generally bought in bullion or bulk form—as coins, in the commodities futures market, indirectly through securities of firms specializing in gold or silver mining, or through mutual funds investing in gold or silver. The little-known metal palladium has been lighting up Wall Street as a potential new energy source. Many experts agree that platinum is perhaps the most desirable because it has the greatest opportunity to yield substantial profits and is the most liquid. Gold is a good investment because it is the world's monetary metal, and if inflation or monetary crisis hits it will be the first to move. Silver is the metal for the long-term investor who is willing to wait for it to go up. *NOTE: Precious metals can move violently in response to news events that could alter supply or demand; platinum and palladium are prime recent examples.*

Table 11-2 provides basics on precious metals in terms of their geographic sources and uses and what news events are likely to affect their prices.

SOURCES OF INFORMATION FOR PRECIOUS METALS

Powell Gold Industry Guide and *The International Mining Analyst*

Published quarterly by Reserve Research Ltd. (181 State Street, Portland, ME 04101, 207/879-0611), they provide information on 100 leading gold, silver, platinum, copper, and aluminum companies in the U.S. and abroad. Coverage of each company includes history, latest earnings and other news, plus 7-year tables of sales, earnings, earnings per share, dividends, stock splits, and number of shares outstanding. Also included are reviews of outlook for prices of gold, silver, platinum, copper, and aluminium.

Precious Metals Data Base

A monthly report published by Moneypower (4257 46th Ave., N., #207, Minneapolis, MN 55422, 612/537-8096) pulls data for all the precious metals into one publication and lists daily spot closes, daily price ratios, monthly averages, 2-year ratio averages, fair dealer prices, and other information for gold, silver, and platinum. It also identifies profitable points at which to swap.

GEMS AND COLLECTIBLES

Precious gems and other collectibles—art, antiques, stamps, Chinese ceramics, and rare books—have attracted investor attention. Although profits are often very high, don't invest in these tangibles without product and market knowledge.

Tangibles are inflation hedges. In the 1970s, oil, gold, U.S. coins, silver, and stamps had the highest compound returns, above 20 percent. From 1980 to 1985, a period of rapid disinflation, financial assets such as bonds, stocks, and Treasury bills had higher returns than every category of tangible assets. In fact, gold and silver suffered huge losses (more than 11 percent) in the early 1980s.

Other Collectibles Information Sources

In addition to the *Wall Street Journal, Money* and *Business Week*, the *Collector/Investor* provides excellent articles on the collectibles market. More specialized periodicals include *American Arts and Antiques, Coin Prices, Coin World, Coins,*

TABLE 11-2: What Drives Strategic Metals

Metal	Sources	Uses	Events
Gold*	South Africa, Chile, Australia	Investment, jewelry, hedge against inflation, dental, ornamentation	Monetary instability, Third World debt default, Middle East confrontation
Silver*	Mexico, USSR, Peru, Canada, Southwest U.S., Australia	Photography, electronics, jewelry, investment, sterling, mirrors	Inflation spurs its use as "poor person's gold"
Platinum*	South Africa, USSR, Canada	Catalytic converters, aerospace industry, oil refining, investment, jewelry, coins	Inflation, use as a conductor in catalytic converters
Palladium*	USSR, Canada, South Africa, Australia	Aerospace industry, dentistry, catalytic converters, possibly nuclear fusion	Government unrest, nuclear fusion news
Aluminum	U.S., USSR, Canada, Japan	Building material, packaging, transportation	Mining strikes, technological replacement, i.e., low-cost tubing
Nickel	USSR, Canada, Australia	Electroplating, stainless and heat-resistant steel, copper alloy	U.S. confrontation with USSR, technological replacement
Copper	U.S., Chile, USSR, Peru, Mexico, Zambia, Zaire, Canada	Electrical tubing and wiring, alloy, construction piping, jewelry, pots and pans	Mining strike in Chile or Peru, political unrest
Lead	U.S., USSR, Canada, Australia	Batteries, solder, gas, additives, ammunition	Europe's increased lead-free gas use, new battery source, industry strikes
Zinc	USSR, U.S., Canada, Australia	Galvanizer in paints, metals, and aluminum, brass alloy	Mining strike

Precious metals, unlike base metals, are in limited supply on a per tonnage of ore basis. Precious metals do not corrode as easily and have high endurance.

Source: Monex International, *A-Mark Precious Metals.*

Linn's Stamp News, Numismatic News, The Sports Collectors' Digest, Antique Monthly, and *Stanley Gibbons' Stamp Catalog.*

Scott Stamp Catalog

The Scott Publishing Company, long involved in the philatelic (stamp) market, publishes the well-known *Scott Stamp Catalog,* which carries price data and pictures with descriptions. Recently, Scott added a *Stamp Market Update,* a quarterly report on current trends and prices featuring prices of major U.S. stamps and popular foreign stamps, information for specialized collectors, investment opportunities and strategies (as stated by recognized experts), and special articles, statistical tables, and graphs.

The *Scott Index* for "fine" stamps is used as a basis for comparison in a study of quality-adjusted rates in stamp auctions.

Kovel's Antiques and Collectibles Price List

An 800-page comprehensive guide to prices of various antiques and collectibles, this is Ralph and Terry Kovel's 23rd edition, published by Crown Publishers, New York.

Leonard's Annual Price Index of Art Auctions

Published by Auction Index Inc. (30 Valentine Park, Newton, MA 02165), it informs you of the shifting "who, what, where, and how much" of every art auction sale conducted in America by the 74 major auction houses during the prior year.

A Guide Book of United States Coins

This is the best seller in the coin hobby, also called the **Red Book,** and features such information as latest price and auction records, official A.N.A Grading Standards, type coin boxes indicating value change from previous year, bullion table for instant updating of gold and silver coin prices. It is published by Western Publishing Co., Inc., M.S. 438, Racine, WI 53401.

World Coins

Published by Krause Publications (700 E. State St., Iola, WI 54990), it provides a comprehensive listing of all world legal tender, current market valuation, and identification numbers plus cross-referencing.

10th Blue Book: Dolls & Values

Published by Jan Foulke (Hobby House Press, Inc., Department CX, 900 Frederick St., Cumberland, MD 21502-3770, 301/759-3770), it contains the descriptions and value estimate ranges of 1,600 antique, collectible, and modern dolls, along with their photographs. The 10th book is the latest edition in the bestselling series known as the "bible" of doll collecting. Its publisher, **Hobby House Press**, publishes numerous books on dolls including:

> *Cloth Dolls*
> *Ginny 1991 Price Guide*
> *French Dolls*
> *Madame Alexander Price Guide for Dolls #16*
> *Collector's Encyclopedia of Dolls, Vol. I and Vol. II*

For their book catalogue, call 301/759-3770, 301/759-4940 Fax. Also, for more about dolls investing, write to the **National Antique Doll Dealers Association**, Box 143, Wellesley Hills, MA 02181.

12

On-Line Data Service and Investment Software

OVERVIEW

The owner of a personal computer (PC) with communication ability and a modem can now dial a data base such as the **Dow Jones News/Retrieval (DJN/R)**. Such data bases are oriented to the analysts and investors and includes financial data, current and historical information on stock quotes, commodity quotes, access to SEC disclosure reports, and much more.

In addition to available data bases for the PC, many software programs facilitate investment analysis. Raw data can either be "downloaded" onto a floppy disk or into your computer memory to save time and be analyzed later, or they can be read directly into a software program designed to perform calculations on the raw data.

This chapter covers automated news/retrieval, on-line computer data bases, and investment computer software.

ON-LINE DATA BASES AND NEWS/RETRIEVAL

Data bases are organized collections of information, both historical and current. Just as hardware is useless without software, PCs are inadequate without news/retrieval capabilities and data bases. Investment analyses require considerable amounts of economic and financial information; the more current it is, the better.

Professional investors are in constant contact with many news sources, and the investors buy or sell securities almost automatically when important events take place. In addition to having access to current news, a PC owner can use this same news to update his or her data base. Currently, Dow Jones's News/Retrieval is the undisputed leader in investment news retrieval software. Its key investor information services are summarized in Table 12-1.

TABLE 12-1: DJN/R Key Information Services

Business News

Dow Jones News   **DJNEWS**
Stories from the Dow Jones News Service wire and selected, condensed stories from the *Wall Street Journal* and *Barron's*.
As recent as 90 seconds and as far back as 90 days. Searched by company, industry, or category.

Business and Finance Report   **BUSINESS**
Continuously updated business and financial news culled from the *Wall Street Journal, Dow Jones News Service*, and other newswires.
Latest news on domestic/international economies. Cross referenced to related information in DJN/R.

Capital Markets & Finacial Futures Report   **CMR**
Newswire has current, comprehensive coverage of fixed-income/financial futures markets around the world.

Text-Search Services   **TEXT**
Wall Street Journal: Full text of articles that appeared or were scheduled to appear in the *Wall Street Journal* since January 1984.
Dow Jones News: Selected Dow Jones News Service wire stories; selected, condensed stories from the *Wall Street Journal* and *Barron's* since June 1979.
Barron's: Full text of articles in *Barron's* since January 1987.
Washington Post: Full text of selected articles from The *Washington Post* since January 1984.
Business Library: Full text of selected articles from *Forbes, Fortune, Money, Inc., American Demographics, Financial World;* full text of the PR Newswire and the Japan Economic Newswire since January 1985.
Business Dateline: Full text of selected articles from more than 140 regional business journals since January 1985.
DataTimes: Full text of articles from 13 regional newspapers, two Associated Press wires, The *Congressional Quarterly,* Gannett News Service, *USA Today.* (DataTimes not included in TEXT ALL Command.)

Japan Economic Daily   **KYODO**
Same-day coverage of Japanese business, financial, political news from Kyodo News Service in Japan.

General News

News/Retrieval World Report   **NEWS**
Continuously updated national and international news from the Associated Press, Dow Jones News Service, and broadcast media.

News/Retrieval Sports Report   **SPORTS**
Continuously updated stories, scores, stats, standings, and schedules for most major sports.

News/Retrieval Weather Report   **WTHR**
Three day Accu-Weather forecasts for more than 100 U.S. and foreign cities.

Company and Industry Statistics and Forecasts

Disclosure Online   **DSCLO**
10-K extracts, company profiles, and other data on over 12,000 publicly held companies from reports filed with SEC and other sources.

Zacks Corporate Earnings Estimator   **EPS**
Consensus earnings-per-share estimates and P/E forecasts for over 4,800 firms. Industry earnings estimates and lists of stocks outperforming or underperforming analysts' forecasts.

Insider Trading Monitor   **INSIDER**
Insider trading information on transactions of 100 shares or more for over 6,500 publicly held companies and nearly 60,000 individuals (corporate directors, officers, or shareholders with more than 10% ownership).

Investext   **INVEST**
Full text of over 20,000 research reports from top brokers, investment bankers, and other analysts.
Covers more than 4,000 U.S. and Canadian companies and 52 industries.
Historical, current, forecasted marketing, and financial information.

Media General Financial Services   **MG**
Detailed financial information on 5,400 companies and 180 industries.
Major categories include: revenue, earnings, dividends, volume, ratio, shareholdings, price changes.
Compare 2 different companies, company vs. industry, or industry vs. industry data on same screen.

MMS Weekly Market Analysis   **MMS**
Weekly survey/analyses of U.S. money market/foreign exchange trends, debt, currency, equity markets. Median monetary/economic indicators forecasts.

Standard & Poor's Online   **SP**
Profiles of 4,700 companies containing earnings, dividends, and market figures for the past four years.
Corporate overviews plus S&P earnings estimates for most major companies.

TABLE 12-1: *continued*

Company Profiles and Reports

Dow Jones QuickSearch   QUICK
One command will generate a complete corporate report drawing information from multiple Dow Jones News/Retrieval sources.

Tracking Service   TRACK
Create customized portfolios of up to 125 companies/industries; automatically track news and quotes.

Quotes and Market Averages

Enhanced Current Quotes   CQE
Minimum 15-minute delay during market hours; quotes on common stocks (with **News Alert** feature).
Preferred stocks, warrants, corporate, and foreign bonds, mutual funds, U.S. Treasury issues, and options.

Historical Quotes   HQ
Daily high, low, close, volume for stock prices and composites. Monthly stock price summaries back to 1979; quarterly summaries back to 1978.

Futures Quotes   FUTURES
Current (10-39 minute delay) and historical quotes for more than 80 commodities from the major North American exchanges updated continuously during market hours. Daily open, high, low, last, settlement prices; daily volume and open interest, lifetime high and low.

Historical Dow Jones Averages   DJA
Historical averages including daily high, low, close, volume available for the last trading year for industrials, transportation, utilities, and 65-stock composite indexes.

Fidelity Investor's Express   FIDELITY
Place trades online for listed securities with Fidelity discount brokerage; organize portfolios/monitor investments with a Fidelity Investor's Express account.

Business Services

Official Airline Guide   OAG
Airline schedules/fares for 600 airlines worldwide. Hotel and motel information.

MCI Mail   MCI
Electronic mail service for sending printed and electronic communications next door or worldwide.

Wall Street Week Online   WSW
Four most recent transcripts of the popular PBS television program Wall Street Week.

General Services

Comp-u-store Online   STORE
An electronic shopping service with more than 250,000 discounted brand-name products.

Academic American Encyclopedia   ENCYC
More than 32,000 carefully researched and concisely written articles covering industry and finance as well as academic subject areas. Updated quarterly.

Peterson's College Selected Service   SCHOOL
Peterson's Guide to two- and four-year colleges and universities. Search by size, entrance difficulty, location, cost, financial aid, and majors.

Cineman Movie Reviews   MOVIES
Reviews of the latest releases as well as thousands of movies dating back to 1926.

Magill Book Reviews   BOOKS
Reviews of recent fiction and non-fiction works with new titles added weekly.

Online Reference Tools

For Your Information   FYI
Free online newsletter for News/Retrieval members. New database announcements, enhancements, rate changes, free-time offers, online user's agreement, and other important information.

Master Menu   MENU
Complete listing of the service's information with instructions on how to access each data base.

News/Retrieval Symbols Directory   SYMBOL
Comprehensive online list of symbols/codes used to access Dow Jones News/Retrieval. Updated daily.

Words of Wall Street   DEFINE
Definitions of over 2,000 business and financial terms used by professional investors.

Source: Dow Jones News/Retrieval *Summary of Information Services.*

WHAT DO ON-LINE DATA BASES OFFER?

Not all data bases offer the same information. Similarities and differences of offerings by various on-line data bases are briefly discussed below.

Numbers

You can get current prices on securities throughout the day. Quotations are generally 15 to 20 minutes behind the market, but by paying more you can also get up-to-the minute quotes.

You can get high, low, and closing stock prices; trading volume; and other technical data going back many years. Corporate financial data—including historical, current, and projected information—also are available.

Depending on the data base, you can also get current and historical data on corporate and municipal bonds, mutual funds, commodities and options; on indexes; and on the state of the general economy.

Information and News

You can get textual information on any company or industry you're interested in, or on the economy as a whole. This information may include a company profile, its product lines, or developments of importance to the industry.

Although this information is accessible in the *Wall Street Journal* and the *Value Line Investment Survey*, the data base makes it available more quickly, covers more companies than Value Line's 1700, and lets you zero in on a particular company or item that you might otherwise miss.

You can also get, shortly after the market's close, not only closing prices but the kind of report and commentary on the day's activity that you will find in tomorrow's paper. When you need to act quickly, getting a jump on the market this way can help.

Analysis and Advice

A few data bases will either analyze their data for you or dispense advice—either their own or that of "experts."

Some data bases provide technical or fundamental analysis on-line. Rather than supply data to be used by your technical or fundamental analysis software, these data bases produce the charts or do the screening on-line.

Telescan, for example, provides not data but graphs of a wide variety of technical and fundamental indicators, with up to 13 years of data on more than 8,000 stocks; 2,000 mutual funds; and 150 market indexes. You can also compare a stock's performance with the performance of the industry group, or the performance of the industry group with any of several overall market averages. All this saves you time, but generally at some loss in control over the output.

CompuServe can screen 46,000 securities to find those that meet criteria you select from the data base's somewhat limited list of criteria; or you can use its new service, **Coscreen,** to screen more thoroughly 9,500 stocks using the Disclosure II data base and 24 screening categories.

Profiteer, available through **The Source,** analyzes the risk and potential profit in investing in the particular stocks, options, convertible bonds, or warrants you may be considering.

Vestor (from Investment Technologies Inc., Metropart, 510 Thornall St., Edison, NJ 08837) evaluates securities for you rather than simply supplying data. Based on its analysis of fundamental and technical data, Vestor produces short- and long-term projections, risk-reward ratios, and rankings and timing signals for buying and selling. You can also screen 4,500 securities—including stocks, options and commodities—for those that meet your selected criteria.

A greater number of data bases relay the analysis and advice of others.

Equalizer, for example, provides access to analysis and recommendations from **Standard & Poor's MarketScope** (a source the pros use).

Dow Jones News/Retrieval provides access to market analysis and recommendations from Standard & Poor's, and the financial press research reports.

The **Independent Investors Forum** (1128 E. Bluff Dr., Penn Yann, NY 14527) takes a different approach, that of a combination newsletter and teleconference. Its staff provides research and recommendations; users ask questions and discuss the pros and cons with the staff and with one another.

Investment Organizer

To organize your investment accounts, **Investment Record** (Claude E. Cleeton, 122 109th Ave., S.E., Bellevue, WA 98004; (206) 451-0293) can track up to 10 accounts, each having up to 150 total investments in 10 categories. It generates two reports: a capital asset statement providing detailed information on all investment assets owned and a personal income statement giving a detailed description of the investor's financial performance—actual and estimated—for the year including yield and tax status.

On-line Trading

The data base will help you place actual buy and sell orders from your computer directly to a broker by sending electronically the same information you would have given your broker by phone. Because fewer hands are involved, the danger of delays or errors is reduced. For example, through **Fidelity Investor's Express,** available on DJN/R, your order goes from your computer directly to the appropriate stock exchange, reviewed only by Fidelity's computer. You can also place your order during non-business hours and have it executed when the market opens.

Spear Securities on **The Source** allows you to place orders after the markets close. In fact, more people seem to be attracted to on-line trading for its convenience over its speed. You can see your portfolio, at any time, updated automatically for new transactions, showing gains and losses, current prices for all holdings and any cash in the account, without having to wait for a monthly statement.

A growing number of discount brokers think data bases make their services more attractive because of the investment data and research investors would miss out on by not using a full-service broker. In addition to the programs offered by Fidelity and Spear, the Equalizer program of Schwab and Co. offers a full range of investment services as well as on-line trading through Max Ule & Co., and Quickway is available through Quick & Reilly.

Only Equalizer has no on-line charge for entering orders or checking up on your account. Fidelity has an $8 per month account fee and time charges of 30 cents per minute in prime time and 10 cents in nonprime time for all baud rates.

Other major sources of data are available for use on-line and are accessible on an interactive, time-share basis. Many of these data bases are now accessible from a personal computer. Table 12-2 provides a list of major on-line computer data bases.

DATA BASES

Some data bases are made for use on large mainframe computers; others can be used with PCs. Not all offer the same information. Data bases are summarized below.

CompuStat Tapes

CompuStat tapes are developed by Investors Management Science Company, a subsidiary of Standard & Poor's Corporation. They are comprehensive in that they:

- Contain 20 years of annual financial data for more than 3,000 industrial companies. Each year's data include more than 120 balance sheet, income statement, and market-related items.
- Have an industrial file that includes company data from the NYSE, AMEX, and the OTC market.
- Have a file on utilities and banks.
- Besides the annual file, they are updated weekly; users can order tapes with quarterly data, also updated weekly.
- Create the **Price-Dividend-Earnings (PDE) tape**, which contains monthly data on per share performance.

NOTE: These tapes are useful for analyzing large numbers of companies in a short time period. Ratios can be created, analyzed, and compared. Trends and regression analyses can be performed. Searches can be implemented for specific kinds of companies. For example, one could read through the tapes and screen for companies meeting certain parameters, such as dividend yield greater than 7 percent, earnings growth greater than 20 percent per year, price/earnings ratio less than 10 times, or market price less than book value.

Continued on page 312.

TABLE 12-2: On-Line Data Base Sampler

Service	What It Offers	Comments
Dow Jones News/Retrieval (DJN/R), P.O. Box 300, Princeton, NJ O8543, (800-522-3567; 609-520-4641), (NJ and Alaska only)	Up-to-the-minute news from Dow Jones sources; includes the *WSJ* full text since 1984; selected stories from Dow Jones News Services since '79; search by company and industry; current and historical quotes on stocks, bonds, mutual funds, options, commodities; detailed stock, company, and insider trading data; earnings estimates; research from S&P and others; on-line trading.	Start-up free with DJ and some other software; free hot-line.
CompuServe 5000 Arlington Centre Blvd., P.O. Box 20212, Columbus, OH 43220 (800-848-8199, except Ohio; 614-457-8600 Ohio and Canada only)	15-minute delayed stock prices; historical data on stocks, bonds, government issues, options; mutual fund price and background information; technical and fundamental data from S&P and Value Line; screening; earnings estimates; economic analysis; portfolio maintenance and on-line trading.	Free hot-line.
The Source Source Telecomputing Corp., 1616 Anderson Rd., McLean, VA 22102 (800-336-3366)	Real-time or 20-minute delayed stock quotes; data on more than 4,300 stocks from Media General, research from Investext; corporate and economic news; commodity prices and news; investment analysis; on-line trading and portfolio management.	Extra charges for Investext, Profiteer; unlimited free use of on-line tutorial; free hotline.
The Equalizer Charles Schwab & Co., Inc., 101 Montgomery St., San Francisco, CA 94104 (800-334-4455)	Access to DJN/R, Warner Computer Systems, S&P Market Scope (for S&P analysis and recommendations); detailed company reports (from several data	Requires Equalizer software; free introductory subscriptions to data bases and on-line time.

TABLE 12-2: *continued*

---

	bases); data on stocks, bonds, options; news; portfolio management; on-line trading in stocks and options with up-to-the-minute price quotes.	
Nite-Line National Computer Network, 1929 Harlem Ave., Chicago, IL 60635 (312-336-3366)	Closing market and historical data on stocks, commodities, indexes, and options; current and historical data on bonds and mutual funds; data goes back 7-1/2 to 12-1/2 years.	Additional charges for extensive historical data.
Telescan Analyzer Telescan, Inc., 10550 Richmond Ave., Suite 250, Houston, TX 77042 (800-324-8353; 713-952-1060)	Graphs for a wide variety of technical and fundamental indicators, including insider trading and industry group anaylsis on more than 8,000 stocks and 2,000 mutual funds (data from 1973); world, national, business, and market news.	Requires an IBM-PC or 100% compatible computer; newsletter every other month.
Warner Computer Systems, Inc., 17-01 Pollitt Ave., Fair Lawn, NJ 07410 (800-336-5376; 201-797-4633)	Descriptions and prices, dividends and earnings since 1975 on 20,000 securities, including stocks, mutual funds, and indexes.	More efficient with investment software from WCS or other software that accesses WCS data automatically.
Commodity Systems, Inc. 200 W. Palmetto Park Rd., Boca Raton, FL 33432 (800-327-0175; 407-392-8663)	Daily update service includes current and historical prices (20 years for most) on more than 200 commodities. Also data on options, futures, industries, and 1,000 securities.	

Interactive Data Corporation Tapes

Interactive Data Corporation provides the same information as the CompuStat tapes, but on a time-share basis.

CRSP Tapes

CRSP tapes are maintained by the University of Chicago's Center for Research in Security Prices (CRSP). Information is oriented to earnings, dividends, stock prices, and dates of mergers, stock splits, stock dividends, and so on. The tapes are extremely useful (data begin in 1926) for historical research on stock performance.

Value Line Tapes

Value Line provides computer tapes of 1,700 companies. They too have market price data as well as financial statement items.

FTC Tapes

The Federal Trade Commission (FTC) has tapes for aggregate industry data.

Federal Reserve Bank of St. Louis Tapes

The Federal Reserve Bank of St. Louis has monetary data tapes, available to analysts.

Chase Econometrics, Citishare Corp., and Nite-Line

These economic consulting firms specialize in financial, business, and economic data.

Value Line and Standard & Poor's

Many old-line financial companies such as **Value Line (Value/Screen,** and **ValuePak)** and **Standard & Poor's** offer their financial data on microcomputer floppy disks with monthly updates.

Disclosure Database

With financial and textual data from SEC documents on over 1,200 companies, **Disclosure Database** also includes more than 250 variables such as company name, address, phone number, financial statements, financial ratios, and weekly prices for each company. (Disclosure Incorporated, 5161 River Rd., Bethesda, MD 20816; (301) 951-1300)

CHOOSING THE RIGHT DATA BASE

Although investment data bases have a lot to offer, they are expensive. In choosing a compatible data base, ask these questions: Is any data base worth its cost to you? Do you want more than just investment information? Is there a data base that offers what you want at an affordable price? Further points to consider are examined in the following sections.

Coverage

The number of securities and companies covered, the depth of financial information, and the availability of historical data vary for different data bases and on-line services; so does the availability of analysis and advice. *NOTE: If you want more than investment information, your choices are limited to four broad data bases:* Dow Jones News/Retrieval, CompuServe, Schwab's Equalizer Service, *and* The Source. *Each of these services has an 800 toll-free number and offers a wide variety of features, including sports, movie reviews, travel information, and discussion groups.*

Data Organization

Even when several services get information from the same data base, each on-line service has its own way of organizing its data for the user. Such organization will determine how difficult it is to get around the data base—especially if you don't do it everyday—and it may also determine how much it costs you to use the data base. *NOTE:* The Source *has a tutorial to its investment services that you can use anytime, free of on-line charges, to familiarize yourself with its procedures and cut your on-line costs.*

Format

Data bases also differ in the way data are accessed. As a result, the time it takes to get the data will be different for each service. For example, getting graphs from **Telescan,** using Telescan software, takes about one-tenth the time it takes on other data bases.

The on-line time required to get specific data also depends on the software you use to get to the data base. Because most investment software will get data from only one or two data bases, it is hard to compare the time required for each data base.

Cost

You pay an hourly fee for the time you spend tapping in to the service's central computer. Each minute you spend using a data base during nonprime hours will cost you money; how much depends on the service. Included in that fee or billed separately is a telecommunications charge, which covers the cost of transporting data from the central computer over a communications network. If you aren't within local reach of a network, you might have to pay long-distance charges.

You'll also have to pay a subscription or start-up fee, separate charges for the phone calls that connect your computer with the data base, and surcharges for access to particular information or analytical tools. Each service has its own method of computing hourly costs. Some have a monthly minimum, and some give new subscribers a few hours of free time or other "gifts."

You also need a modem to connect your computer to your telephone, and communications or investment software—either your choice or the company's own program—to help your computer receive the information. Depending on the type of computer you have, you might also need an interface card or a line cord (or both) to connect your modem with the computer. These add-ons could cost a lot, depending on your preferences and your computer.

Support Services

The availability and quality of data base support services are important factors to consider. For example, if something goes wrong during communications, it is hard to know whether the fault lies with the software, the communications system, or the data base. Use the toll-free number to contact someone who can walk you through the problem.

Before you choose a data base service, try to get hands-on experience with at least a few. Some offer a demonstration diskette with a sample of the kind of material you will get on-line; others offer free sample time. Or, find a friend or a users group with a service that you can try out, and pay whatever costs are involved.

In general, Dow Jones News/Retrieval and Equalizer have the most extensive services for the individual investor. Their hourly charges are also the highest. If you want many of the features of Dow Jones, it is well worth the cost; if not, see whether you can find what you want on CompuServe or The Source. If you want only price quotations, technical analysis, or other specific data, look at other data bases that may fill the need at less cost.

INVESTMENT SOFTWARE

A good investment software package can turn your PC into a valuable tool for practically every step in the investment process—identifying securities to buy and sell, placing orders on-line, and monitoring securities after you buy them.

You can search through data bases containing thousands of stocks for those that meet your own investment criteria, generate scores of market indicators, and perform complex technical analysis on individual securities.

Some programs analyze and create charts of the technical behavior of price movements, and others evaluate the financial data from income statements and balance sheets. Using the **Dow Jones Investment Evaluator,** you can access the Dow Jones News/Retrieval system to obtain information for stocks, bonds, warrants, options, mutual funds, or Treasury issues. Information related to 10-K statements, ratios, earnings growth rates, earnings-per-share forecasts, and so forth, are available for 2,400 companies. The **Dow Jones Market Analyzer,** the **Dow Jones Microscope,** and the **Dow Jones Investor Workshop** all allow access to the Dow

Jones information network. Once the correct data are entered into these software programs, they create standardized analyses from preprogrammed instructions.

Also, new programs are now able to transfer data from a news retrieval service straight into a spreadsheet program such as **Lotus 1-2-3** or Microsoft **Excel**. For example, **Dow Jones Spreadsheet Link** enables corporate planners, investors, researchers, and competitive analysts to extract data from Dow Jones News/Retrieval for extensive analysis with Lotus 1-2-3, **Symphony**, **Multiplan**, or Microsoft's Excel. Each program increases the value of spreadsheets by linking them with key financial data. Programs automatically log on, collect specified data, and enter them into the spreadsheet for further analysis. This saves time and money and allows the individual flexibility to create his or her own financial analysis.

NOTE: Before buying a computer, determine which software programs it will run.

Types of Investment Software

There are three main categories of investment software: portfolio management, fundamental analysis, and technical analysis. In addition, two types of investment software packages deal specifically with fixed-income securities and options and futures (see Table 12-3, starting on page 318, for descriptions of such programs).

Portfolio Management

With portfolio management software you can enter the names of the securities you own or want to follow into one or more portfolios, manually enter current prices or get automatic updates from an on-line service, and generate a variety of portfolio status reports.

The most common report simply shows the portfolio's current status. The report lists each security you own along with information about its type, method of purchase (for cash or on margin), number of shares or units owned, purchase price, current price, and unrealized gain or loss.

Another kind of report conveys vital income tax information. For each security you sell during the tax year, you get the name, number of shares, purchase date, sale date, total cost, total proceeds, and gain or loss. All the information you need to complete your federal income tax return is included in this report.

Other reports reflect dividend and interest income, often providing advance notice of dividends coming due and options expiring.

Fundamental Analysis

Most fundamental analysis software comes in the form of a stock-screening package, which allows you to search through a large group of stocks and identify those meeting criteria you specify.

For example, you might want to identify all stocks listed on the NYSE having a less-than-$35 per share market price, a price/earnings ratio less than the S&P 500 Index, a dividend yield greater than 6 percent, and beta less than 1.5. A stock-screening package can narrow your choices in a few minutes.

Periodically—normally monthly—you receive a data base disk containing up-to-date financial information on a group of stocks.

The amount and type of information available for screening varies with the software package. For example, with **Value Line's Value/Screen Plus**, one data base disk contains information on approximately 1,700 stocks that account for more than 95 percent of the trading activity on all U.S. stock exchanges. The disk contains 37 separate pieces of information for each stock, including historical growth rates, measures of current performance and volatility, and key projections for timeliness and safety.

NOTE: In selecting a stock-screening package compare the number of companies and industries that can be screened, the exchanges on which the stocks are listed, and the frequency with which data are updated. Also check each package for market price, earnings, sales, dividends, assets, liabilities, financial ratios, and proprietary items.

Technical Analysis

Technical analysis software is essentially used for charting. It allows you to plot standard high-low-close-volume bar charts, along with various technical indicators and studies.

Because such software requires the input of extensive information it is wise to compare the kinds of data required by each package under consideration and the sources for such data. For example, if you want to see a basic high-low-close-volume bar chart for General Electric for a 120-day period, the program will require 600 pieces of data. You could always enter the information into the computer piece by piece, but you might prefer a program that can get it from an on-line service (such as the **Dow Jones News/Retrieval**), thus greatly reducing the time it takes to create a chart.

A good program will offer a variety of charting capabilities. In selecting a program, ask five key questions:

1. Which technical indicators and studies can be plotted?

2. Can you plot sophisticated indicators to analyze individual securities and the overall stock market?

3. Are you limited to simple moving-average lines and just a few basic charting tools?

4. Can the program show multiple charts on the same screen so you can compare the activity in two different stocks or examine a number of technical indicators at the same time?

5. Is there an "auto-run" feature? Although programs with this capability are frequently more expensive, they can save a lot of time by allowing you to automatically prepare and print a series of charts you want on a regular basis. You

simply enter the auto-run mode, leave the computer, and return later to pick up your printed charts.

Comparison Shopping

More than 500 investment software packages are on the market. Your local computer store won't help much in sorting through the choices. Because it is specialized, most investment software is sold only through the mail, meaning you'll have to pay several hundred dollars in advance for software that in most cases is not returnable for a refund. Get all the facts before you decide what to buy. Follow these guidelines:

- List the features you believe to be absolutely necessary. Be specific—for example, if you want to break down your stocks by industry group to analyze portfolio diversification, write that down. When you're finished, you'll have a checklist of features to look for as you review actual software.
- Do market research. Look at who's selling what. An excellent user guide is the ***Individual Investor's Guide to Computerized Investing*** compiled by the **American Association of Individual Investors (AAII),** available from International Publishing Corp., 625 N. Michigan Ave., Chicago, IL 60611. Updated annually, the guide contains a description of most investment software packages and financial information services on the market. Refer also to personal computer and financial magazines for their independent ratings and reviews. AAII also publishes ***Computerized Investing Magazine.***
- Request information from each vendor. Match the features offered with those on your checklist to eliminate packages that don't meet your needs.

NOTE: For a nominal amount, many software vendors offer a demonstration package containing a disk and written material illustrating the features of their software packages. Often the cost of the demonstration material is deducted from the cost of the complete package.

TABLE 12-3: Investment Software

Here is a key to the symbols used in the listings that follows on page 319.

B = Bond	NA = Not applicable
C = Current portfolio status	O = Options
CAM = Computer Asset Management	S = Stocks
CS = CompuServe	SP = Standard & Poor's data base
CSI = Commondity Systems, Inc.	T = Treasury issues
D = Dividend and interest income	TE = The Equalizer
Dis = Disclosure data base	TS = The Source
DJN/R = Dow Jones News/Retrieval	VL = Value Line Data Base
F = Ford Investor Services data base	WC = Warner Computer Systems
I = Individual security status	X = Tax year profit/loss
M = Mutual funds	

Continued.

Software for Portfolio Management

Program	Compatible Hardware	Multiple Portfolio	Types Security	Types Report	Data Base Accessed
Dow Jones Market Manager PLUS Dow Jones & Co., P.O. Box 300 Princeton, NJ 08543 (800-522-3567; 609-520-4641)	Apple II series, Apple Macintosh, IBM PC	Yes	S, B, O, M, T	C, I, X, D	DJN/R

Special features/comments: The program flags securities meeting investor's buy/sell limits; sorts dividend and interest reports by tax-exemption codes; provides easy access to DJN/R. Program has three versions for three different levels of investors. The 2.0 version was developed for investment professionals and individual investors. It is for anyone who maintains one or more portfolios. It enables users to minimize tax liability, track commissions, monitor dividends, display reports, and access News Retrieval. Includes tax-lot accounting and automatic price updating. Handles up to 256 portfolios and 1500 securities.

Program	Compatible Hardware	Multiple Portfolio	Types Security	Types Report	Data Base Accessed
Stock Portfolio System Smith Micro Software P.O. Box 7137 Huntington Beach, CA 92615 (714-964-0412)	Apple II, series, Apple Macintosh, IBM PC	Yes	S, B, O, M, T	C, I, X, D	DJN/R, TE, TS

Special features/comments: The program handles margin accounting; produces valuable timing reports; gives advance notice of stocks going long-term, dividends and bond interest coming due, and options expiring.

Program	Compatible Hardware	Multiple Portfolio	Types Security	Types Report	Data Base Accessed
The Isgur Portfolio System 30 Mural St. Richmond Hill, Ontario, Canada L4B 1B5 (416-881-9941)	Apple Macintosh, IBM PC	Yes	S, B, O, M, T	C, I, X	CS, DJN/R,

TABLE 12-3: *continued*

Software for Fundamental Analysis

Program	Compatible Hardware	Stock Exchange Screened	Number of Companies Screened	Number of Items	Data Base Accessed
MarketBase MP Software P.O. Box 37 388 Hillside Ave. Needham Heights, MA 02194 (800-735-0700, 617-449-8460)	IBM	NYSE, AMEX, OTC	4,700	100	—

Special features/comments: MarketBase is an integrated software/data base system that supports fundamental data on over 4,700 companies. Over 100 data elements per company are provided with the ability to use formulas to create 44 additional elements— values and ratios. Users can sort the companies based upon a series of data using up to 17 different criteria to narrow the list of companies to a smaller group, and use a factor weighing function to assign different levels of importance to different data elements, and then sort the whole data base based upon the weighing factor.

Program	Compatible Hardware	Stock Exchange Screened	Number of Companies Screened	Number of Items	Data Base Accessed
The Evaluation Form Investor's Software P.O. Box N Bradenton Beach, FL 33510 (813-778-5515)	Apple II series, IBM PC	NA	NA	NA	NA

Special features/comments: It organizes fundamental stock data; useful for determining under- or overvaluation of a stock's price.

	Platform	Exchanges	Stocks		
Value/Screen II Value Line Publishing 711 Third Ave. New York, NY 10017 (212-687-3965; 800-654-0508)	Macintosh, IBM PC	NYSE, AMEX, OTC	1,700	37	VL

Special features/comments: It transfers data to a spreadsheet program; includes basic portfolio management software. This program covers about 1,700 companies—essentially the companies covered by the **Value Line Investment Survey.** This means that most of the covered stocks will be larger companies, most of which (1,100) are listed on the NYSE. Another 350 companies are NASDAQ, while there are only 90 AMEX stocks in the database. *NOTE: If users are interested in smaller, unlisted companies,* **MarketBase** *is the way to go.*

Compustock A.S. Gibson & Sons, 1412 E. Vineyard Dr., Bountiful, UT 84010 (801-298-4578)	IBM PC	NA	NA	NA	NA

Special features/comments: A stock valuation program that uses historical data to predict prices, earnings, dividends, and total returns; analyzes and predicts the future financial soundness of companies under review; uses graphics to show trends and developing strengths and weaknesses.

Fundamental Investor Savant Corp. 11211 Katy Freeway, Suite 250 Houston, TX 77079 (800-231-9000; 713-973-2400)	IBM PC	NYSE, AMEX, OTC	10,000	300	F, D

Special features/comments: Fundamental/ranking program not only conducts in-depth fundamental analysis but enables user to maintain a fundamental data base of over 35 parameters on up to 2,000 stocks (per floppy disk); calculates an array of financial and market ratios from basic financial information (using spreadsheet-like functions); allows screening of all securities in data according to preselected parameters; can sort stocks on the basis of single or weighted-average parameters. Unlike MarketBase system, users purchase data separately from program. Can automatically access the **Ford Investor Services Database** directly or the **Disclosure Database** available through **Warner.**

Table 12-3: continued

Software for Technical Analysis

Program	Compatible Hardware	Individual Securities	Overall Market Indicators	Number of Data Points	Data Base Accessed
Market Analyzer P.O. Box 300 Princeton NJ 08543 (800-522-3567)	IBM PC	Yes	Yes	1,000	CS, CSI, WC

Special features/comments: An integrated portfolio management program from Dow Jones & Company that includes technical analysis. Program has sorting screening, user-assignable function keys, automated run, spreadsheet interface, portfolio management, and extensive charting capabilities. Program has user-friendly menus; calendar memo and alert function; communications programs for accessing on-line services.

Market Analyzer PLUS P.O. Box 300 Princeton, NJ 08540 (800-522-3567)	Apple Macintosh, IBM PC	Yes	Yes	1,000	DJN/R

Special features/comments: Program collects up to 15 years of historical price and volume data from DJN/R to construct bar charts and point-and-figure charts that reveal underlying trends for individual stocks and the entire market; has sorting, screening, user-assignable function keys, automated run, spreadsheet interface, portfolio management, and extensive charting capabilities.

MetaStock Professional EQUIS International, P.O. Box 26743, Salt Lake City, UT 84126 (801-974-0391; 800-882-3040)	IBM PC	Yes	Yes	1,000	CS, CSI, WC

Special features/comments: It is a general purpose technical charting program for stocks, bonds, commodities, futures, indexes, options and mutual funds. The latest version (2.5) adds Japanese candlestick charts to their chart options. It can plot up to 36 different charts on the screen at one time. The program incorporates over 50 pre-programmed indicators and allows users to build their own indicators using over 70 statistical and mathematical functions. Its option analysis includes the use of the Black-Scholes pricing model.

The Technician
EQUIS International
P.O. Box 26743
Salt Lake City, UT 84126
(801-974-5130;
800-882-3040)

IBM PC　　No　　Yes　　415　　CAM

Special features/comments: Provides wide variety of technical market indicators; includes four to eight years of historical data for each indicator.

Trendline II
Standard & Poor's Corp.,
25 Broadway
New York, NY 10004
(800-852-5200;
212-208-8000)

IBM PC　　Yes　　Yes　　255　　WC

Special features/comments: Loads data and generates charts with extreme rapidity.

Compu Trac
1017 Pleasant St.
New Orleans, LA 70115
(800-535-7990
504-895-1474)

Apple Macintosh　　Yes　　Yes　　1,000　　CS, CSI
IBM PC　　　　　　　　　　　　　　　　WC

Special features/comments: It is a general purpose technical charting program for stocks, bonds, commodities, futures, indexes, options and mutual funds. The latest version provides Japanese candlestick charts along with traditional bar and point and figure charts. The program includes over 60 built-in technical indicators along with the Black-Scholes option pricing model.

Table 12-3: continued

Program	Compatible Hardware	Overall Individual Securities	Number Market Indicators	of Data Points	Data Base Accessed
Technical Investor Savant Corp. P.O. Box 440278 Houston, TX 77244 (800-231-9000)	IBM PC	Yes	Yes	1,000	WC, DJN/R

Special features/comments: Package combines charting with a far-reaching data base of technical measures. The data base is capable of storing up to 40 years of daily high, low, close, and volume information on up to 2,500 securities; information on market indexes is also available. Generates price and volume bar charts; high, low, and close price lines; point-and-figure charts; and much more.

Software for Fixed-Income Securities

Program	Compatible Hardware	Overall Individual Securities	Number Market Indicators	of Data Points	Data Base Accessed
CV Evaluator Beta Systems Co., P.O. Box 1189, Boston, MA 02205 (617-861-1655)	IBM PC				

Special features/comments: Covers 500 convertible bonds and preferreds; provides market quotes, quality rating, betas; calculates and evaluates various yield/conversion values; projects convertible values based on expected price behavior of underlying common stock and interest rates.

| **BondWare** Davidge Data Systems, 12 White St. New York, NY 10013 (212-226-3335) | IBM PC | | | | |

Special features/comments: Integrated package consists of a yield calculator, portfolio analyzer, and bond-swap analyzer; makes yield calculations for all types of fixed-income securities. The portfolio analyzer gives the pre-tax and after-tax effect of liquidating on bond portfolio and purchasing another. In addition to performing a wide variety of yield, price, duration, and return calculations, the program is capable of accessing bond data bases, preparing amortization tables, and generating strip-zero coupon yield charts.

The Bond Swap Analyzer
Technical Data Corp.,
330 Congress St.
Boston, MA 02210
(617-482-3341)

Apple II series,
IBM PC

Special features/comments: Program determines profitability and comparative rates of return from proposed bond-swap transactions; computes prices/yields, durations, accrued interest, and after-tax returns for each issue in a proposed swap transaction; finds comparative yields and net advantage to swapping based on user-specified horizon periods and future yields for the alternative bonds in the swap transactions.

Mortgage-Backed Securities Calculator
Bond-Tech, Inc.,
P.O. Box 192,
Englewood, OH 45322
(513-836-3991)

IBM PC

Special features/comments: Software provides a flexible yet powerful tool for analyzing yield behavior of mortgage-backed securities under a variety of prepayment assumptions; analyzes historical prepayment performance; and permits calculation of yield, semiannual equivalent yield, and modified duration using various assumptions concerning future prepayment experiences.

Software for Options and Futures

Stock Option Analysis
H&H Scientific,
13507 Pendleton St.
Ft. Washington, MD 20744
(301-292-2958)

Apple II series,
IBM PC

Table 12-3: continued

Special features/comments: Program calculates the values of put and call options using popular options valuation techniques; does a series of "what-if" computations for a variety of stock options positions; performs basic options valuation; evaluates various kinds of spreads, straddles, and covered options positions; provides volatility information; can graph expected profit or loss as a function of the underlying stock price. Set up to interface with Dow Jones News/Retrieval to obtain on-line stock and options prices.

Program	Compatible Hardware	Individual Securities	Overall Market Indicators	Number of Data Points	Data Base Accessed
Futuresoft CISCO 327 S. LaSalle St. Suite 1133 Chicago, IL 60604 (800-666-1223; 312-922-3661)	IBM PC				

Special features/comments: Analyzes daily and historical prices on foreign currencies, metals, other futures plus options; calculates some technical indicators. Displays results graphically. Has data management program, five analysis programs, trading model, and plotting program.

| **Commodity Futures Real-Time Charts**
Ensign Software,
7337 Northview
Boise, ID 83704
(208-378-8086; 208-524-0755) | IBM PC | | | | |

Special features/comments: Program aimed at the very serious commodities financial futures trader provides a full range of complicated technical analysis measures using an on-line telecommunications system; is capable of performing dozens of different statistical/technical measures; produces output in statistical/tabular format and real-time and historical charts and graphs.

Warner Options Database
Warner Computer Systems,
1 University Plaza,
Hackensack, NJ 07601
(800-626-4634)

Apple II series,
IBM PC

Special features/comments: Program provides current and historical price information on all options traded in the United States.

Option Valuator
Revenge Software,
P.O. Box 1073,
Huntington, NY 11743
(516-271-9556)

Apple II series
IBM PC

Special features/comments: Program predicts fair market options values and calculates volatility ratios and hedge ratios on both put and call options; plots time-dependent graphs of how options value should change as expiration date approaches; includes an option writer routine, which computes and displays risk–return data for covered writing strategies.

Stock Option Scanner
H&H Scientific,
13507 Pendleton St.
Ft. Washington, MD 20744
(301-292-2958)

Apple II series,
IBM PC

Special features/comments: Options screening program scans on-line price of up to 3,000 stock options, then ranks the top and bottom 50 options according to expected rate of return; spreads, straddles, and hedges can also be ranked; can run analyses for up to 5 preselected scanning criteria. It uses the Black-Scholes model to calculate the fair price of options and has a full Dow Jones News/Retrieval interface.

Investment Software Companies

Following is a list of companies that provide investment software for the investor. These companies offer financial investment software, spreadsheet programs, as well as programs for tax planning, real estate analysis, options, and commodities valuation, etc. Complete product descriptions and pricing information on current investment software programs provided by each company can be found in the *Individual Investor's Guide to Computerized Investing*, 9th edition, available from International Publishing Corporation, 625 N. Michigan Ave., Chicago, IL 60611; (312) 943-7354.

Abacus Software
5370 52nd St. S.E.
Grand Rapids, MI 49512
(800) 451-4319
(616) 698-0330

ADS Associates, Inc.
23586 Calabasas Rd.
Suite 200
Calabasas, CA 91302
(800) 852-3888
(818) 347-9100

Advanced Analysis, Inc.
6370 Pickwick Dr.
Canton, MI 48187
(313) 981-0681

Advanced Investment Software
8101 E. Prentice Ave.
Suite 808
Englewood, CO 80111
(303) 773-8500

Advanced Investment Systems
7031 E. Camelback Rd.
Suite 569
Scottsdale, AZ 85251
(800) 942-9555
(602) 483-9095

Advent Software, Inc.
512 Second St.
San Francisco, CA 94107
(800) 345-0376
(415) 543-7696

AIQ Systems, Inc.
916 Southwood Blvd.
Suite 2C, P.O. Drawer 7530 Incline
Village, NV 89450
(800) 332-2999
(702) 831-2999

American Financial Systems, Inc.
17 Haverford Station Rd.
Haverford, PA 19041
(215) 896-8780

American River Software
1523 Kingsford Dr.
Carmichael, CA 95608
(916) 483-1600

Analytic Associates
4817 Browndeer Lane
Rolling Hills Estates, CA 90274
(213) 541-0418

Analytical Service Associates
21 Hollis Rd.
Lynn, MA 01904
(617) 593-2404

Applied Decision Systems
99 Hayden Ave.
Lexington, MA 02173
(617) 861-7580

Arms Equivolume Corp.
1650 University Blvd.
Suite 300
Albuquerque, NM 87102
(800) 223-2767

Atlantic Systems, Inc.
45 Rockefeller Center
Suite 520
New York, NY 10111
(212) 757-6600

Automated Investments, Inc.
3284 Yonge St.
Suite 401
Toronto, Ontario M4N 3M7
Canada
(416) 489-3500

Automated Reasoning Technologies
2805 Spring Blvd.
Eugene, OR 97403
(800) 289-7638
(503) 342-4454

Berge Software
1200 Westlake Ave. N
Suite 612
Seattle, WA 98109
(206) 284-7610

BKT Systems, Inc.
1408 Providence Hwy.
Norwood, MA 02062
(800) 333-8475
(617) 769-8090

Black River Systems Corp.
4680 Brownsboro Rd.
Building C
Winston-Salem, NC 27106
(800) 841-5398
(919) 759-0600

Blue Chip Software
c/o Britannica Software
345 Fourth St.
San Francisco, CA 94107
(800) 572-2272
(415) 597-5555

BNA Software
1231 25th St., N.W.
Suite 3-200
Washington, DC 20037
(800) 424-2938

Bond-Tech, Inc.
P.O. Box 192
Englewood, OH 45322
(513) 836-3991

Bristol Financial Service, Inc.
15 River Rd.
Suite 254
Wilton, CT 06897
(203) 834-0040

Business Forecast Systems
68 Leonard St.
Belmont, MA 02178
(617) 484-5050

Business Week
Mutual Fund Scoreboard
185 Bridge Plaza N.
Suite 302
Fort Lee, NJ 07024
(800) 553-3575
(201) 461-0040

BV Engineering
2023 Chicago Ave.
Suite B13
Riverside, CA 92507
(714) 781-0252

CableSoft
307 W. Burlington Ave.
Fairfield, IA 52556
(515) 472-8393

California Scientific Software
10141 Evening Star Dr. #6
Grass Valley, CA 95945
(800) 284-8112
(916) 477-7481

Cambridge Planning & Analytic
55 Wheeler St.
Cambridge, MA 02138
(800) 328-3475
(617) 576-6465

CDA, Investment Technologies
1355 Piccard Dr.
Rockville, MD 20850
(800) 232-2285
(301) 975-9600

Charles L. Pack
25303 La Loma Dr.
Los Altos Hills, CA 94022
(415) 949-0887

Charles Schwab & Company, Inc.
101 Montgomery St.
Department S
San Francisco, CA 94104
(800) 334-4455
(415) 627-7000

ChipSoft, Inc.
5045 Shoreham Place
San Diego, CA 92122
(800) 782-1120
(619) 453-8722

CISCO
327 S. LaSalle St.
Suite 1133
Chicago, IL 60604
(312) 922-3661

Coast Investment Software
8851 Albatross Dr.
Huntington Beach, CA 92646
(714) 968-1978

Coherent Software Systems
771 Antony Rd.
Portsmouth, RI 02871
(401) 683-5886

Commodity Exchange, Inc.
Four World Trade Center
Room 7451
New York, NY 10048
(800) 333-2900
(212) 938-7921

Commodity Systems, Inc.
200 W. Palmetto Park Rd.
Boca Raton, FL 33432
(800) 327-0175
(407) 392-8663

Compu-Cast Corporation
1015 Gayley Ave.
Suite 506
Los Angeles, CA 90024
(213) 476-4682

Computer Investing Consultants
9002 Swinburne Court
San Antonio, TX 78240
(512) 681-0491

Computer Science Resources
454 Pine St., Dept. W110
Williamsport, PA 17701
(717) 322-0590

Computer Worksheets, Inc.
4000 Industrial Ave.
Rolling Meadows, IL 60008
(708) 843-0643

Compu Trac, Inc.
1017 Pleasant St.
New Orleans, LA 70115
(800) 535-7990
(504) 895-1474

Compu-Vest Software
545 Fairview Ave.
Glen Ellyn, IL 60137
(708) 469-4437

Concentric Data Systems, Inc.
110 Turnpike Rd.
Westboro, MA 01581
(800) 325-9035
(508) 366-1122

Cyber-Scan, Inc.
Route 4, P.O. Box 247
Buffalo, MN 55313
(612) 682-4150

Cynosure Software
P.O. Box 65
Syracuse, NY 13209
(315) 468-3594

Dantes Financial, Inc.
911 North 1400 E.
Logan, UT 84321
(801) 752-1821

Data Broadcasting Corp.-West
1900 S. Norfolk St.
San Mateo, CA 94403
(800) 367-4670
(415) 377-3597

Data Base Associates
P.O. Box 1838
Honolulu, HI 96805
(808) 926-5854

Data Transmission Network Corp.
9110 W. Dodge Rd.
Suite 200
Omaha, NE 68114
(800) 779-5000
(402) 390-2328

David W. Rettger
5304 Johnson Ave.
Western Springs, IL 60558
phone not given

Decisus, Inc.
9938 Via Pasar,
Suite A
San Diego, CA 92126
(800) 622-6543
(619) 530-4800

Delphi Economics, Inc.
8 Bonn Place
Weshawken, NJ 07087
(800) 873-3574
(201) 867-4303

Denver Data, Inc.
9785 Maroon Circle
Meridian One Suite G-126
Englewood, CO 80112
(303) 790-7327

Diamond Head Software
35 E. Pierson St.
Phoenix, AZ 85012
(602) 277-0316

Disk-Count Software
1751 W. County Rd. B
Suite 107
St. Paul, MN 55113
(800) 333-8776
(612) 633-0730

DollarLink Software
1407 Douglas St.
San Francisco, CA 94131
(415) 641-0721

Donald H. Kraft & Associates
9325 Kenneth Ave.
Skokie, IL 60076
(708) 673-0597

Dow Jones & Company, Inc.
P.O. Box 300
Princeton, NJ 08543
(800) 522-3567
(609) 520-4641

Dun's Marketing Services
3 Silvan Way
Parsippany, NJ 07040
(800) 223-1026
(201) 605-6000 x 3809

Dynacomp, Inc.
The Dynacomp Office Building
178 Phillips Rd.
Webster, NY 14580
(800) 828-6772
(716) 671-6160

Econ
800 E. Ocean Blvd.
Suite 1101
Long Beach, CA 90802
(213) 437-2036

Ecosoft, Inc.
8295 Indy Court
Indianapolis, IN 46214
(800) 952-0472
(317) 271-5551

Electrosonics, Inc.
36380 Garfield
Suite 1
Fraser, MI 48026
(800) 858-8448
(313) 791-0770

Elli-Comp, Inc.
611 Park Ave.
Suite 303
Baltimore, MD 21201
(800) 247-4551
(301) 837-7780

Emerging Market Technologies, Inc.
P.O. Box 420507
Atlanta, GA 30342
(404) 457-2110

EQUIS International
P.O. Box 26743
Salt Lake City, UT 84126
(800) 882-3040
(801) 974-5130

Ergo, Inc.
1419 Wyant Rd.
Santa Barbara, CA 93108
(800) 772-6637
(805) 969-9366

Evans Investment Advisors, Inc.
1725 Eye St. N.W.
Suite 310
Washington, DC 20006
(202) 467-4900

Expert Software
P.O. Box 890967
Houston, TX 77289
(713) 333-2788

FBS Systems, Inc.
P.O. Box 248
Aledo, IL 61231
(309) 582-5628

Financial Data Corp.
P.O. Box 1332
Bryn Mawr, PA 19010
(215) 525-6957

Financial Function, Inc.
400 S. LaSalle St.
P.O. Box 777
Chicago, IL 60605
(800) 346-4678

Finger Tip Systems Corp.
Drawer Y
Buckhannon, WV 26201
(304) 472-7890

FolioWare
74 Hitching Post Rd.
Bozeman, MT 59715
(406) 586-2103

Forbes Magazine
60 5th Ave.
New York, NY 10011
(212) 206-5515

Fossware
1000 Campbell road
Suite 208-626
Houston, TX 77055
(713) 467-3195

Futures Trust USA
815 Hillside Rd.
Hendersonville, NC 28739
(704) 697-0273

Gannsoft Publishing Co.
11670 Riverbend Dr.
Leavenworth, WA 98826
(509) 548-5990

Gates Technologies
P.O. Box 3493
Newport Beach, CA 92663
(phone not given)

G.C.P.I
P.O. Box 790
190 Timber, Dept. #50-E
Marquette, MI 49855
(906) 249-9801

General Optimization
2251 N. Geneva Terrace
Chicago, IL 60614
(312) 248-7300

Genesis Financial Data Services
P.O. Box 49578
Colorado Springs, CO 80949
(800) 642-8860
(719) 260-6111

Good Software Corp.
13601 Preston Rd.
Suite 500W
Dallas, Tx 75240
(800) 272-4663
(214) 239-6085

Granite Mountain Systems
P.O. Box 430
Fair Oaks, CA 95628
(916) 944-2670

Greenstone Software
20 Roehampton Circle
Brampton, Ontario, L6Y 2R4
Canada
(416) 459-8242

Guard Band
138 N. Edinburgh Ave.
Los Angeles, CA 90048
(213) 931-4247

Guru Systems Ltd.
314 E. Holly
Suite 106
Bellingham, WA 98225
(604) 299-1010

H & H Scientific
13507 Pendleton St.
Fort Washington, MD 20744
(301) 292-2958

Halliker's, Inc.
2508 Grayrock St.
Springfield, MO 65810
(800) 288-4266
(417) 882-9697

Halvorson Research Associates
2900 14th St.
Naples, FL 33940
(813) 261-4110

Hamilton Software
6432 E. Mineral Place
Englewood, CO 80112
(303) 795-5572

Harloff, Inc.
26106 Tallwood Dr.
North Olmsted, Oh 44070
(216) 734-7271

Heizer Software
1941 Oak Park Blvd.
Suite 30
Pleasant Hill, CA 94523
(415) 943-7667

Hinson Products
630 S. 26th St.
West Des Moines, IA 50265
(515) 224-4467

HowardSoft
124 Prospect St.
Suite 150
La Jolla, CA 92037
(619) 454-0121

Information Edge, Inc.
96 Lake Dr. West
Wayne, NJ 07470
(800) 334-3669
(201) 305-8440

Inmark Development Corp.
139 Fulton
Suite 810
New York, NY 10038
(212) 406-2299

Institute for Options Research, Inc.
P.O. Box 6586
Lake Tahoe, NV 89449
(800) 334-0854 x 840
(702) 588-3590

Interface Technologies Corp.
6065 Hillcroft
Suite 601
Houston, TX 77081
(800) 922-9049
(713) 523-8422

International Advanced Models, Inc.
P.O. Box 1019
Oak Brook, IL 60522
(708) 369-8461

Intex Solutions, Inc.
161 Highland Ave.
Needham, MA 02194
(617) 449-6222

Investment Software
543 CR 312
Ignacio, CO 81137
(303) 563-9543

INVESTment TECHnology
5104 Utah
Greenville, TX 75401
(800) 833-0269
(214) 455-3255

Investment Tools
P.O. Box 8254
Emeryville, CA 944662
phone not given

J & J Financial Company
9311 San Pedro Ave.
Suite 510
San Antonio, TX 78216
(800) 748-0805
(512) 349-2181

Jerome Technology, Inc.
P. O. Box 403
Raritan, NJ 08869
(201) 369-7503

Larry Rosen Co.
7008 Springdale Rd.
Louisville, KY 40241
(502) 228-4343

Lotus Development Corp.
55 Cambridge Parkway
Cambridge, MA 02142
(800) 554-5501
(617) 225-7058

Market Master
P. O. Box 14111
Columbus, OH 43214
(614) 436-3269

Market Software
24 Balmoral Dr.
Stratham, NH 03885
(603) 772-6353

Market Trend Software
RD #1, Box 193C
Rome, NY 13440
(315) 336-8306

Markex
6192 Oxon Hill Rd.
Suite 401
Oxon Hill, MD 20745
(800) 888-6088 x111
(301) 839-0817

Math Corp.
545 E. Fond du Lac
P. O. Box 361
Ripon, WI 54971
(414) 748-3422

MECA Software, Inc.
327 Riverside Ave.
Westport, CT 06880
(203) 226-2400

Memory Systems, Inc.
P. O. Box 886
Skokie, IL 60076
(708) 674-4833

Mendelsohn Enterprises, Inc.
50 Meadow Lane
Zephyrhills, FL 33544
(813) 973-0496

MESA
P. O. Box 1801
Goleta, CA 93116
(805) 969-6478

MicroApplications, Inc.
P. O. Box 43
71 Oakland Ave.
Miller Place, NY 11764
(516) 821-9355

Micro Code Technologies
501 5th Ave.
22nd Floor
New York, NY 10017
(800) 442-9111
(212) 983-9839

Microsoft Corp.
One Microsoft Way
Redmond, WA 98052
(800) 426-9400
(206) 882-8080

MicroTempo, Inc.
122B N. Bedford St.
Arlington, VA 22201
(703) 243-9603

Micro Trading Software Ltd.
Box 175
Wilton, CT 06897
(203) 762-7820

Mike Burk
829 Old Settlers Trail #3
Hopkins, MN 55343
(800) 325-1344
(612) 939-0076

Miller Associates
P. O. Box 4361
Incline Village, NV 89450
(702) 831-0429

MindCraft Publishing Corporation
52 Domino Dr.
Concord, MA 01742
(800) 888-1660
(508) 371-1660

MoneyCare, Inc.
253 Martens Ave.
Suite 12
Mountain View, CA 94040
(800) 824-9827
(415) 962-0333

Money Tree Software
1753 Wooded Knolls Dr.
Suite 200
Philomath, OR 97370
(503) 929-2140

Money Won
Ten Tower Office Park Dr.
Woburn, MA 01801
(800) 463-6639
(617) 982-0285

Montgomery Investment Group
332 Pine St., Suite 514
San Francisco, CA 94194
(415) 986-6991

MP Software, Inc.
P. O. Box 37
Needham Heights, MA 02194
(800) 735-0700
(617) 449-8460

NAIC Software
P. O. Box 220
1515 E. Eleven Mile Rd.
Royal Oak, MI 48068
(313) 543-0612

New England Software
Greenwich Office Park #3
Greenwich, CT 06831
(203) 625-0062

NewTEK Industries
P. O. Box 46116
Los Angeles, CA 90046
(213) 874-6669

Northfield Information Services, Inc.
99 Summer St.
Suite 1620
Boston, MA 02110
(800) 262-6085
(617) 737-8360

N–Squared Computing
5318 Forest Ridge Rd.
Silverton, OR 97381
(800) 426-3475
(214) 680-1445

Omega Research, Inc.
3900 NW 79th Ave.
Suite 520
Miami, FL 33166
(305) 594-7664

Omni Software Systems, Inc.
146 N. Broad St.
Griffith, IN 46319
(219) 924-3522

Options–80
P. O. Box 471
Concord, MA 01742
(508) 369-1589

OptionVue Systems International, Inc.
175 E. Hawthorn Parkway
Suite 180
Vernon Hills, IL 60061
(800) 733-6610
(708) 816-6610

Oz Software, Inc.
1400 Post Oak Blvd.
Suite 800
Houston, TX 77056
(800) 359-9359
(713) 877-1206

Palisade Corp.
31 Decker Rd.
Newfield, NY 14867
(800) 432-7475
(607) 277-8000

Paperback Software International
2830 Ninth St.
Berkeley, CA 94710
(800) 255-3242
(415) 644-2116

Parsons Software
1230 W. 6th St.
Loveland, CO 80537
(303) 669-3744

P–Cubed, Inc.
a division of Arminius Publications
P. O. Box 1265
Merchantville, NJ 08109
(609) 662-3420

Performance Applications
18321 149th Ave. S.E.
Renton, WA 98058
(206) 226-5921

Performance Technologies, Inc.
4814 Old Wake Forest Rd.
Raleigh, NC 27609
(800) 528-9595
(919) 876-3555

Personal Computer Products
P. O. Box 44445
Washington, DC 20026
(301) 593-2571

Personal Micro Services
1758 Deerpath Court
Suite 1018
Naperville, IL 60565
(708) 420-7108

Personal Money Management
1209 Northwest Hwy.
Suite 203
Garland, TX 75041
(214) 278-7907

Piedmont Software Company
1130 Harding Place
Charlotte, NC 28204
(704) 376-0935

Pine Grove Software
67-38 108th St.
Suite D-1
Forest Hills, NY 11375
(800) 242-9192
(718) 575-9192

Portfolio Software, Inc.
14 Lincoln Ave.
Quincy, MA 02170
(617) 328-8248

Precise Software Corp.
1000 Campbell Road
Suite 208-128
Houston, TX 77055
Phone not given

Precision Investment Services, Inc.
1045 Haro St.
Suite 320
Vancouver, BC V6E 328
Canada
(604) 688-8823

Priori Corp.
P. O. Box 164284
Austin, TX 78716
(800) 677-4674
(512) 331-0114

Programmed Press
599 Arnold Road
West Hempstead, NY 11552
(516) 599-6527

Pro Plus Software, Inc.
2150 E. Brown Road
Mesa, AZ 85203
(602) 461-3296

Pumpkin Software
P. O. Box 4417
Chicago, IL 60680
(708) 416-3530

Quadratron Systems, Inc.
141 Triunfo Canyon Road
Westlake Village, CA 91361
(805) 494-1158

Quant IX Software
5900 N. Port Washington Road
Suite 142
Milwaukee, WI 53217
(800) 247-6354
(414) 961-0669

Radix Research Ltd.
2280 Woodlawn Crescent
Victoria, BC V8R 1P2
Canada
(604) 592-5308

Real–Comp, Inc.
P. O. Box 1210
Cupertino, CA 95015
(408) 996-1160

RealData, Inc.
78 N. Main St.
South Norwalk, CT 06854
(800) 899-6060
(203) 838-2670

Reality Technologies
3624 Market St.
Philadelphia, PA 19104
(800) 346-2024
(215) 387-6055

Realty Software Company
133 Paseo de Granda
Redondo Beach, CA 90277
(213) 372-9419

Research Press, Inc.
4500 W. 72nd Terrace
Box 8137
Prairie Village, KS 66208
(913) 362-9667

Revenge Software
P. O. Box 1073
Huntington, NY 11743
(516) 271-9556

RK Microsystems
17365 Alvin Lane
Brookfield, WI 53045
(414) 786-7333

RLJ Software Applications
306 N. Wolcott St.
Hillsdale, MI 49242
(517) 439-9605

R. Maynard Holt & Company
4400 Belmont Park Terrace
259 King Henry Court
Nashville, TN 37215
(615) 297-0078

Roberts–Slade, Inc.
750 N. 200 West
Suite 301B
Provo, UT 84601
(800) 433-4276
(801) 375-6847

RTR Software, Inc.
19 W. Harget St.
Suite 204
Raleigh, NC 27601
(919) 829-0789

Rugg & Steele, Inc.
6433 Topanga Canyon Blvd.
Suite 108
Canoga Park, CA 91303
(800) 678-3863
(818) 340-0179

Savant Corp.
11211 Katy Freeway
Suite 250
Houston, TX 77079
(800) 231-9900
(713) 973-2400

Scherrer Resources, Inc.
8100 Cherokee St.
Philadelphia, PA 19118
(215) 242-8740

Scientific Consultant Services
20 Stagecoach Road
Selden, NY 11784
(516) 696-3333

Scientific Press, Inc.
651 Gateway Blvd.
Suite 1100
South San Francisco, CA 94080
(800) 451-5409
(415) 583-8840

SCIX Corp. Investment Software
2010 Lacomic St.
Williamsport, PA 17701
(800) 228-6655
(717) 323-3276

Serenson Consulting Service
34 Williams St.
Thomaston, CT 06787
Phone not given

Smith Micro Software, Inc.
P. O. Box 7137
Huntington Beach, CA 92615
(714) 964-0412

Softview, Inc.
1721 Pacific Ave.
Suite 100
Oxnard, CA 93010
(800) 622-6829
(805) 385-5000

Software Advantage Consulting Corp.
38442 Gail
Mt. Clemens, MI 48043
(313) 463-4995

Sorites Group, Inc.
P. O. Box 2939
Springfield, VA 22152
(703) 569-1400

Spectrum Software
P. O. Box 6746
Silver Spring, MD 20906
(301) 946-6002

Spreadsheet Solutions Co.
600 Old Country Road
Garden City, NY 11530
(800) 634-8509
(516) 222-1429

SPSS, Inc.
444 N. Michigan Ave.
Suite 3000
Chicago, IL 60611
(312) 329-3500

Standard & Poor's Corp.
26 Broadway
New York, NY 10004
(212) 208-8581

Strategic Planning Systems, Inc.
21021 Soledad Canyon Road
Suite 504
Santa Clarita, CA 91351
(800) 488-5898
(805) 254-5897

Superior Software
16055 Ventura Blvd.
Suite 725
Encino, CA 91436
(800) 421-3264
(818) 990-1135

Survivor Software Ltd.
11222 La Cienga Blvd.
Suite 450
Inglewood, CA 90304
(213) 410-9527

Systems and Solutions, Inc.
10011 N. Orange Ranch Road
Tucson, AZ 85741
(602) 744-2202

Tech Hackers, Inc.
515 Broadway
3rd Floor
New York, NY 10012
(212) 941-7330

Technical Analysis of Stocks
& Commodities Magazine
3517 S.W. Alaska St.
Seattle, WA 98126
(800) 832-4642
(206) 938-0570

Technical Trading Strategies, Inc.
3333 S. Wadsworth Blvd.
Suite D-318
Lakewood, CO 80227

Techserve, Inc.
P. O. Box 70056
Bellevue, WA 98007
(800) 826-8082
(206) 747-5598

Telemet America, Inc.
325 First St.
Alexandria, VA 22314
(800) 368-2078
(703) 548-2042

Telescan, Inc.
2900 Wilcrest
Suite 400
Houston, TX 77042
(800) 727-4636
(713) 952-1060

Tempo Investment Products, Inc.
4102 Elm Court
Midland, MI 48640
(517) 832-3148

3X USA Corp.
1 Executive Dr.
Fort Lee, NJ 07024
(800) 327-9712
(201) 592-6874

Tick Data, Inc.
720 Kipling St.
Suite 115
Lakewood, CO 80215
(800) 822-8425
(303) 232-3701

Tiger Software
P. O. Box 9491
San Diego, CA 92109
(619) 483-1214

Time Trend Software
337 Boston Road
Billerica, MA 01821
(508) 663-3330

Timeworks
444 Lake Cook Road
Deerfield, IL 60015
(708) 948-9200

Townsend Analytics Ltd.
100 S. Wacker Dr.
Suite 1506
Chicago, IL 60606
(312) 621-0141

Trade, Inc.
100 Iverson St.
Greenville, SC 29615
(803) 268-2579

Trader's Software, Inc.
P. O. Box 2690
Edmond, OK 73083
(405) 348-0544

Trend Index Company
Box 5
Altoona, WI 54720
(715) 833-1234

TRENDPOINT Software
9709 Elrod Rd.
Kensington, MD 20895
(301) 949-8131

Trendsetter
P. O. Box 6481
Santa Ana, CA 92706
(800) 825-1852
(714) 547-5005

Type III, Inc.
1327 Nathan Hale Dr.
Phoenixville, PA 19460
(800) 342-3963
(215) 933-8521

V. A. Denslow & Associates
4151 Woodland Ave.
Western Springs, IL 60558
(708) 246-3365

Value Line Publishing
711 Third Ave.
New York, NY 10017
(800) 654-0508
(212) 687-3965

VM International
370 Altair Way
Suite 156
Sunnyvale, CA 94086
(415) 487-6204

Volkswriter, Inc.
411 Pacific St.
Suite 315
Monterey, CA 93940
(408) 373-4718

Volume Dynamics, Inc.
1923 Hwy. A-1-A,#B-1
Indian Harbor Beach, FL 32937
(407) 777-0369

Wall Street Prophet
1505 Thoreau Dr.
Suwanee, GA 30174
(404) 497-8497

Worden Brothers
111 Cloister Court
Suite 104
Chapel Hill, NC 27514
(919) 490-5250

Zero Base Software
3575 Blvd. St. Laurent
Montreal, Quebec, H2W 2M9
Canada
(514) 982-0055

13

Investment Newsletters and Advisories

Investors often find that a newsletter or two helps them choose a right investment vehicle or decide when to get in and out of an investment. Following is a list of well-known newsletters arranged by investment types.

NEWSLETTERS BY TYPE OF INVESTMENT

Interest Rate

Banxquote
Masterfund Inc.
575 Madison Ave.
New York, NY 10022
(weekly; monthly)

Lists financial institutions with the 20 highest yields for money market accounts and for CDs from 30 days to 5 years.

Income and Safety
The Institute for Econometric Research
3471 N. Federal Hwy.
Fort Lauderdale, FL 33306
(weekly)

Provides a directory of more than 100 taxable and tax-free money funds with a safety rating, a yield projection, and yield for each. Also lists the 10 highest yields for each of 7 kinds of CD accounts from 30 days to 5 years.

The Lyke Report
P.O. Box 290
Glenview, IL 60025
(weekly)

An advisory for CDs.

100 Highest Yields
Advertising News Service Inc.
P.O. Box 08888
North Palm Beach, FL 33408
(weekly)

This newsletter ranks the 20 highest-yielding money market accounts and 20 CDs. It also gives the rate, yield, and compounding methods for each.

General: Stocks, Bonds, and Investment Strategy

The Addison Report
P.O. Box 402
Franklin, MA 02038
(every three weeks; six months)

Quick comments and recommendations on stocks, bonds, commodities.

The Aden Analysis
4425 W. Napoleon Ave.
Metairie, LA 70001
(monthly)

Reports technical comments and recommendations on the economy, currencies, stocks, and bonds.

The Advance Planning Letter
P.O. Box 52852
New Orleans, LA 70152
(every six weeks)

Economic and political opinion followed by a bit of investment counsel.

Alan Shawn Feinstein Insiders Report
41 Alhambra Circle
Cranston, RI 02905
(monthly)

Reports on inside tips; new, unusual, or special investment opportunities.

The Alexander Paris Report
HMR Publishing Inc.
P.O. Box 471
Barrington, IL 60010
(monthly)

An economic commentary and forecast, with detailed analysis but no specific investment selections.

America's Fastest Growing Companies
Financial Data Systems
38 E. 29th St.
New York, NY 10016
(monthly)

Covers model portfolios, company profiles, ratings, and statistics on small companies and emerging industries. Does not make specific buy-and-sell calls.

The Astute Investor
Investor's Analysis, Inc.
P.O. Box 988
Paoli, PA 19301
(every three weeks)

Discusses technical and fundamental developments of the stock market.

The Astute Investor
Route 3
P.O. Box 310-D
Kingston, TN 37763
(monthly)

Screens stocks that meet certain ratios or criteria (such as those priced at a certain percentage below net current assets). A research service rather than an advisory letter.

The Babson Staff Letter
David L. Babson & Co., Inc.
One Memorial Dr.
Cambridge, MA 02142
(semimonthly)

Presents an informative essay on some facet of the market, whether it be "how high is high" or confusion in the computer industry.

Baxter Bulletin
1030 E. Putnam Ave.
Greenwich, CT 06830
(weekly; every six months)

World economic service gives commentary/opinion on international monetary/investment developments.

The Bench Investment Letter
222 Bridge Plaza S.
Fort Lee, NJ 07024
(monthly)

Stock market timing advice based on various indexes and technical signals.

Best's Review
A. M. Best Company Inc.
Ambest Rd.
Oldwick, NJ 08858
(monthly)

Gives Best's Ratings on life, health, property/casualty investment firms.

Better Investing Magazine
National Association of Investors
1515 E. 11 Mile Rd.
Royal Oak, MI 48067
(monthly)

Guides, education, advice on investment techniques for investment clubs. One company is analyzed each month.

BI Research
P.O. Box 301
South Salem, NY 10590
(5 to 8 issues a year, plus periodic portfolio updates)

Detailed research profiles of high-growth or overlooked stocks, with continuing advice on whether to buy more, hold, or sell.

The Bowser Report
P.O. Box 6278
Newport News, VA 23606
(monthly)

Reports buys, sells, trivia, and color on stocks priced below $3 per share.

The Cabot Market Letter
Cabot Farm/Orange St.
P.O. Box 3044
Salem, MA 01970
(semimonthly)

Model portfolios, trends, recommended stocks, market commentary. Concise, readable. Discusses mutual funds.

California Technology Stock Letter
155 Montgomery St.
Suite 1401
San Francisco, CA 94104
(biweekly)

Iconoclastic high-tech publication specializing in West Coast and Rocky Mountain companies. Follows overall market trends.

The Chartist
P.O. Box 3160
Long Beach, CA 90803
(semimonthly; every six months)

Charts various stocks; recommends buys/sells based on technical signals.

Consensus of Insider
P.O. Box 24349
Fort Lauderdale, FL 33307
(biweekly)

Data on selling and buying of stocks by company officials, plus weekly "market-timing modules" that measure indicators such as short selling.

Contrary Investor
Fraser Management Associates
Box 494
Burlington, VT 05402
(fortnightly)

A newsletter espousing the contrarian
theory of investing that reviews and
comments on recommendations and
trends in the traditional investment
community. Also provides broad market-timing recommendations.

The Daily Trader
110 Boggs Lane
Cincinnati, OH 45246
(weekly)

Provides buy-and-sell signals for
stocks and bonds amid detailed economic commentary and yield analysis.

Dawis Investment Service
P.O. Box 524
Northport, NY 11768
(weekly; every six months)

A computerized stock-trading system
based on wave theory.

**Dessauer's Journal of Financial
Markets**
P.O. Box 1718
Orleans, MA 02653
(semimonthly; every six months)

Provides forecasts and opinions on
domestic and international economic
and political matters, with a few securities selections including foreign
stocks.

Dines Letter
James Dine & Company
Box 22
Belvedere, CA 94920
(monthly)

Advisory on stocks, gold, and other
metals, and economics. Combines
technical, psychological, and business
indicators concerning the markets.

Dowbeaters
450 Springfield Ave.
Summit, NJ 07901
(monthly)

Provides a narrow focus stock-picking
sheet, highlighting low-priced shares.

Dow Theory Forecasts
Dow Theory Forecasts, Inc.
7412 Calumet Ave.
Hammond, IN 46324-2692)
(weekly)

A concise, general stock market letter
that lists stock choices, company descriptions, and a regular market commentary. Includes forecasts of the
stock market based on Dow theory.

Dow Theory Letters
P.O. Box 1759
La Jolla, CA 92038
(biweekly)

Probes inner workings of the market,
short-term and longer, and discusses
investments past, present, and future.

Early Warning Forecast
Cahners Publishing Co.
275 Washington St.
Newton, MA 02158
(monthly)

Translates economic indicators into likely events.

The Ehrenkrantz Letter
Ehrenkrantz & King
50 Broadway
New York, NY 10004
(14 issues per year)

Scouts undiscovered stocks and monitors a model portfolio of high-growth equities.

The Elliott Wave Theorist-Investors
P.O. Box 1618
Gainesville, GA 30503
(monthly)

Predicts market direction based on Robert Prechter's theory of super-cycles and lesser waves.

Equity Research Associates
540 Madison Ave.
New York, NY 10022
(semimonthly)

Provides research reports on emerging growth companies.

Fedwatch
Money Market Services
275 Shoreline Dr.
Redwood City, CA 94065
(weekly)

A forecast of the financial markets based on Federal Reserve policy and credit market activity.

Forbes Special Situation Survey
Forbes Investors Advisory Institute
60 Fifth Ave.
New York, NY 10011
(monthly)

A loose-leaf report: Each issue discusses and recommends the purchase of one speculative equity security.

Forecasts & Strategies
Phillips Publishing, Inc.
7811 Montrose Rd.
Potomac, MD 20854
(monthly)

A commonsense approach to investment, taxes, and "financial privacy," with an emphasis on tax avoidance and keeping the government and others out of your financial affairs. Also analyzes new products, such as single-premium, variable-life insurance.

The Garsid Forecast
P.O. Box 1812
Santa Ana, CA 92702
(semimonthly)

Provides a wealth of market-timing signals, based on proprietary methods like the Bell Ringer and the Low-Risk Time Zone.

Global Insight
422 W. Fairbanks Ave.
Suite 300
Winter Park, FL 32789
(quarterly; sometimes monthly)

A newsletter for global stocks and bonds that searches out the best financial opportunities in the international financial market.

Good Money
P.O. Box 363
Worcester, VT 05682
(six times a year)

A rare newsletter devoted to socially motivated investments, lots of unique information if you're looking for "good" and "bad" guys and accept the editors' definitions of same.

The Gordon Market Timer
P.O. Box 938
Englewood Cliffs, NJ 07632
(semimonthly)

Short-, intermediate-, and long-term timing signals in brief.

The Gourgues Report
Harold Gourgues Co., Inc.
Suite 300
3155 Roswell Rd.
Atlanta, GA 30305
(monthly)

Practical investment advice and information for noninstitutional investors.

Graham-Rea Fundamental Values
10966 Chalon Rd.
Los Angeles, CA 90077
(monthly)

Based on the fundamental analysis of the late Ben Graham, it identifies stocks selling at or below quick liquidation value.

The Grandich Letter
4667 Route 9
Suite 12
Howell, NJ 07731
(monthly)

Insight into investments in America by foreigners such as the Japanese.

Grant's Interest Rate Observer
233 Broadway, Suite 4008
New York, NY 10279
(biweekly)

Presents wonderfully creative indexes and statistics and gives advice on fixed-income investments.

The Granville Market Letter Inc.
P.O. Drawer 413006
Kansas City, MO 64141
(46 times a year; six months)

Joe Granville writes colorful market commentaries and offers plenty of stock recommendations.

Growth Stock Outlook
Growth Stock Outlook, Inc.
P.O. Box 15381
Chevy Chase, MD 20815
(semimonthly)

Reports selected stocks with vigorous growth. The growth stock outlook gives specific buy-and-sell recommendations. Charts are detailed, choices well-explained.

Growth Stock Report
82 Wall St.
Suite 1105
New York, NY 10005
(monthly)

Monitors and selects stocks priced
below $10 per share.

Hard Money Digest
3608 Grand Ave.
Oakland, CA 94610
(monthly)

Summarizes and compares opinions
from other newsletters on gold, silver,
interest rates, stocks, and economics.

Harry Browne's Special Reports
P.O. Box 5586
Austin, TX 78763
(ten times a year)

A series of separate reports, updated
regularly, on various investments and
economics.

High Technology Growth Stocks
Fourteen Nason St.
Maynard, MA 01754
(monthly)

Well-researched guide to high-tech
stocks, listing which ones to buy or
which to avoid.

Hi-Tech/Defense Advisory
Oil Statistics Co. Inc.
Babson Park, MA 02157
(monthly, with irregular supplements)

Reports on lesser-known companies
for aggressive/adventurous investors.

High Technology Investments
5925 Kirby
Suite 219
Houston, TX 77005
(monthly)

A computer screen of small high-tech
stocks and occasional in-depth company profiles. The letter has had a good
record over the past several years.

Holt Investment Advisory
Holt Advisory
P.O. Box 2923
West Palm Beach, FL 33402
(semimonthly)

Discusses the economy and stock
market for investors concerned with
long-term capital growth. Serves up
large portions of short-selling recommendations, bond opportunities, and
other beat deflation-and-depression
strategies.

**Howard Ruff's Financial Success
Report**
Target Inc.
6612 Owens Dr.
Pleasanton, CA 94566
(weekly)

Buys and sells, updated in each issue.

The Hulbert Financial Digest
316 Commerce St.
Alexandria, VA 22314
(monthly)

Judges the quality and value of advice
in investment letters. For example, it
provides a list of newsletters that beat
the market over the past five years.

The Hume Moneyletter
P.O. Box 105649
Atlanta, GA 30348
(semimonthly)

Prominent investment experts contribute periodic articles to this well-laid-out letter, which also contains strategies for fast trading.

Income Investor Perspectives
Uniplan, Inc.
3907 N. Green Bay Ave.
Milwaukee, WI 53206
(every three weeks)

Updates on tax-advantaged and income-oriented investments, such as utility stocks and REITs. Useful for safety-and-yield investors.

Indicator Digest
451 Grand Ave.
Palisades Park, NJ 07650
(semimonthly)

A broad-based stock market letter that touches many bases: economic and technical indicators, short sales, model portfolios, and so forth.

Insider Indicator
2230 N.E. Brazee St.
Portland, OR 97212
(semimonthly)

SEC-based buy-and-sell signals on listed and OTC stocks; reports trades by corporate officers and directors.

The Insiders
The Institute for Econometric Research
3471 N. Federal Hwy.
Fort Lauderdale, FL 33306
(semimonthly)

A publication based on the notion that company officials and directors who trade in their own stock "know something". Collects and translates SEC data on buying and selling by insiders and makes recommendations.

Insurance Forum
P.O. Box 245-L
Ellettsville, IN 47429
(monthly)

Provides a list of insurance companies with an A+ rating assigned by Best's Insurance Reports.

InvesTech Market Letter
InvesTech
2472 Birch Glen
Whitefish, MT 59937)
(semimonthly)

A summary and reaction to other letter editors' views. Provides clear technical analysis, and gives stock and mutual fund choices.

Investing Magazine
824 E. Baltimore St.
Baltimore, MD 21298
(monthly)

An advisory for a wide range of stocks, including gold stocks.

Investment Horizons
Investment Information Services
680 N. Lake Shore Dr.
2038 Tower Offices
Chicago, IL 60611
(semimonthly)

An attractive letter for intellectual
investors that follows small companies
not watched extensively by professional analysts. For example, one
issue explains why small utilities can
be better buys than large ones.

The Investment Reporter
133 Richmond St.
W. Toronto
Ontario M5H 3M8, Canada
(semimonthly)

Recommends stocks that are the best
choices for dividend reinvestment.

Investment Values
Orion Publishing Inc.
P.O. Box 517
Mount Kisco, NY 10549
(semimonthly)

A stock-picking sheet with model
portfolios and "perfect investment
stocks."

Investor's Strategist
82 Wass St., Suite 1105
New York, NY 10005
(monthly)

A handsome newsletter that discusses
long-term tax-advantaged investments,
such as cable-TV partnerships and
numismatic coins.

IRRC News for Investors
Investor Responsibility Research
Center
1755 Massachusetts Ave., N.W.
Washington, DC 20036
(monthly)

The leading monitor of corporate
conduct and misconduct, shareholder
resolutions, and other social issues of
interest to investors.

The Janeway Letter
Fifteen E. 80th St.
New York, NY 10021
(weekly)

Comments and sharp opinions on
everything from the stock market to
government farm policy.

JS&A Advisory
P.O. Box 1138
Bloomfield Hills, MI 48303
(every three weeks)

A compilation of excerpts, chiefly
stock picks, taken from various other
letters. Each issue includes one entire
issue of one of the excerpted letters.

Justin Mamis' Insights
P.O. Box 907
Peck Slip Station
New York, NY 10272
(semimonthly)

Provides stock recommendations.

The Kiplinger Washington Letter
Kiplinger Washington Editors, Inc.
1729 H St., N.W.
Washington, DC 20006
(weekly)

Briefings on business trends, pertinent government policies, and information about employment, investments, and interest rates.

The Klein-Wolman Investment Letter
P.O. Box 727
Princeton Junction, NJ 08550
(monthly)

This economic commentary updates the "beat-inflation" strategy developed by the editors 12 years ago when that topic was all the rage.

Kon-Lin Research & Analysis
Five Water Rd.
Rocky Point, NY 11778
(monthly)

The usual market commentary and profiles of a handful of "action stocks" deemed to be priced too low.

LaLoggia's Special Situation Report and Stock Market Forecast
P.O. Box 167
Rochester, NY 14601
(every three weeks; every six months)

Charles LaLoggia is adept at scouting takeover and merger plays, which he discusses following a trenchant opening essay on current market sentiment and activity.

Low-Priced Stock Digest
Idea Publishing Corp.
55 E. Afton Ave.
Yardley, PA 19067
(monthly)

Provides excerpts from comments of many publications that follow stocks priced from one cent to $20 a share.

The Low-Priced Stock Survey
Dow Theory Forecasts, Inc.
7412 Calumet Ave.
Hammond, IN 46324
(semimonthly)

Follows/recommends issues below $30 per share. Many names and selections.

Lynch Municipal Bond Advisory
P.O. Box 25114
Santa Fe, NM 87504
(monthly)

Provides buy-and-sell recommendations. Also reviews, for a fee, the investor's portfolio.

The Lynn Elgert Report
P.O. Box 39485
Phoenix, AZ 85069
(every three weeks)

Provides specific advice/model portfolios for traders and long-term investors. Analyzes broad industry groups.

Market Logic
Institute for Econometric Research
3471 N. Federal Hwy.
Fort Lauderdale, FL 33306
(semimonthly)

Concise, thorough, multifaceted guide predicts market moves, recommends trades. Indicators/research-tools-full.

The Market Mania Newsletter
P.O. Box 1234
Pacifica, CA 94044
(semimonthly)

A little of everything; much diversity in an eight-page stock market letter.

Market Vantage
Orion Publishing Inc.
P.O. Box 517
Mount Kisco, NY 10549
(semimonthly; every three months)

A guide to market timing.

The McKeever Strategy Letter
P.O. Box 4130
Medford, OR 97501
(monthly)

A longer-than-average letter that leads off with essays on economic or market topics before giving advice on stocks, bonds, metals, and currencies.

Medical Technology Stock Letter
P.O. Box 40460
Berkeley, CA 94704
(biweekly)

A solid source of information on bio-technology and other emerging health fields. Provides aggressive investors with timely insight into leading companies in the field.

The Med-Tech Advisor
D. H. Blair & Co. Inc.
44 Wall St.
New York, NY 10005
(monthly)

Provides model portfolios, company profiles, and other information on more speculative medical investments.

MedTech Market Letter
2915 Bissonet
Houston, TX 77005
(semimonthly)

Summarizes company results and prospects in various health care fields.

Merrill Lynch Market Letter
165 Broadway
New York, NY 10080
(semimonthly)

Stock market intelligence, spotlights on industries, explanations of indicators, and other clearly written information from the eminent brokerage firm.

Money & Markets Weiss Research Inc.
P.O. Box 2923
West Palm Beach, FL 33402
(monthly)

A "what's-happening-and-what-to-do-about-it" approach to economic and financial events.

Money Management for Physicians
The Laux Co. Inc.
20 Central Ave.
Ayer, MA 01432
(bimonthly)

Gives specialized advice on professional corporations and other financial topics for doctors and dentists.

New Issues
Institute for Econometric
Research
3471 N. Federal Hwy.
Fort Lauderdale, FL 33306
(monthly)

Has descriptions and no-holds-barred
ratings of initial public offerings.

The Ney Report
P.O. Box 90215
Pasadena, CA 91109
(semimonthly, every six months)

Tracks massive institutional block
trades in high-quality stocks to chart a
course for small investors.

The Nicholson Report
7550 Red Rd.
Coral Gables, FL 33143
(semimonthly; every six months)

Provides well-reasoned discussion of
current stock market events, with
recommendations, model portfolios,
charts, and a market-mood indicator.

Nielsen's Investment Letter
P.O. Box 7532
Olympia, WA 98507
(bimonthly)

A stock-picking and market-timing
publication; recommends buys/sells.

Nourse Investor Reports
P.O. Box 28039
San Diego, CA 92128
(monthly)

A detailed, computerized data screen
of companies and industries for advanced stock players. Lots of ratios
and comparisons.

OTC Growth Stock Watch
P.O. Box 305
Brookline, MA 02146
(monthly)

Fundamental analysis of smaller OTC
companies with an eye on growth
opportunities.

OTC Insight
P.O. Box 127
Moraga, CA 94556
(monthly)

A computerized stock selector for
OTC investors. Includes model portfolios and risk ratings.

OTC Review: Special Situations
110 Pennsylvania Ave.
Oreland, PA 19075
(monthly)

Timely recommendations and model
portfolios with follow-up news on
companies featured in earlier editions.

Penny Stock News
8930 J Oakland Center
Columbia, MD 21045
(weekly)

A comprehensive review of penny
stocks.

Penny Stock Preview
Idea Publishing
55 E. Afton Ave.
Yardley, PA 19067
(monthly)

A catalogue of ads and business reply
postcards by underwriters selling
shares in new penny stock issues.

Pension Investing Strategies
P.O. Box 509
Ridgewood, NJ 07451
(semimonthly)

Updates legislative, tax, and investment developments affecting people with Keoghs or IRAs, or pension plan managers.

Personal Finance
1101 King St.
Suite 400
Alexandria, VA 22134
(semimonthly)

Concise coverage—from stocks to gold and currencies. Advises readers to move quickly when time is right.

The Peter Dag Investment Letter
65 Lakefront Dr.
Akron, OH 44319
(every three weeks)

Provides buy-and-sell signals for stocks, bonds, and metals amid detailed economic commentary and forecasting.

Petroleum Outlook
John S. Herold Inc.
35 Mason St.
Greenwich, CN 06830
(monthly)

An informative, one-stop source of data and news that affect the oil and gas industry's investment outlook.

The Powell Monetary Analyst
Reserve Research Ltd.
181 State St.
Portland, ME 04101
(biweekly)

Oriented toward gold and other hard-money topics; covers South African and non–South African mining stocks. The company also publishes a quarterly directory of mining companies.

The Primary Trend
Arnold Investment Counsel Inc.
700 N. Water St.
Milwaukee, WI 53202
(semimonthly)

Market commentary with stock selections to meet objectives ranging from aggressive to conservative.

Pring Market Review
P.O. Box 338
Washington Depot, CN 06794
(monthly)

A storehouse of charts and trends outdoes most other chart-oriented letters.

The Professional Investor
Lynatrace Inc.
P.O. Box 2144
Pompano Beach, FL 33061
(semimonthly)

Scans listed and OTC issues for buy-and-sell points.

The Professional Tape Reader
P.O. Box 2407
Hollywood, FL 33022
(semimonthly, every six months)

Lists favorable and unfavorable stocks
and mutual funds and provides financial advice, general business news,
and market overview. Also gives advice on gold and bonds.

Professional Timing Service
P.O. Box 7483
Missoula, MT 59807
(monthly)

Times the market on the basis of a
mechanical system called the Supply-
Demand Formula.

The Prudent Speculator
P.O. Box 1767
Santa Monica, CA 90406
(every three weeks)

Uncovers undervalued issues; gives
sell signals—classic stock research.

PSR Prophet
1001-J Bridgeway
P.O. Box 244
Sausalito, CA 94965
(biweekly)

Puts Kenneth Fisher price/sales ratio
theory into daily use.

The Puryear Money Report
45 John St.
New York, NY 10038
(monthly)

Offers brief, general investment commentary as well as a few stock recommendations.

**Reporting on Governments and
Bond and Money Market Letter**
1545 New York Ave., N.E.
Washington, DC 20002
(biweekly; every six months)

The product of a recent merger, this
commentary covers Federal Reserve
and interest-rate matters from Washington and New York perspectives.

The Richland Report
P.O. Box 222
La Jolla, CA 92038
(semimonthly; every six months)

A bland market-timing letter that uses
cycles and oscillators for direction.

**Robert Kinsman's Low-Risk
Growth Letter**
4340 Redwood Hwy.
Suite 150
San Rafael, CA 94903
(monthly)

Recommends investments and model
portfolios for income-oriented readers.
Includes a lot of commonsense investment materials as well.

Ronald Sadoff's Major Trends
6971 N. Beech Tree Dr.
Milwaukee, WI 53209
(monthly)

Keeps score on the monetary, technical, and psychological sides of the
stock market and suggests moves
accordingly.

Savings & Loan Investor
P.O. Box 7163
Long Beach, CA 90807
(semimonthly)

A data base and tip sheet for investors
in S&L stocks.

The Sentinel Investment Letter
Hanover Investment Management
Corp.
P.O. Box 189
New Hope, PA 18938
(monthly)

Overview of the stock market and
economic indicators.

The Sindlinger Digest
P.O. Box E
Wallingford, PA 19086
(weekly)

Analyzes economic and demographic
data and government policy to predict
and explain social trends for the benefit of investors.

Smart Money
The Hirsch Organization Inc.
Six Deer Trail
Old Tappan, NJ 07675
(monthly)

Its mission is "to unearth America's
most undiscovered companies" and
detail why you should buy their stock.

Speculative Ventures
Orion Publishing Inc.
P.O. Box 517
Mount Kisco, NY 10549
(semi-monthly)

Reports and recommendations on
stocks priced below $20 per share.

The Speculator
Money Growth Institute Inc.
37 Van Reipen Ave.
Jersey City, NJ 07306
(semimonthly)

A stock-picking sheet with a focus on
listed stocks priced below $20 per
share. A wealth of names and charts.

*Standard & Poor's Emerging &
Special Situations*
Standard & Poor's Corp.
25 Broadway
New York, NY 10004
(monthly)

Discussions and recommendations on
small-company stocks, mostly those
traded OTC. Also reviews new stocks
issues.

Standard & Poor's The Outlook
Standard & Poor's Corp.
25 Broadway
New York, NY 10004
(weekly)

Forecasts, company and industry por-
traits, and other learned discussions
from the famed rating service. Numerous indexes and statistics.

Staton's Stock Market Advisory
314 Rensselaer Ave.
Charlotte, NC 28203
(every three weeks)

Well-known researcher/analyst gives
clear advice and recommendations.

Street Smart Investing
2651 Strang Blvd.
Yorktown Heights, NY 10598
(biweekly)

Follows stock purchases and tactical moves of the best-known corporate raiders. The premise is that you can profit from arbitrage by following the Icahns and Pickenses.

Systems and Forecasts
Signalert Corp.
150 Great Neck Rd.
Great Neck, NY 11021
(semimonthly)

Technical trading signals for mutual fund switchers and "stock jockeys".

Technical Digest
Woodland Rd.
New Vernon, NJ 07976
(20 issues per year, plus twice-weekly hot-line)

Regular stock/bond market letter for investors; includes charts, commentary, statistics, recommendations, and summaries of other market letters.

Timer Digest
P.O. Box 030130
Fort Lauderdale, FL 33303
(every three weeks)

Features a scorecard on those market timers and gurus you often read about after the stock market takes a big plunge or goes through the roof. A useful monitor for active traders.

Trade Levels
22801 Ventura Blvd.
Suite 115
Woodland Hills, CA 91364
(electronic report daily or printed copy every two weeks)

Provides computerized charts that show uptrends/downtrends in various stocks. Market is divided into sectors such as potential high-flyers and stocks in the most severe downtrends.

Trendway Advisory Service
P.O. Box 7184
Louisville, KY 40207
(semimonthly)

Current analysis of stocks, money markets, and gold, with an eye for waves and other chart patterns.

The Uncommon Stock
Citadel Asset Management, Ltd.
P.O. Box 3039
Colorado Springs, CO 80934
(six times a year)

This tip sheet profiles a handful of obscure stocks that the editors believe show superior potential.

United Business & Investment Report
United Business Service Co.
210 Newbury St.
Boston, MA 02116
(weekly)

Evaluates stock market and other investment trends; notes related federal developments, tables, and advisory comments; and carries regular features such as lists of companies that always pay dividends or never report a loss.

The Value Line Investment Survey
Value Line, Inc.
711 Third Ave.
New York, NY 10017
(weekly)

Loose-leaf booklet covers business activities of major corporations in variety of industries. Many charts and graphs; ranks and updates about 1,700 stocks. Speculates on market's course.

The Value Line New Issues Service
Value Line Inc.
711 Third Ave.
New York, NY 10017
(semimonthly)

Each issue is a package: summary, review of initial public offerings, detailed recommendations on several new stocks. Covers penny and junk stocks and higher-quality issues, at prices starting from $0.01.

The Value Line OTC Special Situations Service
Value Line, Inc.
711 Third Ave.
New York, NY 10017
(semimonthly)

Loose-leaf collection of recommendations/reports on OTC stocks and other issues believed by Value Line to have unusual potential for reasons unrelated to the broad market's direction.

Vickers Weekly Insider Report
Vickers Stock Research Corp.
P.O. Box 59
Brookside, NJ 07926
(weekly)

Reports on stocks being bought/sold by company officers and directors.

Weekly Insider Report
Vickers Stock Research
226 New York Ave.
Huntington, NY 11743
(weekly)

Information on stock transactions of 500 or more shares by corporate officers, directors, and 10% holders who buy/sell shares in their own firms.

The Wellington Letter
1800 Grosvenor Center
733 Bishop St.
Honolulu, HA 96813
(monthly)

Thorough, respected advisory. Covers stocks, bonds, currencies, and metals.

Western Investor Newsletter
Willamette Publishing Inc.
400 S.W. Sixth Ave.
Portland, OR 97204
(semimonthly)

Highlights companies from the West and Northwest.

The Wilsearch Investment Letter
620 South 42nd St.
Boulder, CO 80303
(every three weeks)

The usual market commentary followed by a discourse on a stock or two and a model portfolio.

The Zweig Forecast
P.O. Box 5345
New York, N.Y. 10150
(every three weeks)

Comments on sentiment and other indicators that make for superior stock market performance.

Warrants, Options, and Convertibles

The Ney Option Report
P.O. Box 90215
Pasadena, CA 91109
(semimonthly; every six months)

A letter for option traders, with recommendations and analyses.

RHM Survey of Warrants, Options & Low-Price Stocks
RHM Associates, Inc.
172 Forest Ave.
Glen Cove, NY 11542
(weekly)

Investment advice on warrants, call and put options, and low-priced stocks. Presents tables and charts.

The Stock Option Trading Form
P.O. Drawer 24242
Fort Lauderdale, FL 33307
(monthly)

It looks like a racing form, with puts and calls to buy and sell. There is little explanatory text.

Value Line Options & Convertibles
Value Line, Inc.
711 Third Ave.
New York, NY 10017
(weekly)

Evaluation and analysis of hundreds of convertible bonds, warrants, and options. Probably the preeminent source for active investors.

Commodites

The Addison Report
P.O. Box 402
Franklin, MA 02038
(every three weeks; six months)

Quick comments and recommendations on stocks, bonds, commodities.

The COINfidential Report
P.O. Box 2727
New Orleans, LA 70176
(monthly)

A coin and stock market newsletter and advisory.

Commodity Closeup
(P.O. Box 6
Cedar Falls, IA 50613
(weekly)

Tracks futures prices and trading in financials, metals, grains and meats.

Commodity Service
Dunn & Hargitt, Inc.
22 N. 2nd St.
Box 1100
Lafayette, IN 47902
(weekly)

Charts 34 most actively traded commodities and includes buy-and-sell recommendations.

Commodity Traders Consumer Report
1731 Howe Ave.
Suite 149
Sacramento, CA 95825
(bimonthly)

A wide-ranging look at futures markets, with specific recommendations, plus commentaries and interviews concerning trading strategies.

Dines Letter
James Dine & Company
Box 22
Belvedere, CA 94920
(monthly)

A respected advisory on stocks, gold and other metals, and economics. Combines important technical, psychological, and business indicators concerning the markets.

Dunn & Hargitt Commodity Service
22 N. Second St.
Lafayette, IN 47902
(weekly; every six months)

Charts and action comments for investors and traders in commodities from British pounds to gold, heating oil, and pork bellies.

Gann Angles
245-A Washington St., Suite 2
Monterey, CA 93940
(monthly)

A technical market-timing advisory, heavy on commodities. Based on system devised by W. D. Gann, a turn-of-the-century trader who ascribed price movements to regular mathematical patterns.

Hard Money Digest
3608 Grand Ave.
Oakland, CA 94610
(monthly)

Summary and comparison of opinions from other newsletters on gold, silver, interest rates, stocks, and economics.

The Hume Moneyletter
835 Franklin Court
Marietta, GA 30067
(monthly)

Keeps track of commodity prices.

International Asset Investor
HMR Publishing Co.
P.O. Box 471
Barrington, IL 60010
(monthly)

Comments/statistics on commodities and currencies for investors who put money abroad.

The Kondratieff Wave Analyst
P.O. Box 977
Crystal Lake, IL 60014
(monthly)

Economic commentary and interpretation of trading actions, with much attention to long cycles, and a section on precious metals.

Managed Account Reports
5513 Twin Knolls Rd.
Suite 213
Columbia, MD 21045
(semimonthly)

Alternating reports on futures industry and on the performance of commodity pools. An authoritative source for commodities traders using managed funds. Monitors commodities trading advisers (CTAs), private pools, and public funds.

The McKeever Strategy Letter
P.O. Box 4130
Medford, OR 97501
(monthly)

Longer-than-average letter that leads off with essays on economic or market topics , then gives advise on stocks, bonds, metals, and currencies.

Silver and Gold Report
P.O. Box 510
Bethel, CT 06801
(annual)

Keeps an eye on dealers around the country and publishes an annual survey with comparative prices.

Trendway Advisory Service
P.O. Box 7184
Louisville, KY 40207
(semimonthly)

Current analysis of stocks, money markets, and gold, with an eye for waves and other chart patterns.

Value Forecaster
P.O. Box 50
Pilot Hill, CA 95664
(monthly)

An analysis of COMEX warehouse bullion stocks of silver and other precious metals.

The Wellington Letter
1800 Grosvenor Center
733 Bishop St.
Honolulu, HA 96813
(monthly)

A thorough and respected advisory that covers stocks, bonds, currencies, and metals.

MUTUAL FUND SERVICES, DIRECTORIES, AND NEWSLETTERS

Here are the major sources of information available for making an informed decision about investing your money in mutual funds.

Organizations

Investment Company Institute
1600 M St., N.W.
Suite 600
Washington, DC 20036
(202) 293-7700

The institute is the industry's trade group for both load and no-load funds. It lobbies on behalf of its more than 1,500 member funds and their stockholders while doing trade research and acting as a clearinghouse for industry information.

The Guide to Mutual Funds, published annually by the institute, discusses mutual fund organization and regulation, defines terms used in the industry, and answers common questions about the funds. It also provides addresses, telephone numbers, and information on initial investment requirements, total assets and the like for more than 1,400 funds, which are categorized by investment objective, such as aggressive growth or income. The directory doesn't give performance information.

The Mutual Fund Fact Book, published annually, is designed for investment professionals. The book contains a wealth of facts and statistics that may be useful to more experienced investors.

You can also request copies of the institute's free brochures, including **Money Market Mutual Funds—What Are They?** and **A Translation: Turning Investment-ese Into Investment Ease**.

Magazines

A number of readily available personal finance and business magazines publish charts and analyses of the performance of major mutual funds during the previous year. For example, *Forbes* does its annual mutual fund wrap-up every September. *Kiplinger's Personal Finance Magazine* (formerly, *Changing Times*) publishes its review in October. *Money* generally reviews mutual fund performance twice a year, in the spring and fall.

Directories

The Complete Guide to Closed-End Funds
International Publishing Corporation
625 N. Michigan Ave.
Suite 1920
Chicago, IL 60611
(312) 943-7354

Published annually; provides a description of various fund characteristics; covers 240 closed-end funds on the NYSE, AMEX, and OTC markets.

Donoghue's Mutual Funds Almanac
The Donoghue Organization
P.O. Box 8008
Holliston, MA 01746
(508) 429-5930
(800) 343-5413

Provides a statistical review of 10-year performance of over 2,200 mutual funds, including money market funds.

Frank Cappiello's Closed-End Fund Digest
1280 Coast Village Circle
Suite C
Santa Barbara, CA 93108
(800) 282-2335
(monthly)

Up-to-date information on domestic and foreign closed-end funds, market developments, recommendations, etc.

Handbook for No-Load Fund Investors
No-Load Fund Investor
P.O. Box 283
Hastings-on-Hudson, NY 10706
(914) 693-7420

Lists 10 years of performance data on over 1,200 no-load and low-load funds, including money market funds. Comprehensive coverage of all no-load funds available to the public plus direct marketed low-loads. Provides market timing service and funds news.

The Individual Investor's Guide to No-Load Mutual Funds
The American Association of Individual Investors
625 North Michigan Ave.
Suite 1900
Chicago, IL 60611
(312) 280-0170
(members of the American Association of Individual Investors receive a free copy)

Full-page summaries on over 500 no-load and low-load stock and bond funds. Provides information on ticker symbol, name of portfolio manager, all performance and risk statistics. Association also offers seminars and a 2-hour videocourse on mutual funds.

The Investor's Guide to Closed-End Funds
Thomas J. Herzfeld Advisors, Inc.
P.O. Box 161465
Miami, FL 33116

Contains updates and recommendations on closed-end funds, including foreign ones.

Investor's Guide to Fidelity Funds
John Wiley & Sons
605 Third Ave.
New York, NY 10158
(212) 850-6497

Lists over 100 funds in the Fidelity family with data for past five years.

Investor's Guide to Low-Cost Mutual Funds

Mutual Fund Education Alliance
The Association of No-Load Funds
1900 Erie St., Suite 120
Kansas City, MO 64116
(816) 471-1454

Covers over 260 no-load stock, bond and money market funds.

Mutual Fund Directory
The Investment Company Institute
Probus Publishing Co.
1925 N. Clybourn Ave.
Chicago, IL 60614
(800) 426-1520

Covers over 2,500 stock, bond and money market funds.

Mutual Fund Fact Book
The Investment Company Institute
1775 K St. N.W.
Washington, DC 20006
(202) 293-7700

Contains annually updated facts and figures on the mutual fund industry, including trends in sales, assets, and performance. Also outlines history and growth of the fund industry, its policies, operations, regulation, services, and shareholders.

Mutual Fund Performance Monthly, Current Performance and Dividend Report, and *Management Results*
Wiesenberger Investment Companies
Warren, Gorham & Lamont
210 South St.,
Boston, MA 02111
(617) 423-2020

Provides an alphabetical listing of mutual funds and ranks them in terms of alpha and beta values. Wiesenberger's other reports provide comprehensive information to use in screening a mutual fund, including background, management policy, and financial records for all leading U.S. and Canadian mutual funds.

Mutual Funds Encyclopedia
Dearborn Financial Publishing
520 N. Dearbourn St.
Chicago, IL 60610-4354
(800) 621-9621

Half-page summaries on over 1,100 load and no-load mutual funds with performance data for the past five years.

Mutual Funds Performance Guide
Charles Schwab & Co.
P.O. Box 7780
San Francisco, CA 94120-7780
(800) 526-8600

Lists quarterly return performance for past three months, six months, one year, five years and 10 years for over 500 stock and bond funds.

Mutual Funds Sourcebook
Morningstar Inc.,
53 W. Jackson Blvd.
Chicago, IL 60604
(800) 876-5005
(312) 427-1985

Provides thorough, in-depth information about the operating characteristics, investment holdings, and market behavior of about 1,000 mutual funds.

The 1991 Independent Guide to Vanguard Funds
Fund Family Shareholder Association
328 Flatbush Ave., Suite 106
New York, NY 11238
(718) 636-9813

Full-page descriptions on 55 funds of the Vanguard family give 5 years of performance data.

100% No-Load Mutual Fund Council Member Directory
1501 Broadway, Suite 312
New York, NY 10036
(212) 768-2477

It covers 120 member mutual funds, which are pure no-load funds.

Wiesenberger Investment Companies Service
Warren, Gorham & Lamont
210 South St.
Boston, MA 02111
(617) 423-2020

A publication describing characteristics of various no-load mutual funds. Provides information on name of the manager, policies, services, operations and performance, and risk measures.

Newsletters

Mutual fund investors can find newsletters to be helpful in choosing among hundreds of funds or deciding when to get into and out of an investment. Letters also identify good funds that you haven't heard about elsewhere in print and explain long-term fund performance rankings.

However, before you begin looking for a letter to suit your needs, you should understand that fund publications serve differing objectives. For example, some, such as *Telephone Switch Newsletter* and *Weber's Fund Advisor,* tell you which funds to buy and sell and *when*, according to a rigid trading formula. Unless you intend to follow the system, such letters are useless.

Another group, which includes *Growth Fund Guide, Mutual Fund Letter,* and *United Mutual Fund Selector,* are educational and journalistic enterprises. They run articles (often based on original research) about assorted topics of interest to shareholders, such as how the funds have done through the years or why funds are increasing certain fees and charges.

The third group of letters is largely composed of data bases, in which you can look up scores of funds and their rankings by objectives, time periods, and size. These include *Lipper Analytic Service* (74 Trinity Pl., New York, NY 212-393-1300), *Morningstar's Mutual Fund Values, CDA Mutual Fund Report, Schabacker's Mutual Fund Analysis Guide,* and *Wiesenberger Investment Companies Service*.

Because of intense competition among publishers, most discount their subscription rates for new subscribers. Even better are the short-term trial offers, which may include one free issue. Write or call their toll-free numbers for details or watch for advertisements in financial magazines and newspapers.

The Cabot Market Letter
Cabot Farm/Orange St.
P.O. Box 3044
Salem, MA 01970
(semimonthly)

Provides model portfolios, trend lines, recommended stocks, and market commentary in a concise and readable form. It also discusses mutual funds.

CDA Mutual Fund Report
CDA Investment Technologies
11501 Georgia Ave.
Silver Spring, MD. 20902
(monthly)

A comprehensive directory and data service that rates 850 funds using many parameters, ranks them by short-term and long-term performance, and assigns an overall rating based on a combination of factors.

Donoghue's Moneyletter
The Donoghue Organization
P.O. Box 411
Holliston, MA 01746
(508) 429-5930
(bimonthly)

Report includes a pullout called Fundletter that follows a portfolio of money market funds for "safety, liquidity, yield, and catastrophe-proofing." Tackles bread-and-butter investments like municipal bonds, mutual funds, and bank accounts. Includes wise counsel on current strategies.

Fund Exchange Report
Paul A. Merriman & Associates
1200 Westlake Ave. N.
Seattle, WA 98109-3530
(semiannually)

An updated adjunct to Merriman's fund timing-and-switching service, which is offered for a separate management fee.

Fundline
David H. Menashe & Co.
P.O. Box 663
Woodland Hills, CA 91365
(818) 346-5637
(monthly)

A report on no-load funds with buy-and-sell recommendations.

Growth Fund Guide
Growth Fund Research
P.O. Box 6600
Rapid City, SD 57709
(800) 621-8322
(605) 341-1971)

A 24-page booklet crammed with articles, studies, ratings, and statistics about a small group of select, established no-load funds ranked by the volatility of the stock portfolio.

Income & Safety
The Institute for Econometric
Research
3471 N. Federal Hwy.
Fort Lauderdale, FL 33306
(305) 563-9000 (FL only)
(800) 327-6720
(monthly)

A directory of over 200 mutual funds.
Indicates each fund's primary portfolio holding, yield, minimum investment, services available, and load (if
any). Also recommends "best buys."

Insight
Mutual Fund Investors Association
60 Dedham Ave.
Needham, MA 02192
(800) 444-6342
(monthly)

News and views on Fidelity funds by
a former Fidelity executive for members of MFIA, "the independent association of Fidelity investors."

International Fund Monitor
P.O. Box 5754
Washington, DC 20016
(202) 363-3097
(monthly)
It covers closed-end nation funds.

*Jay Schabacker's Mutual Fund
Investing*
Phillips Publishing Inc.
7811 Montrose Rd.
Potomac, MD 20854
(800) 722-9000
(monthly)

For fund investors less experienced
than the other Schabacker's audiences
this newsletter contains a smorgasbord
of features, model portfolios, question-
and-answer sections, and a brief market commentary.

*Mannie Webb's Sector Fund
Connection*
8949 LaRiviera Dr.
Sacramento, CA 95826
(monthly)

Another switching advisory, covering
several families of no-load funds that
specialize in certain industries.

Mutual Fund Forecaster
The Institute for Econometric
Research
3471 N. Federal Hwy.
Fort Lauderdale, FL 33306
(800) 327-6720
(305) 563-9000)
(monthly)

The institute takes more than 300
mutual funds and projects performance based on a reading of the market
and the fund's characteristics. A directory is included in which performance
measures, one-year income projections, and risk ratings are given.

Mutual Fund Guide
Commerce Clearing House Inc.
4025 W. Peterson Ave.
Chicago, IL 60646
(312) 583-8500
(biweekly)

Covers federal and state rules that govern mutual funds.

The Mutual Fund Letter
Investment Information Services
680 N. Lake Shore Dr.
208 Tower Offices
Chicago, IL 60606
(312) 649-6940
(monthly)

Each issue takes aim at some topic, whether it be creeping charges or an oversupply of sector funds.

Mutual Fund Specialist
Royal R. LeMier & Co.
P.O. Box 1025
Eau Claire, WI 54702
(715) 834-7425
(monthly)

Agglomeration of tables and charts interrupted by brief advisory comments and news tidbits.

Mutual Fund Strategist
Progressive Investing Inc.
P.O. Box 446
Burlington, VT 05402
(802) 658-3513
(monthly)

Timing and trading signals for switchers plus excerpts from rival fund newsletters.

Mutual Fund Trends
Growth Fund Research
P.O. Box 6600
Rapid City, SD 57709
(800) 621-8322
(605) 341-1971)
(monthly)

Chart book designed for low-load and no-load mutual fund investors.

Mutual Fund Values
Morningstar, Inc.
53 West Jackson Blvd.
Chicago, IL 60604
(monthly)

Brings you value-added information such as yields, alpha, beta, R-squared (R^2) and standard deviation. Rates each fund on its risk-adjusted performance and provides "straight-forward "Buy" and "Sell" recommendations.

No-Load Fund Investor
The No-Load Fund Investor Inc.
P.O. Box 283
Hastings-on-Hudson, NY 10706
(914) 693-7420
(monthly)

Largely a data base that updates the yearly handbook, this letter gives you figures on no-load and low-load funds for various periods and some model portfolios and best buys.

No-Load Fund X
DAL Investment Co.
235 Montgomery St.
Suite 662
San Francisco, CA 94104
(800) 452-4455
(415) 866-7979
(monthly)

Presents a system called "following the stars," which coaches you to switch from fund to fund as momentum changes. Ranks over 300 no-load funds.

Performance Guide Publications
P.O. Box 2604
Palos Verdes Peninsula, CA 90274
(monthly)

A timing letter that, like others, tells you to switch into funds that have done well lately, regardless of the fund's objective.

Prime Investment Alert
Prime Financial Associates
P.O. Box 701
Bangor, ME 04401
(monthly)

A brief market commentary followed by fund data and model portfolios.

Quarterly No-Load Mutual Fund Update
American Association of Individual Investors
625 N. Michigan Ave., Suite 1900
Chicago, IL 60611
(312) 280-0170
(quarterly)

Reports performance by quarter over the last year and over the most recent 3-year period of over 500 no-load and low-load mutual funds. Available on disk also as a computerized menu-driven program.

Retirement Fund Advisory
Schabacker Investment Management
8943 Shady Grove Ct.
Gaithersburg, MD 20877
(monthly)

An abridged version of the same company's Switch Fund Advisory (see below), with emphasis on funds suitable for IRA and Keogh investors.

Schabacker's Mutual Fund Analysis Guide
Schabacker Investment Management Inc.
8943 Shady Grove Ct.
Gaithersburg, MD 20877
(monthly)

Comprehensive statistical report and advisory service that, in addition, grades funds on scale from A+ to D.

The Scott Letter
Box 17800
Richmond, VA 23226
(monthly)

A newsletter that places primary emphasis on closed-end funds.

Sector Funds Newsletter
P.O. Box 1210
Escondido, CA 92025
(monthly)

Model portfolios/signals to switch. Emphasizes Fidelity mutual funds.

Switch Fund Advisory
Schabacker Investment Management
8943 Shady Grove Ct.
Gaithersburg, MD 20877
(800) 722-9000
(monthly)

Although the name belies its appeal beyond switching, this is one of the meatier periodicals. Provides performance charts, model portfolios, new recommendations, and risk ratings.

Telephone Switch Newsletter
P.O. Box 2538
Huntington Beach, CA 92647
(800) 950-8765
(714) 898-2588
(monthly)

Provides switching advice and includes a telephone hot line to recommend switching strategies.

Titan Group Research Report
Titan Value Equities Group, Inc.
17852 Seventeenth St., Suite 102
Tustin, CA 92680-2177
(800) 456-6102)
(monthly)

Letter, written by Allan Chiulli, V. P. of Research, features a number of financial products including insurance and real estate partnerships as well as mutual funds. It is for NASD licensed registered representatives only and not to be shown to the general public.

United Mutual Fund Selector
United Business Service
101 Prescott St.
Wellesley Hills, MA 02181
(617) 267-8855
(semimonthly)

This report rates mutual funds, including bond and municipal bond funds. Very well organized and full of performance charts and descriptions of funds, plus industry developments.

Weber's Fund Advisor
Ken Weber Inc.
P.O. Box 92
Bellerose, NY 11426
(monthly)

Switching system is based on the "go-with-the-winner" strategy of rotating into specified funds rising briskly.

Wellington's Worry-Free Investing
(3421 M St., N.W. Suite 1339
Washington, DC 20007
(monthly)

Market forecasts of Bert Dohmen-Ramirez, publisher of the Wellington Letter, applied to mutual funds.

REAL ESTATE: REITS, LIMITED PARTNERSHIPS, AND TAX SHELTERS

Brennan Reports
Valley Forge Office Colony
P.O. Box 882, Suite 200
Valley Forge, PA 19482
(monthly)

Examines tax-advantaged investments such as real estate, single-premium life insurance, oil and gas deals, and other tax shelters. Also coaches you on tax planning.

Brennan's IRA Advisor
Valley Forge Office Colony
P.O. Box 882, Suite 200
Valley Forge, PA 19482
(monthly)

Offshoot of *Brennan Reports* that discusses the ins and outs of unusual IRA investments, such as income real estate limited partnerships.

Diamonds in the Rough
P.O. Box 20161
Tampa, FL 20161
(monthly)
Covers real estate investments and financing.

Eagles in IRAs
Industry Council for Tangible Assets
1701 Pennsylvania Ave., N.W.
Suite 533
Washington, DC 20006

This free booklet contains information on purchasing any denomination of the new U.S. gold (or silver) Eagles for an IRA.

Income Investor Perspectives
Uniplan, Inc.
3907 N. Green Bay Ave.
Milwaukee, WI 53206
(every three weeks)

Updates tax-advantaged and income-oriented investments, such as utility stocks and REITs. Useful for safety-and-yield investors.

John T. Reed's Real Estate Investor's Monthly
342 Bryan Dr.
Danville, CA 94526
(monthly)

Plain talk and cautionary counsel about real estate investment from the writer of many books on real estate ownership.

Oil and Gas Quarterly
1275 Broadway
Albany, NY 12204
(quarterly)

Quarterly newsletter provides specific investment advice and recommendations on oil and gas stocks. Also covers topics in the oil and gas industry.

The Real Estate Digest
P.O. Box 26444
Birmingham, AL 35226
(monthly)

Covers real estate investments, including tax strategies, title insurance, real estate financing, and management.

Real Estate Investing Letter
379 W. Broadway
New York, NY 10012
(monthly)

Covers real estate investments, including tax strategies, depreciation, and real estate syndication.

Real Estate Investor Letter:
A Guide to Prudent Investing
United Media International, Inc.
306 Dartmouth St.
Boston, MA 02116
(monthly)

A guide to real estate investing.

Realty Stock Review
Audit Investments, Inc.
136 Summit Ave., Suite 200
Montvale, NJ 07645
(semimonthly)

Reviews real estate investment trusts (REITs) and other real estate stocks. Includes a rating of REIT securities.

Stanger Register—Partnership
Profiles
Robert A. Stanger and Company
P.O. Box 7490
1129 Broad St.
Shrewsbury, NJ 07701
(monthly)

Investment information, listings, and ranking on public and private partnerships; financial planning ideas, investment product ideas, and articles and features on various investment products, concepts, and strategies.

The Stanger Report: A Guide to
Partnership Investing
Robert A. Stanger & Co.
P.O. Box 7490
1129 Broad St.
Shrewsbury, NJ 07701
(monthly)

A 10-page newsletter with timely, critical articles on limited partnerships, tax shelters, tax reform, and income real estate. Virtually indispensable for serious investors in partnerships of any kind.

Tax Shelter Insider
10076 Boca Entrada Blvd.
Boca Raton, FL 33433
(monthly)

News and commentary on shelters.

Tax Shelter Investment Review
Leland Publishing Co. Inc.
81 Canal St
Boston, MA 02114
(monthly)

Descriptions/advice on partnerships and other real estate investments.

Titan Group Research Report
Titan Value Equities Group, Inc.
17852 Seventeenth St., Suite 102
Tustin, CA 92680-2177
(800) 456-6102
(monthly)

This newsletter, written by Allan Chiulli, Vice President of Research, features a number of financial products, including mutual funds and insurance products as well as real estate partnerships. It is for NASD licensed registered representatives only and not to be shown to the general public.

Important Data Sources

GOVERNMENT SOURCES

Federal Reserve Banks

**Federal Reserve Bank
of Atlanta**
104 Marietta St., N.W.
Atlanta, GA 30303
(404) 521-8500

**Federal Reserve Bank
of Boston**
600 Atlantic Ave.
Boston, MA 02106
(617) 973-3000

**Federal Reserve Bank
of Chicago**
230 South LaSalle St.
Chicago, IL 60690
(312) 322-5322

**Federal Reserve Bank
of Cleveland**
1455 East Sixth St.
Cleveland, OH 44114
(216) 579-2000

**Federal Reserve Bank
of Dallas**
400 South Akard
Dallas, TX 75202
(214) 651-6111

**Federal Reserve Bank
of Kansas City**
925 Grand Ave.
Kansas City, MO 64198
(816) 881-2000

**Federal Reserve Bank
of Minneapolis**
250 Marquette Ave.
Minneapolis, MN 55480
(612) 340-2345

**Federal Reserve Bank
of New York**
33 Liberty St.
New York, NY 10045
(212) 720-5000

**Federal Reserve Bank
of Philadelphia**
10 Independence Mall
Philadelphia, PA 19106
(215) 574-6000

**Federal Reserve Bank
of St. Louis**
411 Locust St.
St. Louis, MO 63102
(314) 444-8444

**Federal Reserve Bank
of Richmond**
701 East Byrd St.
Richmond, VA 23219
(804) 697-8000

**Federal Reserve Bank
of San Francisco**
101 Market St.
San Francisco, CA 94105
(415) 974-2000

Federal Reserve Bulletin

Board of Governors of the Federal Reserve System, Washington, DC 20551

Stock and Commodity Exchanges

American Stock Exchange
86 Trinity Place
New York, NY 10006
(212) 306-1000

MidAmerica Commodity Exchange
444 West Jackson
Chicago, IL 60606
(312) 341-3000

Chicago Board of Options Exchange
400 South LaSalle
Chicago, IL 60605
(312) 786-5600

Midwest Stock Exchange
440 South LaSalle
Chicago, IL 60605
(312) 663-2222

Chicago Board of Trade
141 West Jackson
Chicago, IL 60604
(312) 435-3500

New York Futures Exchange
20 Broad St.
New York, NY 10005
(212) 656-4949
(800) 221-7722

**Commodity Exchange, Inc.
(COMEX)**
4 World Trade Center
New York, NY 10048
(212) 938-2900

New York Mercantile Exchange
4 World Trade Center
New York, NY 10048
(212) 938-2222

Kansas City Board of Trade
4800 Main St., Suite 303
Kansas City, MO 64112
(816) 753-7500

New York Stock Exchange
11 Wall St.
New York, NY 10005
(212) 656-3000

Pacific Stock Exchange
301 Pine St.
San Francisco, CA 94104
(415) 393-4000

Philadelphia Stock Exchange
Philadelphia Board of Trade
1900 Market St.
Philadelphia, PA 19103
(215) 496-5000

U.S. Government Publications

The following U.S. government publications can be requested from the: **Superintendent of Documents**, U.S. Government Printing Office, Washington, DC 20402

> *Business Conditions Digest* (monthly)
> *Business Statistics* (biannual)
> *Economic Indicators* (monthly)
> *Economic Report of the President* (annual)
> *Long Term Economic Growth* (book)
> *Statistical Abstract of the United States* (annual)
> *Statistical Bulletin* (monthly)
> *Survey of Current Business* (monthly)
> *Weekly Business Statistics* (weekly)

The following Federal Reserve System publications can be obtained from: **Federal Reserve System,** Board of Governors, Division of Administrative Services, Washington, DC 20551:

> *Annual Chart Book* (annual)
> *Federal Reserve Bulletin* (monthly)
> *Quarterly Chart Book* (quarterly)

PERIODICALS

Barron's and *Wall Street Journal*
Dow Jones & Company
Subscription Office
200 Burnett Rd.
Chicopee, MA 01021

Business Week
McGraw-Hill, Inc.
1221 Ave. of the Americas
New York, NY 10002

Disclosure Journal
Disclosure Inc.
1450 Broadway
New York, NY 10018

Financial World
Financial World Partners
1450 Broadway
New York, NY 10018

Forbes
60 5th Ave.
New York, NY 10011

Investor's Business Daily
P.O. Box 25970
Los Angeles, CA 90025-9970

Fortune and *Money Magazine*
Time Inc.
Time & Life Bldg.
Rockefeller Center
New York, NY 10020

Kiplinger Personal Finance Magazine (formerly *Changing Times*)
Kiplinger Washington Editors, Inc.
1729 H St. N.W.
Washington, DC 20006

INVESTMENT SERVICES

Dun & Bradstreet
99 Church St.
New York, NY 10017

Standard & Poor's Corporation
345 Hudson St.
New York, NY 10014

Dun's Marketing Division
3 Century Dr.
Parsippany, NJ 07054

Value Line Services
Arnold Bernhard & Co.
5 E. 44th St.
New York, NY 10017

Moody's Investor Service
99 Church St.
New York, NY 10007

ORGANIZATIONS

American Association of Individual Investors (AAII)
625 North Michigan Ave.
Suite 1900
Chicago, IL 60611

National Association of Real Estate Investment Trusts (NAREIT)
1129 Twentieth St., N.W.
Suite 705
Washington, DC 20036

The Investment Company Institute
1600 M St., N.W.
Washington, DC 20036

National Futures Association (NFA)
200 W. Madison St., Suite 1600
Chicago, IL 60606

National Association of Investment Clubs (NAIC)
1515 E. 11 Mile Rd.
Royal Oak, MI 48067

Real Estate Securities and Syndication Institute (RESSI)
430 North Michigan Ave.
Chicago, IL 60611

REGIONAL AND BRANCH OFFICES OF THE SEC

Financial and other data included in registration statements, reports, applications, and similar documents filed with the Commission are available for study in the public reference room in the SEC's main office in Washington, D.C., where copies of these documents also may be obtained. Cost estimates are available from Public Reference Room, Securities and Exchange Commission, Washington, D.C. 20549.

Current annual reports and other periodic reports filed by companies whose securities are listed on the national exchanges are also available for study in the SEC's New York, Chicago, and Los Angeles regional offices (see next section).

Registration statements and subsequent reports filed by companies whose securities are traded over-the-counter and that register under the Securities Exchange Act of 1934 are also available at the New York, Chicago, and Los Angeles offices. SEC filings can be examined at the regional office serving the area in which the issuer's principal office is located. These regional offices are located in Atlanta, Boston, Denver, Fort Worth, Seattle, and Washington.

Prospectuses covering recent public offerings of securities registered under the Securities Act of 1933 may be examined in all regional offices. Broker-dealer and investment adviser registrations, as well as Regulation A notifications and offering circulars, may be examined in the particular regional office in which they were filed.

SEC Regional and Branch Offices

Region 1 New York Regional Office
26 Federal Plaza
New York, NY 10278
(212) 264-1636
Region: New York and New Jersey

Region 2 Boston Regional Office
150 Causeway St.
Boston, MA 02114
(617) 223-2721
Region: Maine, New Hampshire, Vermont, Massachusetts, Rhode Island, and Connecticut

Region 3 Atlanta Regional Office
1375 Peachtree St., N.E.
Suite 788
Atlanta, GA 30367
(404) 881-4768
Region: Tennessee, Virgin Islands, Puerto Rico, North Carolina, South Carolina, Georgia, Alabama, Mississippi, Florida, and Louisiana east of the Atchafalaya River

Miami Branch Office (Region 3)
Dupont Plaza Center
300 Biscayne Blvd. Way, Suite 1114
Miami, FL 33131
(305) 350-5765

Region 4 Securities and Exchange Commission
Everett McKinley Dirksen Bldg.
219 South Dearborn St., Room 1204
Chicago, IL 60604
(312) 353-7390
Region: Michigan, Ohio, Kentucky, Wisconsin, Indiana, Iowa, Minnesota, Missouri,
Kansas City (Kansas), and Illinois

Detroit Branch Office (Region 4)
1044 Federal Bldg.
Detroit, MI 48226
(313) 226-6070

Region 5 Securities and Exchange Commission
411 W. Seventh St.
Fort Worth, TX 76102
(817) 334-3821
Region: Oklahoma, Arkansas, Texas, Louisiana west of the Atchafalaya River, and
Kansas (except Kansas City)

Houston Branch Office (Region 5)
Federal Office and Courts Bldg.
515 Rusk Ave., Room 5615
Houston, TX 77002
(713) 226-4986

Region 6 Denver Regional Office
410 17th St.
Suite 700
Denver, CO 80202
(303) 837-2071
Region: North Dakota, South Dakota, Wyoming, Nebraska, Colorado, New Mexico,
and Utah

Salt Lake Branch Office (Region 6)
Boston Bldg. Suite 810
Nine Exchange Place
Salt Lake City, UT 84111
(801) 524-5796

Region 7 Securities and Exchange Commission
          10960 Wilshire Blvd.
          Suite 1710
          Los Angeles, CA 90024
          (213) 473-4511
Region: Nevada, Arizona, California, Hawaii, and Guam

          San Francisco Branch Office (Region 7)
          450 Golden Gate Ave., Box 36042
          San Francisco, CA 94102
          (415) 556-5264

Region 8 Securities and Exchange Commission
          3040 Federal Building
          915 Second Ave.
          Seattle, WA 98174
          (206) 442-7900
Region: Montana, Idaho, Washington, Oregon, and Alaska

Region 9 Securities and Exchange Commission
          Ballston Center, Tower 3
          4015 Wilson Blvd.
          Arlington, VA 22203
          (703) 557-8201
Region: Pennsylvania, Delaware, Maryland, Virginia, West Virginia, and District of
Columbia
          Philadelphia Branch Office (Region 9)
          William J. Green, Jr. Federal Bldg.
          600 Arch St., Room 2204
          Philadelphia, PA 19106
          (215) 597-2278

U.S. Securities & Exchange Commission, Washington, DC 20549

For:	*Call:*
General information	Office of Public Affairs (202) 272-2650
Investor complaints	Office of Consumer Affairs (202) 523-5516
Filings by registered companies	Public Reference Room (202) 523-5360
Forms and publications	(202) 523-3761

For the *Official Summary,* the monthly publication summarizing all "insider"
security transactions and holdings, contact **Superintendent of Documents,**
Government Printing Office, Washington, D.C. 20402, (202) 783-3238.

14

Investment
Information
Grids

The grids on the following pages list the investment information sources by types in this order: common and preferred stocks, bonds, warrants, convertibles, and mutual funds, and include summaries of types of information or data elements provided.

Information Provided about Common and Preferred Stock

Publications	Recent Price	Price Range Calendar Year	P/E Ratio	Dividend	Yield	Ranking/ Rating	EPS	Beta	Sales	Important Developments Business Summaries	I/S-B/S detailed data
S&P Stock Guide	X	X	X	X	X	X	X		X		
S&P Corporation Records (Stock Reports)	X	X	X	X	X	X	X	X	X	X	X
Value Line Investment Survey	X	X	X	X	X	X	X	X	X	X	X
Moody's Manuals	X	X	X	X	X		X		X	X	

Key to Abbreviations: P/E = Price/Earnings; EPS = Earnings Per Share; I/S = Income Statement; B/S = Balance Sheet

Information Provided about Bonds

Publications	Current Price	P/E Range Calendar Year	Current Yield	Yield to Maturity	Ranking/ Rating	Stock Path Current Price	Stock Path P/E Ratio	Convertible Bonds EPS
Moody's Bond Record	X	X	X	X	X			
S&P Bond Guide	X	X	X	X	X	X	X	X

Key to Abbreviations: P/E = Price/Earnings Ratio; EPS = Earnings Per Share

Information Provided about Convertibles

Publication	Conversion Price (1)	Conversion Ratio (2)	Annual Dividend or Interest (3)	Maturity (4)	Market Price of Convertible (5)	Price of Common Stock (6)	Annual Dividend per Share (7)	Total Dividend (3×7)	Conversion Value (2×5)	Conversion Premium (5×9)	Extra Return (2×8)	Payback Years (10×11)	Current Yield on Convertible (%) (3×5)
Value Line Options and Convertibles	X	X	X	X	X	X	X	X	X	X	X	X	X

Information Provided about Warrants

Publication	Stock to Warrant Ratio (1)	Strike Price (2)	Market Price of Common Stock (3)	Formula Value (4)	Market Price of the Warrant (5)	Premium (6)	Adjusted Premium (7)	Months to Maturity (8)	Price Volatility (9)
Value Line Options and Convertibles	X	X	X	X	X	X	X	X	X

(4) Formula Value = column (1) × [column (3) - column (2)].

(6) Premium = column (5) - column (4).

(7) Adjusted Premium takes into consideration differences in strike prices; it is column (6) divided by column (2).

(9) This Price Volatility measurement is calculated by Value Line. It is the standard deviation of the security's price relative to the standard deviation of the average common stock covered by Value Line.

Information Provided about Mutual Funds

Publications	How Often M.F. Info. Published	Fund Address & Phone #	Investment Objective	Minimum Investment	Front Load/ Initial Sales Charge	Date Fund Established	Total Recent Assets	Special Investor Services	Return Past 1-12 Months	Return Past 3-10 Yrs.	Value of $10,000 Invested
S&P Stock Guide	M		X	X		X	X	X	X	X	X
Money Magazine	A	X	X		X				X	X	
Forbes	A			X	X		X		X	X	
Kiplinger's Personal Finance Magazine (formerly Changing Times)	A								X	X	
Business Week	A	X	X		X		X		X	X	
Barron's	Q		X				X		X	X	X
United M.F. Selector	B	X	X	X	X	X	X		X	X	
Wiesenberger Investment Co. Service	M, Q, A	X	X	X	X	X	X	X	X	X	X
Investor's Directory of No-Load M.F. Assoc.	A	X	X	X		X	X	X			
Individual Investor's Guide to No-Load M.F.	A	X	X	X	X		X	X	X	X	
Morningstar's M.F. Values	B	X	X	X	X	X	X	X	X	X	X

Key to Abbreviations: A = Annually; B = Biweekly; M = Monthly; Q = Quarterly; W = Weekly; R^2 = R-Squared = Coefficient of determination

Information Provided about Mutual Funds (continued)

Summary of Major Holdings	Comparative Returns for Funds & Market	Expense Ratios as % of Assets	Dividends & Capital Gains Distributions	Risk Exposure Rating	Fund Ratings Bull & Bear Mkt.	Ratings of Risk-Adjusted Performances	Beta	Alpha	R²	Standard Deviation	Publications
			X								S&P Stock Guide
	X	X		X	X	X					Money Magazine
	X	X			X						Forbes
				X							Kiplinger's Personal Finance Magazine (formerly Changing Times)
X	X	X		X		X					Business Week
	X		X								Barron's
	X	X									United M.F. Selector
X	X	X	X				X	X			Wiesenberger Investment Co. Service
											Investor's Direcory of No-Load M.F. Assoc.
X		X	X	X	X		X				Individual Investor's Guide to No-Load M.F.
X	X	X	X	X		X	X	X	X	X	Morningstar's Mutual Fund Values

Key to Abbreviations: A = Annually; B = Biweekly; M = Monthly; Q = Quarterly; W = Weekly; R² = R-Squared = Coefficient of determination.

Glossary

Aggressive Growth Fund (also called Maximum Capital Gain, Capital Appreciation, or Small-Company Growth Fund): Type of mutual fund taking greater risk in order to yield maximum appreciation (instead of current dividend income). Typically invests in upstart and high-tech–oriented companies.

American Association of Individual Investors (AAII): An independent, non-profit corporation formed in 1978 for the purpose of assisting individuals in becoming effective managers of their own assets through programs of education, information, and research.

American Classics Index: Index of 30 American classical stamps, equivalent to the Dow Jones 30 Industrial Average for stocks.

American Depository Receipts (ADRs): Security through which foreign stocks are traded in the U.S. markets. Like common stock, each ADR represents a specific number of shares in a specific foreign firm.

American Stock Exchange (AMEX) Market Value Index: Unweighted index of American Stock Exchange (AMEX) stocks. It is computed by adding all of the plus net changes and minus net changes above or below previous closing prices. The sum is then divided by the number of issues listed and the result added to or subtracted from the previous close. It is actually more like an average than an index in that it does not have a base period.

Analytical Information: Available current data in conjunction with projections and recommendations about potential investments.

Annual Report: Formal financial statement issued yearly by a corporation to its shareholders. Includes the president's letter, management's discussion of operations, balance sheet, income statement, statement of cash flows, footnotes, and the audit report.

Ask Price: The lowest price at which a dealer is willing to sell a security.

Asset: Economic resource that is expected to provide benefits to an individual, a business, or an institution. Examples of an asset are cash, accounts receivable, inventory, real estate, and securities.

Averages: Numbers used to measure the general behavior of stock prices by reflecting the arithmetic average price behavior of a representative group of stocks at a given point in time.

Back-End Load (also called Deferred Sales Charges): A fee charged for redeeming mutual fund shares; intended to discourage frequent trading in the fund.

Balanced (Mutual) Fund: A mutual fund that combines investments in common stock, bonds, and, often, preferred stock to provide income and some capital appreciation. Balanced funds tend to underperform all-stock funds in strong bull markets.

Balance Sheet: Condensed statement showing the nature and amount of a company's assets, liabilities, and stockholders' equity as of a given date. A financial photo of what the company owns, what it owes, and the ownership interest.

Barron's: Weekly publication by Dow Jones; the second-most popular source of financial news.

Basis Point: Unit of measure for the change in interest rates for bonds and notes. One basis point equals 1 percent of 1 percent, that is, 0.01 percent; thus 100 basis points = 1 percent.

Bear: One who believes the market will decline.

Bearer Bond: A bond that does not have the owner's name recorded; its coupons can be clipped and cashed by any holder.

Bearish: Expectation of a decline in a stock's price or in the market in general.

Bear Market: A period of declining prices.

Beta: A measure of systematic (nondiversifiable) risk. Shows how the price of a security responds to market forces. In general, the higher the beta, the more risky the security.

Bid and Asked: Often referred to as a quotation or quote. The bid is the highest price a buyer will pay for a security at a given time; the asked is the lowest price a seller will accept at the same time.

Big Board: Popular term for the New York Stock Exchange (NYSE).

Blue Chip: Stock of an investment-grade company of the highest standing.

Bond: Basically an IOU or promissory note of a corporate, municipal, or government debt, expressed in a stipulated face value, a stipulated rate of interest, and a date at which the issuer will pay the holder the face value of the bond.

Bond Ratings: Letter grades that signify investment quality of a bond.

Bond Yield: Summary measure of the return an investor would receive on a bond if it were held to maturity; reported as an annual rate of return.

Book: A notebook used by a stock specialist to record buy orders and sell orders at specified prices, in strict sequence of receipt, as conveyed by other brokers.

Book Value: Stated sum of all a company's assets, minus its liabilities, divided by the number of common shares outstanding, is the book value per common share. Book value of the assets of a company or a security may have little or no significant relationship to market value.

Broker: An agent who for a commission handles the public's orders to buy and sell securities or commodities.

Bull: One who believes the market will rise.

Bull Market: A period of rising prices.

Bullish: Expectation of a rise in a stock's price or in the market in general.

Business Cycle: An indicator of the current state of the economy; the variability in economic activity.

Call: The right to buy 100 shares (usually) of a specified stock at a fixed price per share (the striking price) for a limited time (until expiration).

Callable: A bond issue, all or part of which may be redeemed by the issuing corporation under definite conditions before maturity; also refers to preferred shares that may be retired by the issuing corporation.

Capital Gain (Loss): Profit or loss from the sale of a capital asset; a capital gain may be short-term (one year or less) or long-term (more than one year).

Capital Gains Distribution: Income for investors resulting from net long-term profits of a mutual fund realized when portfolio securities are sold at a gain. These profits from sales of securities are passed on by fund managers to shareholders at least once a year.

Capitalization: Total amount of the various securities issued by a corporation; may include bonds, debentures, preferred, and common stock. Bonds and debentures are usually carried on the books of the issuing company in terms of their par or face value. Preferred and common shares may be carried in terms of par or stated value.

Capital Market: Long-term financial market in which long-term securities such as stocks and bonds are bought and sold.

Capital Stock: All shares, common and preferred, representing ownership of a business.

Cash Flow: (1) Net income plus noncash expenses (e.g., depreciation), minus noncash revenue (e.g., amortization of deferred revenue), yields cash flow from operations. (2) Cash receipts minus cash payments.

Chicago Board of Trade (CBT): Trades commodity futures and futures options.

Chicago Board Options Exchange (CBOE): Organized, national exchange where foreign currency, index, and interest rate options are traded by member for their own accounts and for the accounts of customers.

Chicago Mercantile Exchange (CME): Trades commodity futures and futures options.

Closed-End Mutual Fund: A mutual fund that operates with a fixed number of shares outstanding.

Collateral: Securities or other property pledged by a borrower to secure repayment of a loan.

COMEX: Commodity Exchange, Inc., trades futures and futures options and is located in the Commodity Exchange Center of New York City.

Commission: Broker's fee for buying or selling securities.

Commodity Futures Trading Commission (CFTC): Established in 1974 by the U.S. Congress, it regulates all commodities traded in organized contract markets. It is to commodity futures as the SEC is to securities markets.

Common Stock: Securities representing an ownership interest in a corporation. If the company has also issued preferred stock, both common and preferred have ownership rights, but the preferred normally has prior claim on dividends and, in the event of liquidation, assets. Claims of both common and preferred stockholders are junior to claims of bondholders or other company creditors.

Consolidated Balance Sheet: A balance sheet showing the financial condition of a parent corporation and its subsidiaries.

Convertible (CV): A bond, debenture, preferred share that may be exchanged by the owner for common stock or another security, usually of the same company, in accordance with the terms of the issue.

Coupon Bond: A bearer bond, so called because the annual or semiannual interest payments are made when the coupons attached to the bond are presented to the paying agent.

Covered Options: Options written against stock owned.

Cumulative Preferred: A stock having a provision that if one or more dividends are omitted, the omitted dividends must be paid before dividends may be paid on the company's common stock.

Curb Exchange: Former name of the American Stock Exchange, second largest exchange in the country. The term comes from the market's origin on the streets of downtown New York.

Currency Futures: Futures contracts on foreign currencies; they are traded much like commodities.

Currency Options: Put and call options written on foreign currencies.

Current Yield: Current income a bond provides relative to its prevailing market price.

Data Base: A file containing information on a particular subject or subjects. For example, a data base system has many such files, each devoted to a particular kind of data element, so that one data base may hold all the shareholder names, another all their addresses, another all their Social Security numbers, and so forth.

Dealer: A buyer and seller of securities who maintains an inventory of the issues in which he or she trades, as distinguished from the broker who for a fee acts as the buyer's or seller's agent.

Debenture: A promissory note secured only by the general credit and assets of a company and usually not backed by a mortgage or lien on any specific assets.

Delivery: Transfer of stocks from seller to buyer. The certificate representing shares bought "regular way" on the New York Stock Exchange (NYSE) normally is delivered to the purchaser's broker on the fourth business day after the transaction.

Descriptive Information: Factual data on past behavior of the economy, the stock market, industry, or a given investment vehicle.

Discount Broker: A stockbroker who charges a reduced commission and provides no investment advice.

Discretionary Account: An account in which the customer gives the broker or someone else discretion as to the purchase and sale of securities or commodities including selection, timing, and price to be paid or received. Discretion may be complete or within specific limits.

Distribution: The sale, over a period of time, of a large block of stock without undue depression of the market price.

Diversification: Spreading investments among different companies in different fields. Diversification is also offered by the securities of many individual companies because of the wide range of their activities.

Dividend: Payment designated by a company's board of directors to be distributed pro rata among company shareholders.

Dividend Yield: Return earned on dividend income; dividend yield relates dividends to share price.

Dollar Cost Averaging: A system of buying stocks at regular intervals. A fixed amount regularly invested buys more shares in a low market and fewer in a high market. With long-term averaging, a relatively low price per share results.

Dow Jones Bond Averages: Mathematical averages of closing prices for groups of utility, industrial, and corporate bonds.

Dow Jones Industrial Average (DJIA): A benchmark stock average of 30 blue chip industrial stocks selected for total market value and broad public ownership and believed to reflect overall market activity.

Down Tick (Minus Tick): A transaction of securities executed at a price below that in the preceding transaction. For example, if a stock has been selling at $23 per share, the next transaction is a down tick if it is at $22 1/8.

Dow Theory: A method of analyzing market trends by observing the movement of the Dow Jones industrial and transportation averages. For example, a bull market is supposed to continue as long as one average continues to make new highs that are "confirmed" by the other. A reversal is signaled when one average fails to confirm the other; a bear market is supposed to continue as long as one average makes new lows that are confirmed by the other.

Earnings Per Share (EPS): The amount of annual earnings available to common stockholders, as stated on a per share basis.

Equipment Trust Certificate: A type of security, generally issued by a railroad, to pay for new equipment. Title to the equipment, such as a locomotive, is held by a trustee until the notes are paid off. An equipment trust certificate is usually secured by a first lien on the equipment.

Equity: The ownership interest of common and preferred stockholders in a company. Also refers to the excess value of securities over the debit balance in a margin account.

Ex-Dividend: A synonym for "without dividend." Stocks and registered bonds have record dates for the payment of dividends and interest. The New York Stock Exchange (NYSE) sets dates a few days ahead of each one to allow for the physical transfer of the securities. Investors who buy stocks before this day receive this dividend; investors who buy after it do not.

Exercise: Actual fulfillment of the terms of an option contract. The specified number of shares of the underlying stock are bought or sold at the price predetermined in the option contract.

Exit (Redemption) Fees: Charges assessed upon redemption of mutual fund shares regardless of the length of time the investor has owned the shares.

Expiration: The date the option contract becomes void unless previously exercised. All option contracts expire on the Saturday following the third Friday of the expiration month.

Ex-Rights: Without the rights.

Extra: Short form, of "extra dividend." A dividend in the form of stock or cash in addition to the regular dividend the company has been paying.

Face Value: The amount of the promise to pay that appears on the face of a fixed-income security.

Fair Value: The value of an option, calculated mathematically face value is determined by (1) the striking price of the option, (2) the current price of the underlying stock, (3) the amount of time left until expiration, and (4) the volatility of the underlying stock.

Family of Funds: A group of mutual funds, all with different investment objectives, under the same management company. A shareholder can switch among the funds, sometimes at no charge, as his or her investment objectives and perceptions change.

Federal National Mortgage Association (FNMA, Fannie Mae): A government-sponsored corporation engaged in the buying and selling of FHA, FHDA, or VA mortgages.

Financial Information Services: Services providing historical, financial, market and economic information, and current stock market prices and financial news. Information is obtained through a diskette or an on-line data base with a modem.

Financial Futures: A type of futures contracts in which the underlying commodities are financial assets such as debt securities, foreign currencies, or market baskets of common stocks.

Financial Planner: One engaged in providing personal financial planning services to individuals. A financial planner may be an independent professional or affiliated with a large investment, insurance, accounting, or other institution.

Financial Planning Software: Personal finance computer programs that keep track of income and expenses by budget category, reconcile accounts, store tax records, figure net worth, track stocks and bonds, and print checks and financial reports. Some programs even generate a detailed, long-term personal financial plan that covers college education, investment, and retirement planning. Examples of financial planning software include *Dollars and Sense* and *Managing Your Money*.

Fiscal Year: A corporation's accounting year, which may or may not coincide with a calendar year, either by chance or because of some peculiarity of the company's business. For example, the meat packer's February–January year ends with the most money in hand and the least meat in storage.

Fixed Charges: Expenses a company must meet whether it has earnings or not. Such changes include bond interest, taxes, and royalties.

Fixed-Income Securities: Investment vehicles that provide a fixed periodic return. Examples are debt securities such as bonds.

Form 10-K: A statement filed with the Securities Exchange Commission (SEC) by all firms listed on an exchange.

Front-End Load: Initial sales commission at the time of the purchase of mutual funds. Administration and management fees continue to be charged annually regardless of a fund being a front-end load, back-end load (12b-1), or no-load.

Fundamental Analysis: The process of gathering basic financial, accounting, and economic data on a company and determining whether that company is fairly priced by market standards.

Futures Contract: A commitment to deliver a certain amount of some specified item by some given date in the future.

Futures Market (Futures Exchange): The commodity market that trades futures contracts. It is a self-regulating body that determines conditions for acceptance of members, their trading terms, and their behavior in trading. Examples are Amex Commodity Exchange, The Commodity Exchange, Inc, (COMEX), the New York Mercantile Exchange, the Chicago Board of Trade, and the Chicago Mercantile Exchange.

General Mortgage Bond: A bond secured by a blanket mortgage on a corporation's property, often subordinated to specific pledges against certain properties.

Good-Till-Canceled: A type of order for the purchase or sale of stock or options that remains in effect until order is filled or canceled.

Government Bonds: U.S. government obligations that are regarded as the highest-grade issues in existence.

Government National Mortgage Association (GNMA, Ginnie Mae): Government-owned corporation, that primarily issues pass-through securities. These securities pass through all payments of interest and principal received on a pool of federally insured mortgage loans. GNMA guarantees that all payments of principal and interest will be made on the mortgages on a timely basis.

Growth Fund: A mutual fund that seeks to maximize its return through capital gains. It typically invests in companies whose stocks are expected to rise in value faster than inflation. An example is T. Rowe Price Capital Appreciation Fund.

Growth Stock: Stock of a company with prospects for future growth—a company which over a period of time seems destined to expand materially.

G.T.C. Order: "Good till canceled." A customer's order to a broker to buy or sell securities at a specified price, the order to remain in effect until it is either executed or canceled.

Hardware: The mechanical components of a computer system, such as input and output devices and the central processing unit (CPU).

Hedging: The strategy of protecting oneself against wide market swings by taking both buy and sell positions in a security or commodity.

Holding Company: A corporation that owns the securities of another corporation, in most cases with voting control.

Horizontal Analysis: Time series analysis of financial statements covering more than one accounting period, also called *trend analysis*. It looks at the percentage change in an account over time.

Income Bonds: Bonds that promise to repay principal at a set date, but will pay interest only as it is earned. Often the issuer promises to add any unpaid interest to the face amount of the income bond when it is paid off.

Indenture: A written agreement under which bonds or debentures are issued, setting forth maturity date, interest rate, security, and other terms.

Index: An index weighs changes in prices by the size of the companies affected. Standard & Poor's Index of 400 stocks calculates changes in prices as if all the shares of each company were sold each day, thus giving a giant like General Motors its due influence.

Index Fund: A mutual fund whose primary objective is to match the performance of a particular stock index such as Standard & Poor's 500 Composite Stock Price Index. An example is Vanguard's Index 500 Fund.

Index Options: Index options are option contracts on stock indexes, which measure the value of a group of stocks. Because there is no single underlying asset, covered writing is not possible with stock indexes.

Individual Investor: An individual whose principal concerns in purchasing security are regular dividend income, safety of the original investment, and capital appreciation.

Institutional Investor: An institution such as a mutual fund, bank, insurance company, or pension fund, operating on behalf of a broad client base that trades large blocks of securities.

International Fund: A mutual fund that invests in the stocks and bonds of corporations traded on foreign exchanges. These funds make significant gains when the dollar is falling and foreign stock prices are rising. Some funds invest in many overseas markets, whereas others just concentrate on specific foreign areas. Examples are T. Rowe Price International Stock Fund, T. Rowe Price Europe Fund, Fidelity Pacific Basin Fund, and Fidelity Canada Fund.

Interest Rate Futures: Futures contracts on fixed-income securities.

Interest Rate Options: Put and call options written on fixed-income securities.

In-the-Money: A call option with a striking price less than the market price of the underlying security; a put option with a striking price greater than the market price of the underlying security.

Intrinsic Value: What the premium of an option would be if the price of the underlying stock remained at its current level until expiration.

Investment: The use of money for the purpose of making more money, gaining income or increasing capital, or both where safety of principal is an important consideration.

Investment Banker: Also known as an underwriter. The liaison between a corporation that wants to raise money and the public. An investment banker or syndicate that underwrites a new issue and stands ready to buy the new securities if they cannot be sold to the public.

Investment Company: See: Investment Trust.

Investment Counselor: One professionally engaged in rendering investment advisory and supervisory services.

Investment Letters: Newsletters that provide, on a subscription basis, the analyses and recommendations of various experts in different aspects of investment vehicles.

Investment Trust: A company that invests in other companies after which it sells its own shares to the public. If it is a closed-end company, it sells its shares once and for all. If it is an open-end company, or a mutual fund, it continuously buys and sells its shares.

Issue: (1) Any of a company's securities. (2) The act of distributing company securities.

Junk Bonds: High-risk bonds with low bond ratings that provide high yields.

Leverage: The ratio of dollars controlled in an investment to dollars invested. Buying a stock "on margin," for example, allows an investor to borrow up to half the price of the stock purchase. The ratio of dollars controlled to dollars invested in that case would be 2: 1.

Limited Partnership (Syndicate): A type of partnership in which the limited partner is legally liable only for the amount of his or her initial investment. The general partner (usually the organizer) who operates the syndicate has unlimited financial liability.

Limit Order: A customer's order to a securities broker to buy or sell at a specific price or better.

Liquidation: (1) The process of converting securities or other property into cash, or (2) The dissolution of a company, with cash remaining after sale of its assets and payment of all indebtedness being distributed to the shareholders.

Liquidity: The degree of ease with which a security can be converted into cash.

Listed Stock: The stock of a company that is traded on a national securities exchange and for which a listing application and a registration statement, giving detailed information about the company and its operations, have been filed with the SEC and the exchange itself.

Load: A sales commission charged to purchase shares in many (not all) mutual funds sold by brokers or other members of a sales force. Typically, the charge ranges from 2 percent to 8.5 percent of the initial investment. The charge is added to the net asset value (NAV) per share when determining the offer price.

Load Fund: A mutual fund sold to the public that charges sales commissions, usually called a front-end load, when purchased.

Long: Signifies ownership of securities. An individual "long 100 General Electric" owns 100 shares in that company, as opposed to someone who is "short" (e.g., does not own) 100 shares.

Low-Load Fund: A mutual fund that charges a small commission.

M: Abbreviation for 1,000; used to specify the face value of a $1,000 bond.

Management: The Board of Directors, elected by the stockholders, and the officers of the corporation, appointed by the Board of Directors.

Margin: Amount paid by a customer using credit to buy a security, the balance being advanced by the broker. Under Federal Reserve regulations, initial margin requirements over the past 20 years have ranged from 40 percent up to 100 percent of the purchase price.

Margin Call: A demand on a customer to put up money or securities with the broker. The call is made when a purchase is made or if a customer's equity in a margin account declines below a minimum standard set by an exchange or by the firm.

Market Order: An order by a customer to a broker to buy or sell at the best price available when the order reaches the trading floor.

Market Price: In the case of a security, market price is usually considered the last reported price at which the stock or bond sold.

Market Return: The average return on all stocks, such as those in the S&P 500 Stock Composite Index.

Maturity: The date on which a loan or a bond or debenture comes due and is to be paid off.

Modem: Abbreviated term for Modulator-Demodulator, a device that transforms computer information from binary form to analog form so it can be transmitted and received over telephone lines. Modems can be installed internally in most computers or connected externally through a serial port.

Money Market: Market in which short-term debt securities such as T-bills and certificates of deposit (CDs) are bought and sold.

Money Market (Mutual) Fund: A mutual fund that invests in high-yielding, short-term money market instruments such as U.S. T-bills and commercial paper.

Moody's Investors Services: Publishes a variety of investment reference manuals, including *Moody's Manuals*.

Municipal Bonds: Tax-exempt debt securities issued by states, counties, cities, and other public agencies.

Mutual Fund: A company that uses its capital to invest in other companies. There are two principal types: closed-end and open-end. Shares in closed-end investment trusts are readily transferable in the open market and are bought and sold like other shares. Capitalization of these companies is fixed. Open-end funds sell their own new shares to investors, stand ready to buy back their old shares, and are not listed. Open-end funds are so called because their capitalization is not fixed and they issue more shares as people want them.

Naked: An uncovered options strategy, that is, an investment in which the written options are not matched with a long stock position or a long option position that expires no earlier than the written options. Thereby the loss potential with such a strategy is thereby unlimited. (*See*: Uncovered)

NASDAQ Indexes: Measures of current price behavior of securities sold in the over-the-counter (OTC) market.

National Association of Securities Dealers (NASD): A self-regulatory organization that has jurisdiction over certain broker-dealers who handle over-the-counter (OTC) securities. The NASD requires member broker-dealers to register and conduct examinations for compliance with net capital requirements and other regulations.

Negotiable: Refers to a security, title to which is transferable by delivery when properly endorsed by the owner.

Net Asset Value: A term usually used in connection with investment trusts, meaning net asset value per share. It is common practice for an investment trust to compute its assets daily, or even twice daily, by totaling the market value of all securities owned. All liabilities are deducted, and the balance divided by the number of shares outstanding. The resulting figure is the net asset value per share.

Net Change: The difference between a security's closing price on one day and its closing price on the following day it is traded. For a stock entitled to a dividend on one day but traded "ex-dividend" the next, the dividend is considered in computing the change. For example, if the closing market price of a stock on Monday—the last day it was entitled to receive a $0.50 dividend—was $45 a share, and $44.50 at the close of the next day, when it was "ex-dividend," the price would be considered unchanged. With a split-up of shares, a stock selling at $100 the day before a 2-for-1 split and trading the next day at $50 would also be considered unchanged. If it sold at $51, it would be considered up $1. The net change is ordinarily the last figure in a stock price list.

New Issue: A stock or bond sold by a corporation for the first time. Proceeds may be used to retire outstanding securities of the company, for new plant or equipment, or for additional working capital.

New York Stock Exchange Indexes: Measure of the current price behavior of the stocks traded on the New York Stock Exchange (NYSE).

No-Load Fund: A mutual fund that does not charge a commission when shares are purchased.

Noncumulative: A preferred stock on which unpaid dividends do not accrue. Omitted dividends as a rule, are gone forever.

OCC: Options Clearing Corporation.

Odd Lot: A quantity of stock less than the established 100-share unit or 10-share unit of trading: from 1 to 99 shares for most issues, 1 to 9 for so-called inactive stocks.

Offer: The price at which a person is ready to sell, as opposed to bid, the price at which one is ready to buy.

On-Line Data Base: A service, such as Dow Jones News Retrieval or CompuServe, providing historical, financial, market and economic information or current stock market prices and financial news obtained via modem.

Open-End Fund: A mutual fund from which an investor buys shares and sells them back to the fund. This type of fund offers to sell and redeem shares on a continual basis for an indefinite time period. Shares are purchased at net asset value (NAV) plus commission (if any), and redeemed at NAV less a service charge (if any).

Open Order: An order to buy or sell a security at a specified price. An open order remains in effect until executed or canceled by the customer.

Option: A contract with three features: It allows an investor to reserve the right to buy or sell (1) a specified number of shares of stock (2) at a fixed price per share (3) for a limited time. There are two types of option contracts: call options and put options.

Optionvue Plus: A PC software package for sophisticated options trading. Accurate pricing models are employed for projecting profit/loss scenarios and identifying optimal strategies for the reduction of risk and enhancement of returns. Applies to stock and index options, handles convertible securities and warrants, supports automatic data capture from a variety of sources, and comes with complete, easy-to-use instruction materials. Runs on the IBM PC and all compatibles.

Out-of-the-Money: A term used when the striking price of an option is less than the price of the underlying stock for a call option, or greater than the price of the underlying stock for a put option.

Over-the-Counter (OTC): Securities market characterized by trading through a broker-dealer, usually over the telephone, without using the facilities of an exchange. The securities may or may not be listed on an exchange.

Pacific Stock Exchange (PSE): Handles trading on west coast of U.S.

Paper Profit: An unrealized profit on a security still held. Paper profits become realized profits only when the security is sold.

Participating Preferred: A stock entitled to receive a stated dividend before the common stock and part of any dividend thereafter declared on the common stock.

Par Value: For a stock, the dollar amount assigned each share of stock in the company's charter. For preferred issues and bonds, the value on which the issuer promises to pay dividends.

Passed Dividend: Omission of a regular or scheduled dividend.

Penny Stocks: Low-priced, often highly speculative stocks, that typically sell for $1 or less per share. All penny stocks are traded in the over-the counter (OTC) market.

Point: (1) For shares of stock, a point means $1. For example, if Xerox shares rise 2 points, each share has risen $2. (2) For bonds, a point means $10, since a bond is quoted as a percentage of $1,000. A bond that rises 2 points gains 2 percent of $1,000, or $20, in value. (3) For market averages, a point has intrinsic quality not equivalent to a fixed sum of money.

Portfolio: Holdings of securities by an individual or institution. A portfolio may contain bonds, preferred stocks, and common stocks of various types of enterprises.

Position: A specific instance of a chosen "strategy." For example, an option position is an investment comprised of one or more options.

Precious Metals: Tangible assets such as gold, silver, and platinum.

Preferred Stock: A class of stock with a claim on the company's earnings before payment may be made on the common stock and usually entitled to priority over common stock if the company liquidates. Preferred stockholders are usually entitled to dividends at a specified rate—when declared by the Board of Directors and before payment of a dividend on the common stock—depending on the terms of the issue.

Premium: (1) A market expression carrying the idea of an excess over an expected norm. A preferred stock or bond selling at a premium brings more than its par value. A new issue that rises quickly from its issuing price sells at a premium. When the redemption price of a bond or preferred issue is higher than par, redemption is at a premium. (2) The purchasing or selling price of an option contract.

Price/Earnings (P/E) ratio: Current market price of a stock divided by the 12-month earnings per share.

Primary Distribution: Also called primary offering. The original sale of a company's securities.

Prime Rate: The rate that banks charge their best customers for short-term loans.

Principal: (1) The person for whom a broker executes an order, or a dealer buying or selling for his or her own account. (2) Capital or the face amount of a bond.

Profit Diagram: A graph showing the relationship between the price of a stock and the corresponding profit or loss to an investor.

Profit Margin: A measure of earning capacity after taxes; for example, if a company made $.20 (20 cents) after taxes of each $1 of sales, profit margin would be 20 percent.

Profit Table: A table showing the relationship between the price of a stock and corresponding profit or loss to an investor.

Profit Taking: Selling to take a profit. The process of converting paper profits into cash.

Program Trading: The use of computer software to generate security trading decisions. The software has built-in guidelines that instantaneously trigger buy and sell orders when differences in the prices of the securities are enough to produce profit. Program trading is used by institutional investors, who place buy and sell orders in large blocks of 10,000 or more units. This type of large trade tends to significantly impact the prices of securities in the market. Sometimes, program trading orders reach the trading floors from a number of firms, an impact that can be seen most readily during what is called triple witching hour. The triple witching hour occurs four times annually in the hour prior to the moment (4: 15 P.M. EST, on the third Friday of March, June, September, and December) when stock options, stock index options, and stock index futures expire simultaneously. During this hour, the Dow Jones Industrial Average and other indexes have been known to change drastically.

Prospectus: A circular, required by the Securities Act of 1933, that describes securities being offered for sale. Its purpose is full disclosure, especially of adverse prospects for the issuer. It discloses facts regarding the issuer's operations, management, financial status, any anticipated legal matters that could affect the company, and potential risks of investing in the corporation.

Proxy: Written authorization given by a shareholder to someone else to represent him and vote his shares at a shareholders' meeting.

Proxy Statement: Information the SEC requires most companies to give their stockholders as a prerequisite to solicitation of proxies.

Prudent Person Rule: In some states, the law provides that a fiduciary, such as a trustee, may invest only in a list of securities designated by the state. In other states, the trustee may invest in a security if a prudent person of discretion and intelligence, who is seeking a reasonable income and preservation of capital, would buy it.

Put: This option contract conveys the right to sell 100 shares (usually) of a specified stock at a fixed price per share (the striking price) for a limited time (until expiration).

Puts and Calls: Options that give the right to buy or sell a fixed amount of a certain stock at a specified price within a specified time. A put gives the holder the right to sell the stock; a call, the right to buy the stock. Puts are purchased by those who think a stock might go down. A put obligates the seller of the contract to take delivery of the stock and pay the specified price to the owner of the option within the time limit of the contract. The price specified in a put or call is usually close to the market price of the stock at the time the contract is made. Calls are purchased by those who think a stock might rise. A call gives the holder the right to buy the stock from the seller of the contract at the specified price within a fixed period of time. Put and call contracts are written for 30, 60, or 90 days, or longer. If the purchaser of a put or call does not wish to exercise the option, the price paid for the option becomes a loss.

Quotation (Quote): The highest bid to buy and the lowest offer to sell a security in a given market at a given time. For example, your broker may quote a stock as ''26 1/4 to 26 1/2.'' This means that $26.25 was the highest price any buyer wanted to pay (bid) at the time the quotation was given on the exchange and that $26.50 was the lowest price at which any holder of the stock offered to sell.

''r'': The symbol used in the financial press to indicate that there were no trades on that option today, so there is no last quote to report.

Rally: A brisk rise following a decline in the general price level of the market or of an individual stock.

Real Estate Investment Trust (REIT): A type of closed-end investment company that invests money, obtained through the sale of shares to investors, in various types of real estate.

Realized Yield: The rate of return earned over a period of time that is less than the life of the issue.

Record Date: The date on which a shareholder must be registered on the books of a company to receive a declared dividend or, among other things, to vote on company affairs.

Redemption Price: The price at which a bond may be repurchased before maturity, or a preferred stock retired, at the option of the issuer.

Regional Stock Exchanges: Organized securities exchanges other than the New York Stock Exchange (NYSE) and the American Stock Exchange (AMEX) that deal primarily in securities having a local or regional flavor.

Registered Bond: A bond registered on the books of the issuer's transfer agent. The owner receives the interest by mail rather than by coupon and must endorse the bond to transfer it.

Registered Representative: Also known as customers' broker. A brokerage firm employee who is registered with an exchange or the National Association of

Securities Dealers (NASD) as having met certain requirements before being authorized to serve the firm's public customers.

Registration: Under the Securities Act of 1933, before a public offering may be made of new securities by a company, or of outstanding securities by controlling stockholders—through the mails or in interstate commerce—the securities must be registered and application filed with the SEC by the issuer. The registration statement must disclose pertinent information relating to the company's operations, securities, management, and purpose of the public offering.

Regulation T: Federal guidelines governing the amount of credit that may be advanced by brokers and dealers to customers for the purchase of securities.

Regulation U: Federal regulation governing the amount of credit that may be advanced by a bank to its customers for the purchase of securities.

Reverse Stock Split: A division of shares into a lesser number.

Rights: When a company issues additional stock it often gives current stockholders the right to buy new shares ahead of other buyers in proportion to the number of shares each current holder owns. In general, current stockholders pay less than the public will be asked to pay.

Round Lot: A unit of trading or a multiple thereof. On the New York Stock Exchange (NASD) the unit of trading is generally 100 shares for stocks and $1,000 par value for bonds.

"s": The symbol used in the financial press to indicate that the option does not exist. That is, the options exchange has not opened trading on that option.

Secondary Distribution: Also known as a secondary offering. The resale of a block of stock from a major owner or owners, rather than from the company itself. It is generally sold through an underwriting company or syndicate at a fixed price close to the stock market's valuation of the shares, but without sales commission or odd-lot differential.

Sector Fund: Also called Specialized Fund. A mutual fund that invests in one or two fields or industries (sectors). These funds are risky in that they rise and fall depending on how the individual fields or industries do. An example is Prudential-Bache Utility Fund.

Securities and Exchange Commission (SEC): Established by Congress to help protect investors, the SEC enforces the Securities Exchange Act of 1933, the Securities Exchange Act of 1934, the Trust Indenture Act, the Investment Company Act, the Investment Advisers Act, the Public Utility Holding Company Act, and the amendments to some of these contained in the Securities Acts Amendments of 1964.

Securities Market Indexes: Indexes that measure the value of a number of securities chosen as a sample to reflect the behavior of the general market of investments.

Selling Against the Box: A short sale undertaken to protect a profit in a stock and to defer tax liability to another year. For example, an investor owns 100 shares of ABC Company, which has gone up and which he or she thinks may decline. Consequently, the investor sells the 100 shares "short" and keeps them. If ABC Company stock declines, profit on the short sale is exactly offset by the loss in market value of the stock owned. If ABC Company stock advances, the loss on the short sale is offset by the gain in market value of the stock retained.

Serial Port: A plug that connects a computer to a modem or other external device. Sometimes referred to as an RS-232 port, it is connected to a card that converts the computer's internal parallel communications, which takes place eight bits at a time, to serial communications, one bit at a time.

Shareware: Programs the authors have provided for others to use on a trial basis. If programs are "adopted," users are requested to register or pay a fee, which usually includes technical support. Information about these programs may be obtained from a bulletin board system such as the American Association of Individual Investor's Computerized Investing BBS.

Short: A transaction in which an investor sells borrowed stock, hoping to buy it back at a lower price.

Short Covering: Buying stock to return stock previously borrowed to make delivery on a short sale.

Short Position: Stock sold short and not covered as of a particular date. On the NYSE, a tabulation is issued a few days after the middle of the month listing all issues on the exchange in which there was a short position of 5,000 or more shares, and issues in which the short position had changed by 2,000 or more shares in the preceding month. This tabulation is based on reports of positions on member firms' books. Short position also means the total amount of stock an individual has sold short and has not covered, as of a particular date. Initial margin requirements for a short position are the same as for a long position.

Short Sale: Sale of a stock the seller does not own, in the belief that it can be bought later at a lower price.

Small Investor Index: An index developed by *Money* magazine that measures gains and losses of the average investor. It is based on a portfolio including types of investments held by average small investors.

Software: Programs that instruct a computer which functions to perform.

Sotheby's Art Index: A weighted price index of over 400 individual collectibles grouped into 12 "market baskets" that include paintings, ceramics, and furniture. The index, developed by Jeremy Eckstein, a statistician with Sotheby's in London, appears in *Barron's*.

Specialist: A stock exchange member who undertakes to keep an orderly market in a specified stock by buying or selling on his own account when bids and offers by the public are not matched well enough to maintain an orderly market. The specialist is the broker's broker in the stock in which he specializes and receives commissions for executing other brokers' orders.

Speculation: The act of using funds by a speculator. The safety of principal is a secondary factor.

Speculator: One willing to assume a relatively large risk in the hope of significant gain. The investor's principal concern is to increase capital rather than augment dividend income. A speculator may buy and sell the same day or speculate in an enterprise not expected to be profitable for years. An example of speculation is investing in a penny stock.

Split: Division of the outstanding shares of a corporation into a larger number of shares. A 3-for-1 split by a company with 1,000,000 shares outstanding would result in 3,000,000 shares outstanding. Each holder of 100 shares before the 3-for-1 split would have 300 shares, although his proportionate equity in the company would remain the same, since 100 parts of 1,000,000 are the equivalent of 300 parts of 3,000,000. Ordinarily splits must be voted by directors and approved by shareholders.

Spread Order: A type of order for the simultaneous purchase and sale of two options of the same type (calls or puts) on the same underlying stock. If placed with a ''limit,'' the two options must be traded for a specified price difference or better.

Standard & Poor's Corporation (S&P): Publishes of a variety of financial and investment reports and services, including *Corporation Records, Stock Guide,* and *Bond Guide.*

Standard & Poor's 500 Stock Composite (S&P 500): The 500 Stock Composite Index calculated by Standard & Poor's. It differs from the Dow Jones Industrial Average (DJIA) in several important ways. First, it is a value-weighted, rather than price-weighted, index. This means that the index considers not only the price of a stock but also the number of shares outstanding. That is to say, it is based on the aggregate market value of the stock, i.e., price times number of shares. An advantage of the index over the Dow Jones Industrial Average (DJIA) is that stock splits and stock dividends do not affect the index value. A disadvantage is that large capitalization stocks—those with a large number of shares outstanding—heavily influence the index value. The S&P 500 actually consists of four separate indexes: the 400 industrials, the 40 utilities, the 20 transportation, and the 40 financial.

Stock Dividend: A dividend paid in stock rather than cash. The dividend may be additional shares of the issuing company or shares of another company (usually a subsidiary) held by the company.

Stockholder of Record: A stockholder whose name is registered on the books of the issuing corporation.

Stock Index Futures: Futures contracts written on broad-based measures of stock market performance such as the S&P Stock Index.

Stock Index Option: A put or call option written on a specific market index such as the S&P Stock Index.

Stop Order: This is a type of order for the purchase or sale of stock or options, placed away from the current market price, which becomes a market order if the stock or option trades at the price specified.

Stock Split: A division of shares into a larger number. For example, a 2-for-1 split means two new shares are exchanged for each old share and the price is halved after the split.

Strategy: In options, one of the various kinds of option investments, i.e., long call, covered write, bull spread, and the like.

Street: The New York financial community concentrated in the Wall Street area.

Street Name: Securities held in the broker's name instead of the customer's name are said to be carried in street name. This occurs when the securities have been bought on margin or when the customer wishes the securities to be held by the broker.

Striking Price: This is the fixed price per share specified in the options contract.

Stripped Treasuries: Zero-coupon bonds sold by the U.S. Treasury and created by stripping the coupons from a Treasury bond and selling them separately from the principal.

Switching: Selling one security and buying another.

Syndicate: A group of investment bankers who together underwrite and distribute a new issue of securities or a large block of an outstanding issue.

Tangible Assets: Tangible items of real and personal property that generally have a long life, such as housing and other real estate, automobiles, jewelry, cash, and other physical assets.

Tax Equivalent Yield: The yield on a tax-free municipal bond needs to be looked at on an equivalent before-tax yield basis, because the interest received is not subject to federal income taxes.

Tax-exempt Bond: A bond that pays no federal taxes because it is issued by a state or subordinate division of a state.

Technical Position: The term covering the internal factors affecting the market, as opposed to fundamental forces such as prosperity or recession.

Thin Market: The market for a stock is thin when buying or selling a few shares can affect its price disproportionately in either direction.

Third Market: Trading in the over-the-counter (OTC) market of securities listed on an exchange.

Ticker: The instrument that prints prices and volume of security transactions in cities and towns throughout the U.S. within minutes after each trade on the floor.

Time Value: The amount by which the premium of an option exceeds its intrinsic value. Time value reflects the statistical possibility that the option premium will increase in value rather than finish at zero dollars. If an option is out-of-the-money, then its entire premium consists of time value.

Tips: Supposedly "inside" information on corporate affairs.

Trader: One who buys and sells for his or her own account for short-term profit. Also brokerage firm employees who buy and sell in the over-the-counter (OTC) market.

Trading Post: Trading locations at which stocks assigned to that location are bought and sold on the exchange floor.

Treasury Stock: Stock issued by a company but later reacquired. It may be held in the company's treasury indefinitely, reissued to the public, or retired. Treasury stock receives no dividends and has no vote while held by the company.

Turnover: The volume of business in a security or the entire market. If turnover on the New York Stock Exchange (NYSE) is reported at 3,000,000 shares on a particular day, 3,000,000 shares changed hands. Odd-lot turnover is tabulated separately and ordinarily is not included in reported volume.

12b-1 Fees: Fees of a mutual fund that cover advertising and marketing costs, but do nothing to improve the performance of the fund. Their main purpose is to bring new customers to the fund, and ultimately more money for the fund's management for investment.

Uncovered: An uncovered options strategy, an investment in which the written options are *not* matched with a long stock position or a long option position that expires no earlier than the written options. Thereby the loss potential with such a strategy is unlimited.

Underlying Stock: The stock specified in an options contract, which stock is transferred upon exercise of the options contract.

Underwriter: See: Investment Banker.

Underwriting: The act of buying the securities from the issuing company, thus guaranteeing the company the capital it seeks, and in turn selling the securities at a markup to the investing public or institutions.

Unit Investment Trust: A closed-end investment company in which the proceeds from the sale of original shares are invested in a fixed portfolio of taxable or tax-exempt bonds and held until maturity. Like a mutual fund, a unit investment trust offers to small investors the advantages of a large, professionally selected and diversified portfolio. Unlike a mutual fund, however, its portfolio is fixed; once structured, it is not actively managed.

Unlisted: A security not listed on a stock exchange.

Up Tick: Also called a plus tick. Designates a price higher than that on the preceding transaction in the stock. A stock may be sold short only on an up tick or on a zero-plus tick, a term used for a transaction at the same price as the preceding trade but higher than the preceding different price. A zero-minus tick is a transaction made at the same price as the preceding sale but lower that the preceding different price. A plus sign or a minus sign is displayed throughout the day next to the last price of each company's stock traded at each trading post on the floor of the New York Stock Exchange (NYSE).

Value Averaging: Alternative formula strategy to dollar cost averaging. The idea is to make the *value* of investment holdings go up by some fixed amount (such as $100) each month. It is a little more complex than dollar cost averaging but can usually provide higher returns at lower per-share costs.

Value Line Composite Average: A stock average published by Value Line, which reflects the percentage changes in share price of some 1,700 stocks traded on the New York Stock Exchange (NYSE), American Stock Exchange (AMEX), and over-the-counter (OTC) markets.

Value Line Investment Survey: A weekly subscription service covering some 1,700 of the most widely held stocks.

Vertical Analysis: Financial statement analysis that expresses all other accounts on the financial statement in percentage terms as compared to a base value. For example, in the balance sheet, total assets equals 100%. Each asset is stated as a percentage of total assets.

Volatility: A measure of the amount by which a stock is expected to fluctuate in a given period of time. Stocks with greater volatility exhibit wider price swings and their options are higher in price than less volatile stocks.

Voting Right: A stockholder's right to vote his or her stock in the company affairs. Most common shares have one vote each. Preferred stock usually has the right to vote when preferred dividends are in default. The right to vote may be delegated by the stockholder to another person.

Wall Street Journal: A daily financial newspaper published by Dow Jones.

Warrant: A paper giving its holder the right to buy a security at a set price, either within a specified period or perpetually. A warrant is generally offered with another security as an added inducement to buy.

When Distributed: A security trading in advance of the printing of the certificate.

When Issued: A short form of "when, as, and if issued." The term indicates a conditional transaction in a security authorized for issuance but not yet actually issued. All "when issued" transactions are on an "if" basis, to be settled if and when the actual security is issued and the National Association of Securities Dealers or an exchange rules the transactions are to be settled.

Wilshire 5000 Index: Measure of the total dollar value of 5,000 actively traded stocks, including all those traded on the New York Stock Exchange (NYSE), American Stock Exchange (AMEX), and over-the-counter (OTC) markets.

Write: An investor who sells an option contract not currently held (selling the option short) is said to have written the option.

Yield: Also known as return. The dividends or interest paid by a company expressed as a percentage of the current price—or, if you own the security, of the price you originally paid. The return on a stock is figured by dividing the total of dividends paid in the preceding 12 months by the current market price—or, if you are the owner, the price you originally paid.

Yield to Maturity (YTM): The fully compounded rate of return on a bond, assuming it is held to maturity.

Zero-Coupon Bond: Or, Original Issue Discount (OID) Bond. A bond bought at a deep discount. The interest, instead of being paid out directly, is added to the principal semiannually and both the principal and the accumulated interest are paid at maturity.

Index